Lecture Notes in Computer Science 8047

Commenced Publication in 1973
Founding and Former Series Editors:
Gerhard Goos, Juris Hartmanis, and Jan van Leeuwen

Richard Wilson   Edwin Hancock
Adrian Bors   William Smith (Eds.)

Computer Analysis
of Images and Patterns

15th International Conference, CAIP 2013
York, UK, August 27-29, 2013
Proceedings, Part I

 Springer

Volume Editors

Richard Wilson
Edwin Hancock
Adrian Bors
William Smith
University of York
Department of Computer Science
Deramore Lane
York YO10 5GH, UK
E-mail: {wilson, erh, adrian, wsmith} @cs.york.ac.uk

ISSN 0302-9743   e-ISSN 1611-3349
ISBN 978-3-642-40260-9   e-ISBN 978-3-642-40261-6
DOI 10.1007/978-3-642-40261-6
Springer Heidelberg Dordrecht London New York

Library of Congress Control Number: 2013944666

CR Subject Classification (1998): I.5, I.4, I.2, H.2.8, I.3, H.3

LNCS Sublibrary: SL 6 – Image Processing, Computer Vision, Pattern Recognition,
and Graphics

Typesetting: Camera-ready by author, data conversion by Scientific Publishing Services, Chennai, India

Printed on acid-free paper

Springer is part of Springer Science+Business Media (www.springer.com)

Preface

This volume contains the papers presented at the 15th International Conference on Computer Analysis of Images and Patterns (CAIP 2013) held in York during August 27–29, 2013.

CAIP was first held in 1985 in Berlin, and since then has been organized biennially in Wismar, Leipzig, Dresden, Budapest, Prague, Kiel, Ljubljana, Warsaw, Groningen, Versailles, Vienna, Münster, and Seville.

We received 243 full papers, from authors in 48 countries. Of these 142 were accepted, 39 oral presentation and 103 posters. There were three invited speakers, Rama Chellappa from the University of Maryland, Xiaoyi Jiang from the University of Münster, and Tim Weyrich from University College London.

We hope that participants benefitted scientifically from the meeting, but also got a flavor of York's rich history and saw something of the region too. To this end, we organized a reception at the York Castle Museum, and the conference dinner at the Yorkshire Sculpture Park. The latter gave participants the chance to view large-scale works by the Yorkshire artists Henry Moore and Barbara Hepworth.

We would like to thank a number of people for their help in organising this event. Firstly, we would to thank the IAPR for sponsorship. Furqan Aziz managed the production of the proceedings, and Bob French co-ordinated local arrangements.

June 2013

Edwin Hancock
William Smith
Richard Wilson
Adrian Bors

Organization

Program Committee

Ceyhun Burak Akgül	Vistek ISRA Vision, Turkey
Madjid Allili	Bishop's University, Canada
Nigel Allinson	University of Lincoln, UK
Apostolos Antonacopoulos	University of Salford, UK
Helder Araujo	University of Coimbra, Portugal
Nicole M. Artner	PRIP, Vienna University of Technology, Austria
Furqan Aziz	University of York, UK
Andrew Bagdanov	Media Integration and Communication Center University of Florence, Italy
Antonio Bandera	University of Malaga, Spain
Elisa H. Barney Smith	Boise State University, USA
Ardhendu Behera	University of Leeds, UK
Abdel Belaid	Université de Lorraine - LORIA, France
Gunilla Borgefors	Centre for Image Analysis, Swedish University of Agricultural Sciences, Sweden
Adrian Bors	University of York, UK
Luc Brun	GREYC, ENS, France
Lorenzo Bruzzone	University of Trento, Italy
Horst Bunke	University of Bern, Switzerland
Martin Burger	WWU Münster, Germany
Gustavo Carneiro	University of Adelaide, Australia
Andrea Cerri	University of Bologna, Italy
Kwok-Ping Chan	The University of Hong Kong, SAR China
Rama Chellappa	University of Maryland, USA
Sei-Wang Chen	National Taiwan Normal University, Taiwan
Dmitry Chetverikov	Hungarian Academy of Sciences, Hungary
John Collomosse	University of Surrey, UK
Bertrand Coüasnon	Irisa/Insa, France
Marco Cristani	University of Verona, Italy
Guillaume Damiand	LIRIS/Université de Lyon, France
Justin Dauwels	M.I.T., USA
Mohammad Dawood	University of Münster, Germany
Joachim Denzler	University Jena, Germany
Cecilia Di Ruberto	Università di Cagliari, Italy
Junyu Dong	Ocean University of China, China

Hazim Kemal Ekenel   InterACT Research, Universität Karlsruhe,
                                        Germany
Hakan Erdogan   Sabanci University, Turkey
Francisco Escolano   University of Alicante, Spain
M. Taner Eskil   ISIK University, Turkey
Alexandre Falcão   Institute of Computing - University of
                                        Campinas (Unicamp), Brazil
Chiung-Yao Fang   National Taiwan Normal University, Taiwan
Massimo Ferri   University of Bologna, Italy
Gernot Fink   TU Dortmund University, Germany
Ana Fred   Instituto Superior Tecnico, Portugal
Patrizio Frosini   University of Bologna, Italy
Laurent Fuchs   XLIM-SIC, UMR CNRS 7252, Université de
                                        Poitiers, France
Xinbo Gao   Xidian University, China
Dr. Anarta Ghosh   Research Fellow, Ireland
Georgy Gimelfarb   The University of Auckland, New Zealand
Daniela Giorgi   IMATI Genova, Italy
Dmitry Goldgof   University of South Florida, USA
Rocio Gonzalez-Diaz   University of Seville, Spain
Cosmin Grigorescu   European Patent Office, Brussels
Miguel A Gutiérrez-Naranjo   University of Seville, Italy
Michal Haindl   Institute of Information Theory and
                                        Automation, Czech Republic
Edwin Hancock   University of York, UK
Yll Haxhimusa   Vienna University of Technology, Austria
Vaclav Hlavac   Czech Technical University in Prague,
                                        Czech Republic
Zha Hongbin   Peking University, China
Yo-Ping Huang   National Taipei University of Technology,
                                        Taiwan
Yung-Fa Huang   Chaoyang University of Technology, Taiwan
Atsushi Imiya   IMIT Chiba University, Japan
Xiaoyi Jiang   Universität Münster, Germany
Maria Jose Jimenez   University of Seville, Spain
Martin Kampel   Vienna University of Technology, Computer
                                        Vision Lab, Austria
Nahum Kiryati   Tel Aviv University, Israel
Reinhard Klette   University of Auckland, New Zealand
Andreas Koschan   University of Tennessee, USA
Walter Kropatsch   Vienna University of Technology, Austria
Xuelong Li   University of London, UK
Pascal Lienhardt   SIC Laboratory, France
Guo-Shiang Lin   Da-Yeh University, Taiwan
Agnieszka Lisowska   University of Silesia, Poland

Josep Llados — Computer Vision Center, Universitat Autonoma de Barcelona, Spain

Jean-Luc Mari — Faculté des Sciences de Luminy, Université Aix-Marseille 2, LSIS Laboratory, UMR CNRS 6168, France

Eckart Michaelsen — FGAN-FOM, Germany

Majid Mirmehdi — University of Bristol, UK

Radu Nicolescu — The University of Auckland, New Zealand

Mark Nixon — University of Southampton, UK

Darian Onchis — University of Vienna, Austria

Ioannis Patras — Queen Mary College London, UK

Petra Perner — Institute of Computer Vision and Applied Computer Sciences, Germany

Nicolai Petkov — University of Groningen, The Netherlands

Ioannis Pitas — Aristotle University of Thessaloniki, Greece

Eugene Popov — Nizhegorodsky Architectural and Civil Engineering State University (NNACESU), Russia

Mario J. Pérez Jiménez — University of Seville, Spain

Petia Radeva — Computer Vision Center, Universitat Autònoma de Barcelona, Spain

Pedro Real — University of Seville, Spain

Bodo Rosenhahn — University of Hannover, Germany

Paul Rosin — Cardiff University, UK

Samuel Rota Bulo — Università Ca' Foscari, Italy

Jose Ruiz-Shulcloper — Advanced Technologies Applications Center (CENATAV) MINBAS, Cuba

Robert Sablatnig — Vienna University of Technology, Austria

Hideo Saito — Keio University, Japan

Albert Salah — Bogazici University, Turkey

Gabriella Sanniti Di Baja — Institute of Cybernetics "E. Caianiello", CNR, Italy

Sudeep Sarkar — University of South Florida, USA

Oliver Schreer — Fraunhofer Heinrich Hertz Institute, Germany

Francesc Serratosa — Universitat Rovira i Virgili, Spain

Luciano Silva — Universidade Federal do Parana, Brazil

William Smith — University of York, UK

Mingli Song — Zhejiang University, China

K.G. Subramanian — Universiti Sains Malaysia, Malaysia

Akihiro Sugimoto — National Institute of Informatics, Japan

Dacheng Tao — The Hong Kong Polytechnic University, SAR China

Bernie Tiddeman — University of Wales, Wales

Klaus Toennies — Otto-von-Guericke-Universität, Germany

Javier Toro — Desarrollo para la Ciencia y la Tecnologia, C.A., Venezuela

Table of Contents – Part I

Table of Contents – Part II

Biomedical Imaging:
A Computer Vision Perspective

Xiaoyi Jiang[1,2,3], Mohammad Dawood[1,2], Fabian Gigengack[1,2],
Benjamin Risse[1,4], Sönke Schmid[1,2,3], Daniel Tenbrinck[1,2],
and Klaus Schäfers[2,3]

[1] Department of Mathematics and Computer Science, University of Münster,
Germany
[2] European Institute for Molecular Imaging (EIMI), University of Münster, Germany
[3] Cluster of Excellence EXC 1003, Cells in Motion, CiM, Münster, Germany
[4] Department of Neuro and Behavioral Biology, University of Münster, Germany

Abstract. Many computer vision algorithms have been successfully adapted and applied to biomedical imaging applications. However, biomedical computer vision is far beyond being only an application field. Indeed, it is a wide field with huge potential for developing novel concepts and algorithms and can be seen as a driving force for computer vision research. To emphasize this view of biomedical computer vision we consider a variety of important topics of biomedical imaging in this paper and exemplarily discuss some challenges, the related concepts, techniques, and algorithms.

1 Introduction

The success story of modern biology and medicine is also one of imaging. It is the imaging techniques that enable biological experiments (for high-throughput behavioral screens or conformation analysis) and make the body of humans and animals anatomically or functionally visible for clinical purposes (medical procedures seeking to reveal, diagnose, or examine disease). With the widespread use of imaging modalities in fundamental research and routine clinical practice, researchers and physicians are faced with ever-increasing amount of image data to be analyzed and the quantitative outcomes of such analysis are getting increasingly important. Modern computer vision technology is thus indispensable to acquire and extract information out of the huge amount of data.

Computer vision has a long history and is becoming increasingly mature. Many computer vision algorithms have been successfully adapted and applied to biomedical imaging applications. However, biomedical imaging has several special characteristics which pose particular challenges, e.g.,

- Acquisition and enhancement techniques for challenging imaging situations are needed.
- The variety of different imaging sensors, each with its own physical principle and characteristics (e.g., noise modeling), often requires modality-specific treatment.

R. Wilson et al. (Eds.): CAIP 2013, Part I, LNCS 8047, pp. 1–19, 2013.

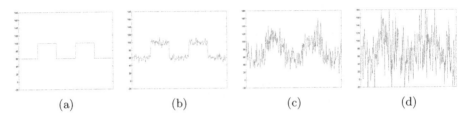

Fig. 1. Illustration of three noise models. (a) Noise-free 1D signal. (b) Signal biased by additive Gaussian noise with $\sigma = 5$. (c) Signal biased by Poisson noise. (d) Signal biased by speckle noise with $\sigma = 5$ and $\gamma = 1$. (from [42])

- It is not seldom that different modalities are involved. Thus, algorithms must be designed to cope with multiple modalities.
- Due to the high complexity of many biomedical image analysis tasks, semi-automatic processing may be unavoidable in some cases. The design of intelligent and user-friendly interactive tools is a challenging task.
- Also the different body organs may require specific treatment.

As an example, the influence of noise modeling is considered. The following noise models are popular:

- Additive Gaussian noise: $f = \mu + \nu$, where μ is the unbiased image intensity and ν is a Gaussian-distributed random variable with expectation 0 and variance σ^2.
- Poisson noise ("photon counting noise"): This type of noise is signal-dependent and appears in a wide class of real-life applications, e.g., in positron emission tomography and fluorescence microscopy.
- Speckle noise: $f = \mu + \nu\mu^{\gamma/2}$ occurs in ultrasound imaging and is of multiplicative nature. Its dependency on the unbiased image intensity μ is controlled by the parameter γ. ν is the same as for additive Gaussian noise.

To illustrate the different characteristics of these noise forms a synthetic 1D signal and its corrupted versions are shown in Figure 1. We can observe that for similar parameters, the appearance of signal-dependent Poisson and speckle noise is in general stronger compared to the additive Gaussian noise. Their processing is thus definitely challenging and pushes the need for accurate data modeling in computer vision.

On the other hand, the special characteristics of biomedical imaging also give extra power to computer vision research. Multimodality can be helpful since they carry complementary information and their combined use may ease some image analysis tasks (e.g., segmentation [25]). Generally, a lot of knowledge specific to a particular application or object type may exist that should be accurately modeled and integrated into algorithms for dedicated processing towards improved performance.

Given the challenges discussed above, biomedical computer vision is far beyond simply adapting and applying advanced computer vision techniques to solve real problems. It is also a wide field with huge potential of developing novel concepts, techniques, and algorithms. Indeed, biomedical imaging can be seen as a driving force for computer vision research.

In this paper this view of biomedical computer vision is emphasized by considering important topics of biomedical imaging: Minimum-cost boundary detection, region-based image segmentation, image registration, optical flow computation, and imaging techniques. Our intention is not to give a complete coverage of these topics, but rather exemplarily focus on typical challenges and the related concepts, techniques, and algorithms. The majority of the given examples is based on our own research and experiences in the respective fields.

2 Minimum-cost Boundary Detection

Quantification is one of the key words in biomedical imaging and requires robust, fast, and possibly automatic image segmentation algorithms. It can be either in the form of boundary detection or alternatively region-based segmentation. Automatic segmentation enables assessment of meaningful parameters, e.g., for diagnosis of pathological findings in clinical environments.

2.1 Live-Wire Techniques

Several paradigms of minimum-cost boundary detection exist in the literature. Among them the live-wire approach was initially introduced by Mortensen *et al.* [37] and Udupa *et al.* [51]. The user interactively picks a seed point on the boundary. Then, a live-wire is displayed in real time from the initial point to any subsequent position taken by the cursor. The entire 2D boundary is specified by means of a set of live-wire segments in this manner. The detection of segments is formulated as a graph searching problem, which finds the globally optimal (minimum-cost) path between an initial start pixel and an end pixel.

Placing seed points precisely on an object boundary may be difficult and tedious. To facilitate seed point placement, a cursor snap mechanism forces the mouse point to the pixel of maximum gradient magnitude within a user-specified neighborhood. The user-friendliness can be further increased by the live lane approach [20]. The user selects only the initial point. Subsequent points are selected automatically as the cursor is moved within a lane surrounding the boundary whose width changes as a function of the speed and acceleration of cursor motion.

Live-wire boundaries are piecewise optimal (between two seed points) and thus provide a balance between global optimality and local control. In contrast to statistical deformable approaches (e.g., [10,11,28]) no training is required. This semi-automatic technique has established itself as a robust and user-friendly method for the extraction of structure outlines for many biomedical applications.

A very fast implementation called live-wire on the fly is described in [19] which avoids unnecessary minimum-cost path computation during segmentation. Another important extension is the 3D generalization proposed in [18] to segment

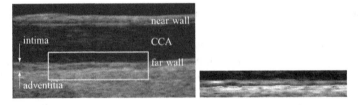

Fig. 2. B-mode CCA image (left) and detected intima and adventitia layer of far wall (right)

3D volume data or time sequences of 2D images. The key idea there is that the user specifies contours via live-wiring on a few slices that are *orthogonal* to the natural slices of the original data. If these slices are selected strategically, then one obtains a sufficient number of seed points in each natural slice which enable a subsequent automatic optimal boundary detection therein.

Live-wire techniques are a good example of designing intelligent and user-friendly interactive segmentation tools. They help to solve complex segmentation tasks by locally and non-extensively integrating the expertises and wishes of domain experts, which in turn also increases the user's faith in the automatic solution.

2.2   Dynamic Programming Based Boundary Detection

Dynamic programming (DP) is a popular technique for boundary detection due to its elegance, efficiency, and guarantee of optimality. One class of detectable boundaries starts from the left, passes each image column exactly once, and ends in the last column. An example is shown in Figure 2 for detecting the intimal and adventitial layers of the common carotid artery (CCA) in B-mode sonographic images [8]. Given an image of n rows and m columns, a total number of $O(n \cdot 3^{m-1})$ potential paths exist. However, the dynamic programming technique gives us an efficient algorithm for exactly finding the minimum-cost path with $O(mn)$ time and space [45].

Another, perhaps even more important, application class deals with closed boundaries. Based on a point p in the interior of the boundary, a polar transformation with p being the central point brings the original image into a matrix, in which a closed boundary becomes one from left to right afterwards. Finally, the detected boundary has to be transformed back to the original image space. This technique works well for star-shaped boundaries[1], particularly including (nearly) convex boundaries. Note that special care must be taken in order to guarantee the closedness of the detected boundary [47].

Typically, DP-based boundary detection assumes strong edges along the boundary and is thus based on gradient computation. In the simplest case the cost function is defined by the sum of gradient magnitudes. In practice, however,

---

[1] A star-shaped boundary is characterized by the existence of a point p such that for each interior point q the segment $\overline{pq}$ lies entirely inside.

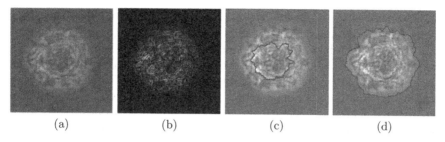

(a)   (b)   (c)   (d)

Fig. 3. (a) Tumor cell ROI; (b) gradient; (c) gradient-based optimal boundary; (d) region-based optimal contour (from [29])

gradient is not always a reliable measure to work with. One such example is the region-of-interest (ROI) of a tumor cell from microscopic imaging shown in Figure 3. Maximizing the sum of gradient magnitude does not produce satisfactory result.

There are only very few works on DP-based boundary detection using non-gradient information [35,53]. A challenge remains to develop boundary detection methods based on region information. A general framework for this purpose is proposed in [29]. A star-shaped contour C can be represented in polar form $r(\theta)$, $\theta \in [0, 2\pi)$. Given the image boundary $B(\theta)$, $\theta \in [0, 2\pi)$, the segmentation task can be generally formulated as one of optimizing the energy function:

$$
E(C) = \int_0^{2\pi} \left[\int_0^{r(\theta)} F_i(\theta, r) dr + \int_{r(\theta)}^{B(\theta)} F_o(\theta, r) dr \right] d\theta \tag{1}
$$

Each region is assumed to be well represented by some model, which can be validated by a model testing function F_i (inside) and F_o (outside), respectively. This problem, however, cannot be solved by dynamic programming since the model parameters have to be estimated by the entirety of inside and outside of C. In [29] an approximation is thus made by *modeling each radial ray separately*, enabling to restrict the model testing functions $F_i(\theta, r)$ and $F_o(\theta, r)$ to a particular radial ray θ instead of the whole image. Then, a dynamic programming solution becomes possible for any representation model and model testing function independent of their form, complexity, and mathematical properties, e.g., differentiability. This universality gives the rather simple scheme of dynamic programming considerable power for real-world applications. In particular, robust estimation methods such as median-based approaches and L_1 norm (see Figure 3d for a related result) are highly desired for improved robustness. Also, sophisticated testing criteria like Fisher linear discriminant and others from machine learning theory provide extra useful options for measuring the separability of two distributions.

The principle of DP-based boundary detection can be extended in various ways. One extension is to simultaneously extract multiple boundaries [8,46], e.g., for detecting a pair of intimal and adventitial boundary in sonographic images (Figure 2). The domain of detectable boundaries can be further enlarged to contain non-star-shaped objects. One such attempt from [30] allows the user to interactively specify and edit the general shape of the desired object by using a so-called rack, which basically corresponds to the object skeleton. The straight-forward extension of the boundary class considered here to 3D is the terrain-like surface $z = f(x, y)$ (height field or discrete Monge surface). Unfortunately, there is no way of extending the dynamic programming solution to the 3D minimum-cost surface detection problem in an efficient manner. An optimal 3D graph search algorithm approach is presented in [32] with low polynomial time for this purpose. Similar to handling closed boundaries, cylindrical (tube-like) surfaces can be handled by first unfolding into a terrain-like surface using cylindrical coordinate transform. In addition to detecting minimum-cost surfaces this algo-rithm can also be applied to sequences of 2D images for temporally consistent boundary detection.

In practice, fast and easy-to-use algorithms like DP-based boundary detection are highly desired. To cite the biologist colleague who provided us the microscopic images used in [29] (see Figure 3): "I have literally tens of thousands of images per experiment" that must be processed within reasonable time. Therefore, further developments like boundary detection based on region information will have high practical impact.

3   Region-Based Image Segmentation

Region-based image segmentation is one of the fundamental problems in biomed-ical imaging for quantitative reasoning and diagnostic. Recently, mathematical tools such as level sets and variational methods led to significant improvements in image segmentation. However, a majority of works on image segmentation implicitly assume the given image to be biased by additive Gaussian noise, for instance the popular Mumford-Shah model [38]. Generally, it still lacks mature treatment of segmenting images with non-Gaussian noise models.

3.1   Discriminant Analysis Based Level Set Segmentation

The popular Chan-Vese (CV) approach [7], which is a special case of the Mumford-Shah formulation, uses a closed contour $\Gamma \subset \Omega$ to separate a given im-age domain Ω into two regions Ω_1, Ω_2. In particular, Γ is implicitly represented by the level sets of a Lipschitz function $\Phi \colon \Omega \to \Re$, i.e., $\Phi(x) < 0$ for $x \in \Omega_1$, $\Phi(x) = 0$ for $x \in \Gamma$, and $\Phi(x) > 0$ for $x \in \Omega_2$. Disregarding regularization of the segmentation area, the CV energy functional is given as:

$$
\begin{aligned}
E_{CV}(c_1, c_2, \Phi) \;=\; & \beta \int_{\Omega} \delta_0(\Phi(x)) \left| \nabla \Phi(x) \right| dx \\
& + \lambda_1 \int_{\Omega} (c_1 - f(x))^2 \, H(\Phi) \, dx \; + \; \lambda_2 \int_{\Omega} (c_2 - f(x))^2 \, (1 - H(\Phi(x))) \, dx
\end{aligned}
\tag{2}
$$

Here f is the perturbed image to be segmented and c_1 and c_2 are constant approximations of f in Ω_1 and Ω_2, respectively. The Heavyside function H is used as indicator function for Ω_1, while δ_0 denotes the one-dimensional δ-Dirac measure.

In case of additive Gaussian noise (cf. Figure 1b) it is shown in [48] that for fixed c_1, c_2, the energy in Eq. (2) gets minimal if Φ partitions the data according to a natural *threshold* $t_{CV} = (c_1 + c_2)/2$ as in clustering where c_1 and c_2 are cluster centers. However, the situation in presence of multiplicative noise is different and the optimal threshold cannot be t_{CV} in this case (see [42] for details). In [48] a discriminant analysis (corresponding to the popular Otsu thresholding method) is thus applied to determine an optimal threshold t_O. Then, a new variational segmentation model is formulated as:

$$E(\Phi) = \frac{1}{2} \int_\Omega \mathrm{sgn}(\Phi(x)) \, (f(x) - t_O) \, dx \; + \; \beta \int_\Omega \delta_0(\Phi(x)) \, |\nabla\Phi(x)| \, dx \quad (3)$$

This approach has been demonstrated to be superior to the Chan-Vese formulation on real patient data from echocardiography, which are known to be perturbed by multiplicative speckle noise.

3.2   Variational Segmentation Framework Incorporating Physical Noise Models

Despite its high popularity the Mumford-Shah formulation has not yet been investigated in a more general context of explicit physical noise modeling. Indeed, only few publications considered the effect of a specific noise model on the results of image segmentation [9,36]. A lot of segmentation problems need a suitable noise model, e.g., positron emission tomography or medical ultrasound imaging. Especially for data with poor statistics, i.e., with a low signal-to-noise ratio, it is important to consider the impact of the present noise model on the segmentation process.

In [42] a general segmentation framework for different physical noise models is presented, which also allows the incorporation of a-priori knowledge by using different regularization terms. For the special case of two-phase segmentation problems, the image domain Ω is partitioned into a background and a target subregion Ω_1 and Ω_2, respectively. An indicator function χ is introduced such that $\chi(x) = 1$ if $x \in \Omega_1$ and 0 otherwise (comparable to the Heavyside function $H(\Phi)$ in Eq. (2)). The data fidelity functions are defined by the negative log-likelihood functions derived from Bayesian modeling:

$$D_i(f, u_i) = -\log p_i(f \mid u_i) \quad \text{for } i \in \{1, 2\} \quad (4)$$

where u_i is a smooth function for each subregion, which is chosen according to the assumed noise model for the given data f. Then, the energy functional for the two-phase segmentation problem is formulated as:

$$E(u_1, u_2, \chi) = \int_\Omega \chi(x) \, D_1(f, u_1) + (1 - \chi(x)) \, D_2(f, u_2) \, dx$$
$$+ \, \alpha_1 R_1(u_1) + \alpha_2 R_2(u_2) + \beta \mathcal{H}^{n-1}(\Gamma) \quad (5)$$

Here $\mathcal{H}^{n-1}(\Gamma)$ is the $(n-1)$-dimensional Hausdorff measure. The regularization terms R_1 and R_2 are used to incorporate a-priori knowledge about the expected unbiased signals, e.g., H^1 seminorm, Fisher information, or TV regularization.

The choice of the probability densities $p_i(f \mid u_i)$ for $i = 1, 2$ crucially depends on the image formation process and hence on the noise model assumed for the data f and the subregion Ω_i. This is the place where physical noise modeling comes into play. In [42] the cases of Poisson and multiplicative speckle noise (cf. Figure 1c and 1d, respectively) have been intensively discussed.

In [50] the influence of three different noise models is investigated using this variational segmentation framework. In particular, shape priors are integrated as regularization term to the framework. It is demonstrated that correct physical noise modeling is of high importance for the computation of accurate segmentation results both in low-level as well as high-level segmentation.

The two approaches discussed above are representative for a variety of segmentation algorithms which fully utilize the knowledge about the specific characteristics of the image data at hand. A better modeling is the prerequisite for improved segmentation accuracy and robustness. This is especially important in biomedical imaging due to the variety of imaging modalities.

4   Image Registration

Image registration [21,34] aims at geometrically aligning two images of the same scene, which may be taken at different times, from different viewpoints, and by different sensors. It is among the most important tasks of biomedical imaging in practice. Given a template image $\mathcal{T} : \Omega \to \Re$ and a reference image $\mathcal{R} : \Omega \to \Re$, where $\Omega \subset \Re^d$ is the image domain and d the dimension, the registration yields a transformation $y : \Re^d \to \Re^d$ representing point-to-point correspondences between $\mathcal{T}$ and $\mathcal{R}$. To find y, the following functional has to be minimized:

$$\min_y \mathcal{D}(\mathcal{M}(\mathcal{T}, y), \mathcal{R}) + \alpha \mathcal{S}(y) \qquad (6)$$

Here, $\mathcal{D}$ denotes the distance functional and the $\mathcal{M}$ transformation model, and $\mathcal{S}$ is the regularization functional. $\mathcal{D}$ measures the dissimilarity between the transformed template image and the fixed reference image. If both images are of the same modality, the sum-of-squared differences (SSD) can be used as a distance functional $\mathcal{D}$. In case of multimodal image registration information-theoretic measures, in particular, mutual information, are popular [39].

The SSD and related dissimilarity measures implicitly assume the intensity constancy between the template and reference image. Thus, we solely search for the optimal geometric transformation. In medical imaging, however, this assumption is not always satisfied. Such a problem instance appears in the context of motion correction in positron emission tomography (PET) [14].

PET requires relatively long image acquisition times in the range of minutes. In thoracic PET both respiratory and cardiac motion lead to spatially blurred images. To reduce motion artifacts in PET, so-called gating based techniques

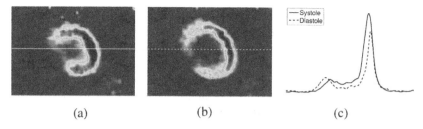

(a)   (b)   (c)

Fig. 4. Coronal slices of the left ventricle in a human heart during systole (a) and diastole (b) and corresponding line profiles (c) are shown for one patient. It can be observed that the maximum peaks in these line profiles vary a lot. (from [24])

were found useful, which decompose the whole dataset into parts that represent different breathing and/or cardiac phases [16]. After gating, each single gate shows less motion, however, suffers from a relatively low signal-to-noise ratio (SNR) as only a small portion of all available events is contained. After gating the data, each gate is reconstructed individually and registered to one assigned reference gate. The registered images are averaged afterwards to overcome the problem of low SNR. Tissue compression and the partial volume effect (PVE) lead to intensity modulations. Especially for relatively small structures like the myocardium the true uptake values are affected by the PVE. An example is given in Figure 4 where a systolic and diastolic slice (same respiratory phase) of a gated 3D dataset and line profiles are shown. Among others, the maximum intensity values of the two heart phases indicate that corresponding points can differ in intensity significantly.

In this situation an image registration mechanism is required which consists of simultaneous geometric transformation (spatially moving the pixels) and intensity modulation (redistributing the intensity values). In gating, all gates are formed over the same time interval. Hence, the total amount of radioactivity in each phase is approximately equal. In other words, in any respiratory and/or cardiac gate no radioactivity can be lost or added apart from some minor changes at the edges of the field of view. This property provides the foundation for a *mass-preserving image registration*. VAMPIRE (Variational Algorithm for Mass-Preserving Image REgistration) [24] incorporates a mass-preserving component by accounting for the volumetric change induced by the transformation y. Based on the integration by substitution theorem for multiple variables we have:

$$\int_{y(\Omega)} \mathcal{T}(x)dx = \int_{\Omega} \mathcal{T}(y(x))|\det(\nabla y(x))|dx \qquad (7)$$

It guarantees the same total amount of radioactivity before and after applying the transformation y to $\mathcal{T}$. Therefore, for an image $\mathcal{T}$ and a transformation y, the mass-preserving transformation model is defined as:

$$\mathcal{M}^{\mathrm{MP}}(\mathcal{T}, y) := \mathcal{T}(y) \cdot \det(\nabla y) \qquad (8)$$

which is used in the registration functional (6) to enable simultaneous geometric transformation and intensity modulation.

In [24] this mass-preserving registration algorithm has been successfully applied to correct motion for dual – cardiac as well as respiratory – gated PET imaging. Motion estimation is also a fundamental requirement for super-resolution computation. More robust motion estimation based on mass-preserving registration thus facilitates improved super-resolution quality [52].

Similar to noise modeling discussed for region-based image segmentation, it is the explicit consideration of the mass-preserving property which enables improved image registration. This is another example of the benefit of accurate modeling in biomedical imaging.

5   Optical Flow Computation

Motion analysis is an important tool in biomedical imaging and optical flow estimation plays a central role in this context [2,22]. The basis of most optical flow algorithms is the brightness constancy[2]:

$$I(x, y, t) = I(x + u, y + v, t + 1) \tag{9}$$

which assumes that when a pixel moves from one image to another, its intensity (or color) does not change. In fact, this assumption combines a number of assumptions about the reflectance properties of the scene, the illumination in the scene, and the image formation process in the camera [2]. Linearizing this constancy equation by applying a first-order Taylor expansion to the right-hand side leads to the fundamental *optical flow constraint* (OFC):

$$u \cdot I_x + v \cdot I_y = -I_t \tag{10}$$

or more compactly:

$$f \cdot \nabla I = -I_t \tag{11}$$

with $f = (u, v)$ and $\nabla I = (I_x, I_y)$, which is used to derive optimization algorithms in a continuous setting.

In practice, however, this popular brightness constancy is not always valid. Other constancy terms have also been suggested including gradient, gradient magnitude, higher-order derivatives, e.g., on the (spatial) Hessian photometric invariants, texture features, and combination of multiple features (see [5] for a discussion). In the following two subsections we briefly discuss two additional variants from the medical imaging perspective.

5.1   Mass-Preserving Optical Flow

The problem of intensity modulations discussed for image registration in the previous section can also be tackled with optical flow techniques. According to

---

[2] For notation simplicity we consistently give the 2D version only. Its extension to n-D cases is straightforward.

the observation that the OFC is very similar to the continuity equation of fluid dynamics, Schunck [44] presented the *extended optical flow constraint* (EOFC):

$$f \cdot \nabla I + I \cdot \text{div}(f) \;=\; -I_t \tag{12}$$

where $\text{div}(f) = u_x + v_y$ is the divergence of f. Optical flow computaton based on EOFC has been studied and compared with ordinary OFC-based methods [4].

Interestingly, the EOFC has a physical interpretation of *mass preservation*. As shown by several researchers [3,12,40], this constraint is equivalent to a total brightness invariance hypothesis. The total brightness is defined as the sum of intensity values of a moving object. Instead of assuming that a point has a constant brightness over time, it is assumed that a moving object has a total brightness constant over time. Combined with a non-quadratic penalization a mass-preserving optical flow method has been applied for cardiac motion correction in 3D PET imaging [13]. In contrast to OFC-based optical flow [15,17], mass-preserving methods reflect better the physical reality of PET imaging.

Note that the idea behind the mass-preserving optical flow and the mass-preserving registration discussed in Section 4 is the same. Indeed, Eq. (12) can also be derived from Eq. (6), see [23]. Both registration and optical flow methods give us a powerful tool for solving mass-preserving motion estimation problems.

5.2   Histogram-Based Optical Flow

Multiplicative speckle noise (cf. Figure 1d) is characteristic for diagnostic ultrasound imaging. The origin of speckle are tiny inhomogeneities within the tissue, which reflect ultrasound waves but cannot be resolved by the ultrasound system. Speckle noise $f = \mu + \nu \mu^{\gamma/2}$ is of multiplicative nature, i.e., the noise variance directly depends on the underlying signal intensity.

The speckle noise has substantial impact on motion estimation. In fact, it turns out that the brightness constancy does not hold any more (see [49] for a mathematical proof). This can be demonstrated by the following simple experiment [49]. Starting from two pixel patches of size 5×5 with constant intensity values $\mu = 150$ and $\eta \in [0, 255]$, a realistic amount of speckle noise was added according to $f = \mu + \nu \mu^{\gamma/2}$ with $\gamma = 1.5$. The resulting pixel patches, denoted by X^{150} and Y^{η}, were compared pixelwise with the squared L_2-distance. Comparison of the two pixel patches was performed 10,000 times for every value of $\eta \in [0, 255]$. The simulation results (average distance of the two pixel patches and standard deviation) are plotted in Figure 5 (left). Normally, one would expect the minimum of the graph to be exactly at the value $\eta = \mu = 150$, i.e., both pixel patches have the same constant intensity before adding noise. However, the minimum of the graph is below the expected value. This discrepancy has been theoretically analyzed in [49], which predicts the minimum at $\eta \approx 141$ for the particular example as can be observed in Figure 5 (left).

In [49] it is argued that the overall distribution within a local image region remains approximately constant since the tissue characteristics remain and thus

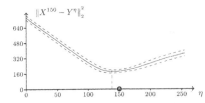 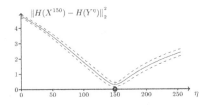

Fig. 5. Left: Average distance between two pixel patches biased by speckle noise. The global minimum is below the correct value of $\eta = 150$. Right: Average distance between the histograms of two pixel patches biased by speckle noise. The global minimum matches with the correct value of $\eta = 150$. In both case the two dashed lines represent the standard deviation of the 10,000 experiments. (from [49])

suggested to consider a small neighborhood around a pixel and compare the local statistics, i.e, local histograms as a discrete representation of the intensity distribution, of the images. This leads to the *histogram constancy constraint*:

$$H(x, y, t) = H(x + u, y + v, t + 1) \tag{13}$$

where H represents the cumulative histogram of the region surrounding the pixel (x, y) at time t. The validity of this new constraint has been mathematically proven in [49] and can also been seen in Figure 5 (right). On ultrasound data the derived histogram-based optical flow algorithm outperforms state-of-the-art general-purpose optical flow methods.

5.3   Periodic Optical Flow

In medical imaging some motion is inherently periodic. For example, this occurs in cardiac gated imaging, where images are obtained at different phases of the periodic cardiac cycle. Another example is in respiratory gated imaging, where the respiratory motion of the chest can also be described by a periodic model. Li and Yang [33] proposed optical flow estimation for a sequence of images wherein the inherent motion is periodic over time. Although in principle one could adopt a frame-by-frame approach to determine the motion fields, a joint estimation, in which all motion fields of a sequence are estimated simultaneously, explicitly exploits the inherent periodicity in image motion over time and can thus be advantageous against the framewise approach.

By applying Fourier series expansion, the components (u, v) at location (x, y) over time are modeled by:

$$u(x, y, t) = \sum_{l=1}^{L} \left[a_l(x, y) \cos \frac{2\pi l}{T} t + b_l(x, y) \sin \frac{2\pi l}{T} t \right] \tag{14}$$

$$v(x, y, t) = \sum_{l=1}^{L} \left[c_l(x, y) \cos \frac{2\pi l}{T} t + d_l(x, y) \sin \frac{2\pi l}{T} t \right] \tag{15}$$

where $a_l(x, y)$, $b_l(x, y)$, $c_l(x, y)$, $d_l(x, y)$ are the coefficients associated with harmonic component l and L is the order of the harmonic representation. This motion model is embedded into the motion estimation for each pair of two successive images and the overall data term of the energy function to be minimized is the sum of all pairwise data terms from the brightness constancy.

While a number of constancy terms have been suggested in computer vision, the popular brightness constancy is dominating. The mass-preserving and histogram-based optical flow computation discussed above exemplarily demonstrate the need of finding suitable constancy terms in particular biomedical imaging scenarios. Periodic optical flow is a new concept and not fully explored yet. In both cases biomedical imaging provides large room for methodological development from a computer vision perspective.

6 Novel Imaging Techniques

Biomedical imaging has a broad range of subjects to be imaged and various imaging modalities. Despite of the enormous progresses there is still substantial room for further development of imaging technology. In the following we exemplarily describe two scenarios.

6.1 PET Imaging of Freely Moving Mice

In an on-going project we aim to track freely moving small animals with high precision inside a positron emission tomograph. Normally, the animals have to be anesthetized during 15-60 minutes of data acquisition to avoid motion artifacts. However, anesthesia influences the metabolism which is measured by PET. To avoid this, the aim of our project is to track awake and freely moving animals during the scan and use the information to correct the acquired PET data for motion. For this task a small animal chamber of $20 \times 10 \times 9$ cm was built (Figure 6) with a pair of stereo cameras positioned on both small sides of the chamber.

Due to the experimental setup highly distorted wide angle lenses have to be used. To reach the required tracking accuracy a high-precision lens distortion correction is crucial. First tests using a simple polynomial model for lens distortion correction lead to deviations from a pinhole camera model of up to 5 pixels. Therefore, more sophisticated methods are needed. Two high-precision lens distortion correction methods are described in [26,27]. In the latter case several images of a harp of wire are acquired and a massive amount of edge points is used to determine the parameters of a 11th grade polynomial distortion function. Both methods require a very accurately manufactured calibration pattern. In [43] another solution is suggested using a planar checkerboard pattern to provide very accurately detectable feature points even under distortion as a calibration pattern. Smoothed thin plate splines are applied to model the mapping between control points, leading to a mean accuracy below 0.084 pixel.

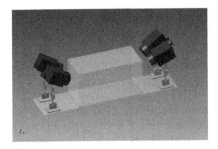 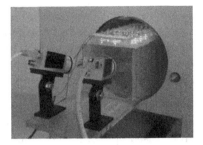

Fig. 6. Camera setup for PET imaging of freely moving mice. Left: Construction model of the animal chamber. Right: Manufactured chamber halfway inserted into a quad-HIDAC PET-scanner (16 cm in diameter). (from [43])

In addition to lens distortion correction we also need to solve other problems like feature detection and stereo vision in order to provide the technical fundament for a motion-corrected reconstruction. It is this bundle of computer vision solutions that will help to further improve the functionality of PET imaging towards imaging of freely moving mice.

6.2   FTIR-Based Imaging Method

The investigation of complex movement patterns of various organisms has become an integral subject of biological research. One of the most popular model organisms to study how the nervous system controls locomotion is Drosophila melanogaster (i.e., fruit fly). Drosophila is a holomethabolous insect. In the larval stage locomotion is confined to 2D, whereas the adult fly moves in two and three dimensions.

Work on freely flying fruit flies is still in its infancy because they form the so-called general multi-index assignment problem, which is nondeterministically polynomial-time hard (NP-hard) [6]. The current solutions are only able to track a small number of subjects for a short period [1,54]. From the computer vision perspective 3D tracking of flying flies is an unsolved challenge. Much efforts are still required to realize highly accurate tracking systems in order to fully meet the need of biological behavior studies.

In contrast, larval crawling occurs in two dimensions at relatively low speed. In principle, larval movement can be documented by a simple camera setup. However, recording of crawling larvae requires high contrast images, which are typically obtained by following sophisticated illumination protocols or dye applications [31]. For conventional, relatively low resolution tracking of larval locomotion, larvae are illuminated by incident or transmitted light and monitored by cameras with appropriate filters. This is technically challenging due to the semi-translucent body of these small animals. In addition, the observation of larvae is complicated by light reflections caused by the tracking surface. Thus, illumination problems aggravate faithful recordings of larval crawling paths and the poor signal to noise ratio complicates subsequent computer-based analysis.

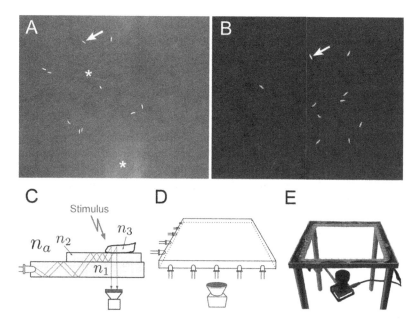

Fig. 7. The FIM setup. (A) Image of 10 larvae (arrow) imaged in a conventional setup. The asterisks denote scratches and reflections in the tracking surface. (B) Image of 10 larvae (arrow) imaged in the FIM setup with high contrast. (C) The principle of frustrated total internal reflection. n_a, n_1, n_2, and n_3 indicate different refractory indices of air, acrylic glass, agar and larvae respectively, an acrylic glass plate is flooded with infrared light (indicated by red lines). The camera is mounted below the tracking table. (D) Schematic drawing of the setup. (E) Image of the tracking table. (from [41])

A novel imaging technique based on frustrated total internal reflection (FTIR) is reported in [41], see Figure 7. Instead of directly illuminating crawling larvae, the frustrated total internal reflection is used to determine the contact surface between the animal and the substrate. In this FIM setup, an acrylic glass plate is flooded with infrared light. Due to the differences in the refractive indices of acrylic glass and air, it is completely reflected at the glass/air boundary (Figure 7C). To provide a moist crawling environment a thin agar layer is added. According to Snell's law, the light enters the agar layer since its refractive index (n_2) is higher than the refractive index of the acrylic glass (n_1). The larvae have an even higher optical density resulting in a higher refractive index (n_3), and thus, reflection is frustrated at the agar/larva interface and light enters the larval body. Here, light is reflected and since the reflection angle is smaller than the critical angle, the light passes through the different layers and can be detected by a camera equipped with an infrared filter (Figure 7D,E). This setup is easy to assemble and does not require cost-intensive equipment. This new imaging approach, named FIM (FTIR-based Imaging Method), provides an unprecedented high contrast view on crawling animals. Even without any background subtraction it generates constant image quality superior to previous setups. In addition, it even allows to image internal organs. FIM is suitable for a wide range of biological applications and a wide range of organisms. Together with optimized tracking software it facilitates analysis of larval locomotion and will simplify genetic screening procedures.

7   Conclusion

Biomedical computer vision is far beyond simply adapting and applying advanced computer vision techniques to solve real problems. Biomedical imaging also poses new and challenging computer vision problems in order to cope with the complex and multifarious reality. In this paper we have exemplarily discussed a number of challenges and the related concepts and algorithms, mainly in the fields of our own research. They are well motivated by the practice. Biomedical imaging is full of such challenges and powerful computer vision solutions will immediately have benefit for the practice.

We need to understand how the domain experts work best with a technical system, which helps to design intelligent and user-friendly interactive tools. In addition, we are forced to have deeper understanding of the sources of signals and images to be processed, i.e., the objects of interest and biomedical devices. Only this way essential knowledge can be included for improved modeling and solution.

Many fundamental assumptions made when developing algorithms for biomedical imaging are shared by different - even non-biomedical - imaging modalities. For instance, the speckle noise model applies to both ultrasound and synthetic aperture radar imaging. Thus, the developed algorithms are of general interest and can be used in manifold application contexts.

Modern biology and medicine is a successful story of imaging. In the past biomedical computer vision has already established a vast body of powerful methods and tools. Continuous well-founded research will further enlarge the spectrum of successfully solved practical problems and thus continue to make a noticable contribution to biology and medicine.

Acknowledgments. The authors were supported by the Deutsche Forschungs-gemeinschaft (DFG): SFB 656 MoBil (project B3, C3), EXC 1003 Cells in Motion – Cluster of Excellence, and DA 1064/3. Thanks go to Kristen Mills at Max Planck Institute for Intelligent Systems, Stuttgart, for providing the microscopic images.

References

1. Ardekani, R., Biyani, A., Dalton, J., Saltz, J., Arbeitman, M., Tower, J., Nuzhdin, S., Tavare, S.: Three-dimensional tracking and behaviour monitoring of multiple fruit flies. J. R. Soc. Interface 10(78), 20120547 (2013)
2. Baker, S., Scharstein, D., Lewis, J.P., Roth, S., Black, M.J., Szeliski, R.: A database and evaluation methodology for optical flow. International Journal of Computer Vision 92(1), 1–31 (2011)

3. Béréziat, D., Herlin, I., Younes, L.: A generalized optical flow constraint and its physical interpretation. In: Proc. of CVPR, pp. 487–492 (2000)
4. Bimbo, A.D., Nesi, P., Sanz, J.L.C.: Optical flow computation using extended constraints. IEEE Trans. on Image Processing 5(5), 720–739 (1996)
5. Bruhn, A.: Variational Optic Flow Computation – Accurate Modelling and Efficient Numerics. Ph.D. thesis, University of Saarland (2006)
6. Burkard, R., Dell'Amico, M., Martello, S.: Assignment Problems. Society for Industrial Mathematics (2009)
7. Chan, T.F., Vese, L.A.: Active contours without edges. IEEE Trans. on Image Processing 10(2), 266–277 (2001)
8. Cheng, D.C., Jiang, X.: Detections of arterial wall in sonographic artery images using dual dynamic programming. IEEE Trans. on Information Technology in Biomedicine 12(6), 792–799 (2008)
9. Chesnaud, C., Réfrégier, P., Boulet, V.: Statistical region snake-based segmentation adapted to different physical noise models. IEEE Trans. on Pattern Anaysis and Machine Intelligence 21(11), 1145–1157 (1999)
10. Cootes, T.F., Edwards, G.J., Taylor, C.J.: Active appearance models. IEEE Trans. on Pattern Analysis and Machine Intelligence 23(6), 681–685 (2001)
11. Cootes, T.F., Taylor, C.J., Cooper, D.H., Graham, J.: Active shape models-their training and application. Computer Vision and Image Understanding 61(1), 38–59 (1995)
12. Corpetti, T., Heitz, D., Arroyo, G., Memin, E., Santa-Cruz, A.: Fluid experimental flow estimation based on an optical-flow scheme. Experiments in Fluids 40(1), 80–97 (2006)
13. Dawood, M., Gigengack, F., Jiang, X., Schäfers, K.: A mass conservation-based optical flow method for cardiac motion correction in 3D-PET. Medical Physics 40(1), 012505 (2013)
14. Dawood, M., Jiang, X., Schäfers, K. (eds.): Correction Techniques in Emission Tomographic Imaging. CRC Press (2012)
15. Dawood, M., Büther, F., Jiang, X., Schäfers, K.P.: Respiratory motion correction in 3-D PET data with advanced optical flow algorithms. IEEE Trans. on Medical Imaging 27(8), 1164–1175 (2008)
16. Dawood, M., Büther, F., Stegger, L., Jiang, X., Schober, O., Schäfers, M., Schäfers, K.P.: Optimal number of respiratory gates in positron emission tomography: A cardiac patient study. Medical Physics 36(5), 1775–1784 (2009)
17. Dawood, M., Kösters, T., Fieseler, M., Büther, F., Jiang, X., Wübbeling, F., Schäfers, K.P.: Motion correction in respiratory gated cardiac PET/CT using multi-scale optical flow. In: Metaxas, D., Axel, L., Fichtinger, G., Székely, G. (eds.) MICCAI 2008, Part II. LNCS, vol. 5242, pp. 155–162. Springer, Heidelberg (2008)
18. Falcão, A.X., Udupa, J.K.: A 3D generalization of user-steered live-wire segmentation. Medical Image Analysis 4(4), 389–402 (2000)
19. Falcão, A.X., Udupa, J.K., Miyazawa, F.K.: An ultra-fast user-steered image segementation paradigm: Live-wire-on-the-fly. IEEE Trans. on Medical Imaging 19(1), 55–62 (2000)
20. Falcão, A.X., Udupa, J.K., Samarasekera, S., Sharma, S., Hirsch, B.E., de Alencar Lotufo, R.: User-steered image segmentation paradigms: Live wire and live lane. Graphical Models and Image Processing 60(4), 233–260 (1998)
21. Fischer, B., Modersitzki, J.: Ill-posed medicine - an introduction to image registration. Inverse Problems 24(3), 034008 (2008)

22. Fleet, D., Weiss, Y.: Optical flow estimation. In: Paragios, N., Chen, Y., Fauregas, O. (eds.) The Handbook of Mathematical Models in Computer Vision, pp. 241–260. Springer (2005)

23. Gigengack, F.: Mass-Preserving Motion Correction and Multimodal Image Segementation in Positron Emission Tomography. Ph.D. thesis, University of Münster (2012)

24. Gigengack, F., Ruthotto, L., Burger, M., Wolters, C.H., Jiang, X., Schäfers, K.P.: Motion correction in dual gated cardiac PET using mass-preserving image registration. IEEE Trans. on Medical Imaging 31(3), 698–712 (2012)

25. Gigengack, F., Ruthotto, L., Jiang, X., Modersitzki, J., Burger, M., Hermann, S., Schäfers, K.P.: Atlas-based whole-body PET-CT segmentation using a passive contour distance. In: Menze, B.H., Langs, G., Lu, L., Montillo, A., Tu, Z., Criminisi, A. (eds.) MCV 2012. LNCS, vol. 7766, pp. 82–92. Springer, Heidelberg (2013)

26. von Gioi, R.G., Monasse, P., Morel, J.M., Tang, Z.: Towards high-precision lens distortion correction. In: Proc. of ICIP, pp. 4237–4240 (2010)

27. von Gioi, R.G., Monasse, P., Morel, J.M., Tang, Z.: Lens distortion correction with a calibration harp. In: Proc. of ICIP, pp. 617–620 (2011)

28. Heimann, T., Meinzer, H.P.: Statistical shape models for 3D medical image segementation: A review. Medical Image Analysis 13(4), 543–563 (2009)

29. Jiang, X., Tenbrinck, D.: Region based contour detection by dynamic programming. In: Hancock, E., Smith, W., Wilson, R., Bors, A. (eds.) CAIP 2013, Part II. LNCS, vol. 8048, pp. 152–159. Springer, Heidelberg (2013)

30. Jiang, X., Große, A., Rothaus, K.: Interactive segmentation of non-star-shaped contours by dynamic programming. Pattern Recognition 44(9), 2008–2016 (2011)

31. Khurana, S., Atkinson, W.L.N.: Image enhancement for tracking the translucent larvae of drosophila melanogaster. PLoS ONE 5(12), e15259 (2010)

32. Li, K., Wu, X., Chen, D., Sonka, M.: Optimal surface segmentation in volumetric images - a graph-theoretic approach. IEEE Trans. on Pattern Analysis and Machine Intelligence 28(1), 119–134 (2006)

33. Li, L., Yang, Y.: Optical flow estimation for a periodic image sequence. IEEE Trans. on Image Processing 19(1), 1–10 (2010)

34. Maintz, J.B.A., Viergever, M.A.: A survey of medical image registration. Medical Image Analysis 2(1), 1–36 (1998)

35. Malon, C., Cosatto, E.: Dynamic radial contour extraction by splitting homogeneous areas. In: Real, P., Diaz-Pernil, D., Molina-Abril, H., Berciano, A., Kropatsch, W. (eds.) CAIP 2011, Part I. LNCS, vol. 6854, pp. 269–277. Springer, Heidelberg (2011)

36. Martin, P., Réfrégier, P., Goudail, F., Guérault, F.: Influence of the noise model on level set active contour segmentation. IEEE Trans. on Pattern Analysis and Machine Intelligence 26(6), 799–803 (2004)

37. Mortensen, E., Morse, B., Barrett, W.: Adaptive boundary detection using 'livewire' two-dimensional dynamic programming. In: IEEE Proc. Computers in Cardiology, pp. 635–638 (1992)

38. Mumford, D., Shah, J.: Optimal approximations by piecewise smooth functions and associated variational problems. Commun. Pure Appl. Math. 42, 577–685 (1989)

39. Pluim, J.P.W., Maintz, J.B.A., Viergever, M.A.: Mutual information based registration of medical images: A survey. IEEE Trans. on Medical Imaging 22(8), 986–1004 (2003)

40. Qiu, M.: Computing optical flow based on the mass-conserving assumption. In: Proc. of ICPR, pp. 7041–7044 (2000)

41. Risse, B., Thomas, S., Otto, N., Löpmeier, T., Valkov, D., Jiang, X., Klämbt, C.: FIM, a novel FTIR-based imaging method for high throughput locomotion analysis. PLoS ONE 8(1), e53963 (2013)
42. Sawatzky, A., Tenbrinck, D., Jiang, X., Burger, M.: A variational framework for region-based segmentation incorporating physical noise models. Journal of Mathematical Imaging and Vision (2013), doi:10.1007/s10851-013-0419-6
43. Schmid, S., Jiang, X., Schäfers, K.: High-precision lens distortion correction using smoothed thin plate splines. In: Hancock, E., Smith, W., Wilson, R., Bors, A. (eds.) CAIP 2013, Part II. LNCS, vol. 8048, pp. 432–439. Springer, Heidelberg (2013)
44. Schunck, B.: The motion constraint equation for optical flow. In: Proc. of ICPR, pp. 20–22 (1984)
45. Sonka, M., Hlavac, V., Boyle, R.: Image Processing, Analysis, and Machine Vision. Cengage Learning, 3rd edn. (2007)
46. Sun, C., Appleton, B.: Multiple paths extraction in images using a constrained expanded trellis. IEEE Trans. on Pattern Analysis and Machine Intelligence 27(12), 1923–1933 (2005)
47. Sun, C., Pallottino, S.: Circular shortest path in images. Pattern Recognition 36(3), 709–719 (2003)
48. Tenbrinck, D., Jiang, X.: Discriminant analysis based level set segmentation for ultrasound imaging. In: Hancock, E., Smith, W., Wilson, R., Bors, A. (eds.) CAIP 2013, Part II. LNCS, vol. 8048, pp. 144–151. Springer, Heidelberg (2013)
49. Tenbrinck, D., Schmid, S., Jiang, X., Schäfers, K., Stypmann, J.: Histogram-based optical flow for motion estimation in ultrasound imaging. Journal of Mathematical Imaging and Vision (2013), doi:10.1007/s10851-012-0398-z
50. Tenbrinck, D., Sawatzky, A., Jiang, X., Burger, M., Haffner, W., Willems, P., Paul, M., Stypmann, J.: Impact of physical noise modeling on image segmentation in echocardiography. In: Proc. of Eurographics Workshop on Visual Computing for Biomedicine, pp. 33–40 (2012)
51. Udupa, J., Samarasekera, S., Barrett, W.: Boundary detection via dynamic programming. In: Visualization in Biomedical Computing 1992, pp. 33–39 (1992)
52. Yan, H., Gigengack, F., Jiang, X., Schäfers, K.: Super-resolution in cardiac PET using mass-preserving image registration. In: Proc. of ICIP (2013)
53. Yu, M., Huang, Q., Jin, R., Song, E., Liu, H., Hung, C.C.: A novel segmentation method for convex lesions based on dynamic programming with local intra-class variance. In: Proc. of ACM Symposium on Applied Computing, pp. 39–44 (2012)
54. Zou, D., Zhao, Q., Wu, H.S., Chen, Y.Q.: Reconstructing 3d motion trajectories of particle swarms by global correspondence selection. In: Proc. of ICCV, pp. 1578–1585 (2009)

Rapid Localisation and Retrieval
of Human Actions with Relevance Feedback

Simon Jones and Ling Shao

The University of Sheffield
{simon.m.jones,ling.shao}@shef.ac.uk

Abstract. As increasing levels of multimedia data online require more sophisticated methods to organise this data, we present a practical system for performing rapid localisation and retrieval of human actions from large video databases. We first temporally segment the database and calculate a histogram-match score for each segment against the query. High-scoring, adjacent segments are joined into candidate localised regions using a noise-robust localisation algorithm, and each candidate region is then ranked against the query. Experiments show that this method surpasses the efficiency of previous attempts to perform similar action searches with localisation. We demonstrate how results can be enhanced using relevance feedback, considering how relevance feedback can be effectively applied in the context of localisation.

1 Introduction

In recent years search engines – such as Google – that operate on textual information have become both mature and commonplace. Efficient and accurate search of multimedia data, however, is still an open research question, and this is becoming an increasingly relevant problem with the growth in use of Internet multimedia data. In order to perform searches on multimedia databases, current technology relies on textual metadata associated with each video, such as keyword tags or the video's description – unfortunately such metadata are often incomplete or inaccurate. Furthermore, even if a textual search engine can locate the correct video, it cannot search within that video to localise specific sub-sequences that the user is interested in.

Compared to this, content-based retrieval systems present a better alternative. Such systems directly search through the content of multimedia objects, avoiding the problems associated with metadata searches. Content-Based Image Retrieval (CBIR) is the primary focus of many researchers. Video retrieval (CBVR) has also been studied [1], but to a far lesser degree. Retrieval of human actions in particular has received relatively little attention in comparison to action recognition, with some notable exceptions in [2,3]. This is perhaps because human actions are particularly difficult to retrieve because only a single query example is provided to search on, but this single query cannot capture the vast intraclass variability of even the simplest of human actions. Additionally, if the

R. Wilson et al. (Eds.): CAIP 2013, Part I, LNCS 8047, pp. 20–27, 2013.

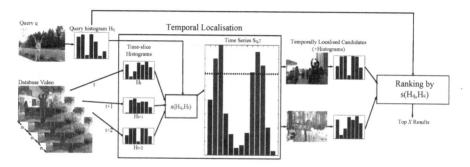

Fig. 1. An overview of the localisation and ranking aspects of our algorithm. Relevance feedback has been omitted for clarity.

query itself is noisy it can be difficult to isolate the relevant features of the action. One method researchers use to overcome this issue is relevance feedback, such as presented in [2].

Finding relevant videos alone is not enough for a practical video retrieval system. It is also necessary to *localise* the relevant segments within longer videos, as in the real world actions of interest are rarely neatly segmented. In the image domain, Rahmani et al. [4] and Zhang et al. [5] have combined retrieval with spatial localisation of objects. In videos, most localisation to date has been performed in a recognition context, such as in [6]. However, more recently Yu et al. [3] have performed human action retrieval combined with localisation.

Our goal is to introduce a time-efficient system for performing human action retrieval, showing how localisation and retrieval can be integrated while maintaining accuracy. We argue that, compared to previous works such as Yu et al.[3] our method is an order of magnitude more efficient in time and space, making it far more practical for real-world searches, while still maintaining practical accuracy. Furthermore, we experiment with the addition of relevance feedback in various forms, demonstrating that even imperfectly localised feedback can be used to significantly improve results. We believe ours is the first work to consider the effect of noisy relevance feedback samples in our experimentation, detailed further in section 3.

2   Localisation and Retrieval

Our foremost consideration in performing video localisation and retrieval is efficiency, as videos are data-intensive and yet searches need to be fast to be practical. In this section, we detail a localisation algorithm. This algorithm has linear complexity with respect to the size of the database, the potential to be further optimised, yet makes little sacrifice in accuracy. We additionally reduce the query time through batch pre-processing of the database to a compact representation. As it is based on local features, our algorithm is scale-invariant, robust against noise and partially viewpoint invariant.

2.1   Pre-processing

In the pre-processing stage it is helpful to consider previous work on human action recognition. Approaches to human action recognition are broken down into two categories based on the feature extraction method: global feature-based methods and local feature-based methods [7]. Global feature based methods, such as [8], consider the whole human shape or scene through time. Local feature-based methods, such as [9,10], discard more potentially salient information, such as the structural information between features, so are generally not as accurate on clean datasets. However, they are typically more robust against noise. Some methods, however, including the spatio-temporal shape context [11] and spatio-temporal pyramid representations [12], are local feature-based but partially retain structural information between features. The localisation technique presented in this work is similar to these structure-retaining representations.

The first step in our approach is to reduce the video database to a compact representation. As we want our algorithm to operate on realistic datasets, we use local features. Features are detected using Dollar's method [10] at a loosely constant rate with respect to time, at multiple spatial and temporal scales. At each detected point, we extract a spatio-temporal cuboid and apply the HOG3D [13] descriptor. We base our choice of detector on a human action classification evaluation study [14], and the descriptor on the experimental results shown in [13]. Next we assign each of the features one of k distinct codewords/clusters, as in the Bag-of-Words method. To achieve this, we first reduce the feature descriptors' dimensionality using principal components analysis. We then perform k-means clustering on the reduced descriptors, and each feature is assigned to one cluster. Each feature is then represented by a single value – its cluster membership.

We then aggregate these features in a way suitable for rapid localisation. While Yu et al.'s fast method [3] for action localisation can often localise the optimal 3D sub-volume, generating a score for each STIP using Random Forests is too expensive for real-world retrieval. Feature voting[6] is another potential scheme, but we have experimentally determined that such methods are only stable when applied to clean datasets. We instead propose to use a BoW-derived approach to video representation, visualised in part of Figure 1. Each database video is divided into time-slices $t \in T$, of n_f frames, and we create a code-word frequency histogram H_t for all the features within each t. Each histogram is normalised, and n_f is chosen to be approximately half the size of the smallest query that can be searched on. The time-slices do not overlap, as preliminary experiments have shown this does not improve accuracy. While this representation is simple, we show through experiments that it captures sufficient information to localise a human action. All of the aforementioned steps can be processed once on the database in batch – this improves the time efficiency of later user searches.

2.2   Search

Previous work [15,16] on human action localisation typically utilise a trained model – this requires several examples of the target action and the accompanying ground truths. This is not possible in a retrieval context, where only a single query example is provided. Some researchers have made attempts to perform image retrieval with spatial localisation [4,5], and one work focuses on spatio-temporal retrieval and localisation of videos [3]. However, all of the aforementioned techniques are computationally complex, making them unsuitable for real-world retrieval. We present a more efficient system below.

To search, the user provides a video example of the human action they want to find. The system performs feature extraction on this query in the manner described in section 2.1, but a single normalised histogram is generated for the entire length of the query, rather than for time-slices. To search for an action within a single video taken from the database, we first use a simple metric to calculate the similarity between each time-slice histogram and the query histogram H_q. This metric is the histogram intersection:

$$s(H_q, H_t) = \sum_{i=1}^{k} min(H_q^i, H_t^i) \qquad (1)$$

If n_f is chosen appropriately, each time-slice t can only, at best, represent a small fraction of the action being searched for, thus H_q and H_t will not be fully correlated. However, we show in our experiments below that the histogram intersection still generates a stronger response generally for relevant time-slices than irrelevant ones. Aggregating s over all $t \in T$ gives a time-series $S_{q,T}$ representing the similarity s of each $t \in T$ to q.

Analysing $S_{q,T}$, it is possible to find candidate regions for the localised action. One possible approach involves finding local peaks in this series. However, such a method proves too sensitive to noise. Our best method applies thresholding and then candidate segmentation. First, any t where $S_{q,t}$ is below a threshold is discarded. This threshold is one standard deviation above the mean over all $S_{q,T}$. Next, we identify false negative time-slices that occur during an action: if time slice t_i and t_{i+2} are candidates, then t_{i+1} is also considered a candidate. False-negative time-slices are often caused by brief interference with the action, such as a person walking in front of the actor as the action is performed. (The assumption is made that even the shortest action will span several time-slices, making the choice of n_f important.) Finally, remaining candidate time slices without neighbours are also discarded, as candidate regions are unlikely to be only n_f frames in length. (N.B. these last two steps are somewhat analogous to the region growing and shrinking methods found in image segmentation.) After this, any temporally contiguous set of time slices remaining are considered to be a single candidate for the action. The computational complexity of the entire localisation process is $O(|T|)$.

Performing these steps on all videos in the database, the system identifies a large set of candidate regions. A single feature frequency histogram H_c is generated over each candidate region, and $s(H_q, H_c)$ is used to rank the candidates by their relevance to the query. The top X of these are returned to the user. The entire process is shown in Figure 1.

3   Relevance Feedback

We can use relevance feedback (RF) to iteratively improve both the ranking and localisation aspects of our algorithm. After an initial search, RF can improve results by combining the original query with user feedback about the quality of the initial results, to generate a more discriminative query. Usually this second, more discriminative query will return better results than the original query. To date, RF has been used mostly in the image retrieval domain [17,18], but has also been applied to human action retrieval in more recent years [2].

In this work, relevance feedback occurs after the localisation and retrieval have been performed once as described above to give an initial ranking of videos. The user provides binary feedback on the relevance of several highly-ranked results, and the histograms associated with these results are used to train new localisation and retrieval algorithms. To improve localisation, we use the feedback histograms and the original query histogram to train an SVM, with the histogram intersection shown in equation 1 as the SVM's kernel. Then, to calculate the relevance of each time slice t, we measure the distance from the SVM's hyperplane to H_t. The rest of the localisation algorithm proceeds as described in §2.2. To improve our ranking with relevance feedback, we replace the histogram intersection shown in equation 1 with a simple query expansion metric that only utilises positive feedback pos. This query expansion takes the following form:

$$D_{t,pos} = min(s(H_p, H_t)|p \in pos\}) \qquad (2)$$

Applying relevance feedback to a system with localisation results in an unusual issue. Results returned to the user are often neither completely irrelevant nor completely relevant – a result may be mostly relevant, but imperfectly localised. In light of this problem, does the user have to manually re-localise the feedback both spatially and temporally before rerunning the query? Two methods of providing feedback are considered in our experiments.

4   Experiments

4.1   Setup

In this section, we describe experiments to demonstrate our algorithm. We use the MSR II human action dataset [19] based on its popular use in other human action localisation works. This dataset consists of 54 videos, totalling approximately 46 minutes of footage, containing 203 total examples of actions. The three classes of action are: handwaving, handclapping and boxing. These actions are performed orthogonally to the camera in a very similar fashion to one other, but the localisation is made more difficult due to various issues such movement of action-unrelated actors in the background and spatially/temporally overlapping actions.

During feature extraction, we extract, on average, 3 features per frame, at 4 different spatio-temporal scales. Because boxing can be performed to either the

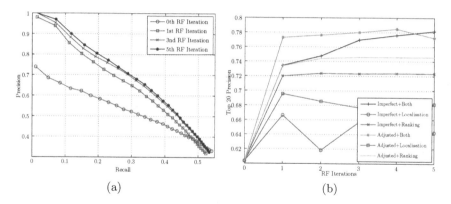

Fig. 2. (a) Precision-recall of localisation+retrieval after having performed relevance feedback iteratively. The improvements of successive RF iterations can be seen clearly here. (b) The precision (% of true positives) of the top 20 results after relevance feedback in different scenarios. We show both imperfect and user-adjusted relevance feedback. We also show the effects of applying relevance feedback to the localisation and ranking algorithms in isolation, to see their contributions to the overall improvement in precision.

left or the right, all features are also mirrored on the y-axis, giving an average of 24 features per frame. In the creation of the feature codebook, we use PCA to retain 95% of the total variance, and for clustering $k = 1000$.

Leave-one-out cross validation is performed, treating each of the 203 actions as the query in turn, averaging results over all runs. We use the following method to determine the accuracy of our localisation: let $L(E, G) = \frac{length(E \cap G)}{length(E \cup G)}$ where E is the temporal extent of the estimated action, and G is the temporal extent of the closest ground truth. An action is considered successfully localised when $L(E, G) \geq 0.5$. To simulate a user's relevance feedback, we use the ground truth to determine up to 5 examples of each of positive and negative feedback.

4.2   Results

Figure 2a shows a precision-recall graph using our optimal setup over the whole MSR II dataset, after various iterations of imperfect relevance feedback. Precision and recall are usually used in the context of binary relevance. To use these metrics with localised results, however, we need a way of determining whether an imperfectly localised result is still relevant. In [3], the authors determined relevance of a result differently for precision and recall. However, we contend that this method creates an unintuitive statistic, which cannot be interpreted in the same way as traditional precision-recall. We use the single, stricter criterion L, defined above for both precision and recall.

The effects of relevance feedback on the precision of the top 20 results is shown in Figure 2b. Only results that satisfy $L(E, G) \geq 0.5$ are considered for positive relevance feedback. Negative relevance feedback is taken from results where $L(E, G) = 0$. We have considered both "imperfect" feedback, unmodified from the results, and user-adjusted feedback, where the spatial and temporal extents of positive feedback are modified to exactly match the ground truth. While user-adjusted feedback performs better, imperfect feedback still shows a significant improvement after one and subsequent rounds of relevance feedback. This could have practical implications for the usability of a retrieval system with localisation. We also consider the effects of applying relevance feedback to only localisation, and only retrieval, to show their individual contribution to the overall improvement in precision.

We ran our experiments using MATLAB R2009a, on a 2.9GHz Core 2 Duo PC, with 4GB RAM, running 32-bit Windows 7. The database is 46 minutes in length, and the mean length of a query video is 5.7 seconds. The average time for a query with and without relevance feedback are 0.298 without relevance feedback, and 0.847 with relevance feedback, excluding offline computational costs. These times are at least an order of magnitude better than previous results. Our algorithm could also potentially be accelerated through programmatic optimisation, or its computational complexity reduced through a search of hierarchical time-slices according to size.

5   Discussion

We have created and demonstrated the use of an efficiency-focused video retrieval system with localisation. Our relatively simple localisation search can still give practical results, but completes in a fraction of the time of any previously reported algorithm. We have additionally looked at the application of relevance feedback in a retrieval context, and have shown that both user-adjusted and imperfect feedback can be used to improve results significantly.

Our proposed method's primary weakness, compared to existing algorithms, lies in its inability to separate spatially-distinct background noise from the results, which may cause incorrect ranking of the candidates. This has not significantly affected our results on the MSR II, but on more complex datasets, such as the HMDB[20] it may become a problem, particularly as the number of actions may decrease accuracy[21]. In future work, we will investigate ways to spatially isolate actions without the performance costs associated with branch-and-bound derived methods. Additionally, further experimentation needs to be done on more complex datasets, such as HMDB [20], to prove the algorithm's general applicability.

References

1. Zhang, H.J., Wu, J., Zhong, D., Smoliar, S.: An Integrated System for Content-based Video Retrieval and Browsing. Pattern Recognition 30(4), 643–658 (1997)
2. Jones, S., Shao, L., Zhang, J., Liu, Y.: Relevance Feedback for Real-World Human Action Retrieval. Pattern Recognition Lett. 33(4), 446–452 (2012)

3. Yu, G., Yuan, J., Liu, Z.: Unsupervised Random Forest Indexing for Fast Action Search. In: Proc. IEEE Conf. Comput. Vision and Pattern Recognition, pp. 865–872 (2011)
4. Rahmani, R., Goldman, S.A., Zhang, H., Krettek, J., Fritts, J.E.: Localized Content Based Image Retrieval. In: ACM SIGMM Int. Conf. Multimedia Inform. Retrieval, pp. 227–236 (2005)
5. Zhang, D., Wang, F., Shi, Z., Zhang, C.: Interactive Localized Content Based Image Retrieval With Multiple-Instance Active Learning. Pattern Recognition 43(2), 478–484 (2010)
6. Ryoo, M., Aggarwal, J.: Spatio-temporal Relationship Match: Video Structure Comparison for Recognition of Complex Human Activities. In: IEEE Int. Conf. Comput. Vision, pp. 1593–1600 (2009)
7. Poppe, R.: A survey on vision-based human action recognition. Image and Vision Computing 28(6), 976–990 (2010)
8. Davis, J.W., Bobick, A.F.: The Representation and Recognition of Human Movement Using Temporal Templates. In: Proc. IEEE Conf. Comput. Vision and Pattern Recognition, p. 928 (1997)
9. Laptev, I.: On Space-Time Interest Points. Int. J. Comput. Vision 64(2-3), 107–123 (2005)
10. Dollar, P., Rabaud, V., Cottrell, G., Belongie, S.: Behavior Recognition via Sparse Spatio-Temporal Features. In: Proc. IEEE Workshop Visual Surveillance and Performance Evaluation Tracking and Surveillance, pp. 65–72 (2005)
11. Shao, L., Du, Y.: Spatio-temporal Shape Contexts for Human Action Retrieval. In: Proc. Int. Workshop Interactive Multimedia Consumer Electronics, pp. 43–50 (2009)
12. Choi, J., Jeon, W.J., Lee, S.-C.: Spatio-temporal pyramid matching for sports videos. In: ACM SIGMM Int. Conf. Multimedia Inform. Retrieval, pp. 291–297 (2008)
13. Kläser, A., Marszałek, M., Schmid, C.: A Spatio-Temporal Descriptor Based on 3D-Gradients. In: Proc. British Mach. Vision Conf., pp. 995–1004 (2008)
14. Shao, L., Mattivi, R.: Feature Detector and Descriptor Evaluation in Human Action Recognition. In: Proc. ACM Int. Conf. Image and Video Retrieval, pp. 477–484 (2010)
15. Kläser, A., Marszalek, M., Schmid, C., Zisserman, A.: Human Focused Action Localization in Video. In: International Workshop on Sign, Gesture, Activity (2010)
16. Sullivan, J., Carlsson, S.: Recognizing and Tracking Human Action. In: Heyden, A., Sparr, G., Nielsen, M., Johansen, P. (eds.) ECCV 2002, Part I. LNCS, vol. 2350, pp. 629–644. Springer, Heidelberg (2002)
17. Tong, S., Chang, E.: Support Vector Machine Active Learning for Image Retrieval. In: Proc. ACM Multimedia, pp. 107–118 (2001)
18. Tao, D., Tang, X., Li, X., Wu, X.: Asymmetric Bagging and Random Subspace for Support Vector Machines-Based Relevance Feedback in Image Retrieval. IEEE Trans. Pattern Anal. Mach. Intell. 28, 1088–1099 (2006)
19. Cao, L., Liu, Z., Huang, T.: Cross-dataset Action Detection. In: Proc. IEEE Conf. Comput. Vision and Pattern Recognition, pp. 1998–2005 (2010)
20. Kuehne, H., Poggio, H.: HMDB: A Large Video Database for Human Motion Recognition. In: IEEE Int. Conf. Comput. Vision (2011)
21. Reddy, K., Shah, M.: Recognizing 50 human action categories of web videos. Mach. Vision and Applicat., 1–11 (2012)

Deformable Shape Reconstruction
from Monocular Video with Manifold Forests

Lili Tao and Bogdan J. Matuszewski

Applied Digital Signal and Image Processing Research Centre
University of Central Lancashire, UK
{lltao,bmatuszewski1}@uclan.ac.uk

Abstract. A common approach to recover structure of 3D deformable scene and camera motion from uncalibrated 2D video sequences is to assume that shapes can be accurately represented in linear subspaces. These methods are simple and have been proven effective for reconstructions of objects with relatively small deformations, but have considerable limitations when the deformations are large or complex. This paper describes a novel approach to reconstruction of deformable objects utilising a manifold decision forest technique. The key contribution of this work is the use of random decision forests for the shape manifold learning. The learned manifold defines constraints imposed on the reconstructed shapes. Due to nonlinear structure of the learned manifold, this approach is more suitable to deal with large and complex object deformations when compared to the linear constraints.

1 Introduction

Deformable shape recovery from a single uncalibrated camera is a challenging, underconstrained problem. The methods proposed to deal with this problem can be divided into three main categories: Low-rank shape models [9], shape trajectory approaches [1,5,6] and template based methods [13]. Most of the existing methods are restricted by the fact that they try to explain the complex deformations using a linear model.

Recent methods have integrated the manifold learning algorithm to regularise the shape reconstruction problem by constraining the shapes as to be well represented by the learned manifold. Using shape embedding as initialisation was introduced in [10]. Hamsici et.al [7] modelled the shape coefficients in a manifold feature space. The mapping was learned from the corresponding 2D measurement data of upcoming reconstructed shapes, rather than a fixed set of trajectory bases.

Contrary to other techniques using manifold in the shape reconstruction, our manifold is learned based on the 3D shapes rather than on 2D observations. The proposed implementation is based on the manifold forest method described in [4]. The main advantage of using manifold forest as compared for example to standard diffusion maps [3] is the fact that in the manifold forest the neighbourhood topology is learned from the data itself rather than being defined by the Euclidean distance. To the best of authors' knowledge, random forests technique has never been applied in the context of non-rigid shape reconstruction. This work is the first to integrate the ideas of manifold forests and deformable shape reconstruction.

R. Wilson et al. (Eds.): CAIP 2013, Part I, LNCS 8047, pp. 28–36, 2013.

1.1 Basic Formulation

Throughout this paper, vectors and matrices are denoted as lower- and upper-case bold letters, whereas sets are represented by calligraphic letters.

We assume that 2D points (features) are obtained from F frames under an orthographic camera projection model. The problem consists of shapes $\mathcal{S} = \{\mathbf{S}_1, \mathbf{S}_2, \ldots \mathbf{S}_F\}$ and camera rotations $\mathcal{R} = \{\mathbf{R}_1, \mathbf{R}_2, \ldots, \mathbf{R}_F\}$ recovery from 2D observations $\mathcal{Y} = \{\mathbf{Y}_1, \mathbf{Y}_2, \ldots, \mathbf{Y}_F\}$, thus can be formulated as the following optimisation problem,

$$\arg\min_{\mathcal{R}, \mathcal{S}} \sum_{t=1}^{F} \|\mathbf{Y}_t - \mathbf{P} \cdot \mathbf{R}_t \cdot \mathbf{S}_t\|^2 \tag{1}$$

where $\mathbf{P}$ represents orthographic camera projection matrix, $\mathbf{Y}_t$ is a $2 \times P$ matrix, and $\mathbf{S}_t \in \mathbb{R}^{3 \times P}$ contains coordinates of P 3D points describing shape in the tth frame. The shape $\mathbf{S}_t$ is represented as a linear combination of $n+1$ (where n is the dimension of the manifold introduced in Section 2.2) unknown but fixed basis shapes $\mathbf{X}_{tl}$: $\mathbf{S}_t = \sum_{l=1}^{n} \theta_{tl} \mathbf{X}_{tl}$. The camera translation has been eliminated by expressing 2D observations $\mathcal{Y}$ with respect to the data points centroid calculated in each observed image.

2 Manifold Forest

Random forests have become a popular method, given their capability to handle high dimensional data, efficiently avoid over-fitting without pruning, and possibility of parallel operation. This section gives a brief review of the randomized decision forests and their use in learning diffusion map manifolds. Although other choices are possible, this paper is focused only on the binary decision forest.

2.1 Randomized Decision Forest

The decision trees in our method are built by making decision in each node of the tree based on randomly selected features. A random decision forest is an ensemble of such decision trees. The trees are different and independent from each other.

Given a set of training data $\mathcal{X}$ with M samples: $\mathbf{X}_i \in \mathcal{X}, i = 1 \ldots M$, where each sample contains $3P$ features. The trees are randomised, by randomly selecting single feature at each internal node. The decision function at the internal node is used to decide whether the data $\mathbf{X}_i$ reaching that node should be assigned to its left or right child node. The threshold α_m of the decision function at node m is selected as result of the maximisation of the information gain:

$$\alpha_m^* = \arg\max_{\alpha_m} I_m \tag{2}$$

with the generic information gain I_m defined as:

$$I_m = H(\mathcal{X}_m) - \sum_{i \in \{L, R\}} \frac{|\mathcal{X}_m^i|}{|\mathcal{X}_m|} H(\mathcal{X}_m^i) \tag{3}$$

where $|.|$ indicate a cardinality for the dataset. $\mathcal{X}_m$ denotes the training data $\mathcal{X}$ reaching node m. $\mathcal{X}_m^L, \mathcal{X}_m^R$ are the subsets assigned to the left and right child nodes of node m.

In the paper it is assumed that data is adequately represented by the Gaussian distribution [4]. In that case the differential entropy $H(\mathcal{X}_m)$ can be calculated analytically as:

$$H(\mathcal{X}_m) = \frac{1}{2}\log(2\pi e |\Lambda|) \tag{4}$$

where Λ is the covariance matrix of $\mathcal{X}_m$. The trees are trained until the number of samples in a leaf is less than the pre-specified limit or the depth of the tree has exceeded the pre-defined depth.

Once the random forest has been trained, the new sample can be simply put through each tree. Depending on the result of the decision function at each internal node, the new data is sent to the left or right child node until it arrives at a leaf. The samples ending up in the same leaf are likely to be statistically similar and are expected to represent the same neighbourhood of the manifold. As such similarity measure is statistical in nature, thus the results is averaged over many decision trees. If the samples end up in the same leaf for the majority of the trees they are consider to be drawn from the similar location on the manifold.

2.2 Forest Model for Manifold Learning

In many problems, data is hard to be represented or analysed due to its high dimensional structure. However, such complex data might by governed by a small number of parameters. The goal of the manifold learning is to find the embedding function, mapping the data set $\mathcal{X}$ form a high, $N = 3P$ dimensional space to a reduced, n dimensional space.

The manifold forests are constructed upon diffusion maps [3] with the neighbourhood topology learned through random forest data clustering. It generates efficient representations of complex geometric structures even when the observed samples are non-uniformly distributed. The diffusion map is a graph based non-linear technique with isometric mapping from original shape space onto a lower dimensional diffusion space.

In the proposed method, the affinity model in manifold learning is built by applying random forest clustering. The data partition is defined based on the leaf node $l(.)$ the input data $\mathbf{X}_i$ would reach. The entries of the affinity matrix $\mathbf{W}^t$ for tree t are calculated as, $W_{ij}^t = e^{-L^t(\mathbf{X}_i, \mathbf{X}_j)}, i,j \in 1\ldots M$, where the distance L is obtained using binary affinity model:

$$L^t(\mathbf{X}_i, \mathbf{X}_j) = \begin{cases} 0 & l(\mathbf{X}_i) = l(\mathbf{X}_j) \\ \infty & \text{otherwise} \end{cases} \tag{5}$$

The binary model is simple and efficient and can be considered to be a parameter-free. However, as affinity matrix calculated based on a single tree is not representative, the ensemble of T trees is used to calculate the more accurate affinity matrix $\mathbf{W}$ by averaging over all affinity matrices from each single tree: $\mathbf{W} = \frac{1}{T}\sum_{t=1}^{T}\mathbf{W}^t$.

Coifman et al. presented a justification behind using normalised graph Laplacian [3] by connecting them to diffusion distance. Each entry of the diffusion operator $\mathbf{G}$ is constructed as $G(X_i, X_j) = W'_{ij}/\Upsilon_{ii}$ with $\Upsilon_{ii} = \sum_j W'_{ij}$. $\mathbf{W}'$ is a renormalised affinity matrix of $\mathbf{W}$ using an anisotropic normalised graph Laplacian, such that $W'_{ij} = W_{ij}/q_i q_j$ with $q_i = \sum_j W_{ij}$, $q_j = \sum_i W_{ji}$. The convergence of optimal embedding Ψ for diffusion maps is proven in [3] and is found via eigen-vectors φ and its corresponding n biggest eigenvalues λ of the operator $\mathbf{G}$, such that $1 = \lambda_0 > \lambda_1 \geq \ldots \geq \lambda_n$,

$$\Psi : \mathbf{X}_i \mapsto [\lambda_1 \varphi_1(\mathbf{X}_i), \cdots, \lambda_n \varphi_n(\mathbf{X}_i)]^T \tag{6}$$

3   Random Forests in 3D Reconstruction

Initialisation: Initial shapes and camera motion are estimated by running a few itera-tion of the optimisation process using the linear method described in [12]. Our method is not significantly sensitive to the initial solution as the method can iteratively update the shapes by projecting them on the learned manifold until convergence.

Mapping Out-of-Sample Points: The manifold forests method briefly described in Section 2 is used to find a meaningful representation of the data, but the mapping Ψ is only able to provide an embedding for the data present in the given training set. Suppose a new shape $\mathbf{S}_t \in \mathbb{R}^N$ becomes available after the manifold had been learned, instead of re-learning the manifold which is computationally expensive, an efficient way is to interpolate the shape onto the lower dimensional feature space. For each new shape, such embedding is calculated based on the Nyström extension [2],

Inverse Mapping: Given a point $\mathbf{b} \in \mathbb{R}^n$ in the reduced space, finding its inverse map-ping $\mathbf{S}_t = \Psi^{-1}(\mathbf{b})$ from the feature space back to the input space is a typical pre-image problem. As claimed in [2], the exact pre-image might not exist if the shape $\mathbf{S}_t$ has not been seen in the training set. However, according to the properties of isometric map-ping, if the points in the reduced space are relatively close, the corresponding shapes in high dimensional space should represent similar shapes since they have small diffusion distances. Based on this, the point $\mathbf{b}_t$ can be approximated as a linear combination of its weighted neighbouring points in feature space, such that $\mathbf{b}_t = \sum_{l=1}^{n+1} \theta_{tl} \mathbf{x}_{tl}$, where $\mathbf{x}_{tl}$ is the lth nearest point of $\mathbf{b}_t$ and the weights θ_{tl} are computed as the barycentric coordinates of $\mathbf{b}_t$. Once the weights are estimated, the shape $\mathbf{S}_t$ can be calculated as well based on a set of weighted training samples $\mathbf{S}_t = \sum_{l=1}^{n+1} \theta_{tl} \mathbf{X}_{tl}$, where the train-ing samples $\mathbf{X}_{tl}$ are the pre-images of $\mathbf{x}_{tl}$, and are equivalent to the basis shapes in Eq.1.

Non-linear Refinement: The cost function is given as,

$$\underset{\{\mathbf{R}_t\},\{\theta_{tl}\}}{\arg\min} \sum_{t=1}^{F} \|\mathbf{Y}_t - \mathbf{P} \cdot \mathbf{R}_t \cdot \mathbf{S}_t\|^2 + \varphi_S \sum_{t=2}^{F} \|\mathbf{S}_t - \mathbf{S}_{t-1}\|^2 + \varphi_R \sum_{t=1}^{F} \varepsilon_{rot}$$

$$\text{with} \sum_{l=1}^{n+1} \theta_{tl} = 1, 0 \leq \theta_t \leq 1 \tag{7}$$

where $\varepsilon_{rot} = \left\| \mathbf{R}_t \cdot \mathbf{R}_t^T - \mathbf{I} \right\|^2$ enforces orthonomality of all $\mathbf{R}_t$. φ_S and φ_R are regu-larisation constants.

However, the underlying problem is that the quality of the optimisation result is strongly depending on the accuracy of initial shapes. To avoid this, we update the basis shapes in each iteration until 2D measurement error is less than the defined threshold (10^{-3} in our case) and the error between two adjacent frames is relatively small.

4   Results and Discussion

A number of experiments were carried out to evaluate the proposed method. Several state-of-the-art algorithms were evaluated and compared in these experiments:
RF: The proposed random forest method; **DM**: The diffusion maps based method. The DM method is similar to the RF except the manifold learning was implemented without random forest. [11]; **MP**: The metric projection method [9]; **PTA**: The discrete cosine transform (DCT) based point trajectory approach [1]; **CSF**: The column space fitting method [5]; **KSFM**: The kernel non-rigid structure from motion approach [6]; **IPCA**: The incremental principal components analysis based method [12].

The data which were used for evaluation include: two articulated face sequences, *surprise* and *talking*, both captured using passive 3-D scanner with 3D tracking of 83 facial landmarks [8]; two surface models, *cardboard* and *cloth* [13]; two human actions, *walking* and *stretch*, and three dance sequences: *dance*, *Indian dance* and *Capoeira* from CMU motion capture database[1]. This paper is not focusing on feature detection and tracking. In the experiments described here the 3D points are known and these were projected onto the image sequences under the orthographic camera model and subsequently used as features. Diffusion maps require training process, so training datasets for two face sequences were taken from the BU-3DFE [14] and for two surface sequences the data were obtained from [13]. Since no separate training data are provided for CMU database, half of each sequence was used for manifold learning and the other half for testing. All the training data has been rigidly co-registered, the same testing data has been used with the methods which do not require training.

4.1   Quantitative Evaluation

Different Number of Bases n: The accuracy of reconstruction is affected by the dimensionality of the reduced space n, corresponding to number of shape basis. The first test looked at the relation between manifold dimensionality and the shape reconstruction error. The 9 sequences were separated into 3 groups: small deformation (*Surprise*, *Talking*, *Cardboard*), large deformation (*Cloth*, *Walking*, *Stretch*) and all the dance sequences representing very large and complex deformations. The forests have been trained with the average 600 number of trees. The results in Fig.1(left) show that with increasing dimension of the reduced space n the shape reconstruction error is reduced. As expected, a higher number of bases is required to describe a complex shape deformation, e.g. dance sequences.

Fig.1(right) shows the comparison results on stretch sequence which were produced by the proposed method and the previous methods. The error calculated for PTA, CSF and KSFM varies with the number of bases and indeed increases for $n>12$ demonstrating that the problem becomes ill-conditions. DM and RF methods are "more stable" as the solution is strongly constrained by the requirement that it belongs to the manifold.

Measurement Data with Noise: In order to assess the performance of the reconstruction methods when the observed data is corrupted by noise, the next experiment

---

[1] The data was obtained from `http://mocap.cs.cmu.edu`

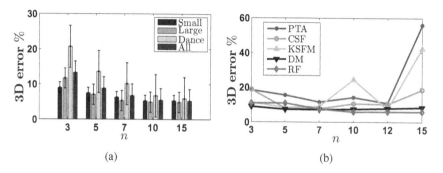

(a)   (b)

Fig. 1. Reconstruction 3D error as a function of the number of bases n. (left) Errors produced by RF. Bars left to right: Group of small deformation sequences, large deformation sequences, all dance sequences, all the sequences; (right) Comparison results on stretch sequence.

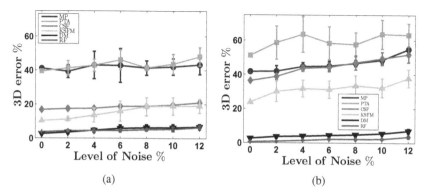

(a)   (b)

Fig. 2. Reconstruction results on *walking* (left) and *capoeira* (right) sequences with Gaussian noise

compared the RF method against previously proposed methods in terms of shape reconstruction error expressed as a function of level of noise in the observed data. We ran 10 trials for each experiment for each level of noise using *walking* and *capoeira* sequences respectively. It can be noticed that although the performance of all six algorithms decreases with the level of noise, two non-linear methods DM and RF are clearly superior and achieve smaller standard deviations, whereas others are quite sensitive with large mean error and error dispersion. Even though RF and DM provide comparable performance in walking, as expected RF outperforms DM in the cases of recovery of more complex deformations, e.g. *capoeira* sequence.

4.2 Qualitative Evaluation

Motion Capture Data: Table 1 shows the 3D reconstruction error for RF, DM, IPCA and KSFM which on average provide better results than other trajectory based methods. The relative normalised means of the 3D error [6] are compared over all frames and all

Table 1. Relative normalised mean reconstruction 3D error in percentages for KSFM, IPCA, DM and RF methods. The optimal number of bases n, for which the 3D errors are shown in the table, is given in brackets for each tested method.

	KSFM	IPCA	DM	RF		
				Initial	No Opt.	Opt.
Surprise	3.81(4)	12.89	3.52(10)	31.54	29.29	**2.41**(15)
Talking	4.98(4)	9.86	3.50(10)	96.57	8.37	**3.43**(10)
Cardboard	27.53(2)	24.45	10.64(10)	26.74	16.06	**9.40**(10)
Cloth	18.06(2)	19.09	2.87(7)	29.67	17.29	**2.54**(7)
Walking	10.29(5)	32.64	**2.65**(9)	35.02	16.31	3.69(15)
IndianDance	23.43(7)	34.40	9.81(10)	29.69	12.82	**5.55**(15)
Capoeira	23.76(7)	40.59	2.58(9)	40.59	29.2	**0.54**(10)
Stretch	7.36(12)	19.18	6.87(6)	26.23	17.08	**5.88**(10)
Dance	23.69(4)	30.58	16.76(7)	26.08	15.30	**11.69**(15)

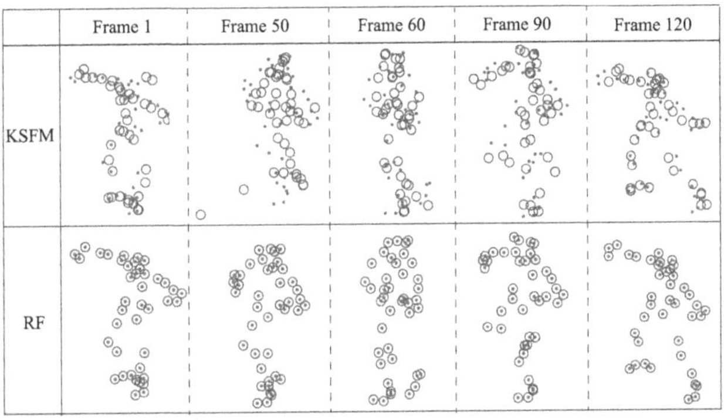

Fig. 3. Reconstruction results on the *Indian Dance* sequence. Reconstructed 3D shapes (circles), with ground truth (dots) are shown.

points. For RF method the initialisation error and the error produced by the proposed algorithm with and without non-linear refinement are presented. The errors shown in the table correspond to the optimal n value selection. This is achieved by running the trials with n varying from 2 to 15. The best selected n value for each tested method is shown in brackets. The reconstructed shapes are aligned using a single global rotation based on Procrustes alignment [1]. As shown in the table, RF has better performance than other methods, especially for the large deformations. Even though the initial error is big, the RF method is still able to provide accurate reconstruction results.

Fig.3 shows three randomly selected reconstructed shapes from the *Indian Dance* sequence using KSFM and RF methods. More comparison results for DM against other methods can be found in [11].

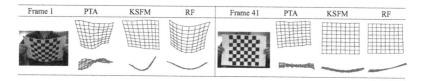

Fig. 4. Selected 2D frames from the video sequence of a paper bending. Front and top views of the corresponding 3D reconstructed results using the proposed method (RF), PTA and KSFM.

Real Data: The algorithms used in the motion capture experiments above are applied to real data in Fig.4. In the video, 81 point features were tracked along 61 frames showing approximately two periods of paper bending movement.

5 Conclusions

In this paper a new approach for monocular reconstruction of non-rigid object is described. The method performs particularly well, when compared to other methods, especially for large and complex deformations. The method combines the ideas of non-linear manifold learning and deformable shape reconstruction. The non-linear manifold has been build upon diffusion maps with random forests used to estimate local manifold neighbourhood topology. The method has the potential to be extended to handle cases with missing data and to be implemented for real time reconstructions. The proposed method shows a significant improvement for the reconstruction of large deformable objects, even though, due to the lack of training data, the manifold is built using only limited number of shapes. Further possible improvements include building a sufficiently dense representation of the manifold by collecting and generating more training data.

References

1. Akhter, I., Sheikh, Y., Khan, S., Kanade, T.: Trajectory space: A dual representation for nonrigid structure from motion. IEEE PAMI 33, 1442–1456 (2011)
2. Arias, P., Randall, G., Sapiro, G.: Connecting the out-of sample and pre-image problems in kernel methods. In: ICPR, pp. 1–8 (2007)
3. Coifman, R., Lafon, S.: Diffusion maps. Appl. Comp. Harm. Anal. 21, 5–30 (2006)
4. Criminisi, A., Shotton, J., Konukoglu, E.: Decision forests: A unified framework for classification, regression, density estimation, manifold learning and semi-supervised learning. Foundations and Trends in Computer Graphics and Computer Vision 7, 81–227 (2012)
5. Gotardo, P., Martinez, A.M.: Computing smooth time-trajectories for camera and deformable shape in structure from motion with occlusion. IEEE PAMI 33, 2051–2065 (2011)
6. Gotardo, P., Martinez, A.M.: Kernel non-rigid structure from motion. In: ICCV, pp. 802–809 (2011)
7. Hamsici, O.C., Gotardo, P.F.U., Martinez, A.M.: Learning spatially-smooth mappings in nonrigid structure from motion. In: Fitzgibbon, A., Lazebnik, S., Perona, P., Sato, Y., Schmid, C. (eds.) ECCV 2012, Part IV. LNCS, vol. 7575, pp. 260–273. Springer, Heidelberg (2012)

8. Matuszewski, B., Quan, W., Shark, L.-K., McLoughlin, A., Lightbody, C., Emsley, H., Watkins, C.: Hi4d–adsip 3d dynamic facial articulation database. Image and Vision Computing 10, 713–727 (2012)
9. Paladini, M., Bue, A., Xavier, J., Stosic, M., Dodig, M., Agapito, L.: Factorization for non-rigid and articulated structure using metric projections. In: CVPR, pp. 2898–2905 (2009)
10. Rabaud, V., Belongie, S.: Linear embeddings in non-rigid structure from motion. In: CVPR, pp. 2427–2434 (2009)
11. Tao, L., Matuszewski, B.J.: Non-rigid strucutre from motion with diffusion maps prior. In: CVPR (2013)
12. Tao, L., Matuszewski, B.J., Mein, S.J.: Non-rigid structure from motion with incremental shape prior. In: ICIP, pp. 1753–1756 (2012)
13. Varol, A., Salzmann, M., Fua, P., Urtasun, R.: A constrained latent variable model. In: CVPR, pp. 2248–2255 (2012)
14. Yin, L., Wei, X., Sun, Y., Wang, J., Rosato, M.: A 3d face expression database for facial behavior research. In: AFGR, pp. 211–216 (2006)

Multi-SVM Multi-instance Learning for Object-Based Image Retrieval

Fei Li[1], Rujie Liu[1], and Takayuki Baba[2]

[1] Fujitsu Research & Development Center Co., Ltd., Beijing, China
{lifei,rjliu}@cn.fujitsu.com
[2] Fujitsu Laboratories Ltd., Kawasaki, Japan
baba-t@jp.fujitsu.com

Abstract. Object-based image retrieval has been an active research topic in recent years, in which a user is only interested in some object in the images. The recently proposed methods try to comprehensively use both image- and region-level features for more satisfactory performance, but they either cannot well explore the relationship between the two kinds of features or lead to heavy computational load. In this paper, by adopting support vector machine (SVM) as the basic classifier, a novel multi-instance learning method is proposed. To deal with the different forms of image- and region-level representations, standard SVM and multi-instance SVM are utilized respectively. Moreover, the relationship between images and their segmented regions is also taken into account. A unified optimization framework is developed to involve all the available information, and an efficient iterative solution is introduced. Experimental results on the benchmark data set demonstrate the effectiveness of our proposal.

Keywords: Object-based image retrieval, support vector machine, multi-instance learning.

1 Introduction

With the explosive growth of the number of digital images, effective and efficient retrieval technique is in urgent need. Since a user usually pays attention to some object instead of the whole image, if only overall characteristics are used for image description, the retrieval performance is often unsatisfactory. To deal with the problem, object-based (or localized content-based) image retrieval is proposed, and much related work has been developed [1], [2].

As an effective approach to describe the relationship between whole and part, multi-instance learning has been widely used in image analysis [3], [4]. In this learning framework, each sample is called a bag, and contains several instances. The available labels are only assigned for bags, and the relationship between bag and instance is that a bag is positive if at least one instance in it is positive, otherwise it is negative. In order to involve object-based image retrieval into the framework of multi-instance learning, images are first segmented into regions, and then images and regions are treated as bags and instances, respectively.

R. Wilson et al. (Eds.): CAIP 2013, Part I, LNCS 8047, pp. 37–44, 2013.

According to the adopted image representation, the existing multi-instance retrieval methods can be divided into two categories. In the first category, only region features are used. To transform region-level multi-instance learning into image-level single-instance learning, MISSL [5] calculates the weighted edges of image-level graph based on region similarities, while EC-SVM [6] maps all the images into a new space spanned by some selected regions. No matter which approach is utilized, some useful information is inevitably lost during the transformation process, and this may influence the final performance. Another usually adopted idea is to directly conduct region-level multi-instance learning, and graph-based methods are often used. In [7], real-valued labels are first assigned to the selected underlying positive regions, and then propagated to the regions of all the database images. GMIL [8] considers the relationship between images and their segmented regions as the fitting constraint of an optimization problem. Since both graph-based learning and multi-instance learning are well involved in a unified framework, it achieves the state-of-the-art performance.

In the other category of methods, both image- and region-level representations are adopted. Although global characteristics cannot effectively describe the user-interested object, some features, especially image-level statistical description of local descriptors, are also useful for image retrieval. Therefore, it is hoped that more satisfactory performance can be obtained by comprehensively utilizing the two kinds of information. In [9], two image-level graphs are constructed, one is directly from image-level features, and the other is from region-level features by a suitable conversion strategy. Then the corresponding propagation matrices are linearly combined and graph-based learning is conducted. Since the two kinds of representations are dealt with separately and only combined via graphs, the available information is not well explored. In the method of multi-graph multi-instance learning [10], both image- and region-level graphs are constructed. To address the problem of their different sizes, the whole learning process is conducted in an optimization framework. And the relationship between images, the relationship between regions, as well as the relationship between images and their segmented regions, are all well involved. Although effective, there are many variables in the optimization problem, and the final solution is obtained by iterative calculation, so its computational load is quite heavy.

In this paper, for exploring both image- and region-level information, we present a novel multi-instance image retrieval method based on support vector machine (SVM). Considering the different forms of the two kinds of features, image-level SVM and region-level multi-instance SVM are adopted respectively. In order to construct two classifiers at the same time, similarly as [10], a unified optimization framework is developed, and the relationship between images and their segmented regions is also involved. Although iterative calculation is still needed to get the final results, since less variables are involved, our proposal is efficient enough for practical applications.

The rest of the paper is organized as follows. Section 2 describes our proposed multi-SVM multi-instance learning method. Our experimental results are presented in Section 3, and it is followed by some conclusions in Section 4.

2 Multi-SVM Multi-instance Learning

In this section, first we explain the ways to represent images by two kinds of features. Then we present the unified optimization framework to construct image-level SVM and region-level multi-instance SVM, and talk about its solution.

2.1 Image Representation

Suppose there are altogether M training images denoted as $\{I_1, I_2, \cdots, I_M\}$, and each image I_m $(m = 1, 2, \cdots, M)$ corresponds to a category label $y_m \in \{-1, 1\}$. After segmentation, image I_m is represented by a set of regions. Let the total number of regions from all the training images be N. When it is unnecessary to point out the corresponding images, the regions are denoted as $\{R_1, R_2, \cdots, R_N\}$. To describe the relationship between image and region, we use $R_n \in I_m$ to indicate that R_n is a region in image I_m. The extracted image- and region-level features are denoted as $\{x_1^I, x_2^I, \cdots, x_M^I\}$ and $\{x_1^R, x_2^R, \cdots, x_N^R\}$, respectively. In this way, image I_m can be described by either a vector x_m^I or a set of vectors $\{x_n^R | R_n \in I_m\}$.

2.2 Optimization Framework

Based on the idea of maximizing the geometric margin, SVM [11] has shown its effectiveness in many fields. With vector-formed image-level features, a linear SVM can be constructed by solving the optimization problem

$$\min_{\mathbf{w}^I, b^I, \xi^I} Q_1 = \min_{\mathbf{w}^I, b^I, \xi^I} \frac{1}{2} \left\| \mathbf{w}^I \right\|^2 + C^I \sum_{m=1}^{M} \xi_m^I \tag{1}$$

s.t. $y_m f(x_m^I) \geq 1 - \xi_m^I, \quad \xi_m^I \geq 0, \quad (m = 1, 2, \cdots, M).$

where $\mathbf{w}^I$ and b^I are classifier parameters and the classification function is defined as $f(x_m^I) = \mathbf{w}^I \cdot x_m^I + b^I$, "·" denotes the inner product of two vectors, ξ_m^I $(m = 1, 2, \cdots, M)$ are slack variables, and $C^I > 0$ is a penalty parameter.

For region-level representation, as each image is described by a set of feature vectors, standard SVM cannot be directly adopted. According to the basic idea of multi-instance learning, the classification results of a bag can be determined by the instance with the maximum classification function value. In this way, multi-instance learning is introduced into the framework of SVM [12], and a linear multi-instance SVM with region-level features can be constructed by

$$\min_{\mathbf{w}^R, b^R, \xi^R} Q_2 = \min_{\mathbf{w}^R, b^R, \xi^R} \frac{1}{2} \left\| \mathbf{w}^R \right\|^2 + C^R \sum_{m=1}^{M} \xi_m^R \tag{2}$$

s.t. $y_m \max_{R_n \in I_m} g(x_n^R) \geq 1 - \xi_m^R, \quad \xi_m^R \geq 0, \quad (m = 1, 2, \cdots, M).$

where $\mathbf{w}^R$ and b^R are classifier parameters and the classification function is defined as $g(x_n^R) = \mathbf{w}^R \cdot x_n^R + b^R$, ξ_m^R $(m = 1, 2, \cdots, M)$ are also slack variables, and $C^R > 0$ is also a penalty parameter.

To avoid separately constructing image-level SVM and region-level multi-instance SVM, a cost item corresponding to the relationship between images and their segmented regions is introduced. Since the classification results can be determined by either image- or region-level features, their corresponding classification function values should be consistent with each other, thus the cost item is defined as

$$Q_3 = \sum_{m=1}^{M} L\left(y_m f(\mathbf{x}_m^I), \ y_m \max_{R_n \in I_m} g(\mathbf{x}_n^R)\right) \tag{3}$$

where $L(x, y)$ is a suitable distance measure. Squared Euclidean distance is usually adopted, but here we only want to involve the distance when the classification results are believable. Considering the characteristic of SVM, larger value of $y_m f(\mathbf{x}_m^I)$ or $y_m \max_{R_n \in I_m} g(\mathbf{x}_n^R)$ indicates more confidence on the result, and only when the value is larger than 1, the corresponding slack variable is 0. Therefore, the measure is defined as

$$L(x, y) = (\max\{x, 1\} - \max\{y, 1\})^2 \tag{4}$$

It should be noted that if $y_m f(\mathbf{x}_m^I) > 1$ and $y_m \max_{R_n \in I_m} g(\mathbf{x}_n^R) < 1$, only the difference between $y_m f(\mathbf{x}_m^I)$ and 1 is considered. This is because the difference between 1 and $y_m \max_{R_n \in I_m} g(\mathbf{x}_n^R)$ has already been embodied by the corresponding slack variable. The case is similar when $y_m f(\mathbf{x}_m^I) < 1$ and $y_m \max_{R_n \in I_m} g(\mathbf{x}_n^R) > 1$.

By taking all the aforementioned issues in a unified framework, the final optimization problem is formulated as

$$\min_{\mathbf{w}^I, b^I, \xi^I, \mathbf{w}^R, b^R, \xi^R} Q_1 + \alpha Q_2 + \beta Q_3$$

$$= \min_{\mathbf{w}^I, b^I, \xi^I, \mathbf{w}^R, b^R, \xi^R} \left[\frac{1}{2} \|\mathbf{w}^I\|^2 + C^I \sum_{m=1}^{M} \xi_m^I + \alpha \left(\frac{1}{2} \|\mathbf{w}^R\|^2 + C^R \sum_{m=1}^{M} \xi_m^R \right) \right.$$

$$\left. + \beta \sum_{m=1}^{M} L\left(y_m f(\mathbf{x}_m^I), \ y_m \max_{R_n \in I_m} g(\mathbf{x}_n^R)\right) \right] \tag{5}$$

$$\text{s.t.} \begin{cases} y_m f(\mathbf{x}_m^I) \geq 1 - \xi_m^I, \quad \xi_m^I \geq 0, \qquad (m = 1, 2, \cdots, M); \\ y_m \max_{R_n \in I_m} g(\mathbf{x}_n^R) \geq 1 - \xi_m^R, \quad \xi_m^R \geq 0, \quad (m = 1, 2, \cdots, M). \end{cases}$$

where α and β are combination coefficients.

2.3   Solution to Optimization Problem

In this paper, the above problem is treated as joint optimization for $\{\mathbf{w}^I, b^I, \xi^I\}$ and $\{\mathbf{w}^R, b^R, \xi^R\}$. In order to solve it, an iterative approach is proposed, in which image-level SVM and region-level multi-instance SVM are constructed respectively, and the details are explained as follows.

Either $\{\mathbf{w}^I, b^I, \xi^I\}$ or $\{\mathbf{w}^R, b^R, \xi^R\}$ can be adopted in the first iteration, and their original values are calculated by (1) or (2).

With fixed $\{\mathbf{w}^R, b^R, \xi^R\}$, the optimization problem (5) is reduced to

$$\min_{\mathbf{w}^I, b^I, \xi^I} \frac{1}{2} \left\| \mathbf{w}^I \right\|^2 + C^I \sum_{m=1}^{M} \xi_m^I + \beta \sum_{m=1}^{M} \left(\max\left\{ y_m f(\mathbf{x}_m^I), 1 \right\} - \Delta_m^R \right)^2 \quad (6)$$

s.t. $\quad y_m f(\mathbf{x}_m^I) \geq 1 - \xi_m^I, \qquad \xi_m^I \geq 0, \qquad (m = 1, 2, \cdots, M).$

where $\Delta_m^R = \max\left\{ y_m \max\limits_{R_n \in I_m} g(\mathbf{x}_n^R), 1 \right\}$. By introducing new variables $\lambda_m^I \ (m = 1, 2, \cdots, M)$, we can further rewrite (6) as

$$\min_{\mathbf{w}^I, b^I, \xi^I, \lambda^I} \frac{1}{2} \left\| \mathbf{w}^I \right\|^2 + C^I \sum_{m=1}^{M} \xi_m^I + \beta \sum_{m=1}^{M} \left(1 + \lambda_m^I - \Delta_m^R \right)^2 \quad (7)$$

s.t. $\quad \begin{cases} y_m f(\mathbf{x}_m^I) \geq 1 - \xi_m^I, \quad \xi_m^I \geq 0, \quad (m = 1, 2, \cdots, M); \\ y_m f(\mathbf{x}_m^I) \leq 1 + \lambda_m^I, \quad \lambda_m^I \geq 0, \quad (m = 1, 2, \cdots, M). \end{cases}$

By changing it to its dual problem, we can solve the problem of quadratic programming efficiently.

While with fixed $\{\mathbf{w}^I, b^I, \xi^I\}$, the optimization problem (5) becomes

$$\min_{\mathbf{w}^R, b^R, \xi^R} \alpha \left(\frac{1}{2} \left\| \mathbf{w}^R \right\|^2 + C^R \sum_{m=1}^{M} \xi_m^R \right) + \beta \sum_{m=1}^{M} \left(\max\left\{ y_m \max\limits_{R_n \in I_m} g(\mathbf{x}_n^R), 1 \right\} - \Delta_m^I \right)^2 (8)$$

s.t. $\quad y_m \max\limits_{R_n \in I_m} g(\mathbf{x}_n^R) \geq 1 - \xi_m^R, \qquad \xi_m^R \geq 0, \qquad (m = 1, 2, \cdots, M).$

where $\Delta_m^I = \max\left\{ y_m f(\mathbf{x}_m^I), 1 \right\}$. To deal with the problem, similarly as [12], for image I_m, a selector variables is defined as

$$S_m = \arg\max_{n: R_n \in I_m} g(\mathbf{x}_n^R) \quad (9)$$

Then (8) can be written as

$$\min_{\mathbf{w}^R, b^R, \xi^R} \alpha \left(\frac{1}{2} \left\| \mathbf{w}^R \right\|^2 + C^R \sum_{m=1}^{M} \xi_m^R \right) + \beta \sum_{m=1}^{M} \left(\max\left\{ y_m g(\mathbf{x}_{S_m}^R), 1 \right\} - \Delta_m^I \right)^2 (10)$$

s.t. $\quad y_m g(\mathbf{x}_{S_m}^R) \geq 1 - \xi_m^R, \qquad \xi_m^R \geq 0, \qquad (m = 1, 2, \cdots, M).$

It can be seen that (10) is with the same form as (6). If the values of S_m $(m = 1, 2, \cdots, M)$ are determined, (10) can also be solved by the aforementioned method. Therefore, the final solution of the original problem (8) can be obtained by iteratively calculating (9) and (10).

So far, only linear SVM is adopted in our proposal. As only the inner product of feature vectors is involved in the dual problem for solving (6) and (8), kernel trick can be easily introduced in our proposed optimization framework, and nonlinear SVM can also be utilized conveniently.

After the iterative process has converged, all the parameters for the two classifiers can be calculated. For a database image I_t with image-level feature $\mathbf{x}_t^I$

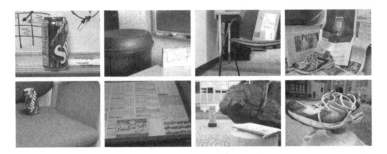

Fig. 1. Example images in the SIVAL data set

and region-level features $\{\mathbf{x}_s^R | R_s \in I_t\}$, the final classification function $h(I_t)$ is determined by combining the two kinds of information together

$$h(I_t) = \omega f(\mathbf{x}_t^I) + (1 - \omega) \max_{R_s \in I_t} g(\mathbf{x}_s^R) \qquad (11)$$

where ω $(0 \le \omega \le 1)$ is a tunable combination parameter and can simply set to 0.5 for convenience. Then the images with the largest values of $h(I_t)$ are returned as the retrieval results.

3   Experimental Results

The proposed method is evaluated on the SIVAL (Spatially Independent, Variable Area, and Lighting) image benchmark, which is widely used for multi-instance learning. It consists of 25 different categories, each includes 60 images. The images in one category contain the same object photographed against highly diverse backgrounds. The object may occur anywhere in the images and may be photographed at a wide-angle or close up. Some example images are shown in Fig. 1. All the images in the data set have been segmented, and each region is represented by a 30-dimensional feature vector.

We conduct 30 independent runs for all the categories in the database. In each category, 8 positive and 8 negative images are randomly selected as training samples. To compare with other methods, we also use the area under the receiver operating characteristic curve (AUC) as the performance measure.

For image representation, the method of locality-constrained linear coding [13] is adopted for constructing image-level features, and the region-level features provided by the data set are directly used after normalization. The parameters in the optimization framework are set as follows. The penalty parameters C^I and C^R are set to 1000. The combination coefficients α and β are set to 1 and 100, respectively. Nonlinear SVMs are constructed in the experiments, in which Gaussian kernel $K(\mathbf{u}, \mathbf{v}) = \exp\left(-\gamma\|\mathbf{u} - \mathbf{v}\|^2\right)$ is adopted, and γ is set to 0.001.

The methods used for comparison include multi-graph multi-instance learning (MGMIL) [10], multi-instance learning based on region-level graph (GMIL) [8], support vector machine with evidence region identification (EC-SVM) [6], as well as image-level semi-supervised multi-instance learning (MISSL) [5]. The average

Table 1. Average AUC values and 95%-confidence intervals over 30 independent runs on the SIVAL data set

	Our proposal	MGMIL	GMIL	EC-SVM	MISSL
FabricSoftenerBox	**99.1±0.5**	95.8±0.7	94.6±0.6	97.9±0.5	97.7±0.3
WD40Can	**95.7±1.0**	92.3±1.0	84.9±1.1	94.3±0.6	93.9±0.9
DataMiningBook	**95.3±0.9**	93.0±0.9	84.8±1.6	75.0±2.4	77.3±4.3
RapBook	**95.1±0.9**	87.0±1.0	77.0±1.7	68.6±2.3	61.3±2.8
GreenTeaBox	**95.1±1.8**	90.4±0.9	93.1±0.8	86.9±2.2	80.4±3.5
CheckeredScarf	94.0±1.0	89.3±0.9	94.0±0.6	**96.9±0.5**	88.9±0.7
AjaxOrange	93.3±1.3	**93.9±0.7**	88.2±1.2	93.8±2.1	90.0±2.1
GoldMedal	**91.2±1.1**	85.3±1.6	80.4±1.7	87.5±1.4	83.4±2.7
FeltFlowerRug	90.6±1.4	89.2±1.2	94.1±0.6	**94.2±0.8**	90.5±1.1
SpriteCan	**90.3±1.0**	79.7±1.4	79.4±1.3	85.4±1.2	81.2±1.5
SmileyFaceDoll	**89.7±1.3**	83.8±1.2	81.1±1.4	84.6±1.9	80.7±2.0
CokeCan	88.8±1.7	89.4±1.4	85.3±0.8	**94.6±0.8**	93.3±0.9
TranslucentBowl	**88.7±1.9**	79.3±1.7	79.6±1.3	74.2±3.2	63.2±5.2
BlueScrunge	**88.7±2.1**	80.4±1.4	73.4±1.8	74.1±2.4	76.8±5.2
JuliesPot	**88.5±2.0**	87.3±1.5	87.1±1.6	67.3±3.3	68.0±5.2
DirtyRunningShoe	86.7±1.6	82.9±1.1	89.5±0.8	**90.3±1.3**	78.2±1.6
CardboardBox	**86.6±1.5**	81.2±1.2	85.0±1.3	85.6±1.6	69.6±2.5
DirtyWorkGloves	81.0±1.9	80.1±1.2	78.1±1.7	**83.0±1.3**	73.8±3.4
Banana	**78.2±2.2**	77.1±0.9	69.5±1.6	69.1±2.9	62.4±4.3
StripedNotebook	77.4±1.7	73.8±1.3	**83.7±1.7**	75.6±2.3	70.2±2.9
CandleWithHolder	76.0±1.9	76.0±1.3	81.0±1.5	**88.1±1.1**	84.5±0.8
Apple	**75.0±2.1**	73.5±1.3	72.7±1.5	68.0±2.6	51.1±4.4
GlazedWoodPot	73.5±1.3	74.9±1.1	**76.4±1.2**	68.0±2.8	51.5±3.3
LargeSpoon	71.8±1.4	**73.7±1.3**	64.3±1.4	61.3±1.8	50.2±2.1
WoodRollingPin	69.7±1.2	70.3±1.2	**72.4±1.9**	66.9±1.7	51.6±2.6
Average	**86.4**	83.2	82.0	81.3	74.8

AUC values and the 95%-confidence intervals for our proposal and the other four methods are listed in Table 1. We can see that the overall performance of our proposal is the best. In all the 25 categories, our proposal achieves highest AUC values on 14 categories. Especially for "RapBook", "TranslucentBowl", and "BlueScrunge", the performance can be improved by more than 8%. MGMIL also adopts both image- and region-level representations. As image-level features can provide additional information, it outperforms GMIL, EC-SVM and MISSL, in which only region features are considered. Comparing MGMIL with our proposal, the main difference is that graph-based learning is involved in MGMIL, while SVM is introduced as the basic classifier in our method. The superior of our proposal demonstrates the advantage of exploring information in the feature space over analyzing relationship between graph nodes.

As far as computational load is concerned, we also compare our proposal with MGMIL. Both the methods develop optimization frameworks based on two kinds of features, but the numbers of involved variables are different. MGMIL wants to calculate the soft labels for images and regions, while our proposal aims to construct effective SVMs. In general, the number of all the images and regions is larger than the number of classifier parameters, hence our proposal often costs less time than MGMIL.

4 Conclusions

In this paper, a novel multi-SVM multi-instance learning method is proposed for object-based image retrieval. According to the two kinds of representations, image-level SVM and region-level multi-instance SVM are adopted respectively. For comprehensively utilizing the available information, a unified optimization framework is developed, and the relationship between images and their segmented regions is also taken into consideration to avoid constructing the two classifiers separately. An iterative approach is introduced to solve the optimization problem. It is demonstrated that our proposal is both effective and efficient for image retrieval.

References

1. Rahmani, R., Goldman, S.A., Zhang, H., Krettek, J., Fritts, J.E.: Localized content based image retrieval. In: Proc. ACM SIGMM Int. Workshop Multimedia Information Retrieval, pp. 227–236 (2005)
2. Zheng, Q.-F., Wang, W.-Q., Gao, W.: Effective and efficient object-based image retrieval using visual phrases. In: Proc. ACM Int. Conf. Multimedia, pp. 77–80 (2006)
3. Chen, Y., Bi, J., Wang, J.Z.: MILES: Multiple-instance learning via embedded instance selection. IEEE Trans. Pattern Analysis and Machine Intelligence 28(12), 1931–1947 (2006)
4. Feng, S., Xu, D.: Transductive multi-instance multi-label learning algorithm with application to automatic image annotation. Expert Systems with Applications 37, 661–670 (2010)
5. Rahmani, R., Goldman, S.A.: MISSL: Multiple-instance semi-supervised learning. In: Proc. Int. Conf. Machine Learning, pp. 705–712 (2006)
6. Li, W.-J., Yeung, D.-Y.: Localized content-based image retrieval through evidence region identification. In: Proc. IEEE Int. Conf. Computer Vision and Pattern Recognition, pp. 1666–1673 (2009)
7. Tang, J., Hua, X.-S., Qi, G.-J., Wu, X.: Typicality ranking via semi-supervised multiple-instance learning. In: Proc. ACM Int. Conf. Multimedia, pp. 297–300 (2007)
8. Wang, C., Zhang, L., Zhang, H.-J.: Graph-based multiple-instance learning for object-based image retrieval. In: Proc. ACM Int. Conf. Multimedia Information Retrieval, pp. 156–163 (2008)
9. Tang, J., Li, H., Qi, G.-J., Chua, T.-S.: Image annotation by graph-based inference with integrated multiple/single instance representations. IEEE Trans. Multimedia 12(2), 131–141 (2010)
10. Li, F., Liu, R.: Multi-graph multi-instance learning for object-based image and video retrieval. In: Proc. ACM Int. Conf. Multimedia Retrieval (2012)
11. Vapnik, V.N.: The Nature of Statistical Learning Theory. Springer, New York (1995)
12. Andrews, S., Tsochantaridis, I., Hofmann, T.: Support vector machines for multiple-instance learning. In: Advances in Neural Information Processing Systems (2002)
13. Wang, J., Yang, J., Yu, K., Lv, F., Huang, T., Gong, Y.: Locality-constrained linear coding for image classification. In: Proc. IEEE Int. Conf. Computer Vision and Pattern Recognition, pp. 3360–3367 (2010)

Maximizing Edit Distance Accuracy with Hidden Conditional Random Fields

Antoine Vinel and Thierry Artières

Université Pierre et Marie Curie (LIP6), Paris, France
{antoine.vinel,thierry.artieres}@lip6.fr

Abstract. Handwriting recognition aims at predicting a sequence of characters from an image of a handwritten text. Main approaches rely on learning statistical models such as Hidden Markov Models or Conditional Random Fields, whose quality is measured through character and word error rates while they are usually not trained to optimize such criterion. We propose an efficient method for learning Hidden Conditional Random Fields to optimize the error rate within the large margin framework.

Keywords: Document Analysis, Conditional Random Fields, Maximum Margin Learning, Handwriting recognition.

1 Introduction

Handwriting recognition (HWR) aims at transforming a raw image of a handwritten document into a sequence of characters and words. HWR systems consist first in performing some preprocessing steps on a sliding window over each text lines, yielding to a sequence of real-valued feature vectors, and second in applying statistical models such as Hidden Markov Models (HMMs) or Conditional Random Fields (CRFs). These systems take as input a T-length sequence of observations $\mathbf{x}$ and output a L-length sequence of characters $\mathbf{y}$ with temporal boundaries. Their accuracy is systematically evaluated from the edit distance which counts the number of character errors (insertions, deletions, and replacement) required to align a predicted string $\mathbf{y}$ and the true string $\mathbf{y}'$ (e.g. the word to recognize), thus ignoring irrelevant eventual temporal boundaries shifts. One can affect various weights to these error types (we used an uniform weighting here). The accuracy of a recognition engine, which will be further denoted by EDA (Edit Distance Accuracy), is defined from the edit distance as follows:

$$\text{accuracy}(\mathbf{y}, \mathbf{y}') = \text{EDA}(\mathbf{y}, \mathbf{y}') = \frac{\text{Hits} - \text{Insertions}}{|\mathbf{y}'|} \tag{1}$$

where Hits denote the number of character that have been well predicted and $|\mathbf{y}'|$ denotes the length (the number of character) of the true string. Most popular approaches rely on HMMs trained with either generative or discriminative criterion such as Maximum Mutual Information (MMI) [1], Minimum Classification Error and variants (MCE, P-MCE) [2–4] and Minimum Phone Error (MPE) [5].

R. Wilson et al. (Eds.): CAIP 2013, Part I, LNCS 8047, pp. 45–53, 2013.

Recently, building on the success of large margin learning ideas (popularized with Support Vector Machines), some works have demonstrated the strong potential of this approach for learning HMMs [7–11]. Most of them focus on optimizing a Hamming distance loss criterion (a frame based error measure wich takes into account the temporal boundaries mismatch) which is simpler to optimize, while their performances are measured with EDA.

Recently, pure discriminative models have been also proposed to deal with sequence labelling tasks. Hidden Conditional Random Fields (HCRFs), which are CRFs [12] powered by hidden states (alike HMMs) [13–15] have been successfully applied to various signal labelling tasks [16, 14, 13, 17–19]. HCRFs are trained either to maximize the conditional likelihood of label sequences given observation sequences or a margin criterion based on a naive zero-one loss (the sentence is completely recognized or not) or at best a Hamming distance loss [20, 16, 21].

This work describes an approach for learning HCRFs with a large margin criterion to maximize the edit distance accuracy. Although this has been often mentioned as a perspective of previous works [22] this extension is not straightforward. We first recall some background on HCRFs, then we detail our algorithm and provide experimental results on two HWR datasets.

2   Background

2.1   HCRF

HCRFs are discriminative graphical models that have been proven useful for handling complex signals like handwriting and speech [13–15]. A common approach consists in using a similar architecture as for HMM systems: a left-right sub-model for every character to be recognized, where all ending states of all sub-models are connected to all starting states. Learning and decoding is performed within this global model. A HCRF defines a conditional probability of a label sequence $\mathbf{y}$ given an observation sequence $\mathbf{x}$ as follows:

$$p(\mathbf{y}|\mathbf{x}, \mathbf{w}) = \sum_{\mathbf{h} \in \mathbf{S}(\mathbf{y})} p(\mathbf{h}|\mathbf{x}, \mathbf{w}) \qquad (2)$$

where $\mathbf{x}$ is a T-length observation sequence $\mathbf{x} = (x_1, ..., x_T)$, $\mathbf{y} = (y_1, ..., y_L)$ is a sequence of L labels (characters), and $\mathbf{h} = (h_1, ..., h_T)$ is a state sequence. Note that L is usually much less than T. The set of all possible labels (resp. hidden states) is denoted by $\mathcal{Y}$ (resp. H). Finally $\mathbf{S}(\mathbf{y})$ denotes the set of all states sequences that match the label sequence $\mathbf{y}$ and $\mathbf{w}$ stands for the HCRF parameter set. The posterior probability of a sequence of states is given by:

$$p(\mathbf{h}|\mathbf{x}, \mathbf{w}) = \frac{\exp\langle \Phi(\mathbf{x}, \mathbf{h}), \mathbf{w} \rangle}{Z(\mathbf{x}, \mathbf{w})} \qquad (3)$$

where $\Phi(., .)$ is a real valued vector, called the joint feature map, which is commonly defined as a sum of local feature map, i.e. $\Phi(\mathbf{x}, \mathbf{h}) = \sum_t \varphi(x_t, h_t, h_{t-1})$, so that all necessary quantities for training and inference may be computed using dynamic programming procedures similar to algorithms used for HMMs (e.g. forward and Viterbi algorithms). The denominator $Z(.)$ is a normalization factor known as the "partition function", and defined by $Z(\mathbf{x}, \mathbf{w}) = \sum_{\mathbf{h} \in H^T} \exp\langle \Phi(\mathbf{x}, \mathbf{h}), \mathbf{w} \rangle$. This term is computationally expensive, and has to be computed at every iteration for each sequence during training.

2.2   Maximum Margin Learning for HCRFs

HCRFs are usually trained to maximize the conditional likelihood. Using a training dataset $\mathcal{B} = \{(\mathbf{x}^i, \mathbf{y}^i) | i = 1, .., N\}$ with N training sequences, the optimal parameter set for the HCRF is defined by :

$$\mathbf{w}^* = \operatorname{argmin}_{\mathbf{w}} \sum_{i=1..N} -\log p(\mathbf{y}^i | \mathbf{x}^i, \mathbf{w}) \qquad (4)$$

Alternatively, the large margin framework was successfully applied to many structured problems [23]. Optimizing a margin criterion has a priori two advantages over maximizing conditional likelihood as in Eq. (4): first, there is no need to compute the costly partition function, second, margin based criterion are known to achieve good generalization. Training resumes to:

$$\begin{cases} \mathbf{w}^* = \operatorname{argmin}_{\mathbf{w}, \xi_i} \frac{1}{2} \|\mathbf{w}\|^2 + C \sum \xi_i \\ \text{such that} \\ \forall (i, \mathbf{y} \neq \mathbf{y}^i), \qquad \delta F(\mathbf{y}^i, \mathbf{y}) \geq 1 - \xi_i \\ \forall i \qquad \qquad \qquad \xi_i \geq 0 \end{cases} \qquad (5)$$

where $\delta F(\mathbf{y}^i, \mathbf{y}) = F(\mathbf{x}^i, \mathbf{y}^i, \mathbf{w}) - F(\mathbf{x}^i, \mathbf{y}, \mathbf{w})$ and $F(\mathbf{x}, \mathbf{y}, \mathbf{w})$ is a discriminant function. Moreover, the standard zero-one loss can be replaced by a penalty term $\Delta(\mathbf{y}, \mathbf{y}^i)$ that fits better the structured output prediction framework (e.g. Hamming distance loss).

The Margin Rescaling (MR) and the Slack Rescaling (SR) frameworks consist in solving the following problem :

$$\begin{cases} \mathbf{w}^* = \operatorname{argmin}_{\mathbf{w}, \xi_i} \frac{1}{2} \|\mathbf{w}\|^2 + C \sum \xi_i \\ \text{such that} \\ \forall i \qquad \qquad \xi_i \geq 0 \\ \quad \text{and} \\ \qquad \qquad \delta F(\mathbf{y}^i, \mathbf{y}) \geq \Delta(\mathbf{y}, \mathbf{y}^i) - \xi_i \text{ (MR case)} \\ \forall (i, \mathbf{y} \neq \mathbf{y}^i), \qquad \text{or} \\ \qquad \qquad \delta F(\mathbf{y}^i, \mathbf{y}) \geq 1 - \frac{\xi_i}{\Delta(\mathbf{y}, \mathbf{y}^i)} \quad \text{(SR case)} \end{cases} \qquad (6)$$

This approach has been used in the past both for generative models (HMMs [21, 20]) and discriminant ones (CRF and HCRFs [23, 16, 21]).

Although $F(\mathbf{x}, \mathbf{y}, \mathbf{w}) = \log p(\mathbf{y}|\mathbf{x}, \mathbf{w})$ would be a natural choice for learning HCRFs, a common and simpler choice is an approximation $F(\mathbf{x}, \mathbf{y}, \mathbf{w}) = \max_{\mathbf{h} \in \mathbf{S}(\mathbf{y})} \langle \Phi(\mathbf{x}, \mathbf{h}), \mathbf{w} \rangle$ which resumes to $F(\mathbf{x}, \mathbf{y}, \mathbf{w}) = \max_{\mathbf{h} \in \mathbf{S}(\mathbf{y})} \log p(\mathbf{y}, \mathbf{h}|\mathbf{x}, \mathbf{w}) \approx \log p(\mathbf{y}|\mathbf{x}, \mathbf{w})$.

The above optimization problems are using as objective an upper bound of the Δ-loss. They may be solved using quadratic programming algorithms. However, since the number of the constraints is exponential in the length of the input, the standard solvers cannot be used easily. Efficient algorithms that overcome this difficulty either rely on an online learning scheme (see section 3.1) or exploit a limited memory algorithm to keep the size of the quadratic program limited [21].

3   Optimization

Our motivation to maximize the edit distance based accuracy (EDA) rather than the Hamming distance accuracy (HDA) comes from the weak correlation between those measures. Indeed, the scatter plot (on figure 1) shows, for each test sequence, a point whose coordinates are the HDA and the EDA. An example of an extreme case is shown on the right part of figure 1 with a high HDA (i.e. 76% of the image's columns are correctly labelled) and a low EDA (25%) suffering from an important number of insertions.

Including the edit distance loss as penalty term $\Delta(\mathbf{y}, \mathbf{y}^i) = d_{\text{edit}}(\mathbf{y}, \mathbf{y}^i)$ is far from being straightforward since the objective function is piecewise constant. All gradient-based algorithms are excluded in favour of contrastive-based [22] or margin-based ones, we investigate these latter methods here.

3.1   Online Learning

The passive-aggressive algorithm [24] solves iteratively a succession of simple quadratic problems. For each iteration n, we pick a new training sequence $(\mathbf{x}^{in}, \mathbf{y}^{in})$ at random, and update the parameter set $\mathbf{w}^n$ as the solution of the following problem (SR case is similar) :

$$\begin{cases} \mathbf{w}^* = \mathbf{argmin}_{\mathbf{w}, \xi} \frac{1}{2}\|\mathbf{w} - \mathbf{w}^{n-1}\|^2 + C\xi \\ \text{s.t. } \delta F(\mathbf{y}^{in}, \hat{\mathbf{y}}^{in}) \geq \Delta(\hat{\mathbf{y}}^{in}, \mathbf{y}^{in}) - \xi \qquad \text{(MR case)} \\ \xi \geq 0 \end{cases} \qquad (7)$$

Note that when there is not any margin violation (i.e. $\xi = 0$) the optimal solution is trivially $\mathbf{w}^n \leftarrow \mathbf{w}^* = \mathbf{w}^{n-1}$. The main interest of this formulation

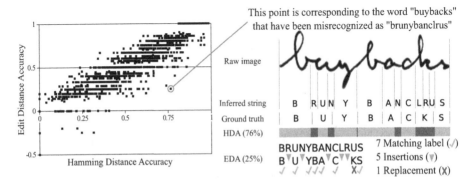

Fig. 1. Relation between Edit Distance Accuracy and Hamming Distance Accuracy EDA vs HDA scatter plot (left) Example of an extreme case (right)

is that in the margin violation case, the optimal solution $\mathbf{w}^*$ can be computed analytically.

$$\mathbf{w}^* = \mathbf{w}^{n-1} + \min(C, \frac{\Delta(\hat{\mathbf{y}}^{in}, \mathbf{y}^{in}) - \langle \delta\Phi(\hat{\mathbf{h}}), \mathbf{w} \rangle}{\|\delta\Phi(\hat{\mathbf{h}})\|^2})\Phi(\mathbf{x}, \hat{\mathbf{h}}) \qquad \text{(MR case) (8)}$$

where $\delta\Phi(\hat{\mathbf{h}})$ is the difference, in the joint feature space, between the most violating hidden state sequence $\hat{\mathbf{h}}^{in}$ and the hidden state sequence $\mathbf{h}^{in}$ matching the ground truth $\mathbf{y}^{in}$.

These quantities are defined according to:

$$\hat{\mathbf{y}}^{in} = \mathbf{argmax}_{\mathbf{y}} \Delta(\mathbf{y}, \mathbf{y}^{in}) - \delta F(\mathbf{y}^{in}, \mathbf{y}) \qquad (9)$$

$$\hat{\mathbf{h}}^{in} = \mathbf{argmax}_{\mathbf{h} \in S(\hat{\mathbf{y}}^{in})} \langle \Phi(\mathbf{x}^{in}, \mathbf{h}), \mathbf{w} \rangle \qquad (10)$$

$$\mathbf{h}^{in} = \mathbf{argmax}_{\mathbf{h} \in S(\mathbf{y}^{in})} \langle \Phi(\mathbf{x}^{in}, \mathbf{h}), \mathbf{w} \rangle \qquad (11)$$

$$\delta\Phi(\hat{\mathbf{h}}) = \Phi(\mathbf{x}^{in}, \mathbf{h}^{in}) - \Phi(\mathbf{x}^{in}, \hat{\mathbf{h}}^{in}) \qquad (12)$$

3.2   Negative Example Selection

Computing the *best negative example for* i^{th} *training sample,* $\hat{\mathbf{h}}^{in}$, requires $\hat{\mathbf{y}}^{in}$ (Eq. (9)). These quantities cannot be computed by dynamic programming routines since the edit distance is not decomposable over the frames. We propose to build incrementally a lattice enclosing a limited number of best hypothesis for which we will compute edit distance.

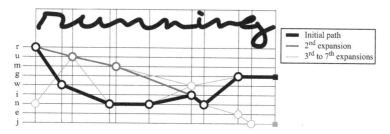

Fig. 2. Hypothesis lattice built for selecting negative example

Inspired by the word-graph algorithm proposed e.g. in [25], we initialize the graph using a standard Viterbi-like algorithm to generate the prediction of the current model. In figure 2 this step corresponds to the boldest black path : the word `rwnning` (starting by the character `r` from frames 1 to 30, `w` from frames 31 to 90, ...), we add a node in the graph for each character (of the decoded string) at its starting time. Then, we iterate what we call expansions of the graph up to a maximum number of expansions E.

Every iteration $e < E$ selects the most likely alternative best path from the beginning of the sequence to one node of the graph. For instance in figure 2, the node `i` was selected for the second expansion yielding a new hypothesis `ruming`.

The E expansions may represent (in the theoretical worst case) a huge number of explored hypothesis (i.e. alternative strings) : $\mathcal{O}(\exp(E))$. The empirical complexity was bounded by $(E/2)^3$. To deal with it, we used an efficient dynamic programming routine to compute $\hat{\mathbf{h}}^{i_n}$ on the graph by factorizing as much as possible the edit distance computation.

This part of our approach differs from MPE [5, 6] by the fact that we use the true EDA (instead of a frame-based "local accuracy" estimation computed from the character overlapping in an hypothesis lattice).

4   Experiments

We performed experiments on two handwritten words datasets. The YAWDa dataset is a home made dataset (freely available at [26]) of 2 400 handwritten words whose character distribution is roughly uniform. We used two versions of this set. In R16 the raw images are rescaled to a 16-pixel height and a frame consists in one column of pixels (resulting in a 16-dimensional feature vector). In R32 the raw images are rescaled to 32-pixels height and every frame is the concatenation of five columns (two "context-columns" on both side of the central frame), leading to 160-dimensional frames. R16 is obviously harder than R32, it allows investigating the behaviour of the methods with "low-informative" data. R32 helps exploring models' behaviour in a "richer-context". We also performed experiments on a 10k words benchmark dataset ($\sim$46k characters) that is extracted from the IAM corpus [27], pre-processing yields nine geometrical frames of computed on a sliding window [28]. As in the YAWDa R32 set, we use augmented frames by including two context frames. As done in [13], we also add the cross-product of all features which guarantees that the model have a representational power at least equal to that of HMMs with one gaussian per state. The final dimension of each frame is 1080. In any case the system's performances are measured as with EDA accuracy. As often done with online algorithms, we

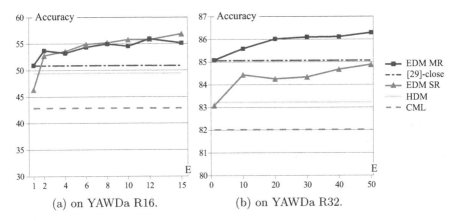

(a) on YAWDa R16.   (b) on YAWDa R32.

Fig. 3. Comparison of HCRF learning criterion w.r.t. the number of expansions

used iterate averaging. This technique use (in the inference process on validation and test set) an average of **w** over some of the last iterations. In our case, we performed averaging over the last iteration over the whole training set.

We first compare on R16 and R32 (fig. 3) the accuracies of few HCRFs trained my maximizing the following learning criterion : the conditional likelihood (CML), a margin based on Hamming Distance (denoted HDM), a margin based on the Edit Distance (denoted EDM) with the Slack or Margin rescaling variants. We also reported the accuracy obtained with a HCRF trained with a method which is pretty similar to [29] by using the "Margin rescaling" approach and using a 1-expansion graph. It differs from the original method in that we do not model stay duration in the states.

EDM approach significantly outperforms the other methods on both datasets. Both strategies of EDM (Margin and Slack Scaling) work well, with a slight advantage for Margin Scaling. The HDM approach performs well too, while slightly less than the EDM with the Margin Scaling strategy. Interestingly, EDM already outperforms the other methods when exploiting a small number of expansions, which means a limited complexity overhead. And the method steadily improves with the number of expansions.

Table 1. Performance comparison on IAM

Models	Specifications	Accuracy
Hidden Markov Model (HMM)	8 states	51.2
	14 states	59.6
HMM trained with Hamming Distance Margin (HDM)	8 states	70.7
	14 states	70.3
Hidden Conditional Random Field (HCRF)	5 states	70.6
HCRF trained with HDM	5 states	72.0
HCRF trained with EDM ([29]-close approach)	5 states	71.1
HCRF trained with EDM Slack Rescaling case	5 states - 5 expansions	72.1
	5 states - 10 expansions	72.4
HCRF trained with EDM Margin Rescaling case	5 states - 5 expansions	72.2
	5 states - 10 expansions	72.9

This table compares a number of methods on the more complex and bigger IAM dataset. All methods have been implemented and tuned by us. These results show that the margin based methods (HDM and EDM) clearly outperform non discriminative and discriminative training of HMMs (HMM and HDM HMMs), standard discriminative training of HCRFs (CML). Moreover margin EDM methods again achieve the best results on this dataset. Although improvement over HDM-HCRF is modest, it must be noticed that all these results are already high on this dataset and that any improvement is very hard to obtain. Finally it must be noticed that we deliberately limited training complexity on this dataset by exploiting a rather small number of expansions to fit our computational power, but one can expect to get even better results by augmenting the number of expansions and training time.

5   Conclusion

We proposed a new algorithm for learning HCRF relying on a max margin criterion to optimize directly the edit distance accuracy in the passive-aggressive framework. We detailed a lattice-based approach allowing a factored computation of the Levenshtein distance for the negative example selection. We finally showed the benefits of this approach on few handwriting labelling tasks with respect to a number of alternative discriminatively learning schemes.

References

1. Woodland, P.C., Povey, D.: Large scale discriminative training of hidden markov models for speech recognition. Computer Speech & Language (1) (2002)
2. Juang, B.H., Katagiri, S.: Discriminative learning for minimum error classification. IEEE Transactions on Signal Processing (12) (1992)
3. Fu, Q., He, X., Deng, L.: Phone-discriminating minimum classification error (p-mce) training for phonetic recognition. In: Interspeech (2007)
4. He, X., Deng, L., Chou, W.: A novel learning method for hidden markov models in speech and audio processing. In: Multimedia Signal Processing. IEEE (2006)
5. Povey, D., Woodland, P.C.: Minimum phone error and i-smoothing for improved discriminative training. In: ICASSP, vol. 1, p. I–105. IEEE (2002)
6. Deng, L., Wu, J., Droppo, J., Acero, A.: Analysis and comparison of two speech feature extraction/compensation algorithms. In: SPL (2005)
7. Cheng, C.-C., Sha, F., Saul, L.K.: Online learning and acoustic feature adaptation in large-margin hidden markov models. JSP (6) (December 2010)
8. Sha, F., Saul, L.K.: Large margin hidden markov models for automatic speech recognition. In: NIPS (2007)
9. Cheng, C.C., Sha, F., Saul, L.K.: A fast online algorithm for large margin training of continuous density hidden markov models. In: Interspeech (2009)
10. Do, T.M.T., Artieres, T.: Maximum margin training of gaussian hmms for handwriting recognition. In: ICDAR, pp. 976–980. IEEE Computer Society (2009)
11. Yu, D., Deng, L., He, X., Acero, A.: Large-margin minimum classification error training for large-scale speech recognition tasks. In: ICASSP (2007)
12. Lafferty, J., McCallum, A., Pereira, F.: Conditional random fields: Probabilistic models for segmenting and labeling sequence data. In: ICML Workshop (2001)
13. Gunawardana, A., Mahajan, M., Acero, A., Platt, J.C.: Hidden conditional random fields for phone classification. In: Interspeech (2005)
14. Do, T.-M.-T., Artieres, T.: Conditional random fields for online handwriting recognition. In: ICFHR (2006)
15. Morency, L.P., Quattoni, A., Darrell, T.: Latent-dynamic discriminative models for continuous gesture recognition. In: CPVR, pp. 1–8. IEEE (2007)
16. Wang, Y., Mori, G.: Max-margin hidden conditional random fields for human action recognition. In: CVPR, pp. 872–879. IEEE (2009)
17. Vinel, A., Do, T.M.T., Artières, T.: Joint optimization of hidden conditional random fields and non linear feature extraction. In: ICDAR (2011)

18. Soullard, Y., Artieres, T.: Hybrid hmm and hcrf model for sequence classification. In: ESANN (2011)
19. Reiter, S., Schuller, B., Rigoll, G.: Hidden conditional random fields for meeting segmentation. In: Multimedia and Expo. IEEE (2007)
20. Taskar, B., Guestrin, C., Koller, D.: Max-margin markov networks. In: NIPS (2003)
21. Do, T.M.T., Artières, T.: Large margin training for hidden markov models with partially observed states. In: ICML (2009)
22. Keshet, J., Cheng, C.-C., Stoehr, M., McAllester, D.A.: Direct error rate minimization of hidden markov models. In: Interspeech (2011)
23. Tsochantaridis, I., Joachims, T., Hofmann, T., Altun, Y.: Large margin methods for structured and interdependent output variables. JMLR (2) (2006)
24. Crammer, K., Dekel, O., Keshet, J., Shalev-Shwartz, S., Singer, Y.: Online passive-aggressive algorithms. Journal of Machine Learning Research (2006)
25. Tran, B.H., Seide, F., Steinbiss, T.: A word graph based n-best search in continuous speech recognition. In: ICSLP (1996)
26. http://YAWDa.lip6.fr/
27. Marti, U.V., Bunke, H.: A full english sentence database for off-line handwriting recognition. In: ICDAR (2002)
28. Marti, U.V., Bunke, H.: Handwritten sentence recognition. In: ICPR (2000)
29. Keshet, J., Shalev-Shwartz, S., Bengio, S., Singer, Y., Chazan, D.: Discriminative kernel-based phoneme sequence recognition. In: Interspeech (2006)

Background Recovery by Fixed-Rank Robust Principal Component Analysis

Wee Kheng Leow, Yuan Cheng, Li Zhang, Terence Sim, and Lewis Foo

Department of Computer Science, National University of Singapore
Computing 1, 13 Computing Drive, Singapore 117417
{leowwk,cyuan,zhangli,tsim,lewis}@comp.nus.edu.sg

Abstract. Background recovery is a very important theme in computer vision applications. Recent research shows that robust principal component analysis (RPCA) is a promising approach for solving problems such as noise removal, video background modeling, and removal of shadows and specularity. RPCA utilizes the fact that the background is common in multiple views of a scene, and attempts to decompose the data matrix constructed from input images into a low-rank matrix and a sparse matrix. This is possible if the sparse matrix is sufficiently sparse, which may not be true in computer vision applications. Moreover, algorithmic parameters need to be fine tuned to yield accurate results. This paper proposes a fixed-rank RPCA algorithm for solving background recovering problems whose low-rank matrices have known ranks. Comprehensive tests show that, by fixing the rank of the low-rank matrix to a known value, the fixed-rank algorithm produces more reliable and accurate results than existing low-rank RPCA algorithm.

Keywords: Background recovery, reflection removal, robust PCA.

1 Introduction

Background recovery is a very important recurring theme in computer vision applications. Traditionally, different approaches have been developed to solve different varieties of the problem. Recent research in **robust principal component analysis** (RPCA) offers a promising alternative approach for solving problems such as noise removal, video background modeling, and removal of shadows and specularity [2,12]. RPCA utilizes the fact that multiple views of a scene contain consistent information about the common background. It constructs a **data matrix** from multiple views and decomposes it into a **low-rank matrix** that contains the background and a **sparse matrix** that captures non-background components. It has been proved that exact solution of RPCA problem is available if the data matrix is composed of a sufficiently low-rank matrix and a sufficiently sparse matrix [2,3,9,13]. Various algorithms have been proposed for solving RPCA problem [6,9,12]. In particular, the methods based on **augmented Lagrange multiplier** (ALM) have been shown to be among the most efficient and accurate methods [9].

R. Wilson et al. (Eds.): CAIP 2013, Part I, LNCS 8047, pp. 54–61, 2013.

In computer vision applications, the non-background components may not be sparse. Moreover, algorithmic parameters need to be fine tuned to yield accurate results [1]. These difficulties are especially pronounced for reflection removal problem, and no work on applying RPCA to reflection removal has been reported so far. Fortunately, these application problems can be framed as one of recovering a **fixed-rank** matrix from the data matrix because the rank of the low-rank matrix is known. This paper proposes a **fixed-rank** RPCA algorithm based on ALM (FrALM) for solving background recovering problems. Comprehensive tests on reflection removal and video background modeling show that FrALM produces more accurate results than does low-rank ALM method (LrALM). Moreover, FrALM can produce optimal or near optimal results over a much wider range of parameter values than does LrALM, making it more reliable for solving computer vision problems whose low-rank matrices have known ranks.

2   Existing RPCA Methods

Robust PCA is a term given to a long line of work that aims to render PCA robust to gross corruption and outliers. Various methods have been proposed including influence function [4], multivariate trimming [7], alternating minimization [8], and random sampling [5]. These methods are either inefficient, having non-polynomial time complexity, or do not guarantee optimal solutions [12].

A recent approach directly decomposes a corrupted data matrix into a low-rank matrix and a sparse matrix. The corruption is assumed to be sparse, but the noise amplitude can be large. Various methods have been proposed such as iterative thresholding [9], proximal gradient [12], accelerated proximal gradient [6], and augmented Lagrange multiplier method (ALM) [9]. In particular, ALM has been shown to be among the most efficient and accurate methods [9]. These methods require tuning of algorithmic parameters [1]. On the other hand, [1] applies Bayesian approach to estimate the algorithmic parameters along with the matrices based on prior distributions of inverse variances.

In our applications, the rank of the low-rank matrix is known. So, we adopt the ALM approach but fix the rank of the low-rank matrix, which provides more specific constraint than do prior distributions. This approach allows our algorithm to converge efficiently and accurately, as for the low-rank ALM method of [9], and is simpler and more efficient than the Bayesian method of [1].

Other methods have been proposed to solve related but different problems. For example, [11] solves low-rank matrix factorization and [10] computes a fixed-rank representation for sparse subspace clustering. They are not directly applicable to our application problem, which is a matrix decomposition problem.

3   Fixed-Rank RPCA

Given an $m \times n$ data matrix $\mathbf{D}$, PCA seeks to recover a low-rank matrix $\mathbf{A}$ from data matrix $\mathbf{D}$ such that the discrepancy or error $\mathbf{E} = \mathbf{D} - \mathbf{A}$ is minimized:

$$\min_{\mathbf{A},\mathbf{E}} \|\mathbf{E}\|_F, \text{ subject to } \operatorname{rank}(\mathbf{A}) \leq r, \ \mathbf{D} = \mathbf{A} + \mathbf{E} \tag{1}$$

where $r \ll \min(m,n)$ is the target rank of $\mathbf{A}$ and $\|\cdot\|_F$ is the Frobenius norm. Eq. 1 can be solved by SVD but the solution will be vastly inaccurate if the error entries in $\mathbf{E}$ are arbitrarily large. Under the conditions that $\mathbf{A}$ is low-rank and $\mathbf{E}$ is sufficiently sparse, Wright et al. [12] show that $\mathbf{A}$ can be exactly recovered by solving the following convex optimization problem:

$$\min_{\mathbf{A},\mathbf{E}} \|\mathbf{A}\|_* + \lambda\|\mathbf{E}\|_1, \text{ subject to } \mathbf{D} = \mathbf{A} + \mathbf{E} \tag{2}$$

where $\|\cdot\|_*$ denotes the nuclear norm and $\|\cdot\|_1$ denotes the 1-norm,

Lin et al. [9] reformulate Eq. 2 using augmented Lagrange multiplier method. Their method (LrALM) uses a matrix $\mathbf{Y}$ and parameter μ to merge the constraint into the objective function, leading to the following revised problem:

$$\min_{\mathbf{A},\mathbf{E}} \|\mathbf{A}\|_* + \lambda\|\mathbf{E}\|_1 + \langle \mathbf{Y}, \mathbf{D} - \mathbf{A} - \mathbf{E} \rangle + \frac{\mu}{2}\|\mathbf{D} - \mathbf{A} - \mathbf{E}\|_F^2 \tag{3}$$

where $\langle \mathbf{U}, \mathbf{V} \rangle$ is the sum of the product of corresponding elements in $\mathbf{U}$ and $\mathbf{V}$, and λ and μ are parameters that need to be specified. An iterative algorithm is applied to determine the $\mathbf{A}$ and $\mathbf{E}$ that minimize Eq. 3.

For reflection removal, a set of reflection images are arranged as column matrices in $\mathbf{D}$. If the images are well aligned such that the transmitted parts are identical, then $\mathbf{A}$ captures the transmitted parts and has a rank of 1. If the reflection is localized, $\mathbf{E}$ is sparse; otherwise, $\mathbf{E}$ is not sparse. Similar characteristics are observed in background modeling of video taken with a stationary camera.

When $\mathbf{E}$ is not sparse, LrALM may not recover accurate results unless the parameter λ is carefully chosen (Section 4). If λ is too large, the trivial solution of $\mathbf{E} = \mathbf{0}$ is obtained, and $\mathbf{A} = \mathbf{D}$, which has a rank larger than the desired low rank. On the other hand, if λ is too small, $\mathbf{E} = \mathbf{D}$ and $\mathbf{A} = \mathbf{0}$, which has a rank of 0. So, the value of λ directly influences the rank of $\mathbf{A}$ recovered by LrALM. Although Zhou et al. [13] prove theoretically that the optimal λ can be set to $1/\sqrt{\max(m,n)}$, this is true only if $\mathbf{A}$ is low-rank and $\mathbf{E}$ is sufficiently sparse. The parameter μ can also affect the accuracy of the recovered $\mathbf{A}$ by influencing the rank of $\mathbf{A}$ (see discussion below).

To overcome the above difficulties, we frame the background recovery problem as one of recovering a low-rank matrix $\mathbf{A}$ with a known rank r:

$$\min_{\mathbf{A},\mathbf{E}} \|\mathbf{E}\|_F, \text{ subject to } \text{rank}(\mathbf{A}) = \text{known } r, \ \mathbf{D} = \mathbf{A} + \mathbf{E}. \tag{4}$$

To solve Eq. 4 robustly, we reformulate it in the same manner as the ALM approach (Eq. 3), with the additional constraint of $\text{rank}(\mathbf{A}) = r$. With $\mathbf{A}$'s rank fixed, it may seem that the term $\|\mathbf{A}\|_*$ in Eq. 3 is redundant. Nevertheless, we choose to keep $\|\mathbf{A}\|_*$ in Eq. 3 and solve for $\mathbf{A}$ using ALM approach so that the convergence and optimality properties proved by Lin et al. [9] are preserved.

Our algorithm (FrALM) adopts the exact ALM approach to solve fixed-rank RPCA problem. It is similar to the low-rank ALM algorithm (LrALM) proposed by Lin et al. [9], except that FrALM fixes the rank of $\mathbf{A}$.

FrALM

Input: D, r, λ

1. $\mathbf{A} = \mathbf{0}$, $\mathbf{E} = \mathbf{0}$.
2. $\mathbf{Y} = \text{sgn}(\mathbf{D})/J(\text{sgn}(\mathbf{D}))$, $\mu > 0$, $\rho > 1$.
3. Repeat until convergence:
4.   Repeat until convergence:
5. $\mathbf{U}, \mathbf{S}, \mathbf{V} = \text{svd}(\mathbf{D} - \mathbf{E} + \mathbf{Y}/\mu)$.
6.   If $\text{rank}(T_{1/\mu}(\mathbf{S})) < r$, $\mathbf{A} = \mathbf{U} T_{1/\mu}(\mathbf{S})\mathbf{V}^{\top}$; otherwise, $\mathbf{A} = \mathbf{U}\mathbf{S}_r\mathbf{V}^{\top}$.
7. $\mathbf{E} = T_{\lambda/\mu}(\mathbf{D} - \mathbf{A} + \mathbf{Y}/\mu)$.
8. $\mathbf{Y} = \mathbf{Y} + \mu(\mathbf{D} - \mathbf{A} - \mathbf{E})$, $\mu = \rho\mu$.

Output: A, E.

In line 2, $\text{sgn}(\cdot)$ computes the sign of each matrix element, and $J(\cdot)$ computes a scaling factor

$$J(\mathbf{X}) = \max\left(\|\mathbf{X}\|_2, \lambda^{-1}\|\mathbf{X}\|_\infty\right) \tag{5}$$

as recommended in [9]. The function T_ϵ in line 7 is a soft thresholding function:

$$T_\epsilon(x) = \begin{cases} x - \epsilon, & \text{if } x > \epsilon, \\ x + \epsilon, & \text{if } x < -\epsilon, \\ 0, & \text{otherwise.} \end{cases} \tag{6}$$

The main difference between FrALM and LrALM lies in Step 6. $\mathbf{S}_r$ is the diagonal matrix of singular values whose diagonal elements above r are set to 0. FrALM fixes $\mathbf{A}$'s rank to the desired rank r if a rank-r matrix is recovered. Otherwise, it behaves in the same manner as LrALM. On the other hand, LrALM allows $\mathbf{A}$'s rank to increase beyond r if μ is too large.

FrALM is algorithmically equivalent to LrALM with a sufficiently small μ that restricts the rank of $\mathbf{A}$ to r. Therefore, the convergence proof of LrALM given in [9] applies to FrALM. Consequently, FrALM can converge as efficiently as LrALM does (Fig. 2(a)). The advantage of FrALM over LrALM is that the user does not have to specify the exact μ that fixes the rank of $\mathbf{A}$ to r.

4 Experiments and Discussions

7 test sets were used to evaluate the performance of FrALM and LrALM on the tasks of reflection removal and video background modeling (Fig. 3, 4). Sets 1 to 3 contained synthetically generated reflection images, and Sets 4 and 5 contained real reflection images. Sets 1 and 4 were corrupted by local reflections whereas Sets 2, 3, and 5 were corrupted by global reflections. Sets 6 and 7 contained video frames of a single moving human and busy traffic junction, respectively.

All the test images were color images of size 200×150 pixels; so $m = 200 \times 150 \times 3 = 90000$. The number of images n in Sets 1 to 7 were respectively, 38, 38, 38, 31, 46, 210, and 250 respectively. Ground truth background images were available for Sets 1 to 6 but not for Set 7. The images were captured with a stationary camera. So the desired rank of the low-rank matrix is 1.

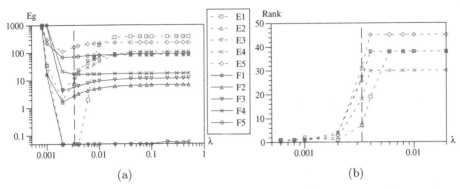

Fig. 1. Performance comparison for reflection removal. (a) Error E_g vs. λ. Error curves above $E_g = 1000$ for very small λ are cropped to reduce clutter. (b) Rank of low-rank matrix recovered by LrALM. (Red dashed lines) LrALM results. Vertical dash lines denote theoretical optimal $\lambda^* = 0.00\dot{3}$. (Blue solid lines) FrALM results.

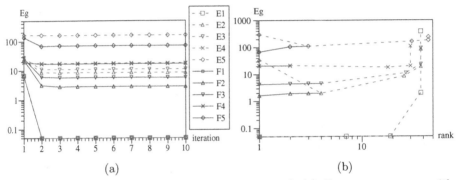

Fig. 2. Performance comparison for reflection removal. (a) Convergence curves with $\lambda = 0.00\dot{3}$. (b) Error vs. rank. Error curves above $E_g = 1000$ for very small λ are cropped to reduce clutter.

LrALM and FrALM were tested on the test sets over a range of λ from 0.0001 to 0.5, including the theoretical optimal λ of $\sqrt{m} = 0.00\dot{3}$, denoted as λ^*, as proved in [13]. The parameters ρ and initial μ were set to the default values of 6 and $0.5/\sigma_1$, where σ_1 is the largest singular value of the initial $\mathbf{Y}$, as for LrALM. The algorithms' accuracy was measured in terms of the mean squared error E_g between the ground truth $\mathbf{G}$ and the recovered $\mathbf{A}$:

$$E_g = \frac{1}{mn} \|\mathbf{G} - \mathbf{A}\|_F^2. \tag{7}$$

Test results show that FrALM converges as efficiently as LrALM (Fig. 2(a)). Since the desired rank of $\mathbf{A}$ is 1, λ has to be sufficiently small for LrALM to produce accurate results (Fig. 1(a)). For Sets 2, 3, and 5 with non-sparse $\mathbf{E}$, the empirical optimal λ (0.002) is smaller than the theoretical λ^* (0.00$\dot{3}$), contrary to the theory of [13]. At this lower λ, the ranks of the optimal $\mathbf{A}$

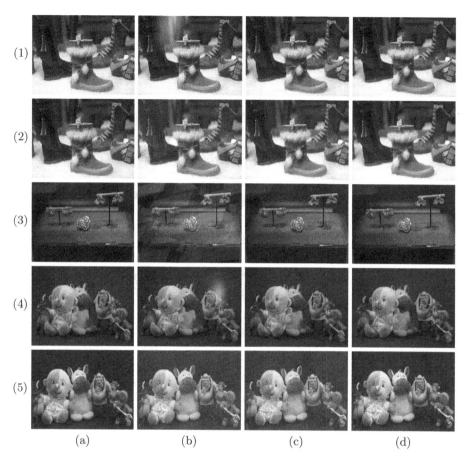

Fig. 3. Sample test results for reflection removal. (a) Ground truth background. (b) Sample input images. (c) LrALM's results. (d) FrALM's results. (1) Set 1: synthetic local reflection. (2) Set 2: synthetic global reflection (light background). (3) Set 3: synthetic global reflection (dark background). (4) Set 4: real local reflection. (5) Set 5: real global reflection. $\lambda = 0.003$ for these test results.

recovered by LrALM are still larger than the known value of 1 (Fig. 1(b)). This shows that LrALM has accumulated higher-rank components in $\mathbf{A}$ and thus over-estimated $\mathbf{A}$. In contrast, FrALM constrains the rank of $\mathbf{A}$ to 1, removing the over-estimation. Consequently, FrALM yields more accurate results than does LrALM, and it returns optimal or near optimal results over a wide range of λ (Fig. 1(a)). We have also verified empirically that reducing the rank of $\mathbf{A}$ to 1 after it is returned by LrALM can reduce over-estimation and improve LrALM's accuracy. However, this post-processing is insufficient for removing the over-estimation entirely and LrALM's error is still larger than that of FrALM.

To investigate the stability of FrALM, we ran it on the test cases at a range of fixed ranks r, with λ set to the empirical optimal of 0.002. FrALM's results were plotted together with LrALM's results obtained in previous tests (Fig. 2(b)).

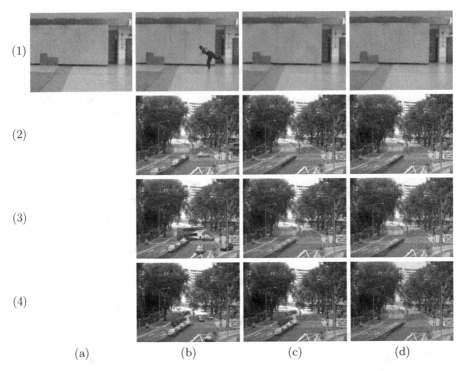

Fig. 4. Sample test results for human and traffic video. (a) Ground truth background. (b) Sample video frames. (c) LrALM's results. (d) FrALM's results. (1) Human motion video. (2–4) Traffic video; ground truth is not available. $\lambda = 0.003$ for these test results.

When r is slightly larger than 1, FrALM's error increases only slightly. when r is larger than the rank of $\mathbf{A}$ recovered (line 6 of algorithm), FrALM reduces to LrALM, and its error simply approaches that of LrALM.

Figure 3 displays sample results for reflection removal obtained at the theoretical λ^*. LrALM's results are good for Sets 1 and 4 whose $\mathbf{E}$ is sparse. For Sets 2, 3, and 5, $\mathbf{E}$ is not sparse and LrALM's results have visually noticeable errors (when the images are viewed at higher zoom factors). In contrast, FrALM obtains good results for all test sets.

Figure 4 shows sample results for video background modeling obtained at the theoretical λ^*. In the video frames where the human and vehicles are moving continuously, LrALM can recover the stationary background well (Fig. 4(1c, 2c)). When the vehicles are moving slowly, $\mathbf{E}$ is not sparse, and LrALM shows signs of inaccuracy (Fig. 4(3c)). When the vehicles stop at the traffic junction for an extended period of time, LrALM regards them as part of the low-rank matrix $\mathbf{A}$ and fails to remove them from $\mathbf{A}$ (Fig. 4(4c)). In contrast, FrALM produces much better overall results than does LrALM (Fig. 4(d)).

5   Conclusions

A fixed-rank RPCA algorithm, FrALM, based on exact augmented Lagrange multiplier method is proposed in this paper. By fixing the rank of the low-rank matrix to be recovered, FrALM removes over-estimation of the low-rank matrix and produces more accurate results than does low-rank ALM method (LrALM). Moreover, FrALM returns optimal or near optimal results over a wide range of λ values, whereas LrALM's accuracy is sensitive to λ. If FrALM is fixed to a desired rank that is larger than the actual rank, then FrALM just reduces to LrALM. These properties make FrALM more reliable and accurate than LrALM for solving computer vision problems whose low-rank matrices have known ranks.

References

1. Babacan, S.D., Luessi, M., Molina, R., Katsaggelos, A.K.: Sparse bayesian methods for low-rank matrix estimation. IEEE Trans. Signal Processing 60(8), 3964–3977 (2012)
2. Candès, E.J., Li, X., Ma, Y., Wright, J.: Robust principal component analysis? Journal of ACM 58(3), 11 (2011)
3. Candès, E.J., Plan, Y.: Matrix completion with noise. In: Proc. IEEE, pp. 925–936 (2010)
4. De la Torre, F., Black, M.: A framework for robust subspace learning. Int. Journal of Computer Vision 54(1-3), 117–142 (2003)
5. Fischler, M., Bolles, R.: Random sample consensus: A paradigm for model fitting with applications to image analysis and automated cartography. Communications of ACM 24(6), 381–385 (1981)
6. Ganesh, A., Lin, Z., Wright, J., Wu, L., Chen, M., Ma, Y.: Fast convex optimization algorithms for exact recovery of a corrupted low-rank matrix. In: CAMSAP (2009)
7. Gnanadesikan, R., Kettenring, J.: A framework for robust subspace learning. Robust Estimates, Residuals, and Outlier Detection with Multiresponse Data (check journal title) 28(1), 81–124 (1972)
8. Ke, Q., Kanade, T.: Robust L1 norm factorization in the presence of outliers and missing data by alternative convex programming. In: Proc. CVPR, pp. 739–746 (2005)
9. Lin, Z., Chen, M., Wu, L., Ma, Y.: The augmented Lagrange multiplier method for exact recovery of corrupted low-rank matrices. Technical Report UILU-ENG-09-2215, UIUC (2009), arXiv preprint arXiv:1009.5055
10. Liu, R., Lin, Z., De la Torre, F., Su, Z.: Fixed-rank representation for unsupervised visual learning. In: Proc. CVPR, pp. 598–605 (2012)
11. Wang, N., Yao, T., Wang, J., Yeung, D.-Y.: A probabilistic approach to robust matrix factorization. In: Fitzgibbon, A., Lazebnik, S., Perona, P., Sato, Y., Schmid, C. (eds.) ECCV 2012, Part VII. LNCS, vol. 7578, pp. 126–139. Springer, Heidelberg (2012)
12. Wright, J., Peng, Y., Ma, Y., Ganesh, A., Rao, S.: Robust principal component analysis: Exact recovery of corrupted low-rank matrices by convex optimization. In: Proc. NIPS, pp. 2080–2088 (2009)
13. Zhou, Z., Li, X., Wright, J., Candès, E.J., Ma, Y.: Stable principal component pursuit. In: Proc. Int. Symp. Information Theory, pp. 1518–1522 (2010)

Manifold Learning and the Quantum Jensen-Shannon Divergence Kernel

Luca Rossi[1], Andrea Torsello[1], and Edwin R. Hancock[2]

[1] Department of Environmental Science, Informatics and Statistics,
Ca' Foscari University of Venice, Italy
{lurossi,torsello}@dsi.unive.it
[2] Department of Computer Science, University of York, YO10 5GH, UK
edwin.hancock@york.ac.uk

Abstract. The quantum Jensen-Shannon divergence kernel [1] was recently introduced in the context of unattributed graphs where it was shown to outperform several commonly used alternatives. In this paper, we study the separability properties of this kernel and we propose a way to compute a low-dimensional kernel embedding where the separation of the different classes is enhanced. The idea stems from the observation that the multidimensional scaling embeddings on this kernel show a strong horseshoe shape distribution, a pattern which is known to arise when long range distances are not estimated accurately. Here we propose to use Isomap to embed the graphs using only local distance information onto a new vectorial space with a higher class separability. The experimental evaluation shows the effectiveness of the proposed approach.

Keywords: Graph Kernels, Manifold Learning, Continuous-Time Quantum Walk, Quantum Jensen-Shannon Divergence.

1   Introduction

Graph-based representations have become increasingly popular due to their ability to characterize in a natural way a large number of systems [2, 3]. Unfortunately, our ability to analyse this wealth of data is severely limited by the restrictions posed by standard pattern recognition techniques, which usually require the graphs to be first embedded into a vectorial space, a procedure which is far from being trivial. Kernel methods [4] provide a neat way to shift the problem from that of finding an embedding to that of defining a positive semidefinite kernel. In fact, once we define a positive semidefinite kernel $k : X \times X \to \mathbb{R}$ on a set X, there exists a map $\phi : X \to H$ into a Hilbert space H, such that $k(x, y) = \phi(x)^\top \phi(y)$ for all $x, y \in X$. Thus, any algorithm can be formulated in terms of the data by implicitily mapping them to H via the well-known kernel trick. As a consequence, we are now faced with the problem of defining a positive semidefinite kernel on graphs rather than computing an embedding. However, due to the rich expressiveness of graphs, this task has also proven to be difficult.

Many different graph kernels have been proposed in the literature [5–7], which are generally instances of the family of R-convolution kernels introduced by

R. Wilson et al. (Eds.): CAIP 2013, Part I, LNCS 8047, pp. 62–69, 2013.

Haussler [8]. The fundamental idea is that of decomposing two discrete objects them and comparing some simpler substructures. For example, Gärtner et al. [5] propose to count the number of common random walks between two graphs, while Borgwardt and Kriegel [6] measure the similarity based on the shortest paths in the graphs. Shervashidze et al. [7], on the other hand, count the number of graphlets, i.e. subgraphs with k nodes. Recently, Rossi et. al [1] introduced a novel kernel where the graph structure is probed through the evolution of a continuous-time quantum walk [9]. The idea underpinning their method is that the interference effects introduced by the quantum walk seem to be enhanced by the presence of symmetrical motifs in the graph [10, 11]. To this end, they define a walk onto a new structure that is maximally symmetric when the original graphs are isomorphic. Finally, the kernel is defined as the quantum Jensen-Shannon divergence [12] between the density operators [13] associated with the walks.

In this paper, we study the separability properties of the QJSD kernel and we apply standard manifold learning techniques [14, 15] on the kernel embedding to map the data onto a low-dimensional space where the different classes can exhibit a better linear separation. The idea stems from the observation that the multidimensional scaling embeddings of the QJSD kernel show the so-called *horseshoe effect* [16]. This particular behaviour is known to arise when long range distances are not estimated accurately, and it implies that the data lie on a non-linear manifold. This is no surprise, since Emms et. al [10] have shown that the continuous-time quantum walk underestimates the commute time related to the classical random walk. For this reason, it is natural to investigate the impact of the locality of distance information on the performance of the QJSD kernel. Given a set of graphs, we propose to use Isomap [14] to embed the graphs onto a low-dimensional vectorial space, and we compute the separability of the graph classes as the distance information varies from local to global. Moreover, we perform the same analysis on a set of alternative graph kernels commonly found in the literature [5–7]. Experiments on several standard datasets demonstrate that the Isomap embedding shows a higher separability of the classes.

The remainder of this paper is organized as follows: Section 2 introduces some basic quantum mechanical terminology, while Section 3 reviews the QJSD kernel. Section 4 illustrates the experimental results and the conclusions are presented in Section 5.

2 Quantum Mechanical Background

Quantum walks are the quantum analogue of classical random walks. In this paper we consider only continuous-time quantum walks, as first introduced by Farhi and Gutmann in [9]. Given a graph $G = (V, E)$, the state space of the continuous-time quantum walk defined on G is the set of the vertices V of the graph. Unlike the classical case, where the evolution of the walk is governed by a stochastic matrix (i.e. a matrix whose columns sum to unity), in the quantum case the dynamics of the walker is governed by a complex unitary matrix i.e., a matrix that multiplied by its conjugate transpose yields the identity matrix. Hence, the evolution of the quantum walk is reversible, which implies that quantum walks are non-ergodic and do not possess a limiting distribution. Using Dirac notation, we denote the basis state corresponding to the walk being at vertex $u \in V$ as $|u\rangle$. A general state of the walk is a complex linear combination of the basis states, such that the state of the walk at time t is defined as

$$|\psi_t\rangle = \sum_{u \in V} \alpha_u(t) |u\rangle \tag{1}$$

where the amplitude $\alpha_u(t) \in \mathbb{C}$ and $|\psi_t\rangle \in \mathbb{C}^{|V|}$ are both complex.

At each instant in time the probability of the walker being at a particular vertex of the graph is given by the square of the norm of the amplitude of the relative state. More formally, let X^t be a random variable giving the location of the walker at time t. Then the probability of the walker being at the vertex u at time t is given by

$$\Pr(X^t = u) = \alpha_u(t)\alpha_u^*(t) \tag{2}$$

where $\alpha_u^*(t)$ is the complex conjugate of $\alpha_u(t)$. Moreover $\alpha_u(t)\alpha_u^*(t) \in [0, 1]$, for all $u \in V$, $t \in \mathbb{R}^+$, and in a closed system $\sum_{u \in V} \alpha_u(t)\alpha_u^*(t) = 1$.

The evolution of the walk is governed by Schrödinger equation, where we take the Hamiltonian of the system to be the graph adjacency matrix A, which yields

$$\frac{d}{dt} |\psi_t\rangle = -iA |\psi_t\rangle \tag{3}$$

Given an initial state $|\psi_0\rangle$, we can solve Equation 3 to determine the state vector at time t

$$|\psi_t\rangle = e^{-iAt} |\psi_0\rangle = \Phi e^{-i\Lambda t} \Phi^\top |\psi_0\rangle , \tag{4}$$

where $A = \Phi\Lambda\Phi^\top$ is the spectral decomposition of the adjacency matrix.

Consider a quantum system that can be in a number of states $|\psi_i\rangle$ each with probability p_i. The system is said to be in the ensemble of (pure) states $\{|\psi_i\rangle, p_i\}$. The density operator (or density matrix) of such a system is defined as

$$\rho = \sum_i p_i |\psi_i\rangle \langle\psi_i| \tag{5}$$

The Von Neumann entropy [13] of a density operator ρ is $H_N(\rho) = -Tr(\rho \log \rho) = -\sum_j \lambda_j \log \lambda_j$, where the λ_js are the eigenvalues of ρ.

With the Von Neumann entropy to hand, we can define the quantum Jensen-Shannon divergence between two density operators ρ and σ as

$$D_{JS}(\rho, \sigma) = H_N\left(\frac{\rho + \sigma}{2}\right) - \frac{1}{2}H_N(\rho) - \frac{1}{2}H_N(\sigma) \tag{6}$$

This quantity is always well defined, symmetric and negative definite [17]. It can also be shown that $D_{JS}(\rho, \sigma)$ is bounded, i.e., $0 \leq D_{JS}(\rho, \sigma) \leq 1$, with equality to 1 if and only if the states ρ and σ have support on orthogonal subspaces.

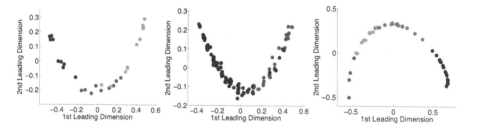

Fig. 1. The MDS embeddings from the QJSD kernel consistently show an horseshoe shape distribution of the points

3   The QJSD Kernel

Given two graphs $G_1(V_1, E_1)$ and $G_2(V_2, E_2)$ we construct a new graph $\mathcal{G} = (\mathcal{V}, \mathcal{E})$ where $\mathcal{V} = V_1 \cup V_2$, $\mathcal{E} = E_1 \cup E_2 \cup E_{12}$, and $(u, v) \in E_{12}$ only if $u \in V_1$ and $v \in V_2$. With this new structure to hand, we define two continuous-time quantum walks $\left| \psi_t^- \right\rangle = \sum_{u \in V} \psi_{0u}^- \left| u \right\rangle$ and $\left| \psi_t^+ \right\rangle = \sum_{u \in V} \psi_{0u}^+ \left| u \right\rangle$ on $\mathcal{G}$ with starting states

$$
\psi_{0u}^- = \begin{cases} +\frac{d_u}{C} & \text{if } u \in G_1 \\ -\frac{d_u}{C} & \text{if } u \in G_2 \end{cases} \qquad \psi_{0u}^+ = \begin{cases} +\frac{d_u}{C} & \text{if } u \in G_1 \\ +\frac{d_u}{C} & \text{if } u \in G_2 \end{cases} \tag{7}
$$

where d_u is the degree of the node u and C is the normalisation constant such that the probabilities sum to one.

We allow the two quantum walks evolve until a time T and we define the average density operators ρ_T and σ_T over this time as

$$
\rho_T = \frac{1}{T} \int_0^T \left| \psi_t^- \right\rangle \left\langle \psi_t^- \right| \, dt \qquad \sigma_T = \frac{1}{T} \int_0^T \left| \psi_t^+ \right\rangle \left\langle \psi_t^+ \right| \, dt \tag{8}
$$

In other words, we have defined two mixed systems with equal probability of being in any of the pure states defined by the quantum walks evolutions.

The quantum Jensen-Shannon kernel $k_T(G_1, G_2)$ between the unattributed graphs G_1 and G_2 is defined as

$$
k_T(G_1, G_2) = D_{JS}(\rho_T, \sigma_T) \tag{9}
$$

where ρ_T and σ_T are the density operators defined as in Eq. 8. Note that this kernel is parametrised by the time T. In [1] the authors we propose to let $T \to \infty$, however, they show that a proper choice of T can yield an increased average accuracy in an SVM classification task.

It can be proved [1] that $0 \leq k_T(G_1, G_2) \leq 1$ and that if G_1 and G_2 are two isomorphic graphs, then ρ_T and σ_T have support on orthogonal subspaces, and as a consequence $k_T(G_1, G_2) = 1$. Note that although the authors are unable to provide a proof that the QJSD kernel is positive semidefinite, both empirical evidence and the fact that the Jensen-Shannon Divergence is negative semidefinite on pure quantum states [17] while the QJSD is maximal on orthogonal states suggest that it might be.

Fig. 2. Sample images of the four selected object from the COIL-100 [18] dataset

3.1 Enhancing the QJSD through Manifold Learning

Figure 1 shows the MDS embedding of the distance matrices associated with the QJSD kernel for the synthetic, MUTAG and COIL datasets. Details on the datasets used in this paper can be found in Section 4. These embeddings clearly suffer from a horseshoe shape effect, which is usually the result of an accurate estimate of the distance between objects only when they are close together, but not when they are far apart [16]. As a consequence, it should be possible to increase the kernel performance by filtering out in some way this long range distance information.

In this paper we propose a simple yet effective way to achieve this goal. Given a set of graphs, we compute the Isomap [14] embedding of the graphs and we evaluate the separability of the graph classes as the distance information varies from local to global. Isomap is a well-known manifold learning technique, which extends classical MDS by incorporating the pairwise geodesic distances between points. To this end, a neighborhood graph is constructed from the original set of points, where each node is connected to its k nearest neighbors in the high-dimensional space. The geodesic distance between two nodes is then defined as the sum of the edge weights along the shortest-path between them. It is known that Isomap suffers from several shortcomings, so further work should focus on experimenting with more robust manifold learning techniques.

The class separability is evaluated in the following way. For each embedding, we perform a 10-fold cross validation using a binary C-SVM with a linear kernel, where we let the value of the SVM regularizer constant C vary over the interval 10^{-3} and 10^3. Then, we take the maximum value of the average classification accuracy as an indicator of the separability. More formally, we look for the Isomap embedding which maximises

$$\arg\max_{d,k} \max_C \alpha \tag{10}$$

where α is the 10-fold cross validation accuracy of the C-SVM, C is the regularizer constant, d is the embedding dimension and k is the number of nearest neighbors. Note that the multi-classification task is solved using majority voting on a set of one-vs-one C-SVM classifiers.

4   Experimental Results

The experiments are performed on four different dataset, namely MUTAG, PPI, COIL [18] and a set of shock graphs. MUTAG is a dataset of 188 mutagenic

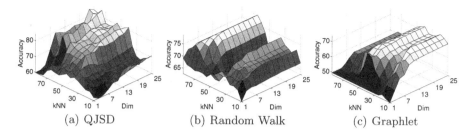

(a) QJSD   (b) Random Walk   (c) Graphlet

Fig. 3. 3D plot of the 10-fold cross validation accuracy on the PPI dataset as the number of the nearest neighbors k and the embedding dimension d vary

aromatic and heteroaromatic compounds labeled according to whether or not they have a mutagenic effect on the Gram-negative bacterium *Salmonella ty-phimurium*. The PPI dataset consists of protein-protein interaction (PPIs) networks related to histidine kinase from two different groups: 40 PPIs from *Acidovorax avenae* and 46 PPIs from *Acidobacteria*. The COIL dataset consists of the 4 objects shown in Figure 2, each with 72 views obtained from equally spaced viewing directions over 360°. For each image, a graph is obtained as the Delaunay triangulation of the Harris corner points. Finally, we select a set of shock graphs, a skeletal-based representation of the differential structure of the boundary of a 2D shape. The 120 graphs are divided into 8 classes of 15 shapes each. Each graph has a node attribute that reflects the size of the boundary feature generating the corresponding skeletal segment. To reflect the presence of attributes, the QJSD kernel is modified by labeling the new connections of the merged graph with the similarity between its two endpoints. To these four datasets, we add a fifth set of 30 synthetically generated graphs, 10 for each class. The graphs belonging to each class were sampled from a generative model with size 12,14 and 16 respectively [19].

Figure 3 shows the 3D plots of the 10-fold cross validation accuracy on the Isomap embeddings of the QJSD, the random walk and the graphlet kernels for the PPI dataset, as the size of the initial neighborhood and the embedding dimension vary. The plots show that for this dataset the QJSD kernel seems to be less sensitive to the locality of the distance information. On the other

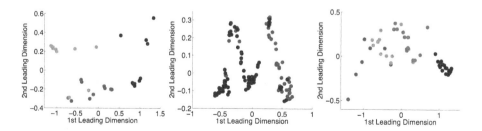

Fig. 4. The optimal two-dimensional Isomap embeddings in terms of separability between the graph classes

Table 1. Maximum classification accuracy on the unattributed graph datasets. Here SP is the shortest-path kernel of Borgwardt and Kriegel [6], RW is the random walk kernel of Gartner et al. [5], while GR denotes the graphlet kernel computed using all graphlets of size 3 described in Shervashidze et al. [7], while the subscript ISO indicates the result after the Isomap embedding. For each dataset, the best performing kernel before and after the embedding is shown in bold and italic, respectively.

Kernel	Synthetic	MUTAG	PPI	COIL	Shock
QJSD	*90.00*	*88.27*	*78.75*	84.44	*67.50*
QJSD$_{ISO}$	**96.67**	**91.96**	**90.69**	**91.53**	**77.50**
SP	80.00	86.08	71.25	85.56	61.67
SP$_{ISO}$	86.67	89.33	87.08	89.17	60.05
RW	86.67	77.02	70.97	79.72	49.17
RW$_{ISO}$	86.67	81.35	82.50	80.97	50.12
GR	86.67	82.92	49.56	*86.67*	39.17
GR$_{ISO}$	90.00	84.53	77.08	87.78	54.17

hand, for the graphlet kernel the maximum accuracy is achieved for a smaller neighborhood, which means that in this case the long range distance information is less accurate.

Figure 4 shows the two-dimensional Isomap embeddings with the highest linear separability for the QJSD kernels on the synthetic dataset, MUTAG and COIL. The result clearly shows the lack of the horseshoe shape distribution of Figure 1. Note, however, that the best embedding is usually found at a dimension higher than two and, as shown in Figure 3, the separability can change significantly as the dimension varies. Figure 4 also shows a clearer separation among the different classes, as highlighted in Table 1, which shows the separability of the data for each kernel and dataset. It is interesting to observe that, with the exception of a few cases, the Isomap embedding always yields an increased separability of the data, independently of the original kernel. It should also be underlined that the QJSD kernel always yields the highest separation, with a maximum classification accuracy above 90% in 4 out of 5 datasets.

5   Conclusions

In this paper, we studied the separability properties of the QJSD kernel and we have proposed a way to compute a low-dimensional embedding where the separation of the different classes is enhanced. The idea stems from the observation that the multidimensional scaling embeddings on this kernel show a strong horseshoe shape distribution, a pattern which is known to arise when long range distances are not estimated accurately. Here we proposed to use Isomap to embed the graphs using only local distance information onto a new vectorial space with a higher class separability. An extensive experimental evaluation has shown the effectiveness of the proposed approach.

Acknowledgments. Edwin Hancock was supported by a Royal Society Wolfson Research Merit Award.

References

1. Rossi, L., Torsello, A., Hancock, E.R.: A continuous-time quantum walk kernel for unattributed graphs. In: Kropatsch, W.G., Artner, N.M., Haxhimusa, Y., Jiang, X. (eds.) GbRPR 2013. LNCS, vol. 7877, pp. 101–110. Springer, Heidelberg (2013)
2. Siddiqi, K., Shokoufandeh, A., Dickinson, S., Zucker, S.: Shock graphs and shape matching. International Journal of Computer Vision 35, 13–32 (1999)
3. Jeong, H., Tombor, B., Albert, R., Oltvai, Z., Barabási, A.: The large-scale organization of metabolic networks. Nature 407, 651–654 (2000)
4. Schölkopf, B., Smola, A.J.: Learning with kernels: Support vector machines, regularization, optimization, and beyond. MIT press (2001)
5. Gaertner, T., Flach, P., Wrobel, S.: On graph kernels: Hardness results and efficient alternatives. In: Schölkopf, B., Warmuth, M.K. (eds.) COLT/Kernel 2003. LNCS (LNAI), vol. 2777, pp. 129–143. Springer, Heidelberg (2003)
6. Borgwardt, K., Kriegel, H.: Shortest-path kernels on graphs. In: Fifth IEEE International Conference on Data Mining, p. 8. IEEE (2005)
7. Shervashidze, N., Vishwanathan, S., Petri, T., Mehlhorn, K., Borgwardt, K.: Efficient graphlet kernels for large graph comparison. In: Proceedings of the International Workshop on Artificial Intelligence and Statistics (2009)
8. Haussler, D.: Convolution kernels on discrete structures. Technical report, UC Santa Cruz (1999)
9. Farhi, E., Gutmann, S.: Quantum computation and decision trees. Physical Review A 58, 915 (1998)
10. Emms, D., Wilson, R., Hancock, E.: Graph embedding using a quasi-quantum analogue of the hitting times of continuous time quantum walks. Quantum Information & Computation 9, 231–254 (2009)
11. Rossi, L., Torsello, A., Hancock, E.R.: Approximate axial symmetries from continuous time quantum walks. In: Gimel'farb, G., Hancock, E., Imiya, A., Kuijper, A., Kudo, M., Omachi, S., Windeatt, T., Yamada, K. (eds.) SSPR&SPR 2012. LNCS, vol. 7626, pp. 144–152. Springer, Heidelberg (2012)
12. Lamberti, P., Majtey, A., Borras, A., Casas, M., Plastino, A.: Metric character of the quantum Jensen-Shannon divergence. Physical Review A 77, 052311 (2008)
13. Nielsen, M., Chuang, I.: Quantum computation and quantum information. Cambridge university press (2010)
14. Tenenbaum, J.B., De Silva, V., Langford, J.C.: A global geometric framework for nonlinear dimensionality reduction. Science 290, 2319–2323 (2000)
15. Czaja, W., Ehler, M.: Schroedinger eigenmaps for the analysis of biomedical data. IEEE Transactions on Pattern Analysis and Machine Intelligence 35, 1274–1280 (2013)
16. Kendall, D.G.: Abundance matrices and seriation in archaeology. Probability Theory and Related Fields 17, 104–112 (1971)
17. Briët, J., Harremoës, P.: Properties of classical and quantum jensen-shannon divergence. Physical review A 79, 052311 (2009)
18. Nayar, S., Nene, S., Murase, H.: Columbia object image library (coil 100). Technical report, Tech. Report No. CUCS-006-96. Department of Comp. Science, Columbia University (1996)
19. Torsello, A., Rossi, L.: Supervised learning of graph structure. In: Pelillo, M., Hancock, E.R. (eds.) SIMBAD 2011. LNCS, vol. 7005, pp. 117–132. Springer, Heidelberg (2011)

Spatio-temporal Manifold Embedding for Nearly-Repetitive Contents in a Video Stream

Manal Al Ghamdi and Yoshihiko Gotoh

Department of Computer Science, University of Sheffield, United Kingdom
{m.alghamdi,y.gotoh}@dcs.shef.ac.uk

Abstract. This paper presents a framework to identify and align nearly-repetitive contents in a video stream using spatio-temporal manifold embedding. The similarities observed in frame sequences are captured by defining two types of correlation graphs: an intra-correlation graph in the spatial domain and an inter-correlation graph in the temporal domain. The presented work is novel in that it does not utilise any prior information such as the length and contents of the repetitive scenes. No template is required, and no learning process is involved in the approach. Instead it analyses the video contents using the spatio-temporal extension of SIFT combined with a coding technique. The underlying structure is then reconstructed using manifold embedding. Experiments using a TRECVID rushes video proved that the framework was able to improve embedding of repetitive sequences over the conventional methods, thus was able to identify the repetitive contents from complex scenes.

Keywords: manifold embedding, synchronisation, inter- and intra-correlations, rushes video.

1 Introduction

In recent years there have been a wide range of audio visual data publicly available, including news, movies, television programmes and meeting records, resulting in various content-management problems. Among these there exist nearly-repetitive video sequences whereby the original material is transformed to nearly, but not exactly, identical contents. Rushes videos, also referred to as pre-production videos, belong to one category of such examples [1]. It is a collection consisting of raw footage, used to produce, *e.g.*, TV programmes [2].

Unlike many other video datasets rushes are unconventional, containing additional contents such as clapper boards, colour bars and empty white shots. They also contain repetitive contents from multiple retakes of the same scene, caused by, *e.g.*, actors' mistakes or technical failures during the production. Although contents are nearly repetitive they may not be totally identical duplicates, sometimes causing inconsistency between retakes. Occasionally some parts of the original sequence may be dropped or extra information may be added at various places, resulting in retakes of the same scene with unequal lengths.

R. Wilson et al. (Eds.): CAIP 2013, Part I, LNCS 8047, pp. 70–77, 2013.

The task of aligning multiple audio visual sequences, potentially from different angles, needs precise synchronisation in both spatial and temporal domains. The majority of previous works employed techniques such as template matching, camera calibration analysis and object tracking. Whitehead *et al.* [3], for example, tracked multiple objects throughout each sequence using a 2D shape heuristic. Temporal correspondence was then computed between frames by identifying the object's location in all views satisfying the epipolar geometry. In [4], the authors required the events to be captured by still cameras with flashes; the binary flash patterns were analysed and matched throughout the video sequence. Tresadern and Reid [5] used a rank constraint on corresponding frame features instead of the epipolar geometry. The synchronisations were defined by searching frame pairs that minimise the rank constraint. However their approach requires prior knowledge on the number of correspondences in the frame sequences.

In this paper we present a spatio-temporal framework to aligning nearly-repetitive contents. Embedded repetitions in the three dimensional (3D) signal, consisting of two spatial and one temporal dimension, are discovered by defining the coherent structure. We depart from the previous extension made on Isomap [1] to spatio-temporal graph-based manifold embedding that captures correlations between repetitive scenes. The intra- and inter-correlations within and between repeated video contents are defined by applying the spatio-temporal extension of the scale-invariant feature transform (SIFT) [6]. It is followed by the modified version of the locality constrained linear coding (LLC) [7], where each spatio-temporal descriptor is encoded by k-nearest neighbours (kNN) based on the geodesic distances, instead of the Euclidean distance. The latter measures the distance between two points as the length of a straight line from one point to the other, whereas on the non-linear manifold, their Euclidean distance may not accurately reflect their intrinsic similarity, which is measured by the geodesic distance. A cluster of intrinsic coordinates are then generated on the embedded space to define the spatial and temporal similarity between repetitions.

The contributions of this study are as follows: Firstly a spatial intra-correlation representation is created for repetitive contents in a video stream. Interest points that have significant local variations in both space and time are extracted and encoded using fewer codebook basis in the high-dimensional feature space. Intra-correlation is derived by constructing a shortest path graph using the kNN with the geodesic distances. Secondly Isomap is extended to estimate the underlying structure of repetitive contents and to define a spatio-temporal inter-correlation in a video stream. Thirdly an unsupervised framework, which does not require prior information or pre-processing steps, for aligning similar contents is presented for multimedia data with repetitions.

2   Spatio-temporal Alignment of Nearly-Repetitive Scenes

In this work we explore a low-dimensional representation of nearly-repetitive contents observed in a video stream. To this end video's semantic structure is defined in the high-dimensional space. The approach consists of two stages. Firstly

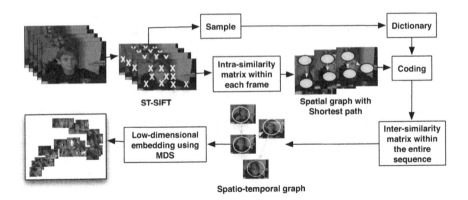

Fig. 1. Processing steps for spatio-temporal alignment of nearly-repetitive contents in a video stream

intra-correlation is captured in the high-dimensional space using the space-time invariant interest points detection and coding scheme (Section 2.1). Application of LCC technique at this stage allows consideration of the locality of the manifold structure. Secondly a manifold representation maps the video sequence to the embedded space (Section 2.2). At this stage the inter-correlation is computed between multiple video scenes using the spatio-temporal kNN graph. We adapted the spatio-temporal Isomap implemented previously by [1] to generate the intrinsic coordinates for each manifold. Generated coordinates are chronologically ordered based on the spatio-temporal similarity and clustered to groups of similar repetitive contents. The entire process of the approach is illustrated in Figure 1.

2.1   Spatio-temporal Video Representation

The framework consists of a space-time extension of SIFT, or ST-SIFT [6], combined with a modified version of the LLC [7]. The coding scheme projects each descriptor into a local coordinate representation produced by max pooling [8].

Spatio-Temporal SIFT. The ST-SIFT algorithm identifies spatially and temporally invariant interest points given a video stream [6]. These points contain the amount of information sufficient to represent the video contents. Unlike other interest points detection schemes, ST-SIFT is able to detect spatially distinctive points with sufficient motion information at multiple scales. To achieve the invariance in both space and time, a spatio-temporal Gaussian and Difference of Gaussian (DoG) pyramids are calculated first. Then the points shared between three spatial and temporal planes (xy, xt and yt) at each scale in the DoG are chosen as interest points.

Coding with Shortest Path Graph. LLC is a coding scheme proposed by Wang *et al.* [7] to project individual descriptors onto their respective local coordinate systems. It translates image descriptors into local sparse codes based on the Euclidean distances and the kNN search. We extended this algorithm to project spatio-temporal descriptors extracted from a video stream into their local linear codes using the geodesic distance and the shortest path graph.

Technically, given the ST-SIFT feature matrix extracted from a video stream with N entries and D dimensions, $i.e.$, $X = \{x_1, \dots, x_N\} \in \mathbb{R}^{D \times N}$, LLC solves the following problem:

$$\min_S \sum_{i=1}^{N} \|x_i - Bs_i\|^2 + \lambda \|d_i \odot s_i\|^2 \quad st. \quad 1^\top s_i = 1, \ \forall i$$

where $\odot$ is the element-wise multiplication, B is a codebook, λ is a sparsity regularisation term and $S = \{s_1, \dots, s_N\} \in \mathbb{R}^{D \times N}$ is a set of codes for X. Furthermore '$1^\top s_i = 1$, $\forall i$' means the shift-invariant requirements for the LLC code. The locality-constrained parameter d_i represents each basis vector with different freedom based on its shortest path to the spatio-temporal descriptor x_i. Intra-correlation in the spatial domain S is derived by firstly constructing a neighbourhood graph based on the geodesic distances between the descriptors and the codebook, then computing the shortest path, performing a kNN search, and finally solving a constrained least square fitting problem.

2.2 Manifold Embedding

High-dimensional representation can be mapped to a spatio-temporal graph where nodes represent frames and edges represent the temporal order (event sequence). We adapted the Isomap extension of [1] to reconstruct the spatio-temporal inter-correlation δ from the intra-correlation S. The algorithm calculates the geodesic distance within the video frames to ensure the shortest path. The algorithm can be summarised in the following three steps:

Step 1. We construct a spatio-temporal neighbourhood graph δ from the intra-correlation matrix S. N nodes represent frames and N edges represent the connection between the frames if they are related. Initially, the geodesic distances between the nodes in δ graph are computed. Then the L spatial neighbours (sn) are defined for each frame x_i using the shortest path:

$$sn_{x_i} = \left\{ x_{i1}, \dots, x_{iL} \ \middle| \ \operatorname*{argmin}_j{}^{L}(\delta_{ij}) \right\}, \quad i = 1, \dots, N$$

where $\operatorname{argmin}_j{}^L$ indicates node indexes for j that give L minimum values of δ_{ij}. Other L chronologically ordered neighbours around each frame x_i are then defined as temporal neighbours (tn):

$$tn_{x_i} = \left\{ x_{i-\frac{L}{2}}, \dots, x_{i-1}, x_{i+1}, \dots, x_{i+\frac{L}{2}} \right\}, \quad i = 1, \dots, N$$

The temporal neighbours of the spatial neighbours $tn_{sn_{x_i}}$ are defined for more coverage:

$$tn_{sn_{x_i}} = \{ tn_{x_{i1}}, \dots, tn_{x_{iL}} \}, \quad i = 1, \dots, N$$

Finally, union between spatial and temporal sets represents the spatio-temporal neighbours *stn*:

$$stn_{x_i} = sn_{x_i} \cup tn_{sn_{x_i}}, \quad i = 1, \ldots, N$$

Step 2. Given the spatio-temporal neighbourhood graph δ, correlation based on the geodesic distances δ_γ is defined by recalculating the shortest path between the neighbouring nodes.

Step 3. The manifold embedding is modelled as a transformation T of the high-dimensional data in terms of correlation δ_γ into a new embedded space D:

$$T : \delta_\gamma \to D$$

The function T is the eigen decomposition of the inter-correlation matrix that minimises the following loss function:

$$L_{projection} = \|\delta - T(\delta)\| = \|\delta - T(\delta_\gamma)\| = \|\delta - (Q \wedge Q^T)\| = \|\delta - (Q_+ \wedge_+^{\frac{1}{2}})\|$$

where Q and $\wedge$ are the eigenvectors and the eigenvalues of δ_γ. To optimise the embedded representation, the m largest eigenvalues in $\wedge$ along the diagonal is defined in $\wedge_+$, and the square root of m columns of Q is defined in Q_+.

3   Experiments

The approach was evaluated using MPEG-1 videos from the NIST TRECVID 2008 BBC rushes video collection [2]. Five video sequences were selected containing drama productions in the following genres: detective, emergency, police, ancient Greece and historical London. In total we had an approximate duration of 82 minutes, sampled at the frame rate of 25 fps (frames per second) and a frame size of 288×352 pixels. Table 1 provides further details of the dataset.

The video representation was created as follows. Firstly, spatio-temporal regions were detected and described from the video cube using the ST-SIFT [6]. For each interest point the descriptor length was 640-dimensional, determined by the number of bins to represent the orientation angles, θ and ϕ, in the sub-histograms. In the spatial pyramid matching step, the LLC codes were computed for each sub-region and pooled together using the multi-scale max pooling to create the pooled representation. We used 4×4, 2×2 and 1×1 sub-regions. The pooled features were then concatenated and normalised using the ℓ^2-norm.

3.1   Evaluation Schema

Each scene from the rushes videos is a line of actions defined by actors' dialogue. They were used as units of evaluation and the purpose of the experiment was to group and align the multiple similar retakes of the same scene. The description of actions for each scene was provided by the NIST for the BBC rushes video

Table 1. The duration, the number of scenes and the number of retakes for each scene

video id	duration (min:sec)	#scenes	#retakes (#retakes/scene)
MS206290	21:03	11	27 (2,1,1,3,5,5,2,2,1,4,1)
MS206370	12:30	7	17 (2,2,2,2,3,4,2)
MS215830	14:55	5	14 (3,3,3,2,3)
MRS044499	12:42	6	10 (2,2,2,1,1,2)
MRS1500072	21:40	10	26 (3,5,1,2,2,3,2,3,3,2)

summarisation task in 2008 [2]. The ground truth was constructed for each video using three human judges at a frame rate of 0.5 fps (one frame per two seconds). The judges were asked to study the video summary and use it to identify the start and the end for each retake. The defined positions for five videos, totalling 39 scenes and 94 retakes, were used as the ground truth.

In the experiments, the approach was compared with the three other simplified alternatives. The first one evaluates the performance of the entire framework. It was a combination of the original 2D SIFT by Lowe [9], LLC coding with the Euclidean distance graph by [7] and spatial Isomap by [10]. The second one evaluates the performance of the intra-correlation step covered by ST-SIFT and LLC with the shortest path graph. It consisted of the 2D SIFT, LLC coding with the Euclidean distance graph and the Isomap-ST, an adapted version of [1]. The third one evaluates the performance of the inter-correlation step covered by the Isomap-ST. For that we combined the ST-SIFT [6] with LLC coding with the shortest path graph and the spatial Isomap.

3.2 Results

Figure 2 presents the average precision and recall for each video using the approach and three alternatives. Graphs were created using the neighbourhood size k as the operating parameter. They indicate that the approach outperformed the conventional techniques with a fair margin. The approach was able to capture the spatio-temporal correlations between retakes in each video sequence. The best result was obtained with video *MRS150072* in Figure 2(e). This video contained outdoor scenes with large variations, characterised by busy backgrounds and lots of movements by actors and objects. On the other hand, Figure 2(a) for video *MS206290* resulted in the lowest performance. It consisted of indoor scenes with crowded people and little moves. Therefore there were few significant changes between the frames to be captured by the ST-SIFT.

Figure 3 illustrates the reconstruction of video sequences, aiming to uncover their nearly-repetitive contents. Retakes from the same scene were mapped close to each other in the manifold resulting in clusters of repetitive contents. The video sequence *MRS044499* presented in the figure contained six scenes with ten retakes (described earlier in Table 1). The left panel of the figure shows the aligned sequences in the 2D space with multiple clusters of frames. Most frames from the same scene were re-positioned and placed close together in the

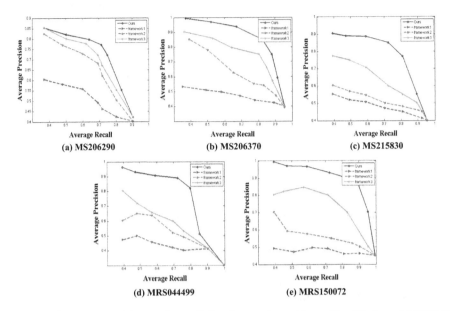

Fig. 2. Average precision and recall for five rushes videos, identified as *MS206290*, *MS206370*, *MS215830*, *MRS044499*, and *MRS150072*. For each video stream, the spatio-temporal alignment method (blue) is compared with three other alternatives.

lower dimensional space. There were many causes, such as camera moves, that could result in discontinuity because such frames did not share sufficient spatial features with others. Consideration of temporal relation in the intra-correlation step alleviated this problem, thus successfully producing a clear video trajectory in the manifold. The contents of one cluster, two retakes of the same scene, are presented in the right panel of the figure.

4   Conclusions and Future Work

This paper presented a framework to aligning nearly-repetitive contents in a video stream using manifold embedding. It utilised LLC with the shortest path graph to densely extract and encode salient feature points from a 3D signal, generating an intra-correlation in the spatial domain. A spatio-temporal graph was derived as a step for manifold embedding that defined the inter-correlation across the video sequence. Experimental results using rushes videos showed that the approach with spatio-temporal representation performed better than the conventional techniques. The contribution of this study may be extended to other applications involving temporal information processing, such as video summarisation and video information retrieval.

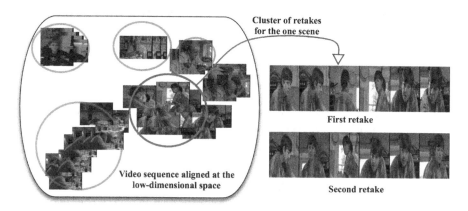

Fig. 3. Video sequence *MRS044499* was aligned in the two-dimensional space using the neighbourhood size of $k = 15$

Acknowledgements. The first author would like to thank Umm Al-Qura University, Makkah, Saudi Arabia for funding this work as part of her PhD scholarship program.

References

1. Chantamunee, S., Gotoh, Y.: Nearly-repetitive video synchronisation using nonlinear manifold embedding. In: Proceedings of ICASSP (2010)
2. Over, P., Smeaton, A.F., Awad, G.: The TRECVID 2008 BBC rushes summarization evaluation. In: ACM TRECVID Video Summarization Workshop (2008)
3. Whitehead, A., Laganiere, R., Bose, P.: Temporal synchronization of video sequences in theory and in practice. In: IEEE Workshop on Motion and Video Computing (2005)
4. Shrestha, P., Weda, H., Barbieri, M., Sekulovski, D.: Synchronization of multiple video recordings based on still camera flashes. In: Proceedings of ACM Multimedia (2006)
5. Tresadern, P.A., Reid, I.D.: Synchronizing image sequences of non-rigid objects. In: Proceedings of BMVC (2003)
6. Al Ghamdi, M., Zhang, L., Gotoh, Y.: Spatio-temporal SIFT and its application to human action classification. In: Fusiello, A., Murino, V., Cucchiara, R. (eds.) ECCV 2012 Ws/Demos, Part I. LNCS, vol. 7583, pp. 301–310. Springer, Heidelberg (2012)
7. Wang, H., Ullah, M.M., Kläser, A., Laptev, I., Schmid, C.: Evaluation of local spatio-temporal features for action recognition. In: Proceedings of BMVC (2009)
8. Serre, T., Wolf, L., Poggio, T.: Object recognition with features inspired by visual cortex. In: Proceedings of CVPR (2005)
9. Lowe, D.G.: Distinctive image features from scale-invariant keypoints. International Journal of Computer Vision (2004)
10. Tenenbaum, J.B., de Silva, V., Langford, J.C.: A global geometric framework for nonlinear dimensionality reduction. Science (2000)

Spatio-temporal Human Body Segmentation from Video Stream

Nouf Al Harbi and Yoshihiko Gotoh

Department of Computer Science, University of Sheffield, United Kingdom
nmalharbi1@sheffield.ac.uk, y.gotoh@dcs.shef.ac.uk

Abstract. We present a framework in which human body volume is extracted from a video stream. Following the line of object tracking-based methods, our approach detect and segment human body regions by jointly embedding parts and pixels. For all extracted segments the appearance and shape models are learned in order to automatically extract the foreground objects across a sequence of video frames. We evaluated the framework using a challenging set of video clips, consisting of office scenes, selected from Hollywood2 dataset. The outcome from the experiments indicates that the approach was able to create better segmentation than recently implemented work.

Keywords: spatio-temporal segmentation, human volume, object tracking.

1 Introduction

Computer vision presents several challenges, the foremost of which is that of automatic interpretation of video streams. The intricate task involves detecting and interpreting video contents and identifying people and other objects, in addition to recognising their movement. Traditionally these tasks are carried out by working with individual video frames. However, the reality of video and its moving language means that there are clues to interpretation beyond any given frame. Specifically these cues can be defined as the motion of objects, the way that individuals and objects interact over time, how time moves within the video, and the event relationships between objects and characters.

To date, various attempts have been made to sort video pixels into groups of similarity, but this has not proven a simple or error-free task. Video segmentation aims to sort pixels into regions of spatio-temporal unity in terms of individual contents and their movements. It is useful for higher level vision tasks such as activity recognition, object tracking across video frames, content-based retrieval and more general image enhancement. However the intricate nature of the segmentation process is related to the temporal coherence of a video clip. The frame-by-frame approach to segmentation generally results in a choppy and unusable end product, since individually segmented frames are difficult to patch back into a video stream due to a lack of coherence in movement. Indeed it is in

R. Wilson et al. (Eds.): CAIP 2013, Part I, LNCS 8047, pp. 78–85, 2013.

the very nature of the process of segmentation developed for still images that it is unable to realise continuity through time.

In this work we explore an approach to extracting three dimensional (3D) human volume, consisting of two spatial and one temporal dimension. Our implementation of video segmentation follows the line of tracking-based methods. It detects and segments human body regions from a video stream by jointly embedding parts and pixels [1]. For all extracted segments the appearance and shape models will be learned in order to automatically identify foreground objects across video frames. It focuses on human contours, in particular, modified from the category independent segmentation work by Lee *et al.* [2]. The approach is evaluated using office scenes selected from the Hollywood2 dataset [3]. The experimental results indicate that the approach was able to create consistently better segmentation than recently implemented work [2].

1.1   Related Work

Recent image segmentation techniques have the possibility of rendering segmentation in real time, though continuity across frames may still present an issue. The consideration of temporal coherence is obviously what needs to be added to the conventional schemes in order to cleanly segment video streams. A mean shift approach was developed by Freedman and Kisilev [4], that used a sample-based method to group frames, ten in their case, into image clusters. They were able to smooth out the segmentation, resulting in elements larger than frames of a moving image, without taking temporal information into account.

The current range of spatio-temporal video segmentation techniques can generally be divided into those that use information from subsequent frames, and those that make use of information from previous frames. Patti *et al.* [5] investigated a Kalman filtering based mechanism, generating more fluid and coherent segmentation. Kalman filtering was able to sort visual information through time, although its causal process could only take past data into account. Paris [6] managed to realise real-time performance using a method based on the Gaussian kernel with mean shift segmentation. The mechanism did not, however, take information from future video frames into the process of analysis.

Techniques that look at both past and future frames are the third category of segmentation [7]. They worked with a video as if it were a 3D space-time volume, making use of a varying mean shift algorithm in order to carry out a segmentation process [8]. One such application was created by Dementhon and Megret [9], who created a lattice with hierarchies, in order to rank and evaluate clusters of space-time in an efficient manner.

Wang *et al.* [10] developed a mechanism for 'tooning' videos based on an anisotropic kernel mean shift. Motion heuristics was yet another scheme for creating smooth layers within a video, as Wang and Adelson [11] segmented a video iteratively using this method. Tracking-based video segmentation methods generally define segments at a frame level; they use motion, colour and spatial relations to determine segmentation in a relatively unified fashion [12,13]. Brendel and Todorovic [14] used contour cues to allow splitting and merging of segments

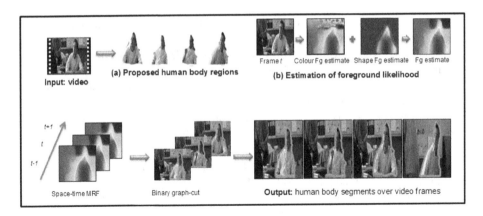

Fig. 1. Two-stage approach to human volume segmentation. A human body detected in the first stage is propagated along video frames in the second stage.

to boost the tracking performance. Finally, interactive object segmentation has recently shown significant progress [15,16,17], producing high quality segmentations driven by user input. We exhibit a similar interactive framework driven by our segmentation.

2   Approach

Our goal is to segment human body volume in an unlabelled video. The approach consists of two main stages (Figure 1). Firstly, human body objects are segmented at a frame level by combining low-level cues with a top-down part-based person detector developed by Maire *et al.* [1], formulating grouped patches. Secondly, detected segments are propagated along the video frames, exploiting the temporal consistency of detected foreground objects using colour models and local shape matching [2]. The final output is a spatio-temporal segmentation of the human body in a video stream. We now describe each stage in turn.

2.1   Estimation of Human Body Region at Frame Level

This stage builds on the graph-based image segmentation technique of Maire *et al.* [1]. It produces a grouping of parts and pixels along the following idea:

- pixels are connected based on low-level cues in order to accomplish region consistency;
- detected parts are bound together when they belong to the same object;
- the regions belonging to a part are included in the foreground, whereas the remaining regions are pushed to the background.

A brief description of the first stage is given below. Further detail should be referred to [1].

Globalisation. The angular embedding (AE) algorithm is used as a globlisation framework [18], which is constrained using a pairwise ordering relationship matrix Θ. Each relationship is assigned a confidence matrix C, which is combined with linear constraints on a solution space of embedding U and complex eigenvectors, $z_0, \ldots, z_{m-1}$, to form the generalised eigenproblem:

$$QPQz = \lambda z$$

where P is a normalised weight matrix and Q is a projector onto the feasible solution space defined by:

$$P = D^{-1}W, \qquad Q = I - D^{-1}U(U^T D^{-1} U)^{-1} U^T$$

D and W are defined based on C and Θ:

$$D = Diag(C1_n), \qquad W = C \bullet e^{i\Theta}$$

where n represent the number of nodes, 1_n is a column vector of ones, I is the identity matrix, $Diag(.)$ is a matrix with an argument on the main diagonal, $\bullet$ stand for the matrix Hadamard product, $i = \sqrt{-1}$ and exponentiation performed element-wise. Eigenvectors $z_0, \ldots, z_{m-1}$ correspond to the largest eigenvalues and transfer the output of pixels and parts into $\mathbb{C}$.

Graph Setup: Pixel and Part Relations. The graph to be used for the image segmentation is constructed using four node types [pixels (p), parts (q), surround (s) and figure/ground prior (f)] within a block structure defined by $n \times n$ matrices, C and Θ. Colour and texture pixel-pixel affinity C_p is determined by examining the contour between the pixels, whereas the geometric compatibility C_q (the part-part affinity) is identified using pairwise part-pose compatibility and poselet detection scores. These part-part detection scores are used to determine increases in repulsion between the part and the surround $[(C_s, \Theta_s)]$; the latter is based on the global surround node (C_f, Θ_f). U is constrained by part embedding equalling the mean embedding of the pixels comprising the part, and requires the part/surround nodes to concur with the pixels assigned to each node.

$$C = \begin{bmatrix} C_p & 0 & 0 & 0 \\ 0 & \alpha \cdot C_q & \beta \cdot C_s & \gamma \cdot C_f \\ 0 & \beta \cdot C_s^T & 0 & 0 \\ 0 & \gamma \cdot C_f^T & 0 & 0 \end{bmatrix}, \qquad \Theta = \Sigma^{-1} \begin{bmatrix} 0 & 0 & 0 & 0 \\ 0 & 0 & -\Theta_s & -\Theta_f \\ 0 & -\Theta_s^T & 0 & 0 \\ 0 & -\Theta_f^T & 0 & 0 \end{bmatrix}$$

Output: Decoding Eigenvectors. The nodes in $\mathbb{C}^m$, which are based on the pixels and parts plugged into the graph according to the eigenvectors, are inherently meaningful; the eigenvectors can be used to identify the region occupied by each human body object in the frame. Each pixel is assigned to a part by solving the equation:

$$p_k \longrightarrow \underset{Q_i}{\mathrm{argmin}} \left\{ \min_{\substack{q_j \in Q_i \\ p_k \in M_j}} \{D(p_k, q_j)\} \right\}$$

where M_j is the region of the image overlapped by a part q_j. Each part is then assigned to a Q_i, which represents the number of confirmed objects detected. Human body segments are then scored for each frame. This step is repeated with a set of $N \times F$, where each N is the number of human body objects per frame and F is the number of frames. These steps result in the set of hypotheses, h, which are then used to identify the spatio-temporal segmentation of human body parts in the entire video stream.

2.2 Spatio-temporal Segmentation of Human from a Video Stream

Each of the hypotheses (h) identified in the previous stage defines a foreground (human body) and a background (surround) model. Each object-like region in each frame is replaced by a human body, following the method of Lee et $al.$ [2]. Pixel-wise segmentation is used to extract the human body segments from the surround in the video stream on a frame-by-frame basis, using the space-time Markov random field (MRF) described below. For each frame, the space-time graph of a pixel is defined, where the pixel is represented by a node and the edge between two nodes equates to the cut between two pixels. Each hypothesis h has an energy function, which can be determined by:

$$E(f, h) = \sum_{i \in S} D_i^h(f_i) + \gamma \sum_{i,j \in N} V_{i,j}(f_i, f_j)$$

where f represents the pixel nodes, $S = \{p_1, \ldots, p_n\}$ is a set of n pixels in the video, and i and j index the pixels in space and time. Each pixel is then assigned to the foreground or background by setting p_i of each pixel to $f_i \in \{0, 1\}$, where $0 =$ background and $1 =$ foreground. The neighbourhood term $V_{i,j}$ is used to enhance smoothness in space and time between the pixels in adjacent frames. Four spatial neighbours are assigned to each pixel per frame. Two temporal neighbours are assigned in the preceding and subsequent frames; each of these is then given an optical flow vector displacement. Neighbouring pixels of the same colour are labelled using standard contrast dependent functions, with the cost of labelling defined by:

$$D_i^h(f_i) = -\log(\alpha \cdot U_i^c(f_i, h) + (1 - \alpha) \cdot U_i^l(f_i, h))$$

where $U_i^c(\cdot)$ is the colour-induced cost, and $U_i^l(\cdot)$ is the local shape match-induced cost. The segments detected in each frame on the basis of their parts and pixels are projected onto other frames by local shape matching, with a spatial extent which defines the location and scale prior to the segment, whose pixels can subsequently be labelled as foreground or background. Optical flow connections are used to maintain frame-to-frame consistency of the background and foreground labelling of propagated segments. For each hypothesis h, the foreground object segmentation of the video can be labelled by using binary graph cuts to minimise the function $E(f, h)$. Each frame is labelled in this way, using a space-time graph of three frames to connect each frame to its preceding and subsequent frames. This is more efficient than segmenting the video as the whole.

sceneclipautoautotrain00405   sceneclipautoautotrain00319

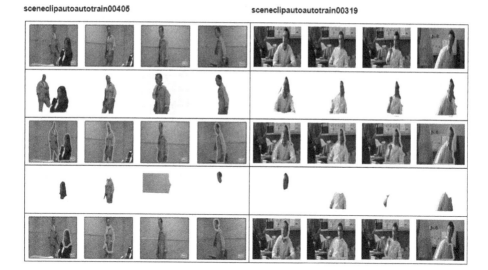

Fig. 2. Sample segmentations. The first row shows key frames from two video clips. The second and the third rows respectively present the results of key segments and the corresponding segmentation using the approach in this paper. The last two rows show the same attempts using the implementation by Lee *et al.* [2]. Best viewed on pdf.

3 Experiments

Dataset. The Hollywood2 dataset [3] holds a total of 69 Hollywood movie scenes, from which ten short video clips were selected for testing the approach. All the selected scenes are set in an office environment, and feature a broad range of motions as well as a variety of temporal changes, thus creating a challenging video segmentation task. The selected clips vary from 30 seconds to 2 minutes in duration, with at least one human present in each shot; there are many shots showing multiple human figures. For each clip, video frames are extracted using a ffmpeg[1] decoder, with a sample rate of one frame per second.

Evaluation Scheme. Accuracy is the commonly used measure for evaluating video segmentation tasks. In this work we adopt the average per-frame pixel error rate [19] for evaluation of the approach. Let F denote the number of frames in the video, and S and GT represent pixels in the segmented region and in the 'groundtruth' across the frame sequence respectively. The error rate is calculated using the exclusive OR operation:

$$E(S) = \frac{|\mathrm{XOR}(S, GT)|}{F}$$

The equation is used under the general hypothesis that object and groundtruth annotation should match.

---

[1] `www.ffmpeg.org/`

Table 1. The average number of incorrectly segmented pixels per frame. The video clip name is in the format of 'sceneclipautoautotrain·····' where '·····' part is shown in the table.

clip name	this paper	Lee *et al.*
00007	1172	1875
00062	9829	42532
00099	6996	20858
00105	10870	13949
00107	2096	6919
00181	1265	9624
00187	8900	19112
00319	520	4659
00405	3400	30513
00431	11585	45361

Results and Discussion. Figure 2 presents sample outcomes of segmentation using (a) the approach in this paper and (b) the recent implementation by Lee *et al.*[2] [2]. It shows that accurate segmentation of humans was made by our approach. Implementation by Lee *et al.* could not extract a complete human body although it discovered some parts.

Quantitative evaluation was conducted using ten video clips from the Hollywood2 dataset. The groundtruth was obtained by manually segmenting each frame into the foreground (humans) and the background (anything else present in the frame). Table 1 shows that the approach produced consistently better segmentation than the one implemented by Lee *et al.* We observed that the typical cause of failed segmentation by our approach was the absence of a human face. On the other hand, segmentation by the latter was unsuccessful especially when there was more than one person present in the scene.

4   Conclusion

In this paper we presented the two-stage approach to spatio-temporal human body segmentation by extracting a human body at a frame level, followed by tracking the segmented regions using colour appearance and local shape matching across the frames. By detecting and segmenting human body parts, we overcame the limitations of the bottom-up unsupervised methods that often oversegmented an object. Using ten challenging video clips derived from the Hollywood2 dataset, we were able to obtain consistently better segmentation results than recent implementations in the field.

---

[2] Program code available from www.cs.utexas.edu/~grauman/research/software.html. We tested their implementation with our office scene dataset. This was perhaps not totally a fair comparison because the purpose of their work was an unsupervised approach to key object segmentation from unlabelled video, where the number of object was restricted to one, while we focused on extraction of human volume.

Acknowledgements. The first author would like to thank Taibah University, Madinah, Saudi Arabia for funding this work as part of her PhD scholarship program.

References

1. Maire, M., Yu, S.X., Perona, P.: Object detection and segmentation from joint embedding of parts and pixels. In: Proceedings of ICCV (2011)
2. Lee, Y.J., Kim, J., Grauman, K.: Key-segments for video object segmentation. In: Proceedings of ICCV (2011)
3. Marszalek, M., Laptev, I., Schmid, C.: Actions in context. In: Proceedings of CVPR (2009)
4. Freedman, D., Kisilev, P.: Fast mean shift by compact density representation. In: Proceedings of CVPR (2009)
5. Patti, A.J., Tekalp, A.M., Sezan, M.I.: A new motion-compensated reduced-order model Kalman filter for space-varying restoration of progressive and interlaced video. IEEE Transactions on Image Processing 7 (1998)
6. Paris, S.: Edge-preserving smoothing and mean-shift segmentation of video streams. In: Forsyth, D., Torr, P., Zisserman, A. (eds.) ECCV 2008, Part II. LNCS, vol. 5303, pp. 460–473. Springer, Heidelberg (2008)
7. Klein, A.W., Sloan, P.P.J., Finkelstein, A., Cohen, M.F.: Stylized video cubes. In: ACM SIGGRAPH/Eurographics Symposium on Computer Animation (2002)
8. Comaniciu, D., Meer, P.: Mean shift: a robust approach toward feature space analysis. IEEE Transactions on Pattern Analysis and Machine Intelligence 24 (2002)
9. DeMenthon, D., Megret, R.: Spatio-temporal segmentation of video by hierarchical mean shift analysis. Technical report, Language and Media Processing Laboratory, University of Maryland (2002)
10. Wang, J., Xu, Y., Shum, H.Y., Cohen, M.F.: Video tooning. ACM Transaction on Graphics 23 (2004)
11. Wang, J.Y.A., Adelson, E.H.: Representing moving images with layers. IEEE Transactions on Image Processing 3 (1994)
12. Khan, S., Shah, M.: Object based segmentation of video using color, motion and spatial information. In: Proceedings of CVPR (2001)
13. Zitnick, C.L., Jojic, N., Kang, S.B.: Consistent segmentation for optical flow estimation. In: Proceedings of ICCV (2005)
14. Brendel, W., Todorovic, S.: Video object segmentation by tracking regions. In: Proceedings of ICCV (2009)
15. Bai, X., Wang, J., Simons, D., Sapiro, G.: Video SnapCut: robust video object cutout using localized classifiers. ACM Transaction on Graphics 28 (2009)
16. Huang, Y., Liu, Q., Metaxas, D.: Video object segmentation by hypergraph cut. In: Proceedings of CVPR (2009)
17. Li, Y., Sun, J., Shum, H.Y.: Video object cut and paste. ACM Transaction on Graphics 24 (2005)
18. Yu, S.X., Shi, J.: Segmentation given partial grouping constraints. IEEE Transactions on Pattern Analysis and Machine Intelligence 26 (2004)
19. Tsai, D., Flagg, M., Rehg, J.M.: Motion coherent tracking with multi-label MRF optimization. In: Proceedings of BMVC (2010)

Sparse Depth Sampling for Interventional 2-D/3-D Overlay: Theoretical Error Analysis and Enhanced Motion Estimation

Jian Wang[1,2], Christian Riess[1], Anja Borsdorf[2], Benno Heigl[2], and Joachim Hornegger[1,3]

[1] Pattern Recognition Lab, Friedrich-Alexander-Universität Erlangen-Nürnberg
[2] Healthcare Sector, Siemens AG, Forchheim
[3] Erlangen Graduate School in Advanced Optical Technologies (SAOT)
jian.wang@cs.fau.de

Abstract. Patient motion compensation is challenging for dynamic 2-D/3-D overlay in interventional procedures. A first motion compensation approach based on depth-layers has been recently proposed, where 3-D motion can be estimated by tracking feature points on 2-D X-ray images. However, the sparse depth estimation introduces a systematic error. In this paper, we present a theoretical analysis on the systematic error and propose an enhanced motion estimation strategy accordingly. The simulation experiments show that the proposed approach yields a reduced 3-D correction error that is consistently below 2 mm, in comparison to a mean of 6 mm with high variance using the previous approach.

Keywords: interventional 2-D/3-D overlay, error analysis, sparse depth sampling, 3-D motion estimation.

1 Introduction

In interventional radiology, pre-operative three-dimensional (3-D) images (e.g. computed tomography (CT) or magnetic resonance angiography (MRA)) can be fused with interventional two-dimensional (2-D) X-ray images (fluoroscopy), which is known as 2-D/3-D overlay. This yields several advantages: 1) the pre-operative planning information in the 3-D images can be displayed on the fluoroscopic images; 2) additional information that is not visible in the fluoroscopic images (e.g. vascular structure and spatial information) can be seen in the overlaid 3-D images. A good 2-D/3-D overlay can shorten the time of the procedure and reduce the radiation dose [1]. Accuracy is the most critical factor for the quality of 2-D/3-D overlay. The proper spatial alignment of a 2-D projection to a 3-D image (e.g. volume) is typically referred to as 2-D/3-D image registration.

2-D/3-D registration is usually performed before the intervention to ensure an accurate overlay at the starting point. However, patient motion during the intervention makes it necessary to correct the registration on the fly. In state-of-the-art applications, the patient motion is usually detected by clinicians and

R. Wilson et al. (Eds.): CAIP 2013, Part I, LNCS 8047, pp. 86–93, 2013.

the correction is triggered by user interaction. However, clinicians have limited time and attention for computer interaction during the treatment [2].

Recently, research work for real-time motion compensation can be found in literature [3–5]. All the approaches either are application specific or rely on specific devices or particular motion models.

Recently, we proposed in [6] a depth-layer-based tracking approach for patient motion compensation. The key innovative contribution of this approach is that the depth information is transferred from 3-D image to 2-D feature points using depth layers, which are the images rendered separately from sub-volumes of different depth intervals. Fig. 1(a) shows how the sub-volumes are generated. Based on the initial registration, the 2-D feature points can be mapped to certain depth intervals by matching them to the depth layers. To the knowledge of the authors, this is the first approach that is capable of estimating real 3-D motion by only tracking 2-D feature points from single-view X-ray images. Since this approach does not rely on a particular device or motion model, and no iterative computation of digitally reconstructed radiographs (DRRs) is involved, it yields a high potential for real-time motion compensation in dynamic 2-D/3-D overlay.

However, depth sampling (quantization) introduces a systematic error in motion estimation. Using fine depth sampling can of course reduce the error, but 3-D structures are rather truncated into several small sub-volumes, and this leads to bad 2-D/3-D matching results; In contrast, the 3-D structures are more likely to be preserved in sub-volumes using coarse depth intervals, i.e. using sparse depth sampling. Therefore, we see a requirement to extend the method to be able to handle the depth error caused by sparse depth sampling.

In this paper, we present a mathematical model of the systematic error introduced by sparse depth sampling. Based on this analysis, we propose a depth correction strategy for motion estimation, which handles the systematic error together with random noise. Quantitative simulation experiments are performed to evaluate the new approach. Qualitative results are shown by an example of motion compensated 2-D/3-D overlay using our approach.

2   Theoretical Error Analysis of Sparse Depth Sampling

In this part, we analyze the systematic error of sparse depth sampling, and set it into relation with the random noise coming from other noise sources.

2.1   The Systematic Error Introduced by Depth Sampling

The principle of 2-D/3-D overlay is to virtually place the 3-D volume at the corresponding position of the patient, so that the volume is rendered as imaged from the X-ray source and fused with the live fluoroscopic image [1]. The projection geometry of a C-arm system is described by a pinhole camera model, as shown in Fig. 1(a). The projection procedure is described by the projection matrix $\mathbf{P} \in \mathbb{R}^{3 \times 4}$, which can be represented as $\mathbf{P} = \mathbf{K}[\mathbf{R}|\mathbf{t}]$, where $\mathbf{K} = \begin{bmatrix} a & & u \\ & a & v \\ & & 1 \end{bmatrix} \in \mathbb{R}^{3 \times 3}$

contains the intrinsic parameters, rotation $\mathbf{R} \in \mathbb{R}^{3\times3}$ and translation $\mathbf{t} \in \mathbb{R}^3$ are known as extrinsic parameters [7]. All the parameters are known during the 2-D acquisition from a calibrated C-arm system.

To simplify the problem, the motion estimation is done in the camera coordinate system, where the origin is located at the camera center $\mathbf{c}$ and the z-axis is aligned with the principal ray direction (L_0 in Fig.1(a)). So that the z component of a 3-D point represents its depth, and the projection matrix in the camera coordinate system is simplified as $\mathbf{P}_c = \mathbf{K}[\mathbf{I}|\mathbf{0}]$.

To analyze the systematic error by depth sampling, we start with a 3-D point $\mathbf{x} = (x, y, z, 1)^{\mathrm{T}}$ (homogeneous coordinates) and its projection $\mathbf{p} = (u_p, v_p, 1)^{\mathrm{T}}$ on the detector plane D (Fig. 1(b)). Given the projection matrix $\mathbf{P}_c$, the 2-D projection point $\mathbf{p}$ can be back-projected to a ray in 3-D [7], denoted as $\mathbf{r}(\mathbf{p}) = \mathbf{v}_r(\mathbf{p}) + \lambda \mathbf{c}$, where $\mathbf{v}_r(\mathbf{p}) = \mathbf{P}_c^+\mathbf{p} = \left(\frac{u_p-u}{a}, \frac{v_p-v}{a}, 1, 0\right)^{\mathrm{T}}$ and λ is a scalar related to the depth of the 3-D point on the ray [7] [6]. In the camera coordinate system, where $\mathbf{c} = (0, 0, 0, 1)$, $\mathbf{r}(\mathbf{p})$ can be further simplified as

$$\mathbf{r}(\mathbf{p}) = \left((\mathbf{v}_r^{xyz}(\mathbf{p}))^{\mathrm{T}}, \lambda\right)^{\mathrm{T}}, \quad \text{with } \mathbf{v}_r^{xyz} = \left(\frac{u_p - u}{a}, \frac{v_p - v}{a}, 1\right)^{\mathrm{T}} \tag{1}$$

Since the 3-D point $\mathbf{x}$ with depth d and the point $\mathbf{x}_E$ with sparsely estimated depth d_E are both on $\mathbf{r}(\mathbf{p})$, it yields $\lambda(\mathbf{x}) = 1/z = 1/d$ and $\lambda(\mathbf{x}_E) = 1/d_E$. The points can be then reformulated as

$$\mathbf{x} \doteq \left((\mathbf{v}_r^{xyz}(\mathbf{p}))^{\mathrm{T}}, 1/d\right)^{\mathrm{T}} \quad \text{and} \quad \mathbf{x}_E \doteq \left((\mathbf{v}_r^{xyz}(\mathbf{p}))^{\mathrm{T}}, 1/d_E\right)^{\mathrm{T}}. \tag{2}$$

Since $\mathbf{v}_r^{xyz}$ is determined by the 2D projection, the representations in Eq. 2 show the geometric relationship between $\mathbf{x}$ and $\mathbf{x}_E$ (as in Fig. 1(b)): they share the same projection but with a shift of $\Delta d = d_E - d$ in depth.

After a rigid motion (rotation $\mathbf{R}_0$ and translation $\mathbf{t}_0$), the new projections of $\mathbf{x}$ and $\mathbf{x}_E$ are $\mathbf{p}'$ and $\mathbf{p}'_E$, respectively, as shown in Fig. 1(b). In this scenario,

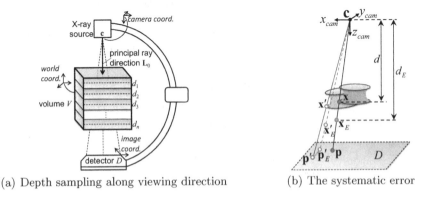

(a) Depth sampling along viewing direction   (b) The systematic error

Fig. 1. Illustration of depth sampling and the systematic error

the points $\mathbf{p}$ and $\mathbf{p}'$ are observations of $\mathbf{x}$ on the 2-D image before and after the motion. Since the estimated 3-D point $\mathbf{x}_E$ and $\mathbf{p}'$ (instead of $\mathbf{p}'_E$) are used in motion estimation [6], the systematic error of one point is introduced by the difference vector between $\mathbf{p}'$ and $\mathbf{p}'_E$, as follows:

$$\mathbf{p}'^{xy} - \mathbf{p}_E^{xy} = a \cdot \frac{d - d_E}{(d \cdot \mathbf{r}_3 \mathbf{v}_r^{xyz} + t_0^z)(d_E \cdot \mathbf{r}_3 \mathbf{v}_r^{xyz} + t_0^z)} \begin{bmatrix} t_0^z & -t_0^x \\ t_0^z & -t_0^y \end{bmatrix} \mathbf{R}_0 \mathbf{v}_r^{xyz} , \quad (3)$$

where $\mathbf{r}_3 \in \mathbb{R}^{1 \times 3}$ is the third row of $\mathbf{R}_0$ and $\mathbf{t}_0 = (t_0^x, t_0^y, t_0^z)^T$. The above 2-D vector corresponds to a line segment $\mathbf{l}_\varepsilon$ connecting $\mathbf{p}'$ and $\mathbf{p}'_E$, which is exactly a segment of the epipolar line of $\mathbf{p}$ under the motion of $[\mathbf{R}_0|\mathbf{t}_0]$ [7]. As Eq. 3 shows, the direction of the vector is only determined by the motion $[\mathbf{R}_0|\mathbf{t}_0]$ and the 2-D projection $\mathbf{p}$. The depth error Δd together with the off-plane motion ($\mathbf{r}_3$ and t_0^z) affects the length of $\mathbf{l}_\varepsilon$. Therefore, the systematic error by sparse depth sampling is not only influenced by the estimation error Δd in depth.

2.2 The Systematic Error in Relation to the Random Noise

In the last section, the mathematical representation of the systematic error is derived. However, all the measurements in the real world are subject not only to systematic error but also to random noise [8]. Therefore, we model the noise from other steps in the whole procedure in [6] (e.g. tracking error) as random noise, which is defined by a uniform distribution. In this section, we analyze the systematic error in Eq. 3 together with random noise, in order to treat them differently to achieve a better motion estimation.

Fig. 2(a) illustrates the systematic error together with random noise in our scenario. After an initial motion estimation using sparse depth sampling as in [6], we can compute the systematic error vector using Eq. 3, which corresponds to the line segment $\mathbf{l}_\varepsilon$ through $\mathbf{p}'_E$ (Fig. 2(a)). The possible maximum length of $\mathbf{l}_\varepsilon$ determined by the depth bounds can be used as an explicit measurement of the the systematic error, denoted as $\mathcal{S}^i$ for $\mathbf{p}'^i_E$ (Fig. 2(b) and 2(c)).

Furthermore, we assume that the random noise can shift a 2-D point towards an arbitrary direction with maximum distance δ_{max}, where direction and distance are uniformly distributed. Therefore, the observation of the projection $\mathbf{p}'$ (denoted as $\tilde{\mathbf{p}}'$) is positioned within a disk-like region with a radius of δ_{max}

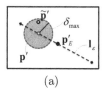
(a)

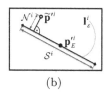
(b)

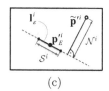
(c)

Fig. 2. (a) Illustration of projection and the errors; (b) the metrics for the "influences" the errors; (c) a case with more significant random noise

(Fig. 2(a)), which reflects the accuracy of the tracking method applied in our procedure. However, $\mathbf{p}'$ and $\delta_{\max}$ are unknowns in practice, there is no explicit measurement for the random noise. Therefore, we again make use of Eq. 3 for the metric of the random noise. Since the in-plane motion can be well estimated initially [6] and the depth error as well as the off-plane motion affects more on the length of the systematic error vector in Eq. 3, the true projection $\mathbf{p}'$ appears near to or on the line $\mathbf{l}_\varepsilon$. Thus, we introduce here the point-to-line distance $\mathcal{N}^i$ (the distance between $\widetilde{\mathbf{p}}'^i$ and $\mathbf{l}^i_E$ in Fig. 2(b)) as the metric for the "influence" of the random noise.

Fig. 2(b) and 2(c) show two examples of error conditions. In Fig.2(b), $\mathcal{N}^i$ is obviously smaller then $\mathcal{S}^i$. If it is mostly the case for other points, we can draw the conclusion that the systematic error is more dominant than the random noise. Contrarily, if $\mathcal{N}^i$ is bigger then $\mathcal{S}^i$ (Fig. 2(c)) for most of the points, the random noise appears more dominant.

3   The Error-Dependent Motion Estimation Strategy

In order to reduce the depth error, we now consider a depth correction step after the initial motion estimation (denoted as $[\hat{\mathbf{R}}_0|\hat{\mathbf{t}}_0]$). It can be performed by solving a least-squares optimization problem as

$$\left\{\hat{d}^i_E\right\} = \underset{\{d'_E\}}{argmin}\left(\sum_i^n \text{dist}\left(\widetilde{\mathbf{p}}'^i, \mathbf{p}'_E(d'^i_E)\right)\right) , \qquad (4)$$

where n is the number of points, $\text{dist}(\cdot, \cdot)$ is the Euclidean distance of the two points and $\mathbf{p}'_E = \mathbf{K}[\hat{\mathbf{R}}_0|\hat{\mathbf{t}}_0]\mathbf{x}_E$. This least-squares optimization helps to find the best fitting corrected depth values based on the estimated motion. We then refine the motion by a follow-up motion estimation using the corrected depths.

However, if the random error is about the same level of or more dominant than the systematic error (e.g. under a small or specific motions causing small systematic error), depth correction can even introduce more error in the motion estimation results (see section 4). The reason is that minimizing $\sum_i^n \text{dist}\left(\widetilde{\mathbf{p}}', \mathbf{p}'_E(d'^i_E)\right)$ in Eq. 4 does not lead to proper fitting depth values 2(c). In contrast, if the random error has an acceptable range (i.e. with reasonable $\delta_{\max}$), it's better to include more points in the motion estimation procedure, so that a globally consistent solution of the motion can be estimated while the effect of the random error is averaged to a minimum.

An error-based motion estimation strategy is therefore proposed according to the influence metrics proposed in section 2.2 and a dominance factor f (Tab. 1). We consider as a strong depth correction criterion if $\bar{\mathcal{S}} > f \cdot \bar{\mathcal{N}}$, we perform depth correction and motion estimation on all points. For the cases not satisfying the strong criterion, we consider as a weak criterion if still some points $\left\{\mathbf{x}^i_E\right\}^{\text{weak}}$ contain dominant systematic error ($\mathcal{S}^i > f \cdot \bar{\mathcal{N}}$) and perform depth correction on $\left\{\mathbf{x}^i_E\right\}^{\text{weak}}$, but still refine the motion using all points. If neither of the criteria are satisfied, we consider all points as random noise dominant (no further correction).

Table 1. The error-dependent motion estimation via dynamic depth correction

---

Inputs 3-D point set with sparse depth estimation $\{\mathbf{x}_E^i\}$, 2-D projections before motion $\{\mathbf{p}^i\}$ and the observed projections after motion $\{\widetilde{\mathbf{p}}'^i\}$.

Initialization Initial estimation of the rigid motion $[\hat{\mathbf{R}}_0|\hat{\mathbf{t}}_0]$ using $\{\mathbf{x}_E^i\}$ and $\{\widetilde{\mathbf{p}}'^i\}$ [6].

Error analysis Based on $[\hat{\mathbf{R}}_0|\hat{\mathbf{t}}_0]$, compute the systematic error vectors for all $\{\mathbf{x}_E^i\}$ using Eq. 3, the systematic error influences $\{\mathcal{S}^i\}$ and the mean influence $\overline{\mathcal{S}}$. Compute the random noise influences $\{\mathcal{N}^i\}$ and the mean influence $\overline{\mathcal{N}}$.

Optimization determination criteria
1. Strong criterion: if $\overline{\mathcal{S}} > f \cdot \overline{\mathcal{N}}$, perform depth correction and motion refinement on all points $\{\mathbf{x}^i\}$;
2. Weak criterion: else if $\max(\mathcal{S}^i) > f \cdot \overline{\mathcal{N}}$, perform depth correction on $\{\mathbf{x}^i\}^{\text{weak}}$ and motion refinement on all points $\{\mathbf{x}^i\}$;
3. Otherwise: no further correction.

---

4   Experiments and Discussion

In this section, we quantitatively evaluate our new approach using point-based simulation experiments. Furthermore, we show the qualitative motion estimation results using a real clinical CT volume with simulated X-ray images.

4.1   Point-Based Simulation Experiments

Point-based simulation is a convenient and established way of evaluating the theoretical-analysis-based algorithms (as in [6]). It allows to neglect the external influences and gives better insights how things behave in the scope of interest. Our point-based simulation set-up is similar as in [6]. The projection parameters of a real C-arm system are applied. 3-D point sets are randomly generated within a bounding box $(20\,\text{cm} \times 20\,\text{cm} \times 30\,\text{cm})$. Random 3-D motions of different scales are generated, which cause 2-D projection errors from about $1\,\text{mm}$ to $13\,\text{mm}$ on the detector plane. Random, uniformly distributed noise with $\delta_{\max} = 4$ pixels (see Sec. 2.2) is added to the 2-D correspondences.

In Fig. 3, results of the test cases using 5- and 10-interval depth sampling are shown. The plots show how the errors caused by a motion, which represent the scale of the 3-D motion, are corrected in 2-D and 3-D. In each plot, the horizontal and vertical axes show respectively the error before and after motion correction. We discuss three important properties of the proposed algorithm.

1. *Error reduction in 2-D and 3-D* – In clinical practice, an error of $2\,\text{mm}$ can be considered acceptable [3]. As shown in Fig. 3, the baseline algorithm [6] often fails to achieve this requirement in 3-D error correction. Conversely, with our proposed depth correction scheme, we consistently yield a 3-D correction error below $2\,\text{mm}$. This shows the fact that the 3D motion (and even the off-plane motion part) can be well estimated using the our proposed approach.

2. *Effects of depth quantization* – Since both examples show sparse depth sampling, where the systematic error causes a significant quantization effect.

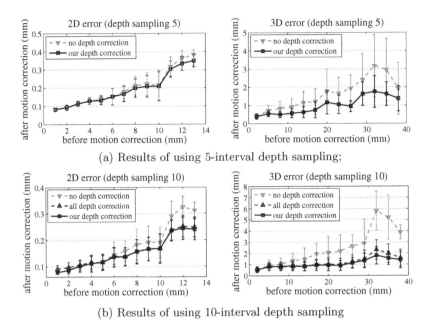

(a) Results of using 5-interval depth sampling;

(b) Results of using 10-interval depth sampling

Fig. 3. Plots of the results of point-based experiments

The quantization effect leads to an uncertainty of the motion estimation. As we can see by comparing the results in Fig. 3(a) and 3(b), 10-interval depth sampling even yields worse results then 5-interval sampling. The results are much more stable (consistently under 2/ts mm) by using our proposed depth correction.

3. *Performance gained by the point selection criteria* – In Fig. 3(b), the estimation results using all points for depth correction, where none of the criteria in Tab. 1 are considered, are shown together with the results using our motion estimation strategy (dominance factor $f = 3$). Obviously, more computation is involved if all points are considered for depth correction. Nevertheless, we can observe better results by using points selection criteria for depth correction.

4.2   Image-Based Experiments

Similar as in [6], a sequence of DRRs is generated from a clinical CT volume under a sequence of rigid motion, where 2-D/3-D overlay is initially registered. 10-layer depth sampling is used for motion compensation. Normalized cross correlation (NCC) based similarity map between the 2-D projection (gradient magnitude) and the 3-D volume (gradient-based rendering [6]), as shown respectively in green, blue and red in Fig. 4 together with the overlays. Fig. 4(a) and 4(b) show the 2-D/3-D overlay without and with our motion estimation approach at frame 19. Due to the patient motion in 2-D projection, the overlay loses 2-D/3-D similarity (green) along the frames. However, our motion compensation approach maintains the high 2-D/3-D similarity. The results clearly show that the 2-D/3-D overlay accuracy is strongly improved using our proposed approach.

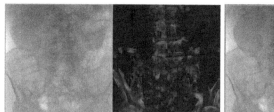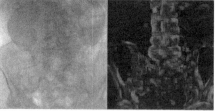

(a) Without motion compensation   (b) With motion compensation

Fig. 4. Motion compensation using sparse depth estimation

5   Conclusion and Future Work

In this paper, a theoretical analysis of the systematic error introduced by sparse depth sampling for motion estimation is presented. An improved motion estimation strategy which handles the depth error is proposed. The experimental results show the improved estimation of 3-D motion in cases of very sparse depth sampling, the 3-D errors are below 2 mm after motion correction.

As an outlook, we will evaluate different tracking methods using the presented error analysis. The theoretical analysis can further help to adapt the tracking methods to X-ray images for our motion compensation framework.

References

1. Rossitti, S., Pfister, M.: 3D road-mapping in the endovascular treatment of cerebral aneurysms and arteriovenous malformations. Interventional Neuroradiology 15(3), 283 (2009)
2. Ruijters, D.: Multi-modal image fusion during minimally invasive treatment. PhD thesis, Katholieke Universiteit Leuven and the University of Technology Eindhoven, TU/e (2010)
3. Brost, A., Liao, R., Strobel, N., Hornegger, J.: Respiratory motion compensation by model-based catheter tracking during ep procedures. Medical Image Analysis 14(5), 695–706 (2010)
4. Ma, Y., King, A.P., Gogin, N., Rinaldi, C.A., Gill, J., Razavi, R., Rhode, K.S.: Real-time respiratory motion correction for cardiac electrophysiology procedures using image-based coronary sinus catheter tracking. In: Jiang, T., Navab, N., Pluim, J.P.W., Viergever, M.A. (eds.) MICCAI 2010, Part I. LNCS, vol. 6361, pp. 391–399. Springer, Heidelberg (2010)
5. Wang, P., Marcus, P., Chen, T., Comaniciu, D.: Using needle detection and tracking for motion compensation in abdominal interventions. In: 2010 IEEE International Symposium on Biomedical Imaging: From Nano to Macro, pp. 612–615. IEEE (2010)
6. Wang, J., Borsdorf, A., Hornegger, J.: Depth-layer based patient motion compensation for the overlay of 3D volumes onto x-ray sequences. In: Proceedings Bildverarbeitung für die Medizin 2013, pp. 128–133 (2013)
7. Hartley, R., Zisserman, A.: Multiple View Geometry in Computer Vision, 2nd edn. Cambridge Univsersity Press (2003)
8. Taylor, J.R.: An Introduction Error Analysis: The Study of Uncertainties in Physical Measurements. University Science Books (1997)

Video Synopsis Based on a Sequential Distortion Minimization Method

Costas Panagiotakis[1], Nelly Ovsepian[2], and Elena Michael[2]

[1] Dept. of Commerce and Marketing,
Technological Educational Institute (TEI) of Crete, 72200 Ierapetra, Greece
cpanag@staff.teicrete.gr
[2] Dept. of Computer Science, University of Crete, P.O. Box 2208, Greece
nelli.ov@hotmail.com, elmich@csd.uoc.gr

Abstract. The main goal of the proposed method is to select from a video the most "significant" frames in order to broadcast, without apparent loss of content by decreasing the potential distortion criterion. Initially, the video is divided into shots and the number of synopsis frames per shot is computed based on a criterion that takes into account the visual content variation. Next, the most "significant" frames are sequentially selected, so that the visual content distortion between the initial video and the synoptic video is minimized. Experimental results and comparisons with other methods on several real-life and animation video sequences illustrate the high performance of the proposed scheme.

Keywords: Video summarization, Key frames, Video synopsis.

1 Introduction

The traditional representation of video files as a sequence of numerous consecutive frames, each of which corresponds to a constant time interval, while being adequate for viewing a file in a movie mode, presents a number of limitations for the new emerging multimedia services such as content-based search, retrieval, navigation and video browsing [1]. Therefore, it is important to segment the video into homogenous segments in content domain and then to describe each segment by a small and sufficient number of frames [2] in order to get a video summarization.

Video summarization algorithms attempt to abstract the main occurrences, scenes, or objects in a clip in order to provide an easily interpreted multimedia synopsis. The videos consist of a sequence of successive images which are called frames and represent scenes in movie-motion. The video summarization algorithms are based on detection of representative frames inside on basic temporal units which are called shots. They are designed to detect the most suitable frames from each shot in order to shorten the video without high distortion. A shot can be defined as a sequence of frames that are or appear to be continuously captured from the same camera. Key frames are the most significant images which

R. Wilson et al. (Eds.): CAIP 2013, Part I, LNCS 8047, pp. 94–101, 2013.
© Springer-Verlag Berlin Heidelberg 2013

are extracted from video footage. They have been used to distinguish videos, summarize them and provide access points [3].

Key frames selection approaches can be classified into basically three categories, namely cluster-based methods, energy minimization-based methods and sequential methods [1,4]. Cluster-based methods take all frames from every shot and classify by content similarity to take key-frame. The disadvantage of these methods is that the temporal information of a video sequence is omitted. The energy minimization based methods extract the key frames by solving a rate-constrained problem. These methods are generally computational expensive by iterative techniques. Sequential methods consider a new key frame when the content difference from the previous key frame exceeds the predefined threshold.

In [5], key frames are computed based on unsupervised learning for video retrieval and video summarization by combination of shot boundary detection, intra-shot-clustering and keyframe "meta-clustering". It exploits the Color Layout Descriptor (CLD) [6], on consecutive frames and compute differences between them define the bounds of each shot. Recently, dynamic programming techniques have been proposed in the literature, such as the MINMAX approach of [7] to extract the key frames of a video sequence. In this work, the problem is solved optimally in $O(N^2 \cdot K_{max})$, where K_{max} is related to the rate-distortion optimization. In [8], a video is represented as a complete undirected graph and the normalized cut algorithm is carried out to globally and optimally partition the graph into video clusters. The resulting clusters form a directed temporal graph and a shortest path algorithm is proposed for video summarization.

Video summarization has been applied by many researchers with multiple approaches. Most of them are dealing with minimizing content features, defining restrictions on distortion, applying simple clustering-based techniques and ignoring temporal variation. In addition, due to its high computational cost ($O(N^3)$ when the number of key frames is proportional to the number of video frames N), most of the prementioned methods have been used to extract a small percentages of initial frames that represent well the visual content but they have not been used to reproduce a video synopsis. Video synopsis is quite important task for video summarization, since it is another short video representation of visual content and video variation. This paper refers to video summarization by the meaning of video synopsis creation. The resulting video synopsis takes into account temporal content variation, shot detection, and minimizes the content distortion between the initial video and the synoptic video. At the same time the proposed method has low computational cost $O(N^2)$. Another advantage of this work is that it can be used under any visual content description.

The rest of the paper is organized as follows: Section 2 gives the problem formulation. Section 3 presents the proposed methodology of the video synopsis creation. segmentation of periodic human motion. The experimental results are given in Section 4. Finally, conclusions and discussion are provided in Section 5.

2   Problem Formulation

The problem of video synopsis belong to video summarization problems. Its goal is to create a new video, shorter than the initial video according to a given parameter α, without significant loss of content between the two videos (the distortion between the original video and the video synopsis is minimized). The ratio between the temporal duration of the video synopsis and the initial video is equal to $\alpha \in [0,1]$. Let N denote the number frames of original video. Then, the video synopsis consists of $\alpha \cdot N$ frames. Therefore, we have to select the $\alpha \cdot N$ representative key frames. The broadcasting of the video synopsis is done with the original frame ratio meaning that the real speed of the new video has been increased by the factor of $\frac{1}{\alpha}$ on average. For example, we have a video with 5 sec duration with 25 frames/sec, so the whole video is consisted of $5 \times 25 = 125$ frames and the given parameter $\alpha = 0.2$ the final video will have $125 \times 0.2 = 25$ frames. In other words, the final duration will be one sec which is 20% of initial video.

Let C_i, $i \in \{1, ..., N\}$ denote the visual descriptor of i-frame of original video. Let $S \subset \{1, ..., N\}$ denote the frames of video synopsis. According to the problem definition, it holds that the number of frames of video synopsis ($|S|$) is equal to $\alpha \cdot N$. Then, the distortion $D(\{1, ..., N\}, S)$ between the original video and video synopsis is given by the following equation:

$$D(\{1, ..., N\}, S) = \sum_{i=1}^{S(1)} d(i, S(1)) + \sum_{i=S(|S|)+1}^{N} d(i, S(|S|)) \tag{1}$$

$$+ \sum_{i=S(1)+1}^{S(|S|)} min_{S(j) \leq i \leq S(j+1)} (d(i, S(j)), d(i, S(j+1)))$$

where $d(i, S(j))$ denotes the distance between the visual descriptor of i-frame and $S(j)$-frame. $S(j)$ and $S(j+1)$ are two successive frames of video synopsis so that $S(j) \leq i \leq S(j+1)$, this means that $S(j)$ is determined by the index i. The first and the second parts of this sum concern the cases that the frame i is located before the first key frame $S(1)$ or after the last key frame $S(|S|)$, respectively. Therefore, the used distortion that is defined by the sum of visual distances between the frame of original video and the "closest" corresponding frame of video synopsis, can be considered as an extension of the definition of Iso-Content Distortion Principle [1] in the domain of shots.

3   Methodology

Fig. 1 illustrates a scheme of the proposed system architecture. The proposed method can be divided into several steps. Initially, we estimate the CLD for each frame of the original video. Next, we performed shot detection (see Section 3.1). Based on the shot detection results and to the given parameter α we estimate the number of frames per shot that the video synopsis (see Section 3.1). Finally, the

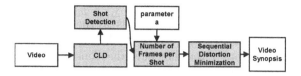

Fig. 1. Scheme of the proposed system architecture

video distortion is sequentially minimized according to the proposed methods resulting to the video synopsis (see Section 3.2).

The proposed method can be executed under any choice or combination of audio/visual content descriptors. Descriptors based on image segmentation results or on camera motion estimation techniques are computational expensive. Moreover, there is not any guarantee that their results will be accurate for any video content variation [1]. To overcome these problems, we adopt the MPEG-7 visual descriptors [6, 9] as appropriate features, such as the Color Layout Descriptor (CLD), a low cost and compact descriptor, which suffices to describe smoothly the changes in visual content of a shot. These descriptors have been successfully used on our prementioned work on key frames extraction problems [1, 4]. The CLD is a compact descriptor that uses representative colors on a grid followed by a DCT and encoding of the resulting coefficients. We used the following semimetric function D to measure the content distance of two CLDs, $\{DY, DCb, DCr\}$ and $\{DY', DCb', DCr'\}$,

$$D = \sqrt{\sum_i (DY_i - DY_i')^2} + \sqrt{\sum_i (DCb_i - DCb_i')^2} + \sqrt{\sum_i (DCr_i - DCr_i')^2},$$

where, (DY, DCb, DCr) represent the ith DCT coefficients of the respective color components [1, 4].

3.1 Shot Detection

This section presents the shot detection method. Shot detection is optional and it is used in order, to ensure that the video synopsis contains frames for each shot and to decrease the computational cost of the proposed sequential algorithms. We perform detection for sharp shot changes only. This is done by using the chi-squared distance between of the lightness histogram of each frame with the next one. This histogram distance has been also successfully used for texture and object categories classification, near duplicate image identification, local descriptors matching, shape classification and boundary detection [10].

Hereafter, we present the method that we have used to compute the number of frames of each detected shot for video synopsis. So, the goal of this section is to find out the percentage of the frames of each shot that are capable enough to represent the whole shot. We have used the metric L_k that is defined with the sum CLD distance between all successive frames in shot k: $L_k = \sum_{i \in SH_k} d(i, i + 1)$, where SH_k denotes the set of frames of shot k. L_k shows the sum of sequential visual changes of shot k. The higher L_k, the higher number of frames have to be selected from shot k. The selected frames (frames of video synopsis) are also called key frames. The number of frames (b_k) in shot k, that is proportional to

L_k, is defined by the following equation: $b_k = \frac{\alpha \cdot N \cdot L_k}{\sum_{k=1}^{|SH|} L_k}$, where $|SH|$ denotes the number of shots. This definition of b_k also satisfies the constraint that the video synopsis should contain $\alpha \cdot N$: $\sum_{k=1}^{|SH|} b_k = \alpha \cdot N$. In the special case of $b_k \leq 1$ which means that all frames of the shot have the same content, we set $b_k = 2$ so that the video synopsis summarizes all of the shots of the video.

3.2 Sequential Distortion Minimization

This section presents the proposed Sequential Distortion Minimization algorithm (SeDiM) for video synopsis creation. This method selects b_k frames for the k shot, so that the distortion between the original video and the video synopsis is sequentially minimized. The ordering of key frames selection corresponds to their significance on content description. The SeDiM method is described hereafter:

Let CAN_k denote the set of candidate frames of shot k for video synopsis. Initially, we set $CAN_k = SH_k$. Let S_k be the frames of video synopsis of shot k. Initially, we set $S_k = \emptyset$. For each shot k, we iteratively select the frame f from CAN_k so that if we include it in set S_k the current video distortion of shot k is minimized (see Equation 2). Next, we remove it from set CAN_k and we add it on set S_k:

$$f = argmin_{u \in CAN_k} \sum_{i \in SH_k} D(SH_k, S_k \cup u) \qquad (2)$$

$$CAN_k = CAN_k - \{f\}, \quad S_k = S_k \cup f$$

When the number of key frames of shot k become b_k, CAN_k is being the empty set ($CAN_k = \emptyset$), since we can not select more frames from this shot. The process continues until the number of key frames of video synopsis become $\alpha \cdot N$.

Concerning the computational cost, this procedure can be implemented in $O(N^2)$. The worst case is appeared when the video consists of one shot. In this case it holds that ($N = |SH_1|$). In the start (fist step), the finding of global minima of $D(\{1, ..., N\}, \emptyset)$ needs $O(N^2)$ (see Equation 1). In the n-step of the method, we have to compute $D(\{1, ..., N\}, S \cup u)$ only when the previous or the next key frame of u is the last key frame that have been added in S in previous step $(n-1)$. Otherwise, it holds that $D(\{1, ..., N\}, S \cup u) = D(\{1, ..., N\}, S)$. This needs $O(\frac{N^2}{n^2})$, since the video content changes "smoothly" in the sense that the selected frames are about equally distributed during the time. Let $T(.)$ denote the computation cost of the algorithm. It holds that $T(1) = O(N^2)$. In the n-step, we have to find the minimum of $D(.,.)$ that can be given in $O(N)$ and to update the specific values of $D(.,.)$ in $O(\frac{N^2}{n^2})$. So, the total computational cost is $O(N^2)$.

In addition, we have proposed a simple variation of SeDiM that is presented hereafter. In this variation, we just assume the first and last frame of each shot as two starting key frames for video synopsis. So, in the case of one-shot, we initialize $S_k = \{SH_k(1), SH_k(|SH_k|)\}$. This algorithm is called SeDiM-IN. The rest of the process is exactly the same with SeDiM. The proposed methods do not guarantee global minima of distortion, since they sequentially minimize the distortion function. SeDiM guarantees global minima of distortion only in the case of $b_k = 1$.

4   Experimental Results

Fig. 2. Snapshots of videos that we have used in the paper

In this section, the experimental results and comparisons with other algorithms are presented. We have tested the proposed algorithm on a data set containing more than 100 video sequences. We selected 10 videos (eight real-life and two synthetic (animation)) videos of different content in order to evaluate the distortion of each algorithm and take results from videos which have different content. The real-life videos have been recording either in indoor or outdoor environments. The ten used videos consist of 69 shots. The number of shots per video varies from one to 22. In addition, the duration of the videos varies from 300 frames to 1925 frames. Fig. 2 depicts shapshots from these videos. The names of the videos are given in the first column of Table 1.

4.1   Comparison to other Algorithms

The proposed methods SeDiM and SeDiM-IN have been compared with the content equidistant and time equidistant algorithms in the same data sets and same set of parameters $\alpha = 0.1$ and $\alpha = 0.3$. Hereafter, we present these two algorithms. The content equidistant algorithm (CEA) is inspired by the work [1], where the iso-content principle has been proposed to estimate the key frames that are equidistant in video content. According to this method, the key frames $\{t_1, t_2, ..., t_{b_k}\}$ in shot k are defined by the following equation:
$m \simeq \sum_{u=1}^{t_1-1} d(u, u+1) \simeq \sum_{u=t_1}^{t_2-1} d(u, u+1) \simeq ... \simeq \sum_{u=t_{b_k}}^{b_k-1} d(u, u+1)$ where
$m = \frac{1}{b_k-1} \sum_{u=1}^{b_k-1} d(u, u+1)$. So, based on the measurement m, first we compute the key frame t_1, next we compute t_2, and so on. Finally we compute t_{b_k}.

The time equidistant algorithm (TEA) is based on equivalent frames in each shot of video by finding key frames as equal intervals in duration of shot. According to this method, the key frame t_i, $i \in \{1, 2, ..., b_k\}$ in shot k is directly defined by the following equation: $t_i = \lfloor \frac{i \cdot |SH_k|}{b_k} \rceil$, where $|SH_k|$ denotes the number of frames of shot k and $\lfloor . \rceil$ denotes the nearest integer function. This is the simplest method for video synopsis creation, since it does not take into account visual changes.

Table 1 depicts the distortion $D(\{1, ..., N\}, S)$ between the original video and video synopsis of SeDiM, SeDiM-IN, CEA, TEA methods under the ten used video sequences with $\alpha = 0.1$ and $\alpha = 0.3$.

Table 1. The distortion $D(\{1, ..., N\}, S)$ between the original video and video synopsis

Dataset	$\alpha = 0.1$ SeDiM	$\alpha = 0.1$ SeDiM-IN	$\alpha = 0.1$ CEA	$\alpha = 0.1$ TEA	$\alpha = 0.3$ SeDiM	$\alpha = 0.3$ SeDiM-IN	$\alpha = 0.3$ CEA	$\alpha = 0.3$ TEA
foreman.avi	19209	**18973**	21814	22069	**6755.1**	6774.1	7738.2	8992.2
coast_guard.avi	**6962.7**	7054.8	7486.6	7079.9	**2521.4**	2562.4	2669.5	4146.4
hall.avi	**3913.8**	3938.8	4309.1	4444.4	**2137**	2141	2228.1	3863
table.avi	**10207**	11578	11529	10928	**4097**	4113.2	4542.4	6046.4
blue.avi	**13826**	14487	14690	16171	**5419**	5494	5736	10631
doconCut.avi	**116420**	122550	142460	148230	**40503**	43602	45412	70521
data.avi	**14635**	15800	17147	15294	**4292**	4303	5058	17260
Wildlife.avi	**27187**	29841	31763	33752	**9052**	9210	10826	12493
MessiVsRonaldo.avi	**74630**	85270	85310	111070	**20971**	22051	23001	40209
FootballHistory.avi	**68434**	79676	80236	95497	**16402**	16842	17323	58503

According to these experiments, SeDiM yields the highest performance results, outperforming the other algorithms, since in 95% of cases (19 out of 20) gives the lowest distortion. SeDiM-IN is the second highest performance method. When $\alpha = 0.3$ is always the second highest performance method. When $\alpha = 0.1$, in 70% of cases is the second highest performance method. In addition, in foreman.avi, SeDiM-IN gives the lowest distortion when $\alpha = 0.1$. SeDiM usually gives less distortion than SeDiM-IN, because the video synopsis of SeDiM-IN contain the first and last frame each shot, without examine if they are appropriate to optimize the summarization of video.

High performance results are also obtained by CEA that is the third highest performance method, especially when $\alpha = 0.3$. We observed that CEA is better method to get video synopsis than TEA because the equal time intervals in the shot don't guarantee that the selected frames from this method have different or same visual content. CEA ensure that the key frames are selected by equal content differences and with this way maintain the distortion of video in low levels. The initial videos and video synopsis results (with $\alpha = 0.1$ and $\alpha = 0.3$) of SeDiM, SeDiM-IN, CEA, TEA methods are given in [1]. It holds that the video synopsis of the proposed schemata describe well the visual content under any type of videos.

5   Conclusion

In this paper, we have proposed a video synopsis creation scheme that can be used in video summarization applications. According to the proposed framework, the problem of video synopsis creation is reduced to the minimization of the distortion between the initial video and the video synopsis. The proposed method sequentially minimizes this distortion, resulting in high performance results under any value of the parameter α that controls the number of frames of the video synopsis. In addition, the proposed scheme can be used under any type of video content description.

---

[1] https://www.dropbox.com/sh/rpysux4oa746jty/B265lHwpAB

Acknowledgments. This research has been partially co-financed by the European Union (European Social Fund - ESF) and Greek national funds through the Operational Program "Education and Lifelong Learning" of the National Strategic Reference Framework (NSRF) - Research Funding Programs: ARCHIMEDE III-TEI-Crete-P2PCOORD and THALIS-UOA- ERASITECHNIS.

References

1. Panagiotakis, C., Doulamis, A., Tziritas, G.: Equivalent key frames selection based on iso-content principles. IEEE Transactions on Circuits and Systems for Video Technology 19, 447–451 (2009)
2. Hanjalic, A., Zhang, H.: An integrated scheme for automated video abstraction based onunsupervised cluster-validity analysis. IEEE Trans. on Circuits and Systems for Video Tech. 9, 1280–1289 (1999)
3. Girgensohn, A., Boreczky, J.S.: Time-constrained keyframe selection technique. Multimedia Tools and Applications 11, 347–358 (2000)
4. Panagiotakis, C., Doulamis, A., Tziritas, G.: Equivalent key frames selection based on iso-content distance and iso-distortion principles. In: IEEE International Workshop on Image Analysis for Multimedia Interactive Services (2007)
5. Hammoud, R., Mohr, R.: A probabilistic framework of selecting effective key frames for video browsing and indexing. In: International Workshop on Real-Time Image Sequence Analysis (RISA 2000), pp. 79–88 (2000)
6. Manjunath, B., Ohm, J., Vasudevan, V., Yamada, A.: Color and texture descriptors. IEEE Trans. on Circuits and Systems for Video Tech. 11, 703–715 (2001)
7. Li, Z., Schuster, G., Katsaggelos, A.: Minmax optimal video summarization. IEEE Trans. Circuits Syst. Video Techn. 15, 1245–1256 (2005)
8. Ngo, C.W., Ma, Y.F., Zhang, H.J.: Video summarization and scene detection by graph modeling. IEEE Trans. Circuits Syst. Video Techn. 15, 296–305 (2005)
9. Kasutani, E., Yamada, A.: The mpeg-7 color layout descriptor: a compact image feature description for high-speed image/video segment retrieval, pp. 674–677 (2001)
10. Pele, O., Werman, M.: The quadratic-chi histogram distance family. In: Daniilidis, K., Maragos, P., Paragios, N. (eds.) ECCV 2010, Part II. LNCS, vol. 6312, pp. 749–762. Springer, Heidelberg (2010)

A Graph Embedding Method Using the Jensen-Shannon Divergence

Lu Bai, Edwin R. Hancock*, and Lin Han

Department of Computer Science, University of York, UK
Deramore Lane, Heslington, York, YO10 5GH, UK
{lu,erh,lin}@cs.york.ac.uk

Abstract. Riesen and Bunke recently proposed a novel dissimilarity based approach for embedding graphs into a vector space. One drawback of their approach is the computational cost graph edit operations required to compute the dissimilarity for graphs. In this paper we explore whether the Jensen-Shannon divergence can be used as a means of computing a fast similarity measure between a pair of graphs. We commence by computing the Shannon entropy of a graph associated with a steady state random walk. We establish a family of prototype graphs by using an information theoretic approach to construct generative graph prototypes. With the required graph entropies and a family of prototype graphs to hand, the Jensen-Shannon divergence between a sample graph and a prototype graph can be computed. It is defined as the Jensen-Shannon between the pair of separate graphs and a composite structure formed by the pair of graphs. The required entropies of the graphs can be efficiently computed, the proposed graph embedding using the Jensen-Shannon divergence avoids the burdensome graph edit operation. We explore our approach on several graph datasets abstracted from computer vision and bioinformatics databases.

1 Introduction

In pattern recognition, graph based object representations offer a versatile alternative way to the vector based representation. The main advantage of graph representations is their rich mathematical structure. Unfortunately, most of the standard pattern recognition and machine learning algorithms are formulated for vectors, and are not available for graphs. One way to overcome this problem is to embed the graph data into a vector space, and then deploy vectorial methods.

However, the vector space embedding presents two obstacles. First, since graphs can be of different sizes, the vectors may be of different lengths. The second problem is that the information residing on the edges of a graph is discarded. In order to overcome these problems, Riesen and Bunke recently proposed a method for embedding graphs into a vector space [1], that bridges the gap between the powerful graph based representation and the algorithms available for the vector based representation. The ideas underpin graph dissimilarity embedding framework were first described in Duin and Pekalska's work [2]. Riesen and Bunke generalized and substantially extended the

---

* Edwin R. Hancock is supported by a Royal Society Wolfson Research Merit Award.

R. Wilson et al. (Eds.): CAIP 2013, Part I, LNCS 8047, pp. 102–109, 2013.

methods to the graph mining domain. The key idea is to use the edit distance from a sample graph to a number of class prototype graphs to give a vectorial description of the sample graph in the embedding space. Furthermore, this approach potentially allows any (dis)similarity measure of graphs to be used for graph (dis)similarity embedding as well. Unfortunately, the edit distance between a sample graph and a prototype graph requires burdensome computations, and as a result the graph dissimilarity embedding using the edit distance can not be efficiently computed for graphs.

To address this inefficiency, in this paper we investigate whether the Jensen-Shannon divergence can be used as a means of establishing a computationally efficient similarity measure between a pair of graphs, and then use such a measure to propose a novel fast graph embedding approach. In information theory the Jensen-Shannon divergence is a nonextensive mutual information theoretic measure based on nonextensive entropies. An extensive entropy is defined as the sum of the individual entropies of two probability distributions. The definition of nonextensive entropy generalizes the sum operation into composite actions. The Jensen-Shannon divergence is defined as a similarity measure between probability distributions, and is related to the Shannon entropy [3]. The problem of establishing Jensen-Shannon divergence measures for graphs is that of computing the required entropies for individual and composite graphs. In [4], we have used the steady state random walk of a graph to establish a probability distribution for this purpose. The Jensen-Shannon divergence between a pair of graphs is defined as the difference between the entropy of a composite structure and their individual entropies. To determine a set of prototype graphs for vector space embedding. We use an information theoretic approach to construct the required graph prototypes [5]. Once the vectorial descriptions of a set of graphs are established, we perform graph classification in the principle component space. Experiments on graph datasets abstracted from bioinformatics and computer vision databases demonstrate the effectiveness and the efficiency of the proposed graph embedding method.

This paper is organized as follows. Section 2 develops a Jensen-Shannon divergence measure between graphs. Section 3 reviews the concept of graph dissimilarity embedding, and shows how to compute the similarity vectorial descriptions for a set of graphs using the Jensen-Shannon divergence. Section 4 provides the experimental evaluations. Finally, Section 5 provides the conclusion and future work.

2   The Jensen-Shannon Divergence on Graphs

In this section, we exploit the Jensen-Shannon divergence for developing a computationally efficient similarity measure for graphs. We commence by defining a Shannon entropy of a graph associated with its steady state random walk. Then we develop the similarity measure for graphs by using the Jensen-Shannon divergence between the graph entropies.

2.1   Graph Entropies

Consider a graph $G(V, E)$ with vertex set V and edge set $E \subseteq V \times V$. The adjacency matrix A for $G(V, E)$ has elements

$$A(i,j) = \begin{cases} 1 \text{ if}(i,j) \in E; \\ 0 \text{ otherwise.} \end{cases} \tag{1}$$

The vertex degree matrix of $G(V, E)$ is a diagonal matrix D with diagonal elements given by $D(v_i, v_i) = d(i) = \sum_{j \in V} A(i, j)$.

Shannon Entropy. For the graph $G(V, E)$, the probability of a steady state random walk on $G(V, E)$ visiting vertex i is $P_G(i) = d(i)/\sum_{j \in V} d(j)$. the Shannon entropy associated with the steady state random walk on $G(V, E)$ is

$$H_S(G) = -\sum_{i=1}^{|V|} P_G(i) \log P_G(i). \tag{2}$$

Time Complexity. *For the graph $G(V, E)$ having $n = |V|$ vertices, the Shannon entropy $H_S(G)$ requires time complexity $O(n^2)$.*

2.2   A Composite Entropy of a Pair of Graphs

To compute the Jensen-Shannon divergence of a pair of random walks on a pair of graphs $G_p(V_p, E_p)$ and $G_q(V_q, E_q)$, we require a method for constructing a composite structure $G_p \oplus G_q$ for the pair of graphs $G_p(V_p, E_p)$ and $G_q(V_q, E_q)$. For reasons of efficiency, we use the disjoint union as the composite structure. According to [6], the disjoint union graph of $G_p(V_p, E_p)$ and $G_q(V_q, E_q)$ is

$$G_{DU} = G_p \cup G_q = \{V_p \cup V_q, E_p \cup E_q\}. \tag{3}$$

Let graphs G_p and G_q be the connected components of the disjoint union graph G_{DU}, and $\rho_p = |V(G_p)|/|V(G_{DU})|$ and $\rho_q = |V(G_q)|/|V(G_{DU})|$. The entropy (i.e. the composite entropy) [7] of G_{DU} is

$$H(G_{DU}) = \rho_p H(G_p) + \rho_q H(G_q). \tag{4}$$

Here the entropy function $H(\cdot)$ is the Shannon entropy $H_S(\cdot)$ defined in Eq.(2).

2.3   The Jensen-Shannon Divergence on Graphs

The Jensen-Shannon divergence between the (discrete) probability distributions $P = (p_1, p_2, \ldots, p_K)$ and $Q = (q_1, q_2, \ldots, q_K)$, associated with the random walks on graphs $G_p(V_p, E_p)$ and $G_q(V_q, E_q)$, is negative definite (**nd**) with the following function:

$$D_{JS}(P, Q) = H_S(\frac{P+Q}{2}) - \frac{H_S(P) + H_S(Q)}{2}. \tag{5}$$

where $H_S(P) = \sum_{k=1}^{K} p_k \log p_k$ is the Shannon entropy of the probability distribution P. Given a pair of graphs $G_p(V_p, E_q)$ and $G_q(V_q, E_q)$, the Jensen-Shannon divergence for them is

$$D_{JS}(G_p, G_q) = H(G_p \oplus G_q) - \frac{H(G_p) + H(G_q)}{2}. \tag{6}$$

where $H(G_p \oplus G_q)$ is the entropy of the composite structure. Here we use the disjoint union defined in Sec.2.2 as the composite structure, and the entropy function $H(\cdot)$ is the Shannon entropy $H_S(\cdot)$ defined in Eq.(2).

Time Complexity. *For a pair of graphs $G_p(V_p, E_p)$ and $G_q(V_q, E_q)$ both having n vertices, computing the Jensen-Shannon divergence $D_{JS}(G_p, G_q)$ defined in Eq. (6) requires time complexity $O(n^2)$.*

3   Graph Embedding Using The Jensen-Shannon Divergence

In this section, we explore how to use the Jensen-Shannon divergence as a means of embedding graph structures into a vector space. We commence by reviewing the definition of the graph dissimilarity embedding.

3.1   Graph Dissimilarity Embedding

In [1], Riesen and Bunke have proposed a graph dissimilarity embedding to embed a sample graph into a vectorial description, they computed the edit distances between the sample graph and a number of prototype graphs. For a sample graph $G_i(V_i, E_i)$ $(i = 1, \ldots, N)$ and a set of prototype graphs $\mathcal{T} = \{\mathcal{T}_1, \ldots, \mathcal{T}_m, \ldots, \mathcal{T}_n\}$, we measure the dissimilarities between $G_i(V_i, E_i)$ and each prototype graph $\mathcal{T}_m \in \mathcal{T}$ as the m-th element of the n-dimensional vectorial description $V(G_i)$ of G_i. The mapping $\varphi_n^{\mathcal{T}}$: $(G_i) \to R^n$ is defined as the function

$$V(G_i) = (d(G_i, \mathcal{T}_1), \ldots, d(G_i, \mathcal{T}_m), \ldots, d(G_i, \mathcal{T}_n)) \tag{7}$$

where $d(G_i, \mathcal{T}_m)$ is the graph dissimilarity measure between $G_i(V_i, E_i)$ and the m-th prototype graph $\mathcal{T}_m$. Riesen and Bunke proposed to use the graph edit distance as the dissimilarity measure. Although, their approach allows any (dis)similarity measure of graphs to be used.

3.2   A Graph Embedding Method Using the Jensen-Shannon Divergence

The novel graph embedding procedure described in Section 3.1 offers us a principled way to develop a new graph embedding approach using the Jensen-Shannon divergence. Consider the sample graph $G_i(V_i, E_i)$ and the set of prototype graphs $\mathcal{T} = \{\mathcal{T}_1, \ldots, \mathcal{T}_m, \ldots, \mathcal{T}_n\}$, we compute the similarity measure between $G_i(V_i, E_i)$ and each prototype graph using the Jensen-Shannon divergence, as a result the mapping $\varphi_n^{\mathcal{T}}$: $(G_i) \to R^n$ defined in Eq.(7) can be re-written as

$$V_{D_{JS}}(G_i) = (D_{JS}(G_i, \mathcal{T}_1), \ldots, D_{JS}(G_i, \mathcal{T}_m), \ldots, D_{JS}(G_i, \mathcal{T}_n)) \tag{8}$$

where $D_{JS}(G_i, \mathcal{T}_m)$ is the Jensen-Shannon divergence between the sample graph $G_i(V_i, E_i)$ and the m-th prototype graph $\mathcal{T}_m$. Since the Jesnen-Shannon divergence between graphs can be efficiently computed, the proposed embedding method are more efficient than the dissimilarity embedding using the costly computed graph edit distance.

3.3   The Prototype Graph Selection

For our approach, the prototype graphs $\mathcal{T} = \{\mathcal{T}_1, \ldots, \mathcal{T}_m, \ldots, \mathcal{T}_n\}$ serve as reference points to transform graphs into real vectors. Hence, the aim of prototype graph selection is to find reference points which result in a meaningful vector in the embedding space. Intuitively, the prototype graphs $\mathcal{T} = \{\mathcal{T}_1, \ldots, \mathcal{T}_m, \ldots, \mathcal{T}_n\}$ should be able to characterize the structural variations present in a set of sample embedded graphs. Furthermore, these prototype graphs should be neither too redundant nor too simple. To locate the prototype graphs we make use of Luo and Hancock's probabilistic model of graph structures described in [8], and develop an information theoretic approach to selecting prototype graphs. By using a two-part minimum description length criterion [9,10,11], these selected prototype graphs trade off the goodness-of-fit to the sample data against their intrinsic complexities. To formalize this idea, we locate the prototype graphs that minimize the overall code-length. The code-length of a set of sample graphs is the average of their *Shannon-Fano code* which is equivalent to the negative logarithm of their likelihood function. The code-length for describing the complexity of the prototype graphs is measured using the approximate von-Neumann entropy [12]. To minimize the overall code length, we develop a variant of EM algorithm where we view both the structure of the prototype graphs and the vertex correspondence information between the sample and prototype graphs as missing data. In the two interleaved steps of the EM algorithm, the expectation step involves recomputing the a posteriori probability of vertex correspondence while the maximization step involves updating both the structure of the prototype graphs and the vertex correspondence information. More details of how we apply the minimum description length criterion and how the EM algorithm work can be found in [5].

4   Experimental Evaluation

In this section, we demonstrate the performance of our proposed method on several graph datasets abstracted from real-world image and bioinformatics databases. These datasets are: ALOI, CMU, MUTAG and NCI109 [13]. The ALOI dataset consists of 54 graphs extracted from selected images of three similar boxes. The CMU dataset consists of 54 graphs extracted from selected images of three similar toy houses. For each object in the ALOI and CMU datasets, there are 18 images captured from different viewpoints. The graphs are the Delaunay triangulations of feature points extracted from the different images using the SIFT detection. The maximum and minimum vertices of the ALOI and CMU datasets are 1288 (max) and 295 (min) for ALOI, and 495 (max) and 27 (min) for CMU. The MUTAG dataset is based on graphs representing 188 chemical compounds, and aims to predict whether each compound possesses mutagenicity. The maximum and minimum number of vertices are 28 and 10 respectively. As the vertices and edges of each compound are labeled with real number, we transform these graphs into unweighted graphs. The NCI109 is based on un weighted graph representing 4127 chemical compounds, and aims to predict whether each sub-set of compound is active in an anti-cancer screen. The maximum and minimum number of vertices are 111 and 4 respectively.

4.1   Experiments on Graph Datasets

Experimental Setup: We evaluate the performance of our proposed graph embedding method using the Jensen-Shannon divergence (DEJS) on the four graph datasets. We compare our method against several alternative graph based learning methods. The comparative methods include a) pattern vectors from coefficients of the Ihara zeta function (CIZF) [14], b) pattern vectors from algebraic graph theory (PVAG) [15], and c) the graph dissimilarity embedding using the edit distance (DEED) [1]. For our method and DEED on each dataset, we randomly divide the graphs into 20 folds and use any 6 folds to learn 6 prototype graphs. We construct the 6 dimensional vector description of each testing graph. For the alternative methods CIZF and PVAG on each dataset, we construct the vectorial description of each testing graph. We then perform 10-fold cross-validation of KNN classifier to evaluate the performance of our method and the alternative methods, using nine folds for training and one fold for testing. All the KNN classifiers and the paraments were performed and optimised on a Weka workbench. We repeat the whole experiment 10 times and report the average classification accuracies in Table 1. We also report the runtime to establish graph feature vectors of each method in Table 1 under Matlab R2011a with an Intel($i5$) 3.2GHz 4-core processor.

Table 1. Experimental Comparisons on Graph Datasets

Data	ALOI	CMU	NCI109	MUTAG	Data	ALOI	CMU	NCI109	MUTAG
DEJS	91.35	100	65.49	80.75	DEJS	2"	1"	2"	1"
CIZF	–	100	67.19	80.85	CIZF	–	2'33"	14"	1"
PVAG	–	62.59	64.59	82.44	PVAG	–	5"	19"	1"
DEED	–	100	63.34	83.55	DEED	–	3h55'	17h49'	49'23"

Experimental Results: On the ALOI dataset which possesses graphs of more than one thousand vertices, our method takes 2 seconds, while DEED takes over one day and even CIZF and PVAG generate overflows on the computation. The runtime of CIZF and PVAG methods are only competitive to our method DEJS on the MUTAG, NCI109 and CMU datasets which possess graphs of smaller sizes. This reveals that our DEJS can easily scale up to graphs with thousands of vertices. DEED can achieve competitive classification accuracies to our DEJS, but requires more computation time. The graph similarity embedding using the Jensen-Shannon divergence measure is more efficient than that using the edit distance dissimilarity measure proposed by Riesen and Bunke. The reason for this is that the Jensen-Shannon divergence between graphs only requires quadratic numbers of vertices.

Furthermore, both our embedding method and DEED also require extra runtime for learning the required prototype graphs. For the ALOI, CMU, NCI109 and MUTAG datasets, the average times for learning a prototype graph are 5 hours, 30 minutes, 15 minutes and 5 minutes respectively. This reveals that for graphs of large sizes, our embedding method may require additionally and potentially expansive computations for learning the prototype graphs. However for graphs of less than 300 vertices, the learning of prototype graphs can still be completed in polynomial time.

4.2 Stability Evaluation

In this subsection, we investigate the stability of our proposed method DEJS. We randomly select three seed graphs from the ALOI dataset. We then apply random edit operations on the three seed graphs to simulate the effects of noise. The edit operations are vertex deletion and edge deletion. For each seed graph, we randomly delete a predetermined fraction of vertices or edges to obtain noise corrupted variants. The feature distance between an original seed graph G_0 and its noise corrupted counterpart G_n is defined as their Euclidean distance, defined as

$$d_{G_0,G_n} = \sqrt{(V_{JS}(G_0) - V_{JS}(G_n))^T (V_{JS}(G_0) - V_{JS}(G_n))} \qquad (9)$$

We show the experimental results in Fig.1 and Fig. 2. Fig.1 and Fig. 2 show the effects of vertex and edge deletion respectively. The x-axis represents 1% to 35% of vertices or edges are deleted, and the y-axis shows the Euclidean distance d_{G_0,G_n} between the original seed graph G_o and its noise corrupted counterpart G_n. From Fig.1 and Fig. 2, there is an approximate linear relationship in each case. This implies that the proposed method possesses ability to distinguish graphs under controlled structural-error.

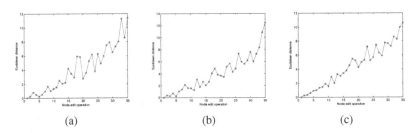

(a)   (b)   (c)

Fig. 1. Stability evaluation vertex edit operation

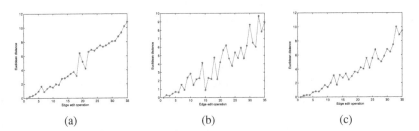

(a)   (b)   (c)

Fig. 2. Stability evaluation edge edit operation

5   Conclusion and Future Work

In this paper, we have shown how to use the Jensen-Shannon divergence as a means of embedding a sample graph into a vector space. We use an information theoretic approach to construct the required prototype graphs. We embed a sample graph into feature space by computing the Jensen-Shannon divergence measure between the sample graph and each of the prototype graphs. We perform 10-folds cross validation associated with KNN classifier to assign the graphs into classes. Experimental results demonstrate the effectiveness and efficiency of the proposed method. Since learning prototype graphs usually requires expensive computation, our further work is to define a fast approach to learn the prototype graphs. This will be useful to define a faster graph embedding method.

Acknowledgments. We thank Dr. Peng Ren for providing the Matlab implementation for the graph Ihara zeta function method.

References

1. Riesen, K., Bunke, H.: Graph Classification and Clustering Based on Vector Space Embedding. World Scientific Press (2010)
2. Pekalska, E., Duin, R.P.W., Paclík, P.: Prototype Selection for Dissimilarity-based Classifiers. Pattern Recognition 39, 189–208 (2006)
3. Martins, A.F., Smith, N.A., Xing, E.P., Aguiar, P.M., Figueiredo, M.A.: Nonextensive Information Theoretic Kernels on Measures. Journal of Machine Learning Research 10, 935–975 (2009)
4. Bai, L., Hancock, E.R.: Graph Kernels from The Jensen-Shannon Divergence. Journal of Mathematical Imaging and Vision (to appear)
5. Han, L., Hancock, E.R., Wilson, R.C.: An Information Theoretic Approach to Learning Generative Graph Prototypes. In: Pelillo, M., Hancock, E.R. (eds.) SIMBAD 2011. LNCS, vol. 7005, pp. 133–148. Springer, Heidelberg (2011)
6. Gadouleau, M., Riis, S.: Graph-theoretical Constructions for Graph Entropy and Network Coding Based Communications. IEEE Transactions on Information Theory 57, 6703–6717 (2011)
7. Köner, J.: Coding of An Information Source Having Ambiguous Alphabet and The Entropy of Graphs. In: Proceedings of the 6th Prague Conference on Information Theory, Statistical Decision Function, Random Processes, pp. 411–425 (1971)
8. Luo, B., Hancock, E.R.: Structural Graph Matching Using the EM Alogrithm and Singular Value Decomposition. IEEE Transactions on Pattern Analysis and Machine Intelligence 23, 1120–1136 (2001)
9. Rissanen, J.: Stochastic Complexity in Statistical Inquiry. World Scientific, Singapore (1989)
10. Rissanen, J.: Modelling by Shortest Data Description. Automatica 14, 465–471 (1978)
11. Rissanen, J.: An Universal Prior for Integers and Estimation by Minimum Description Length. Annals of Statistics 11, 417–431 (1983)
12. Han, L., Hancock, E.R., Wilson, R.C.: Characterizing Graphs Using Approximate von Neumann Entropy. In: Vitrià, J., Sanches, J.M., Hernández, M. (eds.) IbPRIA 2011. LNCS, vol. 6669, pp. 484–491. Springer, Heidelberg (2011)
13. Shervashidze, N., Borgwardt, K.M.: Fast Subtree Kernels on Graphs. In: NIPS, pp. 1660–1668 (2009)
14. Ren, P., Wilson, R.C., Hancock, E.R.: Graph Characterization via Ihara Coefficients. IEEE Transactions on Neural Networks 22, 233–245 (2011)
15. Wilson, R.C., Hancock, E.R., Luo, B.: Pattern Vectors from Algebraic Graph Theory. IEEE Transactions on Pattern Analysis and Machine Intelligence 27, 1112–1124 (2005)

Mixtures of Radial Densities for Clustering Graphs

Brijnesh J. Jain

Technische Universität Berlin, Germany
brijnesh.jain@gmail.com

Abstract. We address the problem of unsupervised learning on graphs. The contribution is twofold: (1) we propose an EM algorithm for estimating the parameters of a mixture of radial densities on graphs on the basis of the graph orbifold framework; and (2) we compare orbifold-based clustering algorithms including the proposed EM algorithm against state-of-the-art methods based on pairwise dissimilarities. The results show that orbifold-based clustering methods complement the existing arsenal of clustering methods on graphs.

Keywords: graphs, clustering, EM algorithm, graph matching.

1 Introduction

Attributed graphs are a versatile and expressive data structure for representing complex patterns consisting of objects and relationships between objects. Examples include molecules, mid- and high-level description of images, instances of relational schemes, web graphs, and social networks.

Despite the many advantages of graph-based representations, statistical learning on attributed graphs is underdeveloped compared to learning on feature vectors. For example, generic state-of-the-art methods for clustering of non-vectorial data are mainly based on pairwise dissimilarity methods such as hierarchical or spectral clustering. One research direction to complement the manageable range of graph clustering methods aims at extending centroid-based clustering methods to attributed graphs [2,3,9,11], which more or less amount in different variants of graph quantization methods. A theoretical justification of these approaches is provided in [8] by means of establishing conditions for optimality and statistical consistency.

Vector quantization, k-means and their variants are not only well-known for their simplicity but also for their deficiencies. Such a statement in the graph domain is difficult to derive, because more advanced generalizations of standard clustering algorithms to graphs are rare and an empirical comparison to state-of-the-art graph clustering methods is missing.

Following this line of research, the contribution of this paper are twofold: (1) we extend mixtures of Gaussians to mixtures of radial densities on graphs and adopt the EM algorithm for parameter estimation on the basis of the orbifold

R. Wilson et al. (Eds.): CAIP 2013, Part I, LNCS 8047, pp. 110–119, 2013.

framework [7]; (2) we compare the performance of clustering methods in orbifolds with state-of-the art clustering based on pairwise dissimilarity data. The results show that clustering in orbifolds constitute a promising alternative and complement existing state-of-the-art graph clustering methods.

2   Graph Orbifolds

The section introduces a suitable representation of attributed graphs by means of the orbifold framework as proposed in [5,7].

Let $\mathbb{E}$ be a p-dimensional Euclidean space. An attributed graph $X = (V, E, \alpha)$ consists of a set V of vertices, a set $E \subseteq V \times V$ of edges, and an attribute function $\alpha : V \times V \to \mathbb{E}$, such that $\alpha(i, j) \neq \mathbf{0}$ for each edge and $\alpha(i, j) = \mathbf{0}$ for each non-edge. Attributes $\alpha(i, i)$ of vertices i may take any value from $\mathbb{E}$.

For simplifying the mathematical treatment, we assume that all graphs are of order n, where n is chosen to be sufficiently large. Graphs of order less than n can be extended to order n by including isolated vertices with attribute zero. This is a merely technical assumption to simplify mathematics. A graph X is completely specified by its matrix representation $\boldsymbol{x} = (\alpha(i, j))$. Let $\mathcal{X} = \mathbb{E}^{n \times n}$ be the Euclidean space of all $(n \times n)$-matrices with elements from $\mathbb{E}$ and let Π^n be the set of all $(n \times n)$-permutation matrices. For each $\boldsymbol{p} \in \Pi^n$ we define a mapping

$$\gamma_{\boldsymbol{p}} : \mathcal{X} \to \mathcal{X}, \quad \boldsymbol{x} \mapsto \boldsymbol{p}^{\mathsf{T}} \boldsymbol{x} \boldsymbol{p}.$$

Then $\mathcal{G} = \{\gamma_{\boldsymbol{p}} : \boldsymbol{p} \in \Pi^n\}$ is a finite group acting on $\mathcal{X}$. For $\boldsymbol{x} \in \mathcal{X}$, the orbit of $\boldsymbol{x}$ is the set defined by $[\boldsymbol{x}] = \{\gamma(\boldsymbol{x}) : \gamma \in \mathcal{G}\}$. Thus, the orbit $[\boldsymbol{x}]$ consists of all possible matrix representations of X obtained by reordering its vertices. We define a graph orbifold by the quotient set

$$\mathcal{X}_{\mathcal{G}} = \mathcal{X}_{\mathcal{G}} = \{[\boldsymbol{x}] : \boldsymbol{x} \in \mathcal{X}\}$$

of all orbits. Its natural projection is given by $\pi : \mathcal{X} \to \mathcal{X}_{\mathcal{G}}, \quad \boldsymbol{x} \mapsto [\boldsymbol{x}]$. In the following, we identify $[\boldsymbol{x}]$ with X and occasionally write $\boldsymbol{x} \in X$ if π projects to X.

In order to mimic Gaussian distributions, we extend the Euclidean norm $\|\cdot\|$ to a metric on $\mathcal{X}_{\mathcal{G}}$ defined by

$$d(X, X') = \min \{\|\boldsymbol{x} - \boldsymbol{x}'\| : \boldsymbol{x} \in X, \boldsymbol{x}' \in X'\}, \tag{1}$$

where $\|\cdot\|$ is the Euclidean distance on $\mathcal{X}$. We call a pair $(\boldsymbol{x}, \boldsymbol{x}') \in X \times X'$ with $\|\boldsymbol{x} - \boldsymbol{x}'\| = d(X, X')$ an optimal alignment of X and X'.

An orbifold function is a mapping of the form $f : \mathcal{X}_{\mathcal{G}} \to \mathbb{R}$. Instead of studying f, it is more convenient to study the lift $f^{\ell} : \mathcal{X} \to \mathbb{R}$ of f satisfying $f^{\ell}(\boldsymbol{x}) = f(\pi(\boldsymbol{x})) = f(X)$ for all $\boldsymbol{x} \in \mathcal{X}$.

3   Mixtures of Radial Densities

This section studies mixtures of radial densities on graphs. Throughout this section, we assume that $(\mathcal{X}, \mathfrak{B}, \lambda)$ is the Lebesgue-Borel measure space. The action of the finite group $\mathcal{G}$ on $\mathcal{X}$ induces the measure space $(\mathcal{X}_\mathcal{G}, \mathcal{B}_\mathcal{G}, \lambda_\mathcal{G})$, where $\mathcal{B}_\mathcal{G} = \{\mathcal{B} \subset \mathcal{X}_\mathcal{G} : \pi^{-1}(\mathcal{B}) \in \mathcal{B}\}$ and $\lambda_\mathcal{G} = \lambda \circ \pi^{-1}$ is the induced quotient measure.

3.1 Radial Densities

Radial densities on graphs are bell-shaped functions of the form

$$h(X|C, \sigma) = a \cdot \exp\left(-\frac{d(X, C)^2}{2\sigma^2}\right),$$

where $a > 0$ is the height of the bell, $C \in \mathcal{X}_\mathcal{G}$ is the graph at the centre of the bell, and $\sigma > 0$ is the width of the bell. The height a scales h to a density and thus is of the form

$$a = \left(\int_{\mathcal{X}_G} h_1(X|C, \sigma)\lambda_\mathcal{G}(dX)\right)^{-1}.$$

Lifting a radial density $h(X|C, \sigma)$ to the Euclidean space $\mathcal{X}$ yields

$$h^\ell(\boldsymbol{x}|C, \sigma) = a \cdot \exp\left(-\frac{\min_{\boldsymbol{c} \in C} \|\boldsymbol{x} - \boldsymbol{c}\|^2}{2\sigma^2}\right) = \max_{\boldsymbol{c} \in C} \ a \cdot \underbrace{\exp\left(-\frac{\|\boldsymbol{x} - \boldsymbol{c}\|^2}{2\sigma^2}\right)}_{=:\phi(\boldsymbol{x}|\boldsymbol{c}, \sigma)}, \quad (2)$$

where $\boldsymbol{x}$ is an arbitrary matrix representation of X and $\phi(\boldsymbol{x}|\boldsymbol{c}, \sigma)$ denotes the radial function on vectors with center $\boldsymbol{c}$ and width σ.

Next, we are interested in those regions of $\mathcal{X}$ at which a radial density $\phi(\boldsymbol{x}|\boldsymbol{c}, \sigma)$ on vectors is maximum. By definition of the lift h^ℓ, this region is the Dirichlet (fundamental) domain of $\boldsymbol{c}$

$$\mathcal{D}_\boldsymbol{c} = \{\boldsymbol{x} \in \mathcal{X} : \|\boldsymbol{x} - \boldsymbol{c}\| \leq \|\boldsymbol{x} - \boldsymbol{c}'\|, \ \boldsymbol{c}' \in C\}.$$

A Dirichlet domain is a convex polyhedral cone [6] with a number of useful properties: (1) members $\boldsymbol{x} \in \mathcal{D}_\boldsymbol{c}$ are optimally aligned with $\boldsymbol{c}$, that is $d(X, C) = \|\boldsymbol{x} - \boldsymbol{c}\|$; (2) each graph X has a representation matrix $\boldsymbol{x}$ in $\mathcal{D}_\boldsymbol{c}$; (3) if $\boldsymbol{x}, \boldsymbol{x}' \in \mathcal{D}_\boldsymbol{c}$ are two distinct matrix representations of the same graph X, then both representations lie on the boundary of $\mathcal{D}_\boldsymbol{c}$; and (4) there is a cross section $s :$ $\mathcal{X}_\mathcal{G} \to \mathcal{X}$ of π such that $\pi(s(X)) = X$.

A cross section s establishes a one-to-one correspondence between the graphs from $\mathcal{X}_\mathcal{G}$ and the elements of $s(\mathcal{X}_\mathcal{G}) \subseteq \mathcal{D}_\boldsymbol{c}$ by selecting a unique representation for each graph from the Dirichlet domain $\mathcal{D}_\boldsymbol{c}$. The subset $s(\mathcal{X}_\mathcal{G}) \subset \mathcal{D}_\boldsymbol{c}$ looks like the Dirichlet domain $\mathcal{D}_\boldsymbol{c}$ itself, except of some holes in the boundary.

Suppose that $h(X|C, \sigma)$ is a radial density on graphs with lift $h^\ell(\boldsymbol{x}|C, \sigma)$. Let $\boldsymbol{c}$ be an arbitrary representation of the center C. Truncating the lift h^ℓ to the Dirichlet domain $\mathcal{D}_\boldsymbol{c}$ yields the density

$$h^t(\boldsymbol{x}|\boldsymbol{c}, \sigma) = \begin{cases} a \cdot \phi(\boldsymbol{x}|\boldsymbol{c}, \sigma) & : \quad \boldsymbol{x} \in \mathcal{D}_\boldsymbol{c} \\ 0 & : \quad \text{otherwise} \end{cases},$$

where the Dirichlet domain $\mathcal{D}_c$ of center c is the support of h^t. This shows that the study of radial densities $h(X|C, \sigma)$ on graphs reduces to the study of truncated radial densities $h^t(\boldsymbol{x}|c, \sigma)$ on a representable region in $\mathcal{D}_c$. The truncated radial density h^t is related to the Gaussian distribution $\mathcal{N}(\boldsymbol{x}|c, \Sigma)$ with mean c and covariance matrix $\Sigma = \sigma^2 \boldsymbol{I}$ as follows:

$$h^t(\boldsymbol{x}|c, \sigma) = \frac{1}{P_c} \cdot \mathcal{N}(\boldsymbol{x}|c, \Sigma), \tag{3}$$

where d is the dimension of $\mathcal{X}$ and $\boldsymbol{x} \in \mathcal{D}_c$. The term P_c is the probability of being in the Dirichlet domain $\mathcal{D}_c$ with respect to the measure λ' defined by some cross section into $\mathcal{D}_c$. Thus, equation (3) shows that studying radial densities on graphs can be reduced to studying truncated Gaussians on vectors with support $\mathcal{D}_c$.

Note that neither the center c nor the squared width σ^2 of a truncated Gaussian coincides with its expectation $\mathbb{E}[\boldsymbol{x}]$ or variance $\mathbb{V}[\boldsymbol{x}]$. The expectation and variance can be obtained from the center and squared width plus an adjustment for the truncation on the distribution.

3.2   Mixture Models of Radial Densities

A mixture model of radial densities on graphs is a probability distribution of the form

$$p(X) = \sum_{j=1}^{K} \pi_j h(X|C_j, \sigma_j), \tag{4}$$

where the parameters π_j are the mixing coefficients of components j with centers C_j and widths σ_j. Lifting the mixture model $p(X)$ to the Euclidean space $\mathcal{X}$ yields

$$p^\ell(\boldsymbol{x}) = \sum_{j=1}^{K} \pi_j h^\ell(\boldsymbol{x}|C_j, \sigma_j), \tag{5}$$

where $\boldsymbol{x}$ is an arbitrarily chosen matrix representation of graph X. Truncation of the lift p^ℓ to a single Dirichlet domain as for radial functions is no longer useful, because different centers C_j may result in different Dirichlet domains regardless of how we choose the particular representations c_j of the centers C_j. Instead, we choose a matrix representation c_j for each center C_j. Next, we truncate the lift h^ℓ of each component j to the Dirichlet domain $\mathcal{D}_j = \mathcal{D}_{c_j}$. In doing so, we obtain a truncated mixture model

$$p^t(\boldsymbol{x}) = \sum_{j=1}^{K} \pi_j h^t(\boldsymbol{x}^j|c_j, \sigma_j), \tag{6}$$

where $\boldsymbol{x}^j \in \mathcal{D}_j$. Note that the argument $\boldsymbol{x}$ of the mixture p^t and the data points $\boldsymbol{x}^j$ represent the same graph. To emphasize that the mixture $p^t(\boldsymbol{x})$ is indeed a function of x, we may think of $x^j = s_j(\pi(x))$, where s_j is a cross section into $\mathcal{D}_j$.

Equation (6) together with equation (3) show that the study of mixtures of radial densities on graphs can be reduced to the study of mixtures of truncated Gaussians on vectors. In contrast to standard mixtures, each component j of a truncated mixture lives in a different region $\mathcal{D}_j$, which requires a transformation of the data points.

3.3   EM Algorithm

Suppose that $\mathcal{S} = (X_1)_{i=1}^{N}$ are N example graphs generated by a mixture model $p(X)$ of radial densities as defined in equation (4). Our goal is to estimate the parameters π_j, C_j, and σ_j^2 on the basis of $\mathcal{S}$ by adopting the EM algorithm for maximizing the log-likelihood

$$\ell(\boldsymbol{\Theta}|\mathcal{S}) = \sum_{i=1}^{N} \ln \sum_{j=1}^{K} \pi_j h(X_i|C_j, \sigma_j),$$

where $\boldsymbol{\Theta} = (\pi_j, C_j, \sigma_j^2)_{j=1}^{K}$. Let c_j be arbitrarily chosen matrix representations of the centers C_j. Lifting and truncating of the log-likelihood $\ell(\boldsymbol{\Theta}|\mathcal{S})$ yields

$$\ell^t(\boldsymbol{\theta}|\mathcal{S}) = \sum_{i=1}^{N} \ln \sum_{j=1}^{K} \pi_j h^t\left(x_i^j|c_j, \sigma_j\right),$$

where $\boldsymbol{\theta} = (\pi_j, c_j, \sigma_j^2)_{j=1}^{K}$ and $x_i^j \in \mathcal{D}_j$ is a representation of the ith-example X_i in $\mathcal{D}_j$.

Since the log-likelihood $\ell^t(\boldsymbol{\theta}|\mathcal{S})$ is differentiable with respect to its parameters in $\mathcal{D}_j$, we can adopt the EM algorithm for mixtures of truncated Gaussians. The E-Step determines the responsibilities γ_{ij} that component j has generated example X_i according to

$$\gamma_{ij} = \frac{\pi_j\, h^t\left(x_i^j \mid c_j, \sigma_j\right)}{\sum\limits_{k} \pi_k\, h^t\left(x_i^k \mid c_k, \sigma_k\right)}. \tag{7}$$

For the M-Step, we arrive at

$$\widehat{c}_j = \frac{1}{N_j} \sum_{i=1}^{N} \gamma_{ij} \left(x_i^j - \delta_{\mathbb{E}}(j)\right) \tag{8}$$

$$\widehat{\sigma}_j^2 = \frac{1}{N_j} \sum_{i=1}^{N} \gamma_{ij} \left(\left\|x_i^j - \widehat{c}_j\right\|^2 - \delta_{\mathbb{V}}(j)\right) \tag{9}$$

$$\widehat{\pi}_j = \frac{N_j}{N}, \tag{10}$$

where $N_j = \sum_{i=1}^{N} \gamma_{ij}$ is the effective number of training graphs assigned to component j, and $\delta_{\mathbb{E}}(j) = \delta_{\mathbb{E}}(c_j, \sigma_j)$ as well as $\delta_{\mathbb{V}}(j) = \delta_{\mathbb{V}}(c_j, \sigma_j)$ are the adjustments for the truncations.

4   Experiments

The goal of our experimental study is to assess the performance of clustering methods based on the graph orbifold framework and compare it against state-of-the-art clustering method based on pairwise dissimilarity data. We considered the following algorithms: (1) EM algorithm for mixtures of radial densities on graphs, (2) k-means for graphs [8], (3) hierarchical clustering using Ward's linkage [15], (4) spectral clustering [12], (5) k-medoids [10], and (6) hierarchical clustering using complete, average, and single linkage. Methods (1)–(3) are orbifold-based and methods (4)–(6) are based on pairwise dissimilarity data. Note that Ward's linkage is considered as an orbifold method though it is based on pairwise dissimilarities, because it computes the cluster mean of graphs for each newly merged cluster.

4.1   Data

We selected subsets of the following training data sets from the IAM graph database repository [14]: Letter (low, medium, high), fingerprint, grec, and coil. In addition, we considered the Monoamine Oxidase (MAO) data set. The *letter* data sets compile distorted letter drawings from the Roman alphabet that consist of straight lines. Lines of a letter are represented by edges and endpoints of lines by vertices. Fingerprint images of the *fingerprints* data set are converted into graphs, where vertices represent endpoints and bifurcation points of skeletonized versions of relevant regions. Edge represent ridges in the skeleton. The distortion levels are low, medium, and high. The *grec* data set consists of graphs representing symbols from noisy versions of architectural and electronic drawings. Vertices represent endpoints, corners, intersections, or circles. Edges represent lines or arcs. The *coil-4* data set is a subset of the coil-100 data set consisting of 4 out of 32 objects that are expected to be recognized easily. The arbitrarily chosen objects correspond to indices 7 (car), 17 (cup), 52 (duck), and 75 (house) of the coil-100 data set (starting at index 1). After preprocessing, the images are represented by graphs, where vertices represent endpoints of lines and edges represent lines. The *mao* data set is composed of 68 molecules, divided into two classes, where 38 molecules inhibit the monoamine oxidase (antidepressant drugs) and 30 do not.These molecules are composed of different chemical elements and are thus encoded as labeled graphs, where nodes represent atoms and edges represent bonds between atoms.[1]

4.2   Experimental Setup

We set the number K of clusters to the number of classes of the respective data sets. All clustering algorithms apply the squared graph metric defined in eq. (1) as underlying dissimilarity function. All graph metrics were approximated using the graduated assignment algorithm [1]. Spectral clustering and k-medoids can

---

[1] `https://brunl01.users.greyc.fr/CHEMISTRY/`

be applied in any distance space, because both methods operate on pairwise dissimilarity data. Ward's clustering, k-means for graphs, and the proposed EM algorithm require the concept of a sample mean, which is generally not available in an arbitrary distance space. By means of the orbifold framework, we estimated sample mean graphs using the incremental arithmetic mean algorithm [4]. The non-hierarchical methods iterate several times through the training set. We terminated these iterative methods after 20 epochs without improvement of the respective error function and recorded the solution where the value of the error function was lowest. To initialize the centroids of the iterative methods, we applied the furthest first method on $3K \log(K)$ randomly chosen elements. To overcome computational issues of the EM algorithm, we substituted the calculation of the adjustment terms by controling the estimated width $\hat{\sigma}_j^2$ according to $\tilde{\sigma}_j^2 = 1/(1 + \exp\left(-\beta \cdot \hat{\sigma}_j^2\right))$, where the slope β is a problem dependent parameter of ψ. The task of the sigmoid is to replace absolute adjustments in a relative manner and to ensure numerical stable solutions which would be sufficient for learning tasks such as clustering.

To assess the quality of the clustering algorithms, we determined its classification accuracy on the respective data sets. Clusters are assigned to classes by solving the corresponding maximum weighted bipartite matching problem. Nodes of the complete bipartite graph represent clusters and classes. Edges connect each cluster $\mathcal{C}$ with each class c weighted by the normalized number of members in $\mathcal{C}$ of class c. We performed scaling parameter selections for EM (β) and spectral clustering (σ^2) as follows: For each data set, we performed a one-dimensional grid-search, where each parameter configuration was tested 10 times. We selected the parameter with best average cost over all 10 runs. We performed 10 trials for each data set. Since each clustering algorithm optimizes an error function, we reported the classification accuracy of the particular trial with lowest error over all 10 trials.

4.3   Results and Discussion

Table 1 and 2 summarize the results. Shown are the classification accuracy *acc* obtained at a trial with lowest error, the average *acc*, maximum *max* and minimum *min* accuracy over all ten trials for each data set. Note that in an unsupervised setting, we are unable to identify the trial with maximum accuracy, when using the error values as criterion for selecting the "best" outcome of a clustering method out of ten trials. We make the following observations taking into account the pre-specified number K of clusters and a limited significance due to the low number trials:

1. Ward's clustering performs best overall. Spectral clustering and the EM algorithm are comparable to Ward's clustering, whereas k-means for graphs and in particular k-medoids are not competitive. Compared to the best results, each cluster method has a performance drop on at least one data set showing that there is no best clustering method. 2. A low error is a good indicator for recovering the class structure for all cluster algorithms. Inspecting the accuracy *acc* at the lowest error and the maximum accuracy *max* attained over all runs, we

Table 1. Classification accuracy of graph clustering algorithms over 10 trials. K denotes the number of clusters. *acc*: accuracy at lowest error. *avg*: average accuracy with standard deviation. *max*: maximum accuracy. *min* minimum accuracy.

data	accuracy	pairwise approaches		orbifold-based approaches		
		Spectral Clustering	k-Medoids	Ward's Clustering	k-Means for graphs	EM for graphs
letter (low)	acc	93.7	82.4	94.5	88.8	93.3
$K = 15$	avg	$93.9^{\pm0.1}$	$73.4^{\pm6.5}$	$94.1^{\pm0.4}$	$80.9^{\pm4.1}$	$91.4^{\pm3.0}$
	max	94.0	82.4	94.5	88.8	93.5
	min	93.7	59.3	93.2	75.5	86.8
letter (medium)	acc	91.1	77.9	92.4	84.9	90.9
$K = 15$	avg	$90.6^{\pm1.8}$	$71.0^{\pm5.4}$	$91.3^{\pm0.7}$	$78.7^{\pm4.9}$	$90.6^{\pm0.3}$
	max	91.6	77.9	92.5	85.1	90.9
	min	85.6	60.4	90.1	68.3	90.3
letter (high)	acc	86.5	55.7	84.9	85.3	90.3
$K = 15$	avg	$84.1^{\pm3.9}$	$47.7^{\pm4.9}$	$82.5^{\pm1.4}$	$75.1^{\pm5.5}$	$85.2^{\pm1.9}$
	max	88.4	55.7	85.5	85.3	90.3
	min	78.9	40.9	78.9	66.0	83.3
fingerprint	acc	61.4	60.8	69.7	63.0	63.2
$K = 4$	avg	$61.4^{\pm0.0}$	$60.0^{\pm5.1}$	$66.6^{\pm2.3}$	$64.6^{\pm1.6}$	$63.0^{\pm0.3}$
	max	61.4	70.4	69.7	66.6	63.2
	min	61.4	54.6	58.7	62.4	62.2
grec	acc	64.7	50.3	69.6	54.5	54.9
$K = 22$	avg	$65.7^{\pm1.2}$	$50.5^{\pm3.4}$	$68.1^{\pm1.3}$	$51.7^{\pm3.1}$	$50.1^{\pm2.3}$
	max	68.5	55.2	70.6	57.3	54.9
	min	64.7	46.2	67.1	45.8	46.5
coil	acc	58.3	44.8	54.2	50.0	64.6
$K = 4$	avg	$59.0^{\pm2.0}$	$42.6^{\pm2.7}$	$51.8^{\pm4.6}$	$46.0^{\pm2.0}$	$51.1^{\pm7.1}$
	max	64.6	46.9	60.4	50.0	64.6
	min	58.3	38.5	44.8	42.7	44.8
mao	acc	73.5	70.6	73.5	72.1	73.5
$K = 2$	avg	$69.7^{\pm7.9}$	$60.0^{\pm6.4}$	$69.6^{\pm8.0}$	$72.8^{\pm1.0}$	$74.1^{\pm5.5}$
	max	80.9	70.6	89.7	75.0	88.2
	min	63.2	55.9	60.3	72.1	66.2

see that *acc* is often close to *max*. 3. Inspecting the letter data sets, where *low*, *medium* and *high* refer to the noise level with which the letters were distorted, we observe that the EM algorithm and k-means are most robust against noise. It is notable that the performance of k-medoids strongly declines with increasing noise level. In contrast to findings in vector spaces (see e.g. [13]), results on graphs do not confirm a common view that k-mediods is more robust than k-means. 4. As shown in Table 2, other hierarchical clustering methods using complete, average, and single linkage were not able to recover the class structure given the fixed number K of clusters.

The good results of Ward's clustering and the EM algorithm suggest that clustering methods relying on the graph orbifold framework complement the collection of existing clustering approaches. The beneficial feature of orbifold-based clustering approaches is the notion of centroid of graphs, which may improve clustering results for some problems and can be used for nearest neighbor classification in a straightforward manner.

5   Conclusion

Graph orbifolds together with lifting and truncating constitute a suitable toolkit to generalize standard clustering methods from vectors to the graphs and to

Table 2. Classification accuracy of hierarchical clustering methods. Results are deterministic.

data	K	Complete	Average	Single
letter (low)	15	69.3	35.7	8.5
letter (medium)	15	63.1	33.7	8.5
letter (high)	15	54.9	22.8	8.5
fingerprint	4	55.6	40.4	40.2
grec	22	47.6	43.0	38.1
coil	4	32.3	28.1	28.1
mao	2	55.9	66.2	55.9

provide geometrical insight into the graph domain. Using this toolkit, we showed that the study of mixtures of radial densities on graphs can be reduced to the study of mixtures of truncated Gaussians, where each truncated component lives in a different region of the Euclidean space. From these findings, we adapted the EM algorithm for parameter estimation. In experiments, we compared clustering methods operating in a graph orbifold against state-of-the-art clustering methods based on pairwise dissimilarities. Results show that clustering in a graph orbifold is a competitive alternative and therefore complement the collection of existing clustering algorithms on graphs.

Open issues with respect to estimating the parameters of a mixture model include a principled approximation of the adjustment terms for truncation, extension to covariances, and a statement to which extent mixtures of radial densities can approximate arbitrary distributions on graphs.

References

1. Gold, S., Rangarajan, A.: A Graduated Assignment Algorithm for Graph Matching. IEEE Transactions on Pattern Analysis and Machine Intelligence 18(4), 377–388 (1996)
2. Gold, S., Rangarajan, E., Mjolsness, A.: Learning with preknowledge: clustering with point and graph matching distance measures. Neural Computation 8(4), 787–804 (1996)
3. Günter, S., Bunke, H.: Self-organizing map for clustering in the graph domain. Pattern Recognition Letters 23(4), 405–417 (2002)
4. Jain, B.J., Obermayer, K.: Algorithms for the Sample Mean of Graphs. In: Jiang, X., Petkov, N. (eds.) CAIP 2009. LNCS, vol. 5702, pp. 351–359. Springer, Heidelberg (2009)
5. Jain, B., Obermayer, K.: Structure spaces. The Journal of Machine Learning Research 10 (2009)
6. Jain, B.J., Obermayer, K.: Large sample statistics in the domain of graphs. In: Hancock, E.R., Wilson, R.C., Windeatt, T., Ulusoy, I., Escolano, F. (eds.) SSPR&SPR 2010. LNCS, vol. 6218, pp. 690–697. Springer, Heidelberg (2010)
7. Jain, B., Obermayer, K.: Maximum Likelihood Method for Parameter Estimation of Bell-Shaped Functions on Graphs. Pat. Rec. Letters 33(15), 2000–2010 (2012)
8. Jain, B.J., Obermayer, K.: Graph quantization. Computer Vision and Image Understanding 115(7), 946–961 (2011)
9. Jain, B.J., Wysotzki, F.: Central clustering of attributed graphs. Machine Learning 56(1), 169–207 (2004)

10. Kaufman, L., Rousseeuw, P.: Clustering by means of medoids. Statistical Data Analysis Based on the L_1-Norm and Related Methods, 405–416 (1987)
11. Lozano, M.A., Escolano, F.: Protein classification by matching and clustering surface graphs. Pattern Recognition 39(4), 539–551 (2006)
12. Ng, A., Jordan, M., Weiss, Y.: On spectral clustering: Analysis and an algorithm. Advances in Neural Information Processing Systems 2, 849–856 (2002)
13. Ng, R.T., Han, J.: Efficient and effective clustering methods for spatial data mining. In: Proceedings of the 20th International Conference on Very Large Data Bases, VLDB 1994, pp. 144–155 (1994)
14. Riesen, K., Bunke, H.: IAM graph database repository for graph based pattern recognition and machine learning. In: da Vitoria Lobo, N., Kasparis, T., Roli, F., Kwok, J.T., Georgiopoulos, M., Anagnostopoulos, G.C., Loog, M. (eds.) S+SSPR 2008. LNCS, vol. 5342, pp. 287–297. Springer, Heidelberg (2008)
15. Ward, J.H.: Hierarchical grouping to optimize an objective function. Journal of the American Statistical Association 58(301) (1963)

Complexity Fusion for Indexing Reeb Digraphs

Francisco Escolano[1], Edwin R. Hancock[2], and Silvia Biasotti[3]

[1] University of Alicante
sco@dccia.ua.es
[2] University of York
erh@cs.york.ac.uk
[3] CNR-IMATI Genova
silvia@ge.imati.cnr.it

Abstract. In this paper we combine different quantifications of heat diffusion-thermodynamic depth on digraphs in order to match directed Reeb graphs for 3D shape recognition. Since different real valued functions can infer also different Reeb graphs for the same shape, we exploit a set of quasi-orthogonal representations for comparing sets of digraphs which encode the 3D shapes. In order to do so, we fuse complexities. Fused complexities come from computing the heat-flow thermodynamic depth approach for directed graphs, which has been recently proposed but not yet used for discrimination. In this regard, we do not rely on attributed graphs as usual for we want to explore the limits of pure topological information for structural pattern discrimination. Our experimental results show that: a) our approach is competitive with information-theoretic selection of spectral features and, b) it outperforms the discriminability of the von Neumann entropy embedded in a thermodynamic depth, and thus spectrally robust, approach.

1 Introduction

This paper is motivated by the hypothesis that mixing the same graph complexity measure over the same shape, represented with different graphs boosts the discrimination power of isolated complexity measures. To commence, there has been a recent effort in quantifying the intrinsic complexity of graphs in their original discrete space. Early attempts have incorporated principles related to MDL (Minimum Description Length) to trees and graphs (see [1] for trees and [2] for edge-weighted undirected graphs). More recently, the intersection between structural pattern recognition and complex networks has proved to be fruitful and has inspired several interesting measures of graph complexity. Many of them rely on elements of spectral graph theory. For instance, Passerini and Severini have applied the quantum (von Neumann) entropy to graphs [3]. We have recently applied thermodynamic depth [5] to the domain of graphs [6] and we have extended the approach to digraphs [7]. However, this latter approach has not been applied to graph discrimination as the one based on approximated von Neumann entropy [4]. Simultaneously, we have recently developed a method for selecting the best set of spectral features in order to classify Reeb graphs

R. Wilson et al. (Eds.): CAIP 2013, Part I, LNCS 8047, pp. 120–127, 2013.

(which summarize 3D shapes) [8]. Besides the spectral features we have evaluated in the latter work the discriminability of three different real functions for building Reeb graphs: geodesic, distance from barycenter and distance from the circumscribing sphere. Feature selection results in two intriguing conclusions: a) heat flow complexity is not one of the most interesting features, and b) the three latter real functions for building Reeb graphs have a similar relevance. The first conclusion seems to discard the use of heat flow based complexity measures for discrimination, at least in undirected graphs, whereas the second conclusion points towards discarding also the analysis of the impact of the representations. In this paper we show that these conclusions are misleading. To commence, when directed graphs are considered, heat-flow complexity information is richer. Secondly, the three functions explored in [8] are far from being orthogonal (they produce very similar graphs). Consequently herein we fuse both lines of research in order to find the best performance achievable only with topological information (without attributes). In Section 2 we present the catalog of real functions we are going to explore. In Section 3 we highlight the main ingredients of heat flow and thermodynamic depth in digraphs. Section 4 is devoted to analyze the result of fusing the directed complexities of several Reeb graphs from the same 3D shape. Finally, in Section 5 we will present our conclusions and future works.

2   Directed Reeb Graphs and Real Functions

The Reeb graph [9] is a well-known topological description that codes in a graph the evolution of the isocontours of a real-valued, continuous function $f : M \to \mathbf{R}$ over a manifold M. In other words, it tracks the origin, the disappearance, the union or the split of the isocontours as the co-domain of the function f is spanned. The nodes of the Reeb graph correspond to the critical points of f while the arcs are associated to the surface portions crossed when going from a critical points to another.

Several algorithms exist for the Reeb graph extraction from triangle meshes [10]; in this paper we adopt a directed version of the Extended Reeb graph (ERG) [11], we name it, the *diERG*. The diERG differs from the ERG in terms of arc orientation. Similarly to the ERG, to build the diERG we sample the co-domain of f with a finite number of intervals, then we characterize the surface in term of critical or regular areas and, finally, we track the evolution of the regions in the graph. Arcs are oriented according to the increasing value of the function. The diERG is then an acyclic, directed graph, a formal proof of this fact can be found in [12]. Figure 1 shows the pipeline of the graph extraction.

Each function can be seen as a geometric property and a tool for coding invariance in the description [13]. When dealing with shape retrieval, the function f has to be invariant from object rotation, translation and scaling. In the large number of functions available in the literature, we are considering:

- the distance from the barycentre B of the object, $Bar(p) = d_E(p, B)$, $p \in M$ and d_E represents the usual Euclidean distance (Figure 2-b);

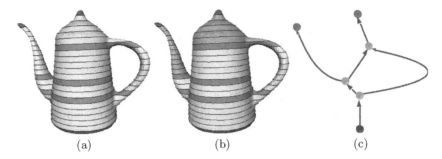

(a)   (b)   (c)

Fig. 1. Pipeline of the diERG extraction. (a) Surface partition and recognition of critical areas; blue areas correspond to minima, red areas correspond to maxima, green areas to saddle areas. (b) Expansion of critical areas to their nearest one. (c) The oriented diERG.

- the distance from the main shape axis v, $MSA(p) = d_E(p, v)$, (Figure 2-c);
- the function $MSANorm(p) = \|v \times (p - B)\|$, $p \in S$, v is the same as above and B is the barycentre (Figure 2-d);
- the average of the geodesic distances defined in [14] (Figure 2-e);
- the first six (ranked with respect to the decreasing eigenvalues), non-constant eigenfunctions of the Laplace-Beltrami operator of the mesh computed according to [15], $LAPL_i, i = \{1, \ldots, 6\}$, (Figure 2(f-i));
- a mix of the first three eigenfunctions of the Laplace-Beltrami operator obtained according to the rule: $MIX_{i+j-2} = (LAPL_i)^2 - (LAPL_j)^2$, $i = \{1, 2\}$, $j = \{2, 3\}$, $i \neq j$ (Figure 2(j-l)).

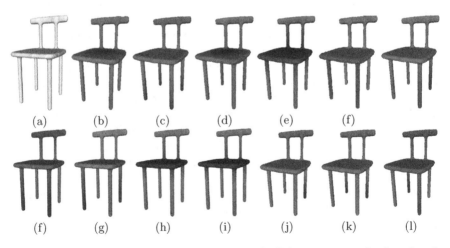

(a)   (b)   (c)   (d)   (e)   (f)

(f)   (g)   (h)   (i)   (j)   (k)   (l)

Fig. 2. The set of real functions in our framework. Colors represent the function, from low (blue) to high (red) values.

Each function reflects either intrinsic or extrinsic shape features. Geodesic-based and Laplacian-based functions are isometry-invariant and therefore pose invariant because they approximate the intrinsic Riemannian metric of the surface [16]. In this way, the graph representation is independent of the different articulations of the objects. On the other hand, the distance from the barycentre highlights the distribution of the object with respect to its barycentre. Therefore such a function is rotation invariant with respect to rotations around the barycentre but sensitive to pose variations. Similarly the distances from the principal shape axis and its orthogonal are independent of axis rotations and independent of axis symmetries.

Mixing the different properties (rigid or isometry invariant) different shape features are kept.

3   Heat Flow Complexity in Digraphs

3.1   The Laplacian of a Directed Graph

A directed graph (digraph) $G = (V, E)$ with $n = |V|$ vertices and edges $E \subseteq V \times V$ is encoded by and adjacency matrix $\mathbf{A}$ where $A_{ij} > 0$ if $i \to j \in E$ and $A_{ij} = 0$ otherwise (this definition includes weigthed adjacency matrices). The outdegree matrix $\mathbf{D}$ is a diagonal matrix where $D_{ii} = \sum_{j \in V} A_{ij}$. The transition matrix $\mathbf{P}$ is defined by $P_{ij} = \frac{A_{ij}}{D_{ii}}$ if $(i, j) \in E$ and $P_{ij} = 0$ otherwise. The transition matrix is key to defining random walks on the digraph and P_{ij} is the probability of reaching node j from node i. Given these definitions we have that $\sum_{j \in V} P_{ij} \neq 1$ in general. In addition, $\mathbf{P}$ is irreducible iff G is strongly connected (there is path from each vertex to every other vertex). If $\mathbf{P}$ is irreducible, the Perron-Frobenius theorem ensures that there exists a left eigenvector ϕ satisfying $\phi^T \mathbf{P} = \lambda \phi^T$ and $\phi(i) > 0 \, \forall i$. If $\mathbf{P}$ is aperiodic (spectral radius $\rho = 1$) we have $\phi^T \mathbf{P} = \rho \phi^T$ and all the other eigenvalues have an absolute value smaller that $\rho = 1$. By ensuring strong connection and aperiodicity we also ensure that any random walk in a directed graph satisfying these two properties converges to a unique stationary distribution.

Normalizing ϕ so that $\sum_{i \in V} \phi(i) = 1$, we encode the eigenvector elements as a probability distribution. This normalized row vector ϕ corresponds to the stationary distribution of the random walks defined by $\mathbf{P}$ since $\phi \mathbf{P} = \phi$. Therefore, $\phi(i) = \sum_{j, j \to i} \phi(j) P_{ji}$, that is, the probability of that the random walk is at node i is the sum of all incoming probabilities from all nodes j satisfying $j \to j$. If we define $\Phi = diag(\phi(1) \dots \phi(n))$ we have the definition of the following matrices:

$$\mathbf{L} = \Phi - \frac{\Phi \mathbf{P} + \mathbf{P}^T \Phi}{2} \quad \text{and} \quad \mathcal{L} = I - \frac{\Phi^{1/2} \mathbf{P} \Phi^{-1/2} + \Phi^{-1/2} \mathbf{P}^T \Phi^{1/2}}{2}, \quad (1)$$

where $\Phi = diag(\phi(1) \dots \phi(n))$, $\mathbf{L}$ is the *combinatorial directed Laplacian* and $\mathcal{L}$ is the *normalized directed Laplacian* [17].

Symmetrizing $\mathbf{P}$ leads to real valued eigenvalues and eigenvectors. In any case, satisfying irreducibility is difficult in practice since sink vertices may arise frequently. A formal trick for solving this problem consists of replacing $\mathbf{P}$ by $\mathbf{P}'$ so that $P'_{ij} = \frac{1}{n}$ if $A_{ij} = 0$ and $D_{ii} = 0$. This strategy is adopted in Pagerank [18] and allows for *teleporting* acting on the random walk to any other node in the graph. Teleporting is modeled by redefining $\mathbf{P}$ in the following way: $\mathbf{P} = \eta\mathbf{P}' + (1 - \eta)\frac{\mathbf{1}\mathbf{1}^T}{n}$ with $0 < \eta < 1$. The new $\mathbf{P}$ ensures both irreducibility and aperiodicity and this allows us to both apply $\mathbf{P}'$ with probability η and to teleport from any node with $A_{ij} = 0$ with probability $1 - \eta$. In [19] a trade-off between large values η (preserving more the structure of $\mathbf{P}'$) and small ones (potentially increasing the spectral gap) is recommended. For instance, in [20], where the task is to learn classifiers on directed graphs, the setting is $\eta = 0.99$. When using the new $\mathbf{P}$ we always have that $P_{ii} \neq 0$ due to the Pagerank masking. Such masking may introduce significant interferences in heat diffusion when the Laplacian is used to derive the heat kernel.

3.2   Directed Heat Kernels and Heat Flow

We commence by reviewing the concept of *heat flow* [6]. Firstly, the spectral decomposition of the diffusion kernel is $\mathbf{K}_\beta(G) = \exp(-\beta\mathcal{L}) \equiv \Psi\Lambda\Psi^T$, where $\Lambda = diag(e^{-\beta\lambda_1}, e^{-\beta\lambda_2}, \ldots, e^{-\beta\lambda_n})$, $\Psi = [\psi_1, \psi_2, \ldots, \psi_n]$, and $\{(\lambda_i, \psi_i)\}_{i=1}^n$ are the eigenvalue-eigenvector pairs of $\Phi - \mathbf{W}$ where $\mathbf{W} = \frac{\Phi\mathbf{P}+\mathbf{P}^T\Phi}{2}$ can be seen as the *weight matrix* of the undirected graph G_u associated with G. Anyway, $K_{\beta_{ij}} = \sum_{k=1}^n \psi_k(i)\psi_k(j)e^{-\lambda_k\beta}$, and $K_{\beta_{ij}} \in [0, 1]$ is the (i, j) entry of a doubly stochastic matrix. Doubly stochasticity for all β implies *heat conservation* in the system as a whole. That is, not only in the nodes and edges of the graph but also in the *transitivity links* eventually established between non-adjacent nodes (if i is not adjacent to j, eventually will appear an entry $K_{\beta_{ij}} > 0$ for β large enough). The total *directed heat* flowing through the graph at a given β *(instantaneous directed flow)* is given by

$$\mathcal{F}_\beta(G) = \sum_{i \to j}^n A_{ij} \left(\sum_{k=1}^n \psi_k(i)\psi_k(j)e^{-\lambda_k\beta} \right) , \qquad (2)$$

A more compact definition of the flow is $\mathcal{F}_\beta(G) = \mathbf{A} : \mathbf{K}_\beta$, where $\mathbf{X} : \mathbf{Z} = \sum_{ij} X_{ij}Z_{ij} = trace(\mathbf{X}\mathbf{Z}^T)$ is the Frobenius inner product. While instantaneous flow for the heat flowing through the edges of the graph, it accounts neither for the heat remaining in the nodes nor for that in the transitivity links. The limiting cases are $\mathcal{F}_0 = 0$ and $\mathcal{F}_{\beta_{max}} = \frac{1}{n}\sum_{i \to j} A_{ij}$ which is reduced to $\frac{|E|}{n}$ if G is unattributed ($A_{ij} \in \{0, 1\} \forall ij$). Defining $\mathcal{F}_\beta$ in terms of $\mathbf{A}$ instead of $\mathbf{W}$, we retain the *directed* nature of the original graph G. The function derived from computing $\mathcal{F}_\beta(G)$ from $\beta = 0$ to β_{max} is the so called *directed heat flow trace*. These traces satisfy the *phase transition principle* [6] (although the formal proof is out of the scope of this paper). In general heat flow diffuses more slowly than in the undirected case and phase transition points (PTPs) appear later. This is due to the constraints imposed by $\mathbf{A}$.

3.3   Thermodynamic Depth Complexity

Let $G = (V, E)$ with $|V| = n$. Then the *directed history of a node* $i \in V$ is $h_i(G) = \{e(i), e^2(i)), \ldots, e^p(i)\}$ where: $e(i) \subseteq G$ is the *first-order expansion subgraph* given by i and all $j : i \to j$. If there are nodes j also satisfying $j \to i$ then these edges are included. If node i is a sink then $e(i) = i$. Similarly $e^2(i) = e(e(i)) \subseteq G$ is the *second-order expansion* consisting on $j \to z : j \in V_{e(i)}, z \notin V_{e(i)}$, including also $z \to j$ if these edges exists and $j \to z$. This process continues until p cannot be increased. If G is strongly connected $e^p(i) = G$, otherwise $e^p(i)$ is the strongly connected component to which i belongs. Thus, every $h_i(G)$ defines a different causal trajectory which may lead to G itself if it is strongly connected. The *depth* of such macro-states relies on the variability of the causal trajectories leading to them. In order to characterize each trajectory we combine the heat flow complexities of its expansion subgraphs by means of defining *minimal enclosing Bregman balls* (MEBB) [21]. Here we use the I-Kullback-Leibler (I-KL) Bregman divergence between traces f and g: $D_F(\boldsymbol{f}||\boldsymbol{g}) = \sum_{i=1}^d f_i \log \frac{f_i}{g_i} - \sum_{i=1}^d f_i + \sum_{i=1}^d g_i$ with convex generator $F(\boldsymbol{f}) = \sum_{i=1}^d (f_i \log f_i - f_i)$.

Given $h_i(G)$, the heat flow complexity trace $\boldsymbol{f}_t = \mathcal{F}(e^t(i))$ for the $t - th$ expansion of i, a generator F and a Bregman divergence D_F, the *causal trajectory* leading to G (or one of its strongly connected components) from i is characterized by the center $\boldsymbol{c}_i \in R^d$ and radius $r_i \in R$ of the MEBB $\mathcal{B}^{c_i, r_i} = \{\boldsymbol{f}_t \in \mathcal{X}_i : D_F(\boldsymbol{c}_i||\boldsymbol{f}_t) \leq r_i\}$ where $\mathcal{X}$ is the set of all causal trajectories for the i−th node. Solving for the center and radius implies finding $\boldsymbol{c}^*$ and r^* minimizing r subject to $D_F(\boldsymbol{c}_i||\boldsymbol{f}_t) \leq r \ \forall t \in \mathcal{X}_i$ with $|\mathcal{X} : i| = T$. Considering the Lagrange multipliers α_t we have that $\boldsymbol{c}^* = \nabla^{-1} F(\sum_{t=1}^T \alpha_t \boldsymbol{f}_t \nabla F(\boldsymbol{f}_t))$. The efficient algorithm in [21] estimates both the center and multipliers. This idea is closely related to Core Vector Machines [22], and it is interesting to focus on the non-zero multipliers (and their support vectors) used to compute the optimal radius. More precisely, the multipliers define a convex combination and we have $\alpha_t \propto D_F(\boldsymbol{c}^*||\boldsymbol{f}_t)$, and the radius is simply chosen as: $r^* = \max_{\alpha_t > 0} D_F(\boldsymbol{c}^*||\boldsymbol{f}_t)$. Given the directed graph $G = (V, E)$, with $|V| = n$ and all the n pairs $(\boldsymbol{c}_i, r_i)$, the *heat flow-thermodynamic depth complexity* of G is characterized by the MEBB $\mathcal{B}^{c,r} = \{\boldsymbol{c}_i \in \mathcal{X}_i : D_F(\boldsymbol{c}||\boldsymbol{c}_i) \leq r\}$. As a result, the *TD depth of the directed graph* is given by $\mathcal{D}(G) = r$.

4   Experiments

In order to compare our method with the technique proposed in [8] we use the same database, SHRECH version used in the Shape Retrieval Contest in [23]. The database has 400 exemplars and 20 classes (20 exemplars per class). For each exemplar we apply the 13 real functions presented in Section 2 and then extract the corresponding Reeb digraphs. Then, each exemplar is characterized by 13 the heat flow complexities (one per digraph). If we map these vectors (bags of complexities) via MDS we found that it is quite easy to discriminate glasses from pliers and fishes. However, it is very difficult to discriminate humans from chairs

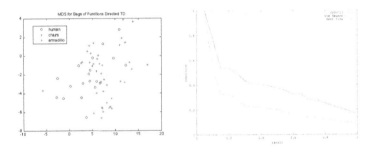

Fig. 3. Experiments. Left: MDS for humans, chairs and armadillos. Right: PR curves.

(see Figure 3-left). The average behavior of these bags of complexities is given by the precision recall (PR) curves. In Figure 3-right we show the PR curves for Feature Selection [8] (CVIU'13), Thermodynamic Depth (TD) with the von Neumann Entropy (here we use the **W** attributed graph induced by the Directed Laplacian) and TD with directed heat flow. Our PR (heat flow) as well as the one of Feature Selection reaches the average performance of attributed methods. The 10-fold CV error for 15 classes reported by Feature Selection is $23, 3\%$. However, here we obtain a similar PR curve for the 20 class problem. Given that Feature Selection relies on a complex offline process, the less computationally demanding heat flow TD complexity for digraphs produces comparable results (or better ones, if we consider that we are addressing the 20 class problem). In addition, heat flow outperforms von Neumann entropy when embedded in TD.

5   Conclusions and Future Work

The main contribution of this paper is the proposal of a method (fusion of digraphs heat flow complexity) which has a similar discrimination power (or even better if we consider the whole 20 classes problem) than Feature Selection and outperforms von Neumann entropy. Future works include the exploration of more sophisticated methods for fusing complexities and more real functions.

Acknowledgements. Francisco Escolano was funded by project TIN2012-32839 of the Spanish Government. Edwin Hancock was supported by a Royal Society Wolfson Research Merit Award.

References

[1] Torsello, A., Hancock, E.R.: Learning Shape-Classes Using a Mixture of Tree-Unions. IEEE Tran. on Pattern Analysis and Mach. Intelligence 28(6), 954–967 (2006)

[2] Torsello, A., Lowe, D.L.: Supervised Learning of a Generative Model for Edge-Weighted Graphs. In: Proc. of ICPR (2008)

[3] Passerini, F., Severini, S.: The von Neumann Entropy of Networks. arXiv:0812.2597v1 (December 2008)

[4] Han, L., Escolano, F., Hancock, E.R., Wilson, R.: Graph Characterizations From Von Neumann Entropy. Pattern Recognition Letters (2012) (in press)

[5] Lloyd, S., Pagels, H.: Complexity as Thermodynamic Depth Ann. Phys. 188, 186 (1988)

[6] Escolano, F., Hancock, E.R., Lozano, M.A.: Heat Diffusion: Thermodynamic Depth Complexity of Networks. Phys. Rev. E 85, 036206 (2012)

[7] Escolano, F., Bonev, B., Hancock, E.R.: Heat Flow-Thermodynamic Depth Complexity in Directed Networks. In: Gimel'farb, G., Hancock, E., Imiya, A., Kuijper, A., Kudo, M., Omachi, S., Windeatt, T., Yamada, K. (eds.) SSPR & SPR 2012. LNCS, vol. 7626, pp. 190–198. Springer, Heidelberg (2012)

[8] Bonev, B., Escolano, F., Giorgi, D., Biasotti, S.: Information-theoretic Selection of High-dimensional Spectral Features for Structural Recognition. Computer Vision and Image Understanding 117(3), 214–228 (2013)

[9] Reeb, G.: Sur les points singuliers d'une forme de Pfaff complètement intégrable ou d'une fonction numérique. Comptes Rendus Hebdomadaires des Séances de l'Académie des Sciences 222, 847–849 (1946)

[10] Biasotti, S., Giorgi, D., Spagnuolo, M., Falcidieno, B.: Reeb graphs for shape analysis and applications. Theoretical Computer Science 392(1-3), 5–22 (2008)

[11] Biasotti, S.: Topological coding of surfaces with boundary using Reeb graphs. Computer Graphics and Geometry 7(3), 31–45 (2005)

[12] Biasotti, S.: Computational Topology Methods for Shape Modelling Applications. PhD Thesis, Universitá degli Studi di Genova (May 2004)

[13] Biasotti, S., De Floriani, L., Falcidieno, B., Frosini, P., Giorgi, D., Landi, C., Papaleo, L., Spagnuolo, M.: Describing shapes by geometrical-topological properties of real functions. ACM Comput. Surv. 40(4), 1–87 (2008)

[14] Hilaga, M., Shinagawa, Y., Kohmura, T., Kunii, T.L.: Topology Matching for Fully Automatic Similarity Estimation of 3D Shapes. In: Proc. of SIGGRAPH 2001, pp. 203–212 (2001)

[15] Belkin, M., Sun, J., Wang, Y.: Discrete Laplace Operator for Meshed Surfaces. In: Proc. Symposium on Computational Geometry, pp. 278–287 (2008)

[16] Bronstein, A.M., Bronstein, M.M., Kimmel, R.: Efficient Computation of Isometry-Invariant Distances Between Surfaces. SIAM J. Sci. Comput. 28(5), 1812–1836 (2006)

[17] Chung, F.: Laplacians and the Cheeger Inequailty for Directed Graphs. Annals of Combinatorics 9, 1–19 (2005)

[18] Page, L., Brin, S., Motwani, R., Winograd, T.: The PageRank Citation Ranking: Bring Order to the Web (Technical Report). Stanford University (1998)

[19] Johns, J., Mahadevan, S.: Constructing Basic Functions from Directed Graphs for Value Functions Approximation. In: Proc. of ICML (2007)

[20] Zhou, D., Huang, J., Schölkopf, B.: Learning from Labeled and Unlabeled Data on a Directed Graph. In: Proc. of ICML (2005)

[21] Nock, R., Nielsen, F.: Fitting the Smallest Enclosing Bregman Ball. In: Gama, J., Camacho, R., Brazdil, P.B., Jorge, A.M., Torgo, L. (eds.) ECML 2005. LNCS (LNAI), vol. 3720, pp. 649–656. Springer, Heidelberg (2005)

[22] Tsang, I.W., Kocsor, A., Kwok, J.T.: Simple Core Vector Machines with Enclosing Balls. In: Proc. of ICLM (2007)

[23] Giorgi, D., Biasotti, S., Paraboschi, L.: SHape Retrieval Contest: Watertight Models Track, http://watertight.ge.imati.cnr.it

Analysis of Wave Packet Signature of a Graph

Furqan Aziz, Richard C. Wilson, and Edwin R. Hancock

Department of Computer Science, University of York, YO10 5GH, UK
{furqan,wilson,erh}@cs.york.ac.uk

Abstract. In this paper we investigate a new approach for characterizing both the weighted and un-weighted graphs using the solution of the edge-based wave equation. The reason for using wave equation is that it provides a richer and potentially more expressive means of characterizing graphs than the more widely studied heat equation. The wave equation on a graph is defined using the Edge-based Laplacian. We commence by defining the eigensystem of the edge-based Laplacian. We give a solution of the wave equation and define signature for both weighted graphs and un-weighted graphs. In the experiment section we perform the proposed method on real world data and compare its performance with other state-of-the-art methods.

Keywords: Edge-based Laplacian, Wave Equation, Gaussian wave packet, Graph Characterization, Weighted graphs.

1   Introduction

Graph clustering is one of the most commonly used problems in areas where data are represented using graphs. Since graphs are non-vectorial, we require a method for characterizing graph that can be used to embed the graph in a high-dimensional feature space for the purpose of clustering. Most of the commonly used method for graph clustering are spectral methods which are based on the eigensystem of the Laplacian matrix associated with the graph. For example Xiao et al [1] have used heat kernel for graph characterization. Wilson et al. [2] have made use of graph spectra to construct a set of permutation-invariant features for the purpose of clustering graphs.

The discrete Laplacian defined over the vertices of a graph, however, cannot link most results in analysis to a graph theoretic analogue. For example the wave equation $u_{tt} = \Delta u$, defined with discrete Laplacian, does not have finite speed of propagation. In [3,4], Friedman and Tillich develop a calculus on graph which provides strong connection between graph theory and analysis. Their work is based on the fact that graph theory involves two different volume measures. i.e., a "vertex-based" measure and an "edge-based" measure. This approach has many advantages. It allows the application of many results from analysis directly to the graph domain.

While the method of Friedman and Tillich leads to the definition of both a divergence operator and a Laplacian (through the definition of both vertex and

R. Wilson et al. (Eds.): CAIP 2013, Part I, LNCS 8047, pp. 128–136, 2013.

edge Laplacian), it is not exhaustive in the sense that the edge-based eigenfunctions are not fully specified. In a recent study we have fully explored the eigenfunctions of the edge-based Laplacian and developed a method for explicitly calculating the edge-interior eigenfunctions of the edge-based Laplacian [5]. This reveals a connection between the eigenfunctions of the edge-based Laplacian and both the classical random walk and the backtrackless random walk on a graph. As an application of the edge-based Laplacian, we have recently presented a new approach to characterizing points on a non-rigid three-dimensional shape[6].

Wave equation provides potentially richer characterisation of graphs than heat equation. Initial work by Howaida and Hancock [7] has revealed some of its potential uses. They have proposed a new approach for embedding graphs on pseudo-Riemannian manifolds based on the wave kernel. However, there are two problems with the rigourous solution of the wave equation; a) we need to compute the edge-based Laplacian, and b) the solution is more complex than the heat equation. Recently we [8] have presented a solution of the edge-based wave equation on a graph. In [9] we have used this solution to define a signature, called the wave packet signature (WPS) of a graph. In this paper we extend the idea of WPS to weighted graphs and experimentally demonstrate the properties of WPS. We perform numerous experiments and demonstrate the performance of the proposed methods on both weighted and un-weighted graphs.

2   Edge-Based Eigensystem

In this section we review the eigenvalues and eigenfunction of the edge-based Laplacian[3][5]. Let $G = (\mathcal{V}, \mathcal{E})$ be a graph with a boundary ∂G. Let $\mathcal{G}$ be the geometric realization of G. The geometric realization is the metric space consisting of vertices $\mathcal{V}$ with a closed interval of length l_e associated with each edge $e \in \mathcal{E}$. We associate an edge variable x_e with each edge that represents the standard coordinate on the edge with $x_e(u) = 0$ and $x_e(v) = 1$. For our work, it will suffice to assume that the graph is finite with empty boundary (i.e., $\partial G = 0$) and $l_e = 1$.

2.1   Vertex Supported Edge-Based Eigenfunctions

The vertex-supported eigenpairs of the edge-based Laplacian can be expressed in terms of the eigenpairs of the normalized adjacency matrix of the graph. Let A be the adjacency matrix of the graph G, and $\tilde{A}$ be the row normalized adjacency matrix. i.e., the $(i,j)th$ entry of $\tilde{A}$ is given as $\tilde{A}(i,j) = A(i,j)/\sum_{(k,j)\in E} A(k,j)$. Let $(\phi(v), \lambda)$ be an eigenvector-eigenvalue pair for this matrix. Note that $\phi(.)$ is defined on vertices and may be extended along each edge to an edge-based eigenfunction. Let ω^2 and $\phi(e, x_e)$ denote the edge-based eigenvalue and eigenfunction. Then the vertex-supported eigenpairs of the edge-based Laplacian are given as follows:

1. For each $(\phi(v), \lambda)$ with $\lambda \neq \pm 1$, we have a pair of eigenvalues ω^2 with $\omega = \cos^{-1}\lambda$ and $\omega = 2\pi - \cos^{-1}\lambda$. Since there are multiple solutions to

$\omega = \cos^{-1}\lambda$, we obtain an infinite sequence of eigenfunctions; if $\omega_0 \in [0, \pi]$ is the principal solution, the eigenvalues are $\omega = \omega_0 + 2\pi n$ and $\omega = 2\pi - \omega_0 + 2\pi n, n \geq 0$. The eigenfunctions are $\phi(e, x_e) = C(e)\cos(B(e) + \omega x_e)$.

2. $\lambda = 1$ is always an eigenvalue of $\tilde{A}$. We obtain a principle frequency $\omega = 0$, and therefore since $\phi(e, x_e) = C\cos(B)$ and so $\phi(v) = \phi(u) = C\cos(B)$, which is constant on the vertices.

2.2   Edge-Interior Eigenfunctions

The edge-interior eigenfunctions are those eigenfunctions which are zero on vertices and therefore must have a principle frequency of $\omega \in \{\pi, 2\pi\}$. Recently we have shown that these eigenfunctions can be determined from the eigenvectors of the adjacency matrix of the oriented line graph[5]. We have shown that the eigenvector corresponding to eigenvalue $\lambda = 1$ of the oriented line graph provides a solution in the case $\omega = 2\pi$. In this case we obtain $|E| - |V| + 1$ linearly independent solutions. Similary the eigenvector corresponding to eigenvalue $\lambda = -1$ of the oriented line graph provides a solution in the case $\omega = \pi$. In this case we obtain $|E| - |V|$ linearly independent solutions. This comprises all the principal eigenpairs which are only supported on the edges.

3   Wave Packet Signatures

Let a graph coordinate $\mathcal{X}$ defines an edge e and a value of the standard coordinate on that edge x. The eigenfunctions of the edge-based Laplacian are

$$\phi_{\omega,n}(\mathcal{X}) = C(e, \omega)\cos\left(B(e, \omega) + \omega x + 2\pi n x\right)$$

The edge-based wave equation is

$$\frac{\partial^2 u}{\partial t^2}(\mathcal{X}, t) = \Delta_E u(\mathcal{X}, t)$$

Let $\mathcal{W}(z)$ be z wrapped to the range $[-\frac{1}{2}, \frac{1}{2})$, i.e., $\mathcal{W}(z) = z - \lfloor z + \frac{1}{2} \rfloor$. For the un-weighted graph, we solve the wave equation assuming that the initial condition is a Gaussian wave packet on a single edge of a graph [9]. The solution for this case becomes

$$u(\mathcal{X}, t) = \sum_{\omega \in \Omega_a} \frac{C(\omega, e)C(\omega, f)}{2}$$

$$\left(e^{-a\mathcal{W}(x+t+\mu)^2} \cos\left[B(e, \omega) + B(f, \omega) + \omega \left\lfloor x + t + \mu + \frac{1}{2} \right\rfloor \right] \right.$$

$$\left. + e^{-a\mathcal{W}(x-t-\mu)^2} \cos\left[B(e, \omega) - B(f, \omega) + \omega \left\lfloor x - t - \mu + \frac{1}{2} \right\rfloor \right] \right)$$

$$+ \frac{1}{2|E|} \left(\frac{1}{4}e^{-a\mathcal{W}(x+t+\mu)^2} + \frac{1}{4}e^{-a\mathcal{W}(x-t-\mu)^2} \right)$$

$$+ \sum_{\omega \in \Omega_c} \frac{C(\omega, e)C(\omega, f)}{4} \left(e^{-aW(x-t-\mu)^2} - e^{-aW(x+t+\mu)^2} \right)$$

$$+ \sum_{\omega \in \Omega_c} \frac{C(\omega, e)C(\omega, f)}{4} \left((-1)^{\lfloor x-t-\mu+\frac{1}{2} \rfloor} e^{-aW(x-t-\mu)^2} \right.$$

$$\left. -(-1)^{\lfloor x+t+\mu+\frac{1}{2} \rfloor} e^{-aW(x+t+\mu)^2} \right)$$

where Ω_a represents the set of vertex-supported eigenvalues and Ω_b and Ω_c represent the set of edge-interior eigenvalues respectively. i.e., π and 2π.

For a weighted graph, we assume a Gaussian wave packet on every edge of the graph, whose amplitude is multiplied by the weight of that particular edge, and solve the wave equation for this case. Let w_{ij} be the weight of the edge (i, j). The solution in this case becomes

$$u(\mathcal{X}, t) = \sum_{(u,v) \in E} w_{i,j} \sum_{\omega \in \Omega_a} \frac{C(\omega, e)C(\omega, f)}{2}$$

$$\left(e^{-aW(x+t+\mu)^2} \cos \left[B(e, \omega) + B(f, \omega) + \omega \left[x + t + \mu + \frac{1}{2} \right] \right] \right.$$

$$\left. + e^{-aW(x-t-\mu)^2} \cos \left[B(e, \omega) - B(f, \omega) + \omega \left[x - t - \mu + \frac{1}{2} \right] \right] \right)$$

$$+ \frac{1}{2|E|} \left(\frac{1}{4} e^{-aW(x+t+\mu)^2} + \frac{1}{4} e^{-aW(x-t-\mu)^2} \right)$$

$$+ \sum_{\omega \in \Omega_c} \frac{C(\omega, e)C(\omega, f)}{4} \left(e^{-aW(x-t-\mu)^2} - e^{-aW(x+t+\mu)^2} \right)$$

$$+ \sum_{\omega \in \Omega_c} \frac{C(\omega, e)C(\omega, f)}{4} \left((-1)^{\lfloor x-t-\mu+\frac{1}{2} \rfloor} e^{-aW(x-t-\mu)^2} \right.$$

$$\left. -(-1)^{\lfloor x+t+\mu+\frac{1}{2} \rfloor} e^{-aW(x+t+\mu)^2} \right)$$

To define signature for both weighted and un-weighted graphs, we use the amplitudes of the waves on the edges of the graph over time. For un-weighted graphs, we assume that the initial condition is a Gaussian wave packet on a single edge of the graph. For this purpose we select the edge $(u, v) \in E$, such that u is the highest degree vertex in the graph and v is the highest degree vertex in the neighbours of u. For weighted graph, we assume a wave packet on every edge whose amplitude is multiplied by the weight of the edge. We define the local signature of an edge as

$$WPS(\mathcal{X}) = [u(\mathcal{X}, t_0), u(\mathcal{X}, t_1), u(\mathcal{X}, t_2), ... u(\mathcal{X}, t_n)]$$

Given a graph G, we define its global wave packet signature as

$$GWPS(G) = hist \left(WPS(\mathcal{X}_1), WPS(\mathcal{X}_2), , ..., WPS(\mathcal{X}_{|E|}) \right) \qquad (1)$$

where hist(.) is the histogram operator which bins the list of arguments $WPS(\mathcal{X}_1), WPS(\mathcal{X}_2), , ..., WPS(\mathcal{X}_{|E|})$.

4   Experiments

In this section we perform an experimental evaluation of the proposed methods on different graphs. These graphs are extracted from the images in the Columbia object image library (COIL) dataset [10]. This dataset contains views of 3D objects under controlled viewer and lighting condition. For each object in the database there are 72 equally spaced views. The objective here is to cluster different views of the same object onto the same class. To establish a graph on the images of objects, we first extract feature points from the image. For this purpose, we use the Harris corner detector [11]. We then construct a Delaunay triangulation (DT) using the selected feature points as vertices of the graph. Figure 1(a) shows some of the object views (images) used for our experiments and Figure 1(b) shows the corresponding Delaunay triangulations.

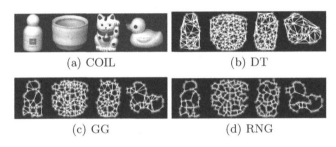

(a) COIL   (b) DT

(c) GG   (d) RNG

Fig. 1. COIL objects and their extracted graphs

We compute the wave signature for an edge by taking $t_{max} = 100$ and $x_e = 0.5$. We take $t = 20$ to allow the wave packet to be distributed over the whole graph. We then compute the GWPS for the graph by fixing 100 bins for histogram. To visualize the results, we have performed principal component analysis (PCA) on GWPS. PCA is mathematically defined [12] as an orthogonal linear transformation that transforms the data to a new coordinate system such that the greatest variance by any projection of the data comes to lie on the first coordinate (called the first principal component), the second greatest variance on the second coordinate, and so on. Figure 2(a) shows the results of the embedding of the feature vectors on the first three principal components.

To measure the performance of the proposed method we compare it with truncated Laplacian, random walk [13] and Ihara coefficients [14]. Figure 2 shows

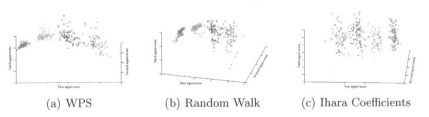

(a) WPS   (b) Random Walk   (c) Ihara Coefficients

Fig. 2. Graph, its digraph, and its oriented line graph

the embedding results for different methods. To compare the performance, we cluster the feature vectors using *k-means clustering* [15]. *k*-means clustering is a method which aims to partition n observations into k clusters in which each observation belongs to the cluster with the nearest mean. We compute *Rand index* [16] of these clusters which is a measure of the similarity between two data clusters. The rand indices for these methods are shown in Table 1. It is clear from the table that the proposed method can classify the graphs with higher accuracy.

Table 1. Experimental results on Mutag dataset

Method	DT	GG	RNG
Wave Kernel Signature	0.9965	0.9511	0.8235
Random Walk Kernel	0.9526	0.9115	0.8197
Ihara Coefficients	0.9864	0.8574	0.7541

We now compare the performance of the proposed method on Gabriel graphs (GG) and relative neighbourhood graphs (RNG) extracted from the same COIL dataset. The Gabriel graph for a set of n points is a subset of Delaunay triangulation, which connects two data points v_i and v_j for which there is no other point v_k inside the open ball whose diameter is the edge(v_i, v_j). The relative neighbourhood graph is also a subset of Delaunay Triangulation. In this case a lune is constructed on each Delaunay edge. The circles enclosing the lune have their centres at the end-points of the Delaunay edge; each circle has a radius equal to the length of the edge. If the lune contains another node then its defining edge is pruned from the relative neighbourhood graph. Figure 1(c) and 1(d) show the GG and RNG of the corresponding COIL object of Figure 1(a) respectively.

The purpose of comparing the performance on GG and RNG is twofold. First, since both the GG and RNG are subset of DT, it allows us to analyze the performance of the proposed method under controlled structure modification. Second, since both GG and RNG reduce the frequency of cycles of smaller length and introduce branches in the graph, it allows us to analyze the performance of the proposed method on non-cyclic graphs. We compute the performance on GG and RNG in the same way as we did for DT. The visual results of the proposed method on GG and RNG are shown in Figure 3(a) and Figure 3(b) respectively. Table 1 compares the performance of the three methods, which shows that the proposed method performs well under controlled structural modification. Note that a drop in the performance of Ihara coefficient is due to the fact that the Ihara coefficients cannot provide a good measure of similarity for the graphs when branches are present.

We now compare the performance of the proposed WPS on weighted graphs. For this purpose, we have selected the same objects from the COIL dataset. We have extracted the Gabriel graphs for each of these view.The edges are weighted with the exponential of the negative distance between two connected vertices, i.e. $w_{ij} = exp[k||x_i x_j||]$ where x_i and x_j are coordinates of corner points i and j in an image and k is a scalar scaling factor. Figure 4(a) shows the clustering result of WPS, while Figure 4(b) shows the clustering result of truncated Laplacian. To

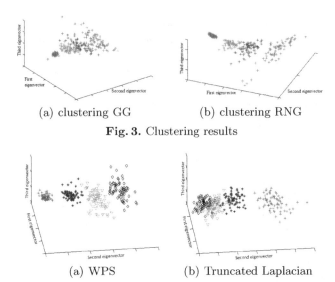

(a) clustering GG   (b) clustering RNG

Fig. 3. Clustering results

(a) WPS   (b) Truncated Laplacian

Fig. 4. Clustering results on Weighted graphs

compare the performance we have computed the rand indices for both methods. The rand index for WPS is 0.9931, while for truncated Laplacian is 0.8855.

Finally we look at the characteristic of the proposed WPS. The histogram distribution of the WPS closely follows Gaussian distribution. Figure 5 shows distribution of WPS of a single view of 3 different objects in COIL dataset and a Gaussian fit for each signature. Figure 6(a) and 6(b) show the values of standard deviation of all the DT and GG respectively of all 72 views of 4 different objects of COIL dataset. Table 2 shows the mean value of the standard deviation and a standard error for each of the 4 objects.

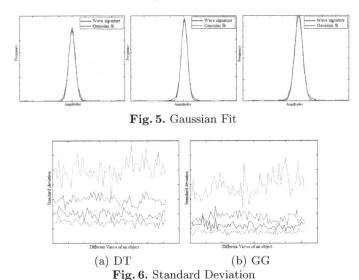

Fig. 5. Gaussian Fit

(a) DT   (b) GG

Fig. 6. Standard Deviation

Table 2. Average value of standard deviation

	Standard Deviation	Standard Error
Object 1	0.1400	1.54×10^{-3}
Object 2	0.0989	6.57×10^{-4}
Object 3	0.0793	5.64×10^{-4}
Object 4	0.0685	4.07×10^{-4}

5   Conclusion and Future Work

In this paper we have used the solution of the wave equation on a graph to characterize both weighted and un-weighted graphs. The wave equation is solved using the edge-based Laplacian of a graph. The advantage of using the edge-based Laplacian over vertex-based Laplacian is that it allows the direct application of many results from analysis to graph theoretic domain. In future our goal is to use the solution of other equations defined using the edge-based Laplacian for defining local and global signatures for graphs.

References

1. Xiao, B., Yu, H., Hancock, E.R.: Graph matching using manifold embedding. In: Campilho, A.C., Kamel, M.S. (eds.) ICIAR 2004. LNCS, vol. 3211, pp. 352–359. Springer, Heidelberg (2004)
2. Wilson, R.C., Hancock, E.R., Luo, B.: Pattern vectors from algebraic graph theory. IEEE Trans. Pattern Anal. Mach. Intell. 27, 1112–1124 (2005)
3. Friedman, J., Tillich, J.P.: Wave equations for graphs and the edge based laplacian. Pacific Journal of Mathematics, 229–266 (2004)
4. Friedman, J., Tillich, J.P.: Calculus on graphs. CoRR (2004)
5. Wilson, R.C., Aziz, F., Hancock, E.R.: Eigenfunctions of the edge-based laplacian on a graph. Linear Algebra and its Applications 438, 4183–4189 (2013)
6. Aziz, F., Wilson, R.C., Hancock, E.R.: Shape signature using the edge-based laplacian. In: International Conference on Pattern Recognition (2012)
7. ElGhawalby, H., Hancock, E.R.: Graph embedding using an edge-based wave kernel. In: Hancock, E.R., Wilson, R.C., Windeatt, T., Ulusoy, I., Escolano, F. (eds.) SSPR & SPR 2010. LNCS, vol. 6218, pp. 60–69. Springer, Heidelberg (2010)
8. Aziz, F., Wilson, R.C., Hancock, E.R.: Gaussian wave packet on a graph. In: Kropatsch, W.G., Artner, N.M., Haxhimusa, Y., Jiang, X. (eds.) GbRPR 2013. LNCS, vol. 7877, pp. 224–233. Springer, Heidelberg (2013)
9. Aziz, F., Wilson, R.C., Hancock, E.R.: Graph characterization using gaussian wave packet signature. In: Hancock, E., Pelillo, M. (eds.) SIMBAD 2013. LNCS, vol. 7953, pp. 176–189. Springer, Heidelberg (2013)
10. Murase, H., Nayar, S.K.: Visual learning and recognition of 3-D objects from appearance. International Journal of Computer Vision 14, 5–24 (1995)
11. Harris, C., Stephens, M.: A combined corner and edge detector. In: Fourth Alvey Vision Conference, Manchester, UK, pp. 147–151 (1988)

12. Jolliffe, I.T.: Principal component analysis. Springer, New York (1986)
13. Gärtner, T., Flach, P.A., Wrobel, S.: On graph kernels: Hardness results and efficient alternatives. In: Schölkopf, B., Warmuth, M.K. (eds.) COLT/Kernel 2003. LNCS (LNAI), vol. 2777, pp. 129–143. Springer, Heidelberg (2003)
14. Ren, P., Wilson, R.C., Hancock, E.R.: Graph characterization via Ihara coefficients. IEEE Tran. on Neural Networks 22, 233–245 (2011)
15. MacQueen, J.B.: Some methods for classification and analysis of multivariate observations, vol. 1, pp. 281–297. University of California Press (1967)
16. Rand, W.M.: Objective criteria for the evaluation of clustering methods. Journal of the American Statistical Association 66, 846–850 (1971)

Hearing versus Seeing Identical Twins

Li Zhang, Shenggao Zhu, Terence Sim, Wee Kheng Leow,
Hossein Najati, and Dong Guo

School of Computing
National University of Singapore
Singapore, 117417
{lizhang,shenggao,tsim,leowwk}@comp.nus.edu.sg,dnguo@fb.com

Abstract. Identical twins pose a great challenge to face recognition systems due to their similar appearance. Nevertheless, even though twins may look alike, we believe they speak differently. Hence we propose to use their voice patterns to distinguish between twins. Voice is a natural signal to produce, and it is a combination of physiological and behavioral biometrics, therefore it is suitable for twin verification. In this paper, we collect an audio-visual database from 39 pairs of identical twins. Three types of typical voice features are investigated, including Pitch, Linear Prediction Coefficients (LPC) and Mel Frequency Cepstral Coefficients (MFCC). For each type of voice feature, we use Gaussian Mixture Model to model the voice spectral distribution of each subject, and then employ the likelihood ratio of the probe belonging to different classes for verification. The experimental results on this database demonstrate a significant improvement by using voice over facial appearance to distinguish between identical twins. Furthermore, we show that by fusion both types of biometrics, recognition accuracy can be improved.

Keywords: identical twins, verification, fusion, Gaussian Mixture Model.

1   Introduction

According to the statistics in [1], twins birth rate has risen from 17.8 to 32.2 per 1000 birth with an average 3% growth per year since 1990. This increase is associated with the increasing usage of fertility therapies and the change of birth concept. Nowadays women tend to bear children at older age and are more likely than younger women to conceive multiples spontaneously especially in developed countries [2]. Although currently identical twins still only represent a minority (0.2% of the world's population), it is worth noting that the total number of identical twins is equal to the whole population of countries like Portugal or Greece. This, in turn, has created an urgent demand for biometric systems that can accurately distinguish between identical twins. Identical twins share the same genetic code, therefore they look very alike. This poses a great challenge to current biometric systems, especially face recognition system. The challenge using facial appearance to distinguish between identical twins has been verified by Sun *et al.* [2] on 93 pairs of twins using a commercial face matcher. Nevertheless,

R. Wilson et al. (Eds.): CAIP 2013, Part I, LNCS 8047, pp. 137–144, 2013.

some biometrics depend not only on the genetic signature but also on the individual development in the womb. Some researchers explored the possibility of using behavior difference, such as expressions and head motion [3] to distinguish between identical twins. Zhang et al. [3] proposed to use exception reporting model to model the head motion abnormality to differentiate twins. They reported the verification accuracy was over 90%, but their algorithm was very sensitive to subject behavior consistence and strongly relied on accurate tracking algorithm. Several researchers showed encouraging results by using fingerprint [4,2], palmprint [5], ear [6] and iris [7,2] to distinguish between identical twins. For example, equal error rate for 4-finger fusion reported by Sun et al. [2] was 0.49, and equal error rate for 2-iris fusion was also 0.49. Despite of the discriminating ability of those biometrics, those biometrics require the cooperation of the subject. Therefore, it is desirable to identify twins in a natural way. In this paper, we propose to utilize voice biometric to distinguish between identical twins and compare voice biometric with facial appearance. Voice is non-intrusive and natural, it does not require explicit cooperation of the subject and is widely available from videos captured by ordinary cam-corders. To the best of our knowledge, we are the first to investigate voice and appearance biometrics at the meantime.

Voice signal usually conveys several levels of information. Primarily, voice signal conveys the words or message being spoken, but on a secondary level, it also conveys information about the identity of the speaker [8]. Voice biometric tries to extract the identity information from the voice and uses it for speaker recognition. Generally speaking, the speaker recognition can be divided into two specific tasks: speaker verification and speaker identification. In speaker verification, the goal is to establish whether a person is who he/she claims to be; whereas in speaker identification, the goal is to determine the identity (name or employee number) of the unknown speaker. In either task the speech can be further divided into text dependent (*i.e.*the speaker is required to talk same phrase) and text independent (*i.e.* the speaker can talk different phrase). Douglas et al. [8] and Sinith et al. [9] proposed to use Mel Frequency Cepstral Coefficients and Gaussian Mixture Model to solve text independent identification problem for general population, i.e. non twins. Dupont et al. [10] and Dean et al. [11] tried to use hidden Markov model to model the distribution of the speaker spectral shape from voice sample and claimed the identity using maximum likelihood of the posterior probabilities belonging to different classes. Both these works demonstrated that the identity of speaker can be well recognized via their voices under the condition that voice samples were in good quality and the gallery size was small, i.e. the number of subjects is small. This conclusion, in turn, brings new hope to use voice biometric to differentiate identical twins, because to distinguish between identical twins, the number of involved subjects was very small *i.e. the number of twins siblings*. In this paper, we are trying to answer those questions as follows:

1. **Can voice be used to distinguish between identical twins? Is it better than appearance based approach? If it is, which voice feature is the best for identical twins?**

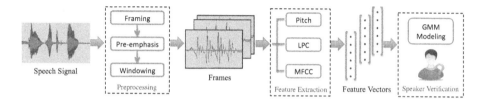

Fig. 1. Flowchart of twin verification using voice

2. Can we combine facial appearance with speech to improve accuracy?

Our work can be divided into three parts: 1) we firstly collected a twin audio-visual database with 39 pairs of identical twins and test the discriminating ability of facial appearance to distinguish between identical twins by using Eigenface [12], Local Binary Pattern [13] and Linear Discriminating Analysis on Gabor wavelet features (Gabor) [14]. 2) We propose to use Gaussian Mixture Model to estimate the spectral shape of each twin subject, an then use the ratio of the probabilities belonging to different twin subjects for verification. Three types of voice features are used: Pitch, LPC and MFCC. 3) We use confidence level fusion to combine the Gabor and MFCC to improve accuracy.

2   Twin Verification Using GMM

2.1   Preprocessing and Feature Extraction

The proposal of our twin verification can be seen in Figure 1. The first step of preprocessing is framing which is to divide audio into successive overlapping frames. The frame size is set to 23 milliseconds in our work, with 50% overlap. The energy in the high frequencies is boosted in each frame to compensates the nonlinear nature of human voice that more energy is located at lower frequencies. A Hamming window is utilized to smooth out the discontinuities at the beginning and the end of the frame. Since silent frames may exist in the speech signal, we filter out these frames using a simple thresholding method. The threshold θ indicates the probability of containing human voice in this frame. If θ is larger than the threshold, we keep this frame; otherwise we throw it away. In our experiments, we set the threshold t0 0.4.

After preprocessing, various acoustic features can be extracted from the frames. We select three kinds of features for testing and comparison purpose, which are Pitch [15], Linear Prediction Coefficients (LPC) [16], and Mel Frequency Cepstral Coefficients (MFCC) [17]. Pitch is a perceptual property of the voice that allows the ordering on a frequency-related scale. MFCC is to map the powers of the frame spectrum onto the mel scale and then uses amplitudes of discrete cosine transform of the list of mel scale as feature. LPC is the coefficients of the linear predictive coding from the frames. In our work, the MFCC coefficient number is set to 13 and the predictor order (i.e., the number of LPC coefficients) is set to 8.

2.2 Modeling Using GMM

For each subject, his/her identity-dependent acoustic spectral distribution is modeled as a weighted sum of M component densities given by the equation

$$p(x) = \sum_{i=1}^{M} w_i b_i(x) \tag{1}$$

where x is the D-dimensional feature vector (In our case, it is Pitch, LCP and MFCC), $b_i(x)$ is the component density and w_i is the mixture weight. Each component density is represented as a Gaussian distribution of the form

$$b_i(x) = \frac{1}{(2\pi)^{D/2}|\Delta_i|^{1/2}} \exp\{-\frac{1}{2}(x - \mu_i)'\Delta_i^{-1}(x - \mu_i)\} \tag{2}$$

with mean vector μ_i and covariance matrix Δ_i. The sum of mixture weights w_i equals to 1. For convenience, we denote mean vectors, covariance matrices and mixture weights as Γ , where $\Gamma = \{w_i, \mu_i, \Delta_i\}, i = 1, ..., M$. Therefore, each speaker is represented by his/her model Γ.

Given the training data in the gallery, we use Expectation Maximization algorithm [18] to estimate the Γ for each subject. In the verification phase, given a test feature vector, ψ, and the hypothesized speaker S, we aim to check whether the hypothesized identity is same to classified identity. We state this task as a basic hypothesis test between two hypotheses:

H0: ψ is from the hypothesized twin speaker S.

H1: ψ is not from the hypothesized speaker S (*i.e.* ψ is from the twin sibling of hypothesized speaker S).

The optimum classification to decide between these two hypotheses is through the likelihood ratio (LR) given by

$$LR = \frac{p(\psi|H0)}{p(\psi|H1)} \tag{3}$$

If $LR > \epsilon$, we accept H0; otherwise, we reject H0. Here, ϵ is the threshold, $p(\psi|H0)$ is the probability density function for the hypothesis subject S for the observed feature vector ψ, and $p(\psi|H1)$ is the probability density function for not being the hypothesis subject S for the observed feature vector ψ.

3   Experiments

3.1   Data and Performance Evaluation

We collected a twins audio-visual database at the Sixth Mojiang International Twins Festival held on 1 May 2010 in China. It includes Chinese, Canadian and

Fig. 2. Some image examples of identical twins

Russian subjects for a total of 39 pairs of twins. Several examples can be seen in Figure 2. For each subject, there are at least three audio recordings, each around 30 seconds. The talking content of those recordings are different. For the first recording, the subjects are required to count the number from one to ten; For the second recording, the subjects are reading a paragraph; For the third recording, the subjects are reciting a poem.

The twin verification performance is evaluated in terms of Twin Equal Error Rate(Twin-EER) which Twin False Accept Rate(Twin-FAR) meets the False Reject Rate (FRR). The Twin-FAR is the ratio between the times that twin imposter is recognized as genuine with the total number of imposter. FRR is the ratio between the times that genuine is recognized as imposter with the total number of the genuine. We also introduce General Equal Error Rate(General-EER) where General False Accept Rate(General-FAR) meets the FRR. The General-FAR is the ratio between the times that general imposter is recognized as genuine with the total number of the non-twin imposter. The purpose of introducing General-FAR is to compare the verification accuracy between twins with non-twins to see the challenge brought by twins.

3.2   Performance of Appearance and Audio Based Approach

We chose three traditional facial appearance approaches, Eigenface, Local Binary Pattern and Gabor, to test the performance of using appearance to distinguish between identical twins. For each twin subject, we randomly select 8 images. The images are then registered by eye positions detected by STASM [19] and resized to to 160 by 128. For Eigenface, we vectorized gray intensity in each pixel as feature and performed PCA to reduce the dimension. For LBP, we divided the image into 80 blocks. For each block, we extract the 59-bins histogram. For Gabor, we used 40 Gabor (5 scales, 8 orientation) filters and set the kernel size for each Gabor filter to 17 by 17. A PCA is performed to reduce the feature dimension for LBP and Gabor. The experimental result is shown in Figure 3(a). From this figure, we can see that identical twins indeed pose a great challenge to appearance based approach. The General-EER of Gabor for general population is around 0.122, while Twin-EER is significantly larger than 0.33. We can also see that there is no huge difference between Intensity, LBP and Gabor for twin verification. The Twin-EERs for them are 0.352 (Intensity), 0.340 (LBP) and 0.338 (Gabor), separately.

For voice based twin verification, we use one of the audio recordings as gallery to train the GMM for each subject. Then, the remaining audio recordings are

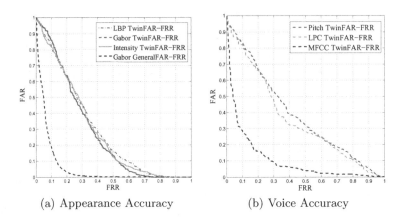

(a) Appearance Accuracy   (b) Voice Accuracy

Fig. 3. Performance comparison between facial appearance and voice biometric

used as probe. For each recording, we divide it into three parts, and each part is acted as single probe. During GMM training, the covariance matrix is assumed to be diagonal and the number of Gaussians is set to 4 for Pitch, 4 for LPC and 5 for MFCC. The number of gaussian is optimized on the test set for better performance. The experimental result is showed in Figure 3(b). Compared with Figure 3(a), it can be clearly seen that twins can be better distinguished via voice than appearance. The Twin-EER for MFCC is 0.171, which is significantly better than appearance (the best for appearance is 0.338). However, not all voice features are better than appearance. The Twin-EERs of pitch and LPC (0.394 for Pitch and 0.366 for LPC) are even larger than appearance based approach. This shows that Pitch and LPC is not discriminating enough for twins.

Moreover, based on the experimental results in [10], the General-EER for speaker verification on general population is around 0.05, which is much smaller than the best (0.171) in twins database. The difference may come from three aspects: 1)insufficient training data in our experiments. In our case, we only use one audio recording around 30 seconds as training, and the talking content is very simple and sometime duplicated. Therefore, it may cannot cover the entire voice spectral pattern. 2) The voice spectral pattern for identical twins may have some overlap. Identical twins share the same genetic code, therefore their voice may share some similarity. 3) Our audio recording is not collected in very clean environment, the environment sound may also degrade our performance. The General-EER reported by [10] was obtained at clean recording room.

4   Fusion of Gabor and MFCC

In this section, we combine the appearance and speech to improve the twin recognition accuracy. We choose Gabor as feature to represent appearance feature; we choose MFCC as feature to represent voice feature. The reason for our choice is trivial, because these two features perform the best in each category

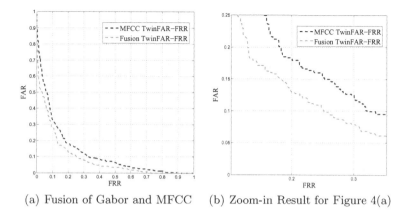

(a) Fusion of Gabor and MFCC   (b) Zoom-in Result for Figure 4(a)

Fig. 4. Performance of Fusion of Gabor and MFCC

in our previous experiment. In multimodal systems, there are three levels of fusion when combining two biometrics. The first is fusion at the feature extraction level. The features for each biometric modality are formed into a new feature. The second is fusion at the confidence level. Each biometric provides a similarity score, and these scores will be combined together to assert the veracity of the claimed identity. The third fusion is at decision level. Each biometric will make one decision and final decision is made based on those decisions.

In our proposal, we use the second fusion strategy. Given a probe and a claim identity, we compute the Euclidean distance of Gabor, denoted as GD, and the likelihood ratio against the claimed identity, denoted LR in Equ 3, separately. The final similarity, FS, is computed as the weighted sum of GD and LR, denoted as $FS = \alpha GD + (1 - \alpha)LR$. Then, we compare the FS against the pre-set threshold ϵ. If $FS > \epsilon$, we accept; otherwise we reject. We conducted the experiments on the whole database, and the performance is showed in Figure 4. From this figure, we can see that when α is set to 0.415, by fusion of Gabor and MFCC the Twin-EER decreases from 0.171(MFCC) to 0.160. We set the α for the best of test performance in our dataset.

5   Conclusion and Future Work

In this work, we collect a moderate size of identical twins database including appearance and voice. We propose to use Gaussian Mixture Model to model the voice spectral pattern for verification. The results verify that voice biometric can be used to distinguish between identical twins and it is significantly better than traditional facial appearance features, including EigenFace, LBP and Gabor; Among various voice features, MFCC has the most discriminating ability. We further prove that the accuracy can be improved via fusion of voice biometric and facial appearance.

In future, we would like to test the robustness of our voice proposal, including the length of training data and environment noise. Even though our current result is very promising, we still hope to collect a larger twin database for our research. We also intend to test the scalability of our voice proposal. Finally, we look forward building a multimodal biometric system to which can work well for general population but also can prevent the evil twin attack.

References

1. Martin, J., Kung, H., Mathews, T., Hoyert, D., Strobino, D., Guyer, B., Sutton, S.: Annual summary of vital statistics: 2006. Pediatrics (2008)
2. Sun, Z., Paulino, A., Feng, J., Chai, Z., Tan, T., Jain, A.: A study of multibiometric traits of identical twins. SPIE (2010)
3. Zhang, L., Ye, N., Marroquin, E.M., Guo, D., Sim, T.: New hope for recognizing twins by using facial motion. In: WACV, pp. 209–214. IEEE (2012)
4. Jain, A., Prabhakar, S., Pankanti, S.: On the similarity of identical twin fingerprints. Pattern Recognition, 2653–2663 (2002)
5. Kong, A., Zhang, D., Lu, G.: A study of identical twins' palmprints for personal verification. Pattern Recognition, 2149–2156 (2006)
6. Nejati, H., Zhang, L., Sim, T., Martinez-Marroquin, E., Dong, G.: Wonder ears: Identification of identical twins from ear images. In: ICPR, pp. 1201–1204 (2012)
7. Daugman, J., Downing, C.: Epigenetic randomness, complexity and singularity of human iris patterns. Proceedings of the Royal Society of London, 1737 (2001)
8. Reynolds, D.A., Rose, R.C.: Robust text-independent speaker identification using gaussian mixture speaker models. IEEE Transactions on Speech and Audio Processing 3(1), 72–83 (1995)
9. Sinith, M., Salim, A., Gowri Sankar, K., Sandeep Narayanan, K., Soman, V.: A novel method for text-independent speaker identification using mfcc and gmm. In: ICALIP, pp. 292–296. IEEE (2010)
10. Dupont, S., Luettin, J.: Audio-visual speech modeling for continuous speech recognition. IEEE Transactions on Multimedia 2(3), 141–151 (2000)
11. Dean, D., Sridharan, S., Wark, T.: Audio-visual speaker verification using continuous fused hmms. In: Proceedings of the HCSNet workshop, pp. 87–92 (2006)
12. Turk, M.A., Pentland, A.P.: Face recognition using eigenfaces. In: CVPR, pp. 586–591. IEEE (1991)
13. Ahonen, T., Hadid, A., Pietikäinen, M.: Face recognition with local binary patterns. In: Pajdla, T., Matas, J(G.) (eds.) ECCV 2004. LNCS, vol. 3021, pp. 469–481. Springer, Heidelberg (2004)
14. Liu, C., Wechsler, H.: Gabor feature based classification using the enhanced fisher linear discriminant model for face recognition. IEEE Transactions on Image processing 11(4), 467–476 (2002)
15. Zatorre, R.J., Evans, A.C., Meyer, E., Gjedde, A.: Lateralization of phonetic and pitch discrimination in speech processing. Science 256(5058), 846–849 (1992)
16. Atal, B.S., Hanauer, S.L.: Speech analysis and synthesis by linear prediction of the speech wave. The Journal of the Acoustical Society of America 50, 637 (1971)
17. Logan, B., et al.: Mel frequency cepstral coefficients for music modeling. In: International Symposium on Music Information Retrieval, vol. 28, p. 5 (2000)
18. Dempster, A.P., Laird, N.M., Rubin, D.B.: Maximum likelihood from incomplete data via the em algorithm. Journal of the Royal Statistical Society, 1–38 (1977)
19. Milborrow, S., Nicolls, F.: Locating facial features with an extended active shape model. In: Forsyth, D., Torr, P., Zisserman, A. (eds.) ECCV 2008, Part IV. LNCS, vol. 5305, pp. 504–513. Springer, Heidelberg (2008)

Voting Strategies
for Anatomical Landmark Localization
Using the Implicit Shape Model

Jürgen Brauer, Wolfgang Hübner, and Michael Arens

Fraunhofer IOSB, Ettlingen / Germany
{juergen.brauer,wolfgang.huebner,michael.arens}@iosb.fraunhofer.de

Abstract. We address the problem of anatomical landmark localization using monocular camera information only. For person detection the
Implicit Shape Model (ISM) is a well known method. Recently it was
shown that the same local features that are used to detect persons, can
be used to give rough estimates for anatomical landmark locations as
well. Though the landmark localization accuracy of the original ISM is
far away from being optimal. We show that a direct application of the
ISM to the problem of landmark localization leads to poorly localized
vote distributions. In this context, we propose three alternative voting
strategies which include the use of a reference point, a simple observation vector filtering heuristic, and an observation vector weight learning
algorithm. These strategies can be combined in order to further increase
localization accuracy. An evaluation on the UMPM benchmark shows
that these new voting strategies are able to generate compact and monotonically decreasing vote distributions, which are centered around the
ground truth location of the landmarks. As a result, the ratio of correct
votes can be increased from only 9.3% for the original ISM up to 42.1%
if we combine all voting strategies.

Keywords: human pose estimation, anatomical landmark localization,
Implicit Shape Model.

1 Introduction

The localization of anatomical landmarks (e.g. hands or hip center) is an essential
preprocessing step in many action recognition approaches. Sliding window-based
person detectors (Dollar et al. [3] provides a survey) are often used for the
initial person detection step. Local feature based methods (Leibe et al. [6]) have
a clear advantage over sliding window based methods in cases where persons
are occluded. For both person detection approaches there are corresponding
anatomical landmark detection approaches. Bourdev and Malik [2] trained SVM
classifiers for body part classification using sets of example image patches that
correspond to a similar 2D (or 3D) pose (called 'poselets'). A multiscale sliding-
window is run over the image and each window is classified by the SVMs, which
is computationally demanding. Müller and Arens [7] reuse local features from an
ISM person detection step to vote for landmark locations which is more efficient

R. Wilson et al. (Eds.): CAIP 2013, Part I, LNCS 8047, pp. 145–153, 2013.
© Springer-Verlag Berlin Heidelberg 2013

in terms of computation time. This approach was recently adopted by Girshick et al. [4] for estimating 3D human poses using depth information provided by the Kinect: instead of assigning each pixel an unique landmark classification as in the original approach (Shotton et al. [8]), a Hough forest is used, where a set of votes is stored at each leaf to directly vote for the location of the landmark. Here we adopt the approach from [7] for landmark localization, i.e. for each landmark we are interested to localize, a single ISM is learned. The contribution of this paper is to provide a set of new voting strategy alternatives in section 2 which allow a much more better localization of landmarks. Further, we provide an evaluation on the UMPM benchmark of each of the new voting strategies and their combination in section 3.

2 Voting Strategies

Original Implicit Shape Model Voting (ORIG-VOT). The basic idea behind the Implicit Shape Model (ISM) (Leibe et al. [6]) is to learn the spatial relationship between local features and an object using training data. For a new image, local features are used to vote for possible object locations according to the learned spatial relationship. More formally, an ISM $\mathcal{I} = (\mathcal{C}, \mathcal{P})$ consists of a set $\mathcal{C}$ (codebook) of prototypical image structures w_i (visual words, codewords) together with a set $\mathcal{P}$ of 3D probability distributions $\mathcal{P} = \{P_1, ..., P_{|\mathcal{C}|}\}$. P_i are 3D distributions, which specify where a visual word w_i is typically located on the object and at which feature scale. Leibe et al. [6] represent these probability distributions in a non-parametric manner by collecting a set $\mathcal{O}_i = \{o_j = (\Delta x_j, \Delta y_j, s_j)^\top : j = 1, ..., Q_i\}$ of sample observation vectors o_j that encode where $(\Delta x_j, \Delta y_j)$ the object center was observed relative to a local feature (matching to word w_i) and at which scale s_j the feature appeared. In Lehmann et al. [5] this non-parametric representation of observation vectors is replaced by Gaussian Mixture Models. In the object detection phase, a set of local features $\mathcal{F} = \{f_k = (f_x, f_y, f_s, d, w_i)^\top : 1 \leq k \leq K\}$ is computed, where f_k is a local feature detected at keypoint location (f_x, f_y) at scale f_s with corresponding descriptor vector d which matches best to word w_i. According to the list of previously learned observation vectors $\mathcal{O}_i$ this feature now casts a vote $v = (v_r, v_x, v_y, v_s)^\top$ according to each previously stored observation vector o_j, where the vote location, scale, and weight v_r is computed by:

$$v_r = \frac{1}{|\mathcal{O}_i|} P(w_i|d) \qquad v_x = f_x + \Delta x \frac{f_s}{s_j} \qquad v_y = f_y + \Delta y \frac{f_s}{s_j} \qquad v_s = \frac{f_s}{s_j} \quad (1)$$

where $P(w_i|d)$ is the probability that descriptor vector d matches to word w_i. With $v_3 = (v_x, v_y, v_s)$ we denote the 3D vote space location, $v_2 = (v_x, v_y)$ the corresponding 2D image vote location, and $\mathcal{V}$ denotes the set of all votes casted by all features. Object instances are then detected by identifying clusters of high vote density in the 3D vote space using a Mean-Shift search.

Reference-Point Voting (RP-VOT). For human pose estimation, we first have to detect persons in the image. The idea of RP-VOT is to exploit knowledge about the person detection location in the landmark localization process. The motivation goes back to the observation that many visual words can appear at very different locations on the human body. For this, it is helpful to include the knowledge about the location where this image structure is observed relative to a reference point (here: person center). For RP-VOT we modify the original voting procedure such that votes are only casted, if the word appears in the detection phase at a similar location relative to the reference point, as in training. We need a description of the location of the word relative to the reference point which is independent from the person's appearance size in the image. More formally, we augment the observation vectors $o_j = (\Delta x_j, \Delta y_j, s_j, h_1)^\top$ such that we record also at which size h_1 (in pixels) we observed the person during training. The word location relative to the object center can then be represented in person height units $a = (-\Delta x_j/h_1, -\Delta y_j/h_1)^\top$ and can be compared with the word location $b = ((f_x - R_x)/h_2, (f_y - R_y)/h_2)^\top$ relative to the reference point (R_x, R_y) during testing where we estimate the person's height to be h_2. For each feature f and observation vector o_j we then cast a vote only, if their location difference is below some threshold, i.e. $\|a - b\|_2 < \theta$. Here we use $\theta = 0.05$ which means that we use the observation vector only if the word's location distance between training and testing is below 5% of the person's height. For the person size estimate we experimented with two approaches: (i) estimating the size from the person's bounding box height, which is a plausible estimate, if the person is upright standing and (ii) estimating the size from the set of local features within the person's bounding box, which is a better choice, if we expect poses, where the person also will show non upright standing poses, as e.g. bending down, or if the person is partially occluded. For estimating the person height from local features we used an ISM as well, where each local feature casts votes for the person height (1D vote space) and the final height estimate is found by applying a 1D Mean Shift with a 1D Gaussian kernel.

Heuristic Voting (H-VOT). In the training phase of ORIG-VOT for each word w_i – which has its keypoint location on the person's segmentation mask – we store an observation vector with its location relative to the person center in $\mathcal{O}_i$. In [6] the person's segmentation mask is automatically retrieved using a motion segmentation by the Grimson-Stauffer background model. For landmark localization we could also allow each word that appears on the person's segmentation mask to store an observation vector for each landmark. Though this means that e.g. a word that appears during training on the feet would store an observation vector for all other landmarks (including the left/right hand, the head, etc.), not only the left/right foot. Therefore, we propose to use a simple but effective heuristic which is to exploit the information, whether the landmark location which we are interested in was within the descriptor region of the feature during training. A vote is generated only if this is the case. This filters for image structures that most probably contain information about the location of the landmark. It is not necessary to augment the observation vectors by this information, since they already contain this information: the landmark location is within the descriptor region of the word during training, if $\sqrt{\Delta x_j^2 + \Delta y_j^2} < s_j$.

Observation Vector Weighting Voting (OW-VOT). A more generic approach – compared to H-VOT – is to treat the problem of choosing observation vectors as a learning problem. For this, each observation vector is provided with an individual weight. The idea is to give an observation vector a large weight if it successfully allows to detect landmarks and to give it a smaller weight if this is not the case. The training of an OW-VOT needs three steps. The training data is split into two equally sized subsets, comparable to the principle of cross-validation. The first set is used to collect the observation vectors. The second set is used to estimate the weights. In the first step, we collect observation vectors as in ORIG-VOT on the first set. In the second step, we iterate on the second set of the training data and augment each observation vector $o_j = (\Delta x_j, \Delta y_j, s_j, h_j, \eta_j)^\top$ by a weight η_j which is initially set to 0. For each sample image from the second set we compute local features f, match them to words, and for each word iterate over all the associated observation vectors. We compute the corresponding vote location v_2 and compare it with the ground truth landmark location t. The weight is increased by $K(\|v_2 - t\|_2, \sigma^2)$ where K is a Gaussian kernel with a standard deviation of $\sigma = 0.1h$, and h is the current person height. This ensures that observation weights are increased stronger if the corresponding vote location is near to the ground truth marker location. In the third step, each weight η_j is normalized by W, i.e. $\eta_j \leftarrow \frac{\eta_j}{W}$, where W is the sum of all observation weights of the word w_i, i.e. $W = \sum_{k=1}^{Q_i} \eta_k$. During voting the vote weight formula in eqn. (1) is then modified by the observation vectors weights, i.e. $v_r = \eta_j P(w_i|d)$. Note that the original vote weight normalization by $\frac{1}{|\mathcal{O}_i|}$ – which was introduced in ORIG-VOT to give each feature the same weight when voting – can be skipped, since the new weights η_j are already normalized to 1. Thus OW-VOT replaces the uniform weighting of all observation vectors by a relative weighting.

Combined Voting Strategy (COMBI-VOT). The three voting strategies (RP,H,OW - VOT) can be combined in order to generate an improved voting strategy COMBI-VOT. RP-VOT and H-VOT mainly act as a filter for observation vectors: each observation vector associated with a detected word is checked for being used during the voting procedure. OW-VOT then further modifies the final vote weights by giving observation vectors larger weights, if they have shown to be appropriate for predicting landmarks.

3   Experiments and Results

Dataset. Aa et al. [1] recently published the new UMPM benchmark[1] which allows for quantitative evaluations of 2D and 3D human pose estimation algorithms. It consists of 30 subjects and a total of approx. 400.000 frames. The dataset is provided with extrinsic and intrinsic camera parameters for all of the four cameras. This allows to project the motion capture data into the image to yield ground truth landmark locations which can be used to train the landmark

---

[1] http://www.projects.science.uu.nl/umpm/

ISMs. Table 1 shows the list of 16 experiments we conducted. In the Xa experiments we used the UMPM codebook, while Xb experiments were conducted using the generic codebook (see Codebook section below). In exp. 5b e.g. we used the generic codebook, trained 15 landmark ISMs using 2 video sequences showing 4 persons performing mainly grabbing objects poses and tested on one video sequence showing one person. In all experiments except 1a+1b test person(s) were different from ISM train data persons.

Table 1. Results for evaluation measures α and β for all landmark localization experiments. [x] specifies the number of persons used for training, or testing respectively. $\emptyset$ specifies the average evaluation measure value for each voting strategy, where we averaged over all experiments 1a-8b.

Exp #	Train videos	Test video	α ORIG	RP	H	OW	COMBI	β ORIG	RP	H	OW	COMBI
1a	[2] p2-chair-2	[1] p1 chair 2	9.8	25.5	18.2	12.9	44.0	44.7	26.3	31.9	35.2	16.4
1b	[2] p2-chair-2	[1] p1 chair 2	8.4	24.4	16.7	11.7	43.5	47.1	26.9	33.5	37.0	16.0
2a	[2] p2-chair-1	[1] p1 chair 2	9.3	21.8	17.8	11.5	37.9	44.1	27.4	30.2	37.3	18.5
2b	[2] p2-chair-1	[1] p1 chair 2	8.6	22.3	17.8	10.9	38.8	46.3	27.1	31.4	39.0	18.0
3a	[4] p2/p3-chair-1	[1] p1 chair 2	8.7	20.9	17.0	11.0	36.7	45.5	28.5	31.1	37.0	17.9
3b	[4] p2/p3-chair-1	[1] p1 chair 2	7.7	21.4	15.9	10.2	37.5	48.3	28.2	33.0	38.9	17.5
4a	[2] p2-grab-1	[1] p1 grab 3	12.0	29.7	21.0	16.4	49.4	38.5	20.1	26.8	30.5	12.1
4b	[2] p2-grab-1	[1] p1 grab 3	10.9	30.5	20.2	14.3	50.3	41.5	19.7	28.9	34.1	12.0
5a	[4] p2/p3-grab-1	[1] p1 grab 3	11.1	29.1	19.8	14.9	48.7	39.9	20.4	27.9	31.5	12.2
5b	[4] p2/p3-grab-1	[1] p1 grab 3	10.0	30.0	18.2	13.3	49.3	42.7	19.8	30.2	34.5	12.1
6a	[2] p3-ball-2	[2] p2 ball 1	9.9	22.4	17.4	13.7	39.3	44.3	26.4	30.5	34.2	15.6
6b	[2] p3-ball-2	[2] p2 ball 1	8.4	22.5	15.0	11.5	39.0	47.5	26.1	33.5	37.0	15.5
7a	[2] p3-free-1	[2] p2 free 1	8.8	22.1	17.5	11.6	38.2	43.7	25.1	30.6	33.6	15.5
7b	[2] p3-free-1	[2] p2 free 1	7.7	22.1	14.9	10.2	38.5	45.6	25.0	32.6	35.8	15.5
8a	[4] p3-free-1/11	[2] p2 free 1	9.5	23.5	18.8	12.4	41.6	42.3	24.5	29.4	32.9	14.8
8b	[4] p3-free-1/11	[2] p2 free 1	8.2	23.1	16.1	10.8	41.4	44.8	24.7	31.4	35.3	14.9
$\emptyset$			9.3	24.5	17.6	12.3	42.1	44.2	24.8	30.8	35.2	15.3

Evaluation Measures. For a good part localization we want the vote distribution to be compact, uni-modal, centered on the ground truth landmark, and monotonically decreasing to the periphery. We use three different evaluation measures (α, β, γ) to assess to which degree this is fulfilled by the different voting strategies:

$$\alpha = \frac{1}{W} \sum_{v \in \mathcal{V}} v_r \delta_r(\|\boldsymbol{v_2} - \boldsymbol{t}\|_2) \quad \text{with} \quad \delta_r(x) = \begin{cases} 1, x \leq r \\ 0, x > r \end{cases} \tag{2}$$

$$\beta = \frac{1}{W} \sum_{v \in \mathcal{V}} v_r \|\boldsymbol{v_2} - \boldsymbol{t}\|_2 / h \tag{3}$$

$$\gamma(d) = \frac{1}{|X_d|} \sum_{(d, \rho(\tilde{l})) \in X_d} \rho(\tilde{l}) \quad \text{with} \quad \rho(\tilde{l}) = \frac{1}{W \lambda(s)} \sum_{v \in \mathcal{V}} v_r K(\|\boldsymbol{v_3} - \tilde{l}\|_2 / \lambda(s)) \tag{4}$$

α measures the ratio of correct vs. total votes casted, weighted by the corresponding vote weights. All votes within a circle of radius r around the ground truth location are considered as correct. Here we use $r = 0.1h$, where h is the person height measured in pixels. h can be estimated from the stick figure ground truth 2D pose by $h = (L_l + L_r)/2 + S + N$, where L_l and L_r are the lengths of the legs, S is the length of the spine and N is the length from the neck to the head. t is the ground truth 2D landmark location, and $W = \sum_{v \in \mathcal{V}} v_r$ is the sum of all vote weights. β measures the mean distance of the votes to the true landmark location, again weighted by the vote weights, such that the distance (to the true location) of a vote with a large weight has higher impact than a distance of a vote with small weight. The distance is computed in relative person height units by dividing through h. γ measures the average vote density in dependence of the distance to the true marker location. For this we sample 3D vote space locations $\tilde{l} = (\tilde{x}, \tilde{y}, \tilde{s})$ on a regular 3D grid and compute the density ρ of the votes at these locations using a (weighted) kernel density estimator with scale-dependent bandwidth $\lambda(s)$. For each vote density sample location $\tilde{l}$, we then compute the distance d of the corresponding 2D vote location v_2 to the true marker location t in person height units, i.e. $d = \|v_2 - t\|/h$ and add a new sample $x = (d, \rho(\tilde{l}))$ of this distance and vote density to a histogram of 100 discretized distance bins X_d ($d = 0.01n$, $0 \le n \le 100$). Fig. 1 shows the average vote density $\gamma(d)$ of all votes within such a bin X_d as a function of the distance d.

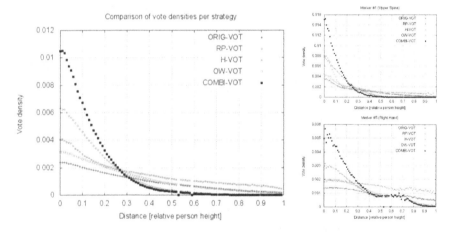

Fig. 1. Vote density as a function of the distance to ground truth landmark location. $\gamma(0.1)$ e.g. specifies the average vote density we find at locations which have a distance of 10% of the person's height to the true marker location. Left: averaged over all experiments and landmarks. Right: averaged over all experiments for landmark 'Upper Spine' (top) and landmark 'Right Hand' (bottom).

Codebooks. Two different codebooks were used for the following experiments. First, a codebook was generated by using 178 of the 272 UMPM video sequences. All video sequences where skipped where persons occurred on which we later tested in the experiments. From 1747 persons images we collected 109458 SURF descriptor vectors of keypoints within a person bounding box. The 128 dimensional descriptor vectors were clustered using RNN clustering [6] resulting in 1315 visual words. The generic codebook was generated using the ETHZ

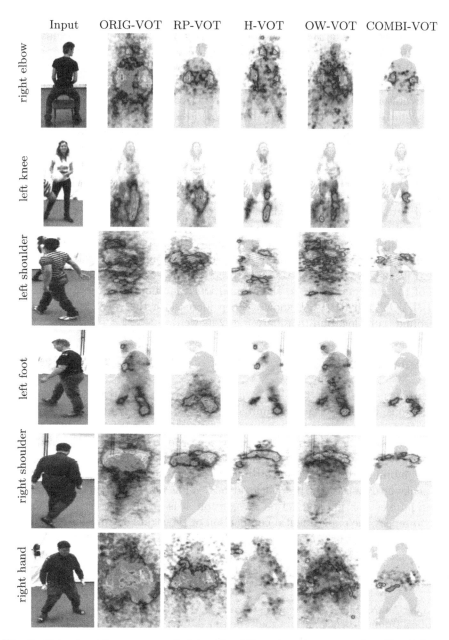

Fig. 2. Vote densities as generated by the different voting strategies. For different landmarks we show the resulting vote density generated by each of the strategy on 6 example person images from the experiments. The original ISM voting strategy yields non focused vote distributions, while especially the combination of the new voting strategies allows a much more focused localization of the landmarks and often shows vote density peaks at the true landmark locations (heat map color encoding: warm colors mean high density).

Pedestrian dataset[2] showing hundreds of different persons in street scenes. From 17721 person images 56234 descriptor vectors were clustered into 843 clusters.

Results. Table 1 shows the results for the evaluation measures α and β for the individual experiments (α,β are specified in %). While only 9.3% of the votes are correct for the ORIG-VOT, RP-VOT can increase the number of correct votes already up to 24.5%. COMBI-VOT can even increase it up to 42.1% correct votes. The (average distance of votes) measure β paints a picture which is consistent with measure α. While the average distance of votes is 44.2% of the person height for ORIG-VOT, COMBI-VOT can reduce this error measure down to 15.3%. The influence of the codebook is only marginal (compare a with b results) which indicates that a generic codebook trained on different person images is appropriate. We expected a larger number of training persons (2 vs. 4) to yield better results, which was slightly the case in exp. 7a vs. 8a and 7b vs. 8b, but not in exp. 4a vs. 5a and 4b vs. 5b, where the performance even slightly dropped. This indicates that a small number of training persons are enough at least when the poses shown in the training phase are similar to the ones in the test phase. Fig. 1 shows the evaluation measure $\gamma(d)$: the new voting strategies locate more of the vote mass near to the ground truth landmark location. Especially, COMBI-VOT and RP-VOT show a steep increase in the vote density near to the ground truth location (compare Fig. 2 as well).

4 Conclusions

In this paper we showed that the original ISM voting strategy produces vote distributions which are clearly limited for usage in the context of landmark localization and as a basis for human pose estimation. We introduced three new alternative vote generation mechanisms which produce much more focused vote distributions and yield higher vote densities near to the true landmark locations. When combining all three voting strategies to a new fourth one, we can see clear vote peaks near to the true marker locations. While our work is in the context of human pose estimation and action recognition, it is highly interesting for future work to repeat the experimental comparison of the strategies presented here on other object categories than humans.

References

1. van der Aa, N., Luo, X., Giezeman, G., Tan, R., Veltkamp, R.: Utrecht multi-person motion (umpm) benchmark: a multi-person dataset with synchronized video and motion capture data for evaluation of articulated human motion and interaction. In: HICV Workshop, in Conj. with ICCV (2011)
2. Bourdev, L., Malik, J.: Poselets: Body part detectors trained using 3D human pose annotations. In: Proc. of ICCV (2009)
3. Dollár, P., Wojek, C., Schiele, B., Perona, P.: Pedestrian detection: An evaluation of the state of the art. PAMI 99(PrePrints) (2011)

---

[2] http://www.vision.ee.ethz.ch/~aess/dataset/

4. Girshick, R., Shotton, J., Kohli, P., Criminisi, A., Fitzgibbon, A.: Efficient regression of general-activity human poses from depth images. In: Proc. of ICCV (2011)
5. Lehmann, A., Leibe, B., van Gool, L.: Prism: Principled implicit shape model. In: Proc. of BMVC, pp. 64.1–64.11 (2009)
6. Leibe, B., Leonardis, A., Schiele, B.: Robust object detection with interleaved categorization and segmentation. IJCV 77, 259–289 (2008)
7. Müller, J., Arens, M.: Human pose estimation with implicit shape models. In: ACM Artemis, ARTEMIS 2010, pp. 9–14. ACM, New York (2010)
8. Shotton, J., Fitzgibbon, A.W., Cook, M., Sharp, T., Finocchio, M., Moore, R., Kipman, A., Blake, A.: Real-time human pose recognition in parts from single depth images. In: CVPR, pp. 1297–1304 (2011)

Evaluating the Impact of Color
on Texture Recognition

Fahad Shahbaz Khan[1], Joost van de Weijer[2], Sadiq Ali[3], and Michael Felsberg[1]

[1] Computer Vision Laboratory, Linköping University, Sweden
fahad.khan@liu.se
[2] Computer Vision Center, CS Dept. Universitat Autonoma de Barcelona, Spain
[3] SPCOMNAV, Universitat Autonoma de Barcelona, Spain

Abstract. State-of-the-art texture descriptors typically operate on grey scale images while ignoring color information. A common way to obtain a joint color-texture representation is to combine the two visual cues at the pixel level. However, such an approach provides sub-optimal results for texture categorisation task.

In this paper we investigate how to optimally exploit color information for texture recognition. We evaluate a variety of color descriptors, popular in image classification, for texture categorisation. In addition we analyze different fusion approaches to combine color and texture cues. Experiments are conducted on the challenging scenes and 10 class texture datasets. Our experiments clearly suggest that in all cases color names provide the best performance. Late fusion is the best strategy to combine color and texture. By selecting the best color descriptor with optimal fusion strategy provides a gain of 5% to 8% compared to texture alone on scenes and texture datasets.

Keywords: Color, texture, image representation.

1 Introduction

Texture categorisation is a difficult task. The problem involves assigning a class label to the texture category it belongs to. Significant amount of variations in images of the same class, illumination changes, scale and viewpoint variations are some of the key factors that make the problem challenging. The task consists of two parts, namely, efficient feature extraction and classification. In this work we focus on obtaining compact color-texture features to represent an image.

State-of-the-art texture descriptors operate on grey level images. Color and texture are two of the most important low level visual cues for visual recognition. A straight forward way to extend these descriptors with color is to operate on separately on the color channels and then concatenate the descriptors. However such representations are high dimensional. Recently, it has been shown that an explicit color representation improves performance on object recognition and detection tasks [1,2]. Therefore, this work explores several pure color descriptors popular in image classification for texture categorisation task.

R. Wilson et al. (Eds.): CAIP 2013, Part I, LNCS 8047, pp. 154–162, 2013.

There exist two main approaches to combine color and texture cues for texture categorisation.

Early Fusion: Early fusion fuses the two cues at the pixel level to obtain a joint color-texture representation. The fusion is obtained by computing the texture descriptor on the color channels. Early fusion performs best for categories which exhibit constancy in both color and shape [1].

Late Fusion: Late fusion process the two visual cues separately. The two histograms are concatenated into a single representation which is then the input to a classifier. Late fusion combines the visual cues at the image level. Late fusion works better for categories where one cue remains constant and the other changes significantly [1]. In this work we analyze both early and late fusion approaches for the task of texture categorisation.

As mentioned above, state-of-the-art early fusion approaches [3] combine the features at the pixel level. Contrary to computer vision, it is well known that visual features are processed separately before combining at a later stage for visual recognition in human brain [4,5]. Recently, Khan et al. [6] propose an alternative approach to perform early fusion for object recognition. The visual cues are combined in a single product vocabulary. A clustering algorithm based on information theory is then applied to obtain a discriminative compact representation. Here we apply this approach to obtain a compact early fusion based color-texture feature representation.

In conclusion, we make the following novel contributions:

- We investigate state-of-the-art color features used for image classification for the task of texture categorisation. We show that the color names descriptor with its only 11 dimensional feature vector provides the best results for texture categorisation.
- We analyze fusion approaches to combine color and texture. Both early and late feature fusion is investigated in our work.
- We also introduce a new dataset of 10 different and challenging texture categories as shown in Figure 1 for the problem of color-texture categorisation. The images are collected from the internet and Corel collections.

2   Relation to Prior Work

Image representations based on color and texture description are an interesting research problem. Significant amount of research has been done in recent years to the solve the problem of texture description [7,8,9,10]. Texture description based on local binary patterns [8] is one of the most commonly used approach for texture classification. Other than texture classification, local binary patterns have been employed for many other vision tasks such as face recognition, object and pedestrian detection. Due to its success and wide applicability, we also use local binary patterns for texture categorisation in this paper[1].

---

[1] We also investigated other texture descriptors such as MR8 and Gabor filters but inferior results were obtained compared to LBP. However, the approach presented in this paper can be applied with any texture descriptor.

Color has shown to provide excellent results for bag-of-words based object recognition [3,1]. Recently, Khan et al. [1,2] have shown that an explicit representation based on color names outperforms other color descriptors for object recognition and detection. However, the performance of color descriptors, popular in image classification, has yet to be investigated for texture categorization task. Therefore, in this paper we investigate the contribution of color for texture categorization. Different from the previous methods [11,12], we propose to use color names as a compact explicit color representation. We investigate both late and early fusion based global color-texture description approaches. Contrary to conventional pixel based early fusion methods, we use an alternative approach to construct a compact color-texture image representation.

3   Pure Color Descriptors

Here we show a comparison of pure color descriptors popular in image classification for texture description.

RGB Histogram [3]: As a baseline, we use the standard RGB descriptor. The RGB histogram combines the three histograms from the R, G and B channels. The descriptor has 45 dimensions.

rg Histogram [3]: The histogram is based on the normalized RGB color model. The descriptor is 45 dimensional and invariant to light intensity changes and shadows.

C Histogram: This descriptor has shown to provide excellent results on the object recognition task [3]. The descriptor is derived from the opponent color space as $\frac{O1}{O3}$ and $\frac{O2}{O3}$. The channels $O1$ and $O2$ describe the color information. Whereas $O3$ channel contains the intensity information in an image. We quantize the descriptor into 36 bins using K-means to construct a histogram.

Opponent-angle Histogram [13]: The opponent-angle histogram proposed by van de Weijer and Schmid is based on image derivatives. The histogram has 36 dimensions.

HUE Histogram [13]: The descriptor was proposed by [13] where hue is weighted by the saturation of a pixel in order to counter the instabilities in hue. This descriptor also has 36 dimensions.

Transformed Color Distribution [3]: The descriptor is derived by normalizing each channel of RGB histogram. The descriptor has 45 dimensions and is invariant to scale with respect to light intensity.

Color Moments and Invariants [3]: In the work of [3] the color moment descriptor is obtained by using all generalized color moments up to the second degree and the first order. Whereas color moment invariants are constructed using generalized color moments.

Hue-saturation Descriptor: The hue-saturation histogram is invariant to luminance variations. It has 36 dimensions (nine bins for hue times four for saturation).

Color Names [14]: Most of the aforementioned color descriptors are designed to achieve photometric invariance. Instead, color names descriptor balances a certain degree of photometric invariance with discriminative power. Humans use color names to communicate color, such as "black", "blue" and "orange". In this work we use the color names mapping learned from the Google images [14].

4   Combining Color and Texture

Here we discuss different fusion approaches to combine color and texture features.

Early Fusion: Early fusion involves binding the visual cues at the pixel level. A common way to construct an early fusion representation is to compute the texture descriptor on the color channels. Early fusion results in a more discriminative representation since both color and shape are combined together at the pixel level. However, the final representation is high dimensional. Constructing an early fusion representation using color channels with a texture descriptor for an image I is obtained as:

$$T_E = [T_R, T_G, T_B],   \tag{1}$$

Where T can be any texture descriptor. Most color-texture approaches in literature are based on early fusion approach [12,3]. Recently, Khan et al. [1] have shown that early fusion performs better for categories that exhibit constancy of both color and shape. For example, the foliage category has a constant shape and color.

Late Fusion: Late fusion involves combining visual cues at the image level. The visual cues are processed independently. The two histograms are then concatenated into a single representation before the classification stage. Since the visual cues are combined at the histogram level, the binding between the visual cues is lost. A late fusion histogram for an image is obtained as,

$$T_L = [H_T, H_C],   \tag{2}$$

Where H_T and H_C are explicit texture and color histograms. Late fusion provides superior performance for categories where one of the visual cues changes significantly. For example, most of the man made categories such as car, motorbike etc. changes significantly in color. Since an explicit color representation is used for late fusion, it is shown to provide superior results for such classes [1].

Portmanteau Fusion: Most theories from the human vision literature suggest that the visual cues are processed separately [4,5] and combined at a later stage for visual recognition. Recently, Khan et al. [6] propose an alternative solution for constructing compact early fusion within the bag-of-words framework. Color and shape are processed separately and a product vocabulary is constructed. A Divisive information theoretic clustering algorithm (DITC) [15] is then applied to obtain a compact discriminative color-shape vocabulary. Similarly, in this work we also aim at constructing a compact early fusion based color-texture representation[2].

Here we construct separate histograms for both color and texture and product histogram is constructed. Suppose that $T = \{t_1, t_2, ..., t_L\}$ and $C = \{c_1, c_2, ..., c_M\}$ represent the visual texture and color histograms, respectively. Then the product histogram is given by

$$TC = \{tc_1, tc_2, ..., tc_S\} = \{\{t_i, c_j\} \mid 1 \leq i \leq L, 1 \leq j \leq M\},$$

where $S = L \times M$. The product histogram is equal to number of texture bins times number of color histogram bins. This leads to high dimensional feature representation. This product histogram is then input to the DITC algorithm to obtain a low dimensional compact color-texture representation. The DITC algorithm works on the class-conditional distributions over product histograms. The class-conditional estimation is measured by the probability distribution $p(R|tc_s)$, where $R = \{r_1, r_2, ..r_O\}$ is the set of O classes. The DITC algorithm works by estimating the drop in mutual information I between the histogram TC and the class labels R. The transformation from the original histogram TC to the new representation $TC^R = \{TC_1, TC_2, ..., TC_J\}$ (where every TC_j represents a group of clusters from TC) is equal to

$$I(R; TC) - I(R; TC^R)$$

$$= \sum_{j=1}^{J} \sum_{tc_s \in TC_j} p(tc_s) KL(p(R|tc_s), p(R|TC_j)), \tag{3}$$

where KL is the Kullback-Leibler divergence between the two distributions defined by

$$KL(p_1, p_2) = \sum_{y \in Y} p_1(y) log \frac{p_1(y)}{p_2(y)}. \tag{4}$$

The algorithm finds a desired number of histogram bins based on minimizing the loss in mutual information between the bins of product histogram and the class labels of training instances. Histogram bins with similar discriminative power are merged together over the classes. We refer to Dhillon et al. [15] for a detail introduction on the DITC algorithm.

5   Experimental Results

To evaluate the performance of our approach we have collected a new dataset of 400 images for color-texture recognition. The dataset consists of 10 different

---

[2] In our experiments we also evaluated PCA and PLS but inferior results were obtained. A comparison of other compression techniques with DITC is also performed by [16].

Fig. 1. Example images from the two datasets used in our experiments. First row: images from the OT scenes dataset. Bottom row: images from our texture dataset.

categories namely: marble, beads, foliage, wood, lace, fruit, cloud, graffiti, brick and water. We use 25 images per class for training and 15 instances for testing. Existing datasets are either grey scale, such as the Brodatz set, or too simple, such as the Outex dataset, for color-texture recognition. Texture cues are also used frequently within the context of object and scene categorisation. Therefore, we also perform experiments on the challenging OT scenes dataset [17]. The OT dataset [17] consists of 2688 images classified as 8 categories. Figure 1 shows example images from the two datasets.

In all experiments a global histogram is constructed for the whole image. We use LBP with uniform patterns having final dimensionality of 383. Early fusion is performed by computing the texture descriptor on the color channels. For late fusion, histograms of pure color descriptor is concatenated with a texture histogram. A non-linear SVM is used for classification. The performance is evaluated as a classification accuracy which is the number of correctly classified instances of each category. The final performance is the mean accuracy obtained from all the categories. We also compare our approach with color-texture descriptors proposed in literature [12,10].

Table 1. Classification accuracy on the two datasets. (a) Results using different pure color descriptors. Note that on both datasets color names being additionally compact provides the best results. (b) Scores using late fusion approaches. On both datasets late fusion using color names provides the best results while being low dimensional.

Method	Size	OT [17]	Texture
RGB	45	43	51
rg	30	39	50
HUE	36	38	43
C	36	39	41
Opp-angle	36	33	27
Transformed color	45	40	41
Color moments	30	42	50
Color moments inv	24	23	34
HS	36	37	42
Color names	11	**46**	**56**

(a)

Method	Size	OT [17]	Texture
RGB LBP	383 + 45	79	74
rg LBP	383 + 30	80	69
HUE LBP	383 + 36	80	74
C LBP	383 + 36	79	73
Opp-angle LBP	383 + 36	79	74
Transformed color LBP	383 + 45	79	72
Color moments LBP	383 + 30	80	74
Color moments inv LBP	383 + 24	23	71
HS LBP	383 + 36	79	72
Color names LBP	383 + 11	**82**	**77**

(b)

5.1   Experiment 1: Pure Color Descriptors

We start by providing results on the pure color descriptors discussed in Section 3. The results are presented in Table 1. On both datasets, the baseline RGB provides improved results compared to several other sophisticated color desccriptors. Among all the descriptors, the color names descriptor provides best results on both datasets. Note that color names being additionally compact, possesses a certain degree of photometric invariance together with discriminative power. It has the ability to encode achromatic colors such as grey, white etc. Based on these results, we propose to use color names as an explicit color representation to combine with texture cue.

5.2   Experiment 2: Fusing Color and Texture

Here, we first show results obtain by late fusion approaches in Table 1. The texture descriptor with 383 dimensions provides a classification score of 77% and 69% respectively. The late fusion of RGB and LBP provides a classification score of 79% and 74%. The STD [12] descriptor provides inferior results of 58% and 67% respectively. The best results are obtained on both datasets using the combination of color names with LBP. Table 2 shows results obtained using early fusion approaches on the two datasets. The conventional pixel based descriptors provide inferior results on both datasets. The LCVBP descriptor [10] provides classification scores of 76% and 53% on the two datasets. By taking the product histogram directly without compression provides an accuracy of 81% and 72% while being significantly high dimensional. It is worthy to mention that both JTD and LCVBP descriptors are also significantly high dimensional. The portmanteau fusion provides the best results among early fusion based methods while additionally being compact in size.

In summary late fusion provides superior performance while being compact on both datasets. Among early fusion based methods portmanteau fusion provides improved performance on both datasets. The best results are achieved using the color names descriptor. Color names having only an 11 dimensional histogram is

Table 2. Classification accuracy using early fusion approaches. Among early fusion approaches, portmanteau fusion provides the best results on both datasets while additionally being compact.

Method	Dimension	OT [17]	Texture
RGBLBP	1149	79	70
CLBP	1149	78	69
OPPLBP	1149	80	70
HSVLBP	1149	78	71
JTD [12]	15625	57	61
LCVBP [10]	15104	76	53
Product	4213	81	72
Portmanteau fusion	**500**	**82**	**73**

compact, possesses a certain degree of photometric invariance while maintaining discriminative power. Note that in this paper we investigate global color-texture representation. Such a representation can further be combined with local bag-of-words based descriptors for further improvement in performance.

6 Conclusions

We evaluate a variety of color descriptors and fusion approaches popular in image classification for texture recognition. Our results suggest that color names provides the best performance for texture recognition. Late fusion is an optimal approach to combine the two cues. Portmanteau fusion provides superior results compared to conventional pixel level early fusion. On scenes and texture datasets, color names in a late fusion settings significantly improve the performance by 5% to 8% compared to texture alone.

Acknowledgments. We acknowledge the support of Collaborative Unmanned Aerial Systems (within the Linnaeus environment CADICS), ELLIIT, the Strategic Area for ICT research, funded by the Swedish Government, and Spanish project TIN2009-14173.

References

1. Khan, F.S., van de Weijer, J., Vanrell, M.: Modulating shape features by color attention for object recognition. IJCV 98(1), 49–64 (2012)
2. Khan, F.S., Anwer, R.M., van de Weijer, J., Bagdanov, A.D., Vanrell, M., Lopez, A.M.: Color attributes for object detection. In: CVPR (2012)
3. van de Sande, K.E.A., Gevers, T., Snoek, C.G.M.: Evaluating color descriptors for object and scene recognition. PAMI 32(9), 1582–1596 (2010)
4. Treisman, A., Gelade, G.: A feature integration theory of attention. Cogn. Psych. 12, 97–136 (1980)
5. Wolfe, J.M.: Watching single cells pay attention. Science 308, 503–504 (2005)
6. Khan, F.S., van de Weijer, J., Bagdanov, A.D., Vanrell, M.: Portmanteau vocabularies for multi-cue image representations. In: NIPS (2011)
7. Lazebnik, S., Schmid, C., Ponce, J.: A sparse texture representation using local affine regions. PAMI 27(8), 1265–1278 (2005)
8. Ojala, T., Pietikainen, M., Maenpaa, T.: Multiresolution gray-scale and rotation invariant texture classification with local binary patterns. PAMI 24(7), 971–987 (2002)
9. Varma, M., Zisserman, A.: A statistical approach to texture classification from single images. IJCV 62(2), 61–81 (2005)
10. Lee, S.H., Choi, J.Y., Ro, Y.M., Plataniotis, K.: Local color vector binary patterns from multichannel face images for face recognition. TIP 21(4), 2347–2353 (2012)
11. Topi Maenpaa, M.P.: Classification with color and texture: jointly or separately? PR 37(8), 1629–1640 (2004)
12. Susana Alvarez, M.V.: Texton theory revisited: A bag-of-words approach to combine textons. PR 45(12), 4312–4325 (2012)

13. van de Weijer, J., Schmid, C.: Coloring local feature extraction. In: Leonardis, A., Bischof, H., Pinz, A. (eds.) ECCV 2006. LNCS, vol. 3952, pp. 334–348. Springer, Heidelberg (2006)
14. van de Weijer, J., Schmid, C., Verbeek, J.J., Larlus, D.: Learning color names for real-world applications. TIP 18(7), 1512–1524 (2009)
15. Dhillon, I., Mallela, S., Kumar, R.: A divisive information-theoretic feature clustering algorithm for text classification. JMLR 3, 1265–1287 (2003)
16. Elfiky, N., Khan, F.S., van de Weijer, J., Gonzalez, J.: Discriminative compact pyramids for object and scene recognition. PR 45(4), 1627–1636 (2012)
17. Oliva, A., Torralba, A.B.: Modeling the shape of the scene: A holistic representation of the spatial envelope. IJCV 42(3), 145–175 (2001)

Temporal Self-Similarity for Appearance-Based Action Recognition in Multi-View Setups

Marco Körner and Joachim Denzler

Friedrich Schiller University of Jena, Computer Vision Group, Jena, Germany
{marco.koerner,joachim.denzler}@uni-jena.de, www.inf-cv.uni-jena.de

Abstract. We present a general data-driven method for multi-view action recognition relying on the appearance of dynamic systems captured from different viewpoints. Thus, we do not depend on 3d reconstruction, foreground segmentation, or accurate detections. We extend further earlier approaches based on *Temporal Self-Similarity Maps* by new low-level image features and similarity measures. *Gaussian Process* classification in combination with *Histogram Intersection Kernels* serve as powerful tools in our approach. Experiments performed on our new combined multi-view dataset as well as on the widely used IXMAS dataset show promising and competing results.

Keywords: Action Recognition, Multi-View, Temporal Self-Similarity, Gaussian Processes, Histogram-Intersection Kernel.

1 Introduction

The automatic recognition of actions from video streams states a very important problem in current computer vision research, as reflected by recent surveys[1]. A variety of possible applications—*e.g. Human-Machine Interaction*, surveillance, *Smart Environments*, entertainment, *etc.*—argues for the emerging relevance of this topic.

As monocular approaches rely on single-view images, they solely perceive 2d projections of the real world and discard important information. Hence, they are likely to suffer from occlusions and ambiguities. As a consequence, the majority of these methods use data-driven methods like *Space-Time Interest Points*[8] instead of model-based representations of the image content. In contrast, existing multi-view action recognition systems try to directly exploit 3d information, *e.g.* by reconstructing the scene or fitting anatomical models, resulting in a far higher complexity.

Having these observations in mind, we propose a method to recognize articulated actions, which meets the following demands: (i) it is designed to be general and not restricted to *human* action recognition, (ii) it avoids expensive dense 3d reconstruction, (iii) it is independent from the camera setup it was learned in, and (iv) it does not rely on foreground segmentation and exact localization.

The rest of this paper is structured as follows: in Sect. 2 we give a short introduction in theory of *Recurrence Plots* and *Temporal Self-Similarity Maps* and

R. Wilson et al. (Eds.): CAIP 2013, Part I, LNCS 8047, pp. 163–171, 2013.

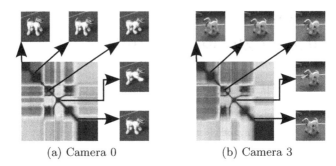

(a) Camera 0   (b) Camera 3

Fig. 1. Two SSMs obtained for a robot dog performing an `stand_kickright` action captured from different viewpoints. Action primitives induce similar local structures in the corresponding SSM even under changes of viewpoint, illumination, or image quality.

motivate their usage. We also suggest to extend the related approach of Junejo *et al.*[7] by new low-level features and distance metrics. Subsequently, Sect. 3 will present our approach to utilize SSMs for multi-view action recognition. Therefore we use a *Gaussian Process* classifier together with the *Histogram Intersection Kernel*, which has been shown to be more suitable for comparison of histograms. In Sect. 4, we show results of our approach on our own new multi-view action recognition dataset as well as on the widely used IXMAS dataset.

1.1 Related Work

Going through the related literature, methods for action recognition can be categorized into three groups: the first kind of approaches tries to reconstruct 3d information or trajectories from the scene[15] or augment these representations by a fourth time dimension[19,5]. Alternatively, relationships between action features obtained from different views are learned by applying transfer learning or knowledge transfer techniques[3,9]. The methods most related to our proposal try to directly model the dynamics of actions within a view-independent framework[7,2]. For a more extensive review about recent work on action recognition we refer to recent reviews[1,14].

2   Temporal Self-similarity Maps

To understand human actions and activities, observers take benefit of their prior knowledge of typical temporal and spatial recurrences in execution of actions. Besides all differences in execution, two actions can be perceived as being *semantically identical* if they share atomic *action primitives* in a similar frequency. Assuming those actions to be instances of deterministic dynamical systems— which can be modeled by differential equations—, Marwan *et al.*[11] presented an intensive discussion about their interpretation utilizing *Recurrence Plots* (RP). This work was further referenced for human gait analysis[2] and—due to their stability in the case of viewpoint changes—for cross-view action recognition[7].

Table 1. Semantic interpretations of patterns shown in SSMs introduced by recorded actions (interpretation of [11]))

Pattern	Interpretation
Homogeneous areas	The corresponding atomic action represents a stationary process
Fading in corners	The recorded action represents a Non-stationary process
Periodic structures	The recorded action contains a cyclic/periodic motion
Isolated points	The recorded action contains an abrupt fluctuation
(Anti-) Diagonal straight lines	The recorded action contains different atomic actions with similar evolutionary characteristics in (reversed) time
Horiz. & vert. lines	No or slow change of states for a given period of time
Bow structures	The recorded action contains different atomic actions with similar evolutionary characteristics in reversed time with different velocities

Given a sequence $\boldsymbol{I}_{1:N} = \{I_1, \ldots, I_N\}$ of images $I_i, 1 \leq i \leq N$, a *temporal Self-Similarity Map* (SSM) is generically defined as a square and symmetric matrix $\boldsymbol{S}_{f,d}^{I_{1:N}} = [d(f(I_i), f(I_j))]_{i,j}$, $\boldsymbol{S}_{f,d}^{I_{1:N}} \in \mathbb{R}^{N \times N}$ of pairwise similarities $d(\cdot, \cdot)$ between low-level image features $f(\cdot)$ computed independently for every sequence frame. In the literature, it has already been shown that SSMs preserve invariants of the dynamic systems they capture[12], they are stable wrt. different embedding dimensions[12,6], invariant under isometric transformations[12] and though not being invariant under projective or affine transformations, SSMs are heuristically shown to be stable under 3d view changes[7]. In Fig. 1, a robot dog performing a stand_kickright action was captured from two viewpoints with different illumination conditions. Apparently, atomic action primitives induce similar structures within the corresponding SSM. It can further be observed, that the local structure of these SSMs reflects the temporal relations between different system configurations over time, as summarized in Tab. 1.

2.1   Image Features

The choice for low-level image features $f(\cdot)$ is of inherent importance and has to suit the given scenario. In the following, we will discuss some possible alternatives.

Intensity Values. The simplest way to convert an image into a descriptive feature vector $f_{\text{int}}(I) \in \mathbb{R}^{M \cdot N}$ is to append its intensities, as proposed for human gait analysis[2]. While this is suitable for sequences with a single stationary actor, it yields large feature vectors and is very sensitive to noise and illumination changes.

Landmark Positions. Assuming to be able to track anatomical or artificial landmarks of the actor over time, their positions $f_{\text{pos}}(I) = (\boldsymbol{x}_0, \boldsymbol{x}_1, \ldots), \boldsymbol{x}_i = (x_i, y_i, z_i)$, can be used to represent the current system configuration[7]. This is sufficient, as long as the tracked points are distributed over moving body parts, but it demands points to be able to be tracked continuously.

Table 2. Exemplary SSMs extracted from recordings of actions from the Aibo dataset using different low-level image features

Table 3. Exemplary SSMs extracted from the same stand_dance1 action from the Aibo dataset using different similarity measures

Feature	Action (perfomed in greeting pose)			
	greeting	scoot right	stretch	dance1
Intensity				
HoG				
HoF				
Fourier				

Similarity Measure	Feature		
	HoG	HoF	Fourier
Euclidean Distance			
Normalized Cross-Correlation			
Histogram Intersection			

Histograms of Oriented Gradients have been shown to give good representations of shape for object detection. For this purpose, the image is subdivided into overlapping cells, where the distribution of gradient directions is approximated by a fixed-bin discretization. These certain local orientation histograms are normalized to the direction of the strongest gradient in order to obtain local rotation invariance. Appending those local gradient histograms gives the final descriptor $f_{\text{HoG}}(I) = (\boldsymbol{h}_0, \boldsymbol{h}_1, \ldots)$, $\boldsymbol{h}_i = (n_i^0, n_i^1, \ldots)$[7].

Histograms of Optical Flows. When analyzing the displacements of each pixel between two succeeding frames, this *optical flow* field represents an early fusion of temporal dynamics. Building a global histogram over discretized flow orientations or appending histograms obtained from smaller subimages yield the HoF descriptor $f_{\text{HOF}}(I)$.

Fourier Coefficients. When computing the 2-dimensional discrete Fourier transform $\hat{a}_{k,l} = \sum_{m=0}^{M-1} \sum_{n=0}^{N-1} I_{m,n} \cdot e^{-2\pi i\left(\frac{mk}{M} + \frac{nl}{N}\right)}$, $0 \leq k \leq M-1, 0 \leq l \leq N-1, \hat{a}_{k,l} \in \mathbb{C}$ of an image patch I, the series of Fourier coefficients $[\hat{a}_{k,l}]$ contains spectral information up to a given cutoff frequency $0 \leq k \leq M_c-1, 0 \leq l \leq N_c-1$ and inherently provides invariance against translation. Since the first Fourier coefficient $\hat{a}_{0,0}$ represents the mean intensity of the transformed image patch I, the Fourier coefficient descriptor $f_{\text{Fourier}} = (\hat{a}_{0,1}, \hat{a}_{0,2}, \ldots, \hat{a}_{1,N_c-1}, \ldots, \hat{a}_{M_c-1,N_C-1})$ is further invariant wrt. global illumination changes. By tuning the cutoff frequencies M_c, N_c, statistical noise can be suppressed as it is represented by higher-order frequencies. Since DFT can be implemented in parallel on modern GPU environments, these features can be computed very efficiently.

A qualitative comparison of these features extracted from different action classes is given in Tab. 2. It can be seen that the HoF feature shows many abrupt changes, while the other SSMs contain more smooth transitions between the certain similarity values. The HoG feature seems to be more sensitive so temporal changes at small time scale, which could be explained by image noise

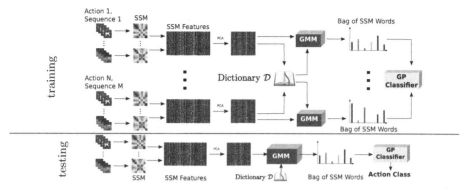

Fig. 2. Outline of the training and testing phase of our approach

and might harm the further processing. Hence, we further concentrate on using the proposed Fourier coefficients, since they are easily and fast to compute and provide some handy invariants by design.

2.2   Similarity Measures

Beside the choice for a suitable image representation $f(\cdot)$, the distance measure $d(\cdot, \cdot)$ plays an important role when computing self-similarities, as qualitatively compared in Tab. 3.

Euclidean Distances. The euclidean distance $d_{\mathrm{eucl}}(\boldsymbol{f}_1, \boldsymbol{f}_2) = \|\boldsymbol{f}_1 - \boldsymbol{f}_2\|_2$ serves as a straightforward way to quantify the similarity between two image feature descriptors $\boldsymbol{f}_1 = f(I_1)$ and $\boldsymbol{f}_2 = f(I_2)$ of equal length, as proposed by [7]. While this is easy to compute, it might be unsuited for histogram data[10], since false bin assignments would cause large errors in the euclidean distance.

Normalized Cross-Correlation. From a signal-theoretical point of view, the image feature descriptors $\boldsymbol{f}_1, \boldsymbol{f}_2$ can be regarded as D-dimensional discrete signals of equal size. Then, the normalized cross-correlation coefficient $d_{\mathrm{NCC}}(\boldsymbol{f}_1, \boldsymbol{f}_2) = \left\langle \frac{f_1}{\|f_1\|}, \frac{f_2}{\|f_2\|} \right\rangle \in [-1, 1]$ measures the cosine of the angle between the signal vectors $\boldsymbol{f}_1$ and $\boldsymbol{f}_2$. Hence, this distance measure is independent from their lengths.

Histogram Intersection. The intersection $d_{\mathrm{HI}}(\boldsymbol{h}_1, \boldsymbol{h}_2) = \sum_{i=0}^{D-1} \min(h_{1,i}, h_{2,i})$ of two histograms $\boldsymbol{h}_1, \boldsymbol{h}_2 \in \mathbb{R}^D$ was shown to perform better for codebook generation and image classification tasks[13]. In case of comparing normalized histograms, the histogram intersection distance is bounded by $[0, +1]$.

3   MVSSM Feature Extraction and Action Topic Model Learning and Classification

As mentioned before, SSMs obtained from videos capturing the identical action from different viewpoints share common patterns. Hence, local feature descriptors suitable for monitoring the structure of those patterns have to be developed in order to use *Multi-View SSM* (MVSSM) representations for action recognition purposes in multi-view environments. Hooked on on the choice for features and the similarity measure used to create the SSM, self-similarity values are expected to become less reliable when moving away from the diagonal, as measuring the similarity gets more difficult. Junejo *et al.*[7] proposed to use a log-polar histogram of intensity gradients extracted on discrete positions at the main diagonal of the SSM to be analyzed, which yields a descriptor of dimension 88. The radius of this histogram, *i.e.* the temporal extend of interest, controls the amount of temporal information taken into account. As an extension, they constructed these histograms at different time scales to catch variations in executions.

Alternatively, we propose to extract 128-dimensional SIFT descriptors at keypoints equally distributed along the diagonal of fused multi-view SSMs. These are scale-invariant by design, as they examine and aggregate the image information on different scale spaces. To reduce the number of dimensions, we further apply PCA to the matrix of descriptor vectors.

Since the number of feature descriptors varies with the size of the SSM, *i.e.* the length of the sequence, and the density of keypoints used for extracting these features, we need to transform this set of features into a fixed-size representation. We used the widely popular *Bag of Visual Words* approach to assign the given action descriptors to representative prototypes identified by a custom cluster algorithm. Choosing an appropriate value for the number of prototypes, the obtained feature histograms are sparse and thus easy to distinguish. Fig. 2 outlines the training and testing phase of our system.

4   Experimental Evaluation

In order to evaluate our multi-view action recognition system, we firstly performed experiments on our own dataset. This dataset contains 10 sequences of each 56 predefined actions performed by SONY AIBO robot dogs simultaneously captured by six cameras.[1]

In our general setup, the dimension of SIFT descriptors extracted along the SSM diagonal was reduced from 128 to 32 by applying PCA. Subsequently, all descriptors from all train sequences were clustered into a mixture of 512 Gaussians to create a *Bag of Self-Similarity Words* (BOSS Words). This is further used to represent each training sequence by a histogram of relative frequencies. These parameters heuristically show best results. While Junejo *et al.*[7] propose to employ a multiclass SVM, this yield a very high complexity in our case, as the AIBO dataset covers a relatively large number of classes to be distinguished. Hence, we use a *Gaussian Process* (GP) classifier combined with a *Histogram Intersection Kernel* $\kappa_{HIK}(\boldsymbol{h}, \boldsymbol{h}') = \sum_{i=0}^{D} \min(h_i, h_i')$, $\boldsymbol{h}, \boldsymbol{h}' \in \mathbb{R}^D$, which can be evaluated efficiently, as recently shown by Rodner *et al.*[16] and Freytag *et al.*[4]. Recognition rates were obtained after 10-fold cross validation.

One of the most important questions concerning multi-view action recognition is the influence of the training and testing camera setup on the overall

---

[1] The complete dataset including labels, calibration data and background images is available at http://www.inf-cv.uni-jena.de/JAR-Aibo.

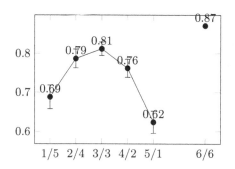

Fig. 3. Results obtained on Aibo dataset: average recognition rates for different $n_{\text{training}}/n_{\text{testing}}$ view partitions

Table 4. Results obtained on IXMAS dataset (cross-view evaluation)

Approach	Description	Rec.
our approach		79%
Junejo *et al.*[7]	HoG[1]	63%
Junejo *et al.*[7]	HOF[1]	67%
Junejo *et al.*[7]	HoG+HoF[1]	74%
Junejo *et al.*[7]	HoG+HoF[2]	80%
Weinland *et al.*[17]	2d Silhouettes	58%
Farhadi *et al.*[3]	2d Silhouettes+OF	69%
Weinland *et al.*[18]	3d HoG[3]	84%

[1]Multi-Scale SSM, [2]Space-Time Interest Points[8]
[3]all views used for training and testing

accuracy. In order to preserve generality, we evaluated our method on disjoint sets for training and testing views. Fig. 3 shows averaged results of experiments, where all 62 possible partitions of views for training and testing where used. As expected, the maximum performance was obtained when dividing the available views into equally-sized subsets. Confusions between semantically related classes only appeared occasionally. In general, we were even able to distinguish identical actions performed in different poses, which argues for the discriminativeness of our modeling scheme. For our experiments we used a standard desktop computer equipped with a Intel(R) Core(TM)2 Quad CPU 2.50 GHz and 8 GB of RAM. Some algorithms were parallelized, *e.g.* the Fourier Transform, SIFT extraction, or GMM modeling. While learning an action model for the whole dataset took about 3 hours, the SSM computation, feature extraction, and classification performed in real-time. Most of the approaches presented before concerning the recognition of actions in multi-view environments focus on cross-view setups, *i.e.* the system is trained on one single view and evaluated on another view. Hence, we adopted the evaluation method of Junejo *et al.*[7] in order to do a fair comparison. We did no further adaptions, especially we did not tune the process parameters to obtain optimal results for this scenario. Tab. 4 shows the resulting recognition rates compared to other not model-based approaches. While Junejo *et al.*[7] used a combination of HoF and HoG features, we can reach similar results using our proposed Fourier descriptors, which are assumed to be computed more efficiently. Furthermore, they enabled their approach to show time-scale invariance by extracting their SSM features on different scales, *i.e.* with distinct radii, while the SIFT features we used for representing SSMs are (time-) scale-invariant by design. By estimating 3d optical flow, Weinland *et al.*[18] obtained slightly higher recognition rates.

5 Summary and Outlook

We presented a framework for creating and evaluation temporal self-similarity maps to employ them for multi-view action recognition. It was pointed out, that the invariance and stability properties of SSMs support our demands on a action recognition system.

We made three contributions: (i) we further extended the method originally presented in [7] by new low-level features and distance metrics, (ii) we applied a Gaussian Process (GP) classifier combined with histogram intersection kernel, which have been shown to be more suitable and efficient for comparing histograms[16,4], and (iii) we used a new extensive dataset for evaluating multi-view action recognition systems, which will be made publicly available.

It is straightforward to augment the *Bag of Self-Similarity Words* modeling scheme by histograms of co-occurrences of vocabulary words in order to improve the descriptive power of this representation. Another important aspect is the direct integration of calibration knowledge into our framework.

References

1. Aggarwal, J.K., Ryoo, M.S.: Human activity analysis: A review. ACM Comput. Surv. 43(3), 16:1–16:43 (2011)
2. Cutler, R., Davis, L.S.: Robust real-time periodic motion detection, analysis, and applications. TPAMI 22(8), 781–796 (2000)
3. Farhadi, A., Tabrizi, M.K.: Learning to recognize activities from the wrong view point. In: Forsyth, D., Torr, P., Zisserman, A. (eds.) ECCV 2008, Part I. LNCS, vol. 5302, pp. 154–166. Springer, Heidelberg (2008)
4. Freytag, A., Rodner, E., Bodesheim, P., Denzler, J.: Rapid uncertainty computation with gaussian processes and histogram intersection kernels. In: Lee, K.M., Matsushita, Y., Rehg, J.M., Hu, Z. (eds.) ACCV 2012, Part II. LNCS, vol. 7725, pp. 511–524. Springer, Heidelberg (2013)
5. Holte, M.B., Chakraborty, B., Gonzalez, J., Moeslund, T.B.: A local 3-D motion descriptor for multi-view human action recognition from 4-D spatio-temporal interest points. Selected Topics in Signal Processing 6(5), 553–565 (2012)
6. Iwanski, J.S., Bradley, E.: Recurrence plots of experimental data: To embed or not to embed? Chaos 8(4), 861–871 (1998)
7. Junejo, I.N., Dexter, E., Laptev, I., Pérez, P.: View-independent action recognition from temporal self-similarities. TPAMI 33(1), 172–185 (2011)
8. Laptev, I., Marszalek, M., Schmid, C., Rozenfeld, B.: Learning realistic human actions from movies. In: CVPR, pp. 1–8 (2008)
9. Liu, J., Shah, M., Kuipers, B., Savarese, S.: Cross-view action recognition via view knowledge transfer. In: CVPR, pp. 3209–3216 (2011)
10. Maji, S., Berg, A.C., Malik, J.: Classification using intersection kernel support vector machines is efficient. In: CVPR, pp. 1–8 (2008)
11. Marwan, N., Romano, M.C., Thiel, M., Kurths, J.: Recurrence plots for the analysis of complex systems. Physics Reports 438(5-6), 237–329 (2007)
12. McGuire, G., Azar, N.B., Shelhamer, M.: Recurrence matrices and the preservation of dynamical properties. Physics Letters A 237(1-2), 43–47 (1997)
13. Odone, F., Barla, A., Verri, A.: Building kernels from binary strings for image matching. IP 14(2), 169–180 (2005)
14. Poppe, R.: A survey on vision-based human action recognition. IVC 28(6), 976–990 (2010)
15. Rao, C., Yilmaz, A., Shah, M.: View-invariant representation and recognition of actions. IJCV 50(2), 203–226 (2002)

16. Rodner, E., Freytag, A., Bodesheim, P., Denzler, J.: Large-scale gaussian process classification with flexible adaptive histogram kernels. In: Fitzgibbon, A., Lazebnik, S., Perona, P., Sato, Y., Schmid, C. (eds.) ECCV 2012, Part IV. LNCS, vol. 7575, pp. 85–98. Springer, Heidelberg (2012)
17. Weinland, D., Boyer, E., Ronfard, R.: Action recognition from arbitrary views using 3D exemplars. In: ICCV, pp. 1–7 (2007)
18. Weinland, D., Özuysal, M., Fua, P.: Making action recognition robust to occlusions and viewpoint changes. In: Daniilidis, K., Maragos, P., Paragios, N. (eds.) ECCV 2010, Part III. LNCS, vol. 6313, pp. 635–648. Springer, Heidelberg (2010)
19. Weinland, D., Ronfard, R., Boyer, E.: Free viewpoint action recognition using motion history volumes. CVIU 104(2), 249–257 (2006)

Adaptive Pixel/Patch-Based Stereo Matching for 2D Face Recognition

Rui Liu[1], Weiguo Feng[1], and Ming Zhu[2]

[1] Department of Electronic Engineering and Information Science, University of Science and
Technology of China, Hefei, China
{liuruin,fwg168}@mail.ustc.edu.cn
[2] Department of Automation, University of Science and Technology of China, Hefei, China
mzhu@ustc.edu.cn

Abstract. In this paper, we propose using adaptive pixel/patch-based stereo matching for 2D face recognition. We don't perform 3D reconstruction but define a measure of the similarity of two 2D face images. After rectifying the two images by epipolar geometry, we match them using the similarity for face recognition. The proposed approach has been tested on the CMU PIE and FERET database and demonstrates superior performance compared to existing methods in real-world situations including changes in pose and illumination.

Keywords: face recognition, adaptive, pixel, patch, stereo matching.

1   Introduction

Although face recognition in controlled environment has been well solved, its performance in real application is still far from satisfactory. The variations of pose, illumination, occlusion and expression are still critical issues that affect the face recognition performance. Existing techniques such as Eigenfaces [1] or Fisherfaces [2] are not robust to these variations. Local features such as local binary patterns (LBP) [3] are then proposed for recognition. Recently, sparse representation-based classification (SRC) [4] has also been proposed and showed very promising results. But these methods degrade gracefully with changes of pose. Previous methods for improving face recognition accuracy under pose variation include [5-10]. In [5], a pose-specific locally linear mapping is learned between a set of non-frontal faces and the corresponding frontal faces. [6] shows that dynamic programming-based stereo matching algorithm (DP-SM) can gain significant performance for 2D face recognition across pose. A learning method is present in [10] to perform patch-based rectification based on locally linear regression.

In our work, we perform recognition by using Adaptive Pixel/Patch-based Stereo Matching (APP-SM) to judge the similarity of two 2D images of faces. Fig. 1 contains a representational overview of our method which consists of the following steps:

First, we build a gallery of 2D face images. Second, we align each probe-gallery image pair using four feature points by calculating the epipolar geometry. Then we

R. Wilson et al. (Eds.): CAIP 2013, Part I, LNCS 8047, pp. 172–179, 2013.

run an adaptive pixel/patch-based stereo algorithm on the image pair. Note that we don't perform 3D reconstruction. Also we discard all the correspondences and the disparities. We only use the matching cost to compute the similarity of two face images. Finally, we identify the probe with the gallery image that produces the max similarity.

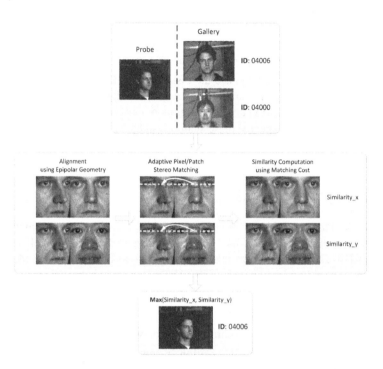

Fig. 1. An overview of our APP-SM method

The paper is organized as follows. Section 2 presents the details of our face recognition method. Section 3 presents and analyses all experiments. Finally, in Section 4, conclusions will be given.

2 Stereo Matching and Face Recognition

2.1 Alignment

Before running the stereo algorithm on the image pair, we first need to rectify them to maintain the epipolar constraint. Generally, eight corresponding points are required to obtain the epipolar geometry. Nevertheless, since the average variation of the depth of the head is small compared to the distance of the camera to the head, and the field of view for the facial image is small, we can simply the model to scaled orthographic projection [11]. Then we only need four feature points to calculate the epipolar geometry.

However, it has been showed in [11] that there can be still considerable variations in disparity between two images under scaled orthographic projection. Traditional linear transformations can only create linear disparity maps, which cannot be used here to align the images accounting for the disparity variations. So in this step, we follow [6] to achieve alignment by solving a non-linear system. For completeness, we briefly review the mainly ideas of solving the epipolar geometry under scaled orthographic projection. Details can be refer to [6].

The epipolar geometry in this scenario is modeled as a tuple: (θ, γ, s, t). Here, θ and γ are the angle of the epipolar lines in the left and right image, respectively. Scaling the right image by s will cause the distance between two epipolar lines in the right image to match the distance in the left image. Translating the image perpendicular to the epipolar lines by t will cause the alignment between the corresponding lines.

In our experiments, we specify these feature points by hand, as in [6]. With four corresponding points, we get a nonlinear system of equations, which we solve in a straightforward way to complete the step of alignment.

2.2   Stereo Matching and Similarity Measure

We propose a stereo algorithm which is appropriate for wide baseline matching of faces. Notice that our approach has been well designed in both pixel and patch level, so that it can handle the problems such as large pose changes and variable illumination.

2.2.1   Pixel Level

Our goal here is to compute the dissimilarity $\widetilde{PI}$ between a pixel at position x_L in the left scanline (row) and a pixel x_R at position in the right scanline (row). Birchfield and Tomasi [12] defined a pixel dissimilarity measure that is insensitive to image sampling:

$$d(x_L, x_R) = \min \left\{ \min_{x_L - \frac{1}{2} \leq x \leq x_L + \frac{1}{2}} \left| \hat{I}_L(x) - I_R(x_R) \right|, \min_{x_R - \frac{1}{2} \leq x \leq x_R + \frac{1}{2}} \left| I_L(x_L) - \hat{I}_R(x) \right| \right\} \quad (1)$$

Here, $x_L = x_R + d, d \in [\Delta_1, \Delta_2]$. I_L and I_R are two discrete one-dimensional arrays of intensity values. $\hat{I}_R$ is the linearly interpolated function between the sample points of the right scanline, and $\hat{I}_L$ is defined similarly.

Based on the Birchfield-Tomasi method, we propose a simple adaptive pixel-based stereo matching algorithm to deal with horizontal slant. It processes a pair of scanlines at a time. Horizontal disparities Δ are assigned to the scanline within a given range $[\Delta_1, \Delta_2]$. The disparities are not assigned to pixels, but continuously over the whole scanline. Given a point x_L in the left scanline and its corresponding point x_R in the right scanline, we have

$$x_L = m \cdot x_R + d \quad (2)$$

m is the horizontal slant, which allows line segments of different length in the two scanlines to correspond adaptively. The values of the horizontal slant which are to be examined are provided as inputs, i.e., $m \in M$, where $M = \{m_1, m_2, ..., m_k\}$, such that $m_1, m_2, ..., m_k \geq 1$.

$$\Delta = (m-1) \cdot x_R + d \tag{3}$$

Δ is the horizontal disparity. The disparity search range $[\Delta_1, \Delta_2]$ is also provided as an input. Then we can find range for d using given range of Δ and Equation (3). In our implementation, we choose Δ and m empirically. With the constraint of runtime and memory consumption, we find $\Delta = [0, 8]$ and $M = \{1, 1.2, ..., 3\}$ performs best.

For i^{th} pixel in the left s^{th} scanline, we simultaneously searched the space of possible disparities and horizontal slants. Then we choose the minimum dissimilarity as the value of $\widehat{PI}(i, s)$. After we obtain the dissimilarity value for each pixel in the left image, we normalise them using Min-Max Normalization method:

$$\widehat{PI}(i, s) = 1 - \frac{\widehat{PI}(i, s) - min(\widehat{PI})}{max(\widehat{PI}) - min(\widehat{PI})} \tag{4}$$

2.2.2 Patch Level

Since matching individual pixel intensities will be very sensitive to noise such as lighting variation, we also compute an adaptive patch-based dissimilarity $\widehat{PA}$ using the local facial features.

For i^{th} pixel in the left s^{th} scanline and j^{th} pixel in the right s^{th} scanline, we compute the dissimilarity $\widehat{PA}(i, s)$ by matching patches around the points (i, s) and (j, s) between images using LBP feature vector (59 dimensions in our experiments).

However, this requires us to account for the effects of slant on patch size. The patch in the left image is fixed-size, while the original patch size in the right image should be determined by the horizontal slant.

We use m to determine the patch size in the right image. For example, if the size of the patch in the left image is fixed at 9×21 , the size of the patch in the right image is therefore $9m \times 21$. We then use interpolation to create a matching patch in the right image and resize it to be the same size as the patch in the left image. Similarly, after we obtain the dissimilarity value for each pixel in the left image, we choose the minimum dissimilarity as the value of $\widehat{PA}(i, s)$ and normalise them as following:

$$\widehat{PA}(i, s) = 1 - \frac{\widehat{PA}(i, s) - min(\widehat{PA})}{max(\widehat{PA}) - min(\widehat{PA})} \tag{5}$$

2.2.3 Similarity Value Computation

For i^{th} pixel in the left s^{th} scanline, a weighted fusion is made to compute the matching cost matrix:

$$MATCH(i, s) = (1 - \alpha) \cdot \widehat{PI}(i, s) + \alpha \cdot \widehat{PA}(i, s) \tag{6}$$

We compute a similarity value $sv(I_1, I_2)$ by making aggregation over all the set of scanlines in the left image. This value tells us how well image I_1 and image I_2 match. Since each similarity is going to be compared to other costs matched over scanlines of potentially different lengths, we use some normalization strategy again:

$$sv(I_1, I_2) = \frac{\sum_s \sum_i MATCH(i,s)}{\sum_s |I_{1,s}| + |I_{2,s}|} \qquad (7)$$

2.3 Face Recognition

Since we do not know which image is left and which image is right in stereo vision, it is better to try both options. We also need to use flip which produces a left-right reflection of the image. Faces are approximately vertically symmetric, so flip is helpful when two views see mainly different sides of the face.

Given two images I_1 and I_2, we define the similarity of the two images as:

$$similarity(I_1, I_2) = \max \begin{cases} sv(I_1, I_2) \\ sv(I_2, I_1) \\ sv(flip(I_1), I_2) \\ sv(I_2, flip(I_1)) \end{cases} \qquad (8)$$

Finally, we perform recognition simply by matching a probe image to the most similar image in the gallery.

3   Experiments

3.1   CMU PIE Database

The CMU PIE [13] database consists of 13 poses of which 9 have approximately the same camera altitude (poses: c34, c14, c11, c29, c27, c05, c37, c25 and c22). For each pose of the same person, there are also 21 images, each with different illumination. We conducted experiments to compare our method APP-SM with the others. The thumbnails used were generated as described in Section 2.1. A number of prior experiments have been done using the CMU PIE database, but somewhat different experimental conditions. We have run our own algorithm under a variety of conditions so that we may compare to these.

First, we only tested on individuals 35-68 from the PIE database to compare our method with six others. Specifically, we selected each gallery pose as one of the 13 PIE poses and the probe pose as one of the remaining 12 poses, for a total of 156 gallery-probe pairs. We evaluated the accuracy of our method in this setting and compared to the results in [6, 7, 9]. Table 1 summarizes the average recognition rates.

Table 1. A comparison on 34 subjects of CMU PIE

Method	Accuracy (%)
Eigenfaces [7]	16.6
FaceIt [7]	24.3
Eigen light-fields (Multi-point norm.) [7]	66.3
DP-SM (Castillo and Jacobs [6])	86.8
Partial Least Squares [9]	90.1
Proposed APP-SM	**92.3**

Then, we evaluated simultaneous variations in pose and illumination, to illustrate that our method can work in more realistic situations. We compare our method to DP-SM [6] which also takes advantage of the stereo algorithm, and Bayesian Face Subregions (BFS) [7] which computes the reflectance and illumination fields from real images. The gallery is frontal pose and illumination. For each probe pose, the accuracy is determined by averaging the results for all 21 different illumination conditions. It can be observed from Fig.2 that our pixel/patch-based synthesizer and normalization strategy provide good robustness to local lighting changes.

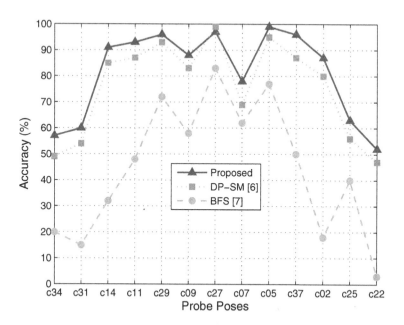

Fig. 2. A comparison with the Method of Castillo et al. [6] and Gross et al. [7]. Gallery pose is frontal (c27) probe. We report the average over the 21 illuminations.

3.2   FERET Database

We also evaluate our method on FERET face image database [14]. This database is one of the largest publicly available databases. It has been used for evaluating face recognition algorithms displays diversity across gender, ethnicity, and age.

Table 2. A comparison on 200 subjects of FERET

Method	bh	bg	bf	be	bd	bc	Avg(%)
Zhang et al. [15]	62.0	91.0	98.0	96.0	84.0	51.0	80.5
Gao et al. [16]	78.5	91.5	98.0	97.0	93.0	81.5	90.0
Sarfraz et al. [8]	92.4	89.7	100	98.6	97.0	89.0	94.5
Mostafa et al. [17]	87.5	98.0	100	99.0	98.5	82.4	94.2
Proposed APP-SM	**92.0**	**94.5**	**100**	**98.8**	**96.0**	**89.5**	**95.1**

In our experiments, we used all 200 subjects at 7 different poses (bh, bg, bf, be, bd, bc). The pose angles range from $+60^0$ to -60^0. The frontal image ba for each subject is used as gallery and the remaining 6 images per subject were used as probes (1,200 totally). Tables 2 shows that our APP-SM performs as well as any prior method based on image comparison. However, it should be noticed that APP-SM needs no training. It is much simpler and more straightforward, which is very important for applications.

4   Conclusion

In this paper, we proposed a method using adaptive pixel/patch-based stereo matching (APP-SM) for 2D face recognition. Compared to existing methods, our APP-SM is simple and performs very well. There is still a lot of room for improvement in our method. For example, some strategies can be pursued to automatically select the parameters. Also it remains a future direction to determine how best to incorporate learning into it.

Acknowledgment. This research was supported by the "Strategic Priority Research Program - Network Video Communication and Control" of the Chinese Academy of Sciences (Grant No. XDA06030900).

References

1. Turk, M.A., Pentland, A.P.: Face recognition using eigenfaces. In: Proceedings 1991 IEEE Computer Society Conference on Computer Vision and Pattern Recognition (91CH2983-5), pp. 586–591 (1991)
2. Belhumeur, P.N., Hespanha, J.P., Kriegman, D.J.: Eigenfaces vs. Fisherfaces: Recognition using class specific linear projection. IEEE Transactions on Pattern Analysis and Machine Intelligence 19, 711–720 (1997)

3. Ahonen, T., Hadid, A., Pietikäinen, M.: Face recognition with local binary patterns. In: Pajdla, T., Matas, J(G.) (eds.) ECCV 2004. LNCS, vol. 3021, pp. 469–481. Springer, Heidelberg (2004)
4. Wright, J., Yang, A.Y., Ganesh, A., Sastry, S.S., Ma, Y.: Robust Face Recognition via Sparse Representation. IEEE Transactions on Pattern Analysis and Machine Intelligence 31, 210–227 (2009)
5. Chai, X., Shan, S., Chen, X., Gao, W.: Locally linear regression for pose-invariant face recognition. IEEE Transactions on Image Processing 16, 1716–1725 (2007)
6. Castillo, C.D., Jacobs, D.W.: Using Stereo Matching with General Epipolar Geometry for 2D Face Recognition across Pose. IEEE Transactions on Pattern Analysis and Machine Intelligence 31, 2298–2304 (2009)
7. Gross, R., Matthews, S.B.I., Kanade, T.: Face recognition across pose and illumination. In: Jain, A.K., Li, S.Z. (eds.) Handbook of Face Recognition. Springer-Verlag New York, Inc. (2005)
8. Sarfraz, M.S., Hellwich, O.: Probabilistic learning for fully automatic face recognition across pose. Image and Vision Computing 28, 744–753 (2010)
9. Sharma, A., Jacobs, D.W.: Ieee: Bypassing Synthesis: PLS for Face Recognition with Pose, Low-Resolution and Sketch. In: 2011 IEEE Conference on Computer Vision and Pattern Recognition, pp. 593–600 (2011)
10. Ashraf, A.B., Lucey, S., Tsuhan, C.: Learning patch correspondences for improved viewpoint invariant face recognition. In: 2008 IEEE Conference on Computer Vision and Pattern Recognition (CVPR), p. 8 (2008)
11. Hartley, R., Zisserman, A.: Multiple View Geometry in Computer Vision. Cambridge University Press (2003)
12. Birchfield, S., Tomasi, C.: A pixel dissimilarity measure that is insensitive to image sampling. IEEE Transactions on Pattern Analysis and Machine Intelligence 20, 401–406 (1998)
13. Sim, T., Baker, S., Bsat, M.: The CMU pose, illumination, and expression database. IEEE Transactions on Pattern Analysis and Machine Intelligence 25, 1615–1618 (2003)
14. Phillips, P.J., Moon, H., Rizvi, S.A., Rauss, P.J.: The FERET evaluation methodology for face-recognition algorithms. IEEE Transactions on Pattern Analysis and Machine Intelligence 22, 1090–1104 (2000)
15. Wenchao, Z., Shiguang, S., Wen, G., Xilin, C., Hongming, Z.: Local Gabor binary pattern histogram sequence (LGBPHS): a novel non-statistical model for face representation and recognition. In: Proceedings of the Tenth IEEE International Conference on Computer Vision, vol. 781, pp. 786–791 (2005)
16. Gao, H., Ekenel, H.K., Stiefelhagen, R.: Pose Normalization for Local Appearance-Based Face Recognition. In: Tistarelli, M., Nixon, M.S. (eds.) ICB 2009. LNCS, vol. 5558, pp. 32–41. Springer, Heidelberg (2009)
17. Mostafa, E.A., Farag, A.A.: Dynamic weighting of facial features for automatic pose-invariant face recognition. In: 2012 Canadian Conference on Computer and Robot Vision, pp. 411–416 (2012)

A Machine Learning Approach
for Displaying Query Results in Search Engines

Tunga Güngör[1,2]

[1] Boğaziçi University, Computer Engineering Department, Bebek,
34342 İstanbul, Turkey
[2] Visiting Professor at Universitat Politècnica de Catalunya, TALP Research Center,
Barcelona, Spain
gungort@boun.edu.tr

Abstract. In this paper, we propose an approach that displays the results of a search engine query in a more effective way. Each web page retrieved by the search engine is subjected to a summarization process and the important content is extracted. The system consists of four stages. First, the hierarchical structures of documents are extracted. Then the lexical chains in documents are identified to build coherent summaries. The document structures and lexical chains are used to learn a summarization model by the next component. Finally, the summaries are formed and displayed to the user. Experiments on two datasets showed that the method significantly outperforms traditional search engines.

1   Introduction

A search engine is a web information retrieval system that, given a user query, outputs brief information about a number of documents that it thinks relevant to the query. By looking at the results displayed, the user tries to locate the relevant pages. The main drawback is the difficulty of determining the relevancy of a result from the short extracts. The work in [14] aims at increasing the relevancy by accompanying the text extracts by images. In addition to important text portions in a document, some images determined by segmenting the web page are also retrieved. Roussinov and Chen propose an approach that returns clusters of terms as query results [12]. A framework is proposed and its usefulness is tested with comprehensive experiments.

Related to summarization of web documents, White et al. describe a system that forms hierarchical summaries. The documents are analyzed using DOM (document object model) tree and their summaries are formed. A similar approach is used in [10] where a rule-based method is employed to obtain the document structures. Sentence weighting schemes were used for identification of important sentences [6,9,16]. In a study, the "table of content"-like structure of HTML documents was incorporated into summaries [1]. Yang and Wang developed fractal summarization method where generic summaries are created based on structures of documents [15]. These studies focus on general-purpose summaries, not tailored to particular user queries. There exist some studies on summarization of XML documents. In [13], query-based summarization is used for searching XML documents. In another study, a machine

R. Wilson et al. (Eds.): CAIP 2013, Part I, LNCS 8047, pp. 180–187, 2013.

learning approach was proposed based on document structure and content [2]. The concept of lexical chains was also used for document summarization. Berker and Güngör used lexical chaining as a feature in summarization [3]. In another work, a lexical chain formation algorithm based on relaxation labeling was proposed [5]. The sentences were selected according to some heuristics.

In this paper, we propose an approach that displays the search results as long extracts. We build a system that creates a hierarchical summary for each document retrieved. The cohesion in the summaries is maintained by using lexical chains. The experiments on standard query sets showed that the methods significantly outperform the traditional search engines and the lexical chain component is an important factor.

2   Proposed Summarization Framework

The architecture of the summarization framework is shown in Fig. 1. The system is formed of four main components. The first component is structure extractor where the document structure is analyzed and converted into a hierarchical representation. The lexical chain builder processes the document content using WordNet and forms the lexical chains. Model builder employs a learning algorithm to learn a summarization model by using the structures and lexical chains. Finally, the summarizer forms the summaries of the documents in a hierarchical representation using the learned model.

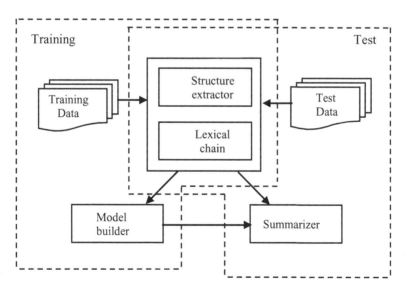

Fig. 1. System architecture

2.1   Extracting Structures of Documents

We simplify the problem of document structural processing by dividing the whole process into a number of consecutive steps. Fig. 2 shows an example web document that includes different types of parts. The first process is extracting the underlying content of the document. We parse a given web document and build its DOM tree using the Cobra open source toolkit [4]. We then remove the nodes that contain non-textual content by traversing the tree. After this process, we obtain a tree that includes only textual elements in the document and the hierarchical relations between them. The result of the simplification process for the document in Fig. 2 is shown in Fig. 3.

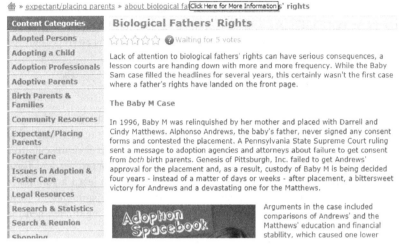

Fig. 2. An example web document

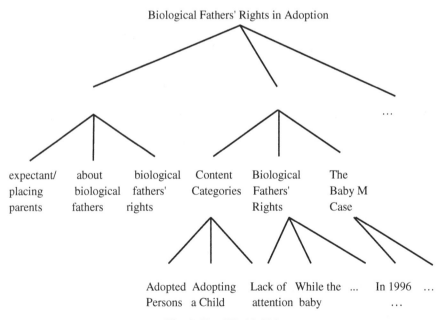

Fig. 3. Simplified DOM tree

The tree structure obtained does not correspond to the actual hierarchical structure. We identify the structure in three steps by using a learning approach. We consider the document structure as a hierarchy formed of sections where each section has a title (heading) and includes subsections. The first step is identification of headings which is a binary classification problem (heading or non-heading). For each textual unit in a document, we use the features shown in Table 1. The second step is determining the hierarchical relationships between the units. We first extract the parent-child relations between the heading units. This is a learning problem where the patterns of heading–subheading connections are learned. During training, we use the actual parent-child connections between headings as positive examples and other possible parent-child connections as negative examples. We use the same set of features shown in Table 1. In the last step, the non-heading units are attached to the heading units. For this purpose, we employ the same approach used for heading hierarchy.

Table 1. Features used in the machine learning algorithm

Heading	<h1> – <h6>
Emphasis	<b>, <i>, <u>, <em>, <strong>, <big>, <small>
Font	<font size>, <font color>, <font face>
Indentation	<center>
Anchor	<a>, <link>
Length	length of the unit (in characters)
Sentence count	number of sentences in the unit
Punctuation	punctuation mark at the end of the unit
Coordinate	x and y coordinates of the unit

3   Identification of Lexical Chains

A lexical chain is a set of terms that are related to each other in some context. We make use of lexical chains in addition to other criteria for summarization. We process all the documents and construct a set of lexical chains from the documents' contents. The idea is forming the longest and strongest chains so that the important relations between different parts of the documents can be captured. To determine the chains, we process the terms by using WordNet [11] to identify different term relations. We consider only the nouns. The documents are parsed using a part-of-speech tagger (http://alias-i.com/lingpipe). The relations we consider are the synonymy, hypernymy, and hyponymy relations. The words are processed and a word is placed in the lexical chain that holds the most number of words with a relation with the candidate word. After the lexical chains are formed, each chain is given a score as follows:

$$score(C) = \sum_{\substack{t_i, t_j \in C \\ i < j}} tscore(t_i, t_j), \ where \tag{1}$$

$$tscore(t_i, t_j) = \begin{cases} value_s \ , & if \ t_i \ and \ t_j \ are \ synonyms \\ value_h \ , & if \ t_i \ is \ a \ hypernym/hyponym \ of \ t_j \\ value_{hh} \ , & if \ t_i's \ and \ t_j's \ hypernyms/hyponyms \ are \ the \ same \\ 0 \ , & otherwise \end{cases}$$

The chain score is calculated by summing up the scores of all pairs of terms in the chain. The score of terms t_i and t_j depends on the relation between them. We use a fixed value for each relation type. As the chains are scored, we select only the strongest chains for summarization. A lexical chain is accepted as a strong chain if its score is more than two standard deviations from the average of lexical chain scores.

4   Learning Feature Weights and Summarization of Documents

In this work, we aim at producing summaries that take into account the structure of web pages and that will be shown to the user as a result of a search query. We use the criteria shown in Table 2 for determining the salience of sentences in a document. For each feature, the table gives the feature name, the formula used to calculate the feature value for a sentence S, and the explanation of the parameters in the formula. The score values of the features are normalized to the range [0,1]. We learn the weight of each feature using a genetic algorithm. As the feature weights are learned, the score of a sentence can be calculated by the equation

$$score(S) = w_l score_l + w_{tf} score_{tf} + w_h score_h + w_q score_q + w_{lc} score_{lc} \quad (2)$$

where w_i denotes the weight of the corresponding feature. Given a document as a result of a query, the sentences in the document are weighted according to the learned feature weights. The summary of the document is formed using a fixed summary size. While forming the summary, the hierarchical structure of the document is preserved and each section is represented by that number of sentences that is proportional to the importance of the section (total score of the sentences in the section).

5   Experiments and Results

To evaluate the proposed approach, we identified 30 queries from the TREC (Text Retrieval Conference) Robust Retrieval Tracks for the years 2004 and 2005. Each query was given to the Google search engine and the top 20 documents retrieved for each query were collected. Thus, we compiled a corpus formed of 600 documents. The corpus was divided into training and test sets with a 80%-20% ratio.

For structure extraction, we used SVM-Light which is an efficient algorithm for binary classification [8]. The results are given in Table 3. Accuracy is measured by dividing the number of correctly identified parent-child relationships to the total number of parent-child relationships. The first row of the table shows the performance of the proposed method. This figure is computed by considering each pair of nodes independent of the others. A stronger success criterion is counting a connection to a node as a success only if the node is in the correct position in the tree. The accuracy under this criterion is shown in the second row, which indicates that the method identified the correct path in most of the cases. The third result gives the accuracy when only the heading units are considered. That is, the last step of the method explained in Section 2 was not performed.

Table 2. Sentence features used in the summarization algorithm

Feature	Feature equation and parameter explanations
Sentence location	$$score_i(S) = \frac{maxs}{sdepth} * \frac{1}{spos}$$ *maxs*: maximum score that a sentence can get *sdepth*: section depth *spos*: location of the sentence within the section
Term frequency-inverse document frequency (tf-idf)	$$score_{tf}(S) = \sum_{t_i \in S} tf(t_i) * log\frac{dnum}{dnum_{t_i}}$$ *tf(t_i)*: term frequency of term t_i in the document *dnum*: number of documents in the corpus *dnum_{t_i}*: number of documents that t_i occurs
Heading	$$score_h(S) = \sum_{t_i \in S} hterm(t_i)$$ *hterm(t_i)*: 1 or 0 depending on whether t_i, respectively, occurs or does not occur in the corresponding heading.
Query	$$score_q(S) = \sum_{t_i \in S} qterm(t_i)$$ *qterm(t_i)*: 1 or 0 depending on whether t_i, respectively, occurs or does not occur in the query
Lexical chain	$$score_{lc}(S) = \sum_{\substack{t_i \in S, \\ t_i \in strong\ chains}} tf(t_i)$$ *tf(t_i)*: term frequency of t_i in the document

We use the document structures identified by the structure extractor component in the summarization process. As lexical chains are formed, we use genetic algorithm to learn the weights of the features. 50 documents selected randomly from the corpus were summarized manually using a fixed summary length. The feature weights were allowed to be in the range of 0-15. After training, we obtained the feature weights as w_l=5, w_{rf}=7, w_h=8, w_q=12, and w_{lc}=11. This shows that query terms are important in determining the summary sentences. The lexical chain concept is also an important tool for summarization. This is probably due to the combining effect of lexical chains in the sense that they build a connection between related parts of a document and it is preferable to include such parts in the summary to obtain coherent summaries.

Table 3. Results of structure extractor

	Accuracy
Document structure	76.47
Document structure (full path)	68.41
Sectional structure	78.11

As the feature weights were determined, we formed the summaries of all the documents in the corpus. For evaluation, instead of using a manually prepared summarization data set, we used the relevance prediction method [9] adapted to a search engine setting. In this method, a summary is compared with the original document. If the user evaluates both of them as relevant or irrelevant to the search query, then we consider the summary as a successful summary.

The evaluation was performed by two evaluators. For a query, the evaluator was given the query terms, a short description of the query, and a guide that shows which documents are relevant results. The evaluator is shown first the summaries of the 20 documents retrieved by the search engine for the query in random order and then the original documents in random order. The user is asked to mark each document or summary displayed as relevant or irrelevant for the query. The results are given in Table 4. We use precision, recall and f-measure for the evaluation as shown below:

$$precision = \frac{|D_{rel} \cap S_{rel}|}{|S_{rel}|} \tag{3}$$

$$recall = \frac{|D_{rel} \cap S_{rel}|}{|D_{rel}|} \tag{4}$$

$$F - measure = \frac{2*precision*recall}{precision+recall} \tag{5}$$

where D_{rel} and S_{rel} denote, respectively, the set of documents and the set of summaries relevant for the query.

The first row in the table shows the performance of the method, where we obtain about 80% success rate. The second row is the performance of the Google search engine. We see that the outputs produced by the proposed system are significantly better than the outputs produced by a traditional search engine. This is due to the fact that when the user is given a long summary that shows the document structure and the important contents of the document, it becomes easier to determine the relevancy of the corresponding page. Thus we can conclude that the proposed approach yields an effective way in displaying the query results for the users.

Table 4. Results of the summarization system

	precision	recall	F-measure
Proposed method	80.76	78.17	79.44
Search engine	63.57	58.24	60.79

6   Conclusions

In this paper, we built a framework for displaying web pages retrieved as a result of a search query. The system makes use of the document structures and the lexical chains extracted from the documents. The contents of web pages are summarized according to the learned model by preserving the sectional layouts of the pages. The experiments on two query datasets and a corpus of documents compiled from the results of the queries showed that document structures can be extracted with 76%

accuracy. In the summarization experiments, we obtained nearly 80% success rates. A comparison with a state-of-the-art search engine has shown that the method significantly outperforms the performance of current search engines.

As a future work, we plan to improve the summarizer component by including new features that can determine the saliency of sentences more effectively. Some semantic features that take into account dependencies between sentences can be used. The methods used in the proposed framework such as structural analysis and lexical chain identification can also be utilized in other related areas. Another future work can be making use of these methods in multi-document summarization or text categorization.

References

1. Alam, H., Kumar, A., Nakamura, M., Rahman, A.F.R., Tarnikova, Y., Wilcox, C.: Structured and Unstructured Document Summarization: Design of a Commercial Summarizer Using Lexical Chains. In: Proc. of the 7th International Conference on Document Analysis and Recognition, pp. 1147–1150 (2003)
2. Amini, M.R., Tombros, A., Usunier, N., Lalmas, M.: Learning Based Summarisation of XML Documents. Journal of Information Retrieval 10(3), 233–255 (2007)
3. Berker, M., Güngör, T.: Using Genetic Algorithms with Lexical Chains for Automatic Text Summarization. In: Proc. of the 4th International Conference on Agents and Artificial Intelligence (ICAART), Vilamoura, Portugal, pp. 595–600 (2012)
4. Cobra: Java HTML Renderer & Parser (2010), http://lobobrowser.org/cobra.jsp
5. Gonzàlez, E., Fuentes, M.: A New Lexical Chain Algorithm Used for Automatic Summarization. In: Proc. of the 12th International Congress of the Catalan Association of Artificial Intelligence (CCIA) (2009)
6. Guo, Y., Stylios, G.: An Intelligent Summarisation System Based on Cognitive Psychology. Information Sciences 174(1-2), 1–36 (2005)
7. Hobson, S.P., Dorr, B.J., Monz, C., Schwartz, R.: Task-based Evaluation of Text Summarisation Using Relevance Prediction. Information Processing and Management 43(6), 1482–1499 (2007)
8. Joachims, T.: Advances in Kernel Methods: Support Vector Learning. MIT (1999)
9. Otterbacher, J., Radev, D., Kareem, O.: News to Go: Hierarchical Text Summarisation for Mobile Devices. In: Proc. of 29th Annual ACM SIGIR Conference on Research and Development in Information Retrieval, pp. 589–596 (2006)
10. Pembe, F.C., Güngör, T.: Structure-Preserving and Query-Biased Document Summarisation for Web Searching. Online Information Review 33(4) (2009)
11. Princeton University, About WordNet (2010), http://wordnet.princeton.edu
12. Roussinov, D.G., Chen, H.: Information Navigation on the Web by Clustering and Summarizing Query Results. Information Processing and Management 37 (2001)
13. Szlavik, Z., Tombros, A., Lalmas, M.: Investigating the Use of Summarisation for Interactive XML Retrieval. In: Proc. of ACM Symposium on Applied Computing (2006)
14. Xue, X.-B., Zhou, Z.-H.: Improving Web Search Using Image Snippets. ACM Transactions on Internet Technology 8(4) (2008)
15. Yang, C.C., Wang, F.L.: Hierarchical Summarization of Large Documents. Journal of American Society for Information Science and Technology 59(6), 887–902 (2008)
16. Yeh, J.Y., Ke, H.R., Yang, W.P., Meng, I.H.: Text Summarisation Using a Trainable Summariser and Latent Semantic Analysis. Information Processing and Management 41(1), 75–95 (2005)

A New Pixel-Based Quality Measure for Segmentation Algorithms Integrating Precision, Recall and Specificity

Kannikar Intawong, Mihaela Scuturici, and Serge Miguet

Université de Lyon, CNRS
Université Lumière Lyon 2, LIRIS UMR5205
5, Av. Pierre Mendès-France, 69676, Bron, France
{kannikar.intawong,mihaela.scuturici,serge.miguet}@univ-lyon2.fr

Abstract. There are several approaches for performance evaluation of image processing algorithms in video-based surveillance systems: Precision/ Recall, Receiver Operator Characteristics (ROC), F-measure, Jaccard Coefficient, etc. These measures can be used to find good values for input parameters of image segmentation algorithms. Different measures can give different values of these parameters, considered as optimal by one criterion, but not by another. Most of the times, the measures are expressed as a compromise between two of the three aspects that are important for a quality assessment: Precision, Recall and Specificity. In this paper, we propose a new 3-dimensional measure (D_{prs}), which takes into account all of the three aspects. It can be considered as a 3D generalization of 2D ROC analysis and Precision/Recall curves. To estimate the impact of parameters on the quality of the segmentation, we study the behavior of this measure and compare it with several classical measures. Both objective and subjective evaluations confirm that our new measure allows to determine more stable parameters than classical criteria, and to obtain better segmentations of images.

Keywords: Segmentation, quality measures, F-measure, Jaccard Coefficient(JC), Percentage of Correct Classification(PCC).

1 Introduction

There is an increasing need for automated processing of massive amounts of visual information generated by video surveillance systems. The goal here is to verify that the automation of a number of tasks for image and video analysis is reliable, in order to reduce human supervision and to assist decision-making. The quantitative performance evaluation methods should make it possible to compare the results provided by different segmentation algorithms. The most commonly used methods in the literature attempt to find a compromise between Precision, Recall (also called Sensitivity) and Specificity. But most widely used representations only consider two of the three indicators: Precision/Recall space and ROC curves (which represent only the Sensitivity=Recall and Specificity).

R. Wilson et al. (Eds.): CAIP 2013, Part I, LNCS 8047, pp. 188–195, 2013.

In the same way, the F-measure is a single value quality measure based on Recall and Precision only, that completely ignores the Specificity of segmentation algorithms.

In the context of segmentation quality evaluation in video surveillance, we observed there are situations where all these measures disagree in the sense that they can give very different values of parameters. In this case, the question we asked ourselves and we tried to answer is "which measure behaves better than others and why"? We compared the optimal parameters given by several of these measures. We propose a segmentation quality measure seeking a compromise between the three indicators above. We show, in a case study, our measure gives more satisfactory results than the most commonly used measures (F-measure, Jaccard coefficient (JC), percentage of correct classification (PCC)).

The outline of the paper is as follows: section 2 presents related work in the fields of performance evaluation of pixel-based segmantation algorithms. Section 3 explains the methodology of evaluation and introduces a new measure which is shown to give more often than the others, better parameters for segmentation algorithms. Experimental results and conclusions are presented in section 4 and 5 respectively.

2   Related Work

Nascimento *et al.* compare in [1] the performance of different segmentation algorithms. They investigate three different approaches: pixel-based, template-based and object-based performance metrics. Here we focus on pixel-based evaluation metrics which compare a classic binary detection with a ground truth. Three measures for quantifying the performances of a classifier are classically used in the literature [2,3]. The most widely used measure is the Percentage of Correct Classification (PCC). PCC does not allow a good quality estimation when the classes are unbalanced (e.g.the scenes where the background represents at least 95% of pixels). This problem is solved by the Jaccard Coefficient (JC) which only considers the foreground. This measure eliminates the consequence of the big volume of true negatives but it does not take into account a bad background detection. Another measure, the Yule Coefficient (YC), tries to avoid the drawbacks of these measures by giving the same weight to the two classes, but it cannot be used for images containing only background.

Several authors have shown the benefit of using two dimensions to describe the behavior of their algorithms: in ROC curves [4], the True Positive Rate (TPR) is plotted against the false positive rate (FPR). For instance, in the case of video surveillance applications, the user can choose the best compromise between probability of miss detections and rate of false alarms. However, in the case of unbalanced classes, ROC curves present weaknesses. In such cases, [5,6] show the advantages of Precision/Recall curves to analyze the behavior of segmentation algorithms. Recall is equal to the TPR used in the ROC curves, but Precision is different from FPR. Two different algorithms might present the same Precision/Recall graph, because they have the same capacity to detect the foreground, but one of them can be less performant than the other if the background is not well detected. In this case, the two algorithms will differ in terms of Specificity. After noting that the TPR dimension used in ROC curves is equal to the Recall dimension of Precision/Recall graphs, we propose to build a quality measure that takes into account the three dimensions involved in the previous two approaches. The 3D generalizarion of ROC curves had already been proposed by [7]. They use a soft decision threshold parameter as a third dimension which helps to take the final binary decision. This is different of our approach but it does not take into account the true negative rate, therefore, in our context of videosurveillance applications, it has the same drawbacks as standard ROC analysis.

3   Evaluation Measure

Our goal is to find the best way to measure the quality of a segmentation algorithm having one or more parameters and to find the best values for these parameters. Most of the authors compare the results of their algorithms to a ground truth which is considered as the ideal segmentation. This ground truth can be obtained from manual segmentations done by human users, but this can be very time-consuming, especially for large video sequences. Alternatively, we can use synthetic sequences where the ground truth is known, since the moving objects are generated by a computer algorithm. This is the method we have used in this paper. The results of any segmentation algorithms vary as a function of the values of different parameters. The best parameters values minimize a distance or maximize the similarity between the segmentation and the ground truth. Several criteria for evaluating this proximity (F-measure, JC, PCC) behave differently, leading to different choices of the best value of the algorithm's parameters.

We consider the segmentation of images divided into two classes: foreground and background. For a given image in a video sequence, we compare the results of a binary segmentation S with the binary image of the ground truth T. A pixel is represented in white if it is part of a moving object (foreground), and black when it belongs to the background. A white pixel in S is called a positive. If it is also white in T, then it is a true positive (TP), whereas if it is black in T, it is a false positive (FP). Symmetrically, a black pixel in S is a negative. If it is also black in T, it is a true negative (TN), while if it is white in T, it is a false negative (FN). We can then define the Precision (PR), Recall (RE) and Specificity (SP) for each image:

$$PR = TP/(TP + FP) \tag{1}$$

$$RE = TP/(TP + FN) \tag{2}$$

$$SP = TN/(TN + FP) \tag{3}$$

A perfect segmentation algorithm calculates an image S identical to the ground truth T. Such an algorithm will give values of Precision, Recall and Specificity equal to 1. The F-measure is the harmonic mean of Precision and Recall.

$$F = 2((PR * RE)/(PR + RE)) \tag{4}$$

Other scalar values as the Percentage of Correct Classification (PCC) or the Jaccard coefficient (JC) can also be defined.

$$PCC = (TP + TN)/(TP + FN + FP + TN) \tag{5}$$

$$JC = TP/(TP + FP + FN) \tag{6}$$

We propose to measure the quality of a segmentation as an Euclidean distance called D_{prs} in the space of the indicators, between the point (PR, RE, SP) and the ideal point $(1, 1, 1)$.

$$D_{prs} = \sqrt{(1 - PR)^2 + (1 - RE)^2 + (1 - SP)^2} \tag{7}$$

This can be seen as a 3D generalization of the use of 2D ROC curves or Precision/Recall diagrams for optimal parameters determination.

4   Experimental Results

In order to evaluate our segmentation quality measure, we segment several videos of the synthetic Visage database [12]. We apply several morphological operations in order to improve the segmentation results and compare the behavior of several quality measures.

In order to segment moving objets we use the hierarchical background modeling technique introduced by [8]. It is considered as one of the best background modeling algorithms in the comparative study proposed by [9]. This method uses coarse level contrast descriptors introduced by [11] whose evolution is represented by mixtures of gaussians. This coarse-level representation is then combined with the classical pixel-based mixture of gaussians [10]. We can thus identify the foreground objects at coarse level, then detail shapes of foreground objects at pixel level. Figure 1 presents some results of background subtraction algorithms.

Object detection by background modeling algorithms, used without postprocessing, very often let appear isolated pixels in the background. They are considered as foreground objects. On the contrary, holes in objects are classified as background. The method most commonly used to overcome these drawbacks is to apply mathematical morphology (erosion, dilation, opening, closing, ...). In our experiments we vary the number of erosions (p) and dilations (q) applied as post-processing of the segmentation. We search the parameter sets giving the best possible values for each of the segmentation quality measures. In many cases, the optimal parameters are significantly different from one measurement to another, and do not coincide with the optimal (subjective) settings provided by a human user.

We calculate the following measures : F-measure, JC, PCC and D_{prs} for all images in a sequence, and for each set of parameters. We evaluate the mathematical morphology (dilations followed by erosions) between $(0, 0)$ and $(10, 10)$

on 10 synthetic videos composed of 1500 frames each (different scenes, sunny or rainy weather, noisy camera). We select the optimal parameters for each frame. F, PCC and JC are quality measures, whose value should be maximized. Instead, D_{prs} is a distance from the ideal situation and its value has to be minimized. It is interesting to note that the criteria may conclude at different optimal sets of parameters. We show in Table 1 and Table 2 a set of experiments for which the different criteria find very different optimal parameters. In Table 1, D_{prs} and PCC exhibit an optimal parameter set equal to (4, 4) whereas F and JC suggest that (10, 10) give better results. In Table 2, F, JC and D_{prs} coincide for choosing (4, 4) as optimal parameter values where PCC finds (1, 1) as being better. In order to illustrate the contribution of Table 2, the graph curves are presented in Figure 3 and Figure 4 and the segmentation results which use optimal parameters determined by the F-measure, JC, PCC and D_{prs} are presented in Figure 5. This first series of experiments show that the optimal parameter selected by D_{prs} are closer to those determined by users.

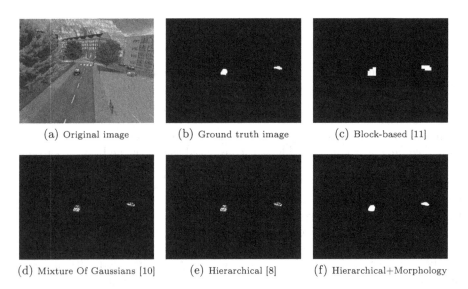

(a) Original image   (b) Ground truth image   (c) Block-based [11]

(d) Mixture Of Gaussians [10]   (e) Hierarchical [8]   (f) Hierarchical+Morphology

Fig. 1. Segmentation results of different background modeling algorithms. Block-based method result is not accurate enough (c). Mixture of Gaussians algorithm is not as reliable as the hierarchical method when illumination/weather conditions change (d), there are plenty of false positives. The background model we use (e) is the intersection of (c) and (d). (f) presents the segmentation with morphological post-treatement.

In order to validate this evaluation, the solution was to refer to what a human user considers as the best solution by a voting system. A website has been developed for presenting the four segmented images using the best parameters chosen by the four compared measures (PCC, F, JC and D_{prs}) (the frames for which the four measures agree are discarded). In these first series of experiments, the new

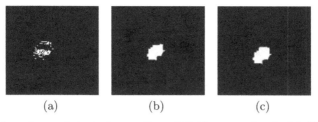

(a)   (b)   (c)

Fig. 2. Number of morphological operations (dilations, erosions): (a) (0, 0) (b) (4,4) (c) (10,10)

Table 1. Comparison of different measures (sunny weather). PCC and D_{prs} give the optimal values corresponding to the (4, 4) pair. Simultaneously, F-measure and JC give the optimal values corresponding to the (10, 10) pair.

Dilation	Erosion	TPR	FPR	Recall	Precision	Standard Measures F measure	PCC	JC	New Measure D_{prs}
0	0	0.3614	0.00042	0.3614	0.6836	0.3003	0.9967	0.2946	0.9554
1	1	0.3818	0.00073	0.3818	0.6738	0.4023	0.9970	0.3881	0.9451
2	2	0.4057	0.00121	0.4057	0.66635	0.4765	0.9971	0.4007	0.9320
3	3	0.4806	0.00124	0.4806	0.6522	0.5064	0.9972	0.4233	0.8684
4	4	0.5176	0.00145	0.5176	0.6497	0.5267	0.9972	0.4684	0.8341
5	5	0.5360	0.00206	0.5360	0.6278	0.5561	0.9971	0.4899	0.8382
6	6	0.5587	0.00242	0.5587	0.5979	0.5668	0.9969	0.5028	0.8458
7	7	0.5703	0.00261	0.5703	0.5858	0.5722	0.9965	0.5089	0.8465
8	8	0.5891	0.00313	0.5891	0.5723	0.5754	0.9961	0.5132	0.8417
9	9	0.5911	0.00362	0.5911	0.5709	0.5879	0.9957	0.5161	0.8416
10	10	0.6018	0.00413	0.3614	0.5612	0.5980	0.9952	0.5165	0.8411

Table 2. Comparison of different measures (noisy camera). F-measure, JC and D_{prs} give the optimal values corresponding to the (3, 3) pair, while only PCC gives the optimal values corresponding to the (1, 1) pair.

Dilation	Erosion	TPR	FPR	Recall	Precision	Standard Measures F measure	PCC	JC	New Measure D_{prs}
0	0	0.3964	0.0005	0.3964	0.6396	0.7493	0.9973	0.3477	0.9645
1	1	0.6096	0.0009	0.6096	0.6500	0.6198	0.9989	0.5134	0.7413
2	2	0.7010	0.0013	0.7010	0.6350	0.6584	0.9987	0.5642	0.6654
3	3	0.7345	0.0017	0.7345	0.6155	0.6615	0.9985	0.5684	0.6517
4	4	0.7500	0.0020	0.7500	0.5986	0.6566	0.9982	0.5623	0.6535
5	5	0.7577	0.0024	0.7577	0.5862	0.6516	0.9979	0.5561	0.6586
6	6	0.7632	0.0029	0.7632	0.5724	0.6436	0.9975	0.5466	0.6674
7	7	0.7678	0.0034	0.7678	0.5602	0.6362	0.9970	0.5376	0.6754
8	8	0.7702	0.0040	0.7702	0.5469	0.6269	0.9965	0.5267	0.6869
9	9	0.7731	0.0046	0.7731	0.5369	0.6204	0.9959	0.5185	0.6945
10	10	0.7744	0.0052	0.7744	0.5296	0.6151	0.9954	0.5125	0.7012

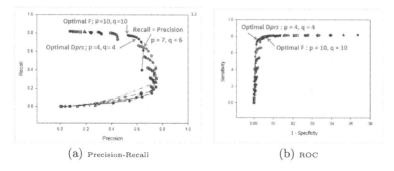

(a) Precision-Recall   (b) ROC

Fig. 3. Conventional 2D representations and graphical interpresentation of optimal parameter values for different measures

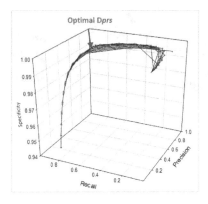

Fig. 4. Precision, Recall, Specificity space

measure appears to give results that are the closest to the human evaluation: D_{prs} collects 37% of votes, PCC receives 29%, and F-measure and JC have a comparable number of votes with only 17%.

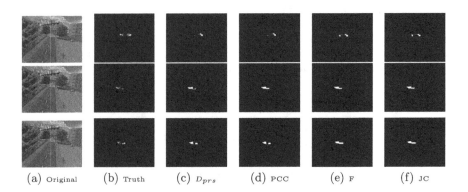

(a) Original   (b) Truth   (c) D_{prs} (d) PCC   (e) F   (f) JC

Fig. 5. Example of optimal segmentations according to different criteria, presented to user for subjective evaluation

5   Conclusions

In this paper we have presented a new measure (D_{prs}) for qualitative evaluation of the segmentation algorithms in complex video surveillance environments. It is an extension of the traditional Precision-Recall methodology and represents a compromise between three indicators: Recall, Precision and Specificity. The third dimension - Specificity - takes into account the correct detection of the background. This measure was compared with other performance measures (F-measure, PCC and JC). It is important to note that each criterion may conclude at different optimal sets of parameters. Experiments show that our measure

D_{prs} seems to give optimal parameters close to those determined by subjective evaluations. Additional experiments should be done on larger scale data, as well as on real data.

References

1. Nascimento, J., Marques, J.: Performance evaluation of object detection algorithms for video surveillance. IEEE Transactions on Multimedia 8, 761–777 (2006)
2. Rosin, P.L., Ioannidis, E.: Evaluattion of Global Image Thresholding for Change Detection. Pattern Recognition Letter 24, 345–2356 (2003)
3. Elhabian, S., El-Sayed, K.: Moving Object Detection in Spatial Domain using Background Removal Techniques - State-of-Art. Recent Patents on Computer Science 1, 32–54 (2008)
4. Gao, X., Boult, T.E., Coetzee, F., Ramesh, V.: Error analysis of background adaptation. In: Computer Vision and Pattern Recognition, vol. 1, pp. 503–510 (2000)
5. Davis, J., Burnside, E., Dutra, I., Page, D., Ramakrishnan, R., Santos Costa, V., Shavlik, J.: View learning for statistical relational learning: With an application to mammography. In: Proceeding of the 19th International Joint Conference on Artificial Intelligence, pp. 677–683 (2005)
6. Davis, J., Goadrich, M.: The Relationship between Precision-Recall and ROC Curves. In: International Conference on Machine Learning, pp. 233–240 (2006)
7. Wang, S., Chang, C.I., Yang, S.C., Hsu, G.C., Hsu, H.H., Chung, P.C., Guo, S.M., Lee, S.K.: 3D ROC Analysis for Medical Imaging Diagnosis. Engineering in Medicine and Biology Society, 7545–7548 (2005)
8. Chen, Y.T., Chen, C.S., Huang, C.R., Hung, Y.P.: Efficient hierarchical method for background subtraction. Pattern Recognition, 2706–2715 (2007)
9. Dhome, Y., Tronson, N., Vacavant, A.: A Benchmark for Background Subtraction Algorithms in Monocular Vision: A Comparative Study. Image Processing Theory Tools and Applications (IPTA), 7–10 (2010)
10. Stauffer, C., Grimson, W.E.L.: Adaptive background mixture models for real-time tracking. In: IEEE Conference on Computer Vision and Pattern Recognition, pp. 246–252 (1999)
11. Huang, C.R., Chen, C.S., Chung, P.C.: Contrast context histogram A discriminating local descriptor for image matching. In: Proceedings of IEEE International Conference on Pattern Recognition, vol. 4, pp. 53–56 (2006)
12. Chateau, T.: Visage Challenge: Video-surveillance Intelligente: Systemes et AlGorithmES (2012), http://visage.univ-bpclermont.fr/?q=node/2

A Novel Border Identification Algorithm Based on an "Anti-Bayesian" Paradigm[*]

Anu Thomas and B. John Oommen[**]

School of Computer Science, Carleton University, Ottawa, Canada: K1S 5B6

Abstract. Border Identification (BI) algorithms, a subset of Prototype Reduction Schemes (PRS) aim to reduce the number of training vectors so that the reduced set (the border set) contains only those patterns which lie near the border of the classes, and have sufficient information to perform a meaningful classification. However, one can see that the true border patterns ("near" border) are not able to perform the task independently as they are not able to always distinguish the testing samples. Thus, researchers have worked on this issue so as to find a way to strengthen the "border" set. A recent development in this field tries to add more border patterns, i.e., the "far" borders, to the border set, and this process continues until it reaches a stage at which the classification accuracy no longer increases. In this case, the cardinality of the border set is relatively high. In this paper, we aim to design a novel BI algorithm based on a new definition for the term "border". We opt to select the patterns which lie at the border of the alternate class as the border patterns. Thus, those patterns which are neither on the true discriminant nor too close to the central position of the distributions, are added to the "border" set. The border patterns, which are *very small* in number (for example, five from both classes), selected in this manner, have the potential to perform a classification which is comparable to that obtained by well-known traditional classifiers like the SVM, and very close to the optimal Bayes' bound.

1 Introduction

The objective of a PRS is to reduce the cardinality of the training set to be as small as possible by selecting some training patterns based on various criteria, as long as the reduction does not significantly affect the performance. Thus, instead of considering all the training patterns for the classification, a subset of the whole set is selected based on certain criteria. The learning (or training) is then performed on this *reduced* training set, which is also called the "Reference" set. This Reference set not only contains the patterns which are closer to the true discriminant's boundary, but also the patterns from the other regions of the space that can adequately represent the entire training set.

---

[*] The authors are grateful for the partial support provided by NSERC, the Natural Sciences and Engineering Research Council of Canada.

[**] *Chancellor's Professor* ; *Fellow: IEEE* and *Fellow: IAPR*. This author is also an *Adjunct Professor* with the University of Agder in Grimstad, Norway.

R. Wilson et al. (Eds.): CAIP 2013, Part I, LNCS 8047, pp. 196–203, 2013.

Border Identification (BI) algorithms, which are a subset of PRSs, work with a Reference set which only contains "border" points. Specializing this criterion, the current-day BI algorithms, designed by Duch [1], Foody [2,3], and Li *et al.* [4], attempt to select a Reference set which contains border patterns derived, in turn, from the set of training patterns. Observe that, in effect, these algorithms also yield reduced training sets. Once the Reference set is obtained, all of these traditional methods perform the classification by invoking some sort of classifier like the SVM, neural networks etc. As opposed to the latter, we are interested in determining border patterns which, in some sense, are neither closer to the true optimal classifier nor to the means, and which can thus better classify the entire training set. Contrary to a Bayesian intuition, these border patterns have the ability to accurately classify the testing patterns, as we shall presently demonstrate. Our method is a combination of NN computations and (Mahalanobis) *multi*-dimensional[1] distance computations which yield the border points that are subsequently used for the purpose of classification. The characterizing component of our algorithm, referred to as ABBI, is that classification can be done by processing the obtained border points by themselves without invoking, for example, a subsequent SVM phase.

How then can one determine the border points themselves? This, indeed, depends on the model of computation - for example, whether we are working within the parametric or non-parametric model. The current paper deals with the former model, where the information about the classes is crystallized in the class-conditional *distributions* and their respective parameters, where the training samples are used to estimate the *parameters* of these models. In this paper, we have shown how the border points can be obtained by utilizing the information gleaned from the estimated distributions. Observe that with regard to classification and testing, all of these computations can be considered to be of a "pre-processing" nature, and so the final scheme would merely be of a Nearest Neighbor(NN)-sort. The details of how this is achieved is described in the paper.

2   A Novel Two-Class "Anti-Bayesian" BI Scheme

The Formal Algorithm. The problem of determining the border points for the parametric model of computation can be solved for fairly complex scenarios. When one examines the existing BI schemes, he observes that the information that has been utilized to procure the border patterns is primarily (and indeed, essentially) distance-based. In other words, the distances between the patterns are evaluated independently, and the border patterns are obtained based on such distances. The patterns obtained in this manner are considered as the new training set, which reduces these BI schemes to be special types of PRSs, but with the border patterns being the Reference set. However, as these border patterns

---

[1] We also have some initial results in which the distance and optimizations are done using lower-dimensional projections, the results of which are subsequently fused using an appropriate fusion technique.

are only the "Near" ones, they do not possess sufficient information to train an efficient classifier. We shall now rectify this.

We now mention a second major handicap associated with the traditional BI schemes. Once they have computed the border points associated with the specific classes, the traditional schemes operate by determining a "classifier" based on the new set. In other words, they have to determine a classifying *boundary* (linear, quadratic or SVM-based) to achieve this classification. As the reader will observe, in our work, we attempt to circumvent this entire phase. Indeed, in our proposed strategy, we merely achieve the classification using the final *small* subset of border points – which entails a significant reduction in computation.

The reader should also observe that this final decision would involve NN-like computations with a *few* points. The intriguing feature of these few points is that they lie close to the boundary and not to the mean, implying an "anti-Bayesian" philosophy [5,6,7].

In order to obtain the border patterns of the distributions ω_1 and ω_2 in an "anti-Bayesian" approach, we make use of the axiom that the patterns that have nearest neighbors from *other* classes *along* with the patterns of the same class fall into a common region - which is, by definition, the overlapped region.

The proposed algorithm has 4 parameters, namely, J, J_1, J_2 and K. First of all, J denotes the number of border points that have to be selected from each class. We understand that in the process of selecting the border points, the training set must be "examined" so as to ignore the patterns which are not relevant for the classification. As this decision is taken based on the border points in and of themselves, we conclude that the patterns which are in the overlapping region are not able to provide an accurate decision, and so these points have to be ignored. Thus, for any X, those patterns with J_2 or more NNs out of the J_1 NNs, which are not from the same class as X, are ignored.

To be more specific, in order to eliminate the overlapping points, we first determine J_1-NNs of every pattern X. If J_2 or more of these NN patterns are from the same class, this pattern X is added to the new training set. Once this step is achieved, we are left with the training points which are not overlapping with any other classes. Thereafter, we evaluate the (Mahalanobis) distance^2(MD) of every pattern of the new training set with respect to the *mean* of both the classes. Both of these phases distinguish our particular strategy. The patterns which are almost equidistant from both the classes, and which are not determined to be overlapping with respect to the other classes, are added to the Border set.

The process of determining the (Mahalanobis) distances with respect to both the classes, is repeated for all the patterns of the new training set, and a decision is made for each pattern based on the difference between these distances.

The two-dimensional view of this philosophy is depicted in Figures 1a - 1c. The border patterns obtained by applying this method are also given in the figure, where the border patterns of class ω_1 are specified by rectangles, and those of class ω_2 are specified by circles. We now make the following observations:

---

^{2} Any well-defined norm, appropriate for the data distribution, can be used to quantify this distance.

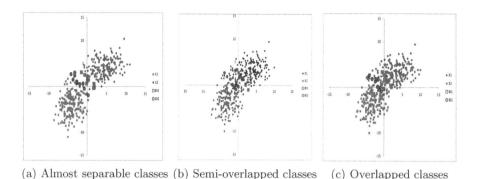

(a) Almost separable classes (b) Semi-overlapped classes   (c) Overlapped classes

Fig. 1. Border patterns for separable and overlapped classes

1. If we examine Figure 1a, we can see that the border patterns that are specified by rectangles and circles are precisely those that lie at the true borders of the classes.
2. However, if the classes are semi-overlapped, then the "more interior" symmetric percentiles, such as the $\langle \frac{2}{3}, \frac{1}{3} \rangle$ can perform a near-optimal classification. This can be seen in Figure 1b. The patterns in this figure have more overlap (the $BD = 1.69$), and the border points chosen are the ones which lie just outside the overlapping region.
3. The same argument is valid for Figure 1c. In the OS-based classification, we have seen that if the classes have a large overlap as in Figure 1c (in this case, $MD = 0.78$), the border patterns again lie outside the overlapped region.

The algorithm for obtaining the border patterns, ABBI, is formally given in Algorithm 1.

Contrary to the traditional BI algorithms, ABBI requires only a *small* number of border patterns for the classification. For example, consider the Breast Cancer data set which contains 699 patterns. A traditional BI algorithms will obtain a border set of around 150 patterns for this data set. Furthermore, once these methods have obtained the border points, they will have to generate a classifier for the new reduced set to achieve the classification. As opposed to this, our method requires only 20 border patterns, and the classification is based on the *five* NN border patterns of the testing pattern.

3   Experimental Results

The proposed method ABBI has been tested on various data sets that include artificial and real-life data sets obtained from the UCI repository [8]. ABBI has also been compared with other well-known methods which include the NB, SVM, and the kNN. In order to obtain the results, ABBI algorithm was executed 50 times with the 10-fold cross validation scheme.

Algorithm 1. ABBI(ω_1, ω_2)

Input:

Data from two classes; ω_1, ω_2, whose means are $\mathbf{M}_1$ and $\mathbf{M}_2$ respectively.
Parameters: J_1, J, J_2, K: Small numbers

Assumption:

Dist computes the distance between two vectors.
DistDiff computes the difference in distances obtained with respect to μ_1 and μ_2

Notation:

NTR_1 and NTR_2 are the new training sets which do not contain points in the overlapped region.

Output:

The classification based only on the Border points

Method:
1: $NTR_1 \leftarrow \emptyset$
2: $NTR_2 \leftarrow \emptyset$
3: Divide points of ω_1 into training and testing sets, TRP_1 and T_1 respectively
4: Divide points of ω_2 into training and testing sets, TRP_2 and T_2 respectively
5: **for all** $X \in TRP_1$ **do**
6:      Compute J_1 NNs of X
7:      If J_2 or more NNs are from class ω_1, $NTR_1 \leftarrow NTR_1 \cup X$
8: **end for**
9: **for all** $X \in TRP_2$ **do**
10:      Compute J_1 NNs of X
11:      If J_2 or more NNs are from class ω_2, $NTR_2 \leftarrow NTR_2 \cup X$
12: **end for**
13: **for all** $X \in NTR_1$ **do**
14:      Dist(X, M_1)
15:      Dist(X, M_2)
16: **end for**
17: **for all** $X \in NTR_2$ **do**
18:      Dist(X, M_1)
19:      Dist(X, M_2)
20: **end for**
21: **for all** $X \in NTR_1$ **do**
22:      DistDiff(X)
23: **end for**
24: **for all** $X \in NTR_2$ **do**
25:      DistDiff(X)
26: **end for**
27: Add J points with minimum DistDiff from NTR_1 and NTR_2 to BI
28: Classify testing points using a K-NN based on the points in BI.

End Algorithm

Artificial Data Sets: For a *prima facie* testing of artificial data, we generated two classes that obeyed Gaussian distributions. To do this, we made use of a Uniform $[0, 1]$ random variable generator to generate data values that follow a Gaussian distribution. The expression $\mathbf{z} = \sqrt{-2ln(u_1)}\ cos(2\pi u_2)$ is known to yield data values that follow $N(0, 1)$ [9]. Thereafter, by using the technique described in [10], one can generate Gaussian random vectors which possess any arbitrary mean and covariance matrix. In our experiments, since this is just for a *prima facie* case, we opted to perform experiments for two-dimensional and three-dimensional data sets. The respective means of the classes were $[\mu_{11}, \mu_{12}]^T$ and $[\mu_{21}, \mu_{22}]^T$ for the two-dimensional data, and $[\mu_{11}, \mu_{12}, \mu_{13}]^T$ and $[\mu_{21}, \mu_{22}, \mu_{23}]^T$

for the three-dimensional data. Further, the corresponding covariance matrices of the two-dimensional classes had the forms:

$$\Sigma_1 = \begin{bmatrix} a^2 & \alpha ab \\ \alpha ab & b^2 \end{bmatrix}, \qquad \Sigma_2 = \begin{bmatrix} b^2 & \alpha ab \\ \alpha ab & a^2 \end{bmatrix}$$

The covariance matrices for the three-dimensional classes had the forms:

$$\Sigma_1 = \begin{bmatrix} a^2 & 0 & \alpha ab \\ 0 & 1 & 0 \\ \alpha ab & 0 & b^2 \end{bmatrix}, \qquad \Sigma_1 = \begin{bmatrix} b^2 & 0 & \alpha ab \\ 0 & 1 & 0 \\ \alpha ab & 0 & a^2 \end{bmatrix}$$

With regard to the cardinality of the data set, each of the classes had 200 instances in the corresponding two and three-dimensional space. For the distance computations, we used the MD, which is based on the means and the covariance matrices Σ_1 and Σ_2. It is based on the correlations between the variables using which different patterns can be identified and analyzed.

In order to not make the chapter too cumbersome, the *specific* details of the values of the μ's, a, b and α (for the means and covariances), are not included here[3]. However, what is crucial to guarantee "repeatability", are the respective values of the BD for each experimental setting, and *these* are clearly specified in every single row.

Experimental Results: Artificial Data Sets. The experimental results obtained for two dimensional artificial data sets can be seen in Table 1 and those for three dimensional artificial data sets can be seen in Table 2.

Table 1. Results of the classification of two dimensional artificial data sets

BD	1NN	3NN	SVM	ABBI
4.52	100	100	100	100
2.94	99.10	99.20	99.25	99.25
1.69	95.30	96.50	97.00	96.40
0.78	84.15	86.05	88.25	88.0
0.45	73.55	75.45	81.50	80.55

Table 2. Results of the classification of three dimensional artificial data sets

Class Nature	Average BD	1NN	3NN	SVM	ABBI
Separated	6.08	100	100	100	100
Semi-overlapped	2.64	96.92	97.67	97.81	95.67
Overlapped	2.42	94.50	95.50	96.50	94.72
Highly overlapped	1.43	83.50	87.23	88.79	85.20

By examining Tables 1 and 2, one can see that ABBI can achieve remarkable classification when compared to that attained by the benchmark classifiers. For

---

[3] These values can be included if requested by the Referees.

example, if we consider the case where the classes are separated by a BD of 1.66 in Table 1, ABBI can achieve a classification accuracy of 95.38%, while the 3NN achieves 97.25%. This is quite fascinating when we consider the fact the ABBI performs the classification based *only 5 samples* from the selected 10 samples from each class, whereas the classification of NN involves the entire training set.

Real-life Data Sets: The data sets [8] used in this study have two classes, and the number of attributes varies from four up to thirty two. The data sets are described in Table 3.

Table 3. The Real-life data sets used in our experiments

Data set	No. Instances	No. Attributes	No. Classes	Attribute Type
WOBC	699	9	2	Integer
WDBC	569	32	2	Real
Diabetes	768	8	2	Integer, Real
Hepatitis	155	19	2	Categorical, Integer, Real
Iris	150	4	3	Real
Statlog (Heart)	270	13	2	Categorical, Real
Statlog (Australian Credit)	690	14	2	Categorical, Integer, Real
Vote	435	16	2	Categorical, Integer

Experimental Results: Real-life Data Sets. The results obtained for the ABBI algorithm are tabulated in Table 4.

Table 4. Classification of Real Data

Data set	kNN	NB	SVM	ABBI
WOBC	96.60	96.40	95.99	95.80
WDBC	96.66	92.97	97.71	92.39
Diabetes	75.26	73.1098	76.70	72.30
Hepatitis	82.58	83.19	82.51	80.27
Iris	95.13	96.00	96.67	94.53
Statlog (Australian Credit)	85.90	87.40	85.51	78.85
Statlog (Heart)	84.40	83.00	85.60	82.50
Vote	94.2857	90.23	94.33	90.76

From the table of results, one can see that the proposed algorithm achieves a comparable classification when compared to the other traditional classifiers, which is particularly impressive because only a very few samples are involved in the process. For example, for the WOBC data set, we can see that the new approach yielded a accuracy of 95.80% which should be compared to the accuracies of the SVM (95.99%), NB (96.40%) and the kNN (96.60%). Similarly, for the Iris data set, ABBI can achieve an accuracy of 94.53%, which is again comparable to the performance of SVM (96.67%), NB (96.00%), and NN (95.13%).

4   Conclusions

The objective of BI algorithms is to reduce the number of training vectors by selecting the patterns that are close to the class boundaries. However, the patterns that are on the exact border of the classes ("near" borders) are not sufficient to perform a classification which is comparable to that obtained based on the centrally located patterns. In order to resolve this issue, researchers have tried to add more patterns ("far" borders) to the "border" set so as to boost the quality of the resultant border set. Thus, the cardinality of the resultant border set can be relatively high. After obtaining such a large border set, a classifier has to be generated for this set, to perform a classification.

In this paper, we have proposed a novel BI algorithm which involves the border patterns selected with respect to a new definition of the term "border". In line with the newly proposed OS-based anti-Bayesian classifiers [5,6,7], we created the "border" set by selecting those patterns which are close to the true border of the *alternate* class. The classification is achieved with regard to *these* border patterns alone, and the size of this set is very small, in some cases, as small as five from each class. The resultant accuracy is comparable to that attained by other well-established classifiers. The superiority of this method over other BI schemes is that it yields a relatively small border set, and as the classification is based on the border patterns themselves , it is computationally inexpensive.

References

1. Duch, W.: Similarity Based Methods: A General Framework for Classification, Approximation and Association. Control and Cybernetics 29(4), 937–968 (2000)
2. Foody, G.M.: Issues in Training Set Selection and Refinement for Classification by a Feedforward Neural Network. In: Proceedings of IEEE International Geoscience and Remote Sensing Symposium, pp. 409–411 (1998)
3. Foody, G.M.: The Significance of Border Training Patterns in Classification by a Feedforward Neural Network using Back Propopation Learning. International Journal of Remote Sensing 20(18), 3549–3562 (1999)
4. Li, G., Japkowicz, N., Stocki, T.J., Ungar, R.K.: Full Border Identification for Reduction of Training Sets. In: Bergler, S. (ed.) Canadian AI 2008. LNCS (LNAI), vol. 5032, pp. 203–215. Springer, Heidelberg (2008)
5. Oommen, B.J., Thomas, A.: Optimal Order Statistics-based "Anti-Bayesian" Parametric Pattern Classification for the Exponential Family. Pattern Recognition (accepted for publication, 2013)
6. Thomas, A., Oommen, B.J.: Order Statistics-based Parametric Classification for Multi-dimensional Distributions (submitted for publication, 2013)
7. Thomas, A., Oommen, B.J.: The Fundamental Theory of Optimal "Anti-Bayesian" Parametric Pattern Classification Using Order Statistics Criteria. Pattern Recognition 46, 376–388 (2013)
8. Frank, A., Asuncion, A.: UCI Machine Learning Repository (2010), http://archive.ics.uci.edu/ml (April 18, 2013)
9. Devroye, L.: Non-Uniform Random Variate Generation. Springer, New York (1986)
10. Fukunaga, K.: Introduction to Statistical Pattern Recognition, 2nd edn. Academic Press, San Diego (1990)

Assessing the Effect of Crossing Databases on Global and Local Approaches for Face Gender Classification

Yasmina Andreu Cabedo, Ramón A. Mollineda Cárdenas,
and Pedro García-Sevilla

Dep. de Lenguajes y Sistemas Informáticos, Universidad Jaume I
{yandreu, mollined, pgarcia}@uji.es

Abstract. This paper presents a comprehensive statistical study of the suitability of global and local approaches for face gender classification from frontal non-occluded faces. A realistic scenario is simulated with cross-database experiments where acquisition and demographic conditions considerably vary between training and test images. The performances of three classifiers (1-NN, PCA+LDA and SVM) using two types of features (grey levels and PCA) are compared for the two approaches. Supported by three statistical tests, the main conclusion extracted from the experiments is that if training and test faces are acquired under different conditions from diverse populations, no significant differences exist between global and local solutions. However, global methods outperform local models when training and test sets contain only images of the same database.

Keywords: Face Gender Classification, Global/Local Representations, Cross-database Experiments, Statistical Study.

1 Introduction

Automated face analysis has been extensively studied over the past decades. Specifically, gender classification has attracted the interest of researchers for its useful applications in many areas, such as, commercial profiling, surveillance and human-computer interaction.

Contrary to what could be thought, gender classification should not be simply considered as a 2-class version of a face recognition problem. While face recognition search for characteristics that make a face unique, gender classification techniques look for common features shared among a group of faces (female or male) [1]. Hence, face recognition solutions are not always suitable for solving gender classification problems.

Although, some researchers employ local descriptions for classifying gender [2,3], most of the published works on face gender classification use global information provided by the whole face [4]. Intuitively, holistic solutions seem to be more likely to achieve higher classification rates, since global characterisations provide configural information (i.e. relations among face parts) as well as featural (i.e. characteristics of the face parts), whereas local descriptors only provide

R. Wilson et al. (Eds.): CAIP 2013, Part I, LNCS 8047, pp. 204–211, 2013.

featural information. However, this has only be tested on single-database experiments. In this work, more realistic scenarios are simulated by using different databases for both training and testing where the acquisition conditions and demographic characteristic vary notably. To the best of our knowledge, in the literature cannot be found a comprehensive study on how realistic conditions affect global and local approaches when classifying gender.

The present paper studies the suitability of global and local approaches for addressing automated gender classification problems of neutral non-occluded faces under realistic conditions. To simulate such conditions, cross-database experiments are performed involving three different databases. A comparison of the performances of three well-known classifiers (1-NN, PCA+LDA and SVM) using two different types of features (grey levels and PCA) is provided. In order to support the discussion of the results, three statistical tests are conducted to better grasp the performance differences.

The rest of this paper is organised as follows: Section 2 presents the methodology adopted for describing the faces and classifying them, Section 3 describes in detail the experiments and the statistical tests, in Section 4 the results are presented as well as discussed and, finally, Section 5 presents the conclusions.

2 Methodology

This study compares the performance in solving gender classification problems of two different approaches (global and local), two types of features (grey levels and PCA) and three different classifiers (1-NN, PCA+LDA and SVM). The methodology followed for performing the experiments has three steps:

Image preprocessing. First of all, the face in the image is detected by the Viola and Jones algorithm [5] implemented in the OpenCV library [6]. Next, the area containing the face is equalized and resized. The interpolation process required for resizing the image uses a three-lobed Lanczos windowed sinc function [7] which keeps the original aspect ratio of the image. It should be noted that no techniques for aligning faces are applied, so in the end unaligned face images are classified.

Feature extraction. Given a preprocessed face image, a global or local approach is followed, as described in Section 2.1, for characterising the face with grey levels or PCA feature vectors, as explained in Section 2.2.

Classification. A trained classifier predicts the gender of a test face using previously extracted features. The classifiers used are detailed in Section 2.3.

2.1 Global and Local Approaches

In this work, faces are described following two approaches: global and local.

The global approach provides configural and featural information by characterizing the face as a whole. In this case, one feature vector is extracted from the area of the image where the face is detected.

The local approach provides featural information by describing overlapping patches of $N \times N$ pixels considered over the face image. From one patch to its neighbour, there is a one pixel shift. A feature vector is extracted from each one of these patches, consequently several feature vectors describe one face. In this approach, the classification methods are based on the concept of neighbourhood which is defined to achieve a higher tolerance towards inaccurate face detections and unaligned faces. Let $N_{i,j}$ be the neighbourhood associated to position (i, j) of the image, then, given a patch $p_{k,l}$ centred at position (k, l), $p_{k,l} \in N_{i,j}$ iff $|i - k| \leq P$ and $|j - l| \leq P$, where P defines how many pixels the neighbourhood spans in each direction.

2.2   Features

Two types of features are used in the experiments: grey levels and Principal Component Analysis.

- **Grey Levels**
  In the global case, the feature vector simply consists of the grey level values of the pixels within the area of the image containing the face. In the local case, one feature vector is formed by the grey level values of the pixels within each patch.

- **Principal Component Analysis (PCA)**
  In the global case, PCA basis are calculated from the grey level value vectors of all the training images. Then, this transformation is applied to all the vectors extracted from the face images of both sets, training and test. In the local case, PCA basis are calculated over the features extracted from each one of the neighbourhoods in the training images. Afterwards, the grey level value vector of each patch is transformed using the PCA transformation associated to their corresponding neighbourhoods.

  In our experiments, the PCA transformation applied retains those eigenvectors accounting for 95% of the variance of the data.

2.3   Classifiers

Three classifiers are tested in the experiments: 1-NN, PCA+LDA and SVM. All of them are well-known classification methods which have been extensively used in automated facial analysis.

- **1-NN**
  In the global case, the classic 1-NN is used. In the local case, a 1-NN classifier per patch's neighbourhood is defined and each of these local classifiers provides a gender estimation for the corresponding patch of a given test face image. Finally, the predicted gender is obtained by majority voting of the local predictions. In both approaches, the metric used is the Square Euclidean distance.

– **PCA+LDA**

Linear Discriminant Analysis (LDA) searches for a linear combination of the features that best discriminates between classes. In the face analysis field, this classifier is most commonly applied over a transformed space, usually Principal Components Analysis (PCA) [3].

In the global case, the standard PCA+LDA is used. In the local case, a local PCA+LDA classifier per patch's neighbourhood is defined which is trained using only the patches that belong to the corresponding neighbourhood. The final predicted class label is obtained by majority voting of the local decisions.

– **SVM**

Support Vector Machine (SVM) is a recognised classifier for its good results in automated face analysis tasks. It is also known that it requires a large amount of time for training purposes. We conducted an experimental study which concluded that the use of local SVMs was not computationally affordable. Therefore, SVM only follows a global approach in the experiments. The SVM implementation with a third degree polynomial kernel provided with LIBSVM 3.0 is employed.

3   Experimental Setup

A number of experiments have been designed to assess how robust are global and local classification models when training and test faces are acquired under different conditions. In order to compare the performance of both approaches, both types of features and the three classifiers previously detailed, an experiment was performed involving each of the possible combinations of those three factors (from now on each combination is referred as *classification model*). These classification models are tested with non-occluded frontal faces from three databases:

– FERET (Facial Recognition Technology Database) [8] contains 12,922 colour images of 512×768 pixels corresponding to 994 peoples faces ranging from ages 10 to 70 and from different races. There are faces from Asians, African-Americans, Hispanics, Caucasians and other races. Our experiments use 2,015 frontal face images. Specifically, 1,173 male and 842 female faces corresponding to 787 different subjects (427 males and 360 females).

– PAL (Productive Aging Lab Face) [9] contains 575 colour images of size 640×480 pixels corresponding to 575 individuals (there is only one image per individual) with ages ranging from 18 to 93. There are 89 African-American faces, 434 Caucasian faces and 52 from other races. All the faces images from this database are used in the experiments.

– AR [10] contains around 4,000 colour images of 768×576 pixels corresponding to 130 people's faces. Images feature frontal view faces with different facial expressions, illumination conditions, and occlusions. Information about the age and race of the subjects is not provided, although after majority sampling the database it can be said that all the individuals are young Caucasian adults. Our experiments use 130 occlusion-free frontal face images with neutral expressions (74 males and 56 females).

In order to simulate realistic conditions, each classification model is evaluated using all possible combinations of these databases for training and testing. Consequently, 72 experiments (8 classification models × 9 data sets) are performed.

When the same database is used for training and testing, 5 repetitions of a 5-fold cross validation technique are implemented. The partition of the database is made by subjects, not by images. Therefore, one subject can only be in the training or test set, but never in both. In cross-database experiments, only one simulation is executed, training with one data set and testing with the other.

For replicating the experiments, it should be noted that after detecting the face in the image, the face area is reduced to 45×36 pixels. In the local approach, the patches covering the image are 7×7 pixels, and the value that defines the neighbourhood size is $P = 2$, resulting in 25 patches per neighbourhood.

3.1   Statistical Tests

Due to the large number of experiments, a detailed comparison of the performances is difficult to provide. In order to ease the comparison task, several tests have been applied to show whether statistical differences exist among the performances of the classifiers. All of these statistical tests are based on a null hypothesis which is assumed certain and they try to prove it to be false.

Firstly, Iman-Davenport test [11] detects differences among the performances of a set of classification models. This statistic's null hypothesis is that all classification models perform equally, with no significant differences. To reject the null hypothesis, the statistic is obtained from the equation: $F_F = \frac{(n-1)\chi_F^2}{n(k-1)-\chi_F^2}$, which follows an F-distribution with $k-1$ and $(k-1)(n-1)$ degrees of freedom. If the F_F statistic is higher than the corresponding value of the F-distribution, the null hypothesis is rejected. Therefore, significant differences among the classification model performances exist.

Secondly, Holm's method [12] is applied to identify statistical differences between the most significant classification model and the remaining models. Holm's null hypothesis assumes that the most significant classification model is statistically superior to the other models. Several hypotheses are checked sequentially, one per each of the models except for the most significant one. For a given significance level α, Holm's method checks if $P_{(i)} < \frac{\alpha}{k-i}$ where $P_{(i)}$ is the P-value of the ith hypothesis and k the amount of classification models. If the condition is met, the corresponding null hypothesis is rejected.

Thirdly, Wilcoxon's Signed Rank test [13] provides pairwise comparisons, so statistical differences between each pair of classification models can be found. This test proceeds by ranking the differences in performance of two models. Let d_i be the difference between the performances of two classification models on the i-th training-test dataset. Then, $d_i \ \forall i$ are ranked according to their absolute

Table 1. Correct gender classification rates (%) obtained in all experiments

Training Data Set	Test Data Set	Global					Local		
		NN			SVM		NN		
		Grey Levels	PCA	PCA+LDA	Grey Levels	PCA	Grey Levels	PCA	PCA+LDA
FERET	FERET	85.31	85.57	91.86	93.66	92.83	92.35	91.29	85.07
	PAL	66.03	64.98	71.25	66.72	62.55	66.03	62.19	60.80
	AR Neutral	79.17	82.31	77.69	81.54	84.62	86.15	86.92	83.08
PAL	FERET	66.53	65.56	75.22	72.99	70.66	63.16	62.07	77.11
	PAL	77.42	77.35	82.72	85.23	85.61	83.73	83.52	73.69
	AR Neutral	81.25	82.31	89.23	92.31	91.54	90.00	90.00	87.69
AR Neutral	FERET	76.02	76.86	80.09	80.83	77.21	78.90	78.90	78.20
	PAL	73.35	72.30	71.43	75.09	70.38	74.39	73.17	65.51
	AR Neutral	83.99	82.46	87.54	90.42	98.15	88.92	89.08	86.31

values. Let R_+ be the sum of the ranks where the 1st model outperforms the 2nd and R_- be the sum of the ranks not included in R_+. In cases where $d_i = 0$, its rank is split evenly between R_+ and R_-. If $d_i = 0$ occurs an odd number of times, one of those ranks is ignored. Being $Z = min(R_+, R_-)$, if Z is less or equal than the Wilcoxon distribution for n degrees of freedom, then the null hypothesis stating that both classification models perform equally is rejected.

These statistical tests were conducted using KEEL data mining software [14].

4   Results and Discussion

Two different analyses of the results are presented in this section: the first one includes all the experiments, whereas the second just cross-database experiments.

Looking at the numerical results of all conducted experiments (shown in Table 1), the first impression is that the classification models using a global SVM or a local classifier obtain higher accuracies than the rest. In order to check whether these performance differences are statistically relevant or not, we applied the three statistical tests previously described which results are shown in Figure 1(a). In Figure 1(a), the table on the left-hand side shows the value of the Iman-Davenport's statistic (F_F) and the corresponding value of the F-distribution; the table in the centre shows the results of the Holm's method with a 95% confidence level where all models above the double line performed significantly worse than the most significant model (marked in bold at the bottom of the table); and the table on the right-hand side shows a summary of Wilcoson's test where the symbol "•" indicates that the classification model in the row significantly outperforms the model in the column, and the symbol "∘" indicates that the model in the column significantly surpasses the model in the row (above the main diagonal with a 90% confidence level, and below it with a 95%).

Iman-Davenport's statistic finds significant differences among the performances of all classification models, which is corroborated by the results of the other two tests. Specifically, Holm's method results indicate that the models

Iman-Davenport's Statistic	Holm's Method	Wilcoxon's Test

Iman-Davenport's Statistic $F_F = 12.18$ $F(7,35)_{0.95} = 2.29$	Holm's Method	Wilcoxon's Test								
			1	2	3	4	5	6	7	8
	1NN-pca-G 0.007143	1NN-grey-G (1)	-		∘	∘	∘	∘	∘	
	1NN-grey-G 0.008333	1NN-pca-G (2)		-	∘	∘	∘	∘	∘	
	PCALDA-L 0.01	PCALDA-G (3)	•	•	-					
	1NN-pca-L 0.0125	SVM-grey-G (4)	•	•		-		•	•	•
	PCALDA-G 0.016667	SVM-pca-G (5)	•				-			•
	SVM-pca-G]0.025	1NN-grey-L (6)	•	•				-		
	1NN-grey-G 0.05	1NN-pca-L (7)							-	
	SVM-grey-G	PCALDA-L (8)			∘					-

(a) Statistical analysis of the accuracies of all experiments

Iman-Davenport's Statistic $F_F = 1.53$ $F(7,35)_{0.95} = 2.29$	Holm's Method	Wilcoxon's Test								
			1	2	3	4	5	6	7	8
	1NN-pca-G 0.007143	1NN-grey-G (1)	-			∘				
	1NN-grey-G 0.008333	1NN-pca-G (2)		-		∘				
	PCALDA-L 0.01	PCALDA-G (3)			-					
	SVM-pca-G 0.0125	SVM-grey-G (4)	•			-				
	1NN-pca-L 0.016667	SVM-pca-G (5)					-			
	PCALDA-G 0.025	1NN-grey-L (6)						-		
	1NN-grey-L 0.05	1NN-pca-L (7)							-	
	1NN-grey-L	PCALDA-L (8)								-

(b) Statistical analysis of the accuracies of only cross-database experiments

Fig. 1. Statistical analyses performed. Holm's results with a 95% significance level (models above the double line performed significantly worse than the most significant model, marked in bold at the bottom). Wilcoxon's summary above the main diagonal with a 90% significance level, and below it with a 95% ("•": model in row outperforms model in column, "∘": model in column outperforms model in row).

using global SVMs (both, with grey levels and PCA features), global PCA+LDA and local 1-NN with grey levels are statistically superior than the rest. In a pairwise comparison, Wilcoxon's test reveals that a global SVM model using grey levels outperforms all classification models except for global PCA+LDA and global SVM with PCA features. In view of the results of this first analysis, a straightforward conclusion would be that global methods are more suitable for dealing with a gender classification problem than local models.

The results of a second analysis of only the cross-database experiments, that is, omitting three experiments that were carried out using the same database for training and testing, are shown in Figure 1(b). In this case, Iman-Davenport's statistic does not find significant differences among classification models. Holm's method only rejects global 1-NN with PCA, indicating that the rest of the models perform statistically equal. The pairwise comparison provided by Wilcoxon's test supports these results, since only a couple of statistical differences are found where global SVM with grey levels outperforms both global 1-NN models.

After these two statistical studies on the performances of all experiments and the cross-database experiments, an interesting fact was discovered: differences among the classification accuracies of the implemented models only exist when single-database experiments are taken into account. In more realistic scenarios, where training and testing images do not share the same acquisition conditions nor the demography of subjects (i.e, simulated with cross-database experiments), no significant differences are found in the performances of the models.

5   Conclusion

This paper has provided a comprehensive statistical study of how suitable global and local approaches are for gender classification under realistic conditions. These circumstances have been simulated by cross-database experiments involving three face image collections with a wide range of ages and races and different acquisition conditions. The comparison has included three classifiers using two different types of features.

The main conclusion drawn from the results is that when addressing gender classification problems from neutral non-occluded faces, global an local approaches achieve statistically equal accuracies. However, if we can ensure similar acquisition condition (i.e., similar to the experiments using the same database for training and testing), global features should be used. As regards the classifiers and features, when the training and test images share the same characteristics, a global SVM using grey levels is more likely to obtain the highest classification accuracies. In other cases, no significant differences were found among the three classifiers studied nor the two types of features considered.

Acknowledgements. This work has been partially funded by Universitat Jaume I through grant FPI PREDOC/2009/20 and projects P1-1B2012-22, and TIN2009-14205-C04-04 from the Spanish Ministerio de Economía y Competitividad.

References

1. Zhao, W., Chellappa, R.: Face Processing: Advanced Modeling and Methods. Academic Press (2006)
2. Shan, C.: Learning local binary patterns for gender classification on real-world face images. Pattern Recognition Letters 33(4), 431–437 (2012)
3. Bekios-Calfa, J., Buenaposada, J.M., Baumela, L.: Revisiting linear discriminant techniques in gender recognition. IEEE PAMI 33(4), 858–864 (2011)
4. Makinen, E., Raisamo, R.: Evaluation of gender classification methods with automatically detected and aligned faces. IEEE PAMI 30(3), 541–547 (2008)
5. Viola, P., Jones, M.: Robust real-time face detection. Int. J. of Computer Vision 57, 137–154 (2004)
6. Bradski, G.R., Kaehler, A.: Learning OpenCV. O'Reilly (2008)
7. Turkowski, K.: Filters for common resampling tasks. In: Graphics Gems I, pp. 147–165. Academic Press (1990)
8. Phillips, P.J., Rizvi, S.A., Rauss, P.J.: The FERET evaluation methodology for face-recognition algorithms. IEEE PAMI 22(10), 1090–1104 (2000)
9. Minear, M., Park, D.: A lifespan database of adult facial stimuli. Behavior Research Methods, Instruments, and Computers 36, 630–633 (2004)
10. Martinez, A., Benavente, R.: The AR face database. Technical report, CVC (1998)
11. Iman, R., Davenport, J.: Approximations of the critical region of the friedman statistic. Communications in Statistics 9, 571–595 (1980)
12. Holm, S.: A simple sequentially rejective multiple test procedure. Scandinavian Journal of Statistics 6, 65–70 (1979)
13. Wilcoxon, F.: Individual comparisons by ranking methods. Biometrics Bulletin 1(6), 80–83 (1945)
14. Alcalá-Fdez, J., Fernandez, A., Luengo, J., Derrac, J., García, S., Sánchez, L., Herrera, F.: KEEL. J. Multiple-Valued Logic and Computing 17(2-3), 255–287 (2011)

BRDF Estimation for Faces from a Sparse Dataset Using a Neural Network

Mark F. Hansen, Gary A. Atkinson, and Melvyn L. Smith

Centre for Machine Vision, Bristol Robotics Laboratory,
University of the West of England & University of Bristol

Abstract. We present a novel five source near-infrared photometric stereo 3D face capture device. The accuracy of the system is demonstrated by a comparison with ground truth from a commercial 3D scanner. We also use the data from the five captured images to model the Bi-directional Reflectance Distribution Function (BRDF) in order to synthesise images from novel lighting directions. A comparison of these synthetic images created from modelling the BRDF using a three layer neural network, a linear interpolation method and the Lambertian model is given, which shows that the neural network proves to be the most photo-realistic.

1 Introduction

The Bi-directional Reflectance Distribution Function (BRDF) describes the relationship between observed intensity at a point on a surface as a function of the incident and reflected angles between the light source and the observer (Fig. 1). BRDFs are commonly used in Computer Generated Imagery (CGI) to provide photo-realistic rendering as well as being used for solving inverse problems associated with shape recovery. A BRDF completely describes the reflectance behaviour of an object under every possible illumination and observation direction assuming no subsurface light transport exists. A discrete representation of the BRDF therefore involves sampling the space in four dimensions (the two angles each to describe incidence and reflectance). As such, this leads to difficulties both in the practicalities of obtaining and using the complete dataset. A BRDF is traditionally measured by using gonio-reflectometers, custom built devices which are expensive [1] and suffer from practical limitations such as angular precision and measurement noise. Some of these limitations can be overcome by employing reflectance models such as Lambertian [2], Phong [3], Torrance-Sparrow [4], Oren-Nayar [5] and more recently a tensor-spline based approach [6], and indeed, these have been used with great success. However, modelling is no substitute for the use of an accurate, image-based BRDF to capture the subtleties of the reflectance properties of an object. In this paper, we present a device which photometrically captures a set of images to create a sparse BRDF, which we then show can realistically model unsampled regions through use of an Artificial Neural Network (ANN).

R. Wilson et al. (Eds.): CAIP 2013, Part I, LNCS 8047, pp. 212–220, 2013.

This paper verifies the capture accuracy of our system and presents progress in obtaining BRDF data from a sparse dataset and using this model to simulate unseen lighting angles photo-realistically via an ANN. The motivation for this work is to show that an accurate BRDF can be modelled from the sparse dataset, and that high speed Near-InfraRed (NIR) capture is suitable for the photometric reconstruction of faces. We make no claim that the modelled BRDF is state-of-the-art for skin reflectance modelling (for examples of such work please refer to [7], [8]), but we are offering a particularly rapid means to acquire sufficient data for photo-realistic rendering.

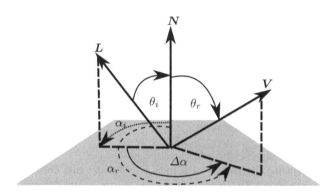

Fig. 1. The four dimensions (zenith incident and reflected angles: θ_i, θ_r and azimuth incident and reflected angles: α_i, α_r) upon which the observed intensity at V (viewer) depends. L is the light source vector, and N is normal to the plane of the reflecting surface. In order to reduce the dimensionality, $\Delta\alpha$, the difference between incident and reflective azimuths is used.

The contributions of this paper are i) to prove the practicality of using NIR for high speed 2.5D data captured in terms of speed and accuracy, compared with a commercial projected pattern scanner and ii) to demonstrate accurate modelling of the BRDF from only five lighting directions via an ANN, which is used to generate photo-realistic images from novel lighting angles.

2   Capture Device

2.1   Hardware

This section details the acquisition device hardware which is based upon the Photoface device presented in [9]. The device, shown in Fig. 2, is designed for practical 3D face geometry capture and recognition. The presence of an individual approaching the device is detected by an ultrasound proximity sensor placed before the archway. This can be seen in Fig. 2(6) towards the left-hand side of the photograph. The sensor triggers a sequence of high speed synchronised frame grabbing and light source switching operations.

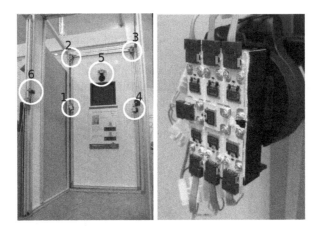

Fig. 2. The NIR geometry capture device (left) and an enlarged image of one of the LED clusters (right). A camera can be seen on the rear panel, above which is located a NIR light source for retro-reflective capture (5). Four other light sources are arranged at evenly spaced angles around the camera (1-4). An ultrasound trigger is located on the left vertical beam of the archway (6).

The aim is to capture six images at a high frame rate: one control image with only ambient illumination and five images each illuminated by one of the NIR light sources in sequence. A captured face is typically 700×850 pixels. Note that the ambient lighting is uncontrolled (for the experiments presented in this paper, overhead fluorescent lights are present). The five NIR lamps are made from a cluster of seven high power NIR LEDs arranged in an 'H'-formation to minimize the emitting area (as can be seen in the right hand side image of Fig 2). The LEDs emit light at $\approx$850nm. The light sources and camera are located approximately 1.2m from the head of the subject with four of the light sources arranged at evenly spaced angles, and one placed as close as possible to the camera to capture retro-reflection.

It was found experimentally that for people walking through the device, a minimum frame rate of approximately 150fps was necessary to avoid significant movement between frames. The device currently operates at 210fps, and it should be noted that it is only operating for the period required to capture the six images. That is, the device is left idle until it is triggered. A monitor is included on the back panel to show the reconstructed face or to display other information.

2.2   Photometric Stereo

The face detection method of Lienhart and Maydt [10] is used to extract the face from the background of the five images. The five intensity images are processed using a MATLAB implementation of a standard Photometric Stereo (PS) method [11, §5.4].

The general equation for PS using five sources for pixel i is

$$
\begin{bmatrix} I_{1,i} \\ I_{2,i} \\ I_{3,i} \\ I_{4,i} \\ I_{5,i} \end{bmatrix} = \rho_i \begin{bmatrix} \mathbf{L}_1^T \\ \mathbf{L}_2^T \\ \mathbf{L}_3^T \\ \mathbf{L}_4^T \\ \mathbf{L}_5^T \end{bmatrix} \mathbf{n}_i
\tag{1}
$$

where ρ_i is the reflectance albedo. The intensity values (I) and light source ($\mathbf{L}$) positions are known, and from these the albedo and surface normal components ($\mathbf{n}$) can be calculated by solving (1) using a linear least-squares method.

3   BRDF Modelling

Traditionally the generation of a BRDF involves illuminating an object from a large number of directions. Traditional PS illuminates an object using three light source directions, and we extend this to five. However this is still a very sparse amount of information from which to generate accurate reflectance information. We therefore explore the use of a traditional linear interpolation of the data, an ANN and the Lambertian reflectance model (which PS assumes) to model the reflectance information from novel lighting angles in order to see how well they can approximate the actual BRDF.

In order to minimise the number of dimensions, we assume that the surface is isotropic. This allows the use of $\Delta\alpha$ rather than the individual α_i, α_r values i.e. it is the difference between the azimuth angles that affects the reflectance, rather the orientation of that difference. While this assumption may not be perfect for human skin, the trade-off between accuracy and complexity makes it appealing.

3.1   Linear Interpolation of BRDF Data

A traditional triangle-based linear interpolation method is used to model the regions between measured points. This method can be expected to work well when the distances between points are not too large and the surface being modelled is relatively uniform and predictable. As the sampled data does not fit this description well, we might expect the results to be poor. Delaunay tessellation is used to fit simplices to the sampled data and these are used to interpolate intensity values for the novel data points given the zenith angle of incidence and reflection (θ_i, θ_r respectively) and the difference in azimuth angle between the incidence and reflection angles ($\Delta\alpha$).

3.2   Neural Network Architecture for BRDF Generation

Gargan & Neelamkavil [12] showed that using an ANN provides excellent approximation performance for a dense BRDF generated using a gonio-reflectometer. Experimenting with different numbers of layers (which affects the ability of the network to either generalise or overfit), they concluded that a three-tier feed-forward backpropagation architecture offers the best performance. The same architecture is used in these experiments, but the novelty is that it is trained with a very sparse dataset instead of the dense BRDF used previously to test whether such good approximation performance is found. Additionally, Gargan & Neelamkavil use an XY parameter space or projected hemispherical space for inputs whereas we use a lower dimensional co-ordinate space which assumes isotropism.

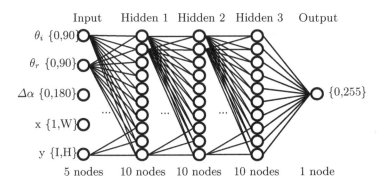

Fig. 3. The architecture of the ANN used to model the BRDF. The inputs θ_i and θ_r are in the range of 0-90 degrees, and $\Delta\alpha$ is in the range 0-180 degrees. x and y give the pixel coordinate and so are in the range of 1 to either the width (W) or height (H). The output is in the range 0-255 for each pixel, so that when all pixels are estimated, a full reflectance image will have been rendered.

The network architecture can be seen in Fig. 3 and was trained using the Levenberg-Marquardt optimisation backpropagation algorithm, taking in the region of 200 epochs to obtain a Mean Square Error (MSE) of 11.58 gray levels and an R value of 0.9598. Using fewer hidden layers generated higher MSEs and lower R-values although training times were faster, while using four layers led to very slightly improved results but at a much higher computational cost. 100,000 image locations (approximately 20% of all data) were chosen at random to provide a representative sample of the whole face surface, and for each location, θ_i, θ_r and $\Delta\alpha$ as well as the x, y co-ordinates were used as inputs.

The reason for including the pixel coordinates is an attempt to allow for the different types of reflectance around the face to be captured (i.e. the reflectance of the skin at the nose tip is different to that of the cheeks). In doing so it is possible to correctly model the behaviour of different skin types when the same θ_i, θ_r and $\Delta\alpha$ are provided without having to label different regions of the face as having different skin types. This provides a means of unsupervised learning that will assist in improving the realism of rendered images.

4 Results

This section first presents results showing the reconstruction accuracy under NIR using a commercially available system as ground truth. Then, to assess the potential of the interpolation and ANN BRDF models, we use re-rendered images from the estimated surface normals obtained by PS. We use the BRDF models to generate images from novel lighting angles to see how well the models can generalise. We compare these images with those generated using the Lambertian reflectance model and show that the ANN produces the most photo-realistic images for unseen lighting angles.

4.1 Surface Reconstruction Using Near-Infrared Photometric Stereo

Fig. 4 shows a reconstruction using NIR light sources for PS, a reconstruction using a commercially available 3D scanner (3dMD [13]) and a map of ℓ_2-distances and angular errors between surface normals at each pixel location. They have been aligned using an Iterative Closest Point (ICP) algorithm[1]. It can be seen that PS offers a very similar level of reconstruction to the commercial scanner – the largest differences occur around regions that are hard to integrate e.g. the lateral edges of the nostril. Median ℓ_2-distance is 0.19 and median angular error (calculated by taking the dot product between corresponding 3dMD and PS vectors) is 11 degrees. These errors appear high, but looking at Fig. 4 (e) (ℓ_2-distance) and (f) (angular error) it is possible to see that overall errors are low, but that discrete areas around difficult to integrate regions where cast shadowing occurs (around the nose and lips) as well as the specularities caused by the eyes have extremely high errors.

4.2 Modelling the BRDF Using Linear Interpolation and a Neural Network, and a Comparison with Lambertian Reflectance

Fig. 5 shows the results of using novel light source directions (i.e. different to the light source directions used by Photoface that have been used to model the reflectance). The first thing to note is that the images produced using the ANN (top row) show a high degree of realism, whereas the interpolated images shown in the second row are noisy and contain many artefacts, presumably due to the sparseness of the BRDF data. The images produced by assuming a Lambertian reflectance clearly show the lighting directions but again lack any real photo-realism.

5 Discussion

The results demonstrated the practicality of using the custom built NIR lamps for PS acquisition. The capture process itself is unobtrusive (most other PS

---

[1] Written by Ajmal Saeed Mian, Computer Science, The University of Western Australia

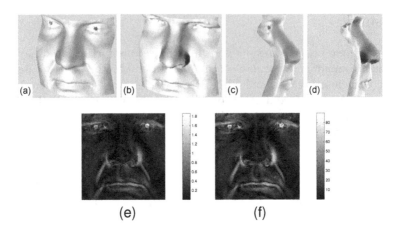

Fig. 4. Reconstructions from the Photoface device (a and c) and 3dMD (b and d) and a map of ℓ_2-distance (e) and angular error (f)

techniques require a sequence of pulsed visible lights), takes only 30ms, and the results generated are accurate and of high resolution.

In terms of BRDF modelling, the results show that photo-realistic images can be synthesised by using an ANN to model the BRDF from a sparse dataset resulting from practical PS acquisition. It offers more realistic results for novel lighting angles than either a linear interpolation based method or Lambertian model. The ANN offers a compact representation of the BRDF and a fast method of synthesising observed intensities from novel lighting directions.

There are some limitations of using a BRDF for modelling skin reflectance, especially under NIR. The BRDF describes the relationship between incident, reflected angles and observed intensity. However, there will be a certain amount of sub-surface scattering (and this will be increased under NIR which penetrates deeper into the skin) which the BRDF is not designed to capture. Also, the BRDF may deviate from actual values as we have used surface normals estimated by PS, but for purposes such as CGI this is not as important as the perceived realism (e.g. avatar generation). We have shown that photo-realistic results are achievable and future work will aim to overcome the Lambertian assumption by incorporating the BRDF model into normal estimates by iteratively enhancing the accuracy of the surface normal representations, which in turn can then be used to generate a more accurate BRDF until convergence is reached. This in turn will reduce distortion in the 3D reconstruction of the surface relief.

6   Conclusion

We have presented a five source NIR, high speed and high resolution 2.5D PS face capture device, which can be used to generate accurate 3D models of human faces. In addition, the five light sources are used to train an ANN to model

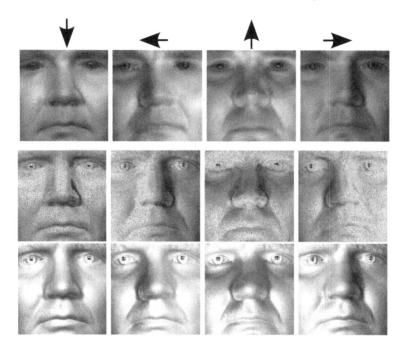

Fig. 5. Synthesised intensity images using estimated surface normals from PS and synthesised light angles (azimuth angles are indicated by arrows. The zenith angle is 15 degrees which is representative of Photoface light sources). Top row: ANN using Photoface surface normals, second row: interpolated Photoface surface normals, bottom row: images generated using the Lambertian reflectance model. A video of the rendering created by the ANN BRDF can be downloaded from www.cems.uwe.ac.uk/~mf-hansen/CAIP13/rerender75.avi

the individual's BRDF. Using this modelled BRDF, photo-realistic results are attained from novel light source directions. Future work will look at the use of the BRDF to improve the 2.5D estimates by replacing the Lambertian assumption in PS, as well as using it as an additional biometric.

References

1. Marschner, S.R., Westin, S.H., Lafortune, E.P.F., Torrance, K.E., Greenberg, D.P.: Image-based BRDF measurement including human skin. In: Proceedings of the 10th Eurographics Workshop on Rendering, pp. 139–152 (1999)
2. Lambert, J.-H.: Photometria, sive de Mensura et gradibus luminis, colorum et umbrae. sumptibus viduae E. Klett (1760)
3. Phong, B.T.: Illumination for computer generated pictures. Communications of the ACM 18(6), 311–317 (1975)
4. Torrance, K.E., Sparrow, E.M.: Theory for off-specular reflection from roughened surfaces. Journal of the Optical Society of America A 57(9), 1105–1112 (1967)

5. Oren, M., Nayar, S.K.: Generalization of the lambertian model and implications for machine vision. International Journal of Computer Vision 14(3), 227–251 (1995)
6. Kumar, R., Barmpoutis, A., Banerjee, A., Vemuri, B.C.: Non-lambertian reflectance modeling and shape recovery of faces using tensor splines. IEEE Transactions on Pattern Analysis and Machine Intelligence 33(3), 533–567 (2011)
7. Debevec, P., Hawkins, T., Tchou, C., Duiker, H.P., Sarokin, W., Sagar, M.: Acquiring the reflectance field of a human face. In: Proceedings of the 27th Annual Conference on Computer Graphics and Interactive Techniques, pp. 145–156 (2000)
8. Ghosh, A., Hawkins, T., Peers, P., Frederiksen, S., Debevec, P.: Practical modeling and acquisition of layered facial reflectance. ACM Transactions on Graphics 27(5), 1–10 (2008)
9. Hansen, M.F., Atkinson, G.A., Smith, L.N., Smith, M.L.: 3D face reconstructions from photometric stereo using near infrared and visible light. Computer Vision and Image Understanding 114(8), 942–951 (2010)
10. Lienhart, R., Maydt, J.: An extended set of haar-like features for rapid object detection. In: IEEE International Conference on Image Processing, vol. 1, pp. 900–903 (2002)
11. Forsyth, D.A., Ponce, J.: Computer Vision: A modern approach. Prentice Hall Professional Technical Reference (2002)
12. Gargan, D., Neelamkavil, F.: Approximating reflectance functions using neural networks. In: Rendering Techniques 1998: Proceedings of the Eurographics Workshop in Vienna, Austria, June 29-July 1, p. 23 (1998)
13. 3dMDface system, http://www.3dmd.com/3dmdface.html (accessed: December 2011)

Comparison of Leaf Recognition by Moments and Fourier Descriptors

Tomáš Suk[1], Jan Flusser[1], and Petr Novotný[2]

[1] Institute of Information Theory and Automation of the ASCR,
Department of Image Processing,
Pod Vodárenskou věží 4, 182 08 Praha 8, Czech Republic
{suk,flusser}@utia.cas.cz
[2] Charles University in Prague, Faculty of Education,
Biology & Environmental Studies Department
M.D. Rettigové 4, 116 39 Praha 1, Czech Republic
petr.novotny@pedf.cuni.cz

Abstract. We test various features for recognition of leaves of wooden species. We compare Fourier descriptors, Zernike moments, Legendre moments and Chebyshev moments. All the features are computed from the leaf boundary only. Experimental evaluation on real data indicates that Fourier descriptors slightly outperform the other tested features.

Keywords: leaf recognition, Zernike moments, Fourier descriptors, Legendre polynomials, Chebyshev polynomials.

1 Introduction

Recognition of plant species by their leaves is an important task in botany. Its automation is at the same time a challenging problem which can be resolved by visual pattern recognition methods. The plant leaves have high intraclass variability and sometimes the leaves of different plants are very similar, which makes this task difficult even for botanists.

Various approaches can be found in the literature. Kumar et al. [1] use a histogram of curvatures. The curvature is computed as a part of a disk with center on a leaf boundary covered by the leaf. The disks of several radii are used. Chen et al. [2] use another type of curvature. Kadir et al. [3] use polar Fourier transformation supplemented by a few color and vein features.

Nanni et al. [4] use the combination of inner distance shape context, shape context and height functions. Wu et al. [5] use simple geometric features as diameter, length, width, area, perimeter, smooth factor, aspect ratio, form factor, rectangularity, narrow factor, convex area ratio, ratio of diameter to perimeter, ratio of perimeter to length plus width and four vein features. The features are evaluated by principal component analysis and neural network. Söderkvist [6] uses similar features as a supplement to geometric moments with support vector machine as a classifier. In [7], Zernike moments are used.

R. Wilson et al. (Eds.): CAIP 2013, Part I, LNCS 8047, pp. 221–228, 2013.

Since the most discriminative information is carried by the leaf boundary (see Fig. 2c), all above-cited papers employ boundary-based features. We decided to objectively compare the most popular ones – Fourier descriptors, Zernike moments, Legendre moments, Chebyshev moments, and a direct use of the boundary coordinates – on a large database of tree leaves.

2   Data Set

In the experiments, we used our own data set named Middle European Woody Plants (MEW 2012 – Fig. 1, [8]). It contains all native and frequently cultivated trees and shrubs of the Central Europe Region. It has 151 botanical species (153 recognizable classes), at least 50 samples per species and a total of 9745 samples (leaves). In the case of compound leaves (Fig. 2b), we considered the individual leaflets separately.

Fig. 1. Samples of our data set (different scale – MEW 2012 scans cleaned for this printed presentation): 1st row – *Acer pseudoplatanus*, *Ailanthus altissima* (leaflet of pinnately compound leaf), *Berberis vulgaris*, *Catalpa bignonioides*, *Cornus alba*, 2nd row – *Deutzia scabra*, *Fraxinus excelsior* (leaflet of pinnately compound leaf), *Juglans regia*, *Maclura pomifera* (male), *Morus alba*, 3rd row – *Populus tremula*, *Quercus petraea*, *Salix caprea*, *Tilia cordata* and *Vaccinium vitis-idaea*.

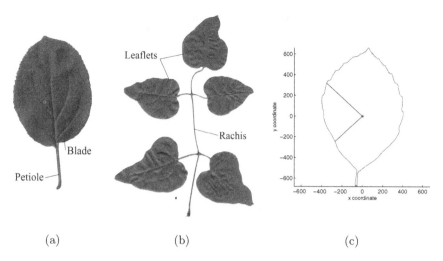

(a)   (b)   (c)

Fig. 2. (a) A simple leaf (*Rhamnus cathartica*). (b) pinnately compound leaf (*Clematis vitalba*). (c) the boundary of the leaf (*Fagus sylvatica*).

3   Method

3.1   Preprocessing

The preprocessing consists namely of the leaf segmentation and boundary detection. The scanned green leaves on white background are first segmented by simple thresholding. The leaves are converted from color to graylevel scale and then we compute the Otsu's threshold [9]. The contours in the binary image are then traced. Only the longest outer boundary of the image is used, the other boundaries (if any) and holes are ignored.

Then we compute the following features: Cartesian coordinates of the boundary points (CB), polar coordinates of the boundary (PB), Fourier descriptors (FD), Zernike moments computed of the boundary image (ZMB), Legendre moments (LM), Chebyshev moments of the first kind (CM1) and that of the second kind (CM2).

All the features need to be normalized to translation and rotation. The normalization to the translation is provided by a subtraction of the centroid coordinates m_{10}/m_{00} and m_{01}/m_{00}, where m_{pq} is a geometric moment. The rotation normalization in the case of the direct coordinates, Legendre and Chebyshev moments is provided so the principal axis coincides with the x-axis and the complex moment c_{21} would have non-negative real part

$$\theta = \frac{1}{2} \arctan\left(\frac{2\mu_{11}}{\mu_{20} - \mu_{02}}\right)$$

$$\text{if } (\mu_{30} + \mu_{12})\cos(\theta) - (\mu_{21} + \mu_{03})\sin(\theta) < 0 \text{ then } \theta := \theta + \pi, \quad (1)$$

where μ_{pq} is a central geometric moment. All the boundary coordinates are multiplied by a rotation matrix corresponding to the angle $-\theta$. The starting point of the coordinate sequence is that one with the minimum x-coordinate. If there is more such points, that one which minimizes y-coordinate is chosen.

3.2   Direct Coordinates

The simplest method is the direct use of the boundary coordinates as the features. To normalize the features with respect to scaling, we resampled the boundaries of all leaves to the constant number of samples n_d. Nearest neighbor interpolation was found slightly better than the linear interpolation for this purpose. Then we used the Cartesian coordinates $a_{2j-1} = x_j/n_o$ and $a_{2j} = y_j/n_o$ as the features, so we have $2n_d$ features together. n_o is the original number of the boundary points, x_j and y_j are the resampled coordinates, $j = 1, 2, \ldots n_d$.

As an alternative, we tried to use the polar coordinates $a_j = \sqrt{x_j^2 + y_j^2}/n_o$ and $\varphi_j = \arctan(y_j/x_j)$, where the angle is used with a lowered weight.

3.3   Fourier Descriptors

The Fourier Descriptors [10] are defined as Fourier transformation of the boundary

$$F(u) = \sum_{k=1}^{n_o} (x_k + iy_k)e^{-2\pi iku/n_o}, \qquad (2)$$

where x_k and y_k are the original boundary point coordinates, n_o is their number, u is the relative frequency (harmonic). We use the descriptors in the range $u = -n_h, -n_h + 1, \ldots n_h$, where n_h is an empiric value common for all leaves, $F(-u) = F(n_o - u)$. After the translation normalization $F(0) = 0$ and it is not further considered.

The scaling invariance can be easily provided by normalization of the amplitudes by the squared boundary length. Another problem is that the magnitude of the amplitude falls quickly with the frequency and we need the appropriate weight of the features in the classifier, therefore we use the normalization $a_u = 10(|u|+1)|F(u)|/n_o^2$. The phase must be normalized to the rotation of coordinates and to the change of the starting point: $\varphi_u = \text{angle}(F(u)) - \vartheta - u\rho$, where $\vartheta = (\text{angle}(F(1)) + \text{angle}(F(-1)))/2$ and $\rho = (\text{angle}(F(1)) - \text{angle}(F(-1)))/2$.

3.4   Zernike Moments

The Zernike moments are frequently-used visual features, see e.g. [11], defined as

$$A_{n\ell} = \frac{n+1}{\pi} \sum_{k=1}^{n_o} R_{n\ell}(r_k)e^{-i\ell\varphi_k}, \qquad (3)$$

where r_k and φ_k are the polar coordinates of the boundary and the radial function $R_{n\ell}(x)$ is a polynomial of the nth degree

$$R_{n\ell}(x) = \sum_{s=0}^{(n-|\ell|)/2} \frac{(-1)^s(n-s)!}{s!((n+|\ell|)/2 - s)!((n-|\ell|)/2 - s)!} x^{n-2s}. \qquad (4)$$

The parameter n is called *order* and ℓ is called *repetition*. Since ZM's were designed for 2D images, we treat the leaf boundary (which is actually 1D information) as a 2D binary image.

This explicit formula becomes numerically unstable for high orders, therefore three recurrence formulas were developed. They are known as Prata method, Kintner method and Chong method, we used the Kintner method [12]. The scaling invariance is provided by a suitable mapping of the image onto the unit disk. The points in the distance κn_o from the centroid are mapped onto the boundary of the unit disk, where κ is a constant found by optimization of the discriminability on the given dataset. The value $\kappa = 0.3$ was determined for MEW2012. The parts of the leaf mapped outside the unit disk are not included into the computation. The moment amplitudes are also normalized both to a sampling density and to a contrast: $a_{n\ell} = |A_{n\ell}|/A_{00}$, the phases are normalized to the rotation as $\varphi_{n\ell} = \mathrm{angle}(A_{n\ell}) - \ell \cdot \mathrm{angle}(A_{31})$.

3.5   Legendre and Chebyshev Moments

The one-dimensional moments can be computed by

$$P_n = \sum_{k=1}^{n_o} (x_k + iy_k) K_n \left(2 \frac{k-1}{n_o - 1} - 1 \right), \tag{5}$$

where x_k, y_k are the boundary coordinates normalized to rotation and starting point by (1). $K_n(x)$ is a Legendre or Chebyshev polynomial. They can be computed by the recurrence formula

$$K_0(x) = 1, \quad K_1(x) = \alpha_0 x, \quad K_n(x) = \alpha_1 x K_{n-1}(x) - \alpha_2 K_{n-2}(x), \tag{6}$$

where $\alpha_0 = 2$ for the Chebyshev polynomials of the second kind otherwise $\alpha_0 = 1$. $\alpha_1 = 2 - \frac{1}{n}$ and $\alpha_2 = 1 - \frac{1}{n}$ for the Legendre polynomials, while $\alpha_1 = 2$ and $\alpha_2 = 1$ for the Chebyshev polynomials.

The amplitude features are used as $a_n = |P_n|/n_o^2$ and the phase features as $\varphi_n = \mathrm{angle}(P_n)$. There is the coefficient $1/n_o^2$ because of the scaling normalization.

3.6   Leaf Size

The leaf size has big intraclass variability – the largest leaf is approximately twice as large as the smallest one. Regardless, the size bears some interesting information, we must use it only with a suitable weight (see the choice of w_s in the next section). When comparing the sizes of two leaves, we must compensate for the resolution of the images if they are different. Then we find diameters $d_m^{(a)}$, $d_m^{(b)}$ of both leaves and define the distance between the leaves as

$$\delta_s(a, b) = 1 - e^{-\frac{\left(d_m^{(a)} - d_m^{(b)} \right)^2}{2 d_m^{(a)} d_m^{(b)}}}. \tag{7}$$

4   Classifier

We use a simple nearest neighbor classifier with optimized weights of individual features. While we can use just L_2 norm for comparison of the amplitude features, the phase features are angles in principle and we have to use special distance

$$\delta_\varphi(\alpha, \beta) = \min(|\alpha - \beta|, 2\pi - |\alpha - \beta|). \tag{8}$$

The distance of two leaves in the feature space is than evaluated

$$d_f(\ell, q) = w_s \delta_s(d_m^{(q)}, d_m^{(\ell)}) + \left(\sum_{k \in S_A} (a_k^{(\ell)} - a_k^{(\ell)})^2 \right)^{\frac{1}{2}} + \\ + w_f \sum_{k \in S_P} w_c(k) \delta_\varphi(\varphi_k^{(\ell)}, \varphi_k^{(q)}), \tag{9}$$

where S_A is the set of all indices, for which a_k is an amplitude feature. Similarly, S_P is the set of all indices, for that φ_k is a phase feature. The weight w_f is constant for a given type of features, while $w_c(k)$ depends on the order of the feature. We use $w_c(k) = 1/|u_k|$ for FD and $w_c(k) = 1/n_k$ for all the moments, where u_k is the current harmonic and n_k is the current moment order. In the case of CB and PB, $w_c(k)$ has no meaning. The parameters and weights of all features were optimized for MEW2012.

In the training phase, the features of all leaves in the data set are computed. In the classification phase, the features of the query leaf are computed, they are labeled by index (q) in Eq. (9), while the features labeled (ℓ) are successively whole data set features. We only consider one nearest neighbor from each species. Where the information whether the leaf is simple or compound is available, only the corresponding species are considered.

5   Results

In the experiments, we divided randomly the leaves of each species in the data set into two halves. One of them was used as a training set and the other half was tested against it. The results are in Tab. 1. The Fourier descriptors slightly outperform the other tested features. The reason of their superiority to moments in this task lies in numerical properties of the features. Since the leaves are similar

Table 1. The success rates (f – boundary features only, s – the leaf size, c – information whether the leaf is simple or compound)

test	CB	PB	FD	ZMB	LM	CM1	CM2
f	64.55%	63.16%	79.88%	69.03%	66.69%	69.13%	74.98%
f & c	67.42%	66.67%	81.84%	72.31%	69.01%	71.92%	77.47%
f & s	74.01%	73.12%	85.43%	78.10%	75.04%	77.38%	77.19%
f & s & c	76.47%	76.16%	86.86%	80.70%	77.31%	80.14%	79.69%

to one another, we need to use high-order features to distinguish them. However, when calculating the high-order moments, floating-point overflow and/or underflow may occur for the orders higher than 60 (even for orthogonal moments calculated by recurrent relations), which leads to a loss of precision. Fourier descriptors are not so prone to overflow/underflow. Although they may also suffer with numerical errors when calculating high-frequency coefficients, the influence of these errors appears to be less significant. Another reason could lie in the shape of the basis functions, which in case of Fourier descriptors can better characterize the shape of most leaves. The direct use of the boundary coordinates, without computing any sophisticated features, produces slightly worse results than both Fourier descriptors and moments. It is also interesting that the leaf size is more important than the information, whether the leaf is simple or compound.

Finally, we compared the performance of the automatic method with the performance of humans. We asked 12 students of computer science to classify the leaves visually. The experiment setup was such that they could see the query leaf and could simultaneously browse the database and compare the query with the training leaves. Unlike the algorithm, they worked with full color images, not with the boundaries only. Each test person classified 30 leaves. The mean success rate was 63% which is far less than the success rate of the algorithm regardless of the particular features used. Hence, the public web-version of our method [13] could be a good leaf recognition tool for non-specialists, which provides them with better performance and higher speed than their sight.

6   Conclusion

We have tested several types of features in a specific task - recognition of wooden species based on their leaves. We concluded that Fourier descriptors are the most appropriate features which can, when combined with the leaf size, achieve the recognition rate above 85%. A crucial factor influencing the success rate is of course the quality of the input image.

In this study, the leaves were scanned in the laboratory. The system is not primarily designed to work with photographs of the leaves taken directly on the tree. In such a case, the background segmentation and elimination of the perspective would have to be incorporated. We encourage the readers to take their own pictures and to try our public web-based application [13].

Acknowledgement. This work was supported by the grant No. P103/11/1552 of the Czech Science Foundation.

References

1. Kumar, N., Belhumeur, P.N., Biswas, A., Jacobs, D.W., Kress, W.J., Lopez, I.C., Soares, J.V.B.: Leafsnap: A computer vision system for automatic plant species identification. In: Fitzgibbon, A., Lazebnik, S., Perona, P., Sato, Y., Schmid, C. (eds.) ECCV 2012, Part II. LNCS, vol. 7573, pp. 502–516. Springer, Heidelberg (2012)

2. Chen, Y., Lin, P., He, Y.: Velocity representation method for description of contour shape and the classification of weed leaf images. Biosystems Engineering 109(3), 186–195 (2011)
3. Kadir, A., Nugroho, L.E., Susanto, A., Santosa, P.I.: Foliage plant retrieval using polar fourier transform, color moments and vein features. Signal & Image Processing: An International Journal 2(3), 1–13 (2011)
4. Nanni, L., Brahnam, S., Lumini, A.: Local phase quantization descriptor for improving shape retrieval/classification. Pattern Recognition Letters 33(16), 2254–2260 (2012)
5. Wu, S.G., Bao, F.S., Xu, E.Y., Wang, Y.X., Chang, Y.F., Xiang, Q.L.: A leaf recognition algorithm for plant classification using probabilistic neural network. In: 7th International Symposium on Signal Processing and Information Technology ISSPIT 2007, p. 6. IEEE (2007)
6. Söderkvist, O.J.O.: Computer vision classiffcation of leaves from swedish trees. Master's thesis, Linköping University (September 2001)
7. Kadir, A., Nugroho, L.E., Susanto, A., Santosa, P.I.: Experiments of Zernike moments for leaf identification. Journal of Theoretical and Applied Information Technology 41(1), 113–124 (2012)
8. MEW2012: Download middle european woods (2012), http://zoi.utia.cas.cz/node/662
9. Otsu, N.: A threshold selection method from gray-level histograms. IEEE Transactions on Systems, Man, and Cybernetics 9(1), 62–66 (1979)
10. Lin, C.C., Chellapa, R.: Classification of partial 2-D shapes using Fourier descriptors. IEEE Transactions on Pattern Analysis and Machine Intelligence 9(5), 686–690 (1987)
11. Flusser, J., Suk, T., Zitová, B.: Moments and Moment Invariants in Pattern Recognition. Wiley, Chichester (2009)
12. Kintner, E.C.: On the mathematical properties of Zernike polynomials. Journal of Modern Optics 23(8), 679–680 (1976)
13. MEWProjectSite: Recognition of woods by shape of the leaf (2012), http://leaves.utia.cas.cz/index?lang=en

Dense Correspondence of Skull Models by Automatic Detection of Anatomical Landmarks

Kun Zhang, Yuan Cheng, and Wee Kheng Leow

Department of Computer Science, National University of Singapore
Computing 1, 13 Computing Drive, Singapore 117417
{zhangkun,cyuan,leowwk}@comp.nus.edu.sg

Abstract. Determining dense correspondence between 3D skull models is a very important but difficult task due to the complexity of the skulls. Non-rigid registration is at present the predominant approach for dense correspondence. It registers a reference model to a target model and then resamples the target according to the reference. Methods that use manually marked corresponding landmarks are accurate, but manual marking is tedious and potentially error prone. On the other hand, methods that automatically detect correspondence based on local geometric features are sensitive to noise and outliers, which can adversely affect their accuracy. This paper presents an automatic dense correspondence method for skull models that combines the strengths of both approaches. First, anatomical landmarks are automatically and accurately detected to serve as hard constraints for non-rigid registration. They ensure that the correspondence is anatomically consistent and accurate. Second, control points are sampled on the skull surfaces to serve as soft constraints for non-rigid registration. They provide additional local shape constraints for a closer match between the reference and the target. Test results show that, by combining both approaches, our algorithm can achieve more accurate automatic dense correspondence.

Keywords: Dense correspondence, anatomical landmarks, skull models.

1 Introduction

Determining dense correspondence between 3D mesh models is a very important task in many applications such as remeshing, shape morphing, and construction of active shape models. Among existing approaches for dense correspondence, non-rigid registration is at present the predominant approach due to its flexibility. Non-rigid registration methods deform a reference mesh to match the target mesh and resample the target by mapping reference mesh vertices to the target surface. They are typically preceded by rigid registration to globally align the sizes, positions, and orientations of the meshes. Various deformable methods have been used including energy minimization [11, 12], mass-spring model [15], local affine transformations [1], trilinear transformation [2], graph and manifold matching [20], octree-splines [6], and thin-plate spline (TPS) [4, 5, 7–10, 14, 18].

R. Wilson et al. (Eds.): CAIP 2013, Part I, LNCS 8047, pp. 229–236, 2013.

Most of these methods are demonstrated on models with simple surfaces such as faces [8, 12, 20], human bodies [1, 15], knee ligaments [6], and lower jaws [2]. TPS is particularly effective for mesh models with highly complex surfaces such as brain sulci [4], lumbar vertebrae [10], and skulls [5, 7, 9, 14, 18]. Skull models are particularly complex because they have holes, missing teeth and bones, and interior as well as exterior surfaces.

Like all non-rigid registration methods, TPS registration of skull models requires known correspondence on the reference and the target, which can be manually marked or automatically detected. The first approach manually marks anatomical landmarks on the reference and the target [5, 9, 14], and uses the landmarks as hard constraints in TPS registration. This approach is accurate, but manual marking is tedious and potentially error prone. The second approach automatically detects surface points on the reference mesh, which are mapped to the target surface. These surface points can be randomly sampled points [7] or distinctive feature points such as local curvature maximals [18], and they serve as soft constraints in TPS registration. This approach is sensitive to noise, outliers, and false correspondences. Turner et al. [18] apply multi-stage coarse-to-fine method to reduce outliers, and forward (reference-to-target) and backward (target-to-reference) registrations to reduce false correspondences. However, there is no guarantee that the correspondences detected anatomically are consistent and accurate, despite the complexity of the method.

This paper presents an automatic dense correspondence algorithm for skull models that combines the strengths of both approaches. First, anatomical landmarks are automatically and accurately detected to serve as hard constraints in TPS registration. They ensure **anatomically consistent correspondence**. The number of such landmarks is expected to be small because automatic detection of anatomical landmarks is a very difficult task (Section 2). Second, control points are sampled on skull surfaces to serve as soft constraints in TPS registration. They provide additional local shape constraints for a **close matching** of reference and target surfaces. Compared to [18], our method also uses multi-stage coarse-to-fine approach, except that our landmark detection algorithm is based on anatomical definitions of landmarks, which ensures the correctness and accuracy of the detected landmarks.

Quantitative evaluation of point correspondence is a challenging task. Most works reported only qualitative results. The quantitative errors measured in [2, 8, 19] are non-rigid registration error instead of point correspondence error. This paper proposes a method for measuring point correspondence error, and shows that registration error is not necessarily correlated to correspondence error.

2   Automatic Craniometric Landmark Detection

In anatomy [16] and forensics [17], craniometric landmarks are feature points on a skull that are used to define and measure skull shapes. Automatic detection of craniometric landmarks is very difficult and challenging due to a form of cyclic definition. Many craniometric landmarks are defined according to the three

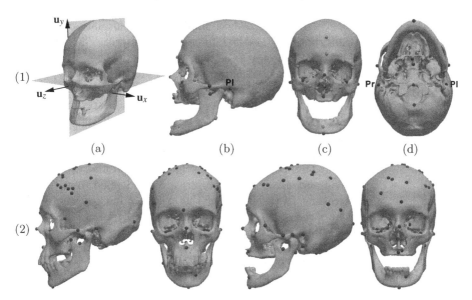

Fig. 1. Skull models and craniometric landmarks. (1) Reference model. (1a) Frankfurt plane (FP) is the horizontal (red) plane and mid-sagittal plane (MSP) is the vertical (green) plane. (1b–1d) Blue dots denote landmarks used for registration and yellow dots denote Landmarks used for evaluation. (2) Detected registration landmarks (blue) and 50 control points (red) on two sample test targets.

anatomical orientations of the skull (Fig. 1(a)): lateral (left-right), anterior-posterior (front-back), and superior-inferior (up-down). These orientations are defined by the *Frankfurt plane* (FP) and the *mid-sagittal plane* (MSP), which are in turn defined as the planes that pass through specific landmarks.

Our automatic landmark detection algorithm is an adaptation of our previous work on automatic identification of FP and MSP [3]. It overcomes the cyclic definition of craniometric landmarks by first mapping known landmarks on a reference model to a target model, and then iteratively refining FP, MSP and their landmarks on the target model. It can be summarized as follows:

Craniometric Landmark Detection Algorithm

1. Register a reference model with known landmarks to the target model.
2. Locate the landmarks on the target based on the registered reference and fit FP and MSP to their landmarks on the target.
3. Repeat until convergence:
   (a) Refine the locations of the FP landmarks on the target, and fit FP to the refined FP landmarks.
   (b) Refine the locations of the MSP landmarks on the target, and fit MSP to the refined MSP landmarks, keeping it orthogonal to FP.

Step 1 registers the reference to the target using Fractional Iterative Closest Point (FICP) [13], a variant of ICP robust to noise, outliers, and missing bones.

Like ICP, FICP iteratively computes the best similarity transformation (scaling, rotation, and translation) that registers the reference to the target. The difference is that in each iteration, FICP computes the transformation using only a subset of reference points whose distances to the target model are the smallest.

After registration, Step 2 maps the landmarks on the reference to the target. First, closest points on the target surface to the reference landmarks are identified. These closest points are the initial estimates of the landmarks on the target, which may not be accurate due to shape variations among the skulls. Next, FP and MSP are fitted to the initial estimates using PCA.

In Step 3, an elliptical landmark region R is identified around each initial estimate. The orientation and size of R are empirically predefined. R varies for different landmark according to the shape of the skull around the landmark. These regions should be large enough to include the landmarks on the target model. Accurate landmark locations are searched within the regions according to their anatomical definitions. For example, the left and right porions (Pl, Pr in Fig. 1) are the most *lateral* points of the roofs of the ear canals [16, 17]. After refining FP landmarks in Step 3(a), FP is fitted to the refined FP landmarks. Next, MSP landmarks are refined in Step 3(b) in a similar manner, and MSP is fitted to the refined MSP landmarks, keeping it orthogonal to FP.

As Step 3 is iterated, the locations and orientations of FP and MSP are refined by fitting to the landmarks, and the landmarks' locations are refined according to the refined FP and MSP. After the algorithm converges, accurate craniometric landmarks are detected on the target model.

In addition to the landmarks on FP and MSP, other landmarks are also detected (Fig. 1). These include points of extremum along the anatomical orientations defined by FP and MSP. These landmarks are detected in a similar manner as the FP and MSP landmarks, first by mapping known landmark regions on the reference to the target, and then searching within the regions for the landmarks according to their anatomical definitions. Test results show that the average landmark detection error is 3.54 mm, which is very small compared to the size of human skulls.

3   Dense Correspondence Algorithm

Our dense correspondence algorithm consists of the following stages:

1. Apply craniometric landmark detection algorithm on the target model.
2. Apply TPS to register the reference to the target with craniometric landmarks as hard constraints.
3. Sample control points on reference surface and map them to target surface.
4. Apply TPS with craniometric landmarks as hard constraints and control points as soft constraints.
5. Resample target surface by mapping reference mesh vertices to the target.

Stage 1 automatically detects craniometric landmarks on the target model. After applying the landmark detection algorithm, the reference model is already rigidly registered to the target model. Stage 2 applies TPS to perform coarse registration with the accurately detected landmarks as hard constraints, which ensure **anatomically consistent correspondence**. Stage 3 randomly selects m reference mesh vertices with the large registration errors as the control points. For each control point, a nearest point on the target surface within a fixed distance and with a sufficiently similar surface normal is selected as the corresponding point. If a corresponding point that satisfies these criteria cannot be found, then the control point is discarded. This approach renders the algorithm robust to missing parts in the target skulls. Stage 4 performs another TPS registration with craniometric landmarks as hard constraints and control points as soft constraints. These constraints ensure **close matching** of reference and target surfaces while maintaining anatomically consistent correspondence. After TPS registration, Stage 5 maps the reference mesh vertices to the target surface in the same manner as mapping of control points in Stage 3.

4   Accuracy of Registration and Correspondence

Registration error E_R measures the difference between the registered reference surface and the target surface. It can be computed as the mean distance between the reference mesh vertices $\mathbf{v}_i^r$ and the nearest surface points $\mathbf{v}_i^t$ on the target:

$$E_R = \left[\frac{1}{n} \sum_{i=1}^{n} \| \mathbf{v}_i^r - \mathbf{v}_i^t \|^2 \right]^{1/2} \tag{1}$$

where n is the number of vertices. This is essentially the error measured in [2, 8, 19], although the actual formulations that they used differ slightly.

Correspondence error, on the other hand, should measure the error in computing point correspondence. One possible formulation of correspondence error is to measure the mean distance between the desired and actual corresponding target points of reference mesh vertices. The desired corresponding point $D(\mathbf{v}_i^r)$ is the ground-truth marked by a human expert, whereas the actual corresponding point $C(\mathbf{v}_i^r)$ is the one computed by dense correspondence algorithm. With this formulation, the correspondence error E_C can be computed as

$$E_C = \left[\frac{1}{n} \sum_{i=1}^{n} \| D(\mathbf{v}_i^r) - C(\mathbf{v}_i^r) \|^2 \right]^{1/2} \tag{2}$$

In practice, it is impossible to manually mark the desired corresponding points of reference mesh vertices accurately on the target mesh surface. An alternative formulation is to measure the mean distance between the desired and actual corresponding target landmarks of reference landmarks $\mathbf{M}_i^r$:

$$E_C = \left[\frac{1}{l} \sum_{i=1}^{l} \| D(\mathbf{M}_i^r) - C(\mathbf{M}_i^r) \|^2 \right]^{1/2} \tag{3}$$

where l is the number of evaluation landmarks. The desired target landmarks are manually marked whereas the actual target landmarks are computed by the dense correspondence algorithm. Given enough landmarks adequately distributed over the entire reference surface, Eq. 3 is a good approximation of Eq. 2.

5   Experiments and Discussions

11 skull models reconstructed from CT images were used in the tests. One of them served as the reference model and the others were target models. For performance comparison, the following methods were tested for dense correspondence:

1. ICP: ICP rigid registration with mesh vertices as corresponding points.
2. FICP: FICP rigid registration with mesh vertices as corresponding points.
3. CP-S: TPS registration with automatically detected control points as soft constraints. This approach was adopted by [7].
4. LM-H: TPS registration with automatically detected craniometric landmarks as hard constraints.
5. LM-S/CP-S: TPS registration with automatically detected craniometric landmarks and control points as soft constraints. This approach is similar to the method of [18], except [18] adopted a more elaborate multi-stage, coarse-to-fine, and forward-backward registration scheme.
6. **LM-H/CP-S**: TPS registration with automatically detected craniometric landmarks as hard constraints and control points as soft constraints. This is our proposed algorithm.
7. MLM-H: TPS registration with manually marked craniometric landmarks as hard constraints. This approach was adopted by [5, 9, 14].

These test cases were equivalent to our algorithm (Case 6) with different stages and constraints omitted. All the TPS registrations were preceded by FICP. The stiffness parameter for TPS soft constraints was set to 0.8 where the algorithms generally performed well. 15 landmarks and 150 control points were used for registration for Cases 3–6, and 30 landmarks for Case 7. More landmarks could be used for Case 7 because they included landmarks that could be accurately marked manually but not detected automatically. 28 other landmarks were used for evaluation. Both registration error and correspondence error were measured.

Test results (Figure 2(a)) show that FICP is more robust than ICP in rigid registration. The registration error of CP-S is smaller than those of LM-S/CP-S and LM-H/CP-S, but its correspondence error is larger. This shows that low registration error does not necessarily imply low correspondence error.

CP-S and LM-S/CP-S use only soft constraints, which are inadequate for ensuring anatomically consistent correspondence. So, their correspondence errors are larger than those of LM-H/CP-S, which also uses registration landmarks as hard constraints. On the other hand, LM-H uses only landmarks, which are insufficient for ensuring close matching of reference and target surfaces, though consistent correspondence is somewhat achieved. So, its correspondence error for registration landmarks E_{CR} is very small, but its correspondence error for evaluation landmarks E_{CE} is large. LM-S/CP-S uses landmarks as soft constraints, which weakens the anatomical consistency of correspondence, though close matching of reference and target surfaces is achieved. Using landmarks as

Algorithm	E_R	E_{CR}	E_{CE}
ICP	2.22	7.09	7.42
FICP	1.97	5.55	6.35
CP-S	1.64	4.15	5.81
LM-H	2.69	3.51	5.94
LM-S/CP-S	1.76	3.68	5.73
LM-H/CP-S	1.76	3.58	5.56
MLM-H	2.42	0.00	4.66

(a)

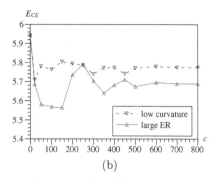

(b)

Fig. 2. Quantitative evaluation. (a) E_R: registration error. E_{CR}, E_{CE}: correspondence errors for registration landmarks and evaluation landmarks, respectively. Units are in mm. (b) Plots of E_{CE} vs. c, number of control points.

hard constraints, our algorithm LM-H/CP-S ensures strong anatomically consistent correspondence. Together with control points as soft constraints, it achieves very low registration error and the lowest correspondence error for evaluation landmarks E_{CE} among the automatic methods (Cases 1–6).

MLM-H uses manually marked landmarks as hard constraints. So, it is not surprising that it has the smallest correspondence errors. Interestingly, its registration error is quite large compared to the other methods. This is because some parts of the skulls lack distinctive surface features for locating both registration and evaluation landmarks (Fig. 1), where most of the registration errors occur.

To investigate the stability of our algorithm LM-H/CP-S, we tested it with varying numbers of control points and two different sampling schemes that are used by existing methods: low curvature [18] and large registration error [5]. Figure 2(b) shows that control points with large registration errors are more effective than those with low curvatures in reducing correspondence error. Compared to the accuracy of LM-H, which uses landmarks only, a small number of control points can already improve correspondence accuracy significantly. After sampling enough control points that cover various parts of the skulls, adding more control points do not reduce correspondence error significantly. This is due to the diminished quality of the additional control points.

6   Conclusions

This paper presents a multi-stage, coarse-to-fine automatic dense correspondence algorithm for mesh models of skulls that combines two key features. First, anatomical landmarks are automatically and accurately detected to serve as hard constraints for non-rigid registration. They ensure **anatomically consistent correspondence**. Second, control points are sampled on the skull surfaces to serve as soft constraints for non-rigid registration. They provide additional local shape constraints to ensure **close matching** of reference and target surfaces. Test results show that, by combining both approaches, our algorithm can achieve more accurate automatic dense correspondence than other automatic algorithms. Our test results also show that low registration error does not always imply low correspondence error. So, both error measures should be used in conjunction to evaluate the accuracy of dense correspondence algorithms.

References

1. Allen, B., Curless, B., Popović, Z.: The space of human body shapes: reconstruction and parameterization from range scans. In: Proc. SIGGRAPH (2003)
2. Berar, M., Desvignes, M., Bailly, G., Payan, Y.: 3D meshes registration: Application to statistical skull model. In: Campilho, A.C., Kamel, M.S. (eds.) ICIAR 2004. LNCS, vol. 3212, pp. 100–107. Springer, Heidelberg (2004)
3. Cheng, Y., Leow, W.K., Lim, T.C.: Automatic identification of frankfurt plane and mid-sagittal plane of skull. In: Proc. WACV (2012)
4. Chui, H., Rangarajan, A.: A new algorithm for non-rigid point matching. In: Proc. CVPR (2000)
5. Deng, Q., Zhou, M., Shui, W., Wu, Z., Ji, Y., Bai, R.: A novel skull registration based on global and local deformations for craniofacial reconstruction. Forensic Science International 208, 95–102 (2011)
6. Fleute, M., Lavallée, S.: Building a complete surface model from sparse data using statistical shape models: Application to computer assisted knee surgery. In: Wells, W.M., Colchester, A.C.F., Delp, S.L. (eds.) MICCAI 1998. LNCS, vol. 1496, pp. 879–887. Springer, Heidelberg (1998)
7. Hu, Y., Duan, F., Zhou, M., Sun, Y., Yin, B.: Craniofacial reconstruction based on a hierarchical dense deformable model. EURASIP Journal on Advances in Signal Processing 217, 1–14 (2012)
8. Hutton, T.J., Buxton, B.F., Hammond, P.: Automated registration of 3D faces using dense surface models. In: Proc. BMVC (2003)
9. Lapeer, R.J.A., Prager, R.W.: 3D shape recovery of a newborn skull using thinplate splines. Computerized Medical Imaging & Graphics 24(3), 193–204 (2000)
10. Lorenz, C., Krahnstöver, N.: Generation of point-based 3D shape models for anatomical objects. Computer Vision and Image Understanding 77, 175–191 (2000)
11. Lüthi, M., Albrecht, T., Vetter, T.: Building shape models from lousy data. In: Yang, G.-Z., Hawkes, D., Rueckert, D., Noble, A., Taylor, C. (eds.) MICCAI 2009, Part II. LNCS, vol. 5762, pp. 1–8. Springer, Heidelberg (2009)
12. Pan, G., Han, S., Wu, Z., Zhang, Y.: Removal of 3D facial expressions: A learningbased approach. In: Proc. CVPR (2010)
13. Phillips, J.M., Liu, R., Tomasi, C.: Outlier robust icp for minimizing fractional RMSD. In: Proc. 3D Digital Imaging and Modeling (2007)
14. Rosas, A., Bastir, M.: Thin-plate spline analysis of allometry and sexual dimorphism in the human craniofacial complex. American J. Physical Anthropology 117, 236–245 (2002)
15. Seo, H., Magnenat-Thalmann, N.: An automatic modeling of human bodies from sizing parameters. In: Proc. ACM SIGGRAPH (2003)
16. Siwek, D.F., Hoyt, R.J.: Anatomy of the human skull, http://skullanatomy.info
17. Taylor, K.T.: Forensic Art and Illustration. CRC (2001)
18. Turner, W.D., Brown, R.E., Kelliher, T.P., Tu, P.H., Taister, M.A., Miller, K.W.: A novel method of automated skull registration for forensic facial approximation. Forensic Science International 154, 149–158 (2005)
19. Wang, Y., Peterson, B.S., Staib, L.H.: Shape-based 3D surface correspondence using geodesics and local geometry. In: Proc. CVPR (2000)
20. Zeng, Y., Wang, C., Wang, Y.: Automated registration of 3D faces using dense surface models. In: Proc. CVPR (2010)

Detection of Visual Defects in Citrus Fruits: Multivariate Image Analysis vs Graph Image Segmentation

Fernando López-García, Gabriela Andreu-García,
José-Miguel Valiente-Gonzalez, and Vicente Atienza-Vanacloig

Instituto de Automática e Informática Industrial. Universidad Politécnica de Valencia
Camino de Vera (s/n), 46022 Valencia, Spain
{flopez,gandreu,jvalient,vatienza}@disca.upv.es
http://www.ai2.upv.es/

Abstract. This paper presents an application of visual quality control in orange post-harvesting comparing two different approaches. These approaches correspond to two very different methodologies released in the area of Computer Vision. The first approach is based on Multivariate Image Analysis (MIA) and was originally developed for the detection of defects in random color textures. It uses Principal Component Analysis and the T^2 statistic to map the defective areas. The second approach is based on Graph Image Segmentation (GIS). It is an efficient segmentation algorithm that uses a graph-based representation of the image and a predicate to measure the evidence of boundaries between adjacent regions. While the MIA approach performs novelty detection on defects using a trained model of sound color textures, the GIS approach is strictly an unsupervised method with no training required on sound or defective areas. Both methods are compared through experimental work performed on a ground truth of 120 samples of citrus coming from four different cultivars. Although the GIS approach is faster and achieves better results in defect detection, the MIA method provides less false detections and does not need to use the hypothesis that the bigger area in samples always correspond to the non-damaged area.

Keywords: Fruit Inspection, Automatic Quality Control, Multivariate Image Analysis, Principal Component Analysis, Unsupervised Methods.

1 Introduction

Quality control in the agro-industry is becoming of paramount importance in order to decrease production costs and increase quality standards. In the packing lines, where external quality attributes are currently inspected visually, machine vision is providing a way to perform this task automatically. The detection of blemishes is one of the most important factors in the commercial quality of fruit. Blemishes in citrus can be due to several causes; medfly egg deposition, green mould by Penicillium digitatum, oleocellosis (rind oil spot), scale, scarring, thrips

R. Wilson et al. (Eds.): CAIP 2013, Part I, LNCS 8047, pp. 237–244, 2013.

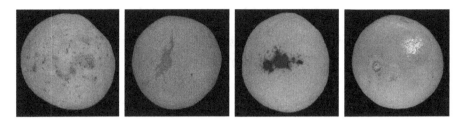

Fig. 1. Some blemishes in citrus. From left to right; scale, thrips scarring, sooty mould and green mould.

scarring, chilling injury, stem injury, sooty mould, anthracnose and phytotoxicity. Figure 1 shows four different types of defects (blemishes) in citrus.

The automatic detection of visual defects in orange post-harvest, performed to classify the fruit depending on their appearance, is a major problem. Species and cultivars of citrus present great unpredictability in colors and textures in both, sound and defective areas. Thus, the inspection system will need frequent training to adapt to the visual features of new cultivars and even different batches within the same cultivar [1]. In addition, as the training process will be performed by non-specialized operators at the inspection lines, we need to select an unsupervised methodology (no labeling process required) that leads to an easy-to-train inspection system. Real-time compliance is also an important issue so that the overall production can be inspected at on-line rates. Thus, approaches with low computational costs are valuable. In the present paper, we study and compare two methods that offer these features, they are unsupervised , easy-to-train and also provide low computational costs in comparison with similar-in-purpose methods in literature.

The first method [2] is based on a Multivariate Image Analysis (MIA) strategy developed in the area of applied statistics [3,4,5]. This strategy differs from traditional image analysis, where the image is considered a single sample from which a vector of features is extracted and then used for classification or comparison purposes. In MIA, the image is considered a sample of size equal to the number of pixels that compose the image. Principal Component Analysis (PCA) is applied to the raw data of pixels and then statistic measures are used to perform the image analysis. The method was originally developed as a general approach for the detection of defects in random color textures, which is a Computer Vision issue where several works have been released recently in literature. We chose this kind of method because it fits the needs for the detection of blemishes (visual defects) in citrus, where sound peel areas and damaged areas are in fact random color textures. With regard to the other literature methods for the detection of defects in random color textures, this method presents the following advantages; it uses one of the simplest approaches providing low computational costs, and also, it is unsupervised and only needs few samples to train the system [2]. In order to better compile defects and parts of defects of different sizes we introduce a multiresolution scheme which minimizes the computational effort. The method is applied at different scales gathering the results in one map of defects. In the paper, we call this method MIA-DDRCT (MIA Defect Detection on Random Color Textures).

The second method we study [6] is a Graph Image Segmentation (GIS) approach which belongs to the set of methods that use a graph representation of the image and a given criteria to segment the image into regions (e.g. [7,8]). It is an efficient segmentation algorithm based on a predicate which is defined to measure the evidence of a boundary between two adjacent regions. This predicate measures inter-regions differences in the neighborhood of boundaries as well as intra-region differences. This way, local and non-local criteria are introduced. We chose this method because it is a recent work on the Computer Vision topic of image segmentation which improves results of previous methods [6]. The GIS method is highly efficient and achieves a running time nearly linear with the number of pixels in the image. Also, it is strictly unsupervised because it does not need to learn about sound or defective areas. If we set the hypothesis that the bigger part in samples correspond to the sound non-damaged area, then the rest of regions will correspond to defects. In this case, we only need to adjust two parameters in the method: $sigma$, which is used to smooth the image before being segmented, and the k value of a threshold function where larger values of k result in larger regions. The hypothesis of the bigger area in samples being the sound area is reasonable and has been used before [1]. In the paper, we call this method EGIS (Efficient Graph Image Segmentation).

Next section shows the experimental work performed to evaluate and compare the approaches. Conclusions are reported in final section.

2   Experimental Work

2.1   Ground Truth

The set of fruit used to carry out the experiments consisted of a total of 120 oranges and mandarins coming from four different cultivars: Clemenules, Marisol, Fortune, and Valencia (30 samples per cultivar). The fruit was randomly collected from a citrus packing house. Five fruits of each cultivar belonged to the extra category, thus, they were fully free of defects. The other 25 fruits of each cultivar fitted secondary commercial categories and had several skin defects, trying to represent the cause of most important losses during post-harvesting (see Section 1).

2.2   MIA-DDRCT Approach

The first step in the experimental work for this approach was to select a set of defect-free samples for each cultivar, in order to build the corresponding model of sound color textures. A total of 64 different sound patches were collected for each cultivar (see Figure 2). We used patches instead of complete samples in order to introduce in the model more different types of sound peels and collect as much as possible the variability of colors and textures.

Fig. 2. Several sound patches of Clemenules cultivar

Then, to tune the parameters, we designed a set of experiments that involved to apply the method to the ground truth of each cultivar and extract the corresponding defect maps, but varying in each experiment; the number of principal eigenvectors chosen to build the reference eigenspace, the percentile used to set the T^2 threshold, and the combination of scales used in the multiresolution scheme. The number of principal eigenvectors were varied in [1, 3, 5, 7, 9, 11, 13, 15, 17, 19, 21, 23, 25, 27], the percentile in [90, 95, 99], and the set of scales in [(0.25,0.12), (0.50, 0.12), (0.50, 0.25), (1.00, 0.12), (1.00, 0.25), (1.00, 0.50), (0.50, 0.25, 0.12), (1.00, 0.25, 0.12), (1.00, 0.50, 0.12), (1.00, 0.50, 0.25), (1.0, 0.50, 0.25, 0.12)]. Thus, a total number of 462 experiments were carried out for each cultivar. To tune the parameters, that is, to select the values that maximize the quality of defect maps, we marked manually the defective areas in the samples and then compared with the achieved defect maps using three measures; Precision, Recall and F-Score.

$$Precision = \frac{tp}{tp + fp}, \quad Recall = \frac{tp}{tp + fn} \tag{1}$$

$$FScore = 2 * \frac{Precision * Recall}{Precision + Recall} \tag{2}$$

where tp (true positives) is the number of pixels marked and correctly detected, fp (false positives) is the number of pixels not marked but detected, and fn (false negatives) is the number of pixels marked but not detected. Precision is a measure of exactness (fidelity), Recall is a measure of completeness, and the F-score combines both through their harmonic mean. Once the set of experiments was carried out for each cultivar, mean values of previous measures were computed. Then, we selected the most balanced result for each cultivar. Table 1 shows the best combination of factors for each cultivar and the corresponding mean values of Precision, Recall and F-Score.

Once the parameters were tuned, from the marked defects and the achieved defect maps we counted the actual defects, the correctly detected defects and the false detections for each cultivar. These results are shown in Table 2 (percentage of false detections is provided with regards to the number of detected defects plus the false detections, that is, the total number of defects extracted by the method).

Table 1. Best combinations of factors (MIA-DDRCT)

Cultivar	#EigenVectors	Percentile	Scales	Precision	Recall	F-Score
Clemenules	11	95	(0.50, 0.25)	0.60	0.61	0.54
Fortune	17	90	(0.50, 0.25)	0.54	0.69	0.56
Marisol	23	90	(0.50, 0.25)	0.62	0.58	0.53
Valencia	27	95	(0.50, 0.12)	0.64	0.67	0.62
T.Mean				**0.60**	**0.64**	**0.56**

Table 2. Detection results on individual defects (MIA-DDRCT)

Cultivar	Defects	Detected	False Detections
Clemenules	238	211 (88.7%)	04 (1.7%)
Fortune	172	159 (92.4%)	10 (5.5%)
Marisol	195	185 (94.9%)	07 (3.5%)
Valencia	138	125 (90.6%)	06 (4.2%)
Total	**743**	**680 (91.5%)**	**27 (3.8%)**

2.3 EGIS Approach

In this approach there is no training stage and also no model of sound color textures is built. Instead, the method tries to segment the sample (the image) into regions in such a way that adjacent regions have a different visual appearance but it remains similar within them. Thus, in order to extract the defects it is necessary to set the hypothesis that bigger regions in samples always correspond to the sound area (the background is not considered).

Since no training is performed, we went directly to tune the parameters of the method for each cultivar. Parameters are *sigma*, which is used to smooth the image before being segmented, and the k value of the threshold function. In [6] the recommended values for *sigma* and k are respectively 0.5 and 500, then, we varied the parameters around these central values. For each cultivar a set of experiments was performed varying *sigma* in [0.25, 0.30, 0.35, 0.40, 0.45, 0.50, 0.55, 0.60, 0.65, 0.70, 0.75], and k in [200, 250, 300, 350, 400, 450, 500, 550, 600, 650, 700, 750], which led to 132 different experiments. As the in previous approach, parameters were tuned by comparing the manually marked defects with regard to those achieved by the method. This comparison was performed again through the measures of Precision, Recall and F-Score. Tables 3 and 4 correspond to Tables 1 and 2 of previous approach. These tables show that the EGIS approach is better in fitting the marked defects and also in defect detection, although it produces more false detections.

A major difference between both approaches arises when we study their timing costs. Using an standard PC, we measured for both methods the mean timing cost of 20 executions performed on the same sample of clemenules cultivar. While the MIA-DDRCT method achieved a mean timing of 588,5 ms, the EGIS method achieved 162.5 ms. Nevertheless and despite the difference, both methods can meet the real-time requirements at production lines (5 pieces per second) since

Table 3. Best combinations of factors (EGIS)

Cultivar	sigma	k	Precision	Recall	F-Score
Clemenules	0.50	350	0.75	0.75	0.71
Fortune	0.45	350	0.72	0.73	0.66
Marisol	0.60	250	0.63	0.65	0.58
Valencia	0.65	450	0.77	0.74	0.72
T.Mean			**0.72**	**0.72**	**0.67**

Table 4. Detection results on individual defects (EGIS)

Cultivar	Defects	Detected	False Detections
Clemenules	238	220 (92.4%)	09 (3.6%)
Fortune	172	164 (95.4%)	12 (6.5%)
Marisol	195	182 (93.3%)	17 (8.2%)
Valencia	138	129 (93.5%)	08 (5.5%)
Total	**743**	**695 (93.5%)**	**46 (6.2%)**

their timing costs can be drastically reduced by using simple and cheap parallelization techniques based on computer clustering. Figure 3 shows the results achieved by both approaches on two different samples.

3   Conclusions

In this paper, we have presented an application of visual quality control in orange post-harvesting comparing two different approaches of Computer Vision. A general approach based on a Multivariate Image Analysis strategy for the detection of defects in random color textures (MIA-DDRCT), and a generic, graph-based and efficient approach to image segmentation (EGIS). Both methods have been compared through an experimental work performed on a ground truth composed by 120 samples of citrus coming from four different varieties.

First, a set of experiments were designed to tune-up the parameters in both methods. For each cultivar, the parameters of the corresponding method were varied in a wide range. This led to an extend number of experiments; 462 for the MIA-DDRCT method and 132 for the EGIS method. Then, the parameters were tuned using Precision, Recall and F-Score, three measures that compare the difference among the defects manually marked and the defects extracted by the methods. Since higher values of these measures were achieved by the EGIS method, we can conclude that this approach fits better the marked defects.

Then, for the best combinations of parameters for each cultivar in both methods, we collected the defect detection results. We counted the actual defects, the correctly detected defects and the false detections. In this case, the EGIS method achieved better performance in the correct detection ratio (93.5% versus 91.5%), while MIA-DDRCT was better providing less false detections (3.8% versus 6.2%). With regards to timing costs, the EGIS method performs 3.6 times

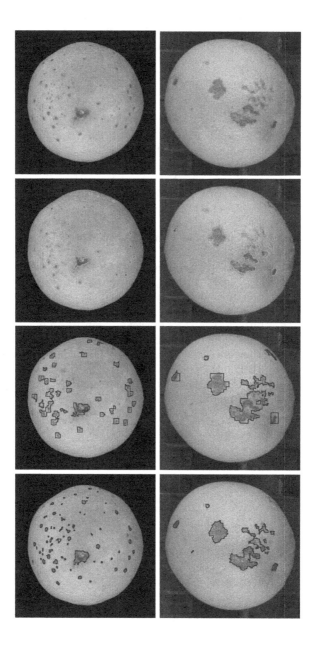

Fig. 3. MIA-DDRCT versus EGIS. From top to bottom; original, manually marked defects, MIA-DDRCT and EGIS results.

faster than MIA-DDRCT, although both methods can easily achieve real-time compliance by introducing simple parallelization techniques. Finally, the MIA-DDRCT approach has the advantage that does not need to use the hypothesis that the bigger area in samples correspond to the sound area, unlike it occurs in EGIS method.

References

1. Blasco, J., Aleixos, N., Moltó, E.: Computer vision detection of peel defects in citrus by means of a region oriented segmentation algorithm. Journal of Food Engineering 81(3), 535–543 (2007)
2. López, F., Prats, J.M., Ferrer, A., Valiente, J.M.: Defect Detection in Random Colour Textures Using the MIA T^2 Defect Maps. In: Campilho, A., Kamel, M.S. (eds.) ICIAR 2006. LNCS, vol. 4142, pp. 752–763. Springer, Heidelberg (2006)
3. Bharati, M.H., MacGregor, J.F.: Texture analysis of images using Principal Component Analysis. In: SPIE/Photonics Conference on Process Imaging for Automatic Control, pp. 27–37 (2000)
4. Geladi, P., Granh, H.: Multivariate Image Analysis. Wiley, Chichester (1996)
5. Prats-Montalbán, J.M., Ferrer, A.: Integration of colour and textural information in multivariate image analysis: defect detection and classification issues. Journal of Chemometrics 21(1-2), 10–23 (2007)
6. Felzenszwalb, P.F., Huttenlocher, D.P.: Efficient Graph-Based Image Segmentation. International Journal of Computer Vision 59(2), 167–181 (2004)
7. Urquhart, R.: Graph theoretical clustering based on limited neighborhood sets. Pattern Recognition 15(3), 173–187 (1982)
8. Zahn, C.T.: Graph-theoretic methods for detecting and describing gestalt clusters. IEEE Transactions on Computing 20(1), 68–86 (1971)

Domain Adaptation Based on Eigen-Analysis and Clustering, for Object Categorization

Suranjana Samanta and Sukhendu Das

V.P. Lab., Dept. of CSE, IIT Madras, India
ssamanta@cse.iitm.ac.in, sdas@iitm.ac.in

Abstract. Domain adaptation (DA) is a method used to obtain better classification accuracy, when the training and testing datasets have different distributions. This paper describes an algorithm for DA to transform data from source domain to match the distribution of the target domain. We use eigen-analysis of data on both the domains, to estimate the transformation along each dimension separately. In order to parameterize the distributions in both the domains, we perform clustering separately along every dimension, prior to the transformation. The proposed algorithm of DA when applied to the task of object categorization, gives better results than a few state of the art methods.

Keywords: Domain Adaptation (DA), non-parametric clustering, eigen-based transformation, object categorization.

1 Introduction

Domain adaptation [1], [2] is a well-known problem in the field of machine learning, with recent applications in many Computer Vision tasks. The basic assumption for most classification and regression techniques is that the training and the testing samples are drawn from the same distribution. For many real-world datasets, the distributions between the training and the testing data are dissimilar, which leads to a poor classification performance. This happens in situations where, the test samples are drawn only from the target domain and typically a large number of training samples are available in the source domain.

In many situations, only a few labeled samples (images) are available for a classification task in the target domain, though plenty of samples are available from the source (or auxiliary) domain. When a small number of labeled training samples are used for learning, then it generally creates an ill-fitting of a model. This is known as small sample size (SSS) problem, where the parameters obtained during the training phase are not generalized for the testing data, leading to high erroneous results during the testing phase.

Domain adaptation (DA) is the process where one can use the training samples available from source domain to aid a classification task. Typically, a large number of samples (instances) from source domain and a few from target domain are available for training in supervised DA. The job of classification is done using

R. Wilson et al. (Eds.): CAIP 2013, Part I, LNCS 8047, pp. 245–253, 2013.

a separate set of test samples obtained only from the target domain. Broadly speaking, there are two types of DA techniques available in the literature: (a) supervised - where we have a very small number of labeled training samples from the target domain and (b) unsupervised - where we have plenty of unlabeled training samples from target domain. Using training samples from both the domains, we expect to built a statistical model, which gives better performance on the testing data available from the target domain.

In the recent past, the problem of transfer learning or DA, has been attempted on applications of various computer vision tasks [1], [2], [3], [4]. Jiang et. al. [5] and Yang et. al. [6] have proposed methods of modifying the existing SVM trained on video samples available from source domain by introducing a bias term between source and target domains during optimization in training the SVM. A transformation matrix has been proposed in [1], which transforms instances from one domain to other. In [7], a domain dependent regularizer has been proposed, which enforces the target classifier to give results similar to the relevant base classifiers on unlabeled instances from target domain. There have been works on unsupervised DA which measures the geodesic distance between source and target domains in Grassmannian manifold [2], [3]. Application of DA on face detection recognition [8] has also been exploited.

In this paper, we use the structural information of clusters present in the dataset for DA. Transformation of data to a different domain becomes simplified if the distribution of the two domains are known or estimated properly. Hence, we group the dataset into Gaussian clusters in both the domains, and propose transformation of clusters from source to target domain using an inter-domain cluster mapping function. Results shown on real-world object categorization datasets reveal the efficiency of the system.

The rest of the paper is organized as follows. Section 2 gives a concise description of the proposed method of clustering and domain transformation. Section 3 presents and discusses the performance of the proposed methodology on real-world datasets. Section 4 concludes the paper.

2   Proposed Method of Domain Adaptation

This paper presents a method of DA, where instances from the source domain are transformed to match the distribution of the target domain. The eigen-analysis of a data is robust to the presence of less number of samples. This has been the major motivation of our work. The proposed method of DA, consists of three main stages - (a) clustering data in both the domains dimension-wise, to represent the data in both the domains using one or multiple number of Gaussian function(s), (b) cross-domain mapping of clusters which helps to determine which cluster in target domain has a similar distribution with a cluster in source domain such that, the particular source domain cluster has distribution similar to the mapped target domain cluster after transformation and (c) Eigen-Domain Transformation (EDT) - to transform a source domain cluster such that its distribution is similar to its mapped target domain cluster. We consider that atleast one training sample per class is present from both source and target domains.

Let $\mathbf{X} \in \Re^{n_s \times D}$ and $\mathbf{Y} \in \Re^{n_t \times D}$ denote the source and the target data having n_s and n_t number of samples respectively. Let, K_s^d and K_t^d be the number of clusters in $\mathbf{X}^d$ and $\mathbf{Y}^d$ respectively. Let $\delta_s^d : \{1, \ldots, K_s^d\}$ and $\delta_t^d : \{1, \ldots, K_t^d\}$ be the sets of cluster-labels of the clusters formed in $\mathbf{X}^d$ and $\mathbf{Y}^d$, where $\mathbf{X}^d$ and $\mathbf{Y}^d$ represents the dth feature of $\mathbf{X}$ and $\mathbf{Y}$ respectively $(d = 1, 2, \ldots, D)$. Let $\mathbf{X}_i^d$ and $\mathbf{Y}_j^d$ denote the ith and j^{th} clusters of $\mathbf{X}^d$ and $\mathbf{Y}^d$ respectively $(i \in \delta_s^d, j \in \delta_t^d)$. The entire process has been explained in the following sub-sections.

2.1   Clustering Using Non-parametric Density Estimation

This step computes the density distribution of data and obtains clusters in both the domains along each dimension separately. To cluster a data along each dimension, we estimate the density of the data using Parzen window estimator. The size of the window is set to $n^{-1/2}$, where n is the number of instances. Next, we detect the peaks and the valleys present in the probability density distribution. All the instances whose probability density falls between two adjacent valley points are clustered together. Since we are clustering the data along each dimension separately, a dataset may have different number of clusters along each dimension. This process is repeated for both source and target domains. A process of smoothing the density distribution may be necessary prior to detection of peaks and valleys.

Initially, we normalize the range of the data in both domains. The problem of small sample size will not affect the method of non-parametric clustering, as the process is performed repeatedly (done for all dimensions separately) using only one dimension at a time. Distribution of dataset can be parameterized by fitting a Gaussian mixture model (GMM) in general. However, due to presence of very few number of samples in target domain, often fitting a GMM produces inaccurate result and is thus avoided.

2.2   Cross-Domain Mapping of Clusters

We define a mapping $F_{S \to T}^d : \delta_s^d \to \delta_t^d$, which maps each cluster in source domain to a cluster in target domain, using KL-divergence measure. If $F_{S \to T}^d(i) = j$, i.e. $\mathbf{X}_i^d$ is mapped to $\mathbf{Y}_j^d$, where $\mathbf{Y}_j^d$ is termed as the 'image cluster' of $\mathbf{X}_i^d$ and $\mathbf{X}_i^d$ is the 'pre-image cluster' of $\mathbf{Y}_j^d$.

Since $n_s \neq n_t$, we calculate the divergence between two cross-domain clusters using the KL-Divergence measure (assuming a Gaussian distribution), which requires the mean and covariance of the two Gaussian distributions. Hence, we assume a univariate Gaussian function over each cluster along a feature dimension. The position of a peak present between the two valleys is considered as the mean of the Gaussian function. The average distance between a pair of valleys on either side of a peak is considered as an approximation of the standard deviation. KL-Divergence ($kldiv$) between two Gaussian distribution is then estimated using the formulation as described in [9]. The cross-domain mapping function, $F_{S \to T}^d$, is calculated as follows:

a. Calculate a dissimilarity matrix $\Lambda^d_{S \to T} \in \Re^{K^d_s \times K^d_t}$, using KL divergence [9] between all pairs of clusters, such that $\Lambda^d_{S \to T}(i,j) = kldiv(\mathbf{X}^d_i, \mathbf{Y}^d_j)$.

b. Calculate the average similarity of each of the clusters in $\mathbf{Y}^d$, with all the source domain clusters as: $\eta^d(j) = \underset{i}{\text{mean}} \left(\Lambda^d_{S \to T}(i,j) \right), \ \forall j \in \delta^d_t$.

c. Using the criterion: if the $\mathbf{Y}^d_j$ is most similar to $\mathbf{X}^d_i$, then $F^d_{S \to T}(i) = j$; calculate $F^d_{S \to T}$ as: $F^d_{S \to T}(i) = \arg\min_j \eta^d_{S \to T}(i,j), \ \forall i \in \delta^d_s$. Here, $F^{-1}_{S \to T}{}^d(i)$ denotes the inverse mapping, which gives the set of 'pre-image clusters' of $\mathbf{Y}^d_j$ in the source domain.

d. Now, if for any $\mathbf{Y}^d_j$ the 'pre-image cluster' set is NULL, then identify a $\mathbf{X}^d_i$ satisfying the following conditions and re-assign the mapping as:

$$F^d_{S \to T}(i) = \arg\min_j \Lambda^d_{S \to T}(i,j) \left| \begin{array}{l} \forall j, \text{ such that } F^{-1}_{S \to T}{}^d(j) \text{ is NULL} \\ \forall i, \text{ such that } |F^{-1}_{S \to T}{}^d(F^d_{S \to T}(i))| > 1 \\ \text{and } \Lambda^d_{S \to T}(i,j) \le \eta^d(j) \end{array} \right.$$

If there remains some cluster in target domain which is outside the range of the function $F^d_{S \to T}$ but have similar distribution to a cluster in source domain, we re-assign the mapping function based on the above equation. Let $\mathbf{X}^d_i$ be a cluster in $\mathbf{X}^d$ and its corresponding 'image cluster' in $\mathbf{Y}^d$ be $\mathbf{Y}^d_j$. Let, there exist another cluster $\mathbf{Y}^d_k$ in $\mathbf{Y}^d$ for which the 'pre-image cluster' set is empty (thus, $kldiv(\mathbf{X}^d_i, \mathbf{Y}^d_j) \le kldiv(\mathbf{X}_i, \mathbf{Y}_k)$). If $\mathbf{X}^d_i$ is quite similar, based on the condition: $kldiv(\mathbf{X}^d_i, \mathbf{Y}^d_k) \le \eta^d(j)$ and the current number of elements in the 'pre-image' set of $\mathbf{Y}^d_j$ is greater than one (there exists at least one more cluster $\mathbf{X}^d_k$ such that $k \ne i$), then according to this step, update the 'image cluster' for $\mathbf{X}^d_i$ to $\mathbf{Y}^d_k$.

2.3   Eigen Domain Transformation (EDT)

This stage describes the process of transferring instances from source to target domain using well-formed clusters formed at the earlier stage. While transformation, we preserve the relative distances between instances of source domain along each of the directions of principal component directions. The relation between the eigen-analysis of a data following Gaussian distribution with the distribution parameters are given in [10] (pp-29). The proposed method of EDT exploits this relation after clustering groups the data following Gaussian distribution. We match the distribution of the source and target clusters in the eigen-space and project it back to get the transformed source cluster.

Let, $(\lambda_i = [\lambda^1_i, \ldots \lambda^D_i], \Phi_i = [\Phi^1_i \ldots \Phi^D_i])$ and $(\gamma_i = [\gamma^1_i \ldots \gamma^D_i], \Psi_i = [\Psi^1_i \ldots \Psi^D_i])$, be the corresponding pair of eigen values/vectors obtained by cluster-wise eigen-analysis of $\mathbf{X}_i$ and $\mathbf{Y}_j$ respectively. Each cluster $\mathbf{X}^d_i, \ i \in \delta^d_s$, of source domain, is transformed to match the distribution of its corresponding 'image cluster' $F^d_{S \to T}(i)$, as determined in the previous stage. If $\overset{\tau}{\mathbf{X}}$ denotes the transformed source domain data, then the eigen analysis of $\overset{\tau}{\mathbf{X}}$ should be identical to that of $\mathbf{Y}$. Let us consider one cluster, $\mathbf{X}_i^d$, whose 'image cluster' is $\mathbf{Y}_j^d$ in the target domain ($F_{S \to T}^d(i) = j$). The steps to obtain $\overset{\tau}{\mathbf{X}}$ are as follows:

1. For each dimension d, do:
   (a) Consider the projection of $\mathbf{X}_i^d$ onto Φ_i^d, denoted by $\hat{\mathbf{X}}_i^d$, which can be obtained by considering the dth dimension of $\mathbf{X}_i\Phi_i$. Similarly, calculate $\hat{\mathbf{Y}}_j^d$ using Ψ_j for target domain. Normalize the range of $\hat{\mathbf{X}}_i^d$.
   (b) Adjust the mean and variance of $\hat{\mathbf{X}}_i^d$ to match that of $\hat{\mathbf{Y}}_i^d$, as: $\tilde{\mathbf{X}}_i^d = \gamma_j^d(\hat{\mathbf{X}}_i^d) + \mu_j^d$; where, μ_j^d is the mean of $\hat{\mathbf{Y}}_j^d$. Since this is a linear operation, the relative distances between instances remain preserved in eigen domain.
   (c) Form $\tilde{\mathbf{X}}^d = [\tilde{\mathbf{X}}_1^d; ...; \tilde{\mathbf{X}}_{K_s^d}^d]^T$, i.e., the dth dimension of $\tilde{\mathbf{X}}$.

2. The transformed source domain data, $\overset{\tau}{\mathbf{X}}$ is estimated using inverse eigen-transformation as: $\overset{\tau}{\mathbf{X}} = \tilde{\mathbf{X}}\Psi^{-1}$ where, $\tilde{\mathbf{X}} = [\tilde{\mathbf{X}}^1 \tilde{\mathbf{X}}^2 ... \tilde{\mathbf{X}}^D]$.

2.4 Result on a Synthetic (toy) Data

To explain the steps of the proposed algorithm, we consider a simple example of data distribution in source and target domains in $\Re^2$. In Fig. 1 (a) the green and the blue points denote the instances from source and target domains respectively. The result of dimension-wise clustering for first and second dimensions are shown in Figs. 1 (b) and (c) respectively. The curves shown on top in green and the blue, denote the density obtained by the Parzen window estimator for source and target domains. The brown and the magenta curves in Figs. 1 (b) & (c) denote the Gaussian distributions modeling the density functions for each cluster in source and target domains respectively. Fig. 1 (d) shows the transformed source domain data in red points obtained using the proposed method, as explained in

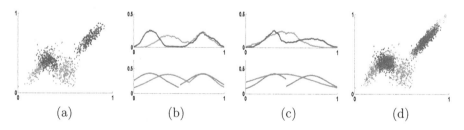

(a)   (b)   (c)   (d)

Fig. 1. Data from source and target domains (in $\Re^2$) are marked in green and blue points in (a) and (d); while transformed source domain data is marked in red in (d). Intermediate results of clustering are shown in (b) and (c) for first and second dimensions respectively. Green and blue (dash) curves denote the density of data in source and target domains. Brown and magenta (dash) curves indicate the Gaussian functions modeling the clusters distributions formed in source and target domains respectively.

previous sub-sections, whose distribution is similar to that of the target domain data. The KL divergence measure with respect to the target domain, for the source and transformed source domains are 9.0179 and 0.5371 respectively.

3   Experimental Results

We evaluate the performance of the proposed method on real world datasets for object categorization. The original Office dataset [1] contains 3 domains: Amazon (A), Dslr (D) and Webcam (W), each having 31 classes of objects. In [2], Office dataset has been merged with Caltech-256 dataset to create four domains, Amazon (A), Caltech (C), Dslr (D) and Webcam (W), with ten classes of objects. A few sample images from the 4 domains are shown in Fig. 2. The size of the image samples in Amazon, DSLR, Webcam and Caltech datasets, are: 300×300, 1000×1000, 500×500 (average size) and $170 \times 104 - 2304 \times 1728$.

Fig. 2. Sample images of two classes of objects taken from four domains

SURF features [11] are extracted and a bag of words (BOW) feature set is calculated with a codebook of size 800, as done in [1], [2]. Two methods of EDT are used for experimentation: (i) class-wise EDT: done for every class separately, and (ii) Unsupervised EDT: done on the entire dataset by considering data from all classes together. In the following, we describe the two sets of experimentation done to exhibit the efficiency of the proposed method of DA.

In the first set of experimentation, we consider the Office dataset [1] with 31 classes. Number of training samples taken are: for target domain 3 samples per class for Amazon/Dslr/Webcam, for source domain 8 samples per class for Webcam/Dslr and 20 samples per class for Amazon. Results obtained using a K-nearest neighbor (k=1) classifier, are averaged over a 10-fold cross validation, which are compared with that reported in [1], [2]. Table 1 shows the classification accuracy (in %-age) of object categorization using different techniques of DA. The 2nd and 3rd columns show the results of metric learning [1] while the 4th and 5th columns show the results of sampling geodesic flow (SGF) [2]. The 6th and 7th columns show the result of our proposed class-wise and unsupervised EDT methods respectively. The proposed EDT gives better performance than the metric learning method given in [1], while the results of SDF [2] outperform the proposed method only in one case.

In second set of experimentations, we consider the object dataset considered in [7], which is a mixture of the office dataset [1] and Caltech - 256 [12]. The

Table 1. Classification accuracy (in %-age) of Office dataset [1] using different techniques of domain adaptation (DA). Best classification accuracy is highlighted in bold.

Domains		Metric Learning [1]		SGF [2]		Proposed EDT	
Source	Target	Asymm	Symm	Unsup.	Semi-sup.	Class-wise	Unsup.
webcam	dslr	25	27	19	37	**41.13**	32
dslr	webcam	30	31	26	36	48.26	**52.22**
amazon	webcam	48	44	39	**57**	50.01	49.00

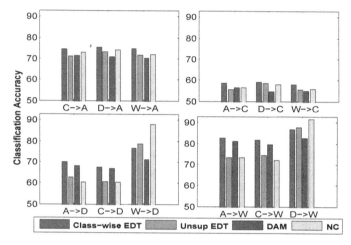

Fig. 3. Classification accuracy done using DA for 12 different cases of object categorization, using the Office+Caltech dataset [2]. Results are grouped into four categories, with an identical target domain and three source domains considered separately.

dataset has four different domains from which we get 12 different pairs of source and target domains. We create different sets of training samples by considering different fractions (0.2, 0.3, ... , 0.7) of the training samples from the target domain. The average classification accuracy is reported with a 10-fold cross validation. In this case, we use SVM with histogram intersection kernel to obtain the classification accuracy. We compare our method with Domain Adaptive Machine (DAM) [7], a supervised technique of DA. Results are shown in Fig. 3.

The mean accuracy over different sets of training samples is reported for all the 12 scenarios of classification using DA. The red and the green bar in Fig. 3 shows the performance of proposed class-wise and unsupervised EDT methods respectively. The blue bar shows the mean accuracy when DAM [7] is used. We also observe the performance of the classifier when samples from both source and target domains are combined together for training. This method is termed as Naive Combination (NC), for which the performance is given by the yellow bar. Class-wise EDT technique gives the best result for 10 DA classification tasks. For two cases, D→W and W→D, NC gives better results. This is due to the fact that the two domains - Dslr and Webcam have similar distribution and application of DA in this case leads to negative transfer.

Another interesting fact for these two tasks is that the unsupervised EDT performs marginally better than the class-wise-EDT, as the available number of training samples are the least among the 12 different classification tasks. Hence, the unsupervised EDT is expected to give better performance as the covariance matrix is estimated more accurately with a larger number of training samples (than in class-wise EDT), leading to less error during eigen-analysis. Hence, the choice between two techniques of EDT (class-wise and unsupervised) for a classification task, should be based on the number of available training samples.

4   Conclusion

We have proposed a new method of domain adaptation and applied it successfully for the task of object categorization. Difference in distributions among the data in source and target domains, is overcome by clustering and then modeling with Gaussian functions. A cross-domain mapping function helps to transform data from source to target domain, using a forward followed by an inverse eigen-transformations. Results show that the proposed method of DA is better than a few state of the art published in the recent past. The work can be extended for handling multiple source domains.

Acknowledgment. This work is supported by TCS India.

References

1. Saenko, K., Kulis, B., Fritz, M., Darrell, T.: Adapting visual category models to new domains. In: Daniilidis, K., Maragos, P., Paragios, N. (eds.) ECCV 2010, Part IV. LNCS, vol. 6314, pp. 213–226. Springer, Heidelberg (2010)
2. Gopalan, R., Li, R., Chellappa, R.: Domain adaptation for object recognition: An unsupervised approach. In: International Conference in Computer Vision, pp. 999–1006 (2011)
3. Grauman, K.: Geodesic flow kernel for unsupervised domain adaptation. In: IEEE Conference on Computer Vision and Pattern Recognition, pp. 2066–2073 (2012)
4. Marton, Z.-C., Balint-Benczedi, F., Seidel, F., Goron, L.C., Beetz, M.: Object categorization in clutter using additive features and hashing of part-graph descriptors. In: Stachniss, C., Schill, K., Uttal, D. (eds.) Spatial Cognition 2012. LNCS (LNAI), vol. 7463, pp. 17–33. Springer, Heidelberg (2012)
5. Jiang, W., Zavesky, E., Fu Chang, S., Loui, A.: Cross-domain learning methods for high-level visual concept classification. In: International Conference on Image Processing, pp. 161–164 (2008)
6. Yang, J., Yan, R., Hauptmann, A.G.: Cross-domain video concept detection using adaptive svms. In: International Conference on Multimedia, pp. 188–197 (2007)
7. Duan, L., Xu, D., Tsang, I.W.H.: Domain adaptation from multiple sources: A domain-dependent regularization approach. IEEE Transaction in Neural Netwetwork Learning System 23(3), 504–518 (2012)

8. Qiu, Q., Patel, V.M., Turaga, P., Chellappa, R.: Domain adaptive dictionary learning. In: Fitzgibbon, A., Lazebnik, S., Perona, P., Sato, Y., Schmid, C. (eds.) ECCV 2012, Part IV. LNCS, vol. 7575, pp. 631–645. Springer, Heidelberg (2012)
9. Penny, W.: Kl-divergences of normal, gamma, dirichlet and wishart densities. Technical report, Wellcome Department of Cognitive Neurology, University College London (2001)
10. Fukunaga, K.: Introduction to Statistical Pattern Recognition, 2nd edn. Academic Press (1990)
11. Bay, H., Ess, A., Tuytelaars, T., Van Gool, L.: Speeded-up robust features (surf). Computer Vision Image Understanding 110(3), 346–359 (2008)
12. Griffin, G., Holub, A., Perona, P.: Caltech-256 object category dataset. Technical Report 7694, California Institute of Technology (2007)

Estimating Clusters Centres Using Support Vector Machine: An Improved Soft Subspace Clustering Algorithm

Amel Boulemnadjel and Fella Hachouf

Laboratoire d' Automatique et de Robotique, Département d' Électronique
Faculté des sciences de l'ingérineur, Université Constantine 1
Route d' Ain el bey, 25000 Constantine, Algérie
meriem.hacini@yahoo.fr, hachouf.fella@gmail.com

Abstract. In this paper, a new approach of soft subspace clustering is proposed. It is based on the estimation of the clusters centres using a multi-class support vector machine (SVM). This method is an extension of the ESSC algorithm which is performed by optimizing an objective function containing three terms: a weighting within cluster compactness, entropy of weights and a weighting between clusters separations. First, the SVM is used to compute initial centres and partition matrices. This new developed formulation of the centres is integrated in each iteration to yield new centres and membership degrees. A comparative study has been conducted on UCI datasets and different image types. The obtained results show the effectiveness of the suggested method.

Keywords: soft, subspace, clustering, SVM, centre.

1 Introduction

Clustering problem concerns the discovery of homogeneous groups of data according to a certain similarity measure. In high dimensional data sets, it is difficult to differentiate between similar data points from dissimilar ones. Clusters are embedded in subspaces of high dimensional data space, and different clusters may exist in different subspaces of different dimensions. The difficulty that conventional clustering algorithms encounter in dealing with high dimensional data sets motivates the concept of subspaces clustering [1]. Subspace clustering is the task of detecting all clusters in all subspaces. This means that a point might be a member of multiple clusters, each existing in a different subspace. This concept is better in handling multidimensional data than other methods. The two main categories of subspace clustering algorithms are hard subspace clustering and soft subspace clustering. Hard subspace clustering methods [2, 3] have been extensively studied for clustering high dimensional data to identify the exact clusters. Soft subspace clustering [4, 5, 6] has become an effective mean of dealing with high dimensional data. It assigns a weight to each dimension to measure its contribution to build a particular cluster. Most clustering techniques

R. Wilson et al. (Eds.): CAIP 2013, Part I, LNCS 8047, pp. 254–261, 2013.

use a distance as a similarity or dissimilarity between objects as a measure to yield clusters. A major weakness of soft subspaces clustering algorithms is that almost all of them are developed based on within- cluster information only or by employing both within-cluster and between- clusters information. Also, most existing soft subspace clustering algorithms contain parameters which are difficult to be determined by users in real-world applications. Many subspaces clustering algorithms have been developed and applied to different areas [7, 8, 9]. Their performance can be further enhanced. In the most recent methods, locally adaptive metrics are developed to avoid the risk of information loss encountered in global dimensionality reduction techniques. Different combinations of dimensions are used via local weighting of features [10]. In [11],the authors propose two types of weights in the clustering process. It is an extension of the K-means algorithm by adding two steps to automatically calculate the two types of subspace weights. Another soft subspace clustering method is proposed in [6] (ESSC) ; employing both within cluster and between cluster information. The optimized objective function is developed by integrating the within- clusters compactness and the between-cluster separation. This objective function contains three terms, the weighting within-cluster compactness, the entropy of weights and the weighting between-cluster separation. This algorithm has a problem of locating clusters centres, in terms of estimating inter and intra clusters' distances. Indeed, errors in estimating distances between centres are amplified through the iterations, which induces a classification low rate and a high processing time. In this paper, we propose a new method for subspace clustering based on enhanced clusters centres estimation. For this purpose a classification step using a multi class support vector machine SVM is performed [12,13]. As an initialization step, the first six parameters of the co-occurrence matrix and the edges are extracted from the original image. An SVM is trained using these features to estimate the clusters centres vi and the membership degree uj of each element. As a processing step the ESSC algorithm uses these values to compute the new ones and produces a new SVM training vector. The classification is performed if the test of centers given by the SVM at two consecutive otherwise the computed v and u by the SVM are injected into the ESSC and so on. Results in different parameters subspace are concatenated (cf. Fig.1). This paper is organized as follows: after an introduction, Section 2 describes the new soft subspace clustering method. The results are discussed in Section 3. Finally some concluding remarks are given in the last section.

2   The Proposed Method

SVM is applied using an arbitrary learning vector T

$$T_{xy} = \{(x_1, y_1), ..., (x_k, y_k)\} \tag{1}$$

Where y_k : the cluster of the input x_k The SVM are trained on the data T_{xy} whith the kernel function k given by :

$$k(x_i y_j) = exp(-\frac{||x_i - y_j||}{2\sigma^2}) \tag{2}$$

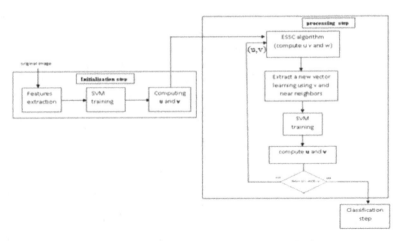

Fig. 1. Flowchart of the proposed method

Where x_i , x_j : data inputs,

σ is a free parameter

The optimal values of σ are retained. They match to the best classification rate. The clusters centers v_{ik} obtained by SVM can be written as:

$$v'_{ik} = \frac{\sum_{l=1}^{N_i} x_{li}}{N_i} = \frac{\sum_{j=1}^{N} w_{ij} x_{jk}}{N_i} \tag{3}$$

Where the membership degrees u' are defined as:

$$\begin{cases} u'_{ij} = 1 \ \ if \ the \ cluster \ of \ the \ pixel \ j \ is \ equal \ to \ i \\ u'_{ij} = 0 \ \ otherwise \end{cases} \qquad i = 1...c; j = 1...N \tag{4}$$

$$J_{ESSC}(v, u, w) = \sum_{i=1}^{c} \sum_{j=1}^{N} u_{ij}^m \sum_{k=1}^{D} w_{ik}(x_{ik} - v_{ik})^2$$

$$+\gamma \sum_{i=1}^{c} \sum_{k=1}^{D} w_{ik} ln w_{ik} - \eta \sum_{i=1}^{c} (\sum_{j=1}^{N} u_{ij}^m) \sum_{k=1}^{D} w_{ik}(v_{ik} - v_{0k})^2$$

$$\tag{5}$$

Where

c: clusters number, N: data size. D: features number. v: cluster center , w: weight matrix, u: fuzzy partition matrix.

Using the Lagrange multiplier u, v and w are deduced to minimize the objective function of $Eq.5$: Using the Lagrange multiplier u, v and w are deduced to minimize the objective function of Eq.5:

$$u_{ij} = \frac{[\sum_{k=1}^{D} w_{ik}(x_{jk} - vik) - \eta \sum_{k=1}^{D} w_{ik}(v_{ik} - v_{0k})^2]^{-\frac{1}{m-1}}}{\sum_{i'=1}^{c} [\sum_{k=1}^{D} w_{ik}(x_{jk} - vik) - \eta \sum_{k=1}^{D} w_{ik}(v_{ik} - v_{0k})^2]^{-\frac{1}{m-1}}} \tag{6}$$

$$v_{ij} = \frac{\sum_{j=1}^{N} u_{ij}^m (x_{jk} - \eta v_{0K})}{\sum_{j=1}^{N} u_{ij}^m (1 - \eta)} \tag{7}$$

$$w_{ik} = \frac{exp(\frac{\sum_{k=1}^{N} u_{ij}^m (x_{jk} - vik) - \eta \sum_{j=1}^{N} u_{ij}^m (v_{ik} - v_{0k})^2}{\gamma})}{\sum_{k'=1}^{D} exp(\frac{\sum_{k=1}^{N} u_{ij}^m (x_{jk} - vik) - \eta \sum_{j=1}^{N} u_{ij}^m (v_{ik} - v_{0k})^2}{\gamma})} \tag{8}$$

In each iteration , the obtained clusters centers v_{ik} and their near neighborhoods detected using an Euclidean distance constitute the new SVM vector training.

$$T_{xy} = \{(v_1, 1), ..., (v_c, c), (x_i, y_i), ..., (x_k, y_k)\} \tag{9}$$

Where
$y_i = \max_{i=1:c} (u_{ij})$ c: number of clusters
k: vector size
The size of the learntng vecior depends on the data size.
The final equations ow u ano f are as follows:

$$u_{ij} = \frac{[\sum_{k=1}^{D} w_{ik}(x_{jk} - \frac{\sum_{j'=1}^{N} u'_{ij'} x_{j'k}}{N_i})^2 - \eta \sum_{k=1}^{D} w_{ik}(\frac{\sum_{j'=1}^{N} u'_{ij'} x_{j'k}}{N_i} - v_{0k})^2]^{-\frac{1}{m-1}}}{\sum_{i'=1}^{c} [\sum_{k=1}^{D} w_{ik}(x_{jk} - \frac{\sum_{j'=1}^{N} u'_{ij'} x_{j'k}}{N_i})^2 - \eta \sum_{k=1}^{D} w_{ik}(\frac{\sum_{j'=1}^{N} u'_{ij'} x_{j'k}}{N_i} - v_{0k})^2]^{-\frac{1}{m-1}}} \tag{10}$$

Where

$$v_{0k} = \frac{\sum_{i=1}^{c} \frac{\sum_{j'=1}^{N} u'_{ij'} x_{j'k}}{N_i}}{c} \tag{11}$$

$$w_{ik} = \frac{exp(\frac{\sum_{k=1}^{N} u_{ij}^m (x_{jk} - \frac{\sum_{j'=1}^{N} u'_{ij'} x_{j'k}}{N_i}) - \eta \sum_{j=1}^{N} u_{ij}^m (\frac{\sum_{j'=1}^{N} u'_{ij'} x_{j'k}}{N_i} - v_{0k})^2}{\gamma})}{\sum_{k'=1}^{D} exp(\frac{\sum_{k=1}^{N} u_{ij}^m (x_{jk} - \frac{\sum_{j'=1}^{N} u'_{ij'} x_{j'k}}{N_i}) - \eta \sum_{j=1}^{N} u_{ij}^m (\frac{\sum_{j'=1}^{N} u'_{ij'} x_{j'k}}{N_i} - v_{0k})^2}{\gamma})} \tag{12}$$

Algorithm.

Initialization step

- Input: Number of clusters C, parameters m, μ and ε.
- Train SVM by input data
- Compute w by using (8)

Processing step
While $|v(t+1) - v(t) \geq \varepsilon|$ **do**

- Compute the partition matrix u using (10)
- Compute the cluster centre matrix v using(7)
- Compute w using (11)
- Extract the vector learning using centres previously computed
- Apply the SVM algorithm.
- Compute the new centres matrix using equations 3 and 4.

endwhile
Clustering step

- Assign each pixel i its potential cluster using the max of memberships degrees.

3 Results and Discussions

The performance of the proposed algorithm has been studied on the six UCI databases [15] given with the specific number of clusters, number of instances and the number of attributes. The normalized mutual information (NMI) metric given by Eq.12 is used to evaluate and compare the performance of the proposed algorithm and ESSC [6]. The higher is the value of NMI, the better is the result of the clustering.

$$NMI = \frac{\sum_{i=1}^{c} \sum_{i=1}^{c} logN. \frac{N_{ij}.Nj}{N_i}}{\sqrt{\sum_{i=1}^{c} \frac{N_i logN_i}{N}} . \sum_{j=1}^{c} N_j log\sqrt{N_j N}} \qquad (13)$$

Where
N_{ij} is the number of agreements between clusters i and true cluster$j$.
N_i is the number of data points in clusters i.
N_j is the number of data points in true cluster j.
All the experiments were implemented on a 2.22 GHz CPU and 2GB RAM. The used database descriptions are given in Table 1. The NMI values are tabulated in Table 2.

It is clear from Table 2 that the NMI value is greater for the proposed algorithm than the ESSC algorithm. Also the iteration number decreases.

For both methods, the evolution norm of clusters centers is plotted against the iterations number. The results are compared to the real norm of clusters centers given by the dataset (Figure.2 green). The clusters centers obtained by

Table 1. UCI datasets

Database name	Clusters number	Number of Instances	Number of Attributes
Abdolan	3	4177	8
Australian	2	690	14
balance	3	625	4
Car	4	946	18
Glass	6 ·	214	9
Heart 1	5	270	13
Heart	2	270	13
Iris	3	150	4
Wine	3	178	13

Table 2. Clustering results Obtained for nine UCI datasets with NMI as metricc

dataset	methods	NMI	iterations
Abdolan	ESSC	0.1639	13
	Proposed method	**0.1811**	7
Australian	ESSC	0.3617	12
	Proposed method	**0.3884**	2
Balance	ESSC	0.2278	4
	Proposed method	**0.2878**	3
Car	ESSC	0.1235	12
	Propdseo method	**0.2265**	3
Glass	ESSC	0.3505	35
	Proposed method	**0.5483**	7
Heart	ESSC	**0.3067**	12
	Proposed method	0.2533	2
Heart1	ESSC	0.1114	16
	Proposed method	**0.1933**	7
Iris	ESSC	0.7419	22
	Proposed method	**0.8642**	4
wine	ESSC	**0.8629**	31
	Proposed method	0.7774	4

the proposed method are closer to the real centers with a minimum number of iterations (Figure.2). The proposed approach has been tested on different types of image to evaluate its performance in image segmentation. The first six parameters of co-occurrence features [15] and the edge detection have been used, namely: contrast, homogeneity, correlation, energy, angular second moment and the entropy. The number of clusters C for Fig 3.A is 5 for the two methods, for Fig 3.B C =6. The obtained images are given in Figure 3. It is noticed that on Figures.3B1 and 3B2, some clusters are merged. On Figure.3B1 some edges of the triangle are missing and some parts of the flower do not appear. The background of the image and the triangle constitute the same cluster. Unlike to Figures.3B1 and 3B2, Figures.3C1 and 3C2 show better shapes. The edge and the leaves of the flower are well defined..

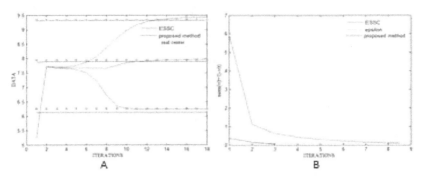

Fig. 2. A:Centres evolution against iterations number: iris dataset, B: Convergence

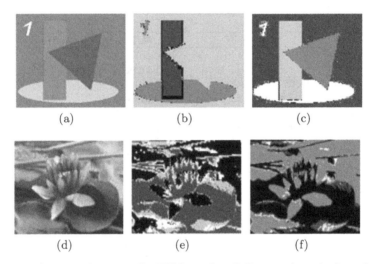

(a)   (b)   (c)

(d)   (e)   (f)

Fig. 3. A: original images; B: ESSC results, C: Proposed method results

4   Conclusion

In this paper a soft subspace clustering is enhanced. New formulations of the membership degrees and centers clusters have been developed. Obtained results have shown the significant improvement of the data clustering. Estimating the center and the membership degree in the initialization step has reduced the number of iterations that made very fast the algorithm convergence. SVM algorithm used in the initialization step has improved the centers location. In a future work, we suggest to use active learning for a better selection of the learning vector, and thus improving the clustering and minimizing the running time.

References

1. Agrawal, R., et al.: Automatic subspace clustering of high dimensional data for data mining applications. In: SIGMOD Record ACM Special Interest Group on Management of Data, pp. 94–105 (1998)

2. Parsons, L., Haque, E., Liu, H.: Evaluating subspace clustering algorithms. In Workshop on Clustering High Dimensional Data and its Applications. In: SIAM Int. Conf. on Data Mining, pp. 48–56 (2004)
3. Yip, K.Y., Cheung, D.W., Ng, M.K.: A practical projected clustering algorithm. IEEE Trans. Knowl. Data Eng. 16(11), 1387–1397 (2004)
4. Chang, H., Yeung, D.Y.: Locally linear metric adaptation with application to semi-supervised clustering and image retrieval. Pattern Recognition 39, 1253–1264 (2006)
5. Liang, B., et al.: A novel attribute weighting algorithm for clustering high-dimensional categorical data. Pattern Recognition 44, 2843–2861 (2011)
6. Deng, Z., et al.: Enhanced soft subspace clustering integrating within cluster and between-cluster information. Pattern Recognition 43, 767–781 (2010)
7. Damodar, R., Janaa, P.K.: A prototype-based modified DBSCAN for gene clustering. Procedia Technology 6, 485–492 (2012)
8. Yang, A., et al.: Unsupervised segmentation of natural images via lossy data compression. Comput. Vis. Image Understand 110, 212–225 (2008)
9. Vidal, R., Tron, R., Hartley, R.: Multiframe motion segmentation with missing data using power factorization and GPCA. Int. J. Comput. Vis. 79, 85–105 (2008)
10. Domeniconi, C., et al.: Locally adaptive metrics for clustering high dimensional data. Data Min. Knowl. Disc. 14, 63–67 (2007)
11. Xiaojun, C., et al.: A feature group weighting method for subspace clustering of high dimensional data. Pattern Recognition 45, 434–446 (2012)
12. Sangeetha, R., et al.: Identifying Efficient Kernel Function in Multiclass Support Vector Machines. International Journal of Computer Applications 28 (2011)
13. Vapnik, V.: An overview of statistical learning theory. IEEE Trans. on Neural Networks (1999)
14. http://archive.ics.uci.edu/ml/
15. Haralick, R., et al.: Textural features for image classification. IEEE Transactions on Systems, Man and Cybernetics 3(6), 610–621 (1973)

Fast Approximate Minimum Spanning Tree Algorithm Based on K-Means

Caiming Zhong[1,2,3], Mikko Malinen[2], Duoqian Miao[1], and Pasi Fränti[2]

[1] Department of Computer Science and Technology, Tongji University,
Shanghai 201804, PR China
[2] Department of Computer Science, University of Eastern Finland, P.O. Box 111,
FIN-80101 Joensuu, Finland
[3] College of Science and Technology, Ningbo University, Ningbo 315211, PR China

Abstract. We present a fast approximate Minimum spanning tree(MST) framework on the complete graph of a dataset with N points, and any exact MST algorithm can be incorporated into the framework and speeded up. It employs a divide-and-conquer scheme to produce an approximate MST with theoretical time complexity of $O(N^{1.5})$, if the incorporated exact MST algorithm has the running time of $O(N^2)$. Experimental results show that the proposed approximate MST algorithm is computational efficient, and the accuracy is close to the true MST.

Keywords: Minimum spanning tree, divide-and-conquer, K-means.

1 Introduction

Given an undirected and weighted graph, the problem of MST is to find a spanning tree such that the sum of weights is minimized. Since MST can roughly estimate the intrinsic structure of a dataset, it has been broadly applied in image segmentation [1], cluster analysis [9], classification [4], manifold learning [8]. However, traditional MST algorithms such as Prim's and Kruskal's algorithm have running time of $O(N^2)$ [3], and for a large dataset a fast MST algorithm is needed.

Recent work to find an approximate MST can be found in [6][7], and the both work apply MSTs to clustering. Wang et al. [7] employ divide-and-conquer scheme to detect the long edges of the MST at an early stage for clustering. Initially, data points are randomly stored in a list, and each data point is connected to its predecessor (or successor), and a spanning tree is achieved. To optimize the spanning tree, the dataset is divided into a collection of subsets with a divisive hierarchical clustering algorithm. The distance between any pair of data points within a subset can be computed by a brute force nearest neighbor search, and with the distances, the spanning tree is updated.

Lai et al. [6] proposed an approximate MST algorithm based on Hilbert curve for clustering. It is a two-phase algorithm: the first phase is to construct an approximate MST of a given dataset with Hilbert curve, and the second phase is to partition the dataset into subsets by measuring the densities of points along

R. Wilson et al. (Eds.): CAIP 2013, Part I, LNCS 8047, pp. 262–269, 2013.

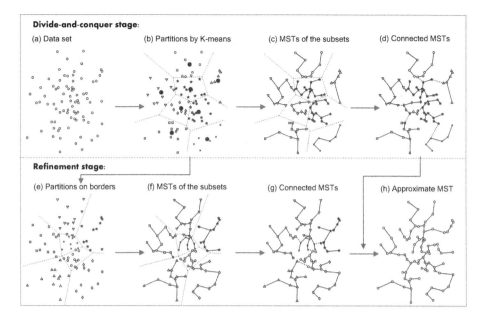

Fig. 1. The scheme of the proposed fast MST algorithm. (a) A given dataset. (b) The dataset is partitioned into $\sqrt{N}$ subsets by K-means. (c) An exact MST algorithm is applied to each subset. (d) MSTs of the subsets are connected. (e) The dataset is partitioned again so that the neighboring data points in different subsets are partitioned into identical partitions. (f) Exact MST algorithm is used again on the secondary partition. (g) MSTs of the subsets are connected. (h) A more accurate approximate MST is produced by merging the two approximate MSTs in (d) and (g) respectively.

the approximate MST with a specified density threshold. However, the accuracy of MST depends on the order of Hilbert Curve and the number of neighbors of a visited point in the linear list.

2 Proposed Method

2.1 Overview of the Proposed Framework

To improve the efficiency of constructing an MST is to reduce the unnecessary comparisons. For example, in Kruskal's algorithm, it is not necessary to sort all $N(N-1)/2$ edges of a complete graph but to find $(1+\alpha)N$ edges with least weights, where $(N-3)/2 \gg \alpha \geq -1/N$. We employ a divide-and-conquer technique to achieve the improvement. The overview of the proposed method is illustrated in Fig. 1.

2.2 Partition Dataset with K-Means

In general, a data point in an MST is connected to its nearest neighbors, which implies that the connections have a locality property. In the divide step, it is therefore expected that the subsets preserve this locality. Since K-means can partition local neighboring data points into the same group, we employ K-means to partition the dataset.

The Number of Clusters K. In our method, the number of clusters K is set to $\sqrt{N}$. There are two reasons for this determination. One is that the maximum number of clusters in some clustering algorithms is often set to $\sqrt{N}$ as a rule of thumb [2]. That means if a dataset is partitioned into $\sqrt{N}$ subsets, each subset will consist of data points coming from an identical genuine cluster, which satisfies the requirement of the locality property when constructing an MST. The other reason is that the overall time complexity of the proposed approximate MST algorithm is minimized if K is set to $\sqrt{N}$, assuming that the data points are equally divided into the clusters.

Divide and Conquer Algorithm. After the dataset is divided into $\sqrt{N}$ subsets by K-means, the MSTs of the subsets are constructed with an exact MST algorithm, such as Prim's or Kruskal's algorithm. The algorithm of K-means based divide and conquer is described as follows:

Divide and Conquer Using K-Means (DAC)
Input: Dataset X;
Output: MSTs of the subsets partitioned from X

1. Set the number of subsets $K = \sqrt{N}$.
2. Apply K-means to X to achieve K subsets $S = \{S_1, \ldots, S_K\}$.
3. Apply an exact MST algorithm to S_i, and its MST $MST(S_i)$ is obtained.

2.3   Combine MSTs of the K Subsets

An intuitive solution to combine MSTs is brute force: for the MST of a cluster, the shortest edge between it and MSTs of other clusters is computed. But this solution is time consuming, and therefore a fast MST-based effective combination is presented.

MST-Based Combination. The neighboring subsets are determined first because the MSTSs of those far away from each other will not be connected. This can be achieved by MST of the centers of the subsets, see Fig. 2. To connect a pair of neighboring subsets efficiently, the nearest point of one subset to the center of the other is selected. For example, a and b are the nearest points to opposite centers respectively, and they are connected.

Consequently, the algorithm of combining MSTs of subsets is summarized as follows:
Combine Algorithm (CA)
Input: MSTs of the subsets partitioned from X: $MST(S_1), \cdots, MST(S_K)$.
Output: Approximate MST of X: MST_1, and MST of the cluster centers: MST_{cen};

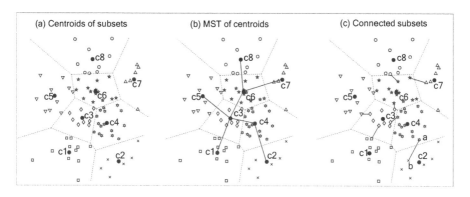

Fig. 2. The combine step of MSTs of the proposed algorithm. In (a), centers of the partitions (c1, ..., c8) are calculated. In (b), a MST of the centers, MST_{cen}, is constructed with an exact MST algorithm. In (c), each pair of subsets whose centers are neighbors with respect to MST_{cen} in (b) is connected.

1. Compute the center c_i of subset S_i, $1 \leq i \leq K$.
2. Construct an MST, MST_{cen}, of $c_1, \cdots, c_K$ by an exact MST algorithm.
3. For each pair of subsets (S_i, S_j) whose centers are connected by an edge of MST_{cen}, discover the edge by **DCE** that connects $MST(S_i)$ and $MST(S_j)$.
4. Combine discovered edges with $MST(S_1), \cdots, MST(S_K)$ to achieve MST_1.

Detect the Connecting Edge (DCE)
Input: A pair of subsets to be connected, (S_i, S_j);
Output: The edge connecting $MST(S_i)$ and $MST(S_j)$;

1. Find data point $a \in S_i$ so that the distance between a and c_j is minimized.
2. Find data point $b \in S_j$ so that the distance between b and c_i is minimized.
3. Select edge $e(a, b)$ as the connecting edge.

2.4 Refine the MST Focusing on Boundaries

However, the accuracy of the approximate MST achieved so far is not enough. The reason is that, when the MST of a subset is built, the data points that lie in the boundary of the subset are considered only within the subset but not across the boundaries. Based on this observation, the refinement stage is designed.

Partition Dataset Focusing on Boundaries. In this step, another complimentary partition is constructed so that the clusters would locate at the boundary areas of the previous K-means partition. We first calculate the midpoints of each edge of MST_{cen}. In most cases, these midpoints lie near the boundaries, and are therefore employed as the initial cluster centers. The dataset is then partitioned by K-means, in which only one iteration is performed for the purpose of focusing on the boundaries. The process is illustrated in Fig. 3.

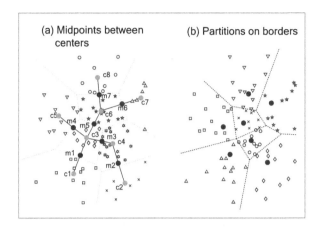

Fig. 3. Boundary-based partition. In (a), the black solid points, $m_1, \cdots, m_7$, are the midpoints of the edges of MST_{cen}. In (b), each data point is assigned to its nearest midpoint, and the dataset is partitioned by the midpoints. The corresponding Voronoi graph is with respect to the midpoints.

Build Secondary Approximate MST. After the dataset has been re-partitioned, the conquer and combine steps similar to those in first stage are used to produce the secondary approximate MST. The algorithm is summarized as follows:

Secondary Approximate MST (SAM)

Input: MST of the subset centers MST_{cen}, dataset X;

Output: Approximate MST of X, MST_2;

1. Compute the midpoint m_i of an edge $e_i \in MST_{cen}$, where $1 \leq i \leq K - 1$.
2. Partition dataset X into $K - 1$ subsets, $S'_1, \cdots, S'_{K-1}$, by assigning each point to its nearest point from $m_1, \cdots, m_{K-1}$.
3. Build MSTs, $MST(S'_1), \cdots, MST(S'_{K-1})$, with an exact MST algorithm.
4. Combine the $K - 1$ MSTs with **CA** to produce an approximate MST MST_2.

2.5   Combine Two Rounds of Approximate MSTs

So far we have two approximate MSTs on dataset X, MST_1 and MST_2. To produce the final approximate MST, we first merge the two approximate MSTs to produce a graph, which has no more than $2(N - 1)$ edges, and then apply an exact MST algorithm on this graph to achieve the final approximate MST of X.

3   Complexity and Accuracy Analysis

3.1   Complexity Analysis

The overall time complexity of the proposed algorithm **FMST**, T_{FMST}, can be evaluated as:

$$T_{FMST} = T_{DAC} + T_{CA} + T_{SAM} + T_{COM} \tag{1}$$

where T_{DAC}, T_{CA} and T_{SAM} are the time complexities of the algorithms **DAC**, **CA** and **SAM** respectively, T_{COM} is the running time of an exact MST algorithm on the combination of MST_1 and MST_2.

DAC consists of two operations: partitioning the dataset X into K subsets and constructing the MSTs of the subsets with an exact MST algorithm. Since $K = \sqrt{N}$, we have $T_{DAC} = O(N^{1.5})$. In **CA**, computing the mean points of the subsets and constructing MST of the K mean points take only $O(N)$ time. For each connected subset pair, determining the connecting edge requires $O(2N \times (K-1)/K)$. The total computational cost of **CA** is therefore $O(N)$.

In **SAM**, Computing $K-1$ midpoints and partitioning the dataset take $O(N \times (K-1))$ time. The running time of Step 3 and 4 is $O((K-1) \times N^2/(K-1)^2) = O(N^2/(K-1))$ and $O(N)$, respectively. Therefore, the time complexity of **SAM** is $O(N^{1.5})$. The number of edges in the graph that is formed by combining MST_1 and MST_2 is at most $2(N-1)$. The time complexity of applying an exact MST algorithm to this graph is only $O(2(N-1)\log N)$. Thus, $T_{COM} = O(N \log N)$.

To sum up, the time complexity of the proposed fast algorithm is $O(N^{1.5})$.

4   Experiments

In this section, experimental results are presented to illustrate the efficiency and the accuracy of the proposed fast approximate MST algorithm. The accuracy of FMST is tested with four datasets: t4.8k [5], MNIST [10], ConfLongDemo [11] and MiniBooNE [11]. Experiments were conducted on a PC with an Intel Core2 2.4GHz CPU and 4GB memory running Windows 7.

4.1   Running Time

From each dataset, subsets with different size are randomly selected to test the running time as a function of data size. The subset sizes of the first two datasets gradually increase with step 20, the third with step 100 and the last with step 1000.

The running time of FMST and Prim's algorithm on the four datasets is illustrated in the first row of Fig. 4. From the results, we can see that FMST is computationally more efficient than Prim's algorithm, especially for the large datasets ConfLongDemo and MiniBooNE. The efficiency for MiniBooNE shown in the rightmost of the second and third row in Fig. 4, however, deteriorates because of the high dimensionality. Although the complexity analysis indicates that the time complexity of proposed FMST is $O(N^{1.5})$, the actual running time may be different because K-means can not produce clusters being of equal size. We analyze the actual processing time by fitting an exponential function $T = aN^b$, where T is the running time and N is the number of data points. The the results are shown in Table 1.

4.2   Accuracy

Suppose E_{appr} is the set of the correct edges in an approximate MST, the edge error rate ER_{edge} is defined as: $ER_{edge} = \frac{N-|E_{appr}|-1}{N-1}$. The second measure is

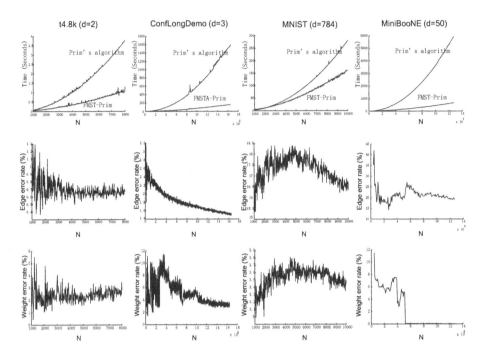

Fig. 4. The results of the test on the four datasets

Table 1. The exponent bs obtained by fitting $T = aN^b$

	t4.8k	MNIST	ConfLongDemo	MiniBooNE
		b		
FMST	1.57	1.62	1.54	1.44
Prim's Alg.	1.88	2.01	1.99	2.00

defined as the differ of the sum of the weights in FMST and the exact MST, which is called weight error rate: $ER_{weight} = \frac{W_{appr} - W_{exact}}{W_{exact}}$, where W_{exact} and W_{appr} are the sum of weights of the exact MST and FMST, respectively.

The edge error rates and weight error rates of the four datasets are shown in the third row of Fig. 4. We can see that both the edge error rate and the weight error rate decrease with the increase of the data size. For datasets with high dimension, the edge error rates are bigger, for example, the maximum edge error rates of MNIST are approximate to 18.5%, while those of t4.8k and ConfLongDemo less than 3.2%. In contrast, the weight error rates decrease when the dimensionality increases. This is one aspect of the curse of dimensionality, *distance concentration*, which means that Euclidean distances between all pairs of points in high dimensional data are tend to be similar.

5   Conclusion

In this paper, we have proposed a fast approximate MST algorithm with a divide and conquer scheme. The time complexity of the proposed algorithm is theoretically $O(N^{1.5})$. Furthermore, any MST algorithm can be incorporated into to the proposed framework to make it more efficient.

References

1. An, L., Xiang, Q.S., Chavez, S.: A fast implementation of the minimum spanning tree method for phase unwrapping. IEEE Trans. Medical Imaging 19, 805–808 (2000)
2. Bezdek, J.C., Pal, N.R.: Some new indexes of cluster validity. IEEE Trans. Systems, Man and Cybernetics, Part B 28, 301–315 (1998)
3. Cormen, T.H., Leiserson, C.E., Rivest, R.L., Stein, C.: Introduction to Algorithms, 2nd edn. The MIT Press (2001)
4. Juszczak, P., Tax, D.M.J., Pękalska, E., Duin, R.P.W.: Minimum spanning tree based one-class classifier. Neurocomputing 72, 1859–1869 (2009)
5. Karypis, G., Han, E.H., Kumar, V.: CHAMELEON: A hierarchical clustering algorithm using dynamic modeling. IEEE Trans. Comput. 32, 68–75 (1999)
6. Lai, C., Rafa, T., Nelson, D.E.: Approximate minimum spanning tree clustering in high-dimensional space. Intelligent Data Analysis 13, 575–597 (2009)
7. Wang, X., Wang, X., Wilkes, D.M.: A divide-and-conquer approach for minimum spanning tree-based clustering. IEEE Trans., Knowledge and Data Engineering 21, 945–958 (2009)
8. Yang, L.: Building k edge-disjoint spanning trees of minimum total length for isometric data embedding. IEEE Trans. Pattern Analysis and Machine Intelligence 27, 1680–1683 (2005)
9. Zhong, C., Miao, D., Wang, R.: A graph-theoretical clustering method based on two rounds of minimum spanning trees. Pattern Recognition 43, 752–766 (2010)
10. http://yann.lecun.com/exdb/mnist
11. http://archive.ics.uci.edu/ml/

Fast EM Principal Component Analysis Image Registration Using Neighbourhood Pixel Connectivity

Parminder Singh Reel[1], Laurence S. Dooley[1], K.C.P. Wong[1], and Anko Börner[2]

[1] Department of Communication and Systems, The Open University, Milton Keynes, United Kingdom
{p.s.reel,laurence.dooley,k.c.p.wong}@open.ac.uk
[2] Optical Sensor Systems, German Aerospace Center (DLR), Berlin, Germany
anko.boerner@dlr.de

Abstract. *Image registration* (IR) is the systematic process of aligning two images of the same or different modalities. The registration of mono and multimodal images i.e., magnetic resonance images, pose a particular challenge due to *intensity non-uniformities* (INU) and noise artefacts. Recent similarity measures including *regional mutual information* (RMI) and *expectation maximisation for principal component analysis* with *MI* (EMPCA-MI) have sought to address this problem. EMPCA-MI incorporates neighbourhood region information to iteratively compute principal components giving superior IR performance compared with RMI, though it is not always effective in the presence of high INU. This paper presents a *modified* EMPCA-MI (*m*EMPCA-MI) similarity measure which introduces a novel pre-processing step to exploit local spatial information using 4-and 8-pixel neighbourhood connectivity. Experimental results using diverse image datasets, conclusively demonstrate the improved IR robustness of *m*EMPCA-MI when adopting second-order neighbourhood representations. Furthermore, *m*EMPCA-MI with 4-pixel connectivity is notably more computationally efficient than EMPCA-MI.

Keywords: Image registration, mutual information, principal component analysis, expectation maximisation algorithms.

1 Introduction

Image Registration (IR) is a vital processing task in numerous applications where the final information is obtained by combining different data sources, as for example in computer vision, remote sensing and medical imaging [1]. The process of IR involves the geometric transformation of a source image in order to attain the best physical alignment with a reference target image. It applies an optimization method to maximize some predefined similarity measure with known transformations between the source and reference image set.

Similarity measures which have been proposed [1] for both mono and multimodal IR can be broadly categorized according to whether they are based on

R. Wilson et al. (Eds.): CAIP 2013, Part I, LNCS 8047, pp. 270–277, 2013.

cross correlation, phase correlation, Fourier techniques or *mutual information* (MI) [2], with MI being well-established in the medical imaging domain [3]. MI is computationally efficient and seeks to form a statistical relationship between the source and reference images [4]. It is however, sensitive to interpolation arte- facts and its performance can be severely compromised when the overlap region between the images is small.

Normalized MI (NMI) [5] was specifically designed to facilitate the sucessful IR of partially overlapping images, though it along with MI is unable to con- sistently and accurately register images containing *intensity non-uniformities* (INU) [6] which is an omnipresent feature in *magnetic resonance images* (MRI) for instance. In contrast, regional MI (RMI) [7] and its variant [8] incorporate neighbourhood features within MI by segmenting an image into several regions for feature extraction to lessen the influence of INU on the resulting IR qual- ity. In computing the associated entropies, these MI-based approaches employ a covariance matrix instead of high-dimensional histograms to reduce data com- plexity, though as the size of a neighbourhood region grows, so the computation overheads commensurately increase [7].

The *expectation maximisation for principal component analysis* with *MI* (EM PCA-MI) algorithm [9] is a recently proposed IR similarity measure, which sig- nificantly reduces the computational cost without loss of IR performance for different mono and multimodalities of the human anatomy [10],[11]. Its per- formance however, can be compromised in the presence of high INU and noise levels [9]. EMPCA-MI achieves dimensionality reduction by iteratively determin- ing the principal component without recourse to solving the complete covariance matrix as in conventional *principal component analysis* (PCA) techniques. As a pre-processing step, EMPCA-MI rearranges the neighbourhood region grayscale data values into vector form so preserving both the spatial and intensity infor- mation of the images.

This paper presents a *modified* EMPCA-MI (*m*EMPCA-MI) similarity mea- sure which uses the difference in grayscale values for direct (*4-pixel*) and indirect (*8-pixel*) neighbourhood relations, instead of rearranging the pixels in the pre- processing stage. This provides the dual advantages of more accurate feature representation for EMPCA and MI computation, and significantly lower compu- tational cost with, as will be evidenced in Section 4, minimal impact upon the corresponding IR performance compared with EMPCA-MI. Quantitative results verify the new pre-processing step adopted in *m*EMPCA-MI provides superior IR performance from both a registration error and computational time perspec- tive for various mono and multimodal test datasets. The remainder of the paper is organized as follows: Section 2 briefly reviews the original EMPCA-MI simi- larity measure before the proposed *m*EMPCA-MI pre-processing step exploiting localised pixel relations is introduced. Section 3 describes the experimental test setup used, while Section 4 presents an IR results analysis of the *m*EMPCA-MI algorithm. Finally, Section 5 provides some concluding comments.

2   The mEMPCA-MI Model

2.1   EMPCA-MI Similarity Measure [9]

EMPCA-MI [9] is a recent similarity measure for IR, which efficiently incorporates spatial information together with MI without incurring high computational overheads. Fig. 1 illustrates the three core processing steps involved in the EMPCA-MI algorithm, namely: input image data rearrangement (highlighted in *yellow*) followed by EMPCA and MI calculation. Both the reference (I_R) and source images (I_S) are pre-processed (*Step I*) into vector form for a given neighbourhood radius r, so the spatial and intensity information is preserved (see Fig. 1(a) and 1(b)). The first P principal components X_R and X_S of the respective reference and source images are then iteratively computed using EMPCA [12] in *Step II*. Subsequently, the MI [3] is calculated between X_R and X_S in *Step III*, with a higher MI value signifying the images are better aligned. In [9], only the first principal component is considered, i.e., $P=1$ since this is the direction of highest variance and represents the most dominant feature in any region.

2.2   New Pre-processing Step

As evidenced in Fig. 1(a), *Step I* of the EMPCA-MI algorithm reorganises the image grayscale values within each neighbourhood region in order to incorporate spatial information. This provides noteworthy IR results [9] when there is neither INU nor noise present, however when there are high levels of INU and noise, the corresponding registration performance can degrade because only a first-order region representation is used which considers each pixel independently without cognisance of any neighbourhood relations. This is reflected in the repetitive patterns in Q_R and Q_S in the neighbouring position of the sliding window (See *Step I*(b) in Fig 1). The rationale behind the proposed mEMPCA-MI pre-processing step is that spatial information within a neighbourhood region can be more accurately characterised as second-order representation, where the relationship between pixels can be exploited instead of just pixel values. To illustrate the new pre-processing step for mEMPCA-MI, consider the example shown in Fig. 1, for a *3 x 3* pixel sliding window ($r=1$) neighbourhood region B (see Fig. 1(a)) which assumes either *4-pixel* (direct neighbours) or *8-pixel* (indirect neighbours) connectivity i.e., $c=4$ and $c=8$ respectively. The resulting single column vector B^* will thus have length $c+1$ as shown in Fig. 1(b), and can be represented as:

$$B_i^* = \begin{cases} B_i - B_5 & i \in [1, c+1]; i \notin [5] \\ B_5 & i \in [5] \end{cases} \qquad (1)$$

Each column vector B^* now represents the differential value of c connected pixels with respect to the centre pixel B_5. Here, mEMPCA-MI pre-processing no longer generates repetitive pattern as in EMPCA-MI, but instead provides unique relative intensity values (See B^* in Fig.1) for the next computational steps in the mEMPCA-MI.

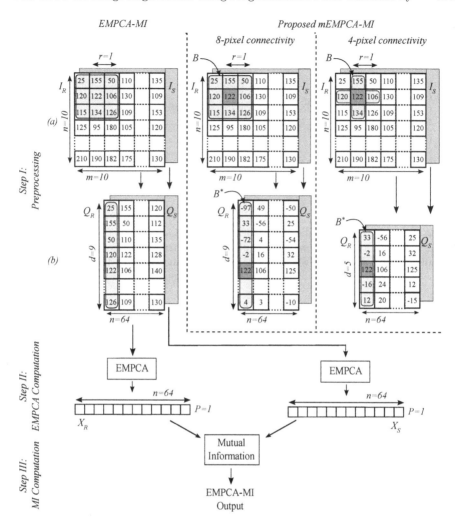

Fig. 1. Illustration of the EMPCA-MI algorithm [9], together with the proposed mEMPCA-MI pre-processing step using neighbourhood 8-pixel and 4-pixel region connectivity for an image pair size of *10* x *10* pixels

Once *Step I* has been completed, the remaining two processing steps of mEMPCA-MI are as in [9]. Fig 2. displays two mEMPCA-MI traces for both 4-pixel and 8-pixel connectivity together with EMPCA-MI with respect to the θ angular rotational transformation parameter for the IR of the multimodal MRI pair T1 and T2. Fig 2(a) shows IR case when there is neither INU nor noise present, while Fig 2(b) reflects the challenging registration of 40% INU and Gaussian noise. It is palpable the mEMPCA-MI traces for both 4-pixel and 8-pixel neighbourhood connectivity provide smoother and higher similarity measure values for the best alignment compared with EMPCA-MI.

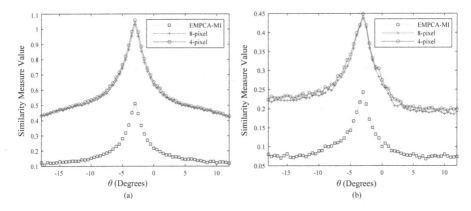

Fig. 2. Similarity measure value traces for EMPCA-MI and mEMPCA-MI (8-pixel and 4-pixel connectivity). (a) shows the angular rotation transformation for MRI T1 and T2 multimodal registration (without INU and noise) and (b) with 40% INU and noise.

Interestingly 4-pixel neighbourhoods are better in both cases, since they exploit the neighbourhood relations with the strongest links leading to a correspondingly higher overall MI value between I_R and I_S. Fig 2 also highlights the smooth convergence of mEMPCA-MI compared with EMPCA-MI with less oscillatory behaviour particularly where 40% INU and noise is present. This is a very useful feature for effective convergence of the ensuing optimization process [1] and ultimately leads to lower IR errors.

3   Experiment Setup

To evaluate the performance of the mEMPCA-MI similarity measure, a series of multimodal IR experiments were undertaken. Multimodal MRI T1 and T2 datasets from BrainWeb Database [13] were chosen due to their challenging characteristics of varying INU and noise artefacts with the corresponding parameter details being defined in Table 1. To simulate a range of applications and analyse the robustness of mEMPCA-MI, both *Lena* and *Baboon* images have also been used with a simulated INU function Z [14]. Finally, Gaussian noise has been added to all the datasets. The IR experiments were classified into four separate scenarios representing monomodal, multimodal and two generic registrations.

Table 1. Dataset Parameter Details

Dataset	Resolution (pixels)	INU	Noise(β)
MRI T1 (T1)	[181 x 217 x 181]	α_{20}=20% INU	Gaussian
MRI T2 (T2)	[181 x 217 x 181]	α_{40}=40% INU	(μ=0.01,
Lena (L)	[256 x 256]		σ^2=0.01)
Baboon (Bb)	[256 x 256]	$Z(x,y)=\dfrac{1}{3.2}(x+y)$ [14]	

Table 2. Registration Error Results for Different *Scenarios*

Scenario No.	I_R	I_S	EMPCA-MI [10] $(r=1,P=1)$) $\Delta X, \Delta Y, \Delta\theta$ (%)	mEMPCA-MI $(r=1,P=1)$ 8-pixel $\Delta X, \Delta Y, \Delta\theta$ (%)	4-pixel $\Delta X, \Delta Y, \Delta\theta$ (%)
1	T1+α_{20}	T1	2.0, 1.3, 0.36	1.26, 0.98, 0.24	1.12. 0.93, 0.21
	T1+α_{40}		4.5, 4.0, 0.42	3.05, 3.21, 0.39	2.96, 3.04, 0.32
	T1+β		6.0, 7.0, 0.52	5.74, 6.58, 0.45	5.41, 6.25, 0.43
	T1+α_{40} + β		8.0, 10.0, 0.58	7.84, 9.59, 0.48	7.45, 9.28, 0.46
2	T1+α_{20}	T2	2.6, 2.6, 0.42	2.05, 1.98, 0.36	1.93, 1.71, 0.32
	T1+α_{40}		4.8, 4.6, 0.62	4.12, 4.27, 0.48	3.98, 4.10, 0.43
	T1+β		6.2, 3.0, 0.46	5.82, 2.32, 0.37	5.68, 2.18, 0.33
	T1+α_{40} + β		9.7, 4.3, 0.62	9.12, 3.28, 0.58	8.99, 3.11, 0.56
3	L+Z	L	0.2, 0.32, 0.21	0.18, 0.28, 0.19	0.16, 0.24, 0.17
	L+β		0.32, 0.50, 0.36	0.29, 0.47, 0.31	0.27, 0.45, 0.29
	L+Z+β		2.0, 5.33, 0.21	1.95, 5.28, 0.20	1.93, 5.26, 0.19
4	Bb+Z	Bb	0.45, 0.70, 0.21	0.32, 0.63, 0.18	0.30, 0.60, 0.16
	Bb+β		0.8, 1.26, 0.21	0.71, 1.14, 0.19	0.69, 1.12, 0.18
	Bb+Z+β		1.4, 1.50, 0.23	1.27, 1.24, 0.22	1.20, 1.22, 0.20

Each experiment involved an initial misregistration of predefined x and y axis translations and rotation θ. The registration process involved partial volume interpolation along with Powell optimization method [2] to iteratively estimate the transformation parameters. The parameter values at which the mEMPCA-MI similarity measure is a maximum then define the final transformation for which the two images are best aligned. The registration error is defined as the difference between the initial and final value for each parameter. All experiments were performed upon an Ubuntu 10.04 (lucid) with 2.93 GHz Intel Core and 3GB RAM, and the assorted algorithms implemented in MATLAB.

4 Results Discussion

Table 2 shows the IR error results for all four *Scenarios* in terms of the percentage translation (ΔX, ΔY) and angular rotational ($\Delta\theta$) errors. To clarify the nomenclature adopted in Table 2; T1+α_{20} for example, represents an MRI T1 image slice with 20% INU, while Bb+Z+β refers to the *Baboon* image with INU and Gaussian noise artefacts. The results confirm the mEMPCA-MI algorithm using both 8-pixel and 4-pixel neighbourhood connectivity consistently provides better registration than the EMPCA-MI model for both mono and multimodal MRI T1 and T2 images, both when there is and is not INU and noise present.

For example, in monomodal IR *Scenario 1* with 40% INU and noise present (T1+α_{40}+β), 8-pixel and 4-pixel connectivity mEMPCA-MI provide percentage errors for the (ΔX, ΔY, $\Delta\theta$) parameters of (*7.84, 9.59, 0.48*) and (*7.45, 9.28, 0.46*) respectively which are both lower than the corresponding EMPCA-MI error (*8.0, 10.0, 0.58*). Similar performance improvements are also evident for *Lena* and *Baboon* images.

Table 3. Average Runtimes (ART) Results (in ms) for Different *Scenarios*

Scenario No.	EMPCA-MI [10] ($r=1,P=1$))	mEMPCA-MI ($r=1,P=1$)	
		8-pixel	4-pixel
1	152	144	95
2			
3	170	156	109
4			

This corroborates the fact that the *m*EMPCA-MI algorithm using both 8-pixel and 4-pixel connectivity in the pre-processing step more accurately reflects neighbourhood spatial information by considering a second-order representation of region pixels values with respect to centre pixel of the sliding window. The results also reveal that the IR error performance of *m*EMPCA-MI with 4-pixel neighbourhood connectivity is consistently lower than 8-pixel connectivity across all four *Scenarios*. Particularly striking, is the performance achieved for the challenging MRI T1 and T2 multimodal registration in *Scenario 2*, in the presence of both INU and noise. This reflects that 4-pixel neighbourhood connectivity exploits the direct pixel relations providing more relevant spatial information about local neighbourhood for subsequent EMPCA and MI computation. In contrast, 8-pixel connectivity also considers weaker indirect neighbours, which marginally reduces the corresponding principal component values leading to a lower MI between the image pair.

Table 3 displays the *average runtimes* (ART) for both EMPCA-MI and *m*EMPCA-MI. While ART is a resource dependent metric, it concomitantly provides an insightful time complexity comparator between similarity measures. As illustrated in Fig. 1, since the data dimensionality of *m*EMPCA-MI with 4-pixel connectivity is reduced to 5 from 9 for both 8-pixel connectivity and EMPCA-MI [12], the corresponding ART values are considerably lower, i.e., *95ms* compared to *144ms* for 8-pixel connectivity and *152ms* for EMPCA-MI to determine only the first principal component for *Scenarios 1* and *2*. A similar trend in the ART values is observed in *Scenarios 3* and *4*, though these datasets have a different spatial resolution compared to *Scenarios 1* and *2*. Overall, the ART results reveal a notable improvement in computational efficiency for *m*EMPCA-MI using 4-pixel neighbourhood connectivity, allied with superior IR robustness to both INU and noise for both mono and multimodal image datasets.

5   Conclusion

This paper has presented a neighbourhood connectivity based modification to the existing *Expectation Maximisation for Principal Component Analysis* with *MI* (EMPCA-MI) similarity measure. Superior and enhanced robust image registration performance in the presence of both INU and Gaussian noise has been achieved by incorporating second-order neighbourhood region information compared with the grayscale value rearrangement in the original EMPCA-MI paradigm. Additionally, the 4-pixel connectivity mEMPCA-MI similarity measure is computationally more efficient compared to both EMPCA-MI and using 8-pixel neighbourhood connectivity.

References

1. Zitová, B., Flusser, J.: Image registration methods: a survey. Image and Vision Computing 21(11), 977–1000 (2003)
2. Pluim, J., Maintz, J., Viergever, M.: Mutual-information-based registration of medical images: a survey. IEEE Transactions on Medical Imaging 22(8), 986–1004 (2003)
3. Collignon, Maes, F., Delaere, D., Vandermeulen, D., Suetens, P., Marchal, G.: Automated multi-modality image registration based on information theory. Imaging 3(1), 263–274 (1995)
4. Viola, P., Wells, W.M.: Alignment by maximization of mutual information. In: Proceedings of the Fifth International Conference on Computer Vision, pp. 16–23. IEEE (June 1995)
5. Studholme, Hill, D., Hawkes, D.J.: An overlap invariant entropy measure of 3D medical image alignment. Pattern Recognition 32(1), 71–86 (1999)
6. Simmons, A., Tofts, P.S., Barker, G.J., Arridge, S.R.: Sources of intensity nonuniformity in spin echo images at 1.5 t. Magnetic Resonance in Medicine 32(1), 121–128 (1994)
7. Russakoff, D.B., Tomasi, C., Rohlfing, T., Maurer Jr., C.R.: Image similarity using mutual information of regions. In: Pajdla, T., Matas, J(G.) (eds.) ECCV 2004. LNCS, vol. 3023, pp. 596–607. Springer, Heidelberg (2004)
8. Yang, C., Jiang, T., Wang, J., Zheng, L.: A neighborhood incorporated method in image registration. In: Yang, G.Z., Jiang, T.-Z., Shen, D., Gu, L., Yang, J. (eds.) MIAR 2006. LNCS, vol. 4091, pp. 244–251. Springer, Heidelberg (2006)
9. Reel, P.S., Dooley, L.S., Wong, K.C.P.: A new mutual information based similarity measure for medical image registration. In: IET Conference on Image Processing (IPR 2012), pp. 1–6 (July 2012)
10. Reel, P.S., Dooley, L.S., Wong, K.C.P.: Efficient image registration using fast principal component analysis. In: 19th IEEE International Conference on Image Processing (ICIP 2012), Lake Buena Vista, Orlando, Florida, USA, pp. 1661–1664. IEEE (September 2012)
11. Reel, P., Dooley, L., Wong, P., Börner, A.: Robust retinal image registration using expectation maximisation with mutual information. In: 38th IEEE International Conference on Acoustics, Speech, and Signal Processing (ICASSP 2013), Vancouver, Canada, pp. 1118–1122. IEEE (May 2013)
12. Roweis, S.: EM algorithms for PCA and SPCA. In: Proceedings of the 1997 Conference on Advances in Neural Information Processing Systems 10, NIPS 1997, pp. 626–632. MIT Press, Cambridge (1998)
13. Collins, D.L., Zijdenbos, A.P., Kollokian, V., Sled, J.G., Kabani, N.J., Holmes, C.J., Evans, A.C.: Design and construction of a realistic digital brain phantom. IEEE Transactions on Medical Imaging 17(3), 463–468 (1998)
14. Garcia-Arteaga, J.D., Kybic, J.: Regional image similarity criteria based on the kozachenko-leonenko entropy estimator. In: IEEE Computer Society Conference on Computer Vision and Pattern Recognition Workshops, CVPRW 2008, pp. 1–8. IEEE (June 2008)

Fast Unsupervised Segmentation Using Active Contours and Belief Functions

Foued Derraz[1], Laurent Peyrodie[2], Abdelmalik Taleb-Ahmed[3],
Miloud Boussahla[4], and Gerard Forzy[1]

[1] Université Nord de France
Faculté Libre de Médicine, Institut Catholique de Lille
46 rue du Port de Lille, France
foued.derraz@icl-lille.fr
[2] Université Nord de France
Haute Etude díngénieur, LAGIS UMR CNRS 8219
46 rue du Port de Lille, France
laurent.peyrodie@hei.fr
[3] Université Nord de France, Lille
Université de Valenciennes, LAMIH UMR CNRS 8201, Valenciennes
taleb@univ-valenciennes.fr
[4] Université Abou Bekr Belkaid, Tlemcen
Telecommunication laboratory

Abstract. In this paper, we study Active Contours (AC) based globally segmentation for vector valued images using evidential Kullback-Leibler (KL) distance. We investigate the evidential framework to fuse multiple features issued from vector-valued images. This formulation has two main advantages: 1) by the combination of foreground/background issued from the multiple channels in the same framework. 2) the incorporation of the heterogeneous knowledge and the reduction of the imprecision due to the noise. The statistical relation between the image channels is ensured by the Dempster-Shafer rule. We illustrate the performance of our segmentation algorithm using some challenging color and textured images.

Keywords: Active Contours, Characteristic function, Evidential Kullback-Leibler distance, Belief Functions, Dempster-Shafer rule.

1 Introduction

Active Contours (AC) models have proven to be very powerful segmentation tools in many computer vision and medical imaging applications [1]. Segmentation based AC models are limited by several challenges mainly related to image noise, poor contrast, weak or missing boundaries between imaged objects, inhomogeneities, etc. One way to overcome these difficulties is to exploit the high level knowledge about usual objects. This will ease the interpretation of low-level cues extracted from images which may be highly beneficial in the segmentation based AC. Statistical knowledge [1] and additional information such as texture

R. Wilson et al. (Eds.): CAIP 2013, Part I, LNCS 8047, pp. 278–285, 2013.

can improve the segmentation based AC models for vector-valued images [2]. Another reason for failed segmentations is due to the local or global minimizer for AC models [3]. To overcome these difficulties, the evidential framework appears to be a new way to improve segmentation based AC models for vector valued images [4,5,6]. The Dempster-Shafer (*DS*) framework [7] has been combined with either a simple thresholding [4], a clustering algorithm [8], a region merging algorithm [5] or with an AC algorithms [6]. In this paper we propose to use the evidential framework [7] to fuse several statistical knowledge as a new descriptor and incorporates this new descriptor in the formulation of the AC models. The fusion of information issued from different feature channels, e.g., color channels and texture offers an alternative to the Bayesian framework [9]. Instead of fusing separated probability densities, the evidential framework allows both inaccuracy and uncertainty. This concept is represented using Belief Functions (*BFs*) [7,10,11,12] which are particularly well suited to represent information from partial and unreliable knowledge. The use of *BFs* as an alternative to the probability in segmentation process can be very helpful in reducing uncertainties and imprecisions using conjunctive combination of neighboring pixels. First, it allows us to reduce the noise and secondly, to highlight conflicting areas mainly present at the transition between regions where the contours occur. In addition, *BFs* have the advantage to manipulate not only singletons but also disjunctions. This gives the ability to represent both uncertainties and imprecisions explicitly . The disjunctive combination allows the transferring of both uncertain and imprecise information on disjunctions [7,12]. Finally, the conjunctive combination is applied to reduce uncertainties due to noise while maintaining representation of imprecise information at the boundaries between areas on disjunctions. In this paper, we highlight the advantage of evidential framework, to define a new descriptor based on the *BFs* to incorporate it in the formulation of the AC models. In Section 2, we review the Dempster-Shafer concept in order to define our evidential descriptor. In section3 we proposed a fast algorithm based split Bregman of our segmentation algorithm. In Section 4, we demonstrate the advantages of the proposed method by applying it to some challenging to some challenging images.

2   Globally Active Contours in Evidential Framework

2.1   Dempster Shafer Rules

The Plausibility (*PL*) and Belief Functions (*BFs*) [7,11], which are both derived from a Mass function (*m*) provide the evidential framework. For the frame of discernment $\Omega_{II} = \{\Omega_1, \Omega_2, ..., \Omega_n\}$, composed of n single mutually exclusive subsets Ω_i, the mass function is defined by $m : 2^\Omega \rightarrow [0, 1]$.

$$m\left(\emptyset\right) = 0$$

$$\sum_{\Omega_i \subseteq \Omega} m\left(\Omega_i\right) = 1$$

$$BFs\left(\Omega\right) = \sum_{\Omega_i \subseteq \Omega_{II}} m\left(\Omega_i\right) \tag{1}$$

$$Pl\left(\Omega\right) = \sum_{\Omega_i \cap \Omega_{II} \neq \emptyset} m\left(\Omega_i\right)$$

When $m\left(\Omega_i\right) > 0$, Ω_i is called a focal element [5,7]. The relation between mass function, BFs and Pel can be described as:

$$m\left(\Omega_i\right) \leq BFs\left(\Omega_i\right) \leq p\left(\Omega_i\right) \leq Pl\left(\Omega_i\right) \tag{2}$$

The independent masses m_j are defined within the same frame of discernment as:

$$m\left(\Omega_{i=\{1,\dots,n\}}\right) = m_1\left(\Omega_{i=\{1,\dots,n\}}\right) \otimes m_2\left(\Omega_{i=\{1,\dots,n\}}\right) \dots m_j\left(\Omega_{i=\{1,\dots,n\}}\right) \otimes \\ \otimes m_m\left(\Omega_{i=\{1,\dots,n\}}\right) \tag{3}$$

where $\otimes$ is the sum of DS orthogonal rule.

The total belief assigned to focal element Ω_i is equal to the belief strictly placed on the foreground region Ω_i. Then Belief Functions (BFs) can expressed as:

$$BFs\left(\Omega_i\right) = m\left(\Omega_i\right) \tag{4}$$

This relationship can be very helpful in the formulation of our AC model.

2.2 Active Contours and Belief Functions

The segmentation based AC models for vector Valued image $\mathbf{I}$ consists of finding one or more regions Ω from $\mathbf{I}$. In Bayesian framework, we search for the domain Ω or the partition of the image $P\left(\Omega\right)$ that maximizes the a posteriori partition probability $p\left(P\left(\Omega\right)|\mathbf{I}\right)$. The Maximum of a-Posteriori of $P\left(\Omega\right)$ can be given by minimizing the criterion as fellows:

$$p\left(P\left(\Omega\right)|\mathbf{I}\right) \propto p\left(\mathbf{I}|P\left(\Omega\right)\right)p\left(P\left(\Omega\right)\right) \tag{5}$$

Therefore, in Bayesian framework, the partitioning probability can be expressed as:

$$\partial\hat{\Omega} = \arg\min\left\{\underbrace{\log\left(\frac{1}{p\left(P\left(\Omega\right)\right)}\right)}_{E_b(\partial\Omega)} + \lambda\underbrace{\log\left(\frac{1}{p\left(\mathbf{I}|P\left(\Omega\right)\right)}\right)}_{E_{data}(\Omega,\mathbf{I})}\right\} \tag{6}$$

In equation (6), the first energy term corresponds to the geometric properties of $P\left(\Omega\right) = \{\Omega_{in}, \Omega_{out}\}$. Ω_{in} and Ω_{out} correspond respectively to the foreground and background region to be extracted. The data-fidelity energy term

$E_{data}(\Omega, \mathbf{I})$ allows us to incorporate statistical properties of the vector valued-image data $\mathbf{I} = \{I_1, ..., I_M\}$.

Our proposed method uses the evidential framework to fuse the knowledge issued from the multiple channels. The expression in (5) can be revisited in evidential framework using BFs with respect to (2):

$$p(P(\Omega)|\mathbf{I}) \geq p(P(\Omega))BFs(P(\Omega)) \qquad (7)$$

In the case of two phase segmentation, we can state that:

$$p(P(\Omega)|\mathbf{I}) \propto p(P(\Omega))BFs(\{\Omega_{in}, \Omega_{out}\}) \qquad (8)$$

Equation (8) is handled because $P(\Omega) = \{\Omega_{in}, \Omega_{out}\}$ is a focal element. When the foreground/background regions are disjoint ($\Omega_{in} \bigcap \Omega_{out} = \emptyset$), then:

$$p(P(\Omega)|\mathbf{I}) \propto p(P(\Omega))BFs(\Omega_{in})BFs(\Omega_{out}) \qquad (9)$$

Intuitively, the best $\partial\Omega$ can be obtained by maximizing the kullback-Leibler distance between BFs associated to the foreground/background region or minimizing the criterion:

$$\partial\hat{\Omega} = \arg\min \left\{ \underbrace{\log\left(\frac{1}{p(P(\Omega))}\right)}_{E_b(\partial\Omega)} + \underbrace{BFs(\Omega_{in})\log\left(\frac{BFs(\Omega_{in})}{BFs(\Omega_{out})}\right)}_{E_{data}(\Omega_{in},\mathbf{I})} - \underbrace{BFs(\Omega_{out})\log\left(\frac{BFs(\Omega_{out})}{BFs(\Omega_{in})}\right)}_{E_{data}(\Omega_{in},\mathbf{I})} \right\} \qquad (10)$$

Similarly to [6], we used the definitions proposed by Appriou in [12] to define mass function for all image channels I_j as:

$$m_{j=\{1,...,M\}}(\Omega_{in/out}) = p_{in/out}^{j=\{1,...,M\}}$$
$$m_{j=\{1,...,M\}}(\Omega) = 1 - p_{in}^{j=\{1,...,M\}} + p_{out}^{j=\{1,...,M\}} \qquad (11)$$
$$m_{j=\{1,...,M\}}(\emptyset) = 0$$

The pdfs p_{in}^j and p_{out}^j are estimated for all channels using the Parzen kernel [13]. Our proposed method uses the total belief committed to foreground or background region. In the next section we propose a fast version of our segmentation algorithm.

3   Fast Algorithm Based on Split Bregman

A fast and accurate minimization algorithm for TV problem is introduced in [3,14]. We propose to perform our segmentation in this new framework and we formulate the variational problem using characteristic function χ:

$$\min_{\chi,d} \ (E\,(\chi,d)) = \int_\Omega |d\,(\mathbf{x})|\,d\mathbf{x} + \lambda_{in} \int_\Omega V_{BFs}^{in}\chi\,(\mathbf{x})\,d\mathbf{x} - \lambda_{out} \int_\Omega V_{BFs}^{out}\chi\,(\mathbf{x})\,d\mathbf{x}$$

$$(12)$$

where the velocity $V_{BFs}^{in/out}$ is calculated using the Eulerian derivative of E_{data} in the direction ξ as follows:

$$\left\langle \frac{\partial E_{data}\,(\Omega_{in/out}\,(t)\,,\mathbf{I})}{\partial t},\xi \right\rangle = \int_{\partial\Omega} V_{BFs}^{in/out}\,\langle \xi\,(s)\,,N\,(s)\rangle\,ds \qquad (13)$$

Where N is an exterior unit normal vector to the boundary $\partial\Omega$, $\langle \varepsilon, N \rangle$ is the Euclidean scalar product, and s is the arc length parametrization. The vectorial function d enforces $d = \nabla\chi$ using the efficient Bregman iteration approach [14] defined as:

$$\begin{cases} (\chi^{k+1},d^{k+1}) = argmin \left\{ \begin{aligned} &\lambda_{in}\int_\Omega V_{BFs}^{in}\chi - \lambda_{out}\int_\Omega V_{BFs}^{out}\chi \\ &+\frac{\mu}{2}\int_\Omega |d - \nabla\chi - b^k|^2 \end{aligned} \right\} \\ b^{k+1} = b^k + \nabla\chi^k - d^{k+1} \end{cases} \qquad (14)$$

The minimizing solution χ^{k+1} is characterized by the optimality condition:

$$\mu\Delta\chi = \lambda_{in}V_{BFs}^{in} - \lambda_{out}V_{BFs}^{out} + \mu div\,(b^k - d^k)\,,\chi \in [0,1] \qquad (15)$$

The minimizing solution is given by soft-thresholding:

$$d^{k+1} = sign(\nabla\chi^{k+1} + b^k)max\,(|\nabla\chi^{k+1} + b^k| - \mu^{-1},0) \qquad (16)$$

Then, the final active contour is given by $\left\{ \mathbf{x} \in \Omega|\,\chi(\mathbf{x})^{final} \geq \frac{1}{2} \right\}$. The two iteration schemes are straightforward to implement. Finally, V_{BFS}^{in} and V_{BFS}^{out} are updated at each iteration using the belief function given in (11) and (4).

4   Results

We introduced an AC model that incorporates BFs as statistical region knowledge. To illustrate and demonstrate the accuracy of our segmentation method, we present some results of our method and compare them to segmentation of vector-valued images done by the traditional AC model and the model proposed in [6]. The three methods are evaluated on 20 color images taken from the Berkeley segmentation datasets [15] using F-measure criterion. Traditional segmentation and the method in [6] are initialized by contour curve around the object to be segmented, our method is free initialization. The segmentation done by the three methods are presented for three challenging images (see Figure.1).

The accuracy of the segmentation is represented in term of Precision/Recall The proposed method give the best segmentation and the F-measure is better then the other methods (see Table.1).

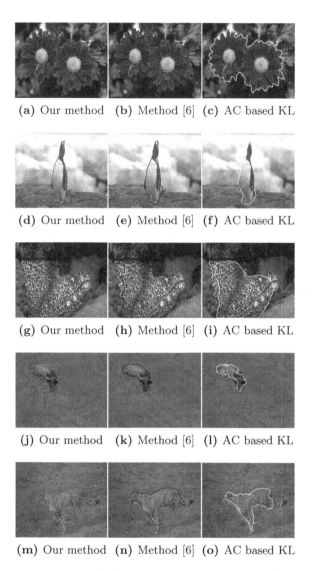

Fig. 1. Images taken from the Berkeley Segmentation benchmark dataset [15]. The from the left to right, en red color segmentation done by our segmentation model, in blue color segmentation done by the model proposed in [6]. In yellow color, the segmentation done by the traditional model based vector valued image and KL distance.

Table 1. Quantitative evaluation of the segmentation using F-measure

Image number	Our method	Method in [6]	Method in [2]
Image:124084	0.93	0.90	0.71
Image:106024	0.94	0.90	0.73
Image:164074	0.88	0.81	0.66
Image:80099	0.92	0.87	0.69
Image:134008	0.88	0.71	0.61

5   Conclusion

We have investigated the use of the evidential framework for AC model using Dempster-Shafer (DS) theory. In particular, we have investigated how to calculate the mass function using Parzen kernel, which represents a difficult task. The results have shown that our proposed approach give the best segmentation for color and textured images. The experimental results show that the segmentation performance is improved by using the three information sources to represent the same image with respect to the use of on information. However, there are some drawbacks of our proposed method. Our method of calculating mass functions is high time consuming when the number of channels increase. Furthermore, the research of other optimal models to estimate mass functions in the DS theory and the imprecision coming from different images channels are an important areas for future research.

References

1. Cremers, D., Rousson, M., Deriche, R.: A review of statistical approaches to level set segmentation: Integrating color, texture, motion and shape. Int. J. Comput. Vision 72(2), 195–215 (2007)
2. Chan, T.F., Sandberg, B.Y., Vese, L.A.: Active contours without edges for vector-valued images. J. of Vis. Communi. and Image Repres. 11, 130–141 (2000)
3. Bresson, X., Esedoglu, S., Vandergheynst, P., Thiran, J.P., Osher, S.: Fast global minimization of the active contour/snake model. J. Math. Imaging Vis. 28(2), 151–167 (2007)
4. Rombaut, M., Zhu, Y.M.: Study of dempster–shafer theory for image segmentation applications. Image and Vision Computing 20(1), 15–23 (2002)
5. Lelandais, B., Gardin, I., Mouchard, L., Vera, P., Ruan, S.: Using belief function theory to deal with uncertainties and imprecisions in image processing. In: Denœux, T., Masson, M.-H. (eds.) Belief Functions: Theory & Appl. AISC, vol. 164, pp. 197–204. Springer, Heidelberg (2012)
6. Scheuermann, B., Rosenhahn, B.: Feature quarrels: The dempster-shafer evidence theory for image segmentation using a variational framework. In: Kimmel, R., Klette, R., Sugimoto, A. (eds.) ACCV 2010, Part II. LNCS, vol. 6493, pp. 426–439. Springer, Heidelberg (2011)
7. Dempster, A.P., Chiu, W.F.: Dempster-shafer models for object recognition and classification. Int. J. Intell. Syst. 21(3), 283–297 (2006)
8. Masson, M.H., Denoeux, T.: Ecm: An evidential version of the fuzzy c. Pattern Recognition 41(4), 1384–1397 (2008)

9. Vannoorenberghe, P., Colot, O., de Brucq, D.: Color image segmentation using dempster-shafer's theory. In: ICIP (4), pp. 300–303 (1999)
10. Cuzzolin, F.: A geometric approach to the theory of evidence. IEEE Trans. on Syst., Man, and Cyber., Part C 38(4), 522–534 (2008)
11. Denoeux, T.: Maximum likelihood estimation from uncertain data in the belief function framework. IEEE Trans. Knowl. Data Eng. 25(1), 119–130 (2013)
12. Appriou, A.: Generic approach of the uncertainty management in multisensor fusion processes. Revue Traitement du Signal 22(2), 307–319 (2005)
13. Parzen, E.: On estimation of a probability density function and mode. The Annals of Mathematical Statistics 33(3), 1065–1076 (1962)
14. Goldstein, T., Bresson, X., Osher, S.: Geometric applications of the split bregman method: Segmentation and surface reconstruction. J. Sci. Comput. 45(1-3), 272–293 (2010)
15. Martin, D.R., Fowlkes, C.C., Malik, J.: Learning to detect natural image boundaries using local brightness, color, and texture cues. IEEE Trans. Pattern Anal. Mach. Intell. 26(5), 530–549 (2004)

Flexible Hypersurface Fitting with RBF Kernels

Jun Fujiki[1] and Shotaro Akaho[2]

[1] Fukuoka University
fujiki@fukuoka-u.ac.jp
[2] National Institute of Advanced Industrial Science and Technology
s.akaho@aist.go.jp

Abstract. This paper gives a method of flexible hypersurface fitting with RBF kernel functions. In order to fit a hypersurface to a given set of points in an Euclidean space, we can apply the hyperplane fitting method to the points mapped to a high dimensional feature space. This fitting is equivalent to a one-dimensional reduction of the feature space by eliminating the linear space spanned by an eigenvector corresponding to the smallest eigenvalue of a variance covariance matrix of data points in the feature space. This dimension reduction is called minor component analysis (MCA), which solves the same eigenvalue problem as kernel principal component analysis and extracts the eigenvector corresponding to the least eigenvalue. In general, feature space is set to an Euclidean space, which is a finite Hilbert space. To consider an MCA for an infinite Hilbert space, a kernel MCA (KMCA), which leads to an MCA in reproducing kernel Hilbert space, should be constructed. However, the representer theorem does not hold for a KMCA since there are infinite numbers of zero-eigenvalues would appear in an MCA for the infinite Hilbert space. Then, the fitting solution is not determined uniquely in the infinite Hilbert space, contrary to there being a unique solution in a finite Hilbert space. This ambiguity of fitting seems disadvantageous because it derives instability in fitting, but it can realize flexible fitting. Based on this flexibility, this paper gives a hypersurface fitting method in the infinite Hilbert space with RBF kernel functions to realize flexible hypersurface fitting. Although some eigenvectors of the matrix defined from kernel function at each sample are considered, we have a candidate of a reasonable solution among the simulation result under a specific situation. It is seen that the flexibility of our method is still effective through simulations.

Keywords: feature space, fitting, kernel PCA, RBF kernel, Hilbert space.

1 Introduction

In the fields of computer vision and machine learning, various nonlinear problems are reduced to linear problems in feature space with feature mappings. For getting such feature mappings, RBF kernel functions are widely used because RBF kernel functions have a great advantage called a *kernel trick* [4]. Since the kernel trick changes a searching problem in feature space into the problem in the

R. Wilson et al. (Eds.): CAIP 2013, Part I, LNCS 8047, pp. 286–293, 2013.

space spanned by sample data, the dimension of searching space also changes from that of feature space to the number of sample data, and then the trick is effective when the dimension of feature space is very large comparing to the number of sample data. In other words, the kernel trick makes high-dimensional problems free from the curse of dimensionality. The justification of kernel trick is guaranteed by the *representer theorem* [7]. The representer theorem ensures that the optimal estimator can be represented by a linear combination of kernel functions evaluated at sample points (functions). When the theorem holds, it changes an estimation in an infinite dimensional feature space corresponding to RBF kernels is change to that in a finite dimensional sample space. This is why RBF kernels are widely used to treat infinite dimension.

One of the purposes of this paper is applying the kernel trick to hypersurface fitting. Wahba [7] gives the representer theorem in the case of regression, which can be regarded as a kind of hypersurface fitting. However, hypersurface fitting based on regression does not have geometrical property. For example, the fitting result is not invariant under any rotation of coordinates. The reason why the fitting is not geometrical is that the fitting has a *special* variable called a *target variable*, and then all variables (coordinates) are not equivalent. This makes the fitting result not be geometrical.

On the other hand, line fitting based on a *principal component analysis (PCA)* is geometrical, that is, the fitting result is invariant under rotation of coordinates. PCA is kernelized as a kernel PCA [3], which is widely utilized in pattern recognition, and a kernel PCA satisfies the representer theorem. The line fitting method based on PCA is extended to nonlinear hypersurface fitting methods [1]. In the extended methods, the fitting hypersurface is represented by an inner product form like $\boldsymbol{a}^\top \boldsymbol{F}(\boldsymbol{x}) = 0$, where $\boldsymbol{F}(\boldsymbol{x})$ is a function of coordinates to represent a set of hypersurfaces. The parameter vector $\boldsymbol{a}$ is estimated so as to minimize the (weighted) sum of $(\boldsymbol{a}^\top \boldsymbol{F}(\boldsymbol{x}))^2$ for observed data, in general.

The extended method means to subtract one-dimensional space of the smallest principal component from feature space. Such a subtraction of the smallest principal component is called a *minor component analysis (MCA)* [6]. From this point of view, to establish a geometrical hypersurface fitting method, the MCA should be given in a kernel formulation such as a kernel MCA (KMCA). However the KMCA does not satisfy the representer theorem. This fact can be explained as following. If the KMCA satisfies the representer theorem, it can be represented as a kernel formulation, and the KMCA corresponding to an infinite dimensional feature space should exist. But in an infinite dimensional feature space, the dimension of eigenspace corresponding to zero-eigenvalue is also infinite. This means that the parameter vector which describes the fitting hypersurface cannot be determined uniquely, and there are infinite possibilities for parameter vectors. This paper gives flexible hypersurface fitting method by utilizing this indeterminacy.

2 Linear Fitting on Feature Space and Its Kernelization

This section reviews linear fitting on feature space, and its kernelization. The fitting criterion is to minimize the sum of square of algebraic errors.

We have D observed points and let $\{x_{[d]}\}_{d=1}^{D}$ be their Euclidean coordinates. Let $a^{\top} F(x) = 0$ be the representation of the set of fitting curve. The result of linear fitting on the feature space, that is, the parameter vector a minimizes $\sum_{d=1}^{D} \left(a^{\top} F_{[d]} \right)^2$ s.t. $\|a\| = 1$, where $F_{[d]} = F(x_{[d]})$. And then, the parameter vector a is the eigenvector corresponding to the minimum eigenvalue of the matrix $\sum_{d=1}^{D} F_{[d]} F_{[d]}^{\top}$.

Here, the kernel function can be represented by inner product as

$$k(x, y) = F(x)^{\top} F(y).$$

We only consider the case that a can be represented by a linear combination of $F_{[d]}$, that is,

$$\underset{(n \times 1)}{a} = \sum_{d=1}^{D} \alpha_{[d]} F_{[d]} = \underset{(n \times D)}{\mathcal{F}} \underset{(D \times 1)}{\alpha}.$$

if the representer theorem holds, it is guaranteed that the global minimum exists in the linear combination, but if not, it is not guaranteed. As explained later, the representer theorem does not hold for hypersurface fitting.

Let $\mathcal{K}$ be a $D \times D$ matrix as $(\mathcal{K})_{ij} = k(x_{[i]}, x_{[j]})$, and let the each column of $\mathcal{K}$ be defined as $\mathcal{K} = \left(\mathcal{K}_{[1]} \cdots \mathcal{K}_{[D]} \right)$. Since $\mathcal{K} = \mathcal{F}^{\top} \mathcal{F}$, there holds $\mathcal{K}_{[d]} = \mathcal{F}^{\top} F_{[d]}$, and $\left(a^{\top} F_{[d]} \right)^2 = \alpha^{\top} \mathcal{K}_{[d]} \mathcal{K}_{[d]}^{\top} \alpha$.

Then the coefficient vector α minimizes

$$\sum_{d=1}^{D} \alpha^{\top} \mathcal{K}_{[d]} \mathcal{K}_{[d]}^{\top} \alpha = \alpha^{\top} \mathcal{K} \alpha. \tag{1}$$

And then, the coefficient vector α is the eigenvector corresponding to the minimum eigenvalue of the matrix $\mathcal{K}$.

2.1 Representer Theorem Does Not Hold

We briefly explain the fact that the representer theorem does not hold in an MCA. The representer theorem ensure that the appropriate a can be represented by a linear combination of $F_{[d]}$, and coefficients of the linear combination is the eigenvector corresponding to the minimum eigenvalue of the matrix $\mathcal{K}$.

Let a be $\mathcal{F}\alpha$, which is a linear combination of $F_{[d]}$. the coefficient vector α satisfies $\lambda \alpha = \mathcal{K} \alpha = \mathcal{F}^{\top} \mathcal{F} \alpha$ for the minimum λ. Then *if $\lambda \neq 0$*, the vector a can be uniquely obtained as a linear combination of $F_{[d]}$ as $a = \mathcal{F}\alpha = \frac{1}{\lambda} \mathcal{F} \mathcal{F}^{\top} \mathcal{F} \alpha$.

However, *if $\lambda = 0$*, there holds $\mathcal{K}\alpha = 0$ implying $a = \mathcal{F}\alpha = 0$, and a should be estimated as 'trivial' linear combination of $F_{[d]}$, then as a result, a is estimated improperly.

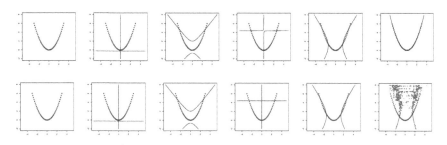

Fig. 1. Quadratic curve fitting for parabola: *with* (top) and *without* (bottom) noises

2.2 Experiments to Check the Representer Theorem

Here, there is the experiment to investigate the feature space for quadratic curve fitting. We generate 50-data from $y = x^2$ of its x-coordinate is chosen uniformly from the interval $x \in [-3.5, 3.5]$. Data are mapped to feature space by feature mapping $\boldsymbol{F} : (x_1, x_2)^\top \mapsto= (x_1^2, x_1 x_2, x_2^2, x_1, x_2, 1)^\top \in \mathbb{R}^6$.

We fit a quadratic curve to data by two-dimensional polynomial kernel. The fitting result of the data with noise is shown in Fig. 1. In the experiment, there holds $\texttt{rank}\,\mathcal{K} \le 6$, and then over sixth eigenvalue of $\mathcal{K}$ should be zero. Let the unit eigenvectors corresponding to the largest six eigenvalues of $\mathcal{K}$ be $\boldsymbol{a}_i$ ($i = 1, \ldots, 6$). Fig. 1 shows the quadratic curve $\boldsymbol{a}_i^\top F(\boldsymbol{x}) = 0$. The results with noises are in the top row and those without noises are in the bottom. The difference between the top and the bottom is the figure corresponded to the sixth eigenvalue. When there are noises, the sixth eigenvalue of $\mathcal{K}$ is not so small ($\texttt{rank}\,\mathcal{K} = 6$), we can compute appropriate $\boldsymbol{a}_6$. To compare with this, when there are no noises, the sixth eigenvalue of $\mathcal{K}$ is theoretically zero ($\texttt{rank}\,\mathcal{K} = 5$), but computed as small value due to round-off error in computation. And then the unreliable eigenvector $\boldsymbol{a}_6$ is computed. In this case, the region $\boldsymbol{a}_6^\top F(\boldsymbol{x}) = 0$ corresponding to sixth eigenvalue in the bottom is drawn by `contour` function provided by statistical software R[2]. It is shown that the curve fitting is failed when there are no noises. Fig. 2 shows equidistant lines of Euclidean distance to the linear space $V_k = \texttt{span}\,\{\boldsymbol{a}_1, \ldots, \boldsymbol{a}_k\}$ in feature space. The results with noises are in the top row and those without noises are in the bottom. The sixth figures of both rows are different. When there are noises, there holds $V_6 = \mathbb{R}^6$ and Euclidean distance is zero for all points. This means the linear space $\{\boldsymbol{x} \mid \boldsymbol{a}_6^\top \boldsymbol{x} = 0\}$, which is the orthogonal complement of $\boldsymbol{a}_6$, is equivalent to V_5.

To compare with this, when there are no noises, there holds $V_6 = V_5 (\ne \mathbb{R}^6)$ since $\boldsymbol{a}_6 = \boldsymbol{0}$ and the fifth and the sixth figures are precisely the same. This means the linear space $\{\boldsymbol{x} \mid \boldsymbol{a}_6^\top \boldsymbol{x} = 0\}$, which is the orthogonal complement of $\boldsymbol{a}_6$, is equivalent to $V_6 = \mathbb{R}^6$.

From the experiment, It can be seen representer theorem does not hold when there are no noises, and the parameter vector $\boldsymbol{a}$ shrinks to zero vector.

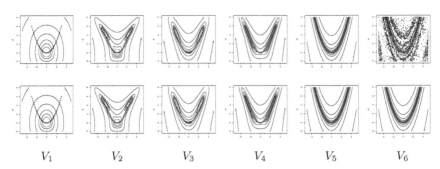

V_1 V_2 V_3 V_4 V_5 V_6

Fig. 2. Equidistant lines from points to V_k: *with* (top) and *without* (bottom) noises

3   Fitting via Hilbert Space

A method of construction of a Hilbert space with RBF kernel functions is proposed by [3], which is known as a kernel PCA (KPCA). The resulting Hilbert space is used for classification, which is called subspace method[5] In this paper, the Hilbert space is used for hypersurface fitting.

To construct a Hilbert space, vectors in $\mathbb{R}^n$ are mapped to square-integrable functions. With RBF kernels, a vector $\boldsymbol{v} \in \mathbb{R}^n$ is mapped to

$$\boldsymbol{v} \mapsto |v\rangle = v(\boldsymbol{x}) = C \exp\left(-\frac{||\boldsymbol{x} - \boldsymbol{v}||^2}{\sigma^2}\right), \quad C = \left(\frac{2}{\pi\sigma^2}\right)^{n/4},$$

and inner product in the Hilbert space is defined as

$$\langle v \,|\, w \rangle = \int v(\boldsymbol{x})w(\boldsymbol{x})d\boldsymbol{x} = \exp\left(-\frac{||\boldsymbol{v} - \boldsymbol{w}||^2}{2\sigma^2}\right).$$

In the definition, a quantity σ is the width parameter of an RBF kernel function.

In the Hilbert space, the representation of hyperplane is $\langle a \,|\, v \rangle = 0$, which is fit to sample points. And the hypersurface fitting is finding the best square-integrable function $a(\boldsymbol{x})$.

We have D observed data $\{\boldsymbol{v}_{[d]}\}_{d=1}^D$ and let $\big|v_{[d]}\big\rangle$ be the image of $\boldsymbol{v}_{[d]}$ on the Hilbert space with RBF kernels. For the data, hyperplane $\langle a \,|\, v \rangle = 0$ is fit in the Hilbert space. The function $|a\rangle$ is estimated as a minimizer of

$$E(a(\boldsymbol{x})) = \sum_{d=1}^D \langle a \,|\, v_{[d]} \rangle \langle v_{[d]} \,|\, a \rangle. \tag{2}$$

As already discussed, the representer theorem does not hold for the hypersurface fitting, but we find appropriate $|a\rangle$ from the linear space spanned by square-integrable functions in the Hilbert space as $|a\rangle = \sum_{d=1}^D \alpha_d \big|v_{[d]}\big\rangle = |\mathcal{V}\rangle \boldsymbol{\alpha}$ where $|\mathcal{V}\rangle = \big(\big|v_{[1]}\big\rangle \cdots \big|v_{[D]}\big\rangle\big)$.

Let $k(\boldsymbol{v}, \boldsymbol{w})$ be a RBF kernel function as $k(\boldsymbol{v}, \boldsymbol{w}) = \langle v \,|\, w \rangle$. And let $\mathcal{K}$ be a $D \times D$-matrix of its ij-components are defined as $(\mathcal{K})_{ij} = \big\langle v_{[i]} \,\big|\, v_{[j]} \big\rangle$.

There holds $\mathcal{K} = \langle \mathcal{V} \, | \, \mathcal{V} \rangle$ for $\langle \mathcal{V} | = \left(|v_{[1]}\rangle \cdots |v_{[D]}\rangle \right)$, and the d-th column of $\mathcal{K}$ is represented as $\mathcal{K}_{[d]} = \langle \mathcal{V} \, | \, v_{[d]} \rangle$. Since there holds

$$\langle a \, | \, v_{[d]} \rangle \langle v_{[d]} \, | \, a \rangle = \boldsymbol{\alpha}^\top \langle \mathcal{V} \, | \, v_{[d]} \rangle \langle v_{[d]} \, | \, \mathcal{V} \rangle \boldsymbol{\alpha} = \boldsymbol{\alpha}^\top \mathcal{K}_{[d]} \mathcal{K}_{[d]}^\top \boldsymbol{\alpha},$$

Eq.(2) is rewritten as

$$\sum_{d=1}^{D} \boldsymbol{\alpha}^\top \mathcal{K}_{[d]} \mathcal{K}_{[d]}^\top \boldsymbol{\alpha} = \boldsymbol{\alpha}^\top \mathcal{K} \boldsymbol{\alpha}$$

without utilizing the mapping to Hilbert space. That is the representation of the energy function that has the same representation as Riemannian space.

4   Experiments: Curve Fitting with RBF Kernel

The curves derived from RBF kernel with $\sigma = 5\sqrt{2}$, is fit to the points on a parabola as the same as the previous experiment. Since the number of data is 50, $\mathcal{K}$ is a 50×50 matrix. Let the unit eigenvectors corresponding to 50 eigenvalues of $\mathcal{K}$ be $|a_i\rangle$ $(i = 1, \ldots, 50)$. Here, small suffix is corresponded to large eigenvalue. Figure 3 shows $\langle a_i \, | \, v \rangle = 0$ (i=1,...,50) drawn by contour function provided by R[2]. The curves sometimes disconnectedly due to round-off error in computation.

From Fig. 3, the eigenvectors corresponding to large eigenvalues (suffix is small) and small eigenvalues (suffix is large) does not correspond to appropriate curve. The curves corresponding to large eigenvalues does not pass through the data, and the curves corresponding to small eigenvalues is complicated though they pass through most of data, that is, overfitting. In the experiment, 15th curve is the best. The way to choose the best eigenvector is one of future works, but the proposed method has a potential to realize good fitting.

Figure 4 shows other fitting results, in which the proposed method works very well.

5   Discussion

This paper gives a flexible hypersurface fitting method for a set of samples from some hypersurface. It is shown by some simulations that our method works well, but it is no easy to choose both the best eigenvector and the width parameter σ systematically. In order to choose both of them, some new criterions must be needed. Nevertheless, our method has worth to be used at first, as we shown in this paper.

Acknowledgment. This work was supported by JSPS KAKENHI Grant Number 25330276.

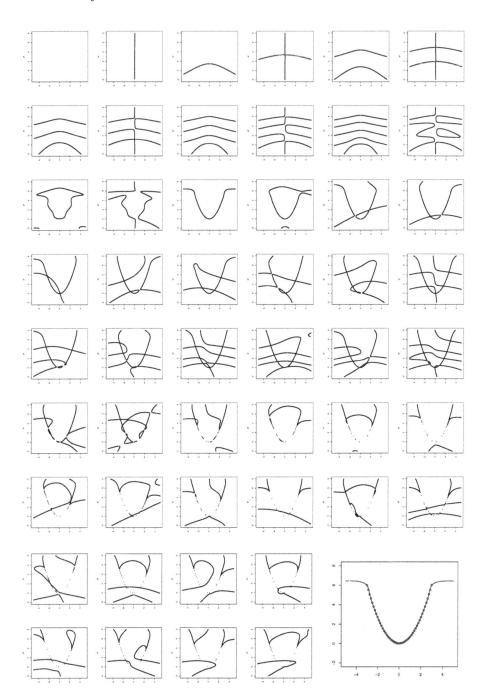

Fig. 3. RBF kernel fitting to points on parabola: Curves correspond to 50-eigenvectors (15th curve is re-shown in bottom right)

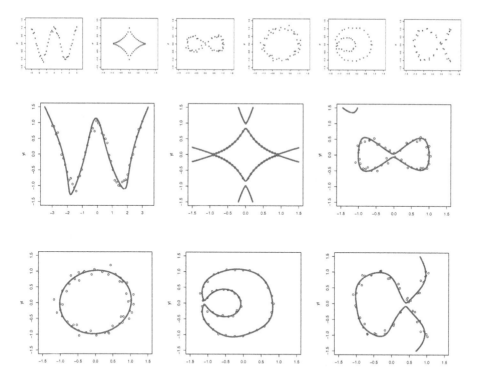

Fig. 4. Examples of flexible fitting: points (top) and results (middle and bottom)

References

1. Fujiki, J., Akaho, S.: Hypersurface fitting via Jacobian nonlinear PCA on Riemannian space. In: Real, P., Diaz-Pernil, D., Molina-Abril, H., Berciano, A., Kropatsch, W. (eds.) CAIP 2011, Part I. LNCS, vol. 6854, pp. 236–243. Springer, Heidelberg (2011)
2. R Development Core Team, R: A language and environment for statistical computing, R Foundation for Statistical Computing, Vienna, Austria (2008) ISBN3-900051-07-0, http://www.R-project.org
3. Schölkopf, B., Smola, A., Müller, K.-R.: Nonlinear component analysis as a kernel eigenvalue problem. Neural Computation 10, 1299–1319 (1998)
4. Schölkopf, B., Smola, A.: Learning with Kernels: Support Vector Machines, Regularization, Optimization, and Beyond. MIT Press (2001)
5. Tsuda, K.: Subspace Classifier in the Hilbert Space. Pattern Recognition Letters 20, 513–519 (1999)
6. Xu, L., Oja, E., Suen, C.: Modified Hebbian learning for curve and surface fitting. Neural Networks 5(3), 441–457 (1992)
7. Wahba, G.: Spline Models for Observational Data. SIAM (1990)

Gender Classification Using Facial Images and Basis Pursuit

Rahman Khorsandi and Mohamed Abdel-Mottaleb

Department of Electrical and Computer Engineering, University of Miami
R.khorsandi@umiami.edu, Mottaleb@miami.edu

Abstract. In many social interactions, it is important to correctly recognize the gender. Researches have addressed this issue based on facial images, ear images and gait. In this paper, we present an approach for gender classification using facial images based upon sparse representation and Basis Pursuit. In sparse representation, the training data is used to develop a dictionary based on extracted features. Classification is achieved by representing the extracted features of the test data using the dictionary. For this purpose, basis pursuit is used to find the best representation by minimizing the l^1 norm. In this work, Gabor filters are used for feature extraction. Experimental results are conducted on the FERET data set and obtained results are compared with other works in this area. The results show improvement in gender classification over existing methods.

Keywords: Gender Classification, Basis Pursuit, Sparse Representation, Facial Images, Gabor Wavelets.

1 Introduction

Gender classification is an important task in social activities and communications. In fact, automatically identifying gender is useful for many applications, *e.g.* security surveillance [4] and statistics about customers in places such as movie theaters, building entrances and restaurants [3]. Automatic gender classification is performed based on facial features [8], voice [10], body movement or gait [23].

Most of the published work in gender classification is based on facial images. Moghaddam *et al.* [16] used Support Vector Machines (SVMs) for gender classification from facial images. They used low resolution thumbnail face images (21×12 pixels). Wu *et al.* [21] presented a real time gender classification system using a Look-Up-Table Adaboost algorithm. They extracted demographic information from human faces. Gollomb *et al.* [8] developed a neural network based gender identification system. They used face images with resolution of 30x30 pixels from 45 males and 45 females to train a fully connected two-layer neural network, SEXNET. Cottrell and Metcalfe [6] used neural networks for face emotion and gender classification from facial images. Gutta and Wechsler [9] used hybrid classifiers for gender identification from facial images. The authors proposed a hybrid approach that consists of an ensemble of RBF neural networks and inductive decision trees. Yu *et al.* [23] presented a study of gender classification based on human gait. They used model-based gait features such as height, frequency and angle between the thighs. Face-based gender classification is still an atractive research area and there is room for developing novel algorithms that are

R. Wilson et al. (Eds.): CAIP 2013, Part I, LNCS 8047, pp. 294–301, 2013.

more roubst, more accurate and fast. In this paper, we will to present a novel method for gender classification based on sparse representation and basis pursuit.

Over the past few years, the theory of sparse representation has been used in various practical applications in signal processing and pattern recognition [7]. A sparse representation of a signal can be achieved by representing the signal as a linear combination of a relatively few base elements in a basis or an overcomplete dictionary [2]. Sparse representation has been used for compression [1], denoising [19], and audio and image analysis [14]. However, its use in recognition and classification is relatively new. Wright *et al.* [20] proposed a classification algorithm for face recognition based on a sparse representation. The reported results for face recognition are encouraging enough to extend this concept to other areas such as gender classification. In addition, Patal *et al.* [17] proposed a face recognition algorithm based on dictionary learning and sparse representation. A dictionary is learned for each class based on given training samples. The test sample is projected onto the span of the training data in each learned dictionary.

The main idea of using sparse representation for recognition and classification is to represent the test data as a linear combination of training data. The set of coefficients of the linear representation is called weight vector. If we assume that there are many subjects in database, the test data will only be related to one of the subjects. Therefore, in sparse representation, the weight vector should be sparse and it is important to find the sparsest solution. To find the weight vector, we use basis pursuit as described in the next section.

In this paper, we present a gender classification system based on 2-D facial images and sparse representation. This paper is organized as follows: In Section 2, we present a brief mathematical explanation of the sparse representation concept and the proposed method based on basis pursuit to obtain the sparsest solution. Section 3 presents experimental results that demonstrate the performance of the proposed method in terms of recognition. Conclusions and future research directions are discussed in Section 4.

2   Classification Based on Sparse Representation

Underdetermined systems appear in different important areas such as signal processing, statistics, pattern recognition and image processing. Sparse representation is a relatively new approach to solve underdetermind systems. In this section, we briefly explain the concept of sparse representation. First, the approach for building a dictionary is introduced. Then, the proposed approach for finding the sparsest solution based on basis pursuit is described. Finally, Gabor wavelets, which we used for extracting the feature vectors, are discussed.

2.1   Building the Dictionary

In the proposed method, a dictionary is built. The dictionary is a matrix where each column is the feature vector of one of the training samples using training data. Assume that there are n_i training data samples for the ith class, where each data sample is represented by a vector of m elements. These vectors are then used to construct the columns of matrix $\mathbf{A}_i$:

$$\mathbf{A}_i = [\mathbf{v}_{i,1}, \mathbf{v}_{i,2}, ..., \mathbf{v}_{i,n_i}] \in \mathbf{R}^{m \times n_i} \tag{1}$$

$\mathbf{v}_{i,j}$, where $j = 1, ..., n_i$, is a column vector that represents the features extracted from the training data sample j of subject i.

It is assumed that a test data from class i can be represented as a linear combination of the training data from that class [20]:

$$\mathbf{y} = \alpha_{i,1}\mathbf{v}_{i,1} + \alpha_{i,2}\mathbf{v}_{i,2} + ... + \alpha_{i,n_i}\mathbf{v}_{i,n_i} \qquad (2)$$

where $\mathbf{y} \in \mathbf{R}^m$ is the feature vector of the test data and the α values are the coefficients corresponding to the training data samples of subject i. Concatenating the matrices $\mathbf{A_i}, i = 1, 2, ..., k$ yields:

$$\mathbf{A} = [\mathbf{A}_1, \mathbf{A}_2, ..., \mathbf{A}_k] \in \mathbf{R}^{m \times n} \qquad (3)$$

where k is the number of subjects and $n = \sum_{i=1}^{k} n_i$. A linear representation for the feature vector of the test data, *i.e.*, $\mathbf{y}$, can then be given as :

$$\mathbf{y} = \mathbf{A}\mathbf{x}_0 \in \mathbf{R}^m \qquad (4)$$

where $\mathbf{x}_0$ is the coefficient vector. By solving this equation for $\mathbf{x}_0$, the class of the test data $\mathbf{y}$ can be identified (as described in the next section).

2.2 Sparse Representation

To solve equation $\mathbf{y} = \mathbf{A}\mathbf{x}$, the number of equations, m, and unknown parameters, n, are important. If $m = n$ the system of equations will be complete and the solution will be unique. However, in recognition and classification, usually there are many subjects or classes, where the test image belongs only to one of the classes and does not belong to the other classes. In addition, the number of extracted features are much less than the training samples. Therefore, the number of equations is less than the number of unknown parameters ($m < n$) and there is no unique solution for the system $\mathbf{y} = \mathbf{A}\mathbf{x}$.

In this formulation, the matrix A is the dictionary that contains the representations of n samples or atoms, where each sample is represented by a feature vector of length m. Since $m < n$, it is an overcomplete matrix. Since dictionary A contains redundancies, it is possible to find $\mathbf{x}$ in an infinite number of ways. Therefore, it is important to introduce a criteria in order to find the best representation (as mentioned later, this criteria is that the solution is the sparsest solution of the equation $\mathbf{y} = \mathbf{A}\mathbf{x}$). When the system $\mathbf{y} = \mathbf{A}\mathbf{x}$ is under determined (*i.e.*, $m < n$), usually the l^2 norm is used and the estimate is expressed as follows:

$$(l^2): \quad \widehat{\mathbf{x}}_2 = argmin\|\mathbf{x}\|_2 \quad Subject\ to \quad \mathbf{y} = \mathbf{A}\mathbf{x} \qquad (5)$$

where $\widehat{\mathbf{x}}_2$ is the solution, which can be obtained simply by computing the pseudo-inverse of $\mathbf{A}$. However, this solution does not contain useful information for recognition. In recognition, the test data belongs to one of the classes represented in the dictionary. Therefore, the obtained answer should be sparse (*i.e.*, only a few elements that correspond to the training samples of the correct class are not zero). The sparsest solution of $\mathbf{y} = \mathbf{A}\mathbf{x}$ can be obtained by minimizing l^0 norm as follows [20]:

$$(l^0): \quad \widehat{\mathbf{x}}_0 = argmin\|\mathbf{x}\|_0 \quad Subject\ to \quad \mathbf{y} = \mathbf{A}\mathbf{x} \qquad (6)$$

where $\|.\|_0$ is the zero norm, which counts the number of non zero elements of $\mathbf{x}$. However, finding the minimum l^0 norm is not an easy task and it becomes harder as the dimensionality increases since we need to use combinatorial search. Furthermore, noise affects the solution because noise magnitude can significantly change the l^0 norm of a vector. In this paper, Basis Pursuit (BP) is used to find the sparsest solution,*i.e.*, the solution vector $\mathbf{x}$ that has the smallest number of non zero elements.

2.3   Sparse Solution Based on Basis Pursuit

Basis pursuit was introduced in the 1970s, and then studied mathematically in the 1990s by Chen and Donoho [5]. To solve the underdetermined system of equations $\mathbf{y} = \mathbf{Ax}$, l^2 minimization is easy to compute, but not useful in recognition. In fact, for recognition purposes, minimizing the l^0 norm provides the best solution since the test data is related to only one of the subjects in the training set. In fact, most of the components of $\mathbf{x}$ should be zero or close to zero. However, the l^0 norm is not a continous function. Since l^0 norm minimization is not a convex optimization problem, it is not easy to obtaine the solution. On the other hand, we can use l^1 norm minization, which is convex, to find $\mathbf{x}$. In the l^1 norm minimization, a cost is assigned to each atom that we use in our representation. Actually, there is no charge for the norm when it gives a zero coefficient. The BP finds the best solution of $\mathbf{x}$ by minimizing the l^1 norm of the $\mathbf{x}$ as follows:

$$\widehat{\mathbf{x}}_1 = argmin \quad \|\mathbf{x}\|_1 \quad subject\ to \quad \mathbf{y} = \mathbf{Ax} \tag{7}$$

Where $\|\mathbf{x}\|_1$ is the l^1 norm. To find $\widehat{\mathbf{x}}_1$, since the nonzero coefficients correspond to columns of the dictionary, it is possible to use the indices of the nonzero components of $\widehat{\mathbf{x}}_1$ to identify the columns of A that are necessary to represent the test image. l^1 norm assigns a cost to each atom that is used in representation. For example, the norm will not be penalized when it gives a zero coefficient, but it should be charged proportionally for small and large coefficients.

Since $\|\mathbf{x}\|_1 = |x_1| + ... + |x_n|$ and we can rewrite equation 7 as:

$$minimize\|\mathbf{x}\|_1 = |x_1| + ... + |x_n| \quad subject\ to \quad \mathbf{y} = \mathbf{Ax} \tag{8}$$

Because $|x_1| + ... + |x_n|$ is a nonlinear function, the optimization problem can not be solved using linear programming methods. To make this function linear, nonlinearities should change to constraints by adding new variables as follow:

$$minimize \quad t_1 + t_2 + ... + t_n \quad subject\ to \tag{9}$$

$$|x_1| \le t_1, \quad .... \quad , |x_n| \le t_n \quad and \quad \mathbf{y} = \mathbf{Ax}$$

Where, $t_1, ..., t_n$ are non-negative constants. In this formulation, the objective function is linear and it is possible to solve this problem using linear programming.

2.4   Using Sparse Representation for Classification

For a test data, $\mathbf{y}$, belonging to the ith class, it is assumed that the non-zero elements of $\widehat{\mathbf{x}_1}$ will correspond to the training data samples from the ith class. However, due to noise and representation errors, there will be extraneous non-zero elements corresponding to training samples from other classes.

In [20], they presented an approach for the decision making step based upon the obtained $\widehat{\mathbf{x}}_1$ by computing the error between $\mathbf{y}$, the original data, and $\widehat{\mathbf{y}}_i$, the approximation obtained through the sparse representation. For each class i and $\mathbf{x} \in \mathbf{R}^n$, vector $\delta_i(\mathbf{x}) \in \mathbf{R}^n$ represents the coefficients that are associated with class i. Using this definition, approximated test data $\widehat{\mathbf{y}}_i$ is given as:

$$\widehat{\mathbf{y}}_i = A\delta_i(\widehat{\mathbf{x}_1}) \tag{10}$$

Recognition was performed by assigning the test data to the class that minimizes the residual between $\mathbf{y}$ and $\widehat{\mathbf{y}}_i$ as follows:

$$\underset{i}{min} \quad r_i(\mathbf{y}) = \|\mathbf{y} - \mathbf{A}\delta_i(\widehat{\mathbf{x}_1})\|_2 \tag{11}$$

where $r_i(\mathbf{y})$ is the residual distance for class i. This signifies that the classification is performed based on the best approximation and least error [20].

Here, we propose a new approach to perform classification using $\widehat{\mathbf{x}}_1$. In gender classification, there are only two classes and the dictionary contains training face images for males and females as representatives of these two classes. The obtained elements of $\widehat{\mathbf{x}}_1$ are the coefficients associated with each training face image and we can divide $\widehat{\mathbf{x}}_1$ into two vectors, $\mathbf{x}_1$ and $\mathbf{x}_2$, where $\mathbf{x}_1$ contains the coefficients associated with males and $\mathbf{x}_2$ contains the coefficients associated with females. $\widehat{\mathbf{x}}_1$ can be written as follows:

$$\widehat{\mathbf{x}}_1 = \begin{bmatrix} \mathbf{x}_1 \\ \mathbf{x}_2 \end{bmatrix}$$

The length of the $\widehat{\mathbf{x}}_1$ is m and the number of training samples for males and females are equal. Hence, the length of $\mathbf{x}_1$ and the length of $\mathbf{x}_2$ is $m/2$.

Let x_{max} be the maximum value of the $\widehat{\mathbf{x}}_1$ elements ($x_{max} = max(\widehat{\mathbf{x}}_1)$). Then, a threshold x_{max}/τ, where ($\tau \geq 1$) is defined. The elements in $\mathbf{x}_1$ and $\mathbf{x}_2$ whose values are more than the threshold are counted. The classification is performed based on the majority vote of the coefficients.

3   Gabor Wavelets

The Gabor filters (kernels) with orientation μ and scale ν are defined as [22]

$$\psi_{\mu,\nu} = \frac{\| k_{\mu,\nu} \|^2}{\sigma^2} e^{\left(\frac{-\| k_{\mu,\nu} \|^2 \| z \|^2}{2\sigma^2}\right)} \left[e^{ik_{\mu,\nu}z} - e^{-\sigma^2/2} \right] \tag{12}$$

where $z = (x, y)$ is the pixel position, and the wave vector $k_{\mu,\nu}$ is defined as $k_{\mu,\nu} = k_\nu e^{i\phi_\mu}$ with $k_\nu = k_{max}/f^\nu$ and $\Phi_\mu = \pi\mu/8$. k_{max} is the maximum frequency, and f is the spacing factor between kernels in the frequency domain. The ratio of the Gaussian window width to wavelength is determined by σ. Considering Eq. 12, the Gabor kernels can be generated from one wavelet, *i.e.*, the mother wavelet, by scaling and rotation via the wave vector $k_{\mu,\nu}$ [13]. In this work, we used five scales, $\nu \in \{0, ..., 4\}$ and eight orientations $\mu \in \{0, ..., 7\}$. We also used $\sigma = 2\pi$, $k_{max} = \pi/2$ and $f = \sqrt{2}$.

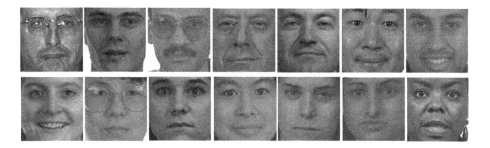

Fig. 1. *Sample images for both males and females in FERET database*

4 Experiments and Results

The FERET database [18] is used to validate the proposed method. Images are frontal faces at a resolution of 256x384 with 256 gray levels. All the images are preprocessed before applying the algorithm. First, the automatic eye-detection method is applied based on the [11] and the distance, d, between the 2 eye corners is measured. Then, the middle point between the 2 eye corners is found and the image is cropped by the size of $2d \times 2d$. Then all images are resized to 128x128. A few sample face images for both male and female subjects are shown in Fig. 1. In this database, there are 250 male subjects and 250 female subjects. As previously stated, in sparse classification, the training samples are used to build a dictionary, which is used during the classification to represent a test sample as a linear combination of the training samples. Since we are using majority voting for making a decision between the two categories, the number of training samples for males and females should be equal. In addition, to compare our results with other methods, especially [12], four experiments are conducted with different number of subjects used for training in each experiment, sizes of: 50, 100, 150 and 200 subjects were used for training. In each experiment, the remaining subjects are used for testing. For instance, when using 200 subjects for training (100 male subjects and 100 female subjects), the other 300 subjects are used for testing. In the feature extraction step, Gabor wavelets are extracted for 8 orientations and 5 spatial frequencies. Finally, using PCA, the number of features used to represent each image is reduced to 128. In the proposed approach, for each test data, the sparsest coefficient vector $\widehat{x_1}$ is obtained based on the basis pursuit. Majority voting is then used to recognize the gender of the test subject. We provide a comparison of the experimental results with other gender classification systems applied to the same dataset. Table. 1 shows the classification rates for 4 different training set sizes. The results of our proposed method (PCA + BP) are compared with the results of the methods proposed by Jain *et al.* [12], in which the authors evaluated their method on the FERET database. They used Independent Component Analysis (ICA) to represent each image as feature vector in a low dimensional subspace. In addition, they used different classifiers such as cosine classifier (COS), linear discriminant classifier (LDA) and the support vector machine (SVM). The best result reported in [12] is 95.67% accuracy using SVM with ICA. Furthermore, the results for conventional sparse representation based classification (SRC)[20] are reported in Table. 1 which show our modification was helpful in gender recognition. The

Table 1. Performance comparison to other gender classification systems based on facial images

Training Set Size	ICA + COS	ICA + LDA	ICA+ SVM	SRC	PCA+BP (Proposed Method)
50	60.67%	64.67%	68.30%	68.88%	68.88%
100	71.67%	73.67%	76.00%	76.00%	76.25%
150	80.33%	83.00%	86.67%	86.85%	88.57%
200	85.33%	93.33%	95.67%	96.33%	97.66%

experimental results in this paper indicate that our proposed method using sparse representation and PCA obtained higher performance of correct classification rate on the same data set. To our best knowledge, better results for gender classification on FERET database is not reported since 2005. Moreover, in [15], authors used 661 images from FERET database, for 248 subjects. The best obtained result for gender classification in that paper is 90% for feature dimension 11,520. However, we obtained a classification rate of 97% for 512 feature dimension and for 500 subjects.

5 Conclusion

In this paper, we presented a method for gender classification, from facial images, using sparse representation. Basis pursuit method was used to formulate the problem in order to find the sparsest solution. The experiments were conducted on the FERET data set containing 500 subjects (250 male and 250 female subjects). Features were extracted using Gabor wavelets, and a dictionary was constructed based on the extracted features from a training set. The rest of the data set was used for testing. We compared the proposed method in this paper with previous methods that used the same data set, performance of our the presented method is better than the previous reported methods. Experiments are encouraging enough for future research on the sparse representation for gender classification. In the future, we plan to apply our method for the fusion of facial and ear features.

References

1. Aharon, M., Elad, M., Bruckstein, A.: K-svd: An algorithm for designing overcomplete dictionaries for sparse representation. IEEE Transactions on Signal Processing 54(11), 4311–4322 (2006)
2. Baraniuk, R., Candes, E., Elad, M., Ma, Y.: Applications of sparse representation and compressive sensing. Proceedings of the IEEE 98(6), 906–909 (2010)
3. Cao, L., Dikmen, M., Fu, Y., Huang, T.S.: Gender recognition from body. In: Proceedings of the 16th ACM International Conference on Multimedia, MM 2008, New York, NY, USA, pp. 725–728 (2008)
4. Chen, D.-Y., Lin, K.-Y.: Robust gender recognition for real-time surveillance system. In: IEEE International Conference on Multimedia and Expo (ICME), pp. 191–196 (July 2010)
5. Chen, S.S., Donoho, D.L., Michael, Saunders, A.: Atomic decomposition by basis pursuit. SIAM Journal on Scientific Computing 20, 33–61 (1998)
6. Cottrell, G.W., Metcalfe, J.: Empath: face, emotion, and gender recognition using holons. In: Proceedings of the 1990 Conference on Advances in Neural Information Processing Systems 3, NIPS-3, San Francisco, CA, USA, pp. 564–571 (1990)

7. Donoho, D.L.: Compressed sensing. IEEE Transaction on Information Theory 52(4) (2006)
8. Golomb, B.A., Lawrence, D.T., Sejnowski, T.J.: Sexnet: A neural network identifies sex from human faces. In: Proceedings Conf. Advances in Neural Information Processing Systems 3, pp. 572–577 (1990)
9. Gutta, S., Wechsler, H.: Gender and ethnic classification of human faces using hybrid classifiers. In: International Joint Conference on Neural Networks, IJCNN 1999, vol. 6, pp. 4084–4089 (1999)
10. Harb, H., Chen, L.: Gender identification using a general audio classifier. In: Proceedings of the International Conference on Multimedia and Expo, ICME 2003, Washington, DC, USA, pp. 733–736 (2003)
11. Hsu, R.-L., Abdel-Mottaleb, M., Jain, A.: Face detection in color images. IEEE Transactions on Pattern Analysis and Machine Intelligence 24(5), 696–706 (2002)
12. Jain, A., Huang, J., Fang, S.: Gender identification using frontal facial images. In: IEEE International Conference on Multimedia and Expo, ICME 2005, p. 4 (July 2005)
13. Liu, C., Wechsler, H.: Gabor feature based classification using the enhanced fisher linear discriminant model for face recognition. IEEE Transactions on Image Processing 11(4), 467–476 (2002)
14. Llagostera Casanovas, A., Monaci, G., Vandergheynst, P., Gribonval, R.: Blind audiovisual source separation based on sparse redundant representations. IEEE Transactions on Multimedia 12(5), 358–371 (2010)
15. Lu, H., Huang, Y., Chen, Y., Yang, D.: Automatic gender recognition based on pixel-pattern-based texture feature. Journal of Real-Time Image Processing 3, 109–116 (2008)
16. Moghaddam, B., Yang, M.-H.: Gender classification with support vector machines. In: Fourth IEEE International Conference on Automatic Face and Gesture Recognition, pp. 306–311 (2000)
17. Patel, V.M., Wu, T., Biswas, S., Phillips, P.J., Chellappa, R.: Dictionary-based face recognition under variable lighting and pose. IEEE Transactions on Information Forensics and Security 7(3), 954–965 (2012)
18. Phillips, P., Moon, H., Rizvi, S., Rauss, P.: The feret evaluation methodology for face-recognition algorithms. IEEE Transactions on Pattern Analysis and Machine Intelligence 22(10), 1090–1104 (2000)
19. Protter, M., Elad, M.: Image sequence denoising via sparse and redundant representations. IEEE Transactions on Image Processing 18(1), 27–35 (2009)
20. Wright, J., Yang, A., Ganesh, A., Sastry, S., Ma, Y.: Robust face recognition via sparse representation. IEEE Transactions on Pattern Analysis and Machine Intelligence 31(2), 210–227 (2009)
21. Wu, B., Ai, H., Huang, C.: Facial image retrieval based on demographic classification. In: Proceedings of the 17th International Conference on Pattern Recognition, ICPR 2004, vol. 3, pp. 914–917 (2004)
22. Yang, M., Zhang, L.: Gabor feature based sparse representation for face recognition with gabor occlusion dictionary. In: Daniilidis, K., Maragos, P., Paragios, N. (eds.) ECCV 2010, Part VI. LNCS, vol. 6316, pp. 448–461. Springer, Heidelberg (2010)
23. Yu, S., Tan, T., Huang, K., Jia, K., Wu, X.: A study on gait-based gender classification. IEEE Transactions on Image Processing 18(8), 1905–1910 (2009)

Graph Clustering through Attribute Statistics Based Embedding

Jaume Gibert[1], Ernest Valveny[2], Horst Bunke[3], and Luc Brun[1]

[1] École Nationale Supérieure d'Ingénieurs de Caen, ENSICAEN
Université de Caen Basse-Normandie, 6 Boulevard Maréchal Juin
14050 Caen, France
{jaume.gibert,luc.brun}@ensicaen.fr
[2] Computer Vision Center, Universitat Autònoma de Barcelona
Edifici O Campus UAB, 08193 Bellaterra, Spain
ernest@cvc.uab.es
[3] Institute for Computer Science and Applied Mathematics, University of Bern,
Neubrückstrasse 10, CH-3012 Bern, Switzerland
bunke@iam.unibe.ch

Abstract. This work tackles the problem of graph clustering by an explicit embedding of graphs into vector spaces. We use an embedding methodology based on occurrence and co-occurrence statistics of representative elements of the node attributes. This embedding methodology has already been used for graph classification problems. In the current paper we investigate its applicability to the problem of clustering color-attributed graphs. The ICPR 2010 Graph Embedding Contest serves us as an evaluation framework. Explicit and implicit embedding methods are evaluated in terms of their ability to cluster object images represented as attributed graphs. We compare the attribute statistics based embedding methodology to explicit and implicit embedding techniques proposed by the contest participants and show improvements in some of the datasets. We then demonstrate further improvements by means of different vectorial metrics and kernel functions on the embedded graphs.

1 Introduction

Clustering, or unsupervised learning, is a key concept in pattern recognition. While the clustering of vectorial pattern representations has reached some level of maturity, the clustering of graphs is still in its infancy [5]. This is due to a number of difficulties that arise especially from the fact that many operations needed in a clustering algorithm, although readily available for vectorial representations, do not exist for graphs (or are at least extremely difficult to accomplish). Examples are the computation of the mean of a set of graphs, or the operation of making two graphs more similar to each other, as needed in kMeans clustering and self-organizing nets, respectively. In order to overcome these problems, a number of approaches have been proposed that relate the graph domain to vector spaces where such operations are easier to perform and plenty of learning machinery

R. Wilson et al. (Eds.): CAIP 2013, Part I, LNCS 8047, pp. 302–309, 2013.
© Springer-Verlag Berlin Heidelberg 2013

is available. Graph embeddings and graph kernels are the main paradigms. The former explicitly assign a feature vector to each graph while the latter implicitly map each graph in a feature space and compute the corresponding scalar product. The relation between graph embeddings and graph kernels is clear since, given an explicit embedding, any kernel function on vectors also defines a graph kernel.

We have previously proposed an explicit embedding approach which is based on extracting features describing the occurrence and co-occurrence of node label representatives in a given graph [4]. Its efficiency and good performance, when compared to state of the art methodologies for graph classification, have been empirically demonstrated. In the current paper, we aim at an evaluation of this embedding methodology for graph clustering. To that end, we make use of the ICPR 2010 Graph Embedding Contest [3]. This contest was organized in order to provide a framework for direct comparison between embedding methodologies for the purpose of graph clustering. Three object image datasets were chosen and converted into graphs, divided into a training and a test set. The participants also received a code with which they could assess their own methodologies in terms of a clustering measure. Object images were first segmented into different regions and a region adjacency graph was constructed. Each node representing a region was attributed with the corresponding relative size and the average RGB color components, while edges remained unattributed.

For the contest, four algorithms were submitted, three explicit embedding methods and an implicit one. Jouili and Tabbone build feature vectors whose distances distribution respect as much as possible that of the corresponding graphs. In particular, they assign a feature vector to every graph by considering the eigenvectors of a positive semidefinite matrix regarding the dissimilarity of graphs [6]. Riesen and Bunke map every graph to a feature vector whose components are the edit distances to a predefined set of prototypes [8]. Their goal is thus to characterize graphs as how they are located with respect to some key graphs in the graph space. Luqman et at. search for particular subgraph structures present in the original graphs. They encode relevant information by quantizing node and edge attributes via the use of fuzzy intervals [7]. Finally, the implicit methodology proposed by Osmanlıoğlu *et al.* maps each node of each graph to a vector space by means of the caterpillar decomposition, and computes a kernel value between two given graphs in terms of a point set matching algorithm based on the Earth Mover's distance [2].

The contribution of the work described in this paper is to evaluate the novel embedding methodology of [4], which was not yet available at the time of the ICPR contest, for the task of clustering and compare it to existing approaches. Besides, the mentioned embedding methodology has been re-formulated in such a way that it can handle color-based attributed graphs. We will show that, in such a way, it constitutes an attractive addition to the set of graph clustering tools currently available. For the purpose of self-completeness, Section 2 of the paper provides a brief introduction to graph embedding using node label occurrence and co-occurrence statistics. Next, Section 3 describes in detail the experimental evaluation and shows how to gain further improvements along this line of research. Finally, Section 4 draws conclusions from this work.

2   Attribute Statistics Based Embedding

The main idea of the embedding methodology used in this work is based on counting the frequency of appearance of the node labels in a given graph and also on the co-occurrence of pairs of node labels in conjunction with edge linkings. The fact that node labels might not be discrete (as it is in the present case) demands for a discretization of the node labelling space and, thus, the selection of a set of representatives. Under the proposed approach, the features are obtained by computing statistics on these representatives in terms of those nodes that have been assigned to each of them. Based on how this assignment from nodes to representatives is made we have two formulations of the embedding approach.

2.1   Hard Assignment

Assume a set of graphs $\mathcal{G} = \{g_1, \ldots, g_N\}$ is given, each being a four-tuple $g_i = (V_i, E_i, \mu_i, \nu_i)$ consisting on a set of nodes V_i, a set of edges $E_i \subseteq V_i \times V_i$, and the corresponding labelling functions μ_i and ν_i. In this work, nodes are labelled with RGB values, thus the labelling function codomain is always the set $[0, 255]^3$ (the relative size attribute is disregarded). Edges remain unlabelled.

From the set of all node labels of all graphs in $\mathcal{G}$ we select some representatives $\mathcal{W} = \{w_1, \ldots, w_n\}$ (see Section 2.3). Given a graph g, each node $v \in V$ is assigned to the closest representative by

$$\lambda_h(v) = \operatorname*{argmin}_{w_i \in \mathcal{W}} \| \mu(v) - w_i \|_2 . \tag{1}$$

Then we extract unary features as occurrences of representatives in the graph by

$$U_i = \#(w_i, g) = | \{v \in V \mid w_i = \lambda_h(v)\} | . \tag{2}$$

Also, co-occurrence features between two representatives are defined as

$$\begin{aligned} B_{ij} &= \#(w_i \leftrightarrow w_j, g) \\ &= | \{(u, v) \in E \mid w_i = \lambda_h(u) \wedge w_j = \lambda_h(v)\} | . \end{aligned} \tag{3}$$

Both the unary features U_i and the binary ones B_i are eventually arranged in a feature vector.

In particular, note that what this formulation is proposing is to build a histogram of the presence of specific features in the graphs. In the present case, we aim at evaluating the presence of each color in every graph, and also the presence of the neighbouring relations of all colors in the graphs. In Section 2.4 we discuss the connections of this approach to other existing graph embedding methodologies.

2.2   Soft Assignment

Assigning nodes to representatives in a hard fashion might lead to weak descriptions because the graph extraction process is usually noisy. However, the embedding methodology used in this work is adaptable for a fuzzy assignment from nodes to representatives which might correct such situations. In particular, each node is represented by a set of probabilities

$$\lambda_s(v) = (p_1(v), \ldots, p_n(v)), \tag{4}$$

where $p_i(v) = P(v \sim w_i)$ is the probability of node v being represented by w_i. The unary features are then the addition of all probabilities for all nodes in the graph g:

$$U_i = \#(w_i, g) = \sum_{v \in V} p_i(v). \tag{5}$$

The fuzzy version of the binary features needs to regard the transition probabilities from one node to the other and thus is defined as

$$B_{ij} = \#(w_i \leftrightarrow w_j, g)$$
$$= \sum_{(u,v) \in E} p_i(u)p_j(v) + p_j(u)p_i(v). \tag{6}$$

2.3   Representative Set Selection

One of the key issues of the embedding methodology is the selection of the set of representatives for the node labels. We can make use of generic clustering approaches independent to the domain such as kMeans, or we can use domain-specific approaches. In addition to using kMeans, we propose in this work a color-based approach that tries to adapt the set of representatives to the inherent RGB structure of the node labelling space.

Generic Approaches. In order to select representatives of the node labels for the hard assignment version of the proposed embedding, we use the kMeans clustering algorithm for different values of the parameter k. This representation will be referred to as *Hard kM*. In Fig. 1(a) we show a sample of node labels with their corresponding original color. Next to it, in Fig. 1(b), the distribution of the $k = 10$ clusters after applying the kMeans algorithm is shown.

For the soft assignment version we use fuzzy kMeans to select the set of representatives, and the probability of each node to belong to a certain representative is defined to be inversely proportional to the Euclidean distance between the considered node and the representative. We will refer to this representations as *Soft kM*.

These two configurations not only depend on how the representative elements are selected, but also on the number of them. This parameter needs to be validated using the training set.

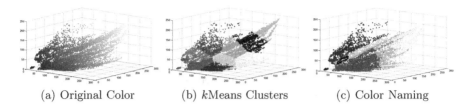

(a) Original Color   (b) kMeans Clusters   (c) Color Naming

Fig. 1. Distributions of the graphs' nodes in the RGB space (best seen in color). (a) Original color of each node. (b) kMeans clusters for $k = 10$. (c) Color naming distribution.

Color-Based Approaches. Due to the spherical arrangement of its clusters, kMeans does not really account for the color distribution of the original node values, grouping for instance node labels of different color into the same cluster. This problem demands for a way of selecting representatives that can adapt in a more accurate manner to the real RGB distribution of the whole set of node attributes (Fig. 1(a)). To do so, we have adopted a color naming approach for which each node label, *i.e.* each point in the RGB space, is assigned to one of the eleven basic colors of the color naming theory.

In particular, we adopted the methodology proposed in [1], where each RGB point is automatically assigned to every color in the color naming scheme with a certain probability. Each node is thus represented with a set of probabilities allowing the use of the soft assignment version of the embedding approach described here. This version is referred to in the text as *Soft Color*. For the hard assignment version, for every node in a given graph, we just pick the color that produces the highest probability value and refer to it as *Hard Color*. Fig. 1(c) shows the resulting 11 clusters after the assignment.

2.4   Relation to other Approaches

An interesting observation to be done regarding the proposed methodology is its connections to other graph characterization approaches. In particular, an appealing consideration is that of its similarity with fingerprint characterization of molecular structures [9]. In this domain, molecules are represented as histograms of the presence of particular subgraph structures, where such substructures are selected based on prior chemical knowledge. The methodology used in this work is related to this one in the sense that, after node attribute discretization, it look for particular substruces in the graph representations such as node appearances and node-edge-node walks.

On the other hand, but strictly related to the former, the explicit embedding of graphs by the presented approach can be reduced to characterize graphs based on walks of length 0 and walks of length 1 with respect to their labelling information. In that sense, it might also be connected to the so-called family of random walk kernels [10].

Table 1. C-index on the test sets under the Euclidean distance: lower index values indicate better clustering results. Comparison with the contest participants. The best results are shown bold face.

Embedding	ALOI	COIL	ODBK	Geometric Mean
Osmanlıoğlu et al.	0.088	**0.067**	0.105	0.085
Jouili and Tabbone	0.136	0.199	0.138	0.155
Riesen and Bunke	**0.048**	0.128	0.132	0.093
Luqman et al.	0.379	0.377	0.355	0.370
Hard kM	0.080	0.160	0.070	0.096
Soft kM	0.068	0.136	0.058	0.081
Hard Color	0.067	0.143	0.061	0.083
Soft Color	0.056	0.121	**0.051**	**0.070**

3 Experimental Evaluation

The three object image datasets that were used in the contest are the ALOI, COIL and OBDK collections. Each of them is representing object images under different angles of rotation and illumination changes. For more details on the datasets, we refer to the contest report [3]. We recall here that a training and a test set are available for each dataset. We use the training set to validate the parameters (number of representative elements) that are eventually used for processing the test set.

Every approach is assessed by computing the C-index clustering measure, and approaches are ranked in terms of the geometric mean of the results on the three datasets. When the embedding is explicit, the clustering index is computed based on the Euclidean distances of the vectorial representations of graphs. When an implicit formulation is given, distances are computed according to the following formula

$$d_{ij} = \sqrt{k_{ii} + k_{jj} - 2k_{ij}} \qquad (7)$$

where k_{ij} is the kernel value between graphs g_i and g_j. Under a kernel function, graphs are implicitly mapped to a hidden feature space where the scalar product is calculated. Formula (7) is the Euclidean distance between the corresponding vectors in such a feature space. Results of the proposed methodologies in comparison with the contest participants are shown in Table 1.

As expected, the *Soft* approaches obtain better results than the hard ones, and the color-based versions improve the generic ones. Compared to the participants methods, the proposed embedding approach ranks second on two databases and first on the third one. This leads to the best geometric mean among all tested methods. Moreover, let us mention the high efficiency of our approach which arises from the fact that we base our embedding method on very simple features with a fast computation.

As already said before, the contest clustering measures are computed based on the Euclidean distances of the embedding representations. In other works, the proposed embedding methodology has been shown to perform better under different vectorial metrics [4]. We thus refine our results by computing the C-index for clustering validation under the L_1 and χ^2 distances. Results of these

Table 2. C-index under different distances and under the k_{χ^2} kernel on the test sets. The best results are shown bold face.

Distance / Kernel	ALOI		COIL	
	Soft kM	*Soft Color*	*Soft kM*	*Soft Color*
L_2	0.073	0.056	0.136	0.121
L_1	0.064	0.060	0.130	0.110
χ^2	**0.031**	0.032	0.066	0.064
k_{χ^2}	0.088	0.083	**3.10e-08**	9.04e-07
	ODBK		Geometric Mean	
	Soft kM	*Soft Color*	*Soft kM*	*Soft Color*
L_2	0.056	0.051	0.083	0.070
L_1	0.063	0.061	0.081	0.074
χ^2	0.033	0.037	0.041	0.042
k_{χ^2}	**8.67e-10**	0.097	**1.33e-06**	1.94e-03

experiments for the *Soft* versions are shown on the first three rows of Table 2 (*Hard* versions are discarded since they do not show as good a performance as the *Soft* ones). The χ^2 distance is providing the best results, ranking best on all datasets, even when compared to the contest participants (we, however, want to point out that a direct comparison to the results obtained by the contest participants would not be fair since we do not know how their algorithms would perform under other metrics). Interestingly, the χ^2 distance extracts the best out of the *Soft kM* versions since it outperforms the *Soft Color* one in two of the three datasets, which does not happen when using the two other metrics.

Finally, in order to relate our methodology to those that provide an implicit embedding of graphs we compute kernel values between embedded graphs as

$$k_d(g_1, g_2) = \exp\left(-\frac{1}{\gamma} d(\phi(g_1), \phi(g_2))\right), \quad \gamma > 0 \tag{8}$$

where $\phi(g_i)$ is the vectorial representation of the graph g_i under the described embedding methodology, and d is the χ^2 metric (L_2 or L_1 could also be used but χ^2 is the one providing the best results when clustering under metrics as discussed above). Distance values for the C-index computation are calculated using Eq. (7). The γ parameter is also validated using the training set. Results for the *Soft* versions are shown on the last row of Table 2.

Although the results for the ALOI database worsen when using the kernel values for both versions of the embedding, the most significant point to highlight from this table is that we obtain almost perfect separation indexes for the COIL dataset under the two *Soft* versions and also for the ODBK under the *Soft kM* one. This makes the geometric means to drastically decrease and demonstrates the embedding methodology we propose in this work being a strong approach for graph clustering.

4   Conclusions

In this work, we have evaluated the color-based explicit graph embedding methodology that accounts for statistics on node label representatives in terms of clustering performance. We have compared it to the approaches that were reported in the ICPR 2010 Graph Embedding Contest and shown that it performs very favorably. Additional improvements are gained by evaluating the embedding method under different metrics and also by the use of kernel functions on the resulting vectors, leading to almost perfect separation results in two of the three contest datasets. Future work on this research line should be directed to assess whether object-wise color quantization provides a better characterization of the color space where the set of node labels can be found.

As a final remark, the authors find of paramount importance that different works appear in the same line as the present, where different pattern recognition methodologies are brought together and compared ones to the others using a unified and clear framework. In this sense, we want to acknowledge the ICPR Graph Embedding Contest organizers for their valuable work.

References

1. Benavente, R., Vanrell, M., Baldrich, R.: Parametric fuzzy sets for automatic color naming. J. Optical Society of America A 25(10), 2582–2593 (2008)
2. Demirci, M.F., Osmanlıoğlu, Y., Shokoufandeh, A., Dickinson, S.: Efficient many-to-many feature matching under the l_1 norm. Computer Vision and Image Understanding 115(7), 976–983 (2011)
3. Foggia, P., Vento, M.: Graph Embedding for Pattern Recognition. In: Ünay, D., Çataltepe, Z., Aksoy, S. (eds.) ICPR 2010. LNCS, vol. 6388, pp. 75–82. Springer, Heidelberg (2010)
4. Gibert, J., Valveny, E., Bunke, H.: Graph embedding in vector spaces by node attribute statistics. Pattern Recognition 45(9), 3072–3083 (2012)
5. Jain, A.K.: Data Clustering: 50 years beyond K-means. Pattern Recognition Letters 31(8), 651–666 (2010)
6. Jouili, S., Tabbone, S.: Graph Embedding Using Constant Shift Embedding. In: Ünay, D., Çataltepe, Z., Aksoy, S. (eds.) ICPR 2010. LNCS, vol. 6388, pp. 83–92. Springer, Heidelberg (2010)
7. Luqman, M.M., Lladós, J., Ramel, J.-Y., Brouard, T.: A Fuzzy-Interval Based Approach for Explicit Graph Embedding. In: Ünay, D., Çataltepe, Z., Aksoy, S. (eds.) ICPR 2010. LNCS, vol. 6388, pp. 93–98. Springer, Heidelberg (2010)
8. Riesen, K., Bunke, H.: Graph Classification and Clustering Based on Vector Space Embedding. World Scientific (2010)
9. Mahé, P., Ueda, N., Akutsu, T., Perret, J.-L., Vert, J.-P.: Graph Kernels for Molecular Structure-Activity Relationship Analysis with Support Vector Machines. Journal of Chemical Information and Modelling, 939–951 (2005)
10. Gärtner, T., Flach, P.A., Wrobel, S.: On graph kernels: Hardness results and efficient alternatives. In: Schölkopf, B., Warmuth, M.K. (eds.) COLT/Kernel 2003. LNCS (LNAI), vol. 2777, pp. 129–143. Springer, Heidelberg (2003)

Graph-Based Regularization of Binary Classifiers for Texture Segmentation

Cyrille Faucheux[1,3,*], Julien Olivier[2,1], and Romuald Boné[2,1]

[1] Université François Rabelais de Tours, Laboratoire d'Informatique
64, Avenue Jean Portalis, 37200 Tours, France
[2] École Nationale d'Ingénieurs du Val de Loire
3, Rue de la Chocolaterie, BP 3410, 41034 Blois CEDEX, France
[3] Cosm'O Laboratory
100, Rue de Suède, 37100 Tours, France
`cyrille.faucheux@etu.univ-tours.fr,`
`{julien.olivier,romuald.bone}@univ-tours.fr`

Abstract. In this paper, we propose to improve a recent texture-based graph regularization model used to perform image segmentation by including a binary classifier in the process. Built upon two non-local image processing techniques, the addition of a classifier brings to our model the ability to weight texture features according to their relevance. The graph regularization process is then applied on the initial segmentation provided by the classifier in order to clear it from most imperfections. Results are presented on artificial and medical images, and compared to an active contour driven by classifiers segmentation algorithm, highlighting the increased generality and accuracy of our model.

Keywords: image segmentation, graph regularization, Haralick texture features, neural networks.

1 Introduction

Developed to overcome some traditional algorithm limitations, non-local image processing approaches, especially graph-based ones [1,2] have recently gained a lot of interest due to the increased flexibility of the data structures involved.

In a previous paper [3], an image segmentation technique that combines two non-local approaches to image processing was proposed. The first one takes advantage of windowed Haralick texture features [4] in order to work with pixel characteristics with a higher level of abstraction than the pixel itself, and therefore more meaningful than raw gray-level intensities. The second approach actually carries out the segmentation task using a graph regularization process that relies on a criteria inspired by the work of Chan and Vese [5] to separate the two textures and partition the image.

---

* This work was partially supported under a research grant of the ANR (1241/2009).

R. Wilson et al. (Eds.): CAIP 2013, Part I, LNCS 8047, pp. 310–318, 2013.
© Springer-Verlag Berlin Heidelberg 2013

One drawback of this segmentation technique comes from applying the Chan and Vese criteria on texture features. Depending on the type of images (acquisition method, content...), some features may be irrelevant, or more relevant than others. This fact cannot be automatically handled by the Chan and Vese criteria, and features must be manually selected in order to obtain the best results. Moreover, unsupervised weighing of the features is impossible.

The aim of this work is to overcome this limitation while keeping the two non-local approaches. To do so, we propose to combine a supervised binary classifier with the graph regularization process used previously. Implemented as a neural network, the classifier takes care of the texture feature relevancy issue by providing an initial classification of the pixels. The graph regularization process from [3], which is designed to handle any multivariate feature, is this time applied on an univariate one, the output of the classifier, in order to correct classification errors and produce a smoothed segmentation.

2 Methodology

2.1 Haralick Texture Features

In order to deal with complex vision problems, the use of pixel features with a higher level of abstraction than raw gray level intensities has now become almost mandatory. Among all texture characterization techniques available in the literature, we have decided to use Haralick features [4]. Several works have shown their efficiency, especially when applied to medical images [6], and can be easily extended to 3D images [7], two of our final goals. Only 10 of the 14 features proposed by Haralick have been used, correlation based ones having been left out due to numerical instability.

2.2 Texture Classification Using Neural Network

The two most studied supervised classifiers are the support vector machine (SVM) [8] and the multi-layer perceptron (MLP) [9]. While the SVM are commonly recognized to be more accurate than the MLP [10], their original design limits them to binary classification problems. Although this is not an issue for the current work, turning this method into a multiclass segmentation one is planned by the authors. The neural network based approach was therefore selected.

The use of a supervised classifier requires the definition of a training set composed of classified texture samples. Depending on the task to be performed, two training set definition schemes are possible.

Interactive Scheme. It is mainly intended to be used for single image segmentation tasks. The user is asked to provide a training set by manually tagging several regions of the image with the expected classes. Given those data, the neural network can be trained and the whole segmentation process conducted. If the result is not as accurate as expected, the user can consolidate the training set by tagging new pixels.

Ground Truth Scheme. If the algorithm is used to regularly process images from the same type, for example produced with the same acquisition technique, a pre-configured MLP can be built upstream and stored in order to be used repeatedly, saving thus some computation time. The training set is then composed from ground truths for one or several images provided by experts.

Once the training set $\mathcal{X}$ is defined, it is divided into two subsets $\mathcal{X}_t$ and $\mathcal{X}_e$, with $|\mathcal{X}_t| = 2|\mathcal{X}_e|$. $\mathcal{X}_t$ will be used by the training algorithm to compute the weights of the neural network, while $\mathcal{X}_e$ is used to evaluate its generalization accuracy. The one with the highest classification rate is selected at the end of the training process.

The MLP used in this paper are composed of 10 inputs – the 10 selected features – and a single output. Each neuron uses a sigmoid activation function and is connected to a bias neuron. The two training subsets can also be used to select the best MLP among several configurations (number of hidden layers, number of hidden neurons per layer, learning-rate...). During our tests, we found that a MLP with a single hidden layer composed of 3 neurons was enough to perform the binary segmentation based on the 10 texture features.

2.3   Regularization of a Binary Graph Function

The classifier is not used to produce an absolute classification: no decision rule is applied on its output. Therefore, the information it returns for an input pattern only represents the likelihood of belonging to one of the two classes. Depending on the content of an image and on the texture features used, the overall result on an image can be quite rough.

The purpose of a regularization process is to perform a bi-criteria optimization: produce a smooth version of a function while keeping it close-enough to its original version. By applying such algorithm on the classifier's output, we manage to obtain a revised version of it, where imperfections are be corrected.

One key element of this work is to take advantage of non-local image processing techniques. Beyond the use of texture features, we want to be able to process pixels that might not be neighbors on the image. It is done by using a graph structure, which allows to efficiently express relations between any pair of pixel in the image.

The graph regularization method we use has been proposed in [3]. It is designed to perform image segmentation using texture features, but is subject to the limitations exposed in the introduction. For this work, we will apply it on an image composed of a single numeric feature: the output of the classifier.

A weighted graph $G = (V, E, w)$ is composed of a set $V = \{V_1 \ldots V_N\}$ of N nodes and a set $E \in V \times V$ of edges. Two nodes u and v that are connected by an edge $(u, v) \in E$ are said to be neighbors. This relation is noted $u \sim v$. The graphs used in our approach are simple (undirected, without loop, with at most one edge between any two nodes). $w : E \mapsto \mathbb{R}$ is a function that associates a real value $w(e)$ (also noted $w_{u,v}$) to each edge $e = (u, v) \in E$.

The type of graph used by the regularization algorithm is called a similarity graph. This is a weighted graph where the weighting function is a similarity measure of each pairs of nodes. Multiple ways to build such graph exist, and correspond to three successive steps: choosing the node set, the edge set, and the similarity measure.

For the choice of the node set, the most obvious approach is to build a pixel adjacency graph (each pixel of the image is represented by a node), but more advanced methods use clustering or segmentation algorithms to already group similar pixels together, building a region adjacency graph [2,11]. While the latter approach can greatly reduce the size of the node set, obtaining such pre-segmentation when working with texture-features is a vast subject, and will therefore not be explored in this paper.

From the point of view of the heuristic used to build the edge set, the best known types of graphs are: fully connected graph, ϵ-neighborhood graph and k-nearest neighbors graph (see [12] for further details). In this paper, it has been decided to work with the ϵ-neighborhood graph, where two nodes are connected together if the distance between them is below a defined threshold. The distance involved in this process is application dependent, and any combination of characteristics (gray level intensity, coordinates...) can be used. The one used here is the Manhattan distance applied on the pixel coordinates with $\epsilon = 1$, which allows to build 4-neighbors graphs.

The similarity measure used by the weighing function is not necessarily linked to the distance used in the previous step, but is also application dependent. We chose to use a constant value of $w_{u,v} = 1$ associated to each edge $(u, v) \in E$, which is enough to allow the regularization process to take place.

The regularization process is actually carried out by solving an optimization problem, which consists in finding a function $f : V \mapsto [0; 1]$ that minimizes the following energy:

$$\mathcal{E}(f, f_0, \lambda) = R_w(f) + \lambda \sum_{u \in V} g(f_0, u) f(u) , \tag{1}$$

$R_w(f)$ being the regularization term, whose purpose is to keep the f function as smooth as possible, while $g(f_0, u)$ is the fitting criteria (inspired by the work of Chan and Vese [5]), which tries to keep the f function as close as possible to f_0, the output of the classifier:

$$R_w(f) = \sum_{u \in V} \sum_{v \sim u} \sqrt{w_{uv}} |f(v) - f(u)| , \tag{2}$$

$$g(f_0, u) = (c_1 - f_0(u))^2 - (c_2 - f_0(u))^2 , \tag{3}$$

where c_1 and c_2 are the average value of f_0 inside ($f \geq 0.5$) and outside ($f < 0.5$) the segmented region. λ expresses the trade-off between regularity of the segmentation and fidelity to the original one provided by the classifier. Due to the simple nature of the "feature vector" actually involved (a single real value), equation (3) presents a simplified version of the fitting criteria proposed in [3] which was designed to work on texture-features.

The optimization problem is then approximated by an iterative Gauss-Jacobi algorithm. The reader can refer to [3] for further details.

3   Experimental Results

The results presented through this section correspond to a measure of the partition distance [13], which is equivalent to the percentage of misclassified pixels according to a ground truth. The ground truth we are referring to are either absolute ones (for artificial images) or obtained by experts (for medical images).

3.1   Artificial Images

In order to validate our method, is has been first applied on artificial images, with an absolute ground truth available.

A set of 16 images was generated, each containing a textured object with a random shape drawn over a textured background. Two examples of such textures are shown in figure 1(b) and 1(c), and the resulting textured object in figure 1(d).

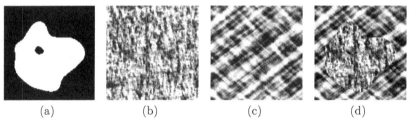

(a)   (b)   (c)   (d)

Fig. 1. (a): random binary object, (b) & (c): examples of textures, (d): resulting textured object

For each image, a classifier is trained using the ground truth (the binary mask used to compose the textures, see figure 1(a)). Then, each image is corrupted by adding white Gaussian noise of varying standard deviation, and processed by the method for different combinations of parameters (λ and number of iterations).

In order to illustrate the benefit of applying a graph regularization algorithm to the output of a binary classifier, the results of our method are compared with the ones obtained by thresholding the raw output of the same classifier. Our method is also compared to the texture-based graph regularization process proposed in [3]. Table 1 presents the results obtained for the three methods for noise level (standard deviation) 8.

Because of the use of a classifier that relies on eager learning, handling high noise levels is impossible since such level of corruption has a high influence on the texture features. Results from this test are therefore exposed considering noise levels 2, 4, 6, 8, 10 and 12.

By comparing the values from the second and fourth column of table 1, we can see that the application of the regularization process on the output of the classifier highly improves the segmentation quality. On the whole test set, it allows to classify correctly up to 13.8% more pixels, with an average improvement of 4.3%. Compared to the texture-based graph regularization method from [3] (third column), our new approach shows an improvement of the segmentation

Table 1. Results (partition distance) for the artificial test set for noise level 8

Image	Classifier only	Texture-based graph regularization method	Our method
1	17.8%	10.2%	**6.9%**
2	15.1%	**7.1%**	10.0%
3	15.0%	9.5%	**6.9%**
4	8.0%	5.4%	**4.1%**
5	4.1%	5.3%	**2.2%**
6	3.9%	6.8%	**3.0%**
7	7.3%	8.2%	**4.5%**
8	11.2%	5.4%	**4.6%**
9	6.3%	4.8%	**3.7%**
10	1.3%	2.6%	**0.9%**
11	17.3%	**14.4%**	15.2%
12	10.2%	5.2%	**4.0%**
13	1.8%	3.7%	**1.4%**
14	2.7%	4.2%	**2.1%**
15	11.9%	6.9%	**4.3%**
16	1.2%	3.5%	**1.2%**
Average	8.4%	6.5%	**4.7%**

quality of 1.9%, and do not require neither a manual selection of relevant texture features nor the definition of an initialization. Moreover, such results are obtained with significantly less regularization iterations: less than 500 for our new method against more than 1000 for the one from [3].

3.2   Medical Images

Because medical imaging is an important source of computer vision challenges, our method is tested against two medical imaging modalities: ultrasonography and confocal microscopy.

Ultrasonography is a technique known to produce particularly noisy images. Hopefully, this noise is also a source of textural information that can be used by our method. Our test set is composed of three ultrasound images of the skin where a lesion (a nevus) can be seen. The classifier is trained using the ground truth of the first image, and the method applied on the two remaining ones. Our method is compared to the texture-based graph regularization method from [3] and to a binary classifier driven active contours technique [6] which uses Haralick texture features, a MLP as a classifier, and the same training scheme. The partition distance is computed for the three methods according to ground truth. Table 2 presents the results for all three methods.

Confocal microscopy is very different to ultrasonography: it generates very clear images. By processing such images, our goal is to illustrate the versatility of our method. A confocal microscope produces a stack of images corresponding

Table 2. Results (partition distance) for the ultrasound test set

Image	Our method	Texture-based graph regularization method	Active contours
2	**1.84%**	2.20%	2.52%
3	**2.0%**	3.19%	4.12%

to different depth. The one used here is a view of the olfactory system of a bee, the bright circular elements being the glomeruli (see figure 2(d)).

The classifier is trained using the ground truth of the first image of the stack, then our method is applied on the following slices. Table 3 presents the partition distance obtained on the test image for some of the slices.

Results for both modalities are illustrated in figure 2.

Table 3. Results (partition distance) for the confocal microscopy test set

Image	Partition distance
2	7.07%
3	8.06%
4	9.05%
8	8.93%

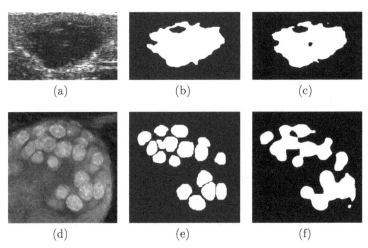

(a)   (b)   (c)

(d)   (e)   (f)

Fig. 2. Top row: ultrasound image #3. Bottom row: confocal microscopy image #2. (a) & (d): Original image. (b) & (e): Ground truth. (c) & (f): Segmentation produced by our method.

4   Conclusion

In this paper, a recent texture-based graph regularization process has been improved. A supervised binary classifier is included in the segmentation process in order to take care of the selection of features. A learning set is first provided by an expert in order to train the classifier, which is then used to provide a raw segmentation of the image. A graph regularization process is finally applied on this initial segmentation to produce the final one.

By including a supervised binary classifier in the segmentation process, we enable it to automatically ponderate relevant texture features. Compared to the initial algorithm, benefits are multiple. First, irrelevant features do not need to be manually deleted, which allows to virtually use any texture characterization technique without the need to worry about its usefulness or uselessness regarding the type of image to be processed. The generic nature of the system has also been improved: a lot more features can be added without risking to minimize their contribution, since the training algorithm will sort them out. Finally, no initialization has to be provided for each image. This fact might be argued since a training set has to be provided, but by turning this algorithm into a system configured for one or several pre-defined tasks, it can easily be rendered parameter-less.

In order to increase the capacity of the process to perform any segmentation task, we intend to incorporate more texture descriptors (Haralick features computed on different co-occurrence matrices, Gabor filters...) in it.

During the design of this algorithm, we chose to implements the classifier as a MLP because of its ability to handle multiclass problems. Research into transforming this binary segmentation algorithm into a multiclass one are already in progress.

References

1. Shi, J., Malik, J.: Normalized cuts and image segmentation. IEEE Transactions on Pattern Analysis and Machine Intelligence 22(8), 888–905 (2000)
2. Ta, V.-T., Lezoray, O., Elmoataz, A.: Graph Based Semi and Unsupervised Classification and Segmentation of Microscopic Images. In: IEEE International Symposium on Signal Processing and Information Technology, pp. 1160–1165 (December 2007)
3. Faucheux, C., Olivier, J., Bone, R., Makris, P.: Texture-based graph regularization process for 2D and 3D ultrasound image segmentation. In: IEEE International Conference on Image Processing (ICIP), pp. 2333–2336 (September 2012)
4. Haralick, R.M., Shanmugam, K., Dinstein, I.: Textural Features for Image Classification. IEEE Transactions on Systems, Man, and Cybernetics 3(6), 610–621 (1973)
5. Chan, T.F., Sandberg, B.Y., Vese, L.A.: Active Contours without Edges for Vector-Valued Images. Journal of Visual Communication and Image Representation 11(2), 130–141 (2000)
6. Olivier, J., Boné, R., Rousselle, J.-J., Cardot, H.: Active Contours Driven by Supervised Binary Classifiers for Texture Segmentation. In: Bebis, G., et al. (eds.) ISVC 2008, Part I. LNCS, vol. 5358, pp. 288–297. Springer, Heidelberg (2008)
7. Tesar, L., Shimizu, A., Smutek, D., Kobatake, H., Nawano, S.: Medical image analysis of 3D CT images based on extension of Haralick texture features. Computerized Medical Imaging and Graphics: The Official Journal of the Computerized Medical Imaging Society 32(6), 513–520 (2008)

8. Vapnik, V.: The nature of statistical learning theory. Springer (1999)
9. Rumelhart, D., Hinton, G., Williams, R.: Learning internal representations by error propagation. In: Parallel Distributed Processing: Explorations in the Microstructure of Cognition. Foundations, vol. 1 (1985)
10. Dal Moro, F., Abate, A., Lanckriet, G.R.G., Arandjelovic, G., Gasparella, P., Bassi, P., Mancini, M., Pagano, F.: A novel approach for accurate prediction of spontaneous passage of ureteral stones: support vector machines. Kidney International 69(1), 157–160 (2006)
11. Trémeau, A., Colantoni, P.: Regions adjacency graph applied to color image segmentation. IEEE Transactions on Image Processing 9(4), 735–744 (2000)
12. von Luxburg, U.: A tutorial on spectral clustering. Statistics and Computing 17(4), 395–416 (2007)
13. Cardoso, J.S., Corte-Real, L.: Toward a generic evaluation of image segmentation. IEEE Transactions on Image Processing 14(11), 1773–1782 (2005)

Hierarchical Annealed Particle Swarm Optimization for Articulated Object Tracking

Xuan Son Nguyen, Séverine Dubuisson, and Christophe Gonzales

Laboratoire d'Informatique de Paris 6 (LIP6/UPMC)
4 place Jussieu, 75005 Paris, France

Abstract. In this paper, we propose a novel algorithm for articulated object tracking, based on a hierarchical search and particle swarm optimization. Our approach aims to reduce the complexity induced by the high dimensional state space in articulated object tracking by decomposing the search space into subspaces and then using particle swarms to optimize over these subspaces hierarchically. Moreover, the intelligent search strategy proposed in [20] is integrated into each optimization step to provide a robust tracking algorithm under noisy observation conditions. Our quantitative and qualitative analysis both on synthetic and real video sequences show the efficiency of the proposed approach compared to other existing competitive tracking methods.

Keywords: particle filter, articulated object tracking, PSO.

1 Introduction

Tracking articulated structures with accuracy and within a reasonable time is challenging due to the high complexity of the problem to solve. For this purpose, various approaches based on particle filtering have been proposed. Among them, one class addresses the complexity issue by reducing the dimensionality of the state space. For instance, some methods add constraints (e.g., physical) to the mathematical models [4, 13], to the object priors [7] or to their interactions with the environment [11]. Relying on the basic assumption that some body part movements are mutually dependent, some learning-based approaches [16, 19] reduce the number of degrees of freedom of these movements.

Alternatively, a second class of methods has been proposed in the literature [5, 9, 12, 14, 17, 18] whose key idea is to decompose the state space into a set of small subspaces where particle filtering can be applied: by working on small subspaces, sampling is more efficient and, therefore, fewer particles are needed to achieve a good performance. Finally, in the class of the optimization-based methods, the approach is to optimize an objective function corresponding to the matching between the model and the observed image features [3, 6, 8]. Recently, Particle Swarm Optimization (PSO) has been reported to perform well on articulated human tracking [10, 20]. Its key idea is to apply evolutionary algorithms inspired from social behaviors observed in wildlife to make the particles evolve following their own experience and the experience of the global population.

R. Wilson et al. (Eds.): CAIP 2013, Part I, LNCS 8047, pp. 319–326, 2013.

In this paper, our approach consists in decomposing the search space into subspaces of smaller dimensions and, then, in exploiting the approach proposed in [20] to search within these subspaces in a hierarchical order. A hierarchical particle swarm optimization has also been introduced in [10]. The main difference between this approach and ours is that we incorporate the sampling covariance and the annealing factor into the update equation of PSO at each optimization step to tackle the problem of noisy observations and cluttered background.

The paper is organized as follows. In Section 2, we briefly recall PSO. Section 3 presents the proposed algorithm. Section 4 reports the results of our experimental evaluation. Finally, Section 5 gives some conclusions and perspectives.

2   Particle Swarm Optimization (PSO)

Let $\mathcal{X}$ denote the state space: our goal is to search for state $\mathbf{x} \in \mathcal{X}$ that maximizes a *cost function* $f : \mathcal{X} \to \mathbb{R}$, with $\mathbf{a} \le \mathbf{x} \le \mathbf{b}$. A swarm consists of N particles, each one representing a candidate state of the articulated object. Denote $\mathbf{x}_{(m)}^{(i)}$ the ith particle at the mth iteration. $\mathbf{x}_{(m)}^{(i)}$ is decomposed into K (object) parts, i.e., $\mathbf{x}_{(m)}^{(i)} = \{\mathbf{x}_{(m)}^{(i),1}, ..., \mathbf{x}_{(m)}^{(i),K}\} \in \mathcal{X}$. Unlike evolutionary algorithms, to each particle in PSO is assigned a velocity $\mathbf{v}_{(m)}^{(i)} = \{v_{(m)}^{(i),1}, ..., v_{(m)}^{(i),K}\} \in \mathcal{X}$ and each particle has the ability to memorize its best state computed so far $\mathbf{s}^{(i)} = \{\mathbf{s}^{(i),1}, ..., \mathbf{s}^{(i),K}\} \in \mathcal{X}$. Let $\mathbf{s}^g$ be the current global best state, i.e., $\mathbf{s}^g = \text{Argmax}\{f(\mathbf{s}^{(i)})\}_{i=1}^{N}$. The evolution of the particles in PSO is described by the following equations:

$$\mathbf{v}_{(m)}^{(i)} = w\mathbf{v}_{(m-1)}^{(i)} + \beta_1 r_1(\mathbf{s}^{(i)} - \mathbf{x}_{(m-1)}^{(i)}) + \beta_2 r_2(\mathbf{s}^g - \mathbf{x}_{(m-1)}^{(i)}) \tag{1}$$

$$\mathbf{x}_{(m)}^{(i)} = \mathbf{x}_{(m-1)}^{(i)} + \mathbf{v}_{(m)}^{(i)} \tag{2}$$

where β_1, β_2 are constants, $r_1, r_2 \sim U(0,1)$ are random numbers drawn from a uniform distribution, w is the inertia weight and $w\mathbf{v}_{(m-1)}^{(i)}$ is the inertial velocity.

PSO has the ability to balance between the local and global search strategies of particles by setting the appropriate values for constants β_1, β_2 and inertia weight w. A large inertia weight results in an exploration of the search space (global search) while a small inertia weight limits the search around the globally best particle (local search). The value of the inertia weight can be fixed as a constant or adaptively changed throughout the search.

In the next section, we introduce our approach, inspired from PSO, and dedicated to articulated object tracking in cluttered environments.

3   Proposed Approach

We propose to exploit the hierarchical nature of the kinematic structure of the articulated object to improve tracking. First, the state space of the target object is decomposed into lower dimensional subspaces. Then, optimal states are searched for in these subspaces in the hierarchical order of the kinematic structure using Partitioned Sampling (PS) [12]. These optimal states are then used to constrain the search in the next subspaces in the hierarchical order.

At time t, let $\mathbf{x}_t^{(i),k}$ (resp. $\mathbf{s}_t^{(i),k}$) denote the kth substate of the ith particle $\mathbf{x}_t^{(i)}$ (resp. the ith particle's best state $\mathbf{s}_t^{(i)}$) and let $\mathbf{s}_t^{\mathbf{g},k}$ be the kth substate of the global best state. Then, at the mth iteration, $\mathbf{x}_{t,(m)}^{(i)} = \{\mathbf{x}_{t,(m)}^{(i),1}, ..., \mathbf{x}_{t,(m)}^{(i),K}\}$, $\mathbf{v}_{t,(m)}^{(i)} = \{v_{t,(m)}^{(i),1}, ..., v_{t,(m)}^{(i),K}\}$ and $\mathbf{s}_{t,(m)}^{(i)} = \{\mathbf{s}_{t,(m)}^{(i),1}, ..., \mathbf{s}_{t,(m)}^{(i),K}\}$. We follow the approach proposed in [20], except that the state and velocity update equations for each subpart k are written as follows:

$$v_{t,(m)}^{(i),k} = r_0 P_{(m-1)} + \beta_1 r_1 (\mathbf{s}_t^{(i),k} - \mathbf{x}_{t,(m-1)}^{(i),k}) + \beta_2 r_2 (\mathbf{s}_t^{\mathbf{g},k} - \mathbf{x}_{t,(m-1)}^{(i),k}) \quad (3)$$

$$\mathbf{x}_{t,(m)}^{(i),k} = \mathbf{x}_{t,(m-1)}^{(i),k} + v_{t,(m)}^{(i),k} \quad (4)$$

$P_{(m-1)} = \alpha_0 * P_{(m-2)}$, $m \geq 2$, is the sampling covariance, with α_0 a constant, and $P_{(0)}$ is a covariance matrix whose diagonal elements are fixed with respect to the model configuration parameters. We propose to compute factors β_1 and β_2 at each iteration m using the annealing principle so that:

$$\beta_1 = \beta_2 = \beta_0 \beta_{max} \left(\frac{\beta_{max}}{\beta_{min}} \right)^{-\frac{m}{M}} \quad (5)$$

where $\beta_0, \beta_{max}, \beta_{min}$ are constants, $0 < \beta_0 \leq 1$, and M is the maximal number of iterations.

By combining PSO and hierarchical search, our approach aims to increase the tracking accuracy and to reduce the computational cost of the tracking algorithm by integrating the benefits of both methods. First, the search efficiency is improved by performing PSO within lower dimensional subspaces, thereby increasing tracking accuracy. Second, since the search is performed in the same way as PS, the number of particles required and thus the computational cost of the tracking algorithm is greatly reduced. Our proposed Hierarchical Annealed based Particle Swarm Optimization Particle Filter (HAPSOPF) is described in Algorithm 1, where $\bar{\mathbf{x}}$ is the estimated state of the object at time slice t, $w(., \mathbf{y})$ is the cost function to be optimized by PSO, and $\mathbf{y}$ is the current observation.

4   Experimental Results

We compare our approach with APF [6], PSAPF [2], APSOPF [20] and HPSO [10]. The *cost function* $w(\mathbf{x}_{t,(m)}^{(i),k}, \mathbf{y})$ to be optimized by PSO measures how well a state hypothesis $\mathbf{x}_{t,(m)}^{(i),k}$ matches the true state w.r.t. the observed image $\mathbf{y}$, and is constructed using histogram and foreground silhouette [6]. An articulated object is described by a hierarchy (a tree) of parts, each part being linked to its parent in the tree by an articulation point. For instance, in the top row of Fig. 1, the blue polygonal parts are the root of the tree and the colored rectangles are the other nodes of the tree. The root is described by its center (x, y) and its

Input: $\{\mathbf{s}_{t-1}^{(i)}\}_{i=1}^{N}$, α_0, β_0, β_{max}, β_{min}, $P_{(0)}$, M (number of iterations)

Output: $\{\mathbf{s}_t^{(i)}\}_{i=1}^{N}$

1 Set $\pi_t^{(i)} = 1$, $i = 1, \ldots, N$

2 **for** $k = 1$ **to** K **do**

3   Sample: $\mathbf{x}_{t,(0)}^{(i),k} \sim \mathcal{N}(\mathbf{s}_{t-1}^{(i),k}, P_{(0)})$, $i = 1, \ldots, N$

4   **for** $m = 0$ **to** M **do**

5   **if** $m \geq 1$ **then**

6   Compute $P_{(m)}$ and update β_1, β_2

7   Carry out the PSO iteration based on Eq. (3) and (4)

8   Evaluate: $f(\mathbf{x}_{t,(m)}^{(i),k}) = w(\mathbf{x}_{t,(m)}^{(i),k}, \mathbf{y})$, $i = 1, \ldots, N$

9   Update $\{\mathbf{s}_t^{(i),k}\}_{i=1}^{N}$ and the k-th part of the global best state $\mathbf{s}_t^{\mathbf{g},k}$

10   Evaluate particle weights: $\pi_t^{(i)} = \pi_t^{(i)} \times w(\mathbf{s}_t^{(i),k}, \mathbf{y})$, $i = 1, \ldots, N$

11 Normalize particle weights: $\bar{\pi}_t^{(i)} = \dfrac{\pi_t^{(i)}}{\sum_{j=1}^{N} \pi_t^{(j)}}$, $i = 1, \ldots, N$

12 **return** $\{\mathbf{s}_t^{(i)}\}_{i=1}^{N}, \bar{\mathbf{x}} = \sum_{i=1}^{N} \bar{\pi}_t^{(i)} \mathbf{s}_t^{(i)}$

Algorithm 1. Our HAPSOPF algorithm

orientation θ whereas the other parts are only characterized by their angle θ. For all algorithms, particles are propagated using a random walk with standard deviations fixed to $\sigma_x = 2$, $\sigma_y = 2$ and $\sigma_\theta = 0.05$. For APSOPF and HAPSOPF, $P_{(0)}$ is a diagonal matrix with the values of σ_x, σ_y and σ_θ. Our comparisons are based on two criteria: estimation errors and computation times.

4.1 Tests on Synthetic Sequences

Video Sequences. We have generated two sets of various synthetic video sequences composed of 200 frames of 640×480 pixels (with ground truth). The video sequences in the first set contain no noise while, in the second set, cluttered background was generated to demonstrate the robustness of the proposed approach. The clutter is made up of polygons and rectangles randomly positioned

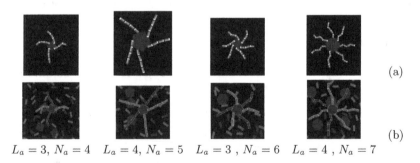

(a)

(b)

$L_a = 3, N_a = 4$ $L_a = 4, N_a = 5$ $L_a = 3, N_a = 6$ $L_a = 4, N_a = 7$

Fig. 1. Synthetic video sequences used for quantitative evaluation (number of arms N_a, length of arms L_a): (a) without clutter and (b) with clutter

in the image. An articulated object is defined by its number N_a of arms, and their length L_a: some examples are given in Fig. 1.

Quantitative Tracking Results. The tracking errors are given by the sum of the Euclidean distances between each corner of the estimated parts and their corresponding corner in the ground truth. We used $M = 3$ layers for PSAPF and APF since it produces stable results for both algorithms, and $M = 3$ maximal iterations for HAPSOPF, HPSO and APSOPF. Table 1 gives the performances of the tested algorithms for sequences without or with noise (cluttered background). In our experiments, tracking in noisy sequences is challenging due to the background. In such cases, the annealing factor helps the particle swarm to follow its own searching strategy without being affected by any wrong guide of the local or global best states. On the contrary, the annealing process of PSAPF forces the particle set to represent one of the modes of the cost function, which causes some parts of the object to get stuck in wrong locations. This problem of annealing approaches was reported in [1]. Moreover, the use of the sampling covariance instead of the inertial velocity of Eq. (1) leads to an efficient exploration of the search space without losing the searching power of PSO. This is validated by our experiments on sequences without cluttered background, where our approach outperforms all the other ones. Fig. 2 gives comparative convergence results (error depending on the number N of particles) and computation times for a synthetic sequence (behaviors are similar for other sequences). Note that our approach converges better and faster than the other methods.

4.2   Tests on Real Sequences

Dataset. We used sequences *S1 Gesture* and *S2 Throwcatch* of the HumanEva-I dataset [15] that include ground truths, thus allowing to evaluate quantitatively our approach. For both sequences, the lower right hands of the subject move quickly, which makes them difficult to track. Moreover, *S2 Throwcatch* contains self-occlusions (hands and torso, left and right hands, left and right legs).

The searching order for PSAPF, HPSO, and HAPSOPF is: torso, head, left thigh, right thigh, left upper arm, right upper arm, left leg, right leg, left forearm,

Table 1. Tracking errors in pixels (average over 30 runs) and standard deviations for synthetic video sequences, N is the number of particles used per filter

		$N_a = 4, L_a = 3$		$N_a = 5, L_a = 4$		$N_a = 6, L_a = 3$		$N_a = 7, L_a = 4$	
	N	50	200	50	200	50	200	50	200
HAPSOPF	without noise	110(2)	106(1)	214(5)	195(2)	243(11)	211(9)	312(7)	271(4)
	noise	204(39)	143(10)	227(56)	175(30)	322(67)	295(60)	553(194)	516(180)
PSAPF	without noise	120(2)	114(1)	238(6)	208(4)	251(7)	218(3)	319(8)	278(4)
	noise	309(109)	221(94)	281(78)	219(48)	432(86)	388(75)	1008(232)	914(213)
HPSO	without noise	125(5)	119(2)	252(9)	227(5)	254(11)	213(6)	382(5)	315(3)
	noise	277(78)	194(65)	245(42)	201(26)	345(27)	295(10)	922(334)	731(259)
APSOPF	without noise	184(3)	169(2)	260(12)	241(10)	265(15)	257(12)	471(30)	439(21)
	noise	254(16)	227(8)	308(33)	291(25)	490(68)	474(47)	817(223)	785(169)
APF	without noise	128(3)	109(2)	246(11)	221(9)	270(13)	236(11)	487(35)	412(24)
	noise	272(9)	258(5)	322(29)	309(18)	440(51)	429(40)	613(174)	592(156)

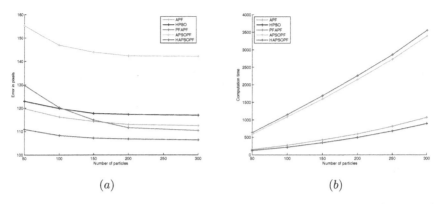

(a) $\qquad\qquad\qquad\qquad\qquad$ (b)

Fig. 2. Comparison tests for convergence and computation time when tracking the object $N_a = 4, L_a = 3$: (a) convergence and (b) computation times (HPSO and our approach give same curves) in seconds

right forearm. For a fair comparison, we fixed the number of evaluations of the weighting function at each frame for all the algorithms to 2000, and tuned parameters {N,M} for each method so that they achieve the best performance while satisfying the above constraint: $\{400, 5\}$ for APF, $\{40, 5\}$ for PSAPF, $\{200, 10\}$ for APSOPF and $\{20, 10\}$ for HPSO and HAPSOPF.

Quantitative Tracking Results. We used the evaluation measure proposed in [15], which is based on Euclidean distances between 15 virtual markers on the human body. Table 2 provides tracking errors and computation times. As can be observed, our approach has the same computation time as HPSO but reduces the estimation error and it outperforms the other approaches on both criteria.

Fig. 3 provides qualitative tracking results. Our approach always outperforms PSAPF and HPSO in cases of self-occlusions (frames 275, 523) or quick movements (frames 160, 387), showing its robustness. Because our approach incorporates the annealing into each searching stage of the hierarchical search, the problem of noisy observations is effectively alleviated. This makes our approach more robust to self-occlusions. The sampling covariance also helps to improve the searching effectiveness by shifting the particle swarm toward more promising regions.

Table 2. Tracking errors for full body in pixels (average over 30 runs)

	HAPSOPF		PSAPF		HPSO		APSOPF		APF	
	Error	Time	Error	Time	Error	Time	Error	Time	Error	Time
S1 Gesture	95(6)	287	99(11)	293	101(9)	287	102(4)	1348	105(2)	1412
S2 Throwcatch	212(10)	557	227(19)	579	232(12)	557	235(7)	2070	240(5)	2184

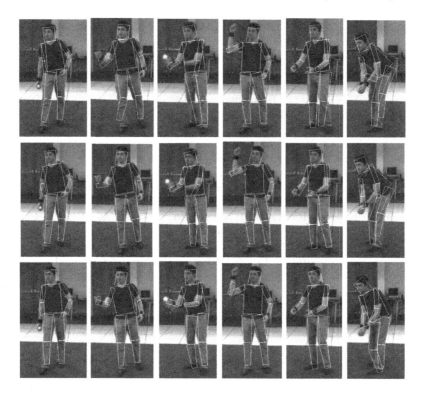

Fig. 3. Tracking results for frames 123,160,275,387,488,523: HPSO (first row), PSAPF (second row), HAPSOPF (third row). The tracking results for the other approaches as well as those for the sequence *S1 Gesture* are not presented due to space constraint.

5   Conclusions and Future Work

In this paper, we have introduced a new algorithm for articulated object tracking based on particle swarm optimization and hierarchical search. We addressed the problem of articulated object tracking in high dimensional spaces by employing a hierarchical search to improve search efficiency. Furthermore, the problem of noisy observation has been alleviated by incorporating the annealing factor terms into the velocity updating equation of PSO. Our experiments on synthetic and real video sequences demonstrate the efficiency and effectiveness of our approach compared to other common approaches, both in terms of tracking accuracy and computation time. Our future work will focus on evaluating the proposed approach in multi-view environments.

References

[1] Balan, A.O., Sigal, L., Black, M.J.: A quantitative evaluation of video-based 3d person tracking. In: PETS, pp. 349–356 (2005)

[2] Bandouch, J., Engstler, F., Beetz, M.: Evaluation of Hierarchical Sampling Strategies in 3D Human Pose Estimation. In: BMVC, pp. 925–934 (2008)

[3] Bray, M., Kollermeier, E., Vangool, L.: Smart particle filtering for high-dimensional tracking. Computer Vision and Image Understanding 106(1), 116–129 (2007)

[4] Brubaker, M., Fleet, D., Hertzmann, A.: Physics-based person tracking using the anthropomorphic walker. International Journal of Computer Vision 87(1-2), 140–155 (2009)

[5] Chang, I.C., Lin, S.Y.: 3D human motion tracking based on a progressive particle filter. Pattern Recognition 43(10), 3621–3635 (2010)

[6] Deutscher, J., Reid, I.: Articulated body motion capture by stochastic search. International Journal of Computer Vision 61(2), 185–205 (2005)

[7] Hauberg, S., Pedersen, K.S.: Stick it! articulated tracking using spatial rigid object priors. In: Kimmel, R., Klette, R., Sugimoto, A. (eds.) ACCV 2010, Part III. LNCS, vol. 6494, pp. 758–769. Springer, Heidelberg (2011)

[8] Hofmann, M., Gavrila, D.: 3D human model adaptation by frame selection and shape-texture optimization. Computer Vision and Image Understanding 115(11), 1559–1570 (2011)

[9] Isard, M.: PAMPAS: real-valued graphical models for computer vision. In: CVPR, pp. 613–620 (2003)

[10] John, V., Trucco, E., Ivekovic, S.: Markerless human articulated tracking using hierarchical particle swarm optimization. Image and Vision Computing 28(11), 1530–1547 (2010)

[11] Kjellstrom, H., Kragic, D., Black, M.: Tracking people interacting with objects. In: CVPR, pp. 747–754 (2010)

[12] MacCormick, J., Isard, M.: Partitioned sampling, articulated objects, and interface-quality hand tracking. In: Vernon, D. (ed.) ECCV 2000. LNCS, vol. 1843, pp. 3–19. Springer, Heidelberg (2000)

[13] Oikonomidis, I., Kyriazis, N.: Full DOF tracking of a hand interacting with an object by modeling occlusions and physical constraints. In: ICCV, pp. 2088–2095 (2011)

[14] Rose, C., Saboune, J., Charpillet, F.: Reducing particle filtering complexity for 3D motion capture using dynamic Bayesian networks, 1396–1401. AAAI (2008)

[15] Sigal, L., Balan, R.: Humaneva: Synchronized video and motion capture dataset and baseline algorithm for evaluation of articulated human motion. Technical report (2009)

[16] Urtasun, R., Fleet, D., Hertzmann, A., Fua, P.: Priors for people tracking from small training sets. In: ICCV, pp. 403–410 (2005)

[17] Wu, Y., Hua, G., Yu, T.: Tracking articulated body by dynamic Markov network. In: ICCV, pp. 1094–1101 (2003)

[18] Xinyu, X., Baoxin, L.: Learning Motion Correlation for Tracking Articulated Human Body with a Rao-Blackwellised Particle Filter. In: ICCV, pp. 1–8 (2007)

[19] Yao, A., Gall, J., Gool, L., Urtasun, R.: Learning probabilistic non-linear latent variable models for tracking complex activities. In: Shawe-Taylor, J., Zemel, R., Bartlett, P., Pereira, F., Weinberger, K. (eds.) Advances in Neural Information Processing Systems 24, pp. 1359–1367 (2011)

[20] Zhang, X., Hu, W., Wang, X., Kong, Y., Xie, N., Wang, H., Ling, H., Maybank, S.: A swarm intelligence based searching strategy for articulated 3D human body tracking. In: CVPRW, pp. 45–50 (2010)

High-Resolution Feature Evaluation Benchmark

Kai Cordes, Bodo Rosenhahn, and Jörn Ostermann

Institut für Informationsverarbeitung (TNT)
{cordes,rosenhahn,ostermann}@tnt.uni-hannover.de

Abstract. Benchmark data sets consisting of image pairs and ground truth homographies are used for evaluating fundamental computer vision challenges, such as the detection of image features. The mostly used benchmark provides data with only low resolution images. This paper presents an evaluation benchmark consisting of high resolution images of up to 8 megapixels and highly accurate homographies. State of the art feature detection approaches are evaluated using the new benchmark data. It is shown that existing approaches perform differently on the high resolution data compared to the same images with lower resolution.

1 Introduction

The detection of features is a fundamental step in many computer vision applications. Standing at the beginning of a processing pipeline, the accuracy of such an application is often determined by the accuracy of the detected features. Thus, the development and the evaluation of feature detectors is of high interest in the computer vision community.

The evaluations of feature detectors and descriptors [1,2,3,4,5,6,7] are based on image pairs showing planar scenes and corresponding homographies which determine the mapping between an image pair. This data serves as ground truth for the accuracy evaluation. The mostly used reference data set is proposed by Mikolajczyk et al. [3]. In this set, a sequence consists of 6 images showing the same scene undergoing different types of distortion, such as scale or viewpoint change, illumination, or coding artefacts. The evaluation criterion for feature detectors is the repeatability. The evaluation protocol counts the number of correctly detected feature pairs. A correctly detected feature pair is determined by using a threshold for the overlap error [3]. The threshold controls the demanded accuracy of the evaluation.

The evaluation benchmark [3] has some deficiencies regarding the images as well as the homographies. The image resolution is only 0.5 megapixels. Many images of the data set are not restricted to a plane which is a violation of the homography assumption as shown in Figure 1. For some images, scene content moves between the capturing process (leaves in the *Trees* sequence). It appears that radial distortion is not considered for the benchmark generation which is another violation of the mapping assumption. For the computation of the ground truth homographies, features are used[1]. This is not desirable because the data is used for the evaluation of feature detectors. Finally, the authors concede that the homographies are *not perfect* [8]. However, the data set is used

---

[1] www.robots.ox.ac.uk/~vgg/research/affine/det_eval_files/
DataREADME

R. Wilson et al. (Eds.): CAIP 2013, Part I, LNCS 8047, pp. 327–334, 2013.
© Springer-Verlag Berlin Heidelberg 2013

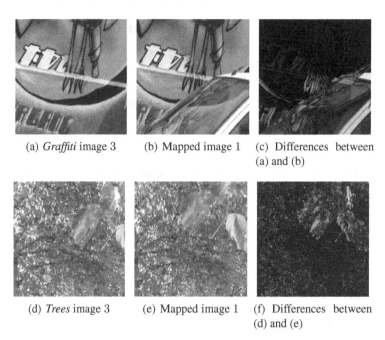

(a) *Graffiti* image 3   (b) Mapped image 1   (c) Differences between (a) and (b)

(d) *Trees* image 3   (e) Mapped image 1   (f) Differences between (d) and (e)

Fig. 1. Part of the mapped images 1 and image 3 of the *Graffiti* sequence (top row) and the *Trees* sequence (bottom row). For the mapping of image 1, the ground truth homographies are used. Large errors occur due to the car in the foreground (*Graffiti*) and the moving leaves because of wind (*Trees*). The bottom part of the *Graffiti* wall indicates a violation of the homography assumption. The error is shown in the images 1(c) and 1(f) (cf. equation (6)).

as ground truth for high-accuracy evaluations, sometimes using very small overlap error thresholds [3,8,9]. Apart from feature evaluation there are applications [10] which use a dense representation of the images. In this case, the mapping errors would spoil the evaluation significantly. Hence, the data set is useless for applications with dense image representations.

Nowadays, consumer cameras provide image resolutions of 8 megapixels or more. The question arises, if feature detector evaluations based on data with 0.5 megapixels are valid for high resolution images. In [3], the evaluated detectors provide scale invariant properties. On the other hand, the localization accuracy of a scale invariant feature may be dependent on the detected scale [11], because its position error in a certain pyramid layer is mapped to the ground plane of the scale space pyramid. In high resolution data, more features are expected to be detected in higher scales of the image pyramid. Thus, a small localization error of a detector may become significant in high resolution image data.

An improved homography benchmark is provided in [12] with image resolutions of 1.5 megapixels per image. In addition, the accuracy of the Mikolajczyk benchmark is slightly increased using a dense image representation instead of image features.

We use the RAW camera data from the images of the data set [12]. The proposed technique exploits the ground truth data from [12] for initializing an evolutionary optimization for the computation of ground truth homographies between image pairs with resolutions of up to 8 megapixels. This technique is called *homography upscaling*. The data is validated using the evaluation protocol invented by [3]. For the comparison between low-resolution and high-resolution benchmark data, the same detectors [3] are evaluated: MSER [13], Hessian-Affine [1], Harris-Affine [8], intensity extrema-based regions (IBR) [14], and edge-based regions (EBR) [15].

The main motivation of this paper is the question if the well known results for the accuracy of feature detectors are still valid for high resolution data. Furthermore, the newly generated high resolution ground truth data set will be provided to the computer vision community for feature detector evaluation or for applications using a dense representation of the images, such as [10].

In the following Section 2, the computation of the new high resolution benchmark is explained. Section 3 shows the accuracy results of the benchmark compared to [12] and the feature evaluation using the repeatability criterion. In Section 4, the paper is concluded.

2 Homography Upscaling

We make use of the RAW image data from [12]. In [12], the benchmark is created using subsampled images of size 1536×1024 (1.5 megapixels). We use the images with the same scene content at higher resolution. The radial distortion is removed in a preprocessing step. Our objective is to create ground truth homographies with image resolutions of up to 3456×2304 (8 megapixels), which is the maximum resolution of the utilized Canon EOS 350D camera.

Since the homography for the image pair at resolution $\mathcal{R}_1$ is approximately known, it can be used for a reasonable initialization for the optimization at resolution $\mathcal{R}_2$ as shown in Section 2.1. The optimization is based on a cost function which computes the mapping error of the homography $H_{\mathcal{R}_2}$ at resolution $\mathcal{R}_2$. The minimization of the cost function is explained in Section 2.2.

2.1 Upscaling a Homography Analytically

Let the homography between two images at resolution $\mathcal{R}_1 = M_{\mathcal{R}_1} \times N_{\mathcal{R}_1}$ be given as $H_{\mathcal{R}_1}$. Then, a point $\mathbf{p}_{\mathcal{R}_1}$ of the first image can be identified in the second image with coordinates $\mathbf{p}'_{\mathcal{R}_1}$ by

$$\mathbf{p}'_{\mathcal{R}_1} = H_{\mathcal{R}_1} \cdot \mathbf{p}_{\mathcal{R}_1} \tag{1}$$

The pixel coordinates of a corresponding image point pair $\mathbf{p}_{\mathcal{R}_1} \leftrightarrow \mathbf{p}'_{\mathcal{R}_1}$ in homogeneous coordinates [16] are normalized to the resolution $\mathcal{R}_0 = [-1; 1] \times [-1; 1]$. This mapping in the left and right image is determined by:

$$\mathbf{p}_{\mathcal{R}_1} = A_{\mathcal{R}_1} \cdot \mathbf{x}_{\mathcal{R}_0} \quad \text{and} \quad \mathbf{p}'_{\mathcal{R}_1} = A_{\mathcal{R}_1} \cdot \mathbf{x}'_{\mathcal{R}_0} \tag{2}$$

with the matrix $A_{\mathcal{R}_1} = \begin{pmatrix} \frac{M_{\mathcal{R}_1}-1}{2} & 0 & \frac{M_{\mathcal{R}_1}-1}{2} \\ 0 & \frac{N_{\mathcal{R}_1}-1}{2} & \frac{N_{\mathcal{R}_1}-1}{2} \\ 0 & 0 & 1 \end{pmatrix}$.

From equations (1) and (2), it follows:

$$A_{\mathcal{R}_1} \cdot x'_{\mathcal{R}_0} = H_{\mathcal{R}_1} \cdot A_{\mathcal{R}_1} \cdot x_{\mathcal{R}_0} \tag{3}$$

The desired homography at image resolution $\mathcal{R}_2 = M_{\mathcal{R}_2} \times N_{\mathcal{R}_2}$ is $H_{\mathcal{R}_2}$. If all image positions from resolutions $\mathcal{R}_1$ and $\mathcal{R}_2$ are normalized to $\mathcal{R}_0$, their coordinates $x_{\mathcal{R}_0}$ are identical (cf. equations (2)):

$$x_{\mathcal{R}_0} = A_{\mathcal{R}_2}^{-1} \cdot p_{\mathcal{R}_2} \quad \text{and} \quad x'_{\mathcal{R}_0} = A_{\mathcal{R}_2}^{-1} \cdot p'_{\mathcal{R}_2} \tag{4}$$

By exchanging $x_{\mathcal{R}_0}$ and $x'_{\mathcal{R}_0}$ in equation (3) with equations (4), it follows:

$$p'_{\mathcal{R}_2} = \underbrace{A_{\mathcal{R}_2} \cdot A_{\mathcal{R}_1}^{-1} \cdot H_{\mathcal{R}_1} \cdot A_{\mathcal{R}_1} \cdot A_{\mathcal{R}_2}^{-1}}_{H_{\mathcal{R}_2}} \cdot p_{\mathcal{R}_2} \tag{5}$$

Hence, the homography $H_{\mathcal{R}_2}$ can be computed by a matrix multiplication consisting of the known matrix $H_{\mathcal{R}_1}$ and the resolutions $M_{\mathcal{R}_1} \times N_{\mathcal{R}_1}$ and $M_{\mathcal{R}_2} \times N_{\mathcal{R}_2}$ of the left and right image, which build the matrices $A_{\mathcal{R}_1}$ and $A_{\mathcal{R}_2}$.

2.2 Optimization Using Differential Evolution

The approximate homography at resolution $\mathcal{R}_2$ is computed from the homography at resolution $\mathcal{R}_1$ as explained in Section 2.1. Due to inaccuracies in $H_{\mathcal{R}_1}$, the matrix $H_{\mathcal{R}_2}$ has to be refined by minimizing a cost function. In the following, we denote the homography in the desired resolution with $H := H_{\mathcal{R}_2}$. Then, the cost function $E(H)$ is [12]:

$$E(H) = \frac{1}{J} \sum_{j=1}^{J} d_{\text{RGB}}(H \cdot p_j, p'_j), \tag{6}$$

using the RGB values of the left and the right image I_1, I_2. The homography H maps a pixel p_j, $j \in [1; J]$ from the left image I_1 to the corresponding pixel p'_j in right image I_2. If the homography is accurate, the color distance $d_{\text{RGB}}(\cdot)$ is small. The color distance $d_{\text{RGB}}(\cdot)$ is determined as:

$$d_{\text{RGB}}(p_i, p_j) = \frac{1}{3} \cdot (|r(p_i) - r(p_j)| + |g(p_i) - g(p_j)| + |b(p_i) - b(p_j)|) \tag{7}$$

using the RGB values $(r(p_i), g(p_i), b(p_i))$ of an image point p_i. For the extraction of the color values, a bilinear interpolation is used. If a mapped point p_j falls outside the image boundaries, it is neglected.

Due to lighting and perspective changes between the images, the cost function is likely to have several local minima. Hence, a Differential Evolution (DE) optimizer is used for the minimization of $E(H)$ with respect to H in the cost function (6). Evolutionary optimization methods have proved impressive performance for parameter estimation challenges finding the global optimum in a parameter space with many local optima. Nevertheless, limiting the parameter space with upper and lower boundaries, increases the performance of these optimization algorithms significantly. For setting the search space boundaries, the approximately known solutions for the homographies at lower resolution are used. With equation (5), the search space centers are computed. Then, a Differential Evolution (DE) optimizer is performed using common parameter settings [17].

3   Experimental Results

For the benchmark generation, 5 sequences are used. Each of the sequences contains 6 images like in the reference benchmark [3]. In Section 3.1, the resulting cost function values of different resolutions are compared. In Section 3.2 the evaluation protocol [3] is performed on the new data.

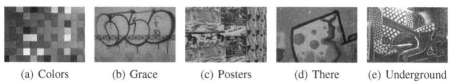

(a) Colors   (b) Grace   (c) Posters   (d) There   (e) Underground

Fig. 2. First images of the input image sequences. The resolution is up to 3456×2304.

3.1   High-Resolution Benchmark Generation

The resulting cost function values $E(\mathtt{H})$ for the resolutions $\mathcal{R}_1 = 1536 \times 1024$ and $\mathcal{R}_2 = 3456 \times 2304$ are shown in Table 1. Two example sequences are selected, *Grace* and *Underground*. Due to the high accuracy of the computed homographies at resolution $\mathcal{R}_2$, $E(\mathtt{H})$ increases only slightly compared to resolution $\mathcal{R}_1$. The generally larger error for the *Underground* sequence is due to the higher amount of light reflection from the surface of the wall. Nevertheless, the accuracies of the new homographies are high.

Table 1. Comparison of cost function values $E(\mathtt{H})$ for the homographies for image resolutions 1536×1024 (cf. [12] for *Grace*) and the new data set with resolution 3456×2304. The resulting cost function values for each image pair are approximately the same.

$E(\mathtt{H})$	Grace					Underground				
	1-2	1-3	1-4	1-5	1-6	1-2	1-3	1-4	1-5	1-6
1.5 megapixels	3.44	4.62	6.02	8.21	9.99	7.23	8.31	12.52	19.07	28.64
8.0 megapixels	3.93	5.20	6.60	8.73	10.46	7.46	8.63	12.67	19.20	28.73

3.2   Repeatability Comparison

To validate the usability of the new data set, the benchmark protocol provided in [3] is used. Like in Section 3.1, we compare results for resolution $\mathcal{R}_1 = 1536 \times 1024$ with $\mathcal{R}_2 = 3456 \times 2304$ for the sequences *Grace* (Figure 4) and *Underground* (Figure 3). Like in the majority of evaluation papers, the overlap error threshold is set to 40 %. The evaluated feature detectors are chosen from the reference paper [3].

Regarding the *Underground* sequence, the results for $\mathcal{R}_2$ are consistent with the results obtained for the smaller resolution $\mathcal{R}_1$. MSER performs best followed by Hessian-Affine and IBR, very similar to the evaluation in [3] for the viewpoint change scenario. But, each of the detectors loose between 1 % and 9 % in repeatability.

For the *Grace* sequence, the results are different for each detector. While Harris-Affine and Hessian-Affine perform like in the *Underground* sequence, MSER and IBR

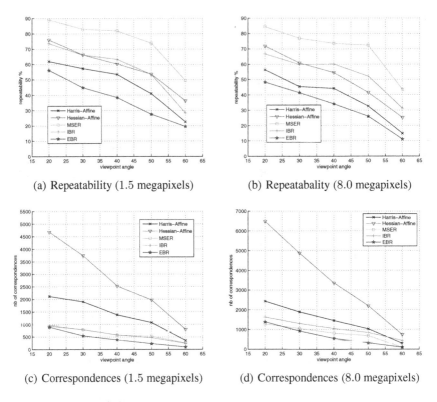

(a) Repeatability (1.5 megapixels)   (b) Repeatability (8.0 megapixels)

(c) Correspondences (1.5 megapixels)   (d) Correspondences (8.0 megapixels)

Fig. 3. Repeatability results (top row) and the number of correctly detected points (bottom row) for the *Underground* sequence with different resolutions

significantly loose repeatability score. The repeatability rate of IBR decreases between 12 % and 15 % and MSER looses up to 25 % for large viewpoint changes. Interestingly, the EBR gains about 4 % for small viewpoint changes, but looses about 5 % for large viewpoint changes. Generally, none of the detectors can really improve their performance using high resolution images.

4   Conclusions

In this paper, high-resolution image data of up to 8 megapixels is presented together with highly accurate homographies. This data can be used as a benchmark for computer vision tasks, such as feature detection. In contrast to the mainly used benchmark, our data provides high-resolution, fully planar scenes with removed radial distortion and a feature independent computation of the homographies. They are determined by the global optimization of a cost function using a dense representation of the images. The optimization is initialized with values inferred from the solution of lower resolution images.

The evaluation shows that none of the standard feature detection approaches can improve in repeatability on higher resolution images. On the contrary, their performance

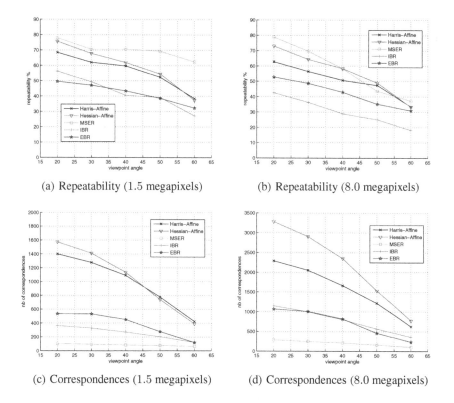

(a) Repeatability (1.5 megapixels)

(b) Repeatability (8.0 megapixels)

(c) Correspondences (1.5 megapixels)

(d) Correspondences (8.0 megapixels)

Fig. 4. Repeatability results (top row) and the number of correctly detected points (bottom row) for the *Grace* sequence with different resolutions

decreases. Dependent on the approach, the repeatability looses up to 25 %, but gains only 4 % in maximum. It follows, that feature detectors should be evaluated using high resolution images. The presented benchmark provides the necessary data to do this.

The data set resulting from this work with all five sequences is available at:
`http://www.tnt.uni-hannover.de/project/feature_evaluation/`
The provided resolutions include versions with 1.5 megapixels, 3 megapixels, 6 megapixels, and 8 megapixels for each sequence.

References

1. Mikolajczyk, K., Schmid, C.: Scale & affine invariant interest point detectors. International Journal of Computer Vision (IJCV) 60, 63–86 (2004)
2. Mikolajczyk, K., Schmid, C.: A performance evaluation of local descriptors. IEEE Transactions on Pattern Analysis and Machine Intelligence (PAMI) 27, 1615–1630 (2005)
3. Mikolajczyk, K., Tuytelaars, T., Schmid, C., Zisserman, A., Matas, J., Schaffalitzky, F., Kadir, T., Gool, L.V.: A comparison of affine region detectors. International Journal of Computer Vision (IJCV) 65, 43–72 (2005)
4. Schmid, C., Mohr, R., Bauckhage, C.: Comparing and evaluating interest points. In: IEEE International Conference on Computer Vision (ICCV), pp. 230–235 (1998)

5. Schmid, C., Mohr, R., Bauckhage, C.: Evaluation of interest point detectors. International Journal of Computer Vision (IJCV) 37, 151–172 (2000)

6. Haja, A., Jähne, B., Abraham, S.: Localization accuracy of region detectors. In: IEEE Conference on Computer Vision and Pattern Recognition (CVPR), pp. 1–8 (2008)

7. Tuytelaars, T., Mikolajczyk, K.: Local invariant feature detectors: a survey. Foundations and Trends in Computer Graphics and Vision, vol. 3 (2008)

8. Mikolajczyk, K., Schmid, C.: An affine invariant interest point detector. In: Heyden, A., Sparr, G., Nielsen, M., Johansen, P. (eds.) ECCV 2002, Part I. LNCS, vol. 2350, pp. 128–142. Springer, Heidelberg (2002)

9. Förstner, W., Dickscheid, T., Schindler, F.: Detecting interpretable and accurate scale-invariant keypoints. In: IEEE International Conference on Computer Vision (ICCV), Kyoto, Japan, pp. 2256–2263 (2009)

10. Mobahi, H., Zitnick, C., Ma, Y.: Seeing through the blur. In: IEEE Conference on Computer Vision and Pattern Recognition (CVPR), pp. 1736–1743 (2012)

11. Brown, M., Lowe, D.G.: Invariant features from interest point groups. In: British Machine Vision Conference (BMVC), pp. 656–665 (2002)

12. Cordes, K., Rosenhahn, B., Ostermann, J.: Increasing the accuracy of feature evaluation benchmarks using differential evolution. In: IEEE Symposium Series on Computational Intelligence (SSCI) - IEEE Symposium on Differential Evolution (SDE). IEEE Computer Society (2011)

13. Matas, J., Chum, O., Urban, M., Pajdla, T.: Robust wide baseline stereo from maximally stable extremal regions. British Machine Vision Conference (BMVC) 1, 384–393 (2002)

14. Tuytelaars, T., Gool, L.V.: Wide baseline stereo matching based on local, affinely invariant regions. In: British Machine Vision Conference (BMVC), pp. 412–425 (2000)

15. Tuytelaars, T., Van Gool, L.: Content-based image retrieval based on local affinely invariant regions. In: Huijsmans, D.P., Smeulders, A.W.M. (eds.) VISUAL 1999. LNCS, vol. 1614, pp. 493–500. Springer, Heidelberg (1999)

16. Hartley, R.I., Zisserman, A.: Multiple View Geometry, 2nd edn. Cambridge University Press (2003)

17. Price, K.V., Storn, R., Lampinen, J.A.: Differential Evolution - A Practical Approach to Global Optimization. Natural Computing Series. Springer, Berlin (2005)

Fully Automatic Segmentation of AP Pelvis X-rays via Random Forest Regression and Hierarchical Sparse Shape Composition

Cheng Chen and Guoyan Zheng

Institute for Surgical Technology and Biomechanics, University of Bern,
CH-3014, Bern, Switzerland
cheng.chen@istb.unibe.ch, guoyan.zheng@ieee.org

Abstract. Knowledge of landmarks and contours in anteroposterior (AP) pelvis X-rays is invaluable for computer aided diagnosis, hip surgery planning and image-guided interventions. This paper presents a fully automatic and robust approach for landmarking and segmentation of both pelvis and femur in a conventional AP X-ray. Our approach is based on random forest regression and hierarchical sparse shape composition. Experiments conducted on 436 clinical AP pelvis x-rays show that our approach achieves an average point-to-curve error around 1.3 mm for femur and 2.2 mm for pelvis, both with success rates around 98%. Compared to existing methods, our approach exhibits better performance in both the robustness and the accuracy.

Keywords: image segmentation, visual feature selection, shape model.

1 Introduction

Segmenting anatomical regions such as the femur and the pelvis is an important task in the analysis of conventional 2D X-ray images, which benefits many applications such as disease diagnosis [1,2], operation planning/intervention [3], 3D reconstruction [4,5], and so on. Traditionally, manual segmentation of X-ray images is both time-consuming and error-prone. Therefore, automatic methods are beneficial both in efficiency and accuracy. However, automatic segmentation of X-ray images face many challanges. The poor and non-uniform image constrast, along with the noise, makes the segmentation very difficult. Occlusions such as the overlap between bones make it difficult to identify local features of bone contours. Furthermore, the existence of implants drastically interferes with the appearance. Therefore, conventional segmentation techniques [1,3], which mainly depend on local image features such as the edge information, cannot provide satisfactory results, and model based segmentation techniques are often adopted [5,6]. However, model based methods suffer from the requirement of proper initialization, which is typically done manually, and the limited converging region, leading to unsatisfactory results.

R. Wilson et al. (Eds.): CAIP 2013, Part I, LNCS 8047, pp. 335–343, 2013.

To overcome these challanges, machine learning-based methods has gained more and more interests in medical image segmentation. In [7], Zhou and Comaniciu introduced the so-called shape regression machine to segment in real time the left ventricle endocardium from an echocardiogram of an apical four chamber view. In [8], Zheng et al. proposed marginal space learning to automatically localize the heart chamber from 3D CT. More recently, random forest regression has been used to automatically localize organs from 3D volumetric data such as CT or MRI [9,10]. However, in comparison with 3D data, 2D X-ray images pose more challenges because of the poor image quality caused by projection overlap of surrounding soft and hard tissues. In [2], Lindner et al. introduced a regression voting method in combination with a constrained local model (CLM) framework for automatic segmentation of proximal femur from conventional x-ray radiographs without occlusion.

In this paper, we propose a new fully automatic method for femur and pelvis segmentation in anteroposterior (AP) X-ray images. The contributions of this paper include: (A) A hierarchical landmark detection framework where a set of globally detected landmarks are used for image normalization and another set of locally detected landmarks are utilized for shape optimization; and (b) The exploitation of the recently proposed sparse shape composition model.

2   The Proposed Approach

2.1   Landmarks and Shape Models

We define X-ray landmarks hierarchically in two different levels, as shown in Fig. 1. The first level, *global landmarks*, contains one group of 22 landmarks $\mathcal{G} = \{L_1^{\mathcal{G}}, ..., L_{22}^{\mathcal{G}}\}$ defined on anatomically important positions over the whole image (Fig. 1(a)). The second level, *local landmarks* consists of two different groups: left femur $\mathcal{LF} = \{L_1^{\mathcal{LF}}, ..., L_{59}^{\mathcal{LF}}\}$ with 59 local landmarks (Fig. 1(b)), and left pelvis $\mathcal{LP} = \{L_1^{\mathcal{LP}}, ..., L_{97}^{\mathcal{LP}}\}$ with 97 local landmarks (Fig. 1(c)).

Shapes are defined by the ordered landmarks in the same group. For example, an instance of "global shape" $y^{\mathcal{G}}$ is defined by $y^{\mathcal{G}} = [l_1^{\mathcal{G}}, ... l_{22}^{\mathcal{G}}] \in \mathbb{R}^{44}$, where $l_i^{\mathcal{G}}$ is the location of landmark $L_i^{\mathcal{G}}$ in the image. For each landmark group, there

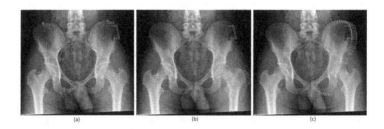

Fig. 1. (a): Global landmarks. (b): Local landmarks defining the left femur shape. (c): Local landmarks defining the left pelvis shape.

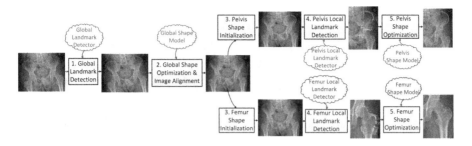

Fig. 2. Workflow on a test image. Rectangles represent different steps. Clouds represent different pre-trained models.

is an associated statistical shape model. We denote $\mathcal{M}^{\mathcal{G}}$, $\mathcal{M}^{\mathcal{LF}}$, $\mathcal{M}^{\mathcal{LP}}$ as the shape models for $\mathcal{G}$, $\mathcal{LF}$ and $\mathcal{LP}$, respectively. Shape models specify the prior distribution of landmark positions in the correponding landmark group.

2.2   Workflow

Fig. 2 shows the workflow of our method given a test image I.

(1) Global landmark detection. First, we launch landmark detector for the global landmarks, which produces response images $\{R(I)_1^{\mathcal{G}}, ..., R(I)_{22}^{\mathcal{G}}\}$. The detailed definition of response image will be given in Section 2.3.

(2) Global shape optimization and global image alignment. The response images $\{R(I)_i^{\mathcal{G}}\}$, together with the global shape model $\mathcal{M}^{\mathcal{G}}$, are used for a shape optimization process which finds the optimal global shape, as well as the similarity transform (rigid+scale) with regard to the shape model. Then, the image and global landmark positions are transformed by this similarity transform, which compensates for the global translation, rotation and scaling. Note in Fig. 2 how the erroneous landmark detections are corrected by the shape optimization.

(3) Local Shape initialization. The left femur shape $y^{\mathcal{LF}}$ and the left pelvis shape $y^{\mathcal{LP}}$ (i.e. the corresponding landmark positions) are initialized based on the positions of the 22 global landmarks derived in the previous step.

(4) Local landmark detection. Local landmarks are detected, which generates the response images $\{R(I)_1^{\mathcal{LF}}, ..., R(I)_{59}^{\mathcal{LF}}\}$ and $\{R(I)_1^{\mathcal{LP}}, ..., R(I)_{97}^{\mathcal{LP}}\}$.

(5) Local shape optimization. With the initialized shape $y^{\mathcal{LF}}$ from step (3), the landmark response images $\{R(I)_i^{\mathcal{LF}}\}$ from step (4), and the shape model $\mathcal{M}^{\mathcal{LF}}$, this final step searches for the optimal femur shape. The same process is repeated for the pelvis.

In short, we use global shape to compensate for the global image pose as well as to initialize the local shapes, and this (steps (1)-(2)) needs to be done only once for an image. After the global alignment is done, the local landmark detection in step (4) only has to be done in limited image region without considering large scale/rotation variance, which speeds up the detection.

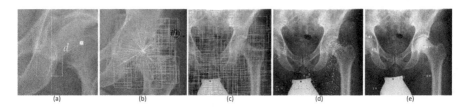

Fig. 3. The landmark detection algorithm. (a): A patch sampled around the ground-truth landmark. (b): Patches sampled for training. (c): For a new image, patches sampled over the image. (d): Each patch produces a prediction of landmark position. (e): The response image is calculated by combining individual predictions.

2.3   Landmark Detection

We have a separate detector for each landmark. During training, in each training image, we sample a set of rectangular patches[1] around the ground-truth landmark position which is known. Each patch is represented by its visual feature $f \in \mathbb{R}^{d_f}$ and the displacement vector $d \in \mathbb{R}^2$ from the patch center to the landmark (Fig 3(a)). Let us denote all the sampled patches in all training images as $\{P_i = (f_i, d_i)\}_{i=1,...,N}$ (Fig. 3(b)). The goal is then to learn a mapping function $\phi : \mathbb{R}^{d_f} \mapsto \mathbb{R}^2$ from the feature space to the displacement vector space. Principally, any regression method can be used. In this paper, similar to [9,2], we utilize the random forest regressor [11].

Once the regressor is trained, given a new image, as in Fig. 3(c), we randomly sample a another set of patches $\{P'_j = (f'_j, c'_j)\}_{j=1,...,N'}$ all over the image (or an ROI), where f'_j and c'_j are the visual feature and center coordinate of the patch P'_j, respectively. Through the trained mapping ϕ, we can calculate the predicted displacement $d(P'_j) = \phi(f'_j)$, and then $d(P'_j) + c'_j$ is the prediction of the landmark location by a single patch P'_j (Fig. 3(d)). The individual predictions are very noisy, but when combined, they approach an accurate prediction $l^\star$:

$$l^\star = \frac{1}{N'} \sum_j \left(\phi(f'_j) + c'_j \right) \tag{1}$$

In practice, the output of random forest regressor $d(P_j)$ is not a single value, but a distribution[2]. Similarly to Eq. (1), we add up the predicted distributions, getting a single distribution (as in Fig. 3(e)), which is called the *response image*.

In our method, we use the multi-level HoG (Histogram of Oriented Gradient) [13] as our feature for image patches, and we use a feature selection algorithm propose in [14] to efficiently select only the most relevant feature components.

---

[1] We use 1000 patches per image for both training and testing in our implementation.
[2] The raw output of the random forest regressor is the displacement vectors on the leave where the test feature vector falls, from which we fit a gaussian distribution.

Table 1. The algorithm of shape optimization

Input: Initial shape y_0, landmark response images $\{R(I)_i\}_{i=1,\ldots,K}$, shape model $\mathcal{M}$
Output: Optimal shape y^*, pose transform matrix T
Procedure:
1. Initialize $y = y_0$, T = the optimal similarity transform from y to shape model $\mathcal{M}$
2. Update shape y by locally moving each landmark in the ascend direction in the corresponding response image
3. Regularize shape y by the shape model $\mathcal{M}$.
4. Update pose T by the optimal similarity transform from y to shape model $\mathcal{M}$
5. Repeat steps 2 to 4 until convergence. Then $y^* = y$

2.4 Shape Optimization

In this section we present our method which searches for the optimal shape in steps (2) and (5) of Section 2.2. Prior to the shape optimization, we have the response images $\{R(I)_i\}_{i=1,\ldots,K}$ for K landmarks, the initial shape $y_0 \in \mathbb{R}^{2K}$, and a shape model $\mathcal{M}$. The task is then to find the optimal shape $y^* \in \mathbb{R}^{2K}$, starting from the initial shape y_0, constrained both by the image cue encoded in the response images, and the prior information encoded in the shape model.

The procedure is shown in Table 1. Basically, starting from the initial shape, we update the shape iteratively. In each iteration, we perform three actions: update the shape by moving each local landmark to a better position according to response images, regularize the shape by the shape model, and update the shape pose. These steps are straightforward except the shape regularization, which regularizes the locally updated shape by the shape model to remove noise (step 3 in Table 1). Traditionally, this can be done by the Active Shape Model [15] based on PCA (Principal Component Analysis). In this paper, we instead employ the recently proposed shape model based on sparse representation [12]. Here we briefly explains this method.

The shape model consists of a set of pre-aligned training shapes $\{y_i\}_{i=1,\ldots,N}$. For each new shape y' to be regularized, after a transformation T (which is evaluated separately in step 4 of Table 1), it should be approximated by a linear combination involving only a small subset of the training shapes, plus a sparse error:

$$T(y') \approx Yx + e = \begin{bmatrix} Y & I \end{bmatrix} \begin{bmatrix} x \\ e \end{bmatrix} = Y'x' \tag{2}$$

where $Y' = [Y, I]$, and $x' = \begin{bmatrix} x^\top, e^\top \end{bmatrix}^\top$. In Eq. (2), both the linear coefficients x and the error e are sparse. Therefore, the composite coefficient x' is also sparse. Our goal becomes to solve the following L_1-regularized least squares problem:

$$x'_{\text{opt}} = \arg\min_{x'} \left(\|T(y') - Y'x'\|_2^2 + \lambda \|x'\|_1 \right) \tag{3}$$

where λ is a parameter controlling the importance of the sparsity constraint. There are a number of solvers for Eq. (3), and we employ the method using truncated Newton interior-point method.

The intepretation of Eq. (2) is clear: the shape y' should be approximated (with a transformation T) as a linear combination of only a small number of "basis", which can either be the training shapes, or standard basis of the $\mathbb{R}^{2K}$ space. The contribution from the training shapes represents the "true" part of shape y' that is consistent to the shape model, and the contribution from the standard basis accomodates large but sparse errors (noises). Therefore, after we get the optimal x'_{opt} by Eq. (3), we decompose x'_{opt} by $x'_{opt} = \left[x^\top_{opt}, e^\top_{opt} \right]^\top$ as in Eq. (2), discard the e_{opt} which corresponds to the noises, and the regularized shape is given by back-projecting the "true" part of the shape:

$$y'_{\text{regularized}} = T^{-1}(Y x_{opt}) \qquad (4)$$

Thus we complete the shape regularization step in Table 1.

3 Experiments

3.1 Data

We conduct experiments using a collection of 436 AP radiographs from our clinical partner. A considerable part of these images are post-operative x-ray radiographs after trauma or joint replacement surgery, which significantly increases the challenge due to large variation of femur/pelvis appearance and the presence of implants. From these 436 images, we randomly select 100 images for training, and the other 336 images are used for testing purpose. For the training images, we manually annotate all the (global and local) landmarks.

3.2 Results on Femur/Pelvis Segmentation

We implemented our segmentation algorithm on the 336 test images, and Fig. 4 shows examples done with our method. We can see that our method achieves excellent performance despite of chanllenges such as significant variation of appearance, poor image contrast, or implants. Note that 115 of the 336 test images (34%) have different types of implants, which reflects the challenge of our dataset.

For quantitative evaluation, from the 336 test images, we randomly choose 192 images, on which we manually annotated the left femur and left pelvis contour. The error of segmentation is thus calculated by the average point-to-curve distance between the points on the segmented shape and the annotated contour. Since the images are stored in Dicom format, we know the pixel resolution of each image and therefore the error is expressed in the physical unit of millimeter, which is shown in Table 2. We can see that our method achieves an average error of 1.3 mm for femur segmentation, and 2.2 mm for pelvis segmentation.

Evaluated on all the 192 annotated test images, our method succeeded in 189 for femur segmentation, with a success rate of 98.4%. A segmentation is classified as successful if the average point-to-curve distance is smaller than 4 mm. For pelvis segmentation, 19 images out of the 192 do not contain complete pelvis structure (as in Fig. 4(d)) and are naturally excluded from the evaluation. Among

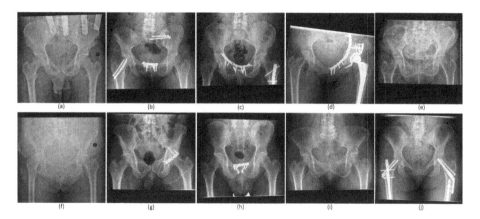

Fig. 4. Segmentation examples done with our method. Yellow: prlvis; green: femur.

the 173 valid images for pelvis, our method succeeded in 169 with a success rate of 97.7%.

Our method takes around 5 minutes to process one image with an unoptimized Matlab implementation.

3.3   Evaluation of the Sparse Shape Composition Model

To evaluate the effectiveness of our shape model, we compare with the PCA based shape model (as in [2]), for which the result is shown in Table 3. Comparing Table 3 with Table 2, we see that our shape model outperforms the PCA based one.

Note that the result reported here is not directly comparable with that of [2] due to several reasons. First, we perform both femur and pelvis segmentation, while [2] only segments femur. Second, we model the femur contour details such as the lesser trochanter, and these details are missing in [2] which uses a simplfied model. Third and most importantly, in part of our test images the regions to be segmented are occluded by implants (see Fig. 4).

Table 2. Quantitative result of our method

Anatomy	Success rate	Median	Min.	Max.	Mean	Std.	97.5th percentile
Femur	98.4%	1.2	0.6	3.4	1.3	0.6	2.7
Pelvis	97.7%	2.1	1.0	3.7	2.2	0.5	3.4

Table 3. Quantitative evaluation using the PCA based shape model

Anatomy	Success rate	Median	Min.	Max.	Mean	Std.	97.5th percentile
Femur	97.1%	1.3	0.6	3.6	1.4	0.6	3.0
Pelvis	95.4%	2.4	1.2	3.8	2.5	0.6	3.5

4   Conclusions

We have proposed a new fully-automatic method for left femur and pelvis segmentation in conventional X-ray images. Our method features a hierarchical segmentation framework and a shape model based on sparse representation. Experiments show that our method achieves good results, and that the different contributions (feature selection, shape model) indeed improve the performance. Although we demonstrate our method using the left femur and left pelvis, our method can be readily extended to the right side. In the future, we are also interested in extending our method into 3D data.

Acknowledgements. This work was partially supported by the Swiss National Science Foundation via Project 51NF40-144610.

References

1. Chen, Y., Ee, X., Leow, W.-K., Howe, T.S.: Automatic extraction of femur contours from hip X-ray images. In: Liu, Y., Jiang, T.-Z., Zhang, C. (eds.) CVBIA 2005. LNCS, vol. 3765, pp. 200–209. Springer, Heidelberg (2005)
2. Lindner, C., Thiagarajah, S., Wilkinson, J.M., Wallis, G.A., Cootes, T.F.: Accurate fully automatic femur segmentation in pelvic radiographs using regression voting. In: Ayache, N., Delingette, H., Golland, P., Mori, K. (eds.) MICCAI 2012, Part III. LNCS, vol. 7512, pp. 353–360. Springer, Heidelberg (2012)
3. Gottschling, H., Roth, M., Schweikard, A., Burgkart, R.: Intraoperative, fluoroscopy-based planning for complex osteotomies of the proximal femur. IJMRCAS 1(3), 33–38 (2005)
4. Baka, N., Kaptein, B.L., Bruijne, M., van Walsum, T., Giphart, J.E., Niessen, W.J., Lelieveldt, B.P.: 2D-3D shape reconstruction of the distal femur from stereo x-ray imaging using statistical shape model. Med. Image Anal. 15(6), 840–850 (2001)
5. Dong, X., Zheng, G.: Automatic extraction of proximal femur contours from calibrated x-ray images using 3D statistical models: an in vitro study. IJMRCAS 5(2), 213–222 (2009)
6. Cristinacce, D., Cootes, T.: Automatic feature localization with constrained local models. Pattern Recognition 41(19), 3054–3067 (2008)
7. Zhou, S.K., Comaniciu, D.: Shape regression machine. In: Karssemeijer, N., Lelieveldt, B. (eds.) IPMI 2007. LNCS, vol. 4584, pp. 13–25. Springer, Heidelberg (2007)
8. Zheng, Y., Barbu, A., Georgescu, B., Scheuering, M., Comaniciu, D.: Four-chamber heart modeling and automatic segmentation of 3-D cardiac CT volumes using marginal space learning and steerable features. IEEE T. Med. Imaging 27(11), 1668–1681 (2008)
9. Pauly, O., Glocker, B., Criminisi, A., Mateus, D., Möller, A.M., Nekolla, S., Navab, N.: Fast multiple organ detection and localization in whole-body MR Dixon sequences. In: Fichtinger, G., Martel, A., Peters, T. (eds.) MICCAI 2011, Part III. LNCS, vol. 6893, pp. 239–247. Springer, Heidelberg (2011)
10. Criminisi, A., Shotton, J., Robertson, D., Konukoglu, E.: Regression forests for efficient anatomy detection and localization in CT studies. In: MCV 2010, pp. 106–117 (1201)

11. Gall, J., Lempitsky, V.: Class-specific Hough forests for object detection. In: CVPR, pp. 1022–1029 (2009)
12. Zhang, S., Zhan, Y., Dewan, M., Huang, J., Metaxas, D.N., Zhou, X.S.: Sparse shape composition: a new framework for shape prior modeling. In: CVPR (2011)
13. Dalal, N., Triggs, B.: Histograms of oriented gradients for human detection. In: CVPR, vol. I, pp. 886–893 (2005)
14. Chen, C., Yang, Y., Nie, F., Odobez, J.M.: 3D human pose recovery from image by efficient visual feature selection. CVIU 115(3), 290–299 (2011)
15. Cootes, T.F., Taylor, C.J.: Active shape models-'smart snakes'. In: BMVC (1992)

Language Adaptive Methodology
for Handwritten Text Line Segmentation

Subhash Panwar[1], Neeta Nain[1], Subhra Saxena[2], and P.C. Gupta[3]

[1] Deptt. of Computer Engineering, Malaviya National Institute of Technology Jaipur
[2] School of Engineering and Technology, Jaipur National University, Jaipur
[3] Deptt. of Computer Scinece and Informatics, University of Kota, Kota

Abstract. Text line segmentation in handwritten documents is a very challenging task because in handwritten documents curved text lines appear frequently. In this paper, we have implemented a general line segmentation approach for handwritten documents with various languages. A novel connectivity strength parameter is used for deciding the groups of the components which belongs to the same line. oversegmentation is also removed with the help of depth first search approach and iterative use of the CSF. We have implemented and tested this approach with English, Hindi and Urdu text images taken from benchmark database and find that it is a language adaptive approach which provide encouraged results. The average accuracy of the proposed technique is 97.30%.

Keywords: Handwritten text recognition, Line Segmentation, Connected component, Connectivity strength function.

1 Introduction

Text line segmentation of handwritten documents is much more difficult than that of printed documents. Unlike the printed documents which have approximately straight and parallel text lines, the lines in handwritten documents are often un-uniformly skewed and curved. Moreover, the spaces between handwritten text lines are often not obvious compared to the spaces between within-line characters, and some text lines may interfere with each other. Therefore many text line detection techniques, such as projection analysis [7] [5], Hough transform [6] and K-nearest neighbour connected components (CCs) grouping [9], are not able to segment handwritten text lines successfully and also still a uniform approach to handle all kind of challenges is not available. Figure 1 shows an example of unconstrained handwritten document. Text document image segmentation can be roughly categorized into three classes: top-down, bottom-up, and hybrid. Top-down methods partition the document image recursively into text regions, text lines, and words/characters with the assumption of straight lines. Bottom-up methods group small units of image (pixels, CCs, characters, words, etc.) into text lines and then text regions. Bottom-up grouping can be viewed as a clustering process, which aggregates image components according to proximity and does not rely on the assumption of straight lines. Hybrid methods

R. Wilson et al. (Eds.): CAIP 2013, Part I, LNCS 8047, pp. 344–351, 2013.

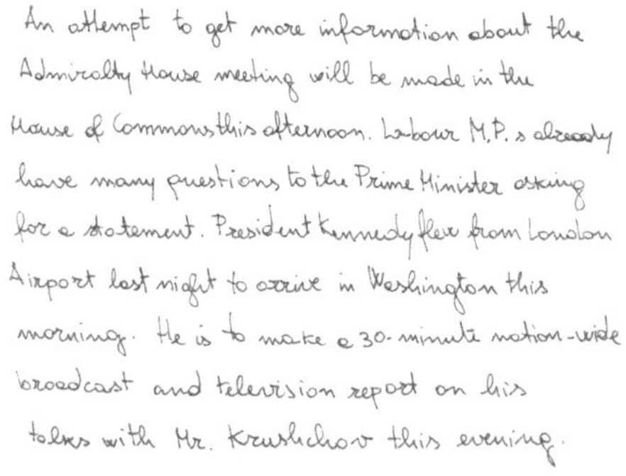

Fig. 1. Example image of a general handwritten text paragraph from IAM dataset [4]

combine bottom-up grouping and top-down partitioning in different ways.

All the three approaches have their advantages and disadvantages. Top-down methods work well for typed text where the text lines are relatively horizontal, but it does not perform well on curved and overlapping text lines. The performance of bottom-up grouping relies on some heuristic rules or artificial parameters, such as the between-component distance metric for clustering. On the other hand, hybrid methods are complicated in computation, and the design of a robust combination scheme is non-trivial.

In graph representation of image as each component is represented as vertex and the distance calculated between the CC is represented as an edge with weight. Then, we may find out the minimum spanning tree of the given image, and thus the segmentation is made as by comparing with pre determined distance which may be an inter word distance or intra word distance [8] .

In [1] authors use the image meshing for line detectioin locally in the presence of multi-orientation of lines. Wigner-Villey distribution and projection histogram is used to determine the local orientation. This local orientation is then enlarged to limit the orientation in the neighbourhood.

In [2] the text line is segmented using Affinity Propogation. They first estimate the local orientation at each primary component to build a sparse similirity graph then use a shortest path algorithm to compute similirities between non-neighbouring components. Affinity propagnation and Breadth-first-search are used to obtain coarse text lines.

In [3], the line segmentation algorithm is based on locating the optimal succession of text and gap areas within veritcal zones by applying Viterbi algorithm and a text line seperator drawing technique is applied and finally the connected components are assigned to text lines.

We are proposing an effective bottom-up grouping method for text line segmentation for unconstrained handwritten text documents. Our approach is based on minimal spanning tree (MST), grouping of CCs, and the connectivity strength function (CSF).

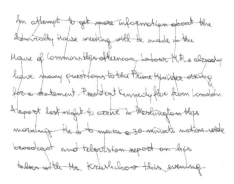

Fig. 2. *MST* generated for the text paragraph shown in Figure 1, the green pixels mark the centroids of every connected component, and the red lines depict the edges of the *MST* of the graph of the connected components of the same figure

2   The Proposed Line Segmentation Method

In this paper, we first extract the *CC*s from the image (binarized). To construct a line from these *CC*s, calculate the centroid of every *CC* as depicted in Figure 2 with green coloured pixels. Using these centroids of *CC*s as vertices (graph), calculate the cost matrix of the given graph, where the cost of the edge is the distance between two vertices. The *MST* is then calculated for the graph as shown in Figure 2. The *MST* as shown in Figure 2, also have some mis-qualified words linked with the line words which are not part of the same line. For removing such connections (edges) from the *MST*, we further use a connectivity strength function as explained below which is very useful in deciding the groups of the components which belongs to the same line. Thus the mis-aligned edges are removed from the *MST* and we generate the correct forest of the *CC*s.

The Connectivity Strength Function *CSF* is derived as, let there be two connected components C_1 and C_2 having centroids as (x_1, y_1) and (x_2, y_2), respectively. The minimum distance (d) between the two components is

$$d = \sqrt{(x_2 - x_1)^2 + (y_2 - y_1)^2}$$

and the vertical distance Y_d is

$$y_d = (y_2 - y_1)$$

then the *CSF* is defined as

$$CSF = \frac{|d - y_d|}{y_d}$$

For each pair of connected component in the *MST* compute the value of *CSF*. The decision for grouping the components depends on *CSF* as

$$CSF = \begin{cases} 0 & \text{belongs to different lines.} \\ \infty & \text{belongs to same line.} \end{cases}$$

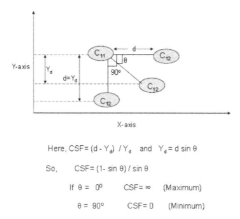

Here, CSF= (d - Y_d) / Y_d and Y_d = d sin θ

So,   CSF= (1- sin θ) / sin θ

If θ = 0°   CSF= ∞   (Maximum)

θ = 90°   CSF= 0   (Minimum)

Fig. 3. Illustration of boundary values of CSF

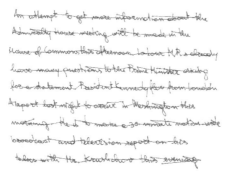

Fig. 4. Forest remains after removing the week edges from Figure 1 using CSF

where, $CSF = 0$, only when $d = y_d$, means the two components have the minimum connectivity strength as they are orthogonal and hence belongs to different lines, which are almost parallel. And the $CSF = \infty$, only when $y_d = 0$. This means the connectivity between the two components is the strongest as they both belong to the same line. The angle between the two components is zero aligning them on the same line as shown in Figure 3.

Thus, after applying the CSF rules on Figure 1 we remove the mis-aligned components from the text lines and generate the forest of given document image as shown in Figure 4. Where our forest is defined as a group of trees. Where every tree is a text line. Text lines are over segmentation in a single iteration of CSF . To overcome such situation we apply same process on forest treating each tree of forest as a single node and find the connected graph and apply CSF approach. Finally we get the forest having a single tree for every single text line as shown in Figure 4 . Figure 5(a) shows an example of hindi handwritten

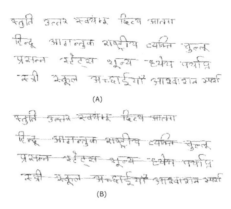

(A)

(B)

Fig. 5. (a) Example image of a hindi handwritten document. (b) Forest remains after applying CSF.

document. Figure 5(b) shows the result using proposed approach. The complete process can be enumerated as shown in Algorithm 1.

3   Experimental Results

The experiments are done on various variety of handwritten document images including different languages as hindi, english and urdu. To cover all the cases such as skewed lines, curved lines and touching line, some images are randomly selected from the large IAM[4] database of handwritten document and some are generated from different writers with different languages. The various cases are enumerated below.

1. Curved lines: Figure 6(A) shows an example of a curved handwritten lines. The projection profile techniques [7] for such curved lines fails completely in such line segmentations. Also Figure 6(B) shows the result that the MST generated which when used by clustering techniques [9] using inter word distance for line segmentation will also give erroneous result. This shortcoming of existing techniques is overcome by the application of CSF on which gives the correct result. Figure 7(a) shows an example of urdu handwritten document with curved lines. Figure 7(b) shows the result using proposed approach.

2. Skewed lines: An example image of handwritten document with skewed lines is shown in Figure 8(A); and after finding the MST of given example image, we apply the CSF and find the exact forest of the text line which is shown in Figure 8(B). Here also the traditional methods would fail.

   Again it is ascertained that the CSF improves the accuracy of line segmentation in presence of skewed line in the documents.

Algorithm 1. Text Line Segmentation.

Ensure: F- Forest of text lines.

Require: I- Text document binarized image with background as 0.

Compute connected components (CC_i)s using 8-connectivity.

Compute centroids for all CC_is.

$\{(c_x, c_y) = (\frac{1}{M} \sum x_j, \frac{1}{M} \sum y_j)$, where $x_j, y_j \in CC_i$; M is the number of pixels in i^{th} $CC.\}$

$\{$Compute cost matrix $d_{m,n}$ of CCs$\}$

$d_{i,j} = \sqrt{(x_i - x_j)^2 + (y_i - y_j)^2}$.

Scan the CC using DFS of G (graph) using cost matrix$d_{m,n}$

$\{\forall V$ (vertex) $\in G$ with $V_{degree} \geq 2 \in$ DFS sequence, apply CSF.$\}$

if $(V_{degree} \geq 2)$ **then**

    $y_d = (y_2 - y_1)$.

    $CSF = \frac{|d - y_d|}{y_d}$.

    $\{\forall CC$ connected with this $V.\}$

end if

Calculate Th_{CSF} $\{Th_{CSF}$=Minimum vertical distance between two $CC_i\}$

Remove the week edges where ever $CSF \leq Th_{CSF}$.

Compute centroids and cost metrix for Forest F.

$\{\forall$ tree $T_i \in F$ are treated as vertex of the graph$\}$

Remove the week edges where ever $CSF \approx 0$.

Return(F) $\{$Finally remains a forest having the trees for every single line.$\}$

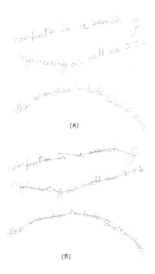

(A)

(B)

Fig. 6. (A) Example image of curved lines in handwritten text document. (B) Forest remains after applying CSF.

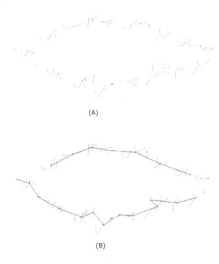

(A)

(B)

Fig. 7. (a) Example image of a urdu handwritten document. (b) Forest remains after applying CSF.

(A)

(B)

Fig. 8. (A) Example image of a skewed lines in handwritten text document. (B) Forest remains after applying CSF.

The experimental results of the proposed line segmentation approach shows that proposed CSF improves line segmentation accuracy significantly in all the cases. The proposed method was also compared with other state-of-the-art methods in experiments on a large database of IAM[4], handwritten documents data set and its superiority was demonstrated. The accuracy rate of the proposed text line segmentation method is summarized in Table 1.

Table 1. Accuracy rate of proposed text line segmentation using CSF

Line types	Total no. of lines	Accurate detected lines	Accuracy rate
Printed lines	320	320	100
Skewed lines	2600	2520	96.92
Curved lines	1750	1670	95.42

4   Conclusions

In this paper, a language adaptive approach for handwritten text line segmentation with CSF has been presented and applied to the IAM dataset and documents collected from different writers with different languages as Hindi english and urdu. The proposed text line segmentation approach with the novel use of CSF has the advantage of language adaptivity with highly curve and skewed text lines. From the experiments, 97.30% average accuracy were observed in the system. The results obtained by this segmentation is a forest of lines. It shows that the proposed system is capable of locating accurately the text lines in images and documents. Future work mainly concerns the sequential arrangement of all lines of forest according to appearing in paragraph so that the sequential stroke is sent to next step of recognition system.

References

1. Ouwayed, N., Belaid, A.: A general approach for multi-oriented text line extraction of handwritten documents. IJDAR 15(4), 297–314 (2012)
2. Kumar, J., et al.: Handwritten Arabic text line segmentation using affinity propagation. In: DAS 2010, pp. 135–142 (2010)
3. Papavassiliou, V., et al.: Handwritten document image segmentation into text lines and words. Pattern Recognition 43, 369–377 (2010)
4. Marti, U., Bunke, H.: The IAM-database: An English Sentence Database for Offline Handwriting Recognition. Int. Journal on Document Analysis and Recognition, IJDAR 5, 39–46 (2002)
5. Likforman Sulem, L., Zahour, A., Taconet, B.: Text line segmentation of historical documents: A survey. IJDAR 9, 123–138 (2007)
6. Likforman-Sulem, L., Hanimyan, A., Faure, C.: A Hough based algorithm for extracting text lines in handwritten documents. In: Proc. 3rd Int. Conf. on Document Analysis and Recognition, pp. 774–777 (1995)
7. Zamora-Martinez, F., Castro-Bleda, M.J., Espaa-Boquera, S., Gorbe-Moya, J.: Unconstrained offline handwriting recognition using connectionist character N-grams. In: The 2010 International Joint Conference on Neural Networks (IJCNN), July 18-23, pp. 1–7 (2010)
8. Yin, F., Liu, C.-L.: Handwritten Chinese text line segmentation by clustering with distance metric learning. Pattern Recognition (Elsevier) 42(12), 3146–3157 (2009)
9. Kumar, M., Jindal, M.K., Sharma, R.K.: K-nearest neighbour Based offline Handwritten Gurumukhi Character Recognition. In: International IEEE Conference on Image Information Processing (ICHP 2011), vol. 1, pp. 7–11 (2011)

Learning Geometry-Aware Kernels in a Regularization Framework

Binbin Pan[1] and Wen-Sheng Chen[2]

[1] Shenzhen University
pbb@szu.edu.cn
[2] Shenzhen University
chenws@szu.edu.cn

Abstract. In this paper, we propose a regularization framework for learning geometry-aware kernels. Some existing geometry-aware kernels can be viewed as instances in our framework. Moreover, the proposed framework can be used as a general platform for developing new geometry-aware kernels. We show how multiple sources of information can be integrated in our framework, allowing us to develop more flexible kernels. We present some new kernels based on our framework. The performance of the kernels is evaluated on classification and clustering tasks. The empirical results show that our kernels significantly improve the performance.

1 Introduction

There has recently been a surge of interest in learning algorithms that are aware of the geometric structure of the data. These algorithms have been successfully applied to pattern recognition, image analysis, data mining etc.. Kernel function, defining the similarity between the data in Reproducing Kernel Hilbert Space (RKHS), can capture the structure of the data. Thus, the use of kernels for learning the geometric structure of the data has received a significant amount of attention. Such kernels are called as geometry-aware kernels. Algorithms for learning geometry-aware kernels can be roughly classified into two categories.

Algorithms in the first category only explore the geometric structure of the data, ignoring other source of information. Kondor and Lafferty propose Diffusion Kernels which are originated from the heat equation on geometric manifold and are aware of the data geometry [1]. Smola and Kondor show that the spectrum of graph Laplacian can be passed through various filter functions leading to a family of geometry-aware kernels [2]. Some examples of kernels are given, including Regularized Laplacian Kernel, Diffussion Kernel, Random Walk Kernel and Inverse Cosine Kernel. Some well-known algotihms for dimensionality reduction of manifold can be unified in a kernel perspective [3]. These algothrithms can be interpreted as kernel PCA with specifically constructed Gram matrices. Also, researchers focus on learning geometry-aware kernels for nonlinear dimensionality reduction [4,5]. These methods are unsupervised and well-suited to task of dimensionality reduction. However, they may not give satisfactory performance on supervised tasks.

R. Wilson et al. (Eds.): CAIP 2013, Part I, LNCS 8047, pp. 352–359, 2013.
© Springer-Verlag Berlin Heidelberg 2013

The second category learns kernels from multiple sources of information which include data geometry, side information and so on. Sindhwani et. al. show how the standard kernels can be adapted to incorporate data geometry while retaining out-of-sample extension [6]. Song et. al. show a variant of Maximum Variance Unfolding that is aware of the data geometry and side information [7]. Learning geometry-aware kernels from the nonparametric transforms of graph Laplacian are discussed in semi-supervised learning scenario [8]. Some studies focus on learning nonparametric geometry-aware kernels with the help of manifold regularization [9]. Comparing with the algorithms in the first category, these methods are more suitable for supervised tasks since the task related information is incorporated into them.

In this paper, we present a general framework for learning geometry-aware kernels. Our framework involves an optimization problem which minimizes a divergence between the learnt kernel matrix and a given prior matrix, along with some regularization term. Some existing geometry-aware kernels can be unified in our framework. Furthermore, new geomerty-aware kernels can be developed. We will show how to integrate multiple sources of information within the framework, leading to a family of algorithms by choosing various divergence, prior matrix and regularization term. Empirical results indicate that our algorithms significantly improve the performance.

2   The Regularization Framework

2.1   Problem Formulation

Given a prior kernel matrix K_0, we investigate how to learn geometry-aware kernel from the prior kernel matrix and the geometric structure of the data. We formulate the learning problem as follows:

$$\min_{K} D(K, K_0) + \gamma \Omega(K)$$
$$s.t. \ \ K \succeq 0, \tag{1}$$

where $D(\cdot, \cdot)$ is the divergence between two matrices, $\Omega(\cdot)$ is a regularization term, $\gamma > 0$ is the regularization trade-off, $K \succeq 0$ means K is a positive semi-definite matrix. The regularizer $\Omega(K)$ should measure the complexity of preserving the geometric structure.

If $D(K, K_0)$ and $\Omega(K)$ are convex functionals with respect to K, then (1) is a convex optimization problem with global minima. However, the positive semi-definiteness constraint makes the problem not easy to solve. Some papers reformulate their problems with such constraint as semi-definite programmings, leading to algorithms involving expensive computation [4]. In this paper, we adopt Bregman divergence to measure the discrepancy between the matrices. As we will see later, this divergence is well-suited to positive semi-definite matrices.

2.2   Choosing $D(\cdot, \cdot)$

We choose $D(\cdot, \cdot)$ as the Bregman divergence. Let $\mathcal{F} : \Delta \to \mathbb{R}$ be a continuously-differentiable real-valued and strictly convex function defined on a closed convex set Δ. The Bregman divergence associated with $\mathcal{F}$ for $K, K_0 \in \Delta$ is:

$$D_{\mathcal{F}}(K, K_0) = \mathcal{F}(K) - \mathcal{F}(K_0) - \text{tr}((K - K_0)\nabla\mathcal{F}(K_0)^T). \qquad (2)$$

The Bregman divergence represents a class of distance and divergence. For instance, if $\mathcal{F}(K) = \|K\|_F^2$, then the resulting Bregman divergence is the squared Frobenius norm $\|K - K_0\|_F^2$. When choosing $\mathcal{F}(K) = \text{tr}(K \log K - K)$, then $\nabla\mathcal{F}(K) = \log K$ and the corresponding Bregman divergence becomes the von Neumann divergence:

$$D_{\mathcal{F}}(K, K_0) = \text{tr}(K \log K - K \log K_0 - K + K_0). \qquad (3)$$

If we choose $\mathcal{F}(K) = -\text{LogDet}K$, then the gradient is $\nabla\mathcal{F}(K) = -K^{-1}$. The corresponding Bregman divergence is LogDet divergence:

$$D_{\mathcal{F}}(K, K_0) = \text{tr}(KK_0^{-1}) - \log\det(KK_0^{-1}) - n. \qquad (4)$$

2.3   Choosing $\Omega(\cdot)$

The regularization term $\Omega(\cdot)$ is chosen as a manifold regularization [10] which can exploit the geometric structure. Given a data set $X = \{x_1, \cdots, x_n\}$, we can build a weighted undirected graph with adjacency matrix W to describe the local neighborhood relations between the data points. The entries $W_{ij} > 0$ if the ith and jth data points are neighbors, otherwise $W_{ij} = 0$. The neighbor relations can be defined in terms of symmetric nearest neighbors or an ϵ-ball distance criterion. The non-zero weights in W can be chosen as $W_{ij} = 1$, or according to a heat kernel $W_{ij} = \exp(-\|x_i - x_j\|^2/t)$ where $t > 0$.

Suppose that the data were sampled from a smooth manifold which is approximated by a graph $\mathcal{G}$. We seek a nonlinear mapping ϕ which embeds the graph $\mathcal{G}$ to a RKHS so that connected points stay as close together as possible. Mathematically, we need to minimize

$$\sum_{i,j} \|\frac{\phi(x_i)}{\sqrt{D_{ii}}} - \frac{\phi(x_j)}{\sqrt{D_{jj}}}\|^2 W_{ij} = \text{tr}(KL), \qquad (5)$$

where K is the kernel matrix upon X associated with ϕ, i.e., $K_{ij} = \phi(x_i)^T \phi(x_j)$, $L = I - D^{-\frac{1}{2}}WD^{-\frac{1}{2}}$ is the normalized Laplacian matrix, D is diagonal matrix with entries $D_{ii} = \sum_j W_{ji}$. Thus, the regularization term $\Omega(K) = \text{tr}(KL)$.

2.4   Algorithm

The kernel learning problem with manifold regularization is

$$\min_{K} \mathcal{F}(K) - \mathcal{F}(K_0) - \text{tr}((K - K_0)\nabla\mathcal{F}(K_0)^T) + \gamma\text{tr}(KL)$$
$$s.t.\ \ K \succeq 0. \qquad (6)$$

Problem (6) is a convex programming since the Bregman divergence is convex with respect to the first parameter. Ignoring the positive semi-definiteness constraint and setting the derivative with respect to K to zero, we have

$$\nabla \mathcal{F}(K) - \nabla \mathcal{F}(K_0) + \gamma L = 0. \tag{7}$$

The solution is derived in closed-form:

$$K = (\nabla \mathcal{F})^{-1}(\nabla \mathcal{F}(K_0) - \gamma L). \tag{8}$$

We will show how the positive semi-definiteness constraint can be satisfied automatically by choosing various kinds of Bregman divergence. Specifically, we present the following kernels:

$$K = K_0 - \frac{\gamma}{2} L \qquad \text{(squared Frobenius norm)} \tag{9}$$

$$K = \exp(\log K_0 - \gamma L) \qquad \text{(von Neumann divergence)} \tag{10}$$

$$K = (K_0^{-1} + \gamma L)^{-1} \qquad \text{(LogDet Divergence)} \tag{11}$$

A small γ should be set to ensure the positive semi-definiteness of Equation (9). Note that the eigenvalues of L are no more than 2. Equation (10) is positive definite since the exponent $\log K_0 - \gamma L$ is a symmetric matrix and the matrix exponential converts symmetric matrix back into a positive definite matrix. Equation (11) is positive definite because of the positive definiteness of K_0 and L.

3   Discussions

3.1   Relation to Related Work

We present that some geometry-aware kernels can be unified in our framework.

Diffusion Kernel. We choose that $K_0 = I$ in Equation (10), which means no prior similarity information in K_0. We have $\log I = O$, where O is the zero matrix, then the solution is

$$K = \exp(-\gamma L). \tag{12}$$

Equation (12) is the diffusion kernel proposed in [1].

Regularized Laplacian Kernel. Setting $K_0 = I$ in Equation (11), we arrive at that

$$K = (I + \gamma L)^{-1}. \tag{13}$$

This is the Regularized Laplacian Kernel presented in [2].

1-Step Random Walk Kernel. Given $K_0 = I$ in Equation (9), we yield the following kernel

$$K = I - \frac{\gamma}{2}L. \tag{14}$$

When choosing $\gamma \leq 1$, K is positive semi-definite. It becomes the 1-Step Random Walk Kernel proposed in [2].

Sindhwani's Work. Note that Equation (11) is the Gram matrix of the kernel proposed in [6]. Given new test data, we can compute the out-of-sample extension in Equation (11) by enlarging K_0 with additional test data and setting $\tilde{L} = \text{diag}(L, O)$. The resulting formulation is the same as the kernel function presented in [6]. Therefore, we reinterpret Sindhwani's work in our regularization framework.

3.2   Integrating Multiple Sources of Information

The data geometry is incorporated with the manifold regularization. Other source of information could be integrated by the special choice of K_0. If K_0 is chosen as the identity matrix, we only use the geometric information, ignoring other source of information.

When choosing K_0 as the Gram matrix generated by Gaussian or linear kernel, we integrate the information of ambient space. When the manifold assumption does not hold or holds to a lesser degree, the incorporation of ambient space maybe yield a better solution. Being able to trade off the ambient space and manifold space may be important in practice.

The supervised information can be integrated by defining K_0 as the ideal kernel:

$$K_0 = yy^T, \tag{15}$$

where $y \in \mathbb{R}^n$ is a vector of $\{0, -1, +1\}$ labels, 0 means the data point is unlabeled. Ideal kernel indicates whether two given training points belong to the same class or not. Since the manifold regularization brings the geometric structure of the unlabeled data into the ideal kernel, the learnt geometry-aware kernel generalizes to unlabeled data.

4   Experiments

We perform experiments on clustering and classification tasks. We use the von Neumann divergence (Equation (10)) and choose various prior kernel matrix, leading to three algorithms: Manifold Regularized Gaussian Kernel (MR-Gaussian), Manifold Regularized Linear Kernel (MR-Linear) and Manifold Regularized Ideal Kernel (MR-Ideal). Comparisons are made with Diffusion Kernel (Equation (12)), Gaussian kernel κ_G and linear kernel κ_L:

$$\kappa_G(x, y) = \exp(-\|x - y\|^2/t), \tag{16}$$
$$\kappa_L(x, y) = \langle x, y \rangle, \tag{17}$$

where $t > 0$ is the width of Gaussian kernel.

4.1 Classification

We consider the transductive learning where the test data are available in advance before the classifier is learned. The classification experiments are designed using USPS dataset which contains 16×16 grayscale images of handwritten digits. We select challenging tasks where the digits are similar: 2 vs 3, and 5 vs 6. The first 400 images for each digit were taken to form the dataset. Training data are normalized to zero mean and unit variance. The same processing settings are applied to the test data. The parameter of Gaussian kernel is tuned via 2-fold cross validation. The trade-off γ in (10) is fixed to 10. We compute accuracy using 1-norm soft margin SVM classifier where the regularization parameter $C = 1$. The results are averaged over 20 runs.

The number of training data per digit is fixed to be 10 and the total number of each digit is changed within the set of $\{25, 50, 100, 200, 400\}$. We wish to see how the accuracies vary with the accurate and inaccurate manifolds. The averaged performance are tabulated in Table 1 and 2. The accuracies of Gaussian and linear kernels change tinily with different total number of data. Since these two kernels do not consider the geometric structure of the data, the incremental data have little influence to the performance. The Diffusion Kernel performs unstably. The performance of MR-Gaussian and MR-Linear are unsatisfactory with 25 data, but improved as more and more data are available. So do the MR-Ideal. This is in accord with our conjecture. When the total number of data is very limited, the recovered manifold is inaccurate. Thus, the kernel with this inaccurate information yields worse performance. But once the data are enough to reconstruct the manifold, our algorithms give higher accuracies.

Table 1. Accuracy (%) of 2 vs 3 task (#training=10). The best results are highlighted.

# data	Gaussian	Linear	Diffusion	MR-Gaussian	MR-Linear	MR-Ideal
25	91.33±5.23	**92.50±4.70**	91.17±4.36	79.83±11.67	82.17±15.72	90.17±5.67
50	90.06±3.88	**91.06±2.99**	89.69±5.97	84.81±9.66	87.50±6.80	88.38±7.49
100	89.31±6.64	91.31±3.07	90.25±7.95	90.08±5.47	**93.97±3.29**	91.00±5.89
200	88.30±6.63	90.84±2.69	91.37±9.53	94.49±2.19	**95.96±1.88**	95.04±3.30
400	88.74±5.67	90.90±2.80	82.45±16.01	96.07±0.68	**97.04±1.08**	96.56±0.85

Table 2. Accuracy (%) of 5 vs 6 task (#training=10). The best results are highlighted.

# data	Gaussian	Linear	Diffusion	MR-Gaussian	MR-Linear	MR-Ideal
25	88.00±8.19	92.83±4.22	89.67±9.48	74.50±10.56	78.17±12.26	**94.67±6.70**
50	87.94±11.65	93.44±4.37	91.88±6.63	88.06±10.61	**95.75±3.57**	95.13±5.21
100	89.14±9.79	94.08±2.91	90.64±11.64	92.14±7.38	**97.39±1.71**	96.28±4.80
200	91.01±4.16	93.92±2.98	84.87±13.47	93.59±10.92	**98.63±0.69**	95.25±9.57
400	90.86±4.36	93.47±2.86	76.14±13.51	97.82±2.18	**98.94±0.70**	98.09±1.06

4.2   Clustering

The MNIST dataset is used for clustering. This dataset contains 28×28 grayscale images of handwritten digits. We also take the first 400 images for each digit to form the dataset. The data are normalized to zero mean and unit variance. The parameter of Gaussian kernel is fixed to 10^4. The trade-off γ in (10) is also fixed to 10. We use the kernel k-means algorithm and evaluate the performance by computing Normalized Mutual Information (NMI) and clustering accuracy. For two random variable A and B, the NMI is defined as:

$$\text{NMI} = \frac{I(A, B)}{\sqrt{H(A)H(B)}}, \tag{18}$$

where $I(A, B)$ is the mutual information between the random variables A and B, $H(A)$ is the Shannon entropy of A. High NMI value indicates that the cluster and true labels match well. The clustering accuracy is defined as:

$$\text{Accuracy} = \frac{\sum_{i=1}^{n} \delta(y_i, map(c_i))}{n}, \tag{19}$$

where n is the number of data, y_i denotes the true label and c_i denotes the corresponding cluster label, $\delta(y, c)$ is a function that equals 1 if $y = c$ and equals 0 otherwise. map($\cdot$) is a permutation function that maps each cluster label to a true label. This optimal matching can be found with the Hungarian algorithm. We run kernel k-means on the dataset 10 times with random initialization, then average the NMI and Accuracy values.

The experiment is designed to investigate the impact of the number of manifold on the performance. Since each digit can be viewed as a submanifold in the input space, we vary the number of digits within the set of $\{2, 3, \cdots, 10\}$. We firstly adopt digits 1 and 2 for evaluation, then add another digit one by one. The results are shown in Figure 1. As the number of digits increases, the performance of all algorithms tend to degenerate, because the mixture of manifolds complicates the problem. Our MR-Gaussian outperforms other two algorithms in almost all cases, except for one situation. This demonstrates that the incorporation of manifold structure provides advantages in clustering.

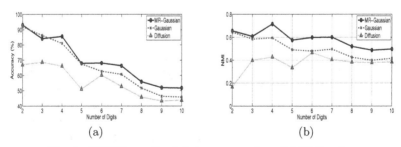

(a)   (b)

Fig. 1. MNIST results. (a) Accuracy values (b) NMI values.

5   Conclusions

We present a regularization framework for learning geometry-aware kernels. Our framework includes some existing geometry-aware kernels. Furthermore, we develop new geometry-aware kernels by integrating other source of information. In future research, we will study how to incorporate more sources of information into our framework by defining more flexible regularization term.

Acknowledgement. This work is partially supported by Natural Science Foundation of SZU (grant no. 00035693), NSF of China (61272252) and Science & Technology Planning Project of Shenzhen City (JC201105130447A).

References

1. Kondor, R.I., Lafferty, J.: Diffusion kernels on graphs and other discrete input spaces. In: Proceedings of the 19th Annual International Conference on Machine Learning, pp. 315–322 (2002)
2. Smola, A.J., Kondor, R.: Kernels and regularization on graphs. In: Schölkopf, B., Warmuth, M.K. (eds.) COLT/Kernel 2003. LNCS (LNAI), vol. 2777, pp. 144–158. Springer, Heidelberg (2003)
3. Ham, J., Lee, D., Mika, S., Schölkopf, B.: A kernel view of the dimensionality reduction of manifolds. In: Proceedings of the 21st Annual International Conference on Machine Learning, pp. 47–54 (2004)
4. Weinberger, K., Sha, F., Saul, L.: Learning a kernel matrix for nonlinear dimensionality reduction. In: Proceedings of the 21st Annual International Conference on Machine Learning, pp. 839–846 (2004)
5. Lawrence, N.D.: A unifying probabilistic perspective for spectral dimensionality reduction: Insights and new models. The Journal of Machine Learning Research 12, 1609–1638 (2012)
6. Sindhwani, V., Niyogi, P., Belkin, M.: Beyond the point cloud: from transductive to semi-supervised learning. In: Proceedings of the 22nd International Conference on Machine Learning, pp. 824–831 (2005)
7. Song, L., Smola, A., Borgwardt, K., Gretton, A.: Colored maximum variance unfolding. Advances in Neural Information Processing Systems 20, 1385–1392 (2008)
8. Zhu, X., Kandola, J., Ghahramani, Z., Lafferty, J.: Nonparametric transforms of graph kernels for semi-supervised learning. Advances in Neural Information Processing Systems 17, 1641–1648 (2005)
9. Zhuang, J., Tsang, I., Hoi, S.: A family of simple non-parametric kernel learning algorithms. The Journal of Machine Learning Research 12, 1313–1347 (2011)
10. Belkin, M., Niyogi, P., Sindhwani, V.: Manifold regularization: A geometric framework for learning from labeled and unlabeled examples. The Journal of Machine Learning Research 7, 2399–2434 (2006)

Motion Trend Patterns for Action Modelling and Recognition

Thanh Phuong Nguyen, Antoine Manzanera, and Matthieu Garrigues

ENSTA-ParisTech, 828 Boulevard des Maréchaux, 91762 Palaiseau CEDEX, France
{thanh-phuong.nguyen,antoine.manzanera,
matthieu.garrigues}@ensta-paristech.fr

Abstract. A new method for action modelling is proposed, which combines the trajectory beam obtained by semi-dense point tracking and a local binary trend description inspired from the Local Binary Patterns (LBP). The semi dense trajectory approach represents a good trade-off between reliability and density of the motion field, whereas the LBP component allows to capture relevant elementary motion elements along each trajectory, which are encoded into mixed descriptors called Motion Trend Patterns (MTP). The combination of those two fast operators allows a real-time, on line computation of the action descriptors, composed of space-time blockwise histograms of MTP values, which are classified using a fast SVM classifier. An encoding scheme is proposed and compared with the state-of-the-art through an evaluation performed on two academic action video datasets.

Keywords: Action Recognition, Semi dense Trajectory field, Local Binary Pattern, Bag of Features.

1 Introduction

Action recognition has become a very important topic in computer vision in recent years, due to its applicative potential in many domains, like video surveillance, human computer interaction, or video indexing. In spite of many proposed methods exhibiting good results on academic databases, action recognition in real-time and real conditions is still a big challenge. Previous works cannot be evoked extensively, we refer to [1] for a comprehensive survey. In the following, we will concentrate on the two classes of method most related to our work: trajectory based modelling, and dynamic texture methods.

An important approach for action representation is to extract features from point trajectories of moving objects. It has been considered for a long time as an efficient feature to represent action. Johansson [2] showed that human subjects can perceive a structured action such as walking from points of light attached to the walker's body. Messing et al. [3], inspired by human psychovisual performance, extracted features from the velocity histories of keypoints using KLT tracker. Sun et al. [4] used trajectories of SIFT points and encoded motion in three levels of context information: point level, intra-trajectory context and

R. Wilson et al. (Eds.): CAIP 2013, Part I, LNCS 8047, pp. 360–367, 2013.

inter-trajectory context. Wu et al. [5] used a dense trajectory field obtained by tracking densely sampled particles driven by optical flow. They decomposed the trajectories into camera-induced and object-induced components using low rank optimisation. Then a set of global measures coming from the theory of chaotic dynamical systems are used to describe the action. Wang et al. [6] also used a dense trajectory field. They encoded the action information using histograms of the differential motion vectors computed along the boundary of the moving objects. Those works have shown the benefits of using dense motion features with respect to the sparse approaches, when using histogram based action descriptors.

On the other hand, the LBP representation [7] was introduced for texture classification. It captures local image structure thanks to a binary sequence obtained by comparing values between neighbouring pixels. Due to its nice properties in terms of contrast invariance and computation time, LBP is very attractive for many applications, including action recognition. Zhao and Pietikäinen proposed an extension (LBP-TOP) [8] to dynamic texture by computing LBP on Three Orthogonal Planes (TOP), that was used by Kellokumpu et al. [9] in 3d spacetime to represent human movement. In another approach [10], they used classical LBP on temporal templates (MEI and MHI, 2d images whose appearance is related to motion information). In these methods, the action is modelled using Hidden Markov Model to represent the dynamics of the LBPs. Recently, Yeffet and Wolf proposed LTP (Local Trinary Patterns) [11] that combines the effective description of LBP with the flexibility and appearance invariance of patch matching methods. They capture the motion effect on the local structure of self-similarities considering 3 neighbourhood circles at different instants. Kliper-Gross et al. extended this idea to Motion Interchange Patterns [12], which encodes local changes in different motion directions.

In this paper, we present a novel representation of human actions based on elementary motion elements called Motion Trend Patterns (MTP), that capture local trends along trajectories obtained by semi-dense point tracking. It combines the effective properties of the two previously presented techniques. The semi dense point tracking allows to obtain a large number of trajectories with a much smaller computational cost than fully dense tracking. We encode local direction changes along each trajectory using an LBP based representation. The combination of these approaches allows a real-time, on-line computation of action descriptors. The remaining of the paper is organised as follows: Section 2 summarises the computation of semi-dense trajectories. Section 3 details our elementary motion element, the MTP descriptor. Section 4 introduces the action modelling and its application to recognition. The last sections are dedicated to experiments, evaluation and discussion.

2   Semi Dense Beam of Trajectories

Trajectories are compact and rich information source to represent activity in video. Generally, to obtain reliable trajectories, the spatial information is dramatically reduced to a small number of keypoints, and then it may be hazardous to compute statistics on the set of trajectories. In this work we use the semi dense point tracking method [13] which is a trade-off between long term tracking and dense optical flow, and allows the tracking of a high number of weak keypoints in a video in real-time, thanks to its high level of parallelism. Using GPU implementation, this method can handle 10 000 points per frame at 55 frames/s on 640 × 480 videos. In addition, it is robust to sudden camera motion changes thanks to a dominant acceleration estimation. Figure 1 shows several actions represented by their corresponding beams of trajectories.

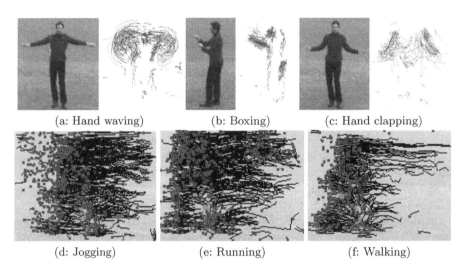

|(a: Hand waving)|(b: Boxing)|(c: Hand clapping)|

|(d: Jogging)|(e: Running)|(f: Walking)|

Fig. 1. Actions from the KTH dataset represented as beams of trajectories. For actions (d-f), only the most recent part of the trajectory is displayed.

3   Motion Trend Patterns

We describe hereafter our MTP descriptor for action modelling. The input of the MTP is the previously described beam of trajectories, and no appearance information is used. An MTP descriptor is produced for every frame and for every point which belongs to a trajectory. It has two components: the motion itself, represented by the quantised velocity vector, and the motion local trend, represented by polarities of local direction changes.

3.1   Encoding of Motion

Let $\overrightarrow{p_i}$ be the 2d displacement of the point between frames $i-1$ and i. The first part of the encoding is simply a dartboard quantisation of vector $\overrightarrow{p_i}$ (see Fig. 2). In our implementation, we used intervals of $\pi/6$ for the angles and 2 pixels for the norm (the last interval being $[6, +\infty[$), resulting in 12 bins for the angle, 4 bins for the norm.

3.2   Encoding of Motion Changes

Inspired by LBP, we encode elementary motion changes by comparing the motion vector $\vec{p_i}$ with its preceding and following velocities along the trajectory: $\{\overrightarrow{p_{i-1}}, \overrightarrow{p_{i+1}}\}$. Encoding the sign of the difference can be applied to the 2 components: (1) the norm, where it relates to tangential acceleration, and (2) the direction, where it relates to concavity and inflexion. The two can be encoded in a binary pattern. It turned out from our experiments that the use of the norm did not improve the results with respect to using the direction only, and then we only consider direction changes in MTP proposed hereafter.

Motion Trend Patterns (MTP): The local direction trend is encoded by the signs of the 2 differences between the direction $\angle \vec{p_i}$ and the directions of its 2 preceding and following motion vectors. This encoding corresponds to the local trend of the motion direction in terms of concavity and inflexion, as illustrated by Fig. 3, which shows the 4 possible configurations of MTP, for a fixed value of the quantised motion vector.

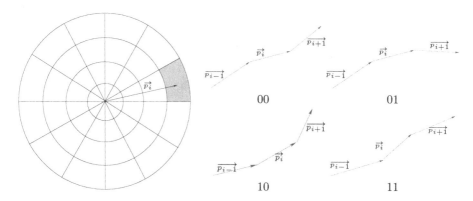

Fig. 2. Dartboard quantisa-tion of the motion vector

Fig. 3. Possible configurations of MTPs

3.3   Properties of Our Descriptor

Several good properties of our action descriptor can be pointed out:

– *Low computation cost.* It is based on the semi dense beam of trajectories whose computation is very fast [13]. Thanks to the low complexity of LBP-based operators, the calculation of MTPs is also very fast and then our system is suitable for action recognition in real-time.
– *Invariance to monotonic changes of direction.* It inherits from LBPs their invariance to monotonic changes, which in our case correspond to changes in the curvature of concavities and inflexions.
– *Robustness to appearance variation.* By design of the weak keypoints de-tection, which is normalised by the contrast, the descriptor must be robust against illumination change and should not depend much on the appearance of the moving objects.

4 Modelling and Recognition of Actions

Motion Words and Action Representation
The MTP descriptors represent elementary motion elements, or *motion words*. The number of different motion words is 48×2^2. Following hierarchical bag-of-features approach [14], we model an action by the space-time distribution of motion words: let B be the 3d space-time bounding box of the action. Histograms of MTPs are calculated in B and in sub-volumes of B, using regular pyramidal sub-grids, and the different histograms are concatenated as shown on Fig. 4. In our experiments we used 3 different sub-grids: $1 \times 1 \times 1$, $2 \times 2 \times 2$ and $4 \times 4 \times 4$, resulting in 73 histograms.

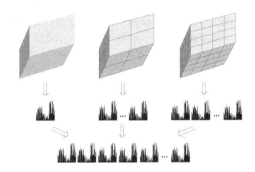

Fig. 4. Action modelling by concatenation of MTP histograms

Classification
To perform action classification, we choose the SVM classifier of Vedaldi et al. [15] which approximates a large scale support vector machines using an explicit feature map for the additive class of kernels. Generally, it is much faster than non linear SVMs and it can be used in large scale problems.

5 Experiments

We evaluate our descriptor on two well-known datasets. The first one (KTH) [16] is a classic dataset, used to evaluate many action recognition methods. The second one (UCF Youtube) [17] is a more realistic and challenging dataset.
Extraction of Semi-Dense Trajectories. We have studied the influence of the extraction of semi-dense trajectories on the performance of our model. We changed the parameters of the semi dense point tracker [13] to modify the number of trajectories obtained on the video. What we observe is that as long as the average matching error does not increase significantly, more we have trajectories, the better is the recognition rate. The improvement can be raised up to 5-6 % for KTH dataset. Table 1 shows the recognition rate obtained on this dataset, for different average number of tracked trajectories. In our experiments, the average number is set to 5 000 for a good result.

Table 1. Recognition rate on the KTH dataset in function of the number of trajectories

Mean number of trajectories per video	1 240	2 700	3 200	5 271	7 763
Recognition rate	87.5	88.33	90	**92.5**	90.83

Table 2. Confusion matrix on KTH dataset

	Box.	Clap.	Wave	Jog.	Run.	Walk.
Boxing	97.5	2.5	0	0	0	0
Clapping	7.5	92.5	0	0	0	0
Waving	0	2.5	97.5	0	0	0
Jogging	0	0	0	95.0	2.5	2.5
Running	0	0	0	12.5	82.5	5.0
Walking	0	0	0	10.0	0	90.0

Table 3. Comparison with other methods on KTH dataset

Method	Result	Method	Result
Our method	92.5	[11]	90.17
[18]	82.36	[12]	93.0
[19]	88.38	[9]	93.8
[10]	90.8	[17]	90.5
[6]	95.0		

Experiments on KTH Dataset. The KTH dataset contains 25 people for 6 actions (running, walking, jogging, boxing, hand clapping and hand waving) in 4 different scenarios (indoors, outdoors, outdoors with scale change and outdoors with different clothes). It contains 599 [1] videos, of which 399 are used for training, and the rest for testing. As designed by [16], the test set contains the actions of 9 people, and the training set corresponds to the 16 remaining persons.

Table 2 shows the confusion matrix obtained by our method on the KTH dataset. The ground truth is read row by row. The average recognition rate is 92.5 % which is comparable to the state-of-the-art, including LBP-based approaches (see Table 3). We recall that unlike [9,10], which works on segmented boxes, our results can be obtained on line on unsegmented videos, using a preprocessing step to circumscribe the interest motions in space-time bounding boxes. The main error factor comes from confusion between jogging and running, which is a typical problem in reported methods. Table 6 presents the recognition rates obtained separately by the different components of our method: motion only, MTP only and both components (motion words). Clearly, quantised motion provides more information than the MTP component, but combining these complementary components allows to improve by 2 % the recognition rate.

Experimentation on UCF Youtube Dataset. This dataset [17] contains 1 600 video sequences with 11 action categories. Each category is divided into 25 groups sharing common appearance properties (actors, background, or other). Following the experimental protocol proposed by the authors [17], we used 9 groups out of the 25 as test and the 16 remaining groups as training data. This dataset is much more challenging than KTH because of its large variability in terms of viewpoints, backgrounds and camera motions. Table 4 shows the confusion matrix obtained by our method; our mean recognition rate (65.63 %) is comparable to recent methods (see Table 5).

---

[1] It should contain 600 videos but one is missing.

Table 4. Confusion matrix on UCF. Ground truth (by row) and predicted (by column) labels are: basketball, biking, diving, golf swing, horse riding, soccer juggling, swing, tennis swing, trampoline jumping, volleyball spiking, walking with dog.

48.98	0	2.05	0	0	8.16	14.28	10.20	0	16.33	0
0	70.21	0	0	8.51	0	17.02	0	2.13	0	2.12
4.92	0	90.16	0	0	1.64	0	0	0	0	3.28
0	0	3.70	83.33	0	7.41	3.71	0	0	1.85	0
1.64	4.92	0	0	73.77	4.92	0	1.64	0	4.92	8.20
0	0	5.26	8.77	1.75	64.91	7.02	1.75	0	1.75	8.77
1.96	5.88	0	0	0	7.84	56.86	1.96	11.76	5.88	7.84
1.64	4.92	0	1.64	1.64	1.64	0	78.69	3.28	1.64	4.92
0	0	0	0	0	9.10	13.64	15.91	56.82	0	4.54
11.36	0	6.82	4.54	6.82	2.27	0	4.54	0	59.10	4.54
4.348	15.22	0	4.38	8.69	2.17	17.39	4.35	2.17	2.17	39.13

Table 5. Comparison on UCF Youtube

Our method	[20]	[21]	[17]	[22]
65.63		64	64	71.2	56.8

Table 6. Experimentation on KTH using different components

Motion	Motion changes	Motion words
90.42	84.58	92.5

6   Conclusions

We have presented a new action model based on semi dense trajectories and LBP-like encoding of motion trend. It allows to perform on line action recognition on unsegmented videos at low computational complexity.

For the future, we are interested in using other variants of LBP operator. A temporal multi-scale approach for MTP encoding will also be considered. Furthermore, we will address the effects of moving camera in the performance of our model, in order to deal with uncontrolled realistic videos.

Acknowledgement. This work is part of an ITEA2 project, and is supported by french Ministry of Economy (DGCIS).

References

1. Aggarwal, J., Ryoo, M.: Human activity analysis: A review. ACM Comput. Surv. 43, 16:1–16:43 (2011)
2. Johansson, G.: Visual perception of biological motion and a model for its analysis. Perception and Psychophysics 14, 201–211 (1973)
3. Messing, R., Pal, C., Kautz, H.A.: Activity recognition using the velocity histories of tracked keypoints. In: ICCV 2009, pp. 104–111 (2009)
4. Sun, J., Wu, X., Yan, S., Cheong, L.F., Chua, T.S., Li, J.: Hierarchical spatio-temporal context modeling for action recognition. In: CVPR, pp. 2004–2011 (2009)

5. Wu, S., Oreifej, O., Shah, M.: Action recognition in videos acquired by a moving camera using motion decomposition of lagrangian particle trajectories. In: ICCV, pp. 1419–1426 (2011)

6. Wang, H., Kläser, A., Schmid, C., Liu, C.L.: Action recognition by dense trajectories. In: CVPR, pp. 3169–3176 (2011)

7. Ojala, T., Pietikäinen, M., Mäenpää, T.: Multiresolution gray-scale and rotation invariant texture classification with local binary patterns. PAMI 24, 971–987 (2002)

8. Zhao, G., Pietikainen, M.: Dynamic texture recognition using local binary patterns with an application to facial expressions. PAMI 29, 915–928 (2007)

9. Kellokumpu, V., Zhao, G., Pietikäinen, M.: Human activity recognition using a dynamic texture based method. In: BMVC (2008)

10. Kellokumpu, V., Zhao, G., Pietikäinen, M.: Texture based description of movements for activity analysis. In: VISAPP (2), 206–213 (2008)

11. Yeffet, L., Wolf, L.: Local trinary patterns for human action recognition. In: ICCV, pp. 492–497 (2009)

12. Kliper-Gross, O., Gurovich, Y., Hassner, T., Wolf, L.: Motion interchange patterns for action recognition in unconstrained videos. In: Fitzgibbon, A., Lazebnik, S., Perona, P., Sato, Y., Schmid, C. (eds.) ECCV 2012, Part VI. LNCS, vol. 7577, pp. 256–269. Springer, Heidelberg (2012)

13. Garrigues, M., Manzanera, A.: Real time semi-dense point tracking. In: Campilho, A., Kamel, M. (eds.) ICIAR 2012, Part I. LNCS, vol. 7324, pp. 245–252. Springer, Heidelberg (2012)

14. Lazebnik, S., Schmid, C., Ponce, J.: Beyond bags of features: Spatial pyramid matching for recognizing natural scene categories. In: CVPR, pp. 2169–2178 (2006)

15. Vedaldi, A., Zisserman, A.: Efficient additive kernels via explicit feature maps. PAMI 34, 480–492 (2012)

16. Schuldt, C., Laptev, I., Caputo, B.: Recognizing Human Actions: A Local SVM Approach. In: ICPR, pp. 32–36 (2004)

17. Liu, J., Luo, J., Shah, M.: Recognizing realistic actions from video "in the wild". In: CVPR, pp. 1996–2003 (2009)

18. Tabia, H., Gouiffès, M., Lacassagne, L.: Motion histogram quantification for human action recognition. In: ICPR, pp. 2404–2407 (2012)

19. Mattivi, R., Shao, L.: Human action recognition using lbp-top as sparse spatio-temporal feature descriptor. In: Jiang, X., Petkov, N. (eds.) CAIP 2009. LNCS, vol. 5702, pp. 740–747. Springer, Heidelberg (2009)

20. Lu, Z., Peng, Y., Ip, H.H.S.: Spectral learning of latent semantics for action recognition. In: ICCV, pp. 1503–1510 (2011)

21. Bregonzio, M., Li, J., Gong, S., Xiang, T.: Discriminative topics modelling for action feature selection and recognition. In: BMVC, pp. 1–11 (2010)

22. Wang, S., Yang, Y., Ma, Z., Li, X., Pang, C., Hauptmann, A.G.: Action recognition by exploring data distribution and feature correlation. In: CVPR, pp. 1370–1377 (2012)

On Achieving Near-Optimal "Anti-Bayesian" Order Statistics-Based Classification for Asymmetric Exponential Distributions

Anu Thomas and B. John Oommen*

School of Computer Science, Carleton University, Ottawa, Canada : K1S 5B6

Abstract. This paper considers the use of Order Statistics (OS) in the theory of Pattern Recognition (PR). The pioneering work on using OS for classification was presented in [1] for the Uniform distribution, where it was shown that optimal PR can be achieved in a counter-intuitive manner, diametrically opposed to the Bayesian paradigm, i.e., by comparing the testing sample to a few samples *distant from the mean* - which is distinct from the optimal Bayesian paradigm. In [2], we showed that the results could be extended for a few *symmetric* distributions within the exponential family. In this paper, we attempt to extend these results significantly by considering asymmetric distributions within the exponential family, for some of which even the closed form expressions of the cumulative distribution functions are not available. These distributions include the Rayleigh, Gamma and certain Beta distributions. As in [1] and [2], the new scheme, referred to as Classification by Moments of Order Statistics (CMOS), attains an accuracy very close to the optimal Bayes' bound, as has been shown both theoretically and by rigorous experimental testing.

Keywords: Classification using Order Statistics (OS), Moments of OS.

1 Introduction

Class conditional distributions have numerous indicators such as their means, variances etc., and these indices have, traditionally, played a prominent role in achieving pattern classification, and in designing the corresponding training and testing algorithms. It is also well known that a distribution has many other characterizing indicators, for example, those related to its Order Statistics (OS). The interesting point about these indicators is that some of them are quite unrelated to the traditional moments themselves, and in spite of this, have not been used in achieving PR. The amazing fact, demonstrated in [3] is that OS can be used in PR, and that such classifiers operate in a completely "anti-Bayesian" manner, i.e., by only considering *certain* outliers of the distribution.

---

* *Chancellor's Professor* ; *Fellow: IEEE* and *Fellow: IAPR*. This author is also an *Adjunct Professor* with the University of Agder in Grimstad, Norway. The work of this author was partially supported by NSERC, the Natural Sciences and Engineering Research Council of Canada.

R. Wilson et al. (Eds.): CAIP 2013, Part I, LNCS 8047, pp. 368–376, 2013.

Earlier, in [1] and [2], we showed that we could obtain optimal results by an "anti-Bayesian" paradigm by using the OS. Interestingly enough, the novel methodology that we propose, referred to as Classification by Moments of Order Statistics (CMOS), is computationally not any more complex than working with the Bayesian paradigm itself. This was done in [1] for the Uniform distribution and in [2] for certain distributions within the exponential family. In this paper, we attempt to extend these results significantly by considering asymmetric distributions within the exponential family, for some of which even the closed form expressions of the cumulative distribution functions are not available. Examples of these distributions are the Rayleigh, Gamma and certain Beta distributions. Again, as in [1] and [2], we show the completely counter-intuitive result that by working with a *very few* (sometimes as small as two) points *distant* from the mean, one can obtain remarkable classification accuracies, and this has been demonstrated both theoretically and by experimental verification.

2   Optimal OS-Based Classification: The Generic Classifier

Let us assume that we are dealing with the 2-class problem with classes ω_1 and ω_2, where their class-conditional densities are $f_1(x)$ and $f_2(x)$ respectively (i.e, their corresponding distributions are $F_1(x)$ and $F_2(x)$ respectively)[1]. Let ν_1 and ν_2 be the corresponding *medians* of the distributions. Then, classification based on ν_1 and ν_2 would be the strategy that classifies samples based on a *single* OS. We can see that for all symmetric distributions, this classification accuracy attains the Bayes' accuracy.

This result is not too astonishing because the median is centrally located close to (if not exactly) on the mean. The result for higher order OS is actually far more intriguing because the higher order OS are not located centrally (close to the means), but rather distant from the means. In [2], we have shown that for a large number of distributions, mostly from the exponential family, the classification based on *these* OS again attains the Bayes' bound. These results are now extended for asymmetric exponential distributions.

3   The Rayleigh Distribution

The pdf of the Rayleigh distribution, whose applications are found in [4], with parameter $\sigma > 0$ is $\varphi(x, \sigma) = \frac{x}{\sigma^2} e^{-x^2/2\sigma^2}, x \geq 0$ and the cumulative distribution function is $\Phi(x) = 1 - e^{-x^2/2\sigma^2}, x \geq 0$. The mean, the variance and the median of the Rayleigh distribution are $\sigma\sqrt{\frac{\pi}{2}}, \frac{4-\pi}{2}\sigma^2$ and $\sigma\sqrt{ln(4)}$, respectively.
Theoretical Analysis: Rayleigh Distribution - 2-OS. The typical PR problem involving the Rayleigh distribution would consider two classes ω_1 and ω_2 where the class ω_2 is displaced by a quantity θ, and the values of σ are σ_1 and

---

[1] Throughout this section, we will assume that the a priori probabilities are equal.

σ_2 respectively. We consider the scenario when $\sigma_1 = \sigma_2 = \sigma$. Consider the distributions $f(x, \sigma) = \frac{x}{\sigma^2} e^{\frac{-x^2}{2\sigma^2}}$ and $f(x - \theta, \sigma) = \frac{x-\theta}{\sigma^2} e^{\frac{-(x-\theta)^2}{2\sigma^2}}$. In order to do the classification based on CMOS, we shall first derive the moments of the 2-OS for the Rayleigh distribution. The expected values of the first moments of the two OS can be obtained by determining the points where the cumulative distribution function attains the values of $\frac{1}{3}$ and $\frac{2}{3}$ respectively. Let u_1 be the point for the percentile $\frac{2}{3}$ of the first distribution, and u_2 be the point for the percentile $\frac{1}{3}$ of the second distribution. Then, $\int_0^{u_1} \frac{x}{\sigma^2} e^{-x^2/2\sigma^2} dx = \frac{2}{3} \implies u_1 = \sigma\sqrt{2 \ln(3)}$ and $u_2 = \theta + \sigma\sqrt{2\ln\left(\frac{3}{2}\right)}$.

Theorem 1. *For the 2-class problem in which the two class conditional distributions are Rayleigh and identical, the accuracy obtained by CMOS deviates from the optimal Bayes' bound as the solution of the transcendental equality* $\ln\left(\frac{x}{x-\theta}\right) = \frac{-\theta^2 + 2\theta x}{2\sigma^2}$ *deviates from* $\frac{\theta}{2} + \frac{\sigma}{\sqrt{2}}\left(\sqrt{\ln(3)} + \sqrt{\ln\left(\frac{3}{2}\right)}\right)$.

Proof. The proof of the theorem can be found in [4]. □

Remark: Another way of comparing the approaches is by obtaining the error difference created by the CMOS classifier when compared to the Bayesian classifier. The details of this can be found in [4].

Theorem 2. *For the 2-class problem in which the two class conditional distributions are Rayleigh and identical, the accuracy obtained by using 2-OS CMOS deviates from the classifier which discriminates based on the distance from the corresponding medians as* $\frac{\theta}{2} + \sigma\sqrt{\ln(4)}$ *deviates from* $\frac{\theta}{2} + \frac{\sigma}{\sqrt{2}}\left(\sqrt{\ln(3)} + \sqrt{\ln\left(\frac{3}{2}\right)}\right)$.

Proof. The proof is omitted here but can be seen in [4]. □

Experimental Results: Rayleigh Distribution - 2-OS. The CMOS classifier was rigorously tested for a number of experiments with various Rayleigh distributions having the identical parameter σ. In every case, the 2-OS CMOS gave almost the same classification as that of the Bayesian classifier. The method was executed 50 times with the 10-fold cross validation scheme. The test results are tabulated in Table 1. The results presented justify the claims of Theorems 1 and 2.

Table 1. A comparison of the accuracy of the Bayesian and the 2-OS CMOS classifier for the Rayleigh Distribution

θ	3	2.5	2	1.5	1
Bayesian	99.1	97.35	94.45	87.75	78.80
CMOS	99.1	97.35	94.40	87.70	78.65

Theoretical Analysis: Rayleigh Distribution - k-OS. We have seen from Theorem 1 that for the Rayleigh distribution, the moments of the 2-OS are sufficient for a near-optimal classification. As in the case of the other distributions, we shall now consider the scenario when we utilize other k-OS. Let u_1 be the point for the percentile $\frac{n+1-k}{n+1}$ of the first distribution, and u_2 be the point for the percentile $\frac{k}{n+1}$ of the second distribution. Then, $\int_0^{u_1} \frac{x}{\sigma^2} e^{-x^2/2\sigma^2} dx =$

$$\frac{n+1-k}{n+1} \implies u_1 = \sigma\sqrt{2 \ln\left(\frac{n+1}{k}\right)} \text{ and } u_2 = \theta + \sigma\sqrt{2 \ln\left(\frac{n+1}{n+1-k}\right)}.$$

Theorem 3. *For the 2-class problem in which the two class conditional distributions are Rayleigh and identical, a near-optimal Bayesian classification can be achieved by using symmetric pairs of the n-OS, i.e., the $n - k$ OS for w_1 and the k OS for w_2 if and only if $\sqrt{\ln\left(\frac{n+1}{k}\right)} - \sqrt{\ln\left(\frac{n+1}{n+1-k}\right)} < \frac{\theta}{\sigma\sqrt{2}}$. The classification obtained by CMOS deviates from the optimal Bayes' bound as the solution of the transcendental equality $\ln\left(\frac{x}{x-\theta}\right) = \frac{-\theta^2+2\theta x}{2\sigma^2}$ deviates from*

$$\frac{\theta}{2} + \frac{\sigma}{\sqrt{2}}\left[\sqrt{\ln\left(\frac{n+1}{k}\right)} + \sqrt{\ln\left(\frac{n+1}{n+1-k}\right)}\right].$$

Proof. The proof of this theorem is omitted here, but is included in [4]. □

Experimental Results: Rayleigh Distribution - k-OS. The CMOS method has been rigorously tested with different possibilities of the k-OS and for various values of n, and the test results are given in Table 2. The Bayesian approach provides an accuracy of 82.15%, and from the table, it is obvious that some of the considered k-OSs attains the optimal accuracy and the rest of the cases attain near-optimal accuracy. Also, we can see that the Dual CMOS has to be invoked if the condition stated in Theorem 3 is not satisfied.

Table 2. A comparison of the accuracy of the Bayesian(i.e., 82.15%) and the k-OS CMOS classifier for the Rayleigh Distribution by using the symmetric pairs of the OS for different values of n (where $\sigma = 2$ and $\theta = 1.5$)

No.	Order(n)	Moments	OS_1	OS_2	CMOS	CMOS/ Dual CMOS
1	Two	$\left(\frac{2}{3}, \frac{1}{3}\right)$	$\sigma\sqrt{\left(2 \ln\left(\frac{3}{1}\right)\right)}$	$\theta + \sigma\sqrt{\left(2 \ln\left(\frac{3}{2}\right)\right)}$	82.05	CMOS
2	Four	$\left(\frac{5-i}{5}, \frac{i}{5}\right), 1 \le i \le \frac{n}{2}$	$\sigma\sqrt{\left(2 \ln\left(\frac{5}{2}\right)\right)}$	$\theta + \sigma\sqrt{\left(2 \ln\left(\frac{5}{3}\right)\right)}$	82.0	CMOS
3	Six	$\left(\frac{7-i}{7}, \frac{i}{7}\right) 1 \le i \le \frac{n}{2}$	$\sigma\sqrt{\left(2 \ln\left(\frac{7}{1}\right)\right)}$	$\theta + \sigma\sqrt{\left(2 \ln\left(\frac{7}{6}\right)\right)}$	81.6	Dual CMOS
4	Eight	$\left(\frac{9-i}{9}, \frac{i}{9}\right), 1 \le i \le \frac{n}{2}$	$\sigma\sqrt{\left(2 \ln\left(\frac{9}{4}\right)\right)}$	$\theta + \sigma\sqrt{\left(2 \ln\left(\frac{9}{5}\right)\right)}$	82.15	CMOS

Details of when the original OS-based criteria and when the Dual criteria are used, are found in [4]. These are omitted here in the interest of space.

4 The Gamma Distribution

The Gamma distribution is a continuous probability distribution with two parameters - a, a shape parameter and b, a scale parameter. The pdf of the Gamma distribution is $\frac{1}{\Gamma(a)\,b^a}\,x^{a-1}e^{\frac{-x}{b}}$; $a > 0$, $b > 0$, with mean ab and variance ab^2 where a and b are the parameters. Unfortunately, the cumulative distribution function does not have a closed form expression [5,6,7].

Theoretical Analysis: Gamma Distribution. The typical PR problem invoking the Gamma distribution would consider two classes ω_1 and ω_2 where the class ω_2 is displaced by a quantity θ, and in the case analogous to the ones we have analyzed, the values of the scale and shape parameters are identical. We consider the scenario when $a_1 = a_2 = a$ and $b_1 = b_2 = b$. Thus, we consider the distributions: $f(x, 2, 1) = xe^{-x}$ and $f(x - \theta, 2, 1) = (x - \theta)e^{-(x-\theta)}$.

We first derive the moments of the 2-OS, which are the points of interest for CMOS, for the Gamma distribution. Let u_1 be the point for the percentile $\frac{2}{3}$ of the first distribution, and u_2 be the point for the percentile $\frac{1}{3}$ of the second distribution. Then, $\int_0^{u_1} x\,e^{-x}dx = \frac{2}{3} \implies ln(u_1) - 2u_1 = ln\left(\frac{1}{3}\right)$ and $ln(u_2 - \theta) - 2(u_2 - \theta) = ln\left(\frac{1}{3}\right) - ln(\theta)$. The following results hold for the Gamma distribution.

Theorem 4. *For the 2-class problem in which the two class conditional distributions are Gamma and identical, the accuracy obtained by CMOS deviates from the accuracy attained by the classifier with regard to the distance from the corresponding medians as* $1.7391 + \frac{\theta}{2}$ *deviates from* $1.6783 + \frac{\theta}{2}$.

Proof. The proof of this theorem can be found in [4].   □

Experimental Results: Gamma Distribution - 2-OS. The CMOS classifier was rigorously tested for a number of experiments with various Gamma distributions having the identical shape and scale parameters $a_1 = a_2 = 2$, and $b_1 = b_2 = 1$. In every case, the 2-OS CMOS gave almost the same classification as that of the classifier based on the central moments, namely, the mean and the median. The method was executed 50 times with the 10-fold cross validation scheme. The test results are tabulated in Table 3.

Table 3. A comparison of the accuracy with respect to the median and the 2-OS CMOS classifier for the Gamma Distribution

n	4.5	4.0	3.5	3.0	2.5	2.0	1.5
Median	94.83	94.25	92.74	90.77	86.51	80.15	72.64
CMOS	95.01	94.49	92.92	90.43	85.99	79.54	72.34

Theorem 5. *For the 2-class problem in which the two class conditional distributions are Gamma and identical, a near-optimal Bayesian classification can be achieved by using certain symmetric pairs of the n-OS, i.e., the $(n-k)^{th}$ OS for ω_1 (represented as u_1) and the kth OS for ω_2 (represented as u_2) if and only if $u_1 < u_2$.*

Proof. The proof of this theorem is included in [4].   □

Experimental Results: Gamma Distribution - k-OS. The CMOS method has been rigorously tested for numerous symmetric pairs of the k-OS and for various values of n, and a subset of the test results are given in Table 4. Experiments have been performed for different values of θ, and we can see that the CMOS attained near-optimal Bayes' bound. Also, we can see that the Dual CMOS has to be invoked if the condition stated in Theorem 5 is not satisfied.

Table 4. A comparison of the k-OS CMOS classifier when compared to the Bayes' classifier and the classifier with respect to median and mean for the Gamma Distribution for different values of n. In each column, the value which is near-optimal is rendered bold.

No.	Classifier	Moments	$\theta = 4.5$	4.0	3.5	3.0	2.5	2.0
1	Bayes	-	97.06	95.085	93.145	90.68	86.93	81.53
2	Mean	-	96.165	94.875	92.52	88.335	83.105	77.035
3	Median	-	90.04	93.57	92.735	90.775	86.275	80.115
4	2-OS	$\left(\frac{2}{5}, \frac{1}{5}\right)$	95.285	93.865	92.87	90.61	86.085	79.48
5	4-OS	$\left(\frac{4}{5}, \frac{1}{5}\right)$	95.905	94.605	93.11	89.57	84.68	22.125
6	4-OS	$\left(\frac{3}{5}, \frac{2}{5}\right)$	95.185	93.675	92.82	**90.855**	86.02	**80.32**
7	6-OS	$\left(\frac{5}{7}, \frac{1}{7}\right)$	96.405	**95.01**	92.125	88.005	17.29	23.565
8	6-OS	$\left(\frac{6}{7}, \frac{2}{7}\right)$	95.47	94.11	**93.135**	90.16	85.495	79.55
9	6-OS	$\left(\frac{4}{7}, \frac{3}{7}\right)$	95.135	93.625	92.78	90.745	**86.135**	80.165
10	8-OS	$\left(\frac{8}{9}, \frac{1}{9}\right)$	**96.815**	94.895	91.555	13.095	19.41	24.06
11	8-OS	$\left(\frac{7}{9}, \frac{2}{9}\right)$	95.8	94.445	93.11	89.885	84.81	78.535
12	8-OS	$\left(\frac{5}{9}, \frac{4}{9}\right)$	95.135	93.625	92.735	90.7	86.085	80.045

5   The Beta Distribution

The Beta distribution is a family of continuous probability distributions defined in $(0,1)$ parameterized by two shape parameters α and β. The distribution can take different shapes based on the specific values of the parameters. If the parameters are identical, the distribution is symmetric with respect to $\frac{1}{2}$. Further, if $\alpha = \beta = 1$, $B(1,1)$ becomes $U(0,1)$. The pdf of the Beta distribution is $f(x; \alpha, \beta) = \frac{\Gamma(\alpha+\beta)}{\Gamma(\alpha)\,\Gamma(\beta)}\, x^{\alpha-1}(1-x)^{\beta-1}$. The mean and the variance of the distribution are $\frac{\alpha}{\alpha+\beta}$ and $\frac{\alpha\beta}{(\alpha+\beta)^2\,(\alpha+\beta+1)}$ respectively. We consider the case when $\alpha = \beta > 1$. Earlier, in paper [3], when we first introduced the concept of CMOS-based PR, we had analyzed the 2-OS and k-OS CMOS for the Uniform distribution, and had provided the corresponding theoretical analysis and the experimental results. We had concluded that, for the 2-class problem in which the two class conditional distributions are Uniform and identical, CMOS can, indeed, attain the optimal Bayes' bound. So, in this paper, to avoid repetition, we skip the analysis for the Beta distribution, B(1,1), as this case reduces to the analysis for Uniform U(0,1). Thus, we reckon that the first of these cases (i.e., when $\alpha = 1$ and $\beta = 1$) as being closed. We also discussed the symmetric Beta distribution when the values of the shape parameters α and β are identical in [4]. In this paper, we now move on to the unimodal Beta distribution characterized by the shape parameters $\alpha > 1$ and $\beta > 1$, $\alpha \neq \beta$.

Theoretical Analysis: Beta Distribution $(\alpha > 1, \beta > 1)$ **- 2-OS.** Consider the two classes w_1 and w_2 where the class w_2 is displaced by a quantity θ. In this section, we consider the case when the shape parameters take the values $\alpha > 1$ and $\beta > 1$, and for the interest of preciseness[2], we consider the case when $\alpha = 2$ and $\beta = 5$. Then, the distributions are $f(x, 2, 5) = 30x(1 - x)^4$ and $f(x - \theta, 2, 5) = 30(x - \theta)(1 - x + \theta)^4$.

We first derive the moments of the 2-OS, namely o_1 and o_2 where o_1 represents the point for the percentile $\frac{2}{3}$ of the first distribution, and o_2 represents the point for the percentile $\frac{1}{3}$ of the second distribution. Then, $\int_0^{o_1} 30x(1 - x)^4 dx = \frac{2}{3}$ and $\int_0^{o_2} 30(x - \theta)(1 - x + \theta)^4 dx = \frac{1}{3}$.

These positions o_1 and o_2 can be obtained by making use of the built-in functions available in standard software packages as $o_1 = 0.34249$ and $o_2 = \theta + 0.1954$. Thus, our aim is to show that the classification based on these points can attain near optimal accuracies when compared to the accuracy obtained by the classifier with regard to the medians, the most central points of the distributions.

Theorem 6. *For the 2-class problem in which the two class conditional distributions are $Beta(\alpha, \beta)$ $(\alpha > 1, \beta > 1)$ and identical with $\alpha = 2$ and $\beta = 5$, the accuracy obtained by CMOS deviates from the accuracy attained by the classifier with regard to the distance from the corresponding medians as the areas under the error curves deviate from the positions $0.26445 + \frac{\theta}{2}$ and $0.2689 + \frac{\theta}{2}$.*

Proof. The proof of this theorem is omitted here, but can be found in [4].   □

Experimental Results: Beta Distribution $(\alpha > 1, \beta > 1)$ **- 2-OS.** The CMOS has been rigorously tested for various Beta distributions with 2-OS. For each of the experiments, we generated 1,000 points for the classes w_1 and w_2 characterized by $B(x, 2, 5)$ and $B(x - \theta, 2, 5)$ respectively. We then performed the classification based on the CMOS strategy and with regard to the medians of the distributions. In every case, CMOS was compared with the accuracy obtained with respect to the medians for different values of θ, as tabulated in Table 5. The results were obtained by executing each algorithm 50 times using a 10-fold cross-validation scheme. The quality of the classifier is obvious.

Table 5. A comparison of the accuracy of the 2-OS CMOS classifier with the classification with respect to the medians for the Beta Distribution for different values of θ

θ	0.4	0.45	0.5	0.55	0.6	0.65	0.7	0.75	0.8
Median	89.625	92.9	94.3	95.525	97.3	97.975	98.375	99.05	99.15
CMOS	89.475	92.775	94.525	95.75	97.3	98.05	98.375	99.2	99.225

---

[2] Any analysis will clearly have to involve specific values for α and β. The analyses for other values of α and β will follow the same arguments and are not included here.

Theoretical Analysis: Beta Distribution $(\alpha > 1, \beta > 1)$ **-** k**-OS.** We have seen in Theorem 6 that the 2-OS CMOS can attain a near-optimal classification when compared to the classification obtained with regard to the medians of the distributions. We shall now prove that the k-OS CMOS can also attain almost indistinguishable bounds for some symmetric pairs of the n-OS. The formal theorem, proven in [4], follows.

Theorem 7. *For the 2-class problem in which the two class conditional distributions are* $Beta(\alpha, \beta)$ $(\alpha > 1, \beta > 1)$ *and identical with* $\alpha = 2$, $\beta = 5$, *a near-optimal classification can be achieved by using certain symmetric pairs of the* n*-OS, i.e., the* $(n-k)^{th}$ *OS for* ω_1 *(represented as* o_1*) and the* k^{th} *OS for* ω_2 *(represented as* o_2*) if and only if* $o_1 < o_2$*. If* $o_1 > o_2$*, the CMOS classifier uses the* Dual *condition, i.e., the* k *OS for* ω_1 *and the* $n-k$ *OS for* ω_2*.*

$\square$

Experimental Results: Beta Distribution $(\alpha > 1, \beta > 1)$ **-** k**-OS.** The CMOS method has been rigorously tested for certain symmetric pairs of the k-OS and for various values of n, and the test results are given in Table 6. From the table, we can see that CMOS attained a near-optimal Bayes' accuracy when $o_1 < o_2$. Also, we can see that the Dual CMOS has to be invoked if $o_1 > o_2$.

Table 6. A comparison of the k-OS CMOS classifier when compared to the classifier with respect to means and medians for the Beta Distribution for different values of n. The scenarios for the *Dual* condition are specified by "(D)".

No.	Classifier	Moments	$\theta = 0.35$	0.45	0.55	0.65	0.75	0.85
1	Mean	-	85.325	92.575	96.55	98.3	99.4	99.475
2	Median	-	86.675	92.775	95.525	97.975	99.05	99.275
3	2-OS	$\left(\frac{2}{3}, \frac{1}{3}\right)$	86.2	92.575	95.75	98.05	99.2	99.275
4	4-OS	$\left(\frac{4}{5}, \frac{1}{5}\right)$	85.375	92.525	96.225	98.225	99.325	99.475
5	4-OS	$\left(\frac{3}{5}, \frac{2}{5}\right)$	86.475	**92.775**	95.6	98.05	99.125	99.275
6	6-OS	$\left(\frac{6}{7}, \frac{1}{7}\right)$	85.2 (D)	92.425	**96.475**	**98.35**	99.45	99.625
7	6-OS	$\left(\frac{5}{7}, \frac{2}{7}\right)$	86.125	92.625	96.0	98.075	99.2	99.275
8	6-OS	$\left(\frac{4}{7}, \frac{3}{7}\right)$	86.55	**92.775**	95.525	97.975	99.125	**99.75**

6   Conclusions

In this paper, we have shown that optimal classification for symmetric distributions and near-optimal bound for asymmetric distributions can be attained by an "anti-Bayesian" approach, i.e., by working with a *very few* (sometimes as small as two) points *distant* from the mean. This scheme, referred to as CMOS, Classification by Moments of Order Statistics, operates by using these points determined by the *Order Statistics* of the distributions. In this paper, we have proven the claim for some distributions within the exponential family, and the theoretical results have been verified by rigorous experimental testing. Our results for classification using the OS are both pioneering and novel.

References

1. Thomas, A., Oommen, B.J.: Optimal "Anti-Bayesian" Parametric Pattern Classification Using Order Statistics Criteria. In: Alvarez, L., Mejail, M., Gomez, L., Jacobo, J. (eds.) CIARP 2012. LNCS, vol. 7441, pp. 1–13. Springer, Heidelberg (2012)

2. Thomas, A., Oommen, B.J.: Optimal "Anti-Bayesian" Parametric Pattern Classification for the Exponential Family Using Order Statistics Criteria. In: Campilho, A., Kamel, M. (eds.) ICIAR 2012, Part I. LNCS, vol. 7324, pp. 11–18. Springer, Heidelberg (2012)

3. Thomas, A., Oommen, B.J.: The Fundamental Theory of Optimal "Anti-Bayesian" Parametric Pattern Classification Using Order Statistics Criteria. Pattern Recognition 46, 376–388 (2013)

4. Oommen, B.J., Thomas, A.: Optimal Order Statistics-based "Anti-Bayesian" Parametric Pattern Classification for the Exponential Family. Pattern Recognition (accepted for publication, 2013)

5. Krishnaih, P.R., Rizvi, M.H.: A Note on Moments of Gamma Order Statistics. Technometrics 9, 315–318 (1967)

6. Tadikamalla, P.R.: An Approximation to the Moments and the Percentiles of Gamma Order Statistics. Sankhya: The Indian Journal of Statistics 39, 372–381 (1977)

7. Young, D.H.: Moment Relations for Order Statistics of the Standardized Gamma Distribution and the Inverse Multinomial Distribution. Biometrika 58, 637–640 (1971)

Optimizing Feature Selection through Binary Charged System Search*

Douglas Rodrigues[1], Luis A.M. Pereira[1], Joao P. Papa[1], Caio C.O. Ramos[2], Andre N. Souza[3], and Luciene P. Papa[4]

[1] UNESP - Univ Estadual Paulista, Department of Computing, Bauru, Brazil
{markitovtr1,caioramos,lucienepapa}@gmail.com,
papa@fc.unesp.br
[2] UNESP - Univ Estadual Paulista, Depart. of Electrical Engineering, Bauru, Brazil
andrejau@feb.unesp.br
[3] University of São Paulo, Polytechnic School, São Paulo, Brazil
[4] Faculdade Sudoeste Paulista, Department of Health, Avaré, Brazil

Abstract. Feature selection aims to find the most important information from a given set of features. As this task can be seen as an optimization problem, the combinatorial growth of the possible solutions may be inviable for a exhaustive search. In this paper we propose a new nature-inspired feature selection technique based on the Charged System Search (CSS), which has never been applied to this context so far. The wrapper approach combines the power of exploration of CSS together with the speed of the Optimum-Path Forest classifier to find the set of features that maximizes the accuracy in a validating set. Experiments conducted in four public datasets have demonstrated the validity of the proposed approach can outperform some well-known swarm-based techniques.

Keywords: Feature Felection, Charged System Search, Evolutionary Optimization.

1 Introduction

Feature Selection is a challenging task which aims selecting a subset of features in a given dataset. Working only with relevant features can reduce the training time and improve the prediction performance of classifiers. A simple way to handle feature selection is performing an exhaustive search, if the dimensions (features) is not too large. However, this problem is known to be NP-hard and the computational load may become intractable [1].

Recently, several works have employed meta-heuristic algorithms based on biological behavior and physical systems to deal with feature selection as an optimization problem. In such context, Kennedy and Eberhart [2] proposed a binary version of the traditional Particle Swarm Optimization (PSO) algorithm in order to handle binary optimization problems. Further, Firpi and Goodman [3]

---

* The authors would like to thank FAPESP grants #2009/16206-1, #2011/14094-1 and #2012/14158-2, CAPES and also CNPq grant #303182/2011-3.

R. Wilson et al. (Eds.): CAIP 2013, Part I, LNCS 8047, pp. 377–384, 2013.

extended BPSO to the context of feature selection. Some years later, Rashedi et al. [4] proposed a binary version of the Gravitational Search Algorithm (GSA) called BGSA for feature selection, and Ramos et al. [5] presented their version of the Harmony Search (HS) for the same purpose in the context of theft detection in power distribution systems. Nakamura et al. [6] introduced their version of Bat Algorithm (BA) for binary optimization problems, called BBA.

Kaveh and Talatahari [7] proposed an optimization algorithm called Charged System Search (CSS), which is based on the interactions between electrically charged particles. The idea is that an electrical field of one particle generates an attracting or repelling force over other particles. This interaction is defined by physical principles such as Coulomb, Gauss and Newtonian laws. The authors have shown interesting results of CSS when compared with some well-known approaches, such as PSO and Genetic Algorithms.

In this paper, we propose a binary version of the Charged System Search for feature selection purposes called BCSS, in which the search space is modeled as a m-cube, where m stands for the number of features. The main idea is to associate for each charged particle a set of binary coordinates that denote whether a feature will belong to the final set of features or not, and the function to be maximized is the one given by a supervised classifier's accuracy. As the quality of the solution is related with the number of charged particles, we need to evaluate each one of them by training a classifier with the selected features encoded by the particles' quality and also to classify an evaluating set. Thus, we need a fast and robust classifier, since we have one instance of it for each charged particle. As such, we opted to use the Optimum-Path Forest (OPF) classifier [8,9], which has been demonstrated to be so effective as Support Vector Machines, but faster for training.

The proposed algorithm has been compared with Binary Bat Algorithm, Binary Gravitational Search Algorithm, Binary Harmony Search and the Binary Particle Swarm Optimization using several public datasets, being one of them related with non-technical losses detection in power distribution systems. The remainder of the paper is organized as follows. In Section 2 we revisit the Charged System Search approach and we present the proposed methodology for binary optimization using CSS. The methodology and the experimental results are discussed in Sections 3 and 4, respectively. Finally, conclusions are stated in Section 5.

2   Charged System Search

The governing Coulomb's law is a physics law used to describe the interactions between electrically charged particles. Let a charge be a solid sphere with radius r and uniform density volume. The attraction force F_{ij} between two spheres i and j with total charges q_i and q_j is defined by:

$$F_{ij} = \frac{k_e q_i q_j}{d_{ij}^2}, \tag{1}$$

where k_e is a constant called the Coulomb constant and d_{ij} is the distance between the charges.

Based on aforementioned definition, Kaveh and Talatahari [7] have proposed a new metaheuristic algorithm called Charged System Search (CSS). In this algorithm, each Charged Particle (CP) on system is affected by the electrical fields of the others, generating a resultant force over each CP, which is determined by using the electrostatics laws. The CP interaction movement is determined using Newtonian mechanics laws. Therefore, Kaveh and Talatahari [7] have sumarized CSS over the following definitions:

– Definition 1: The magnitude of charge q_i, with $i = 1, 2, ..., n$, is defined considering the quality of its solution, i.e. objective function value $fit(i)$:

$$q_i = \frac{fit(i) - fitworst}{fitbest - fitworst}, \tag{2}$$

where $fitbest$ and $fitworst$ denote, respectively, the so far best and the worst fitness of all particles. The distance d_{ij} between two CPs is given by the following equation:

$$d_{ij} = \frac{\|\boldsymbol{x}_i - \boldsymbol{x}_j\|}{\left\|\frac{\boldsymbol{x}_i - \boldsymbol{x}_j}{2} - \boldsymbol{x}_{best}\right\| + \epsilon}, \tag{3}$$

in which $\boldsymbol{x}_i$, $\boldsymbol{x}_j$ and $\boldsymbol{x}_{best}$ denote the positions of the ith, jth and the best current CP respectively, and ϵ is a small positive number to avoid singularities.

– Definition 2: The initial position $x_{ij}(0)$ and velocity $v_{ij}(0)$, for each jth variable of the ith CP, with $j = 1, 2, \ldots, m$, is given by:

$$x_{ij}(0) = x_{i,min} + \theta(x_{i,max} - x_{i,min}) \tag{4}$$

and

$$v_{ij}(0) = 0, \tag{5}$$

where $x_{i,max}$ and $x_{i,min}$ represents the upper and low bounds respectively, and $\theta \sim U(0, 1)$.

– Definition 3: For maximization problem, the probability of each CP moves toward others CPs is given as follow:

$$p_{ij} = \begin{cases} 1 \text{ if } \frac{fit(j) - fitworst}{fit(i) - fit(j)} > \theta \vee fit(i) > fit(j), \\ 0 \text{ otherwise} \end{cases} \tag{6}$$

– Definition 4: The value of the resultant force acting on a CP j is defined as:

$$r = 0.1 \max(x_{i,max} - x_{i,min}) \tag{7}$$

$$F_j = q_j \sum_{j, i \neq j} \left(\frac{q_i}{r^3} \cdot d_{ij} \cdot c_1 + \frac{q_i}{d_{ij}^2} \cdot c_2 \right) p_{ij}(\boldsymbol{x_i} - \boldsymbol{x_j}), \tag{8}$$

where $c_1 = 1$ and $c_2 = 0$ if $d_{ij} < r$, otherwise $c_1 = 0$ and $c_2 = 1$.
- *Definition 5*: The new position and velocity of each CP is given by

$$\boldsymbol{x}_j(t) = \theta_{j1} \cdot k_a \cdot F_j + \theta_{j2} \cdot k_v \cdot \boldsymbol{v}_j(t-1) + \boldsymbol{x}_j(t-1) \tag{9}$$

and

$$\boldsymbol{v}_j(t) = \boldsymbol{x}_j(t) - \boldsymbol{x}_j(t-1), \tag{10}$$

where $k_a = 0.5(1 + \frac{t}{T})$ and $k_v = 0.5(1 - \frac{t}{T})$ are the acceleration and the velocity coefficients respectively, being t the actual iterations and T the maximum number of iterations.
- *Definition 6*: A number of the best so far solutions is saved using a Charged Memory (CM). The worst solutions are excluded from CM, and better new ones are included to the CM.

2.1 BCSS: Binary Charged System Search

In this paper we propose the Binary Charged System Search (BCSS) for feature selection, in which each CP can change its position only to binary values. Therefore, we propose some modifications in the traditional CSS as follows:

- The Equation 4 is replaced for a function which initializes randomly each CP vector with binary values (0 or 1), where 0 stand for absence and 1 for presence of feature.
- In order to compute the distance between two binary CP vectors, we employ a Hamming distance function $\mathcal{H}(\cdot, \cdot)$. Thus the Equation 3 is changed to

$$d_{ij} = \frac{\mathcal{H}(\boldsymbol{x}_i, \boldsymbol{x}_j)}{\mathcal{H}((\boldsymbol{x}_i \& \boldsymbol{x}_j), \boldsymbol{x}_{best}) + \epsilon}, \tag{11}$$

where $\&$ performs the logical AND between two vectors.
- In the traditional CSS, Kaveh et al. [7] proposed use an HS-based algorithm to correct the position of a CP which surpass the upper or lower bounds. In case of the BCSS for feature selection, as the new solution should be always 0 or 1, we employ a sigmoid function in order to restrict the new solutions to only binary values:

$$S(x_{ij}) = \frac{1}{1 + e^{-x_{ij}}}. \tag{12}$$

$$x_{ij} = \begin{cases} 1 \text{ if } S(x_{ij}) > \theta, \\ 0 \text{ otherwise.} \end{cases} \tag{13}$$

Therefore, Equation 13 can provide only binary values for each CP coordinates. In addition the search space is modelled as a m-dimensional boolean lattice, where the CPs moves across the corners of a hypercube.

3   Methodology

Suppose we have a fully labeled dataset $\mathcal{Z} = \mathcal{Z}_1 \cup \mathcal{Z}_2 \cup \mathcal{Z}_3 \cup \mathcal{Z}_4$, in which $\mathcal{Z}_1$, $\mathcal{Z}_2$, $\mathcal{Z}_3$ and $\mathcal{Z}_4$ stand for training, learning, validating, and test sets, respectively. The idea is to employ $\mathcal{Z}_1$ and $\mathcal{Z}_2$ to find the subset of features that maximize the accuracy over $\mathcal{Z}_2$, being such accuracy the fitness function. Therefore, each agent (bat, CP, particle, etc.) is then initialized with random binary positions and the original dataset is mapped to a new one which contains the features that were selected in this first sampling. Further, the fitness function of each agent is set as the recognition rate of a classifier over $\mathcal{Z}_2$ after training in $\mathcal{Z}_1$. As soon as the agent changes its position, a new training in $\mathcal{Z}_1$ followed by classification in $\mathcal{Z}_2$ needs to be performed. As the reader can see, such formulation requires a fast training and classification steps. This is the reason why we have employed the Optimum-Path Forest (OPF) classifier [8,9], since it is a non-parametric and very robust classifier.

However, in order to allow a fair comparison, we have added a third set in the experiments called validating set ($\mathcal{Z}_3$): the idea is to establish a threshold that ranges from 10% to 90%, and for each value of this threshold we marked the features that were selected at least a minimum percentage of the runnings (10 times) over a learning process in $\mathcal{Z}_1$ and $\mathcal{Z}_2$, as aforementioned. For instance, a threshold of 40% means we choose the features that were selected at least 40% of the runnings. For each threshold, we computed the fitness function over the validation set $\mathcal{Z}_3$ to evaluate the generalization capability of the selected solution. Thus, the final subset will be the one that maximizes the curve over the range of values, i.e., the features that maximize the accuracy over $\mathcal{Z}_3$. Further, these selected features are then applied to assess the accuracy over $\mathcal{Z}_4$. Notice the fitness function employed in this paper is the accuracy measure proposed by Papa et al. [8], which is capable to handle unbalanced classes. Notice we used 30% of the original dataset for $\mathcal{Z}_1$, 20% for $\mathcal{Z}_2$, 20% for $\mathcal{Z}_3$, and 40% for $\mathcal{Z}_4$. These percentages have been empirically chosen.

4   Experimental Results

4.1   Dataset

In this work we have employed four datasets, in which three of them have been obtained from LibSVM repository[1], and NTL refers to a dataset obtained from a Brazilian electrical power company frequently used to detect thefts in power distributions systems. Table 1 presents all datasets and their main characteristics.

4.2   Experiments

In this section we discuss the experiments conducted in order to assess the robustness of BCSS against with BBA, BGSA, BHS (Binary Harmony Search) and

---

[1] http://www.csie.ntu.edu.tw/~cjlin/libsvmtools/datasets/

Table 1. Description of the datasets used in this work

Dataset	# samples	# features	# classes
Australian	690	14	2
Diabetes	768	8	2
NTL	3182	8	2
Vehicle	846	18	4

BPSO for feature selection. Table 2 presents the parameters employed for each evolutionary-based technique. Notice for all techniques we employed 30 agents with 100 iterations. These parameters have been empirically set.

Table 2. Parameters setting of metaheuristic algorithms

Technique	Parameters
BBA	$\alpha = 0.9$, $\gamma = 0.9$
BGSA	$G_0 = 100$
BHS	HMCR$= 0.9$
BPSO	$c_1 = 2.0$, $c_2 = 2.0$, w$= 0.7$

Figure 1a shows the OPF accuracy curve for Australian dataset, in which BBA, BCSS and BGSA achieve the maximum value of the fitness function equals to 87.20%, with a threshold equal, 40%, 80% and 70% respectively. Figure 1b displays the results for Diabetes dataset. We can see that BBA, BCSS, BGSA and BPSO have achieved the same effectiveness (around 61.5%), while BHS did not perform very well. Actually, although BHS has selected the same number of features, its accuracy over $\mathcal{Z}_4$ was about 2.32% less accurate than the others approaches, as we can see in Table 3, which displays the accuracy over $\mathcal{Z}_4$ and also the threshold over $\mathcal{Z}_3$ for all datasets.

Figures 2a and 2b display the curves over $\mathcal{Z}_3$ for Vehicle and NTL datasets, respectively. From Figure 2a we can see that the maximum accuracy over $\mathcal{Z}_3$ has been obtained by BHS with a threshold of 40%, and with respect to NTL dataset BBA and the proposed BCSS have achieved 95% with a threshold of 30%, while the remaining techniques needed a threshold of 50% to reach such accuracy.

Table 4 displays the mean execution times for all techniques. The fastest approach has been BHS, followed by BPSO and BGSA. Although the proposed technique has required a considerable computational effort, it is not so different than BBA and BGSA. From Table 3, we can see that BCSS has been the most accurate approach together with other techniques for Australian, Diabetes and NTL datasets, and has been the sole more effective approach for Vehicle dataset.

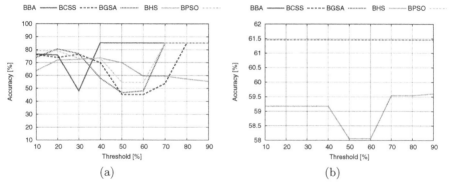

Fig. 1. OPF accuracy curve over $\mathcal{Z}_3$ for (a) Australian and (b) Diabetes datasets

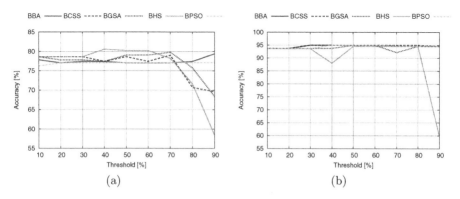

Fig. 2. OPF accuracy curve over $\mathcal{Z}_3$ for (a) Vehicle and (b) NTL datasets

Table 3. Classification accuracy over $\mathcal{Z}_4$ with the best subset of features selected over $\mathcal{Z}_3$

Dataset	BBA		BCSS		BGSA		BHS		BPSO	
	$\mathcal{Z}_3$	$\mathcal{Z}_4$	$\mathcal{Z}_3$	$\mathcal{Z}_4$	$\mathcal{Z}_3$	$\mathcal{Z}_4$	$\mathcal{Z}_3$	$\mathcal{Z}_4$	$\mathcal{Z}_3$	$\mathcal{Z}_4$
Australian	40.0%	**87.20%**	80.0%	**87.20%**	70.0%	**87.20%**	30.0%	66.85%	70.0%	**87.20%**
Diabetes	10.0%	**67.82%**	10.0%	**67.82%**	10.0%	**67.82%**	10.0%	65.50%	10.0%	**67.82%**
NTL	30.0%	**95.49%**	30.0%	**95.49%**	50.0%	94.55%	50.0%	89.33%	40.0%	**95.49%**
Vehicle	90.0%	77.09%	70.0%	**78.47%**	50.0%	76.44%	40.0%	77.92%	20.0%	76.90%

5   Conclusions

We have proposed a binary version of the well-known continuous-valued Charged System Search, which was derived in order to position the charged particles to binary coordinates.

We conducted experiments against several metaheuristic algorithms to show the robustness of the proposed technique and also its good generalization

Table 4. Mean computational load in seconds

Dataset	BBA	BCSS	BGSA	BHS	BPSO
Australian	115.9	119.3	115.1	5.13	98.40
Diabetes	137.03	139.7	135.0	5.95	136.6
NTL	2305.2	2337.4	2310.4	99.81	2223.7
Vehicle	184.0	186.9	181.0	7.98	182.0

capability. We have employed four datasets to accomplish this task, in which BCSS has been compared against BBA, BGSA, BPSO and BHS. The proposed algorithm has obtained the best results together with other techniques for three datasets, and has been the more effective approach for one dataset.

References

1. Guyon, I., Elisseeff, A.: An introduction to variable and feature selection. J. Mach. Learn. Res. 3, 1157–1182 (2003)
2. Kennedy, J., Eberhart, R.C.: A discrete binary version of the particle swarm algorithm. In: IEEE International Conference on Systems, Man, and Cybernetics, vol. 5, pp. 4104–4108 (1997)
3. Firpi, H.A., Goodman, E.: Swarmed feature selection. In: Proceedings of the 33rd Applied Imagery Pattern Recognition Workshop, pp. 112–118. IEEE Computer Society, Washington, DC (2004)
4. Rashedi, E., Nezamabadi-pour, H., Saryazdi, S.: BGSA: binary gravitational search algorithm. Natural Computing 9, 727–745 (2010)
5. Ramos, C., Souza, A., Chiachia, G., Falcão, A., Papa, J.: A novel algorithm for feature selection using harmony search and its application for non-technical losses detection. Computers & Electrical Engineering 37(6), 886–894 (2011)
6. Nakamura, R.Y.M., Pereira, L.A.M., Costa, K.A., Rodrigues, D., Papa, J.P., Yang, X.-S.: BBA: A binary bat algorithm for feature selection. In: Proceedings of the XXV SIBGRAPI - Conference on Graphics, Patterns and Images (2012) (accepted for publication)
7. Kaveh, A., Talatahari, S.: A novel heuristic optimization method: charged system search. Acta Mechanica 213(3), 267–289 (2010)
8. Papa, J.P., Falcão, A.X., Suzuki, C.T.N.: Supervised pattern classification based on optimum-path forest. International Journal of Imaging Systems and Technology 19(2), 120–131 (2009)
9. Papa, J.P., Falcão, A.X., Albuquerque, V.H.C., Tavares, J.M.R.S.: Efficient supervised optimum-path forest classification for large datasets. Pattern Recognition 45(1), 512–520 (2012)

Outlines of Objects Detection by Analogy

Asma Bellili[1], Slimane Larabi[1], and Neil M. Robertson[2]

[1] University of Sciences and Technology Houari Boumediene, Computer Science Department, BP 32 El Alia, Algiers, Algeria
slarabi@usthb.dz
[2] Edinburgh Research Partnership in Engineering and Mathematics, School of Engineering and Physical Sciences, Heriot-Watt University, Edinburgh, EH14 4AS, UK
n.m.robertson@hw.ac.uk

Abstract. In this paper we propose a new technique for outlines of objects detection. We exploit the set of contours computed using the image analogies principle. A set of artificial patterns are used to locate contours of any query image, each one permits the location of contours corresponding to a specific intensity variation. We studied these contours and a theoretical foundation is proposed to explain the slow motion of these contours around regions boundaries. Experiments are conducted and the obtained results are presented and discussed.

Keywords: Segmentation, Object outline, Analogy, Contour, Multi-Scale.

1 Introduction

Image segmentation is considered as an important task in many computer vision applications. It consist of partitioning an image into meaningful regions including objects. Despite that there are many image segmentation methods proposed in the literature [5], [16], this problem remains an active topic for two reasons: first, results of the proposed techniques are still far from what the human can achieve; second, segmentation is a critical step for many applications.

Image analogies constitutes a natural means of specifying filters and image transformations. Assuming that the transformation between two images A and A' is "learned", image analogies is defined as a method of creating an image filter which allows to recover by analogy from any given different image B the image B' in the same way as A' is related to A [6], [9]. Rather than selecting from among myriad different filters and their settings, a user can simply supply an appropriate exemplar (along with a corresponding unfiltered source image) and say, in effect, "Make it look like this". Ideally, image analogies should make it possible to learn very complex and non-linear image filters [9].

Image analogies has been largely used in many applications such as texture synthesis [2], curves synthesis [10], super resolution [8], image colorization, image enhancement and artistic filters [14], [15]. This new technique has been also used

R. Wilson et al. (Eds.): CAIP 2013, Part I, LNCS 8047, pp. 385–392, 2013.

in supervised medical image segmentation [11] consisting in finding by analogies the same colored regions in medical images as those processed by the expert.

Recent work has been published and concerns contour detection by image analogies which attempts to locate contours as humans do [12]. A set of training images (artificial patterns) are proposed, producing several images of contours, at varying intensity levels. Each one is obtained applying the corresponding pattern (see figures in Table 1).

We present in this paper what can be achieved with these contours for outlines of objects detection. We note that the motion of these contours from one pattern to another is implicitly related to regions boundaries, similar to those required for segmentation. A fast motion is present when the considered part of image does not contain objects or regions. However, this motion is slow and the contours are sometimes static around regions boundaries. We prove theoretically this property in this paper and it serves as the basis for a new approach to outlines of objects detection. In section 2 we present a review of the contour detection by image analogy [12]. We propose in section 3 a theoretical foundation of our method. Section 4 is devoted to the experiments conducted on different images.

Table 1. Illustrative contours located using a selection (four) of the 14 artificial patterns. Note the increase of intensity around the located contours from left to right.

2 Contour Detection Using Images Analogies: A Review [12]

The problem addressed in [12] is how to do for automatic location of contours on the query image I_B giving the result S_B in the same way as this is done for (I_A, S_A) where I_A is an initial image whose contours are manually located giving the synthesized image noted S_A (see figure 1).

Using the Image Analogy technique, each pixel q of I_B is classified (contour pixel or not) using the knowledge inferred from (I_A, S_A). The best match p^* of q is searched in I_A using the neighbourhoods $N(p)$, $N(q)$ of p and q. For this, p^* must verify the minimal value of the similarity measure $S_m(q, p)$ between $N(p)$, $N(q)$ pixels. A kernel $K(m \times m)$ is used in this measure in order to give high weight for pixels of four main directions (horizontal, vertical and two diagonals).

The main result is that if the training pair of images (I_A, S_A) and the query one I_B are taken from the same scene, the location of contour pixels of I_B is

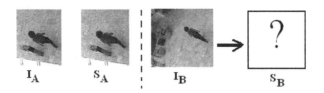

Fig. 1. Contour detection by analogy: the basic principle

done with success. However when I_B is from a different scene, the location of contour pixels cannot be done without the loss of many candidates. To locate all contour pixels, a set of constraints must be verified in the neighbours $N(p)$, $N(q)$. To avoid this, a set of pairs of artificial patterns (I_A, S_A) are proposed instead of hand drawn contours. The pattern I_A is composed by a shape with intensity F_A (Foreground) and a background with intensity G_A. The pattern S_A is the same as I_A, in addition, the contour is highlighted. The values of (G_A, F_A) are chosen so as for any query pixel q, the values of (G_B, F_B) representing the average of intensities of $N(q)$ regions verify the required constraints. The set of patterns $P_1, P_2, ..., P_{14}$ (see figure 2) are characterised by the values of G_A, F_A (background and foreground intensities):
$(0, 32)$, $(0, 64)$, $(0, 96)$, $(0, 128)$, $(0, 160)$, $(0, 192)$, $(0, 224)$, $(64, 192)$, $(64, 224)$, $(96, 224)$, $(128, 224)$, $(160, 224)$, $(192, 224)$, $(208, 240)$.

For each pattern (I_A, S_A) and for a query image I_B, only a set of contour pixels q will be localized such as the intensities of the neighbouring pixels in $N(q)$ verify a defined constraint related to (I_A, S_A) . We obtain then 14 images of contours corresponding to the 14 patterns (see figures in table 1).

Fig. 2. Artificial patterns (I_A, S_A)

3   Outlines of Objects Detection

The use of artificial patterns allows locating contours of any query image I_B and provides the images: $S_{B,1}, ..., S_{B,n}$ where n is the number of artificial patterns ($n = 14$). The computed contours are different from $S_{B,i}$ to $S_{B,i+1}$. Figures of table 2 illustrate the contours computed using the patterns P_3 and P_4. We note that inside of regions, contours are moving quickly from one pattern to another, and around region boundaries they are moving slowly or are steady.

First, we introduce the property of object boundaries, we prove it theoretically in the next. Finally, we describe our method for outlines of object detection based on this property.

Table 2. Contours located using the patterns P_3 and P_4

Property of Region's Boundary. *Contours extracted by image analogy are more stable at regions boundaries and are unstable for others parts of image.*
Proof.
We prove that if the contour is moving slowly, this implies that there is boundary defined as a gradual changing of intensity between neighbouring pixels. Let q be a contour pixel detected by the pattern P_i but not detected by the next one P_{i+1}, q' a contour pixel detected by the pattern P_{i+1} but not detected by the previous pattern P_i. Let G_{A^i}, F_{A^i} be the intensities of the two regions (background and foreground) of the pattern P_i.
If q is detected by the pattern P_i then the values G_B , F_B associated to $N(q)$ verify (see figure 3) [12]: $F_B \geq G_{B^i} + \delta l$ and $G_{A^i} < G_B \leq G_{B^i}$, where $G_{B^i} = (F_{A^i} + G_{A^i})/2$ and δl is the minimum intensity between two different regions.
   As P_i and P_{i+1} are successive patterns, this means that whether $((F_{A^i} = F_{A^{i+1}})$ and $(G_{A^{i+1}} = G_{A^i} + 2\delta l))$ or $((G_{A^i} = G_{A^{i+1}})$ and $(F_{A^{i+1}} = F_{A^i} - (2\delta l)))$. We consider in this proof that $(G_{A^i} = G_{A^{i+1}})$, the same reasoning is also valid for other cases. If q is not detected using the pattern P_{i+1}, then F_B is necessarily lower than $G_B^{i+1} + \delta l$ where $G_{B^{i+1}} = (G_{A^{i+1}} + F_{A^{i+1}})/2)$, otherwise it will be detected by the pattern P_{i+1}. The belonging interval of F_B is then: $[G_{B^i} + \delta l, G_{B^{i+1}} + \delta l]$ (see figure 3). We assume that q is located as a contour pixel using the pattern P_i, and let q' be the neighbouring to p where G'_B, F'_B are the averages of intensities associated to $N(q')$. Now if we assume that q' is located by the pattern P_{i+1} and not detected by the pattern P_i, this means that the contour is steady (or moving slowly). We get from the previous result: $G_{B^i} + \delta l < F_B < G_{B^i} + 2\delta l$ and $G_{B^{i+1}} + \delta l < F'_B$. This is possible if $F'_B \geq G_{B^i} + 2\delta l$ and $G_{B^{i+1}} > G'_B > G_{B,i}$.
   Let $dist = 1$ be the distance between the two pixels q and q' (see figure 4). Without loss of generality, we can write: $G'_B = (5 \times F_B + 5 \times G_B)/10$ and $F'_B = (10 * F_B + 5 * F''_B)/15$ such as F''_B is the average intensity of neighboring pixels to $N(q)$ and $m = 5$ is the size of the neighborhoods $N(p), N(q)$.
   As $F'_B \geq G_{B^i} + 2\delta l$ and $G'_B < G_{B^{i+1}}$. The analysis of these relations gives the condition : $F''_B > 3G_{B^i} - 2F_{B^i} + 6\delta l$. However, as $F_B < G_{B^{i+1}} + \delta l$, $N(q')$ must then verify: $F''_B > G_{B^{i+1}} + \delta l$. Also, as $G'_B = (F_B + G_B)/2$, and $G_{B^{i+1}} + \delta l \geq F_B \geq G_{B^{i+1}}$, then $G_{B^i} \leq G_B < G_{B^{i+1}}$. Then, to locate q' as a contour pixel, a minimal difference of luminance intensity between F_B and F''_B in $N(q')$ equal to δl

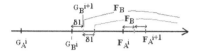

Fig. 3. Possible values of F_B in case where q is detected using only by one pattern

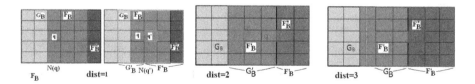

Fig. 4. Example of contour motion with $dist = 1, 2, 3$, $N(q)$, $N(q')$ are illustrated in red and green colors

must be verified. We note also the presence of a graduate changing of luminance intensities between G_B, G'_B, F'_B and F''_B. For the case $dist = 2$ and applying the same reasoning (see figure 4), we obtain: $G'_B = F_B$ and $F'_B = (5F_B + 10F''_B)/15$. As $F'_B \geq G_{B^i} + 2\delta l$ and $G_{B^{i+1}} > G'_B > G^i_B$, we get : $(2F''_B + F_B)/3 \geq G_{B^i} + 2\delta l$. This implies that: $2F''_B \geq 3G_{B^i} + 6\delta l - F_B$, we get : $F''_B \geq G_{B^{i+1}} + \delta l$ thus: $F''_B \geq G'_B + \delta l$. When $dist = 3$ (see figure 4), we have: $G'_B = F_B$ and $F'_B = F''_B$. As $F'_B \geq G_{B^i} + 2\delta l$, we get the same relation: $F''_B \geq G'_B + \delta l$. Otherwise, if q' isn't detected by the pattern P_{i+1}, this means that there is no intensity variation in the neighbourhood of q.

3.1 Outline of Objects Detection: The Algorithm

We define the *energy* of contour as the number of times it is located using successive patterns with slow motion. We proved in previous subsection that when a contour is moving slowly and then with high energy, this means that it corresponds to object outline (border).

4 Results

We present in this section results obtained by applying our method to real images of BSD [4]. Firstly, we illustrate in table 3 the evolution of the contour located using artificial patterns. We can see that the located contour using P_7, P_8, P_9 is steady around object boundary except the central left part where the contour is moving fast (3 pixels from one pattern to another). For the patterns P_{10}, P_{11}, P_{12}, contours are moving fast from one pattern to other due to the absence of object boundary.

We applied our method using different values of energy defined as the number of times where the contours is steady or with slow motion. The increasing of energy value allows producing most significant contours corresponding to high

---

Algorithm 1. Object Outlines Detection

Extract Contours C_j^i using all patterns P_i
for Each successive patterns P_i, P_{i+1} **do**
    for Each contour C_j^i **do**
        Find the contour C_k^{i+1} neighbouring to C_j^i with $(dist < 3)$, $energy(C_k^{i+1}) + +$
    end for
end for
Select contours of given energy

Table 3. Contour's evolution using the patterns $P_7, P_8, P_9, P_{10}, P_{11}$

difference of intensities of related regions. Figures of table 4 illustrate the results obtained for energy equal to 3 and 4.

To measure the quality of outlines located, we used the ratios - precision, recall computed using the numbers of pixels found in the automatic contours vs the correct (hand-drawn) ones. For the data set BSD500 [4], for each image, five hand drawn contours are available as ground truth.

Depending of the used energy, which is synonymous to resolution level, the Precision and Recall have different values. More the energy increases, more precision increases because only the pixels contours corresponding to high difference of intensity are located and then the number of false candidates decreases. However, the recall decreases because the number of located outline pixels decreases. Figure 5 illustrates the values of Precision/Recall for Energy=1. These results

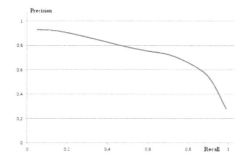

Fig. 5. Precision-Recall values for BSD dataset when Energy=1

Table 4. (*Left to right*): original image, located outlines with energy equal to 3 and 4

are similar to those of Arbelaez et al [4]. For high Recall values, our Precision is better and the difference reaches 20%. However for low Recall values, our Precision values are near from the values of Arbelaez et al [4], the difference is around 3%.

5   Conclusion and Future Work

We proposed in this paper a new technique for Object Outlines Detection based on image analogy. In the first part, we presented a review of contour detection by image analogy technique and then we gave a theoretical explanation of the steady contour motion corresponding to boundary object. The proposed algorithm has been applied to Weizmann and BSD datasets and the obtained results are presented. The obtained results are promising knowing that only intensity is used for this approach. We plan to add new attributes in the stage of contour detection e.g. color in order to locate the contours which may be missing using the current approach.

References

1. Alpert, S., Galun, M., Basri, R., Brandt, A.: Image Segmentation by Probabilistic Bottom-Up Aggregation and Cue Integration. In: Proceedings of the IEEE Conference on Computer Vision and Pattern Recognition (June 2007)

2. Ashikhmin, M.: Fast texture transfer. IEEE Computer Graphics and Applications 23(4), 38–43 (2003)
3. Alpert, S., Galun, M., Basri, R., Brandt, A.: Image Segmentation by Probabilistic Bottom-Up Aggregation and Cue Integration, In. In: Proceedings of the IEEE Conference on Computer Vision and Pattern Recognition (2007)
4. Arbelaez, P., Maire, M., Fowlkes, C., Malik, J.: Contour Detection and Hierarchical Image Segmentation. IEEE Transactions on Pattern Analysis and Machine Intelligence 33(5), 898–916 (2011)
5. Cheng, H.D., Jiang, X.H., Sun, Y., Wang, J.L.: Color image segmentation: advances and prospects. Pattern Recognition 34, 2259–2281 (2001)
6. Cheng, L., Vishwanathan, S.V.N., Zhang, X.: Consistent image analogies using semi-supervised learning. In: IEEE Conference on Computer Vision and Pattern Recognition, CVPR 2008 (2008)
7. De Winter, J., Wagemans, J.: Segmentation of object outlines into parts: A large-scale integrative study. Cognition 99, 275–325 (2006)
8. Freeman, W.T., Pasztor, E.C., Carmichael, O.T.: Learning Low-Level Vision. International Journal of Computer Vision 40(1) (2000)
9. Hertzmann, A., Jacobs, C.E., Oliver, N., Curless, B., Seitz, S.M.: Image analogies. In: SIGGRAPH Conference Proceedings, pp. 327–340 (2001)
10. Hertzmann, A., Oliver, N., Curless, B., Seitz, S.M.: Curve analogies. In: Proc. 13th Eurographics Workshop on Rendering, Pisa, Italy, pp. 233–245 (2002)
11. Lackey, J.B., Colagrosso, M.D.: Supervised segmentation of visible human data with image analogies. In: Proceedings of the International Conference on Machine Learning; Models, Technologies and Applications (2004)
12. Larabi, S., Robertson, N.M.: Contour detection by image analogies. In: Bebis, G., Boyle, R., Parvin, B., Koracin, D., Fowlkes, C., Wang, S., Choi, M.-H., Mantler, S., Schulze, J., Acevedo, D., Mueller, K., Papka, M. (eds.) ISVC 2012, Part II. LNCS, vol. 7432, pp. 430–439. Springer, Heidelberg (2012)
13. Martin, D., Fowlkes, C., Tal, D., Malik, J.: A Database of Human Segmented Natural Images and its Application to Evaluating Segmentation Algorithms and Measuring Ecological Statistics. In: Proc. 8th Int'l Conf. Computer Vision (2001)
14. Sykora, D., Burianek, J., Zara, J.: Unsupervised colorization of black-and-white cartoons. In: Proceedings of the 3rd Int. Symp. Non-photorealistic Animation and Rendering, pp. 121–127 (2004)
15. Wang, G., Wong, T., Heng, P.: Deringing cartoons by image analogies. ACM Transactions on Graphics 25(4), 1360–1379 (2006)
16. Zhanga, H., Frittsb, J.E., Goldmana, S.A.: Image segmentation evaluation: A survey of unsupervised methods. Computer Vision and Image Understanding 110(2), 260–280 (2008)

PaTHOS: Part-Based Tree Hierarchy for Object Segmentation

Loreta Suta[1], Mihaela Scuturici[1], Vasile-Marian Scuturici[2], and Serge Miguet[1]

[1] Université de Lyon - LIRIS
Université Lumière Lyon 2
5, Avenue Pierre Mendès-France
69676 Bron Cedex France
{Mihaela.Scuturici,Loreta.Suta,Serge.Miguet}@univ-lyon2.fr
[2] Université de Lyon - LIRIS
INSA de Lyon
7 Bd Jean Capelle
69621 Villeurbanne cedex France
Marian.Scuturici@insa-lyon.fr

Abstract. The problem we address in this paper is the segmentation and hierarchical grouping in digital images. In terms of image acquisition protocol, no constraints are posed to the user. At first, a histogram thresholding provides numerous segments where a homogeneity criterion is respected. Segments are merged together using similarity properties and aggregated in a hierarchy based on spatial inclusions. Shape and color features are extracted on the produced segments. Tests performed on Oxford Flower 17 [8] show that our method outperforms a similar one and allow the relevant object selection from the hierarchy. In our case, this approach represents the first stage towards flower variety identification.

Keywords: segmentation, hierarchical grouping, plant recognition.

1 Introduction

The swift growth of innovative technologies in the field of smartphone applications generated new possibilities for exploiting multimedia data. Users can take photos of objects and use them to search over the internet for complementary information (e.g. Google Goggles - for landmarks, artwork, wine, logos, Leafsnap, [16] and Folia, [15] - to identify leaf species, etc.). This implies the recognition of the photographed object. There are situations whereas recognition to be effective we need a segmentation step as accurate as possible.

In the case of flower species recognition, [11] investigated a new segmentation algorithm and compared the results to those obtained by [3] claiming that recognition was improved by 4% due to a better segmentation. To our knowledge, there are several applications attempting to recognize flower species nevertheless remaining an active research field. Moreover, retrieving flower variety is even

R. Wilson et al. (Eds.): CAIP 2013, Part I, LNCS 8047, pp. 393–400, 2013.

more challenging. We are also aware that a single photo may be insufficient to identify the specie and even less the variety of a flower. From a botanical point of view, plant recognition should furthermore take into account plant morphology such as features based on the appearance or the external form of a plant. The study of vegetative parts (roots, stems and leaves) as well as the reproductive parts (inflorescences, flowers, fruits and seeds) are crucial for plant variety identification.

The purpose of this paper is object segmentation on multiple level of detail. A hierarchical aggregation describes an image in its constituent objects. Thus, the analysis of plant morphology becomes accessible in contrast with classical approaches. In particular, we are interested in plant recognition tasks based on images of flowers and/or inflorescences, [14]; therefore an accurate segmentation is an essential step.

The remainder of the paper is organized as follows: section 2 presents related work. Section 3 describes our hierarchical approach for natural image segmentation and relevant object selection is presented in section 4. Experimental results are shown in section 5 followed by conclusions and future work in section 6.

2   Related Work

A wide variety of image segmentation methods have been recently proposed focusing on particular object types (cars, birds, horses, plants, etc.). In the field of flower segmentation, authors explore background/foreground separation techniques, [1] and [12], or combine them with geometrical models, [2] and [10], and superpixel segmentation, [11], [3] and [13].

Bottom-up methods use uniformity conditions in order to form image segments which are merged together respecting homogeneity criteria such as similar color properties, spatial structure, texture, etc. The object results from the aggregation of several components. For example, the components of a plant can be the flower, the leaves and the stem. According to the level of detail we would like to study, this approach offers multiple detail levels. In [5] the authors propose an image segmentation technique based on a high-performance contour detector. Oriented watershed procedure creates regions from the oriented contour signal. Image segmentation is achieved by agglomerative clustering with a method that transforms contours into a hierarchy of regions. [9] uses hierarchical grouping for object localization. Segments are generated using [4] while a greedy algorithm merges similar regions based on size and appearance features. In [7] and [6] a novel multiscale image segmentation method is introduced. The ramp transform detect ramp discontinuities and seeds for all regions while a region growing technique creates the desired segmented parts which can be organized as a tree representation. Segmentation is independent of object properties, parameters and initialization; contrariwise region growing technique may produce false associations.

We focused on hierarchical approaches since our purpose is plant morphology analysis (sepals, petals, stamens, etc.). It will be an intermediate step towards object semantics: a complex object having several regions of different colors will be represented as a more complex hierarchical structure than a uniform color region which will be represented as a single node in the hierarchy.

3   Segmentation and Hierarchical Grouping

The target of our segmentation method is to group pixels using spatial criteria to build a tree-like representation of the input image where each node describes objects. Figure 1 presents the main stages of our approach: input image (1), segmentation using color uniformity criterion filter (2), segment merging and aggregation into a hierarchy (3), feature extraction (4) and relevant object selection (5).

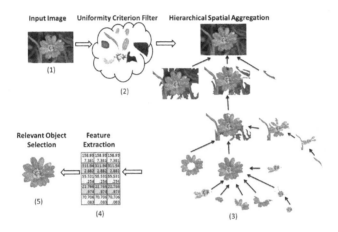

Fig. 1. The diagram of the proposed method describing the main steps

Our segmentation method is presented in Algorithm 1. It takes an image as input and a number of bins. Each bin corresponds to a color range (or a color histogram bin) generating a segmentation of the input image. For every colour channel of the input image and for each possible bin we build a new binary image *binaryImg*. This image will set to 1 all the pixels corresponding to the bin and to 0 the others (lines 5-11).

Pixels are grouped satisfying the color homogeneity criterion (line 12, call to the function *segmentation*). Pseudo-objects - hereby denoted segments - are detected using an edge detection filter. A large number of segments are created characterized by similar colors and kept in the list $\mathcal{O}$ (line 12). The same segments can be found several times in the list (under slightly different forms) due to color transitions caused by illumination.

Starting from the list $\mathcal{O}$ we organize the segments in a hierarchical structure using the following steps (*build_tree* from line 15):

Algorithm 1. "PaTHOS"

Require: Image I; number of bins for each color channel $BinCount$.
Ensure: Object hierarchy $\mathcal{H}$.
1: $\mathcal{O} \leftarrow \emptyset$
2: **for** $color = 0 \rightarrow I.channels$ **do**
3:      **for** $i = 0 \rightarrow BinCount - 1$ **do**
4:          $binaryImg \leftarrow$ new Image
5:          **for all** $pixel \in I$ **do**
6:              **if** $(0 \leq pixel[color] < (i+1) * 255/BinCount)$ **then**
7:                  $binaryImg[pixel] = 1$
8:              **else**
9:                  $binaryImg[pixel] = 0$
10:             **end if**
11:         **end for**
12:         $\mathcal{O} \leftarrow \mathcal{O} \cup segmentation(binaryImg)$
13:     **end for**
14: **end for**
15: $\mathcal{H} \leftarrow build\_tree(\mathcal{O})$
16: **return** $\mathcal{H}$

- Inclusion relationship: a segment o_1 is included in the segment o_2 if all the pixels from o_1 are found in o_2; we denote this relation as $o_1 \subseteq o_2$
- Equality relationship (for identical segments): two segments o_1 and o_2 are equal (identical) if $o_1 \subseteq o_2$ and $o_2 \subseteq o_1$
- Merging: two identical segments o_1 and o_2 are merged in a single one (o_1);
- Child-parent relationship: the segment $o_1 \in \mathcal{O}$ is the direct child of $o_2 \in \mathcal{O}$ if $\quad \neg \exists \ o_3 \in \mathcal{O} | o_1 \subset o_3 \subset o_2$

The resulting tree $\mathcal{H}$ characterise the content of the image I. Segments from several partitions of I contribute to the construction of this tree.

4   Relevant Object Selection

After the segmentation process, we obtain a hierarchy of multiple segments. Among them, there are one or several objects similar to the object of interest that we would like to find automatically. In our case, the object of interest is the flower. Other segments in the hierarchy represent either parts of the background or insignificant sub-parts or super-parts of the object of interest. For example, a single petal is a part of the flower that we obtain in the hierarchy due to the homogeneity of its color. However, we consider it less significant in comparison with the entire flower.

We noticed that many segments in the segmentation hierarchy are irrelevant objects. Thus, we supposed that they share common features which are different of the segments of interest (irregular edges, color, position, etc.). We perform a supervised learning using a C4.5 decision tree in order to choose relevant segment(s) (Figure 1 - (5)) from the hierarchy. Unlike other supervised learning algorithms such as SVM (Support Vector Machine) or neural networks, a decision tree provides comprehensible decision rules involving the most discriminant features which are reusable in subsequent tasks or embedded systems.

In order to perform supervised learning of correct and incorrect parts of the segmentation hierarchy, the segments are labeled as *correct/incorrect* segmentations. We add a new attribute, *GoodSegmentation* which is set to "yes" if the segmentation is correct and to "no" if the segmentation is incorrect. In order to automatically label the segments as correct/incorrect we rely on the ground truth and the accuracy defined in information retrieval. All the segments with $accuracy \geq t$ are considered as correct (GoodSegmentation = "Yes") while the segments where $accuracy < t$ are considered incorrect (GoodSegmentation = "No"). Here, t represents a threshold fixed at 0.85 (see section 5 for details).

For each segment, we also extract the following features: shape (perimeter, area, Hu moments), color (normalized entropy and standard deviation), roundness, eccentricity, minimum bounding box, gravity center and diameter. We apply a C4.5 decision tree algorithm, in order to predict the qualitative attribute GoodSegmentation. As we will see in section 5, the decision tree provides several decision rules allowing to choose the correct segments with a 77% success rate.

5 Experimental Results

5.1 Segmentation

As a hierarchical implementation, our method returns one object from several found in a digital image, see figure 2. This is an advantage that most of other approaches do not provide ([1], [3], etc.). It represents a relevant property as, in recognition tasks, methods take only one object in order to recognize it. The last column in figure 2 shows three possible flowers in the original image (corresponding to foreground objects), but only one is selected as being relevant. This disfavor our approach in comparative tests.

Fig. 2. Flower segmentation results: top row - original images; bottom row - our segmentations. Note that for images containing multiple objects, we obtain each object separately unless a spatial correlation exists.

Tests were performed on Oxford Flowers 17, [8], with 848 images which dispose of ground truth segmentations. Applying the proposed segmentation method, we obtain 5958 segments (one or several segments organized in a hierarchy per image). Subsequently, the decision tree indicates 2089 correct segments (Good-Segmentation = "Yes"), corresponding to the relevant objects (hereby flowers). In order to estimate the quality of our segmentation, we compare our results to the contour-based tree segmentation approach presented in [6]. As their method produces similar results without specifying correct segmentations, the user has to indicate the one corresponding to the object of interest. We chose their best result for each image according to the maximum value of the accuracy - compared to the ground truth. Table 1 presents the average Hausdorff distance between the segmented objects and the groundtruth. Best segmentation is achieved in case of minimum distance. Table 1 show a small advantage of our method compared to [6].

Table 1. Performance evaluation of the segmentation results on Oxford Flowers 17

Method	Hausdorff Distance
Tree segmentation	35.34
Our method	30.71

5.2   Relevant Object

In order to choose the relevant object of each segmented image, we performed a supervised learning using C4.5 decision tree in order to learn the GoodSegmentation attribute values ("Yes"/"No"). 5958 segments were labeled using a threshold $t = 0.85$ on the accuracy value. In order to choose the best value of parameter t, we varied the threshold value with a 0.05 step. For an accuracy rate higher than 0.85, the correct segments can be identified with a success rate of 77%. Best segmentation results are achieved for accuracy rates above 0.94 but with much less available data (not enough correct segments available). The supervised learning of correct segments was performed in cross validation: 10 validations with stratified sampling on "Good Segmentation" column, which gives a more realistic estimate of the error rate.

Decision rules based on the extracted features for correct/incorrect segmentation labeling are presented in figure 3. The confusion matrix shows 4588 accurately classified segments from a total of 5958 segments resulting in an error rate of 22%. Figure 4 presents two segments with different accuracy values belonging to the same original image. Both images were initially labeled as correct. Due to the supervised learning the bottom-right image is labeled as incorrect which proves the necessity of such validation.

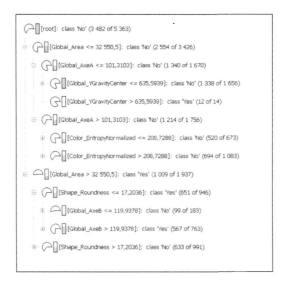

Fig. 3. Decision rules

Fig. 4. Results relevant object choice (first row - original and groundtruth image; second row - correct and incorrect segmentation after classification)

6   Conclusions and Future Work

In this paper we presented a hierarchical grouping segmentation model. At first, a histogram thresholding provides numerous segments where a homogeneity criterion is respected. Segments are merged and aggregated in a hierarchy via spatial inclusions. Shape and color features are extracted on the produced segments.

Supervised learning applied on features and accuracy labels segments into correct/incorrect segmentations and, therefore, allows the choice of relevant objects. Tests have been conducted on Oxford Flowers 17 in order to compare our results with a similar state-of-the-art method.

Future work includes the development of new features based on the hierarchy that may complement classical ones in the process of object selection. Our target is to employ the presented segmentation approach in plant recognition tasks extending our research towards flower variety identification.

Acknowledgements. This work has been supported by the French National Agency for Research with the reference ANR-10-CORD-005 (REVES project).

References

1. Rother, C., Kolmogorov, V., Blake, A.: GrabCut: Interactive Foreground Extraction using Iterated Graph Cuts. ACM Transactions on Graphics 23, 309–314 (2004)
2. Nilsback, M.-E., Zisserman, A.: Delving Deeper into the Whorl of Flower Segmentation. Image and Vision Computing 28(6), 1049–1062 (2010)
3. Chai, Y., Lempitsky, V., Zisserman, A.: BiCoS: A Bi-level Co-Segmentation Method for Image Classification. In: IEEE International Conference on Computer Vision, pp. 2579–2586 (2011)
4. Felzenszwalb, P.F., Huttenlocher, D.P.: Efficient Graph-Based Image Segmentation. International Journal on Computer Vision 59(2), 167–181 (2004)
5. Arbelaez, P., Maire, M., Fowlkes, C., Malik, J.: Contour Detection and Hierarchical Image Segmentation. IEEE Transactions on Pattern Analysis and Machine Intelligence 33(5), 898–916 (2011)
6. Akbas, E., Ahuja, N.: From Ramp Discontinuities to Segmentation Tree. In: Zha, H., Taniguchi, R.-i., Maybank, S. (eds.) ACCV 2009, Part I. LNCS, vol. 5994, pp. 123–134. Springer, Heidelberg (2010)
7. Todorovic, S., Ahuja, N.: Unsupervised Category Modeling, Recognition, and Segmentation in Images. IEEE Transactions on Pattern Analysis and Machine Intelligence 30(12), 2158–2174 (2008)
8. Oxford Flowers 17 (2011), http://www.robots.ox.ac.uk/~vgg/data/bicos/
9. van de Sande, K., Uijlings, J., Gevers, T., Smeulders, A.: Segmentation as Selective Search for Object Recognition. In: IEEE International Conference on Computer Vision, pp. 1879–1886 (2011)
10. Cerutti, G., Tougne, L., Vacavant, A., Coquin, D.: A Parametric Active Polygon for Leaf Segmentation and Shape Estimation. In: International Symposium on Visual Computing, pp. 202–213 (2011)
11. Angelova, A., Zhu, S., Lin, Y.: Image segmentation for large-scale subcategory flower recognition. In: IEEE Workshop on the Applications of Computer Vision, pp. 39–45 (2013)
12. Kumar, N., Belhumeur, P.N., Biswas, A., Jacobs, D.W., John Kress, W., Lopez, I.C., Soares, J.V.B.: Leafsnap: A computer vision system for automatic plant species identification. In: Fitzgibbon, A., Lazebnik, S., Perona, P., Sato, Y., Schmid, C. (eds.) ECCV 2012, Part II. LNCS, vol. 7573, pp. 502–516. Springer, Heidelberg (2012)
13. Chai, Y., Rahtu, E., Lempitsky, V., Van Gool, L., Zisserman, A.: TriCoS: A tri-level class-discriminative co-segmentation method for image classification. In: Fitzgibbon, A., Lazebnik, S., Perona, P., Sato, Y., Schmid, C. (eds.) ECCV 2012, Part I. LNCS, vol. 7572, pp. 794–807. Springer, Heidelberg (2012)
14. Singh, G.: Plants Systematics: An Integrated Approach. Science Publishers (2004)
15. Folia (2011), http://liris.cnrs.fr/reves/index.php
16. Leafsnap (2011), http://leafsnap.com/

Tracking System with Re-identification Using a Graph Kernels Approach

Amal Mahboubi[1], Luc Brun[1],
Donatello Conte[2], Pasquale Foggia[2], and Mario Vento[2]

[1] GREYC UMR CNRS 6072, Equipe Image ENSICAEN
6, boulevard Maréchal Juin F-14050 Caen, France
amal.mahboubi@unicaen.fr , luc.brun@ensicaen.fr
[2] Dipartimento di Ingegneria dell'Informazione, Ingegneria Elettrica e Matematica
Applicata
Università di Salerno, Via Ponte Don Melillo, 1 I-84084 Fisciano (SA), Italy
{dconte,pfoggia,mvento}@unisa.it

Abstract. This paper addresses people re-identification problem for visual surveillance applications. Our approach is based on a rich description of each occurrence of a person thanks to a graph encoding of its salient points. People appearance in a video is encoded by bags of graphs whose similarities are encoded by a graph kernel. Such similarities combined with a tracking system allow us to distinguish a new person from a re-entering one into a video. The efficiency of our method is demonstrated through experiments.

Keywords: Visual surveillance, Graph Kernel, Re-identification.

1 Introduction

Re-identification is a recent field of study in pattern recognition. The purpose of re-identification is to identify object/person coming back onto the field view of a camera. Such a framework may be extended to the tracking of object/persons on a network of cameras.

Methods dealing with the re-identification problem can be divided into two categories. A first group is based on building a unique signature for object. Features used to describe signatures are different: regions, Haar-like features, interest points [1], [2]. The second group of methods [3], [4] does not use a single signature for the object, but the latter is represented by a set of signatures. Thus, the comparison between objects takes place between two sets of signatures rather than between two individual signatures.

The basic idea of our work starts from the consideration that there are few works that exploit relationships between the visual features of an object. Furthermore, our work combines both approaches by describing a person both with a global descriptor over several frames and a set of representative frames. More precisely, the principle of our approach is to represent each occurrence of a person at time t by a graph representation called a t-prototype (Section 2). A kernel

R. Wilson et al. (Eds.): CAIP 2013, Part I, LNCS 8047, pp. 401–408, 2013.

between t-prototypes (Section 3) is proposed in order to encode the similarity between two persons based on their appearance on a single frame.

The design of the proposed kernel in Section 3 is based on a previous kernel [6] devoted to image indexation. However for people re-identification, tracking problems have to be addressed in order to cover the re-identification investigations. Within our framework a person is not characterized by a single image but by a sequence of images encoding its appearance along several frames. This new proposal (as shown by the dotted box in Figure 1) is described in section 4 and 5. The global appearance of a person over a video, is described by a bag of t-prototypes (Section 4) and global features of the bag computed on representative t-prototypes. The temporal window over which is build a bag of t-prototypes is called the history tracking window (HTW). Kernels between bags of t-prototypes are proposed in Section 4.1 in order to measure the similarity of two persons on several frames. Such kernels are used within our tracking system (Section 5) in order to determine if an entering person is a new person or a re-entering one. The efficiency of the proposed approach is evaluated through experimental results in section 6.

2   T-Prototype Construction

The first step of our method consists to separate subjects from the background. To that end, we use binary object masks [5] defined by a foreground detection with shadow removals. Each moving person within a frame is thus associated to a mask that we characterize using SIFT key point detectors. Such key points provide a fine local characterization of the image inside the mask which is robust against usual image transformations such as scales and rotations. Each key-point is represented by its x and y coordinates, scale, orientation and 128 numbers (the descriptors) per color channel. In order to contextualize the information encoded by SIFT points we encode them by a mutual k nearest neighbor graph $G = (V, E, w)$ where V corresponds to the set of SIFT points, E to the set of edges and w is a weight function defined over V and defined as the scale of appearance of the corresponding vertex. The set of edges E is defined from the key point coordinates x and y: one edge (v, v') belongs to E if v belongs to the k nearest neighbors of v' while v' belongs to the k nearest neighbors of v. The degree of each vertex is thus bounded by k. For a given vertex u, we take into account the local arrangement of its incident vertices by explicitly encoding the sequence of its neighbors encountered when turning counterclockwise around it. This neighborhood $\mathcal{N}(u) = (u_1, ..., u_n)$ is thus defined as an ordered set of vertices. The first vertex of this sequence u_1 is arbitrary chosen as the upper right vertex. The set $\{\mathcal{N}(u)\}_{u \in V}$ is called the bag of oriented neighborhoods (BON). The node u is called the central node.

3   Kernel between T-Prototypes

Our kernel between t-prototypes (eq. 5) is based on a previous contribution [6] within the image indexation framework. This kernel is based on the description of each graph by a finite bag of patterns. Such an approach consists to: i) define the bag of patterns from each graph, ii) define a minor kernel between patterns, iii) convolve minor kernels into a major one in order to encode the similarity between bags. SIFT points being local detectors, we consider that the more relevant information of a t-prototype corresponds to the local oriented neighborhood of its vertices. We thus define the bag of patterns of a t-prototype as its BON (section 2). The minor kernel between oriented neighborhoods is defined as follows:

$$K_{seq}(u,v) = \begin{cases} 0 & if \ |\mathcal{N}(u)| \neq |\mathcal{N}(v)| \\ \prod_{i=1}^{|\mathcal{N}(u)|} K_g(u_i, v_i) \ otherwise \end{cases} \tag{1}$$

where $K_g(u,v)$ is a RBF kernel between features of input vertices defined by a tuning parameter σ and the Euclidean distance $d(.,.)$ between feature values: $K_g(x,y) = e^{-\frac{d(\mu(x),\mu(y))}{\sigma}}$.

Eq. 1 corresponds to the same basic idea that the heuristic used to compute the graph edit distance between two nodes [7] where the similarity between two nodes is enforced by a comparison of their neighborhoods.

Note that $K_{seq}(.,.)$ corresponds to a tensor product kernel and is hence definite positive. However, due to acquisition noise or small changes between two images, some SIFT points may be added or removed within the neighborhood of some vertices. Such an alteration of the neighborhood's cardinal may drastically change the similarity between key points. Indeed, according to equation (1), two points with a different neighborhood's cardinal have a similarity equal to 0. Equation (1) induces thus an important sensibility to noise. In order to overcome this drawback, we introduce a rewriting rule on oriented neighborhoods. Given a vertex v, the rewriting of its oriented neighborhood denoted $\kappa(v)$ is defined as: $\kappa(v) = (v_1, ..., \hat{v_i}, ..., v_{l_v})$ where $\hat{v_i} = argmin_{j \in \{1,...,l_v\}} w(v_j)$ is the neighbor of v with lowest weight.

This rewriting is iterated leading to a sequence of oriented neighborhoods $(\kappa^i(v))_{i \in \{0,...,D_v\}}$, where D_v denotes the maximal number of rewritings. The cost of each rewriting is measured by the cumulative weight function CW defined by:

$$\begin{cases} CW(v) & = 0 \\ CW(\kappa^i(v)) = w(v_i) + CW(\kappa^{i-1}(v)) \end{cases} \tag{2}$$

where v_i is the vertex removed between $\kappa^{i-1}(v)$ and $\kappa^i(v)$.

Kernel between Oriented Neighborhoods: Our kernel between two oriented neighborhoods is defined as a convolution kernel between the sequence of rewritings of each neighborhood, each rewriting being weighted by its cumulative cost:

$$K_{rewriting}(u,v) = \sum_{i=1}^{D_v} \sum_{j=1}^{D_u} K_W(\kappa^i(u), \kappa^j(v)) * K_{seq}(\kappa^i(u), \kappa^j(v)) \tag{3}$$

where kernel K_W penalizes costly rewritings corresponding to the removal of important key-points. Such a kernel is defined as follows:

$$K_W(\kappa^i(u), \kappa^j(v)) = e^{-\frac{CW(\kappa^i(u)) + CW(\kappa^j(v))}{\sigma'}} \quad \text{where } \sigma' \text{ is a tuning variable.} \tag{4}$$

The number of rewritings (D_v) for each vertex v corresponds to a compromise between an over simplification of its oriented neighborhood (large D_v) and the corruption of equation 3 by non relevant vertices which may appear in only one of two similar oriented neighborhoods. This number has been empirically set to half the cardinal of v's neighborhood [6].

Graph Kernel: Taking into account central nodes, our final kernel between two vertices u and v is defined as follows: $K(u,v) = K_g(u,v)K_{rewriting}(u,v)$

Our final kernel between two graphs is defined as a convolution kernel between both BONs:

$$K_{graph}(G_1, G_2) = \sum_{u \in V_1} \sum_{v \in V_2} \varphi(u)\varphi(v)K(u,v) \qquad (5)$$

The weighting function φ encodes the relevance of each vertex and is defined as an increasing function of the weight: $\varphi(u) = e^{-\frac{1}{\sigma'(1+w(u))}}$

4   People Description

The identification of a person by a single t-prototype is subject to errors due to slight changes of the pose or some errors on the location of SIFT points. Assuming that the appearance of a person remains stable on a set of successive frames, we describe a person at instant t by the set of its t-prototypes computed on its HTW window. The description of a person, by a set of t-prototypes provides an implicit definition of the mean appearance of this person over HTW. Let $\mathcal{H}$ denotes the Hilbert space defined by K_{graph} (equation 5). In order to get an explicit representation of this mean appearance, we first use K_{graph} to project the mapping of all t-prototypes onto the unit-sphere of $\mathcal{H}$. This operation is performed by normalizing our kernel [8]. Following [8], we then apply a one class ν-SVM on each set of t-prototypes describing a person. From a geometrical point of view, this operation is equivalent to model the set of projected t-prototypes by a spherical cap defined by a weight vector w and an offset ρ both provided by the ν-SVM algorithm. These two parameters define the hyper plane whose intersection with the unit sphere defines the spherical cap. T-prototypes whose projection on the unit sphere lies outside the spherical cap are considered as outliers. Each person is thus encoded by a triplet (w, ρ, S) where S corresponds to the set of t-prototypes and (w, ρ) are defined from a one class ν-SVM. The parameter w indicates the center of the spherical cap and may be intuitively understood as the vector encoding the mean appearance of a person over its HTW window. The parameter ρ influence the radius of the spherical cap and may be understand as the extend of the set of representatives t-prototypes in S.

4.1   People's Kernel

Let $P_A = (w_A, \rho_A, S_A)$ and $P_B = (w_B, \rho_B, S_B)$ denote two triplets encoding two persons A and B. The distance between A and B is defined from the angle between vectors w_A and w_B defined by [8] as follows:

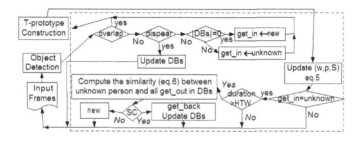

Fig. 1. Algorithm steps

$d_{sphere}(w_A, w_B) = arccos\left(\frac{w_A^T K_{A,B} w_B}{\|w_A\|\|w_B\|}\right)$ where $\|w_A\|$ and $\|w_B\|$ denote the norms of w_A and w_B in $\mathcal{H}$ and $K_{A,B}$ is a $|S_A| \times |S_B|$ matrix defined by $K_{A,B} = (K_{norm}(t,t'))_{(t,t')\in S_A \times S_B}$, where K_{norm} denotes our normalized kernel. Based on d_{sphere}, the kernel between A and B is defined as the following product of RBF kernels:

$$K_{change}(P_A, P_B) = e^{\frac{-d^2_{sphere}(w_A, w_B)}{2\sigma^2_{moy}}} e^{\frac{-(\rho_A - \rho_B)^2}{2\sigma^2_{origin}}} \tag{6}$$

Where σ_{moy} and σ_{origin} are tuning variables.

5   Tracking System

Our tracking algorithm uses four labels 'new', 'get_out', 'unknown' and 'get_back' with the following meaning: *new* refers to an object classified as new, *get-out* represents an object leaving the scene, *unknown* describes a query object (an object recently appeared, not yet classified) and *get-back* refers to an object classified as an old one.

Unlike our previous work [5], where we used a training data set to model each object and the re-identification was triggered by an edit graph distance. in this paper, we are using online learning and the re-identification is performed using the similarity (eq.6) between each unknown person and all the get_out persons. The general architecture of our system is shown in Figure 1. All masks detected in the first frame of a video are considered as new persons. Then a mask detected in frame $t + 1$ is considered as matched if there is a sufficient overlap between its bounding box and a single mask's bounding box defined in frame t. In this case, the mask is affected to the same person than in frame t and its graph of SIFT points is added to the sliding HTW window containing the last graphs of this person. If one mask defined at frame t does not have any successor in frame $t + 1$, the associated person is marked as get_out and its triplet $P = (w, \rho, S)$ (Section 4) computed over the last $|HTW|$ frames is stored in an output object data base model noted DB_S. In the case of a person corresponding to an unmatched mask in frame $t + 1$, the unmatched person is initially labeled as 'get_in'. When a 'get_in' person is detected, if there is no 'get_out' persons we classify this 'get_in' person immediately as new. This 'get_in' person is then tracked along the video using the previously described protocol. On the other hand, if there is at least one 'get_out' person we should delay the identification of this 'get_in' person which is thus labeled as 'unknown'. This 'unknown' person is then tracked on $|HTW|$ frames in order to obtain its description by a triplet (w, ρ, S). Using this description we compute the value of kernel K_{change} (equation 6) between this unknown person and all get_out persons contained in our database. Similarities between the unknown person and get_out ones are sorted in decreasing order so that the first get_out person of this list corresponds to the best candidate for a re identification. Our criterion to map an unknown person to a get_out one, and thus to classify it as get_back is based both on a threshold on the maximum similarity values max_{ker} and a threshold on the standard deviations σ_{ker} of the list of similarities. This criterion called, SC is defined as $max_{ker} > th_1$ and $\sigma_{Ker} > th_2$, where th_1 and th_2 are experimentally fixed thresholds. Note that, SC is reduced to a fixed threshold on max_{ker} when the set of get_out persons is reduced to two elements. An unknown person whose SC criterion is false is labeled as a new person. Both new and get_back persons are tracked between frames until they get_out from the video and reach the get_out state.

Classically, any tracking algorithm has to deal with many difficulties such as occlusions. The type of occlusions examined in this paper is limited to the case where bounding boxes overlap. An occlusion is detected when the spatial overlap between two bounding boxes is greater than an experimentally fixed threshold while each individual box remains detected. If for a given object an occlusion is detected, the description of this object is compromised. Thus a compromised object is only tracked and its triplet (w, ρ, S) is neither updated nor stored in DB_S. At identification time, the model of the unknown person is matched against each get-out person from DB_S.

6   Experiments

The proposed algorithm has been tested on v01, v05, v04 and v06 video sequences of the PETS'09 S2L1 [9] dataset. Each sequence contains multiple persons. To compare our framework with previous work, we use the well-known metrics Sequence Frame Detection Accuracy ($SFDA$), Multiple Object Detection Accuracy ($MODA$) and Multiple Object Tracking Accuracy ($MOTA$) described in [11]. Note that such a measure does not allow to take into account the fact that the identification of a person may be delayed. Since our method identifies a person only after HTW frames, we decided not to take into account persons with an unknown status in the $MODA$ and $MOTA$ measures until these persons are identified as get_back or new (Section 5).

In our first experiment we have evaluated how different values of the length of HTW may affect the re-identification accuracy. The obtained results show that, v01 and v05 perform at peak efficiency for HTW=35. V04 and v06 attain their optimum at HTW=20.

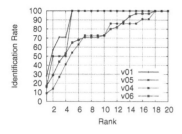

Fig. 2. CMC curves

Table 1. Evaluation results

View	MODA of[10]	MODA	MOTA	SFDA
v01	0.67	0.91	0.91	0.90
v05	0.72	0.75	0.75	0.80
v04	0.61	0.2799	0.2790	0.47
v06	0.75	0.506	0.505	0.64

To validate our method of re-identification we used the Cumulative Matching Characteristic (CMC) curves. The CMC curve represents the percentage of times the correct identity match is found in the first n matches. Figure 2 shows the CMC curves for the four views. We can see that the performance of v01 is much better than that of v05, v06 and v04. We attribute this to the high detection accuracy in v01. Figure 2 shows that if we focus on the first 5 matches, we find that for v04 and v06 a score of 54% and 65% respectively is obtained, while for v01 and v05 it attains 100%.

In order to compare our results to the state of the art's methods we used the exhaustive comparison of 13 methods defined in [9]; where a quantitative performance evaluation of the submitted results by contributing authors of the two PETS workshops in 2009 on PETS'09 S2.L1 dataset was performed. Using the metrics MODA, MOTA, MODP, MOTP SODA and SFDA described in [11], the submitted results of [10] outperform all other methods. We hence only compare our results to this best method. The left column of Table 1 shows the best results [10] obtained by methods described in [9] on each video. As shown by the two left-most data columns of Table 1, our method obtains lower result than that of [10] for v04 and v06. This may be explained by the fact that v04 and v06 have persistent group cases. Indeed the case where two or more existing objects at time t become too spatially close at time $t + 1$ and then merge together to become a one detected object at time $t + 1$ is not considered here as an occlusion, but rather as a group. Since such case is not addressed by this paper, v04 and v06 results need to be interpreted with caution. Due to the frequent group cases in v04 and v06 we missed a lot of persons in the scene. However, our method obtains better result than that of [10] for v01 and v05. These results set forth the relevance of the proposed re-identification algorithm since we have only occlusion cases.

7 Conclusion

In this paper, we presented a new people re-identification approach based on graph kernels. Our graph kernel between SIFT points includes rewriting rules on oriented neighborhood in order to reduce the lack of stability of the key point detection methods. Furthermore, each person in the video is defined by a set of graphs with a similarity measure between sets which removes outliers. Our tracking system is based on a simple matching criterion to follow one person along a video. Person's description and kernel between these descriptions is used to remove ambiguities when one person reappears in the video. Such a system may be easily extended to follow one person over a network of camera. People are prone to occlusions by others nearby. However, a re-identification algorithm for an individual person is not suitable for solving the groups cases. A further study with more focus on groups is therefore suggested.

References

1. Hamdoun, O., Moutarde, F., Stanciulescu, B., Steux, B.: Person re-identification in multi-camera system by signature based on interest point descriptors collected on short video sequences. In: ICDSC 2008, pp. 1–6 (2008)
2. Ijiri, Y., Lao, S., Han, T.X., Murase, H.: Human Re-identification through Distance Metric Learning based on Jensen-Shannon Kernel. In: VISAPP 2012, pp. 603–612 (2012)
3. Truong Cong, D.-N., Khoudour, L., Achard, C., Meurie, C., Lezoray, O.: People re-identification by spectral classification of silhouettes. International Journal of Signal Processing 90, 2362–2374 (2010)
4. Zhao, S., Precioso, F., Cord, M.: Spatio-Temporal Tube data representation and Kernel design for SVM-based video object retrieval system. Multimedia Tools Appl. (55), 105–125 (2011)
5. Brun, L., Conte, D., Foggia, P., Vento, M.: People Re-identification by Graph Kernels Methods. In: Jiang, X., Ferrer, M., Torsello, A. (eds.) GbRPR 2011. LNCS, vol. 6658, pp. 285–294. Springer, Heidelberg (2011)
6. Mahboubi, A., Brun, L., Dupé, F.-X.: Object Classification Based on Graph Kernels. In: HPCS-PAR, pp. 385–389 (2010)
7. Fankhauser, S., Riesen, K., Bunke, H.: Speeding up Graph Edit Distance Computation through Fast Bipartite Matching. In: Jiang, X., Ferrer, M., Torsello, A. (eds.) GbRPR 2011. LNCS, vol. 6658, pp. 102–111. Springer, Heidelberg (2011)
8. Desobry, F., Davy, M., Doncarli, C.: An Online Kernel Change Detection Algorithm. IEEE Transaction on Signal Processing 53, 2961–2974 (2005)
9. Ellis, A., Shahrokni, A., Ferryman, J.: PETS 2009 and Winter PETS 2009 Results, a Combined Evaluation. In: 12th IEEE Int. Work. on Performance Evaluation of Tracking and Surveillance, pp. 1–8 (2009)
10. Berclaz, J., Shahrokni, A., Fleuret, F., Freyman, J.M., Fua, P.: Evaluation of probabilistic occupancy map people detection for surveillance systems. In: 11th IEEE Int. Work. on Performance Evaluation of Tracking and Surveillance, pp. 55–62 (2009)
11. Kasturi, R., Goldgof, D., Soundararajan, P., Manohar, V., Garofolo, J., Bowers, R., Boonstra, M., Korzhova, V., Zhang, J.: Framework for performance evaluation of face, text, and vehicule detection and tracking in video: Data, metrics, and protocol. IEEE Transaction on Pattern Analysis and Machine Intelligence 31(2), 319–336 (2009)

Recognizing Human-Object Interactions Using Sparse Subspace Clustering

Ivan Bogun and Eraldo Ribeiro

Computer Vision Laboratory,
Florida Institute of Technology
Melbourne, Florida, U.S.A.
ibogun2010@my.fit.edu,
eribeiro@fit.edu

Abstract. In this paper, we approach the problem of recognizing human-object interactions from video data. Using only motion trajectories as input, we propose an unsupervised framework for clustering and classifying videos of people interacting with objects. Our method is based on the concept of sparse subspace clustering, which has been recently applied to motion segmentation. Here, we show that human-object interactions can be seen as trajectories lying on a low-dimensional subspace, and which can in turn be recovered by subspace clustering. Experimental results, performed on a publicly available dataset, show that our approach is comparable to the state-of-the-art.

Keywords: human-object interaction, action classification, human motion, sparse subspace clustering, subspace decomposition.

1 Introduction

Recognizing human-object interactions from videos is a hard problem that has been receiving renewed attention by the computer-vision community. The problem's complexity comes from large degree of variations present in both the appearance of objects and the many ways people interact with them. Current solutions differ mostly in terms of the type of input data used by algorithms, which ranges from low-level features such as optical flow to human-centered features such as spatio-temporal volumes.

The state-of-the-art is represented by the weakly supervised method described by Prest et al. [1], which combines part-based human detector, tracking by detection, and classification into a single framework. This method reports the best results on most datasets. Other representative solutions include the work of Gupta et al. [2], which uses a histogram-based model to account for appearance information, and trajectories for representing motion. Their classification approach is based on a Bayesian network. They introduce interaction features such as time of the object grasp, interaction start, and interaction stop, which are learned from velocity profiles. Motion trajectories were also used by Filipovych and Ribeiro [3] for recognizing interactions by matching trajectories of hand motion using a robust sequence-alignment method.

R. Wilson et al. (Eds.): CAIP 2013, Part I, LNCS 8047, pp. 409–416, 2013.

Fig. 1. Examples of interactions and annotated trajectories in dataset from [2]

In this paper, we look at the problem of human-object interaction recognition in light of recent developments in sparse subspace clustering [4]. Here, we show that such interactions can be seen as trajectories lying on a low-dimensional subspace. We propose an unsupervised framework for interaction recognition that uses sparse subspace clustering (Section 2). We compare our method to the state-of-the art (Section 3).

2   Our Method

2.1   Trajectory Extraction and Pre-processing

We commenced by annotating the videos from Gupta et al. [2]. Currently, video datasets of human-object interactions are either not publicly available, such as the *Coffee and Cigarretes* used by Laptev and Pérez [5] and by Prest et al. [1], or are unannotated, as in the case of dataset provided by Gupta et al. [2]. Videos in Gupta et al. are short sequences (i.e., 3–10 seconds long) of a single person performing interactions such as drinking from a cup, answering the phone, making a phone call, spraying, pouring from a cup, and lighting a torch. Our annotation is as follows: on every 3rd frame of the videos, we extract the position (i.e., the centroid of the bounding box) of the left hand, torso, head, right hand, and the object associated with the interaction. Figure 1 shows samples of these trajectories superimposed on frames from the input videos.

In our interaction-classification method, each video is represented by five trajectories that we extracted manually by linearly interpolating between the previously annotated keyframes. These trajectories are termed $\mathcal{T}^h$, $\mathcal{T}^r$, $\mathcal{T}^l$, $\mathcal{T}^t$, and $\mathcal{T}^o$, for head, left hand, right hand, torso, and object, respectively. While automatic trajectory extraction is indeed desirable, it is not the focus of this paper, and we decided that assuming trajectory availability would suffice. The extracted trajectories were resampled to become both contiguous and of equal length (i.e., from $t_{\min} = 3$ to $t_{\max} = 100$).

We further pre-processed each video to normalize trajectories with respect to the head location, and to remove potential bias that may exist towards right-handed subjects. Because the head motion is not relevant for the interactions in the dataset, the mean location of the head trajectory was subtracted from the other four trajectories. For example, let $\mathcal{T}^h = \{\mathbf{x}_1^h, \ldots, \mathbf{x}_N^h\}$ be the trajectory of length N frames that describes the head motion. Its mean is given by:

$$\bar{\mathbf{x}}^h = \frac{1}{N} \sum_{i=1}^{N} \mathbf{x}_i^h. \tag{1}$$

Here, $\bar{\mathbf{x}}^h = (\bar{x}^h, \bar{y}^h)^\mathsf{T}$ is a centroid location that we can use to flip trajectories horizontally and thus account for left-right hand symmetry. For each trajectory j in the video, the registered trajectory points are given by:

$$\hat{\mathbf{x}}_i^j = \left(|x_i^j - \bar{x}^h|, \, y_i^j - \bar{y}^h \right)^\mathsf{T}, \quad \forall i. \tag{2}$$

This normalization reduces bias towards right-handed people as well as noise associated with the object being placed at random locations on the table. Hereafter, we assume that all trajectories have been normalized using this procedure.

2.2   Video Representation

As we clarify in the next section, we want each video to be represented by a single feature vector. However, simply stacking all trajectories to form a raw feature vector would lead to incorrect results as trajectories associated with the non-interacting hand do not provide valuable information, and we do not want to use these trajectories for classification. To detect the hand that is more likely to be interacting with the object, we calculate the correlation between the object trajectory and the trajectory of each hand using p-values. We use χ^2 (chi-square) statistical test as a correlation measure. The trajectory having the smallest p-value is selected as the one performing the interaction, i.e.:

$$\mathcal{T} = \underset{\mathcal{T}' \in \{\mathcal{T}^l, \mathcal{T}^r\}}{\arg\min} \; p\left(\chi^2(\mathcal{T}^o, \mathcal{T}') \right), \tag{3}$$

where the $p(.)$ returns the p-value. Now, that we have determined the trajectory corresponding to the interacting-hand, we represent a video by its feature vector:

$$\mathbf{f} = \begin{bmatrix} \mathcal{T} \\ \mathcal{T}^o \end{bmatrix}. \tag{4}$$

Finally, given a set $\mathcal{V} = \{v_1, \ldots, v_M\}$ of M videos containing human-object interactions, we can stack their corresponding feature vectors to form a large matrix $Y = (\mathbf{f}_1, \ldots, \mathbf{f}_M) \in \mathbb{R}^{2N \times M}$, where N is the size of normalized trajectories.

2.3   Interaction Motion as Sparse Subspace Separation

Our method is based on the Subspace Clustering algorithm (SSC) proposed by Elhamifar and Vidal [4]. An earlier version of the SSC algorithm was applied to motion segmentation by casting the segmentation as a problem of subspace separation [6]. The motion-segmentation approach in Rao et al. [6] is based on two observations: the motion data lies in the union of low-dimensional spaces and the fact the dataset satisfies the *self-expressiveness* property. According to Elhamifar and Vidal [4], a dataset is self-expressive if each data point in a union of subspaces can be reconstructed by a combination of other points in the dataset. Let c_i be such a representation for video i, then the sparsest representation of y_i via the set $\{y_j | j \neq i\}$ is given as follows:

$$\min. \quad ||c_i||_0 \tag{5}$$
$$\text{s.t.} \quad y_i = Y c_i, \tag{6}$$
$$c_{ii} = 0, \tag{7}$$

where $||x||_0 = \#\{i | x_i \neq 0\}$. Equation 5 enforces sparsity in coefficients while Equation 6 takes care of self-expressiveness. Equation 7 restricts the representation such that it does not contain any part of the original vector itself. This problem turns out to be non-convex and NP-hard [7]. Nevertheless, recent developments in the optimization field have provided heuristics that are able to find relaxed solutions that are sparse [8]. More specifically, the relaxed version of Equation 5 replaces the l_0-norm with the l_1-norm, which is known to prefer sparse solutions [9]. With the norm replacement, the relaxation can be written in matrix notation as follows:

$$\min. \quad ||C||_1 \tag{8}$$
$$\text{s.t.} \quad Y = YC, \tag{9}$$
$$\text{diag}(C) = 0, \tag{10}$$

where $\text{diag}(C)$ denotes diagonal entries of C. Relaxed versions of Equations 8 to 10 are able to find solutions only when the data lies perfectly on the union of subspaces. We follow Rao et al. [6] and assume that the data can be decomposed into a noise-free component and a noise component, i.e.:

$$Y = Y_{\text{perfect}} + Z. \tag{11}$$

Here, Z is the noise and Y_{perfect} is the clean data, which lies in the union of the subspaces. Thus, the problem becomes:

$$\min. \quad ||C||_1 + \frac{\lambda_z}{2}||Z||_F^2 \tag{12}$$
$$\text{s.t.} \quad Y = YC + Z, \tag{13}$$
$$\text{diag}(C) = 0, \tag{14}$$

where $||Z||_F = \sqrt{\sum_{i=1}^{m} \sum_{j=1}^{n} |z_{ij}|^2}$ and λ_z is a regularization parameter. For parameter settings, Elhamifar and Vidal [4] suggest to set $\lambda_z = \alpha_z / \mu_z$, where $\alpha_z > 1$ and μ_z is defined by $\mu_z = \min_i \max_{i \neq j} |\mathbf{y}_i^T \mathbf{y}_j|$.

After coefficient matrix C is found, SSC clusters trajectories using spectral clustering. SSC gave state-of-the art results on the Hopkins-155 dataset [10]. Combined with nice theoretical properties [11] and the momentum gained by the success of sparse optimization problems [12], we believe that SSC can be useful in classifying human actions and interactions.

2.4 Why Should We Care about Sparsity?

Let $Y \in \mathbb{R}^{m \times n}$ be the data set. The Sparse Subspace Clustering algorithm is seeking for the sparsest representation for every $y_i \in Y, i = 1, \ldots, n$

$$\min. \quad ||c_i||_1 \tag{15}$$
$$\text{s.t.} \quad y_i = Y c_i, \tag{16}$$
$$c_{ii} = 0, \tag{17}$$

which can be seen as a limit $\lambda \to \infty$ of the following:

$$\min. \quad ||c_i||_1 + \lambda ||y_i - Y c_i||_2^2$$

$$\text{s.t. } c_{ii} = 0.$$

Let c_{-i} be c_i without c_{ii}. Similarly, define Y_{-i} as Y without its i-th row. Then, the problem can be cast as:

$$\min. \, ||c_{-i}||_1 + \lambda ||y_i - Y_{-i} c_{-i}||_2^2.$$

The latter is problem where we are trying to find the sparsest approximation of y_i using Y_{-i} in the form $y_{-i} = \sum_{j=1}^{m} Y_{-i,j} c_{-ij}$. It can be shown that SVM can be reformulated to solve it [13]. On the other hand, Girosi [14] has shown that, for noiseless data, the solution given by sparse approximation corresponds exactly to the solution given by SVM. Moreover, non-zero coefficients of c_{-i} correspond to support vectors.

Limited amount of support vectors correspond to the bounded VC dimension of the dataset, which is shown to define generalization ability; the result, due to Vapnik [13], shows the connection between generalized error and the number of support vectors, i.e.:

$$E[P(\text{error})] \leq \frac{E[\#\text{of support vectors}]}{\# \text{ of training examples}}. \tag{18}$$

This leads to the connection between sparsity and the ability to extract the most important samples from the dataset, which in turn leads to the proper partitioning of the samples via SSC.

3   Experimental Evaluation

In this section, we experiment with the SSC algorithm in an unsupervised approach for actor-object interaction recognition based on the trajectory data. Our experiments were designed with an emphasis on trying to answer the following two questions: (i) Can human-object interactions be seen as body and object trajectories that lie in a low-dimensional space? (ii) What is the role of interaction localization (i.e., segmentation) in recognition?

Here, we run the SSC algorithm[1] in two settings: (a) With complete trajectories (i.e., from the first to the last frame of the input videos), and (b) With trajectories corresponding only to interaction frames (i.e., frames where the interaction starts and ends)[2]. Confusion matrices resulting from these experiments are given in Figures 2(a) and 2(b), and present classification rates of 74.1% and 81.48%, respectively. As a point of comparison, we note that Gupta et al. [2] report accuracy of 93.34% while Prest et al. [1] report an average classification of 93%. However, in addition to being completely supervised, these approaches use additional data to train a HOG-based object detector, while our method is unsupervised given trajectories and their parameters. As reported in Gupta et al. [2], interaction such as lighting and pouring, dialing and lighting have similar trajectories, thus can be hardly distinguished by motion cues alone. This behavior is also observed in our results. The test videos and demo code for our method are available online.[3]

Our results suggest that segmentation of interaction trajectories can be seen as a special case of motion segmentation, and consequently, the space of such trajectories consists of a union of low-dimensional subspaces. Our results imply that, if two interactions lie on different subspaces, motion information alone is able to distinguish between them. However, if the interactions lie on the same subspace then appearance information should be used for classification.

In our second experiment, the higher classification rates suggest that interaction localization (i.e., segmentation of start and end of actions) is a goal worth pursuing. The results agree with the intuition that removing unnecessary parts of trajectories, we can improve the value of information necessary for recognition.

4   Conclusion and Future Work

We presented an unsupervised approach for the recognition of actions involving people interacting with objects. Our method uses motion-trajectory data as input. We demonstrated that the SSC algorithm is applicable to the problem. We showed that motion data from human-object interactions can indeed be considered to lie in a low-dimensional space. Whenever this is not the case, additional information such as appearance is needed to improve classification.

---

[1] Code provided by Elhamifar and Vidal [15], which uses the CVX Convex Programming package [16].

[2] These parameters were also manually annotated.

[3] Test videos and code are available on `https://github.com/ibogun/interaction`

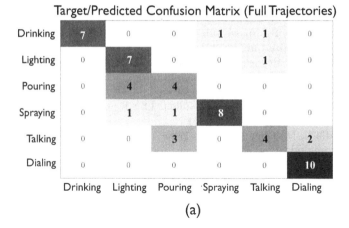

Fig. 2. Confusion matrices. (a) full trajectories, (b) localized trajectories.

A main drawback of our work is the use of manual trajectory annotation. This issue can be addressed by implementing a method for tracking and detection [1]. Another direction is to investigate how to use the classification labels provided by our method in a fully supervised setting.

References

[1] Prest, A., Schmid, C., Ferrari, V.: Weakly supervised learning of interactions between humans and objects. TPAMI 34(3), 601–614 (2012)
[2] Gupta, A., Kembhavi, A., Davis, L.S.: Observing human-object interactions: Using spatial and functional compatibility for recognition. TPAMI 31(10), 1775–1789 (2009)

[3] Filipovych, R., Ribeiro, E.: Robust sequence alignment for actor-object interaction recognition: Discovering actor-object states. CVIU 115(2), 177–193 (2011)

[4] Elhamifar, E., Vidal, R.: Sparse subspace clustering: Algorithm, theory, and applications. arXiv preprint arXiv:1203.1005 (2012)

[5] Laptev, I., Pérez, P.: Retrieving actions in movies. In: ICCV, pp. 1–8 (2007)

[6] Rao, S., Tron, R., Vidal, R., Ma, Y.: Motion segmentation in the presence of outlying, incomplete, or corrupted trajectories. TPAMI 32(10), 1832–1845 (2010)

[7] Meka, R., Jain, P., Caramanis, C., Dhillon, I.S.: Rank minimization via online learning. In: ICML, pp. 656–663 (2008)

[8] Ma, S., Goldfarb, D., Chen, L.: Fixed point and bregman iterative methods for matrix rank minimization. Mathematical Programming 128(1-2), 321–353 (2011)

[9] Robert Tibshirani. Regression shrinkage and selection via the lasso. Journal of the Royal Statistical Society Series B, 267–288 (1996)

[10] Tron, R., Vidal, R.: A benchmark for the comparison of 3-d motion segmentation algorithms. In: CVPR, pp. 1–8. IEEE (2007)

[11] Soltanolkotabi, M., Candes, E.J.: A geometric analysis of subspace clustering with outliers. The Annals of Statistics 40(4), 2195–2238 (2012)

[12] Chandrasekaran, V., Sanghavi, S., Parrilo, P.A., Willsky, A.S.: Sparse and low-rank matrix decompositions. In: IEEE CCC, pp. 962–967 (2009)

[13] Vapnik, V.: The nature of statistical learning theory. Springer (1999)

[14] Girosi, F.: An equivalence between sparse approximation and support vector machines. Neural computation 10(6), 1455–1480 (1998)

[15] Elhamifar, E., Vidal, R.: Sparse subspace clustering. In: CVPR, pp. 2790–2797. IEEE (2009)

[16] Inc. CVX Research. CVX: Matlab software for disciplined convex programming, version 2.0 beta (September 2012), http://cvxr.com/cvx

Scale-Space Clustering on the Sphere

Yoshihiko Mochizuki[1], Atsushi Imiya[2], Kazuhiko Kawamoto[3], Tomoya Sakai[4], and Akihiko Torii[5]

[1] Faculty of Science and Engineering, Waseda University
3-4-1 Ohkubo, Shinjuku-ku, Tokyo, 169-8555, Japan
[2] Institute of Management and Information Technologies, Chiba University
[3] Academic Link Center, Chiba University
Yayoicho 1-33, Inage-ku, Chiba, 263-8522, Japan
[4] Department of Computer and Information Sciences, Nagasaki University
Bunkyo-cho 1-14, Nagasaki 852-8521, Japan
[5] Department of Control Engineering, Tokyo Institute of Technology
Ookayama, 1-12-1, Meguro-ku, Tokyo, 153-8550, Japan

Abstract. We present an algorithm for scale-space clustering of point cloud on the sphere using the methodology for the estimation of the density distribution of the points in the linear scale space. Our algorithm regards the union of observed point sets as an image defined by the delta functions located at the positions of the points on the sphere. A blurred version of this image has a deterministic structure which qualitatively represents the density distribution of the points in a point cloud on a manifold.

1 Introduction

The linear scale-space theory [1] provides a dimension-independent observation theory of input data [2,3]. As an extension of scale-space-based clustering of point cloud on a plane and a curved manifold [6], we develop a framework to extract the clusters in a point cloud on the sphere, and to evaluate their statistical significance or cluster validity. Regarding the density function as a greyscale image, we can estimate the density function in the scale space and identify the point correspondences by the scale-space analysis of image structure.

There are two types of clustering methodologies: (i) supervised clustering and (ii) unsupervised clustering. Furthermore, there are metric based and non-metric-based clustering methods. In this paper, we focus on unsupervised metric-based clustering using scale-space analysis of point cloud. Although in typical metric-based clustering, data are assumed to be points in a flat space, data sometimes lie on a curved manifold. The graph-Laplacian-based method is a powerful method to deal with data on a manifold expressing data as an undirected weighted graph using metric in the data space. On the other hand, the scale-space-based clustering [2,3,4] estimates the number of clusters from hierarchical expression of data derived by scale-space analysis of a point cloud.

R. Wilson et al. (Eds.): CAIP 2013, Part I, LNCS 8047, pp. 417–424, 2013.

2   Mathematical Preliminaries

A vector $\boldsymbol{x} \in \mathbb{S}^3$ is expressed as $\boldsymbol{x} = \boldsymbol{x}(\phi, \theta) = (\cos\phi\sin\theta, \sin\phi\sin\theta, \cos\theta)^\top$ using spherical coordinates (ϕ, θ), where $\phi \in [0, 2\pi)$, $\theta \in [0, \pi]$. The scale image of an image $f(\boldsymbol{x}, \tau)$ on $\mathbb{S}^2$ is the solution of the linear spherical heat equation

$$\frac{\partial}{\partial\tau} f(\boldsymbol{x}, \tau) = \Delta_{\mathbb{S}^2} f(\boldsymbol{x}, \tau) = \left[\frac{1}{\sin\theta} \frac{\partial}{\partial\theta} \left(\sin\theta \frac{\partial}{\partial\theta} \right) + \frac{1}{\sin^2\theta} \frac{\partial^2}{\partial\phi^2} \right] f(\boldsymbol{x}, \tau), \quad (1)$$

for $f(\boldsymbol{x}, 0) = f(\boldsymbol{x})$. The scale space image $f(\boldsymbol{x}, \tau)$ of scale τ is expressed as

$$f(\boldsymbol{x}, \tau) = \sum_{l=0}^{\infty} \sum_{m=-l}^{l} \left(e^{-l(l+1)\tau} c_l^m \right) Y_l^m(\boldsymbol{x}), \ c_l^m = \int_{\mathbb{S}^2} f(\boldsymbol{x}) \overline{Y_l^m(\boldsymbol{x})} d\sigma, \quad (2)$$

for $d\sigma = \sin\theta d\theta d\phi$, where Y_l^m is the spherical harmonic function of the degree l and the order m. Equation (2) is re-expressed as

$$f(\boldsymbol{x}, \tau) = \int_{\mathbb{S}^2} f(\boldsymbol{x}) K(\boldsymbol{x}, \boldsymbol{y}, \tau) d\sigma = K_\tau *_{\mathbb{S}^2} f(\boldsymbol{x}), \ \boldsymbol{x}, \boldsymbol{y} \in \mathbb{S}^2 \quad (3)$$

using the spherical heat kernel

$$K(\boldsymbol{x}, \boldsymbol{y}, \tau) = \sum_{l=0}^{\infty} \sum_{m=-l}^{l} e^{-l(l+1)\tau} Y_l^m(\boldsymbol{x}) Y_l^m(\boldsymbol{y}) = \frac{1}{4\pi} \sum_{l=0}^{\infty} (2l+1) e^{-l(l+1)\tau} P_l^0(\cos\Theta),$$
$$(4)$$

for $\cos\Theta = \boldsymbol{x}(\phi, \theta)^\top \boldsymbol{y}(\phi', \theta') = \cos\phi\cos\phi' + \sin\phi\sin\phi'\cos(\theta - \theta')$, where $P_l^0(t)$ is the associated Legendre function of the degree l and the order 0 [9,10].

Setting $\boldsymbol{n} = (0, 0, 1)^\top$ to be the north pole, the impulse function on $\mathbb{S}^2$ can be defined similarly to one in Euclidean space.

Definition 1. *For an arbitrary test function f on $\mathbb{S}^2$, the impulse function $\delta_{\mathbb{S}^2}(\boldsymbol{x})$ can be defined as the function which satisfies the relation*

$$\int_{\mathbb{S}^2} f(\boldsymbol{x}) \delta_{\mathbb{S}^2}(\boldsymbol{x}) d\sigma = f(\boldsymbol{x}) *_{\mathbb{S}^2} \delta_{\mathbb{S}^2}(\boldsymbol{x}) = \delta_{\mathbb{S}^2}(\boldsymbol{x}) *_{\mathbb{S}^2} f(\boldsymbol{x}) = f(\boldsymbol{n}). \quad (5)$$

For a function $f(\boldsymbol{x})$ and the matrix $\boldsymbol{R} \in \mathrm{SO}(3)$, the function $g(\boldsymbol{x}) = f(\boldsymbol{R}^\top \boldsymbol{x})$ represents a rotated function of f. The north pole $\boldsymbol{n} = (0, 0, 1)^\top$ is moved to $\boldsymbol{n}' = \boldsymbol{R}\boldsymbol{n}$ and the relationship $f(\boldsymbol{n}) = g(\boldsymbol{n}')$ is satisfied. When $f(\boldsymbol{x}(\phi, \theta))$ is constant for any ϕ, the rotated function of f is identical to f for any $\boldsymbol{R} \in \mathrm{SO}(3)$ which satisfies $\boldsymbol{n}' = \boldsymbol{R}\boldsymbol{n}$. Using this property, we define the rotation of functions on the sphere.

Definition 2. *For the function $f(\boldsymbol{x}(\phi, \theta))$ which is constant for any ϕ and the rotation matrix $\boldsymbol{R} \in \mathrm{SO}(3)$ which moves the north pole $(0, 0, 1)^\top$ to $\boldsymbol{p}$, we write the function rotated by $\boldsymbol{R}$ as $f(\boldsymbol{x} \sim \boldsymbol{p}) = f(\boldsymbol{R}^\top \boldsymbol{x})$.*

For a point set on the sphere, by substituting each point for an impulse function, we can have the function associated with a point set.

Definition 3. *For a set of points $\mathcal{P}$ on the sphere, the spherical image of $\mathcal{P}$ is*

$$f(\boldsymbol{x}) = [\mathcal{P}](\boldsymbol{x}) = \sum_{\boldsymbol{p} \in \mathcal{P}} \delta_{\mathbb{S}^2}(\boldsymbol{x} \sim \boldsymbol{p}). \tag{6}$$

We call $f(\boldsymbol{x}) = [\mathcal{P}](\boldsymbol{x})$ a probability density function (PDF) on the sphere.

Definitions 1 and 2 imply $K_\tau *_{\mathbb{S}^2} \delta_{\mathbb{S}^2}(\boldsymbol{x} \sim \boldsymbol{p}) = K(\boldsymbol{x} \sim \boldsymbol{p}, \boldsymbol{n}, \tau)$. Therefore, setting $G(\boldsymbol{x}, \tau) = K(\boldsymbol{x}, \boldsymbol{n}, \tau)$, we have the relations

$$f(\boldsymbol{x}, \tau) = \sum_{\boldsymbol{p} \in \mathcal{P}} G(\boldsymbol{x} \sim \boldsymbol{p}, \tau), \quad \nabla_{\mathbb{S}^2} f(\boldsymbol{x}, \tau) = \sum_{\boldsymbol{p} \in \mathcal{P}} \nabla_{\mathbb{S}^2} G(\boldsymbol{x} \sim \boldsymbol{p}, \tau), \tag{7}$$

where $\nabla_{\mathbb{S}^2} = \left(\overline{\partial_\phi}, \partial_\theta \right)^\top$, for $\overline{\partial_\phi} = \frac{1}{\sin\theta} \frac{\partial}{\partial\phi}$ and $\partial_\theta = \frac{\partial}{\partial\theta}$. We call $f(\boldsymbol{x}, \tau) = [\mathcal{P}](\boldsymbol{x}, \tau)$ the *generalised PDF (GPDF)* after the scale-space theory [8].

For PDF $f(\boldsymbol{x})$ on the sphere, the derivative of $f(\boldsymbol{x})$ describes the differential geometric features. A primitive geometric feature of the GPDF is the extension of stationary point $\{\boldsymbol{x} \mid \nabla_{\mathbb{S}^2} f(\boldsymbol{x}) = 0\}$, where the spatial gradient vanishes. The stationary point can be classified into three types based on the combination of the signs of the eigenvalues of the Hessian matrix $\boldsymbol{H}_f = \nabla_{\mathbb{S}^2} \nabla_{\mathbb{S}^2}^\top f$, where

$$\nabla_{\mathbb{S}^2} \nabla_{\mathbb{S}^2}^\top = \begin{pmatrix} \overline{\partial_\phi}^2 & \overline{\partial_\phi}\partial_\theta \\ \partial_\theta\overline{\partial_\phi} & \partial_\theta^2 \end{pmatrix} = \begin{pmatrix} \frac{\partial^2}{\partial\theta^2} & \frac{1}{\sin\theta}\frac{\partial^2}{\partial\theta\partial\phi} - \frac{\cot\theta}{\sin\theta}\frac{\partial}{\partial\phi} \\ \frac{1}{\sin\theta}\frac{\partial^2}{\partial\theta\partial\phi} - \frac{\cot\theta}{\sin\theta}\frac{\partial}{\partial\phi} & \frac{1}{\sin^2\theta}\frac{\partial^2}{\partial\phi^2} + \cot\theta\frac{\partial}{\partial\theta} \end{pmatrix}. \tag{8}$$

We denote the signs of the eigenvalues as $(\pm, \pm)$. Sign $(-,-)$ means that the point on f is a local maximum. A local maximum of a PDF is called the *mode* in probability theory and statistics.

3   Structural Simplification and Mode Tree Construction

The trajectory of the stationary point [8]

$$S(\tau) = \left\{ \boldsymbol{x}(\tau) = \boldsymbol{x}(\phi(\tau), \theta(\tau)) \in \mathbb{S}^2 \mid \nabla_{\mathbb{S}^2} f(\boldsymbol{x}, \tau) = 0 \right\} \tag{9}$$

in the scale space is called the stationary curve in the scale-space theory. Since $\nabla_{\mathbb{S}^2} f = 0$ and $f_\tau = \Delta_{\mathbb{S}^2} f$, we have the relationship

$$\boldsymbol{H}_f \frac{d}{d\tau} f(\boldsymbol{x}(\tau), \tau) = -\nabla_{\mathbb{S}^2} \Delta_{\mathbb{S}^2} f(\boldsymbol{x}(\tau), \tau). \tag{10}$$

If the scale is sufficiently small, the generalised PDF f consists of $|\mathcal{P}|$ small blobs of spherical heat kernels. As the scale increases, the blobs merge with each other into large ones, and the modes at their peaks disappear one after another [11,12]. Since $\boldsymbol{n} = arg\{\nabla_{\mathbb{S}^2} G(\boldsymbol{x}) = 0\}$, we have the relation $\boldsymbol{p} = arg\{\nabla_{\mathbb{S}^2} G(\boldsymbol{x} \sim \boldsymbol{p}) = 0\}$. Moreover, since the function $f(\boldsymbol{x}, \tau) = \sum_{\boldsymbol{p} \in \mathcal{P}} G(\boldsymbol{x} \sim \boldsymbol{p}, \tau)$ is asymptotically equivalent to $f(\boldsymbol{x}, \tau) = G(\boldsymbol{x} \sim \boldsymbol{q}, \tau)$ for $\boldsymbol{q} = \frac{\sum_{\boldsymbol{p} \in \mathcal{P}} \boldsymbol{p}}{|\sum_{\boldsymbol{p} \in \mathcal{P}} \boldsymbol{p}|}$, we have the relation $\boldsymbol{q} = (\cos\phi^* \sin\theta^*, \sin\phi^* \sin\theta^*, \cos\theta^*)$ for $\lim_{\tau \to \infty} \theta(\tau) = \theta^*$ and $\lim_{\tau \to \infty} \phi(\tau) = \phi^*$.

Let $\mathcal{P}$ be a set of points, $f = [\mathcal{P}]$, and $N = |\mathcal{P}|$. Let τ_i be selected scale values, where $\tau_i < \tau_{i+1}$ for $i = 0, 1, \ldots, M$ with $\tau_0 = 0$. The mode tree M corresponding to f is defined as follows.

- Each node in M has three values: the node ID i, a scale value τ and a location vector $\boldsymbol{x}$, is denoted by $(\tau, i, \boldsymbol{x})$.
- M has N leaf nodes. Each node has a unique ID in $\{0, \ldots, N-1\}$. The scale values of the all leaf nodes are 0 and each location is defined by $\mathcal{P}$.
- Parent of a node whose scale is τ_i is a node whose scale is τ_{i+1} for $i < M-1$.
- A node whose scale and location are τ and $\boldsymbol{p}$, respectively, is one of the local maxima of the function $f(\boldsymbol{x}, \tau)$ at $\boldsymbol{x} = \boldsymbol{p}$.

We denote a set of nodes whose scale is τ by M_τ. The algorithm 1 constructs the mode tree. In this, the leaf nodes (at the scale 0) correspond to the input points. All nodes at a scale are moved according to the scale image of the next scale. When some node points are concentrated to a point, they are merged into a new node whose ID is inherited from the point which remains as isolated point in the scale space. Figure 1 shows an example of construction of a tree.

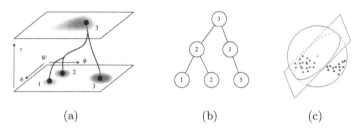

(a)   (b)   (c)

Fig. 1. Mode tree and node merging. (a) Trajectory of three modes in scale space. Each plane represents the spherical space in spherical coordinates on the different scale. (b) The mode tree. Each circle and the number in it represent a node in the tree and its ID, respectively. (c) The linear separability for point set on the spherical space.

4   Deterministic Structure and Critical Scale

Since the random features of a point cloud are filtered out as the scale increases, and deterministic features emerge, the deterministic structure of a point cloud is established from coarse to fine. Therefore, this scale-space hierarchy of clusters [1,11] provides us with the multi-resolution approach to scale selection for the clustering. There presumably exists a critical lower bound of scale, above which the structure is deterministic and the clusters are valid, and below which the structure is stochastic and the clusters are invalid. Therefore, detection of the critical scale is achieved by observing the decay of the number of clusters with respect to the scale [5]. We define the lifitime as the scale at which a new cluster appears.

Definition 4. *The lifetime of the cluster is defined as the scale at which the cluster disappears with increasing scale.*

Furthermore, we define the linear separability for point set on the spherical space as shown in Fig. 1(c).

Algorithm 1. Mode tree construction

Input: A point set $\mathcal{P} = \{\,\boldsymbol{p}_i \in \mathbb{S}^2\,\}_{i=0}^{N-1}$, $f = [\mathcal{P}]$ and scales
$\quad\quad t_0 = 0 < t_1 < \cdots < t_M$
Output: Mode tree
Let M be a graph with N nodes, $\{\,(t_0, i, \boldsymbol{p}_i)\,\}_{i=0}^{N-1}$.
$i \leftarrow 1$
while $i < M$ **do**
$\quad$ // Update local maxima for the next scale
$\quad$ **for** $n = (t_i, j, \boldsymbol{p}) \in \mathsf{M}_{t_i}$ **do**
$\quad\quad$ Calculate the maximised point $\boldsymbol{p}'$ of $\boldsymbol{p}$ on the function $f(\boldsymbol{x}, t_{i+1})$.
$\quad\quad$ Add a node $(t_{i+1}, j, \boldsymbol{p}')$ to M adjacent to node n.
$\quad$ // Marge absorbed maxima
$\quad$ **for** $n = (t_{i+1}, j, \boldsymbol{p}) \in \mathsf{M}_{t_{i+1}}$ **do**
$\quad\quad$ $\mathcal{N} \leftarrow \{\,(t_{i+1}, k, \boldsymbol{q}) \in \mathsf{M}_{t_{i+1}} \mid \boldsymbol{q} = \boldsymbol{p}\,\}$
$\quad\quad$ Find $m \in \mathcal{N}$ whose displacement is the smallest.
$\quad\quad$ All nodes $\mathcal{N} \setminus m$ are removed from M and their child nodes are
$\quad\quad$ connected to be adjacent to m.
$\quad$ $i \leftarrow i + 1$
Output M as a tree whose leaf nodes are M_{τ_0}.

Definition 5. *Let $\mathcal{P}$ and $\mathcal{Q}$ be point sets on $\mathbb{S}^2$. $\mathcal{P}$ and $\mathcal{Q}$ are linearly separable if there exists a plane through the origin of the sphere, which separates the space $\mathbb{R}^3$ into two subsets $\mathbb{R}^3_-$ and $\mathbb{R}^3_+$, such that $\mathcal{P} \subset \mathbb{R}^3_{\pm}$ and $\mathcal{Q} \subset \mathbb{R}^3_{\mp}$.*

5   Experimental Results

We show an example shown in Fig. 2. The set consists of three clusters with 3000 points, which can be separated by a curve with the appearance of a baseball stitching. Figure 2(c) shows the graph of the number of maxima. The set can be successfully separated into two clusters in the mode tree.

Fig. 3 (a) shows the spherical image generated by the dioptric image shown in Fig. 3 (b). Our aim is to detect spatial lines captured in the spherical image. Since spatial lines are projected to the great circles in the spherical image [7], We use the spherical Hough transform for spherical images [13,14] which detects the great circles from sample points on a spherical image. Since the voting space of the spherical Hough transform is the unit sphere, the votes yield a point cloud on the sphere [13]. Therefore, line detection is achieved by detecting mean points in clusters of a point cloud on the spherical voting space.

To apply the spherical clustering, we extend the voting space to the sphere duplicating all points $\boldsymbol{x}$ as the antipodal points $-\boldsymbol{x}$. As a result of constructing the mode tree of the point cloud, Fig. 4 (d) shows the graph of the number of modes at each scale. From symmetry of the extended points, the modes are also symmetry at any scales and we can divide the mode tree into two subtrees. From this geometric property of the mode tree, we use the modes in the north hemisphere

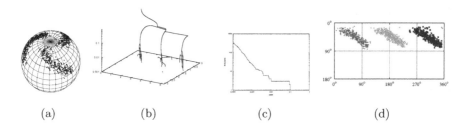

(a)   (b)   (c)   (d)

Fig. 2. Clustering of a linearly non-separable point set on the sphere in three-dimensional Euclidean space. (a) point cloud with clusters, each of which has randomly generated 2000 points on the sphere. (b) Number of maxima at each scale. Using the life time, we can estimate the number of clusters in a point cloud on the sphere. (c) The mode tree of the point set. (d) The clustered point set at the scale of 0.1.

(a)   (b)

Fig. 3. Spherical image captured by Fish-eye-lens camera system. (a) Image on unit sphere transformed from (b). (b) Image acquired by fish-eye-lens camera system.

to estimate clusters of the point cloud generated voting. In the graph, there are some stable intervals in which the number of points does not change. The first three these stable intervals of scales are $[0.00337, 0.00526]$, $[0.00925, 0.0134]$ and $[0.01587, 0.02907]$. These intervals are shaded regions on the graph. The number of modes in these intervals are 36, 20 and 10 respectively. The clustering results in these intervals are shown in Fig. 4 (d).

Figures 5 (a), (b) and (c) are means of the clustr detected from point cloud on spherical voting space using spherical scale-space clustering. Furthermore, Figs 5 (d), (e) and (f) illustrate detected lines. The results show that the method can detect parameters of lines from dioptric images.

6   Conclusions

We introduced an algorithm for scale-space-based clustering for point clouds on the sphere regarding the union of given point sets as an image of a finite sum of the delta functions located at the positions of the points on the sphere.

The principal advantage of the scale-space-based analysis for the point-set analysis is that deterministic features of the point set can be observed at higher scales even if the positions of the points are stochastic. This property can be

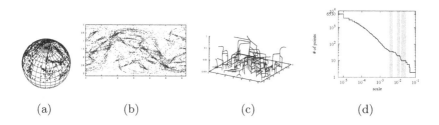

(a)   (b)   (c)   (d)

Fig. 4. Voting points obtained for the N-point randomized Hough Transform (NPRHT)[13,14]. (a) and (b) Point set on the spherical accumulato space. (c) Mode tree. (d) Numbers of mode.

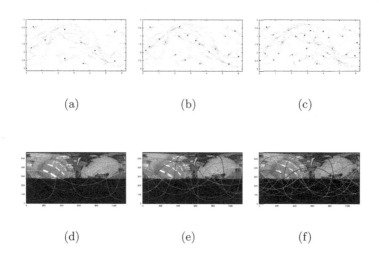

(a)   (b)   (c)

(d)   (e)   (f)

Fig. 5. Detected means nd lines. (a) Means detected from 1587 clusters. (b) Means detected from 925 clusters. (c) Means detected from 337 clusters. (d) Lines detected from 1587 clusters. (e) Lines detected from 925 clusters. (f) Lines detected from 337 clusters.

qualitatively explained using an image of dots. Our method is capable of finding the deterministic correspondences of points and clusters at sutable scales, analysing the distribution of the points in scale space.

References

1. Witkin, A.P.: Scale space filtering. In: Proc. 8th IJCAI, pp. 1019–1022 (1983)
2. Griffin, L.D., Colchester, A.: Superficial and deep structure in linear diffusion scale space: Isophotes, critical points and separatrices. Image and Vision Computing 13, 543–557 (1995)
3. Nakamura, E., Kehtarnavaz, N.: Determining number of clusters and prototype locations via multi-scale clustering. Pattern Recognition Letters 19, 1265–1283 (1998)
4. Loog, M., Duistermaat, J.J., Florack, L.M.J.: On the Behavior of Spatial Critical Points under Gaussian Blurring (A Folklore Theorem and Scale-Space Constraints). In: Kerckhove, M. (ed.) Scale-Space 2001. LNCS, vol. 2106, pp. 183–192. Springer, Heidelberg (2001)
5. Sakai, T., Imiya, A., Komazaki, T., Hama, S.: Critical scale for unsupervised cluster discovery. In: Perner, P. (ed.) MLDM 2007. LNCS (LNAI), vol. 4571, pp. 218–232. Springer, Heidelberg (2007)
6. Sakai, T., Imiya, A.: Unsupervised cluster discovery using statistics in scale space. Engineering Applications of Artificial Intelligence 22, 92–100 (2009)
7. Franz, M.O., Chahl, J.S., Krapp, H.G.: Insect-inspired estimation of egomotion. Neural Computation 16, 2245–2260 (2004)
8. Zhao, N.-Y., Iijima, T.: A theory of feature extraction by the tree of stable viewpoints. IEICE Japan, Trans. D J68-D, 1125–1135 (1985) (in Japanese)
9. Kim, G., Sato, M.: Scale space filtering on spherical pattern. In: Proc. ICPR 1992, pp. 638–641 (1992)
10. Chung, M.K.: Heat kernel smoothing on unit sphere. In: Proc. 3rd IEEE ISBI: Nano to Macro, pp. 992–995 (2006)
11. Kuijper, A., Florack, L.M.J., Viergever, M.A.: Scale space hierarchy. Journal of Mathematical Imaging and Vision 18, 169–189 (2003)
12. Minnotte, M.C., Scott, D.W.: The mode tree: A tool for visualization of nonparametric density features. Journal of Computational and Graphical Statistics 2, 51–68 (1993)
13. Torii, A., Imiya, A.: The randomized-Hough-transform method for great-circle detection on sphere. Pattern Recognition Letters 28, 1186–1192 (2007)
14. Mochizuki, Y., Torii, A., Imiya, A.: N-Point Hough transform for line detection. Journal of Visual Communication and Image Representation 20, 242–253 (2009)

The Importance of Long-Range Interactions to Texture Similarity

Xinghui Dong and Mike J. Chantler

The Texture Lab
School of Mathematical and Computer Sciences
Heriot-Watt University
Edinburgh, UK
{xd25,m.j.chantler}@hw.ac.uk

Abstract. We have tested 51 sets of texture features for estimating the perceptual similarity between textures. Our results show that these computational features only agree with human judgments at an average rate of 57.76%. In a second experiment we show that the agreement rates, between humans and computational features, increase when humans are not allowed to use long-range interactions beyond 19×19 pixels. We believe that this experiment provides evidence that humans exploit long-range interactions which are not normally available to computational features.

Keywords: Texture Features, Texture Similarity, Perceptual Similarity, Long-Range Interactions, Evaluation.

1   Introduction

Although computed texture similarity is widely used for texture classification and retrieval, human "perceptual similarity" is difficult to acquire and estimate. Halley [1] derived a perceptual similarity matrix for a large texture database of 334 textures, and Clarke et al. [2] compared these data with similarity matrices obtained by 4 computational feature sets and found that these did not correlate well.

Traditionally, computational features are divided into: filtering-based [3], structural [4], statistical [5], and model-based [6] features. According to Parseval's theorem [7], filtering operations in the spatial domain are equivalent to those in the frequency domain when the variances of filtered images are used. In this case, linear filtering based features, with the exception of quadrature filters which are designed to capture local phase, only use power spectrum information. However, phase is believed to encode the "structure" information in images [8]. As a result, these approaches are unlikely to be able to capture texture structure. Texton-based features are a form of vector quantization and normally work by clustering in pixel neighborhood space. Computational cost and feature space sparsity both severely limit the size of the neighborhood. Generally, statistical features also extract only local statistics again largely for reasons of computational cost. Similarly, model-based features utilize only a small neighborhood

R. Wilson et al. (Eds.): CAIP 2013, Part I, LNCS 8047, pp. 425–432, 2013.

although the recursive structures have the potential to encode long-range interactions. However, the majority of published features either work in the power spectrum, or only exploit higher-order information from relatively small (i.e. 19×19 or less) local neighborhoods. However, the more interesting aperiodic structures in textures are represented by phase spectra data and features with small spatial extent cannot encode these long-range interactions.

In order to examine the abilities of computational features to estimate perceptual similarity, we have benchmarked 51 sets of features but we have found that these do not agree well with humans' perceptual judgments, even if a multi-pyramid scheme is employed. We believe this may be because the majority of texture features do not encode long-range higher-order information, such as continuity as expressed by the Gestalt law of "good continuation" [9]. Furthermore, Polat et al. [10] found that the interactions might be attributed to grouping collinear line segments into smooth curves after they studied the lateral interactions between spatial filters. As Spillmann et al. stated, classical receptive-field models can only explain local perceptual effects but are unable to explain some global perceptual phenomenon, such as the perception of illusory contours [11], which is believed to result from long-range interactions.

The most direct hypothesis is that the features that we have investigated cannot exploit these long-range interactions and hence these produce estimates of similarity that are not consistent with human judgments. Unfortunately, it is difficult to test this hypothesis directly by "adding" long-range interactions to textures as such actions invariably change local features or 1st- or 2nd-order statistics. However, it is relatively simple to prevent humans from using long-range interactions. In this situation, humans are likely to make judgments that are more similar to the computational results if our hypothesis holds true. Hence, we performed two additional pair-of-pairs experiments and their results show that humans are more inclined to make judgments that coincide with the feature data when long-range interactions are not available to the observers. These results indicate that the features that we have examined do not exploit long-range interactions.

In the next section, a series of evaluation experiments is conducted that compare human and computational similarity. The effect of removing long-range interactions on perceptual similarity is investigated in section 3. Finally, in section 4, conclusions are drawn.

2   Evaluating Texture Features for Estimating Perceptual Similarity

In this section, we carry out a series of evaluation experiments for examining the abilities of 51 sets of different computational features to estimate perceptual similarity as obtained from free-grouping [1, 12] and pair-of-pairs [12] experiments respectively. Multi-pyramid decomposition is used to increase the spatial extent of the computational features and 6 pyramid levels are used. The computational similarity is compared with perceptual similarity and the agreement rate is used to measure the estimation ability of each set of features.

2.1   Capturing Perceptual Similarity

Halley [1] obtained a perceptual similarity matrix for the *Pertex* texture database of 334 textures using free grouping. However, for more than 200 textures this sorting-based method is very time-consuming and hence only 30 participants were used. In order to augment these data, a new set of perceptual similarity judgments were obtained using the pair-of-pairs method, in which two pairs of textures were displayed simultaneously in each trial and the participant was required to decide which pair is more similar [12].

2.2   Estimating Perceptual Similarity Using Computational Features

Spatial extent is an important impact factor of features that capture visual structure and is normally limited by computational considerations. Multi-resolution analysis is often used to enhance the performance of features because such techniques allow larger spatial extent to be considered. In our study, a simple multi-pyramid perceptual similarity estimation scheme is proposed. Firstly, each texture image is decomposed into 5 Gaussian pyramid [13] sub-bands. Next, each sub-band is individually normalized to have an average intensity of 0 and standard deviation of 1 in order to remove the influence of 1st- and 2nd-order gray level properties. Feature extraction is performed to obtain a feature vector from each sub-band independently. In addition, all 5 feature vectors are combined into an additional feature vector. Thus, in total 6 feature vectors are generated for each texture. Finally, a distance matrix is computed from all 334 sub-band images on every pyramid level. Although the Euclidean distance (see Equation (1)) is a simple but popular metric, it is not suitable for measuring the distance between two histograms. Therefore, the Chi-square statistic (see Equation (2)) and the Euclidean distance are used for histogram-based features and the rest respectively. Each distance matrix is first normalized to the range of [0, 1] and is then converted to a similarity matrix. As a result, six similarity matrices are obtained for each method and are used as the estimation of perceptual similarity.

$$Euclidean(x, y) = \sqrt{\Sigma_i(x_i - y_i)^2} \tag{1}$$

$$\chi^2(x, y) = \frac{1}{2}\Sigma_i \frac{(x_i - y_i)^2}{x_i + y_i} \tag{2}$$

In our research, 51 sets of features were used to estimate perceptual similarity. Due to space limitations, we list and reference these in the paper's supplementary material.

2.3   Comparing Computational and Perceptual Similarity

We use agreement rate (%) to measure the consistency between the computational features and human judgments. When perceptual judgments from pair-of-pairs experiments [12] are used as the ground-truth, it is separately computed on each pyramid level as shown below:

(a) Accumulate the choice (left or right) decisions made by all 20 participants for 1000 pair-of-pairs trials, and label these as HCF_L and HCF_R respectively. The difference between these two figures is computed and normalized:

$$HCD_i = \frac{HCF_L - HCF_R}{20}, i = 1, 2, ..., 1000; \tag{3}$$

(b) For each trial, label the computational similarities of the left and right pairs as FS_L and FS_R respectively, and compute their difference as

$$FCD_i = FS_L - FS_R, i = 1, 2, ..., 1000; \tag{4}$$

(c) Compute the criterion to decide whether the computational features and human decisions are consistent for each trial:

$$IsAgreed_i = (HCD_i * FCD_i > 0) \,||\, ((HCD_i == 0) \,\&\&\, (FCD_i == 0)), i = 1, 2, ..., 1000; \tag{5}$$

(d) Finally compute the percentage agreement rate:

$$Agreement\ Rate\ (\%) = \sum_{i=1}^{1000} IsAgreed_i * 100/1000. \tag{6}$$

In total, six agreement rates are obtained for each approach.

Since only 1000 pairs of pairs were examined in the pair-of-pairs experiment, we can only consider these when the perceptual similarity matrix [1, 12] is used as the ground-truth, in order to obtain consistent evaluation results for these two ground-truth datasets. As a result, step (a) above is replaced by step (a1) below.

(a1) For each pair-of-pairs trial, label the perceptual similarities of the left and right pairs as HS_L and HS_R respectively, and compute their difference as

$$HCD_i = HS_L - HS_R, i = 1, 2, ..., 1000. \tag{7}$$

However, the other three steps are kept constant.

2.4   Results

The average agreement rates (%) of the humans' perceptual pair-of-pairs judgments against 51 sets of computational features computed at 6 resolutions are displayed in Figure 1(a). In addition a second set of human data obtained by free grouping and Isomap analysis (8D-ISO) is also shown for comparison purposes. The 8D-ISO data provides the highest agreement rate at 73.9% providing validation of the pair-of-pairs data and an indication of the variability of human performance. However, the performance of the computational features is much lower (average agreement rates lie in the range 48.58% to 63.38%). Figure 1(b) provides a similar plot in which the same computational features are compared against the 8D-ISO human data. The highest and lowest performances (58.55% and 48.85%) were provided by MRSAR and SVR, respectively. It can be seen that two curves in Figure 1(a) and 1(b) are similar. In both cases the performance of the 51 computational features is poor when compared against the two sources of human data.

In order to investigate the failure of the computational features further, 80 pairs of pairs of textures were selected in which the disagreement between computer and human judgments was greatest. These were used in the experiment described in the next section.

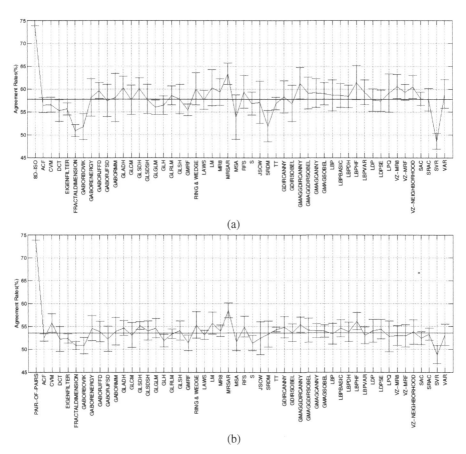

Fig. 1. The average agreement rates (%) of computational features with perceptual pair-of-pairs judgments (a), 8D-ISO data (b), and corresponding standard deviations (error bars) over 6 resolutions. In (a) and (b), the black solid lines illustrate the overall average agreement rates (57.76% and 53.59%), over all 51 methods and 6 resolutions.

Table 1. Pairwise t-test ($\alpha = 0.05$) results, where $r \geq 0.5$ means that the strong effect is obtained. POP_O, POP_N and POP_R: probabilities that the participants chose "Left" throughout 80 trials in original, non-randomized and randomized pair-of-pairs experiments respectively.

t-test	t	p	r	df	Significant
POP_O vs. POP_N	-1.12	0.27	0.21	28	No
POP_O vs. POP_R	-4.73	0.00	0.67	28	Yes
POP_N vs. POP_R	2.74	0.02	0.67	9	Yes

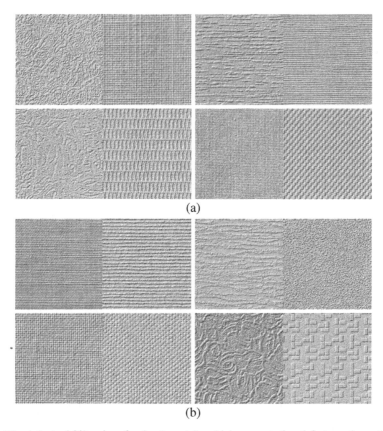

(a)

(b)

Fig. 2. The 4 (out of 80) pairs of pairs (rows) in which computational features have the most difficulty agreeing with human judgments: (a) most participants think that the right pairs are more similar in the original (POP_O) and the non-randomized (POP_N) pair-of-pairs but they change their minds in the randomized pair-of-pairs (POP_R), and (b) most participants always think the left pairs are more similar throughout all three versions of pair-of-pairs

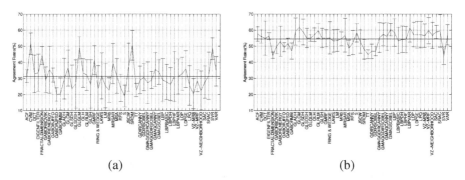

(a)   (b)

Fig. 3. Average agreement rates between each method and perceptual judgments in POP_O and POP_R, along with standard deviations (error bars) over 6 resolutions. The black solid lines illustrate the overall average rates: (a) 31.28% and (b) 54.67%, on 51 methods and 6 resolutions.

3   The Effect of Removing Long-Range Interactions

We hypothesize that one possible reason for the computational features producing results that do not agree with human perceptual judgments is that the features compute higher order spatial statistics only on small neighborhoods. Thus, these cannot exploit the long-range interactions that humans have been shown to be capable of using for other tasks. Unfortunately, it is difficult to introduce long-range interactions to real texture images or generate synthetic textures that with controlled long-range interactions that do not affect local and/or 1st-/2nd-order statistics. As an alternative, we designed an experiment in which the human observers were prevented from using long-range interactions. We were inspired by Field et al. [9] who showed that humans can recognize an object in one image by using long-range interactions even although a grid has been imposed on top of it. Hence given a "blocked" texture image we can remove the original long-range interactions by randomizing the position of the blocks. Experiments were performed using "non-randomized blocked" and "randomized blocked" textures respectively. The former was designed to provide a control to understand the effect of superimposing the grid onto images. Note that the grid was provided in order to lessen the effect of local discontinuities at randomized blocked edges. The size of each block was set at 19×19 which is the largest neighborhood used by computational features (excluding filtering-based features). Two modified pair-of-pairs (POP_N and POP_R) experiments were designed using non-randomized and randomized blocked images respectively. All other conditions were kept the same as for the original pair-of-pairs (POP_O) experiment.

Three pairwise t-tests were conducted on the 3 sets of results (see Table 1). There is no significant difference between the choices participants have made in the original (POP_O) and the blocked but non-randomized (POP_N) experiments. However, the results of the randomized experiment (POP_R) against both the original (POP_O) and the blocked but non-randomized (POP_N) show significant changes. In both cases the randomized blocked experiment provides increased agreements with the computational features. That is, when humans are provided with images containing the original long-range interactions (i.e. either the original, or the blocked but non-randomized images), they disagree significantly more with the computational results compared with when these long-range interactions have been removed. For example, in Figure 2(a) most participants judge that the right pairs are more similar in POP_O and POP_N but change their minds in POP_R. The average agreement rates between each computational approach and perceptual judgments in POP_O and POP_R over 6 resolutions, are plotted in Figure 3(a) and 3(b). It can be seen that the participants have agreed more with the features when they have not been able to use long-range interactions.

4   Conclusions

In this paper, we examined the abilities of 51 feature sets to estimate perceptual similarity as estimated using free-grouping and pair-of-pairs experiments. Even though five different pyramid resolutions were used in order to enhance the feature sets' spatial extents, the results did not agree well with humans' perceptual judgments. The average agreement rates of 57.76% and 53.59% were obtained over all methods and resolutions. Obviously, enhancing spatial extent alone is not enough for capturing the complexity of human perception.

In a second experiment, 80 of the most difficult pairs of pairs of images from experiment one, were selected for further investigation. These were "blocked" and then the position of the blocks within an image was randomized in order to remove, or at least reduce, the ability of observers to exploit long-range interactions in the textures. The results of the second experiment showed that the block-randomized images produced significantly different results from the original experiment, while the blocked but non-randomized images did not. When human observers are allowed to use long-range interactions in textures, they agree significantly less with the computational feature-based results. Thus we hypothesize that long-range interactions are important when humans judge the similarity of textures and that the 51 feature sets that we tested do not use this important information.

Acknowledgements. We would like to acknowledge the support of the Life Sciences Interface theme of Heriot-Watt University.

References

1. Halley, F.: Perceptually Relevant Browsing Environments for Large Texture Databases. PhD Thesis, Heriot Watt University (2011)
2. Clarke, A.D.F., Halley, F., Newell, A.J., Griffin, L.D., Chantler, M.J.: Perceptual Similarity: A Texture Challenge. In: BMVC 2011, pp. 120.1–120.10. BMVA Press (2011)
3. Randen, T., Husøy, J.H.: Filtering for Texture Classification: A Comparative Study. IEEE Transactions on PAMI 21, 291–310 (1999)
4. Varma, M., Zisserman, A.: A Statistical Approach to Material Classification Using Image Patch Exemplars. IEEE Transactions on PAMI 31, 2032–2047 (2009)
5. Unser, M.: Sum and Difference Histograms for Texture Classification. IEEE Transactions on PAMI 8(1), 118–125 (1986)
6. Mao, J., Jain, A.K.: Texture classification and segmentation using multiresolution simultaneous autoregressive models. Pattern Recognition 25(2), 173–188 (1992)
7. Parseval's Theorem, http://mathworld.wolfram.com/ParsevalsTheorem.html
8. Oppenheim, A.V., Lim, J.S.: The Importance of Phase in Signals. Proceedings of the IEEE 69(5), 529–541 (1991)
9. Field, D.J., Hayes, A., Hess, R.F.: Contour integration by the human visual system: evidence for a local "association field". Vision Research 33, 173–193 (1993)
10. Polat, U., Sagi, D.: The Architecture of Perceptual Spatial Interactions. Vision Research 34, 73–78 (1994)
11. Spillmann, L., Werner, J.S.: Long-range interactions in visual perception. Trends in Neurosciences 19, 428–434 (1996)
12. Clarke, A.D.F., Dong, X., Chantler, M.J.: Does Free-sorting Provide a Good Estimate of Visual Similarity. In: Predicting Perceptions, pp. 17–20 (2012)
13. MatlabPyrTools-v1.4, http://www.cns.nyu.edu/~lcv/software.php

Unsupervised Dynamic Textures Segmentation

Michal Haindl and Stanislav Mikeš

Institute of Information Theory and Automation
of the ASCR, Prague, Czech Republic
{haindl,xaos}@utia.cz

Abstract. This paper presents an unsupervised dynamic colour texture segmentation method with unknown and variable number of texture classes. Single regions with dynamic textures can furthermore change their location as well as their shape. Individual dynamic multispectral texture mosaic frames are locally represented by Markovian features derived from four directional multispectral Markovian models recursively evaluated for each pixel site. Estimated frame-based Markovian parametric spaces are segmented using an unsupervised segmenter derived from the Gaussian mixture model data representation which exploits contextual information from previous video frames segmentation history. The segmentation algorithm for every frame starts with an over segmented initial estimation which is adaptively modified until the optimal number of homogeneous texture segments is reached. The presented method is objectively numerically evaluated on the dynamic textural test set from the Prague Segmentation Benchmark.

Keywords: dynamic texture segmentation, unsupervised segmentation.

1 Introduction

Many automated static or dynamic visual data analysis systems build on the segmentation as the fundamental process which affects the overall performance of any analysis. Visual scene regions, homogeneous with respect to some usually textural or colour measure, which result from a segmentation algorithm are analysed in subsequent interpretation steps. Dynamic texture-based (DT) image segmentation is an area of novel research activity in recent years and several algorithms were published in consequence of all this effort. Different published methods are difficult to compare because of incompatible assumptions (grayscale, fixed or known number of regions, segmentation or retrieval, constant shape and/or location of texture regions, etc.), lack of a comprehensive analysis together with accessible experimental data. Gray scale dynamic texture segmentation or retrieval was addressed in few papers [1–5], while colour texture retrieval based on VLBP [6] or DT segmentation [7], based on the geodesic active contour algorithm and partial shape matching to obtain partial match costs between regions of subsequent frames, were addressed to even lesser extent. However all available published results indicate that the ill-defined dynamic texture

R. Wilson et al. (Eds.): CAIP 2013, Part I, LNCS 8047, pp. 433–440, 2013.

segmentation problem is far from being satisfactorily solved. Spatial interaction models and especially Markov random fields-based models are increasingly popular for texture representation [8, 9], etc. Several researchers dealt with the difficult problem of unsupervised segmentation using these models see for example [10–13] or [14] which is also generalized to dynamic textures and addressed in this paper.

The contribution of the paper is a novel unsupervised dynamic multispectral texture segmentation method with unknown and variable number of texture classes, and regions (with dynamic texture) which can in addition change their location as well as their shape. Thus the method relaxes most of the alternative approaches [1–5] limitations (gray-scale textures, fixed or known number of regions, fixed regions shape and locations) which prevent their practical applications.

The outline of this paper is as follows. Section 2 presents our Markovian multispectral texture representation. Section 3 outlines the unsupervised segmenter, followed by the experimental verification in the subsequent Section 4 and concluding Section 5.

2   Dynamic Texture Representation

Dynamic multispectral textures would require a four dimensional (4D) model or some of its lower dimensional approximation such as a set of spectrally factorized 3D models. However we assume to model each dynamic texture frame separately and thus a 3D static smooth textural model is sufficient for its adequate representation. We assume that single multispectral frame textures can be locally modeled using a 3D simultaneous causal auto-regressive random field model (AR3D). This model can be expressed as a stationary causal uncorrelated noise driven 3D auto-regressive process [15]:

$$Y_r = \gamma X_r + e_r \ , \tag{1}$$

where $X_r = [Y_{r-s}^T : \forall s \in I_r^c]^T$ is a vector of the contextual neighbours Y_{r-s}, I_r^c is a causal neighbourhood index set of the model with the cardinality $\eta = card(I_r^c)$, $\gamma = [A_1, \ldots, A_\eta]$ is the $d \times d\eta$ parameter matrix containing parametric sub-matrices A_s for each contextual neighbour Y_{r-s}, d is the number of spectral bands, e_r is a white Gaussian noise vector with zero mean and a constant but unknown covariance, and $r, r-1, \ldots$ is a chosen direction of movement on the image index lattice I. The selection of an appropriate model support (I_r^c) is important to obtain good texture representation for realistic texture synthesis but less important for adequate texture segmentation which works only with site specific parameters. Both, the optimal neighbourhood as well as the Bayesian parameters estimation of the AR3D model can be found analytically under few additional and acceptable assumptions using the Bayesian approach (see details in [15]). The local model parameters can be advantageously evaluated using the recursive Bayesian parameter estimator for every DT frame as follows:

$$\hat{\gamma}_{r-1}^T = \hat{\gamma}_{r-2}^T + \frac{V_{x(r-2)}^{-1} X_{r-1} (Y_{r-1} - \hat{\gamma}_{r-2} X_{r-1})^T}{(1 + X_{r-1}^T V_{x(r-2)}^{-1} X_{r-1})} , \tag{2}$$

where the data accumulation matrix is

$$V_{x(r-1)} = \sum_{k=1}^{r-1} X_k X_k^T + V_{x(0)} . \tag{3}$$

Thus the parameter matrix estimate can be easily upgraded after moving to a new lattice location $(r - 1 \longrightarrow r)$. The model is very fast, hence the local texture for each pixel can be represented by four directional parametric vectors corresponding to four distinct models. Each vector contains local estimations of the AR3D model parameters. These models have identical contextual neighbourhood I_r^c but they differ in their major movement direction (top-down, bottom-up, rightward, leftward), i.e.,

$$\tilde{\gamma}_{r,o}^T = \{\hat{\gamma}_{r,o}^t, \hat{\gamma}_{r,o}^b, \hat{\gamma}_{r,o}^r, \hat{\gamma}_{r,o}^l\}^T , \tag{4}$$

where $o = 1, \ldots, n$ is the DT frame number.

3 Gaussian Mixture Segmenter

Multispectral texture segmentation is done by clustering in the AR3D parameter space Θ_o defined on the lattice I for every frame o where

$$\Theta_{r,o} = \tilde{\gamma}_{r,o}^T \tag{5}$$

is the decorrelated parameter vector (4) computed for the lattice location r (the frame index is further left out to simplify notation). We assume that this parametric space can be represented using the Gaussian mixture model with diagonal covariance matrices due to the previous CAR parametric space decorrelation. The Gaussian mixture model for AR3D parametric representation is as follows:

$$p(\Theta_r) = \sum_{i=1}^{K} p_i \, p(\Theta_r \,|\, \nu_i, \Sigma_i) , \tag{6}$$

$$p(\Theta_r \,|\, \nu_i, \Sigma_i) = \frac{|\Sigma_i|^{-\frac{1}{2}}}{(2\pi)^{\frac{d}{2}}} \, e^{-\frac{(\Theta_r - \nu_i)^T \Sigma_i^{-1} (\Theta_r - \nu_i)}{2}} . \tag{7}$$

The mixture model equations (6),(7) are solved using a modified EM algorithm. The algorithm is initialised, for the first DT frame, using ν_i, Σ_i statistics estimated from the corresponding rectangular subimages obtained by regular division of the input texture mosaic. An alternative initialisation can be random choice of these statistics. For each possible couple of rectangles the Kullback Leibler divergence

$$D\left(p(\Theta_r \,|\, \nu_i, \Sigma_i) \,\|\, p(\Theta_r \,|\, \nu_j, \Sigma_j)\right) =$$
$$\int_{\Omega} p(\Theta_r \,|\, \nu_i, \Sigma_i) \, \log\left(\frac{p(\Theta_r \,|\, \nu_i, \Sigma_i)}{p(\Theta_r \,|\, \nu_j, \Sigma_j)}\right) d\Theta_r \tag{8}$$

is evaluated and the most similar rectangles, i.e.,

$$\{i, j\} = \arg\min_{k,l} D\left(p(\Theta_r \mid \nu_l, \Sigma_l) \,\|\, p(\Theta_r \mid \nu_k, \Sigma_k)\right) \tag{9}$$

are merged together in each step. This initialization results in K_{ini} subimages and recomputed statistics ν_i, Σ_i. $K_{ini} > K$ where K is the optimal number of textured segments to be found by the algorithm. All the subsequent DT frames are initialized either from the corrected statistics $\hat{\nu}_{i,o-1}, \hat{\Sigma}_{i,o-1}$ for $i = 1, \ldots, K$ computed from the trimmed segmented regions in the previous frame $o - 1$ or with random parameter values $\hat{\nu}_{i,o-1}, \hat{\Sigma}_{i,o-1}$ $i = K + 1, \ldots, K_{ini}$ for possibly newly (re)appearing regions. Two steps of the EM algorithm are repeating after initialisation. The components with smaller weights than a fixed threshold $(p_j < \frac{0.1}{K_{ini}})$ are eliminated. For every pair of components we estimate their Kullback Leibler divergence (8). From the most similar couple, the component with the weight smaller than the threshold is merged to its stronger partner and all statistics are actualised using the EM algorithm. The algorithm stops when either the likelihood function has negligible increase $(\mathcal{L}_t - \mathcal{L}_{t-1} < 0.05)$ or the maximum iteration number threshold is reached.

The parametric vectors representing texture mosaic pixels are assigned to the clusters according to the highest component probabilities, i.e., Y_r is assigned to the cluster ω_j if

$$\pi_{r,j} = max_j \sum_{s \in I_r} w_s \, p(\Theta_{r-s} \mid \nu_j, \Sigma_j) \, , \tag{10}$$

where w_s are fixed distance-based weights, I_r is a rectangular neighbourhood and $\pi_{r,j} > \pi_{thre}$ (otherwise the pixel is unclassified). The area of single cluster blobs is evaluated in the post-processing thematic map filtration step. Regions with similar statistics are merged. Thematic map blobs with area smaller than a given threshold are attached to its neighbour with the highest similarity value. Finally, the resulting region classes are remapped to ensure their between frame consistency.

4   Experimental Results

The algorithm was tested on the natural colour dynamic textural mosaics from the Prague Texture Segmentation Data-Generator and Benchmark [16]. The benchmark (http://mosaic.utia.cas.cz) test mosaics with varying layouts and each cell texture membership are randomly generated and filled with dynamic colour textures from the Dyntex database [17]. The benchmark ranks segmentation algorithms according to a chosen criterion. The benchmark has implemented the majority of segmentation criteria used for both supervised or unsupervised algorithms evaluation. Twenty seven evaluation criteria (see their definition in [16]) are categorized into four groups: region-based (5+5), pixel-wise (12), consistency measures (2), and clustering comparison criteria (3) and permit detailed and objective study of any segmentation method properties. Tab.1 compares

Table 1. Dynamic A benchmark results for DTAR3D+EM (e+pp), DTAR3D+EM (pp), DTAR3D+EM; (Benchmark criteria [16]: **CS = correct segmentation; OS = over-segmentation; US = under-segmentation; ME = missed error; NE = noise error; O = omission error; C = commission error; CA = class accuracy; CO = recall - correct assignment; CC = precision - object accuracy; I. = type I error; II. = type II error; EA = mean class accuracy estimate; MS = mapping score; RM = root mean square proportion estimation error; CI = comparison index; GCE = Global Consistency Error; LCE = Local Consistency Error; dD = Van Dongen metric; dM = Mirkin metric; dVI = variation of information**). Arrows directions denote the required criterion motion, the criteria rank numbers are down-sized on the right with the average rank besides the method label. The bold numbers are the best criterion values, while italic numbers are the worst criterion values.

| | Benchmark – Dynamic A | | |
	DTAR3D+EM e+pp (1.33)	DTAR3D+EM pp (1.86)	DTAR3D+EM (2.62)
↑ CS	**92.68** ¹	60.75 ²	*60.12* ³
↓ OS	*39.47* ³	20.37 ²	**14.78** ¹
↓ US	0.00 ¹	0.00 ¹	0.00 ¹
↓ ME	**0.00** ¹	*35.77* ²	*35.77* ²
↓ NE	**0.00** ¹	36.52 ²	*36.76* ³
↓ O	3.23 ¹	10.07 ²	*11.08* ³
↓ C	13.25 ²	**12.45** ¹	*14.56* ³
↑ CA	**87.03** ¹	81.26 ²	*80.10* ³
↑ CO	**92.68** ¹	84.42 ²	*83.69* ³
↑ CC	*94.01* ³	**95.85** ¹	95.18 ²
↓ I.	**7.32** ¹	15.58 ²	*16.31* ³
↓ II.	*1.32* ³	**0.76** ¹	0.89 ²
↑ EA	**92.80** ¹	89.01 ²	*88.30* ³
↑ MS	**89.07** ¹	82.41 ²	*81.35* ³
↓ RM	**2.56** ¹	*5.54* ³	5.21 ²
↑ CI	**93.07** ¹	89.56 ²	*88.86* ³
↓ GCE	**11.13** ¹	12.39 ²	*13.51* ³
↓ LCE	**7.02** ¹	11.03 ²	*12.21* ³
↓ dD	**7.27** ¹	11.68 ²	*12.37* ³
↓ dM	**4.95** ¹	6.36 ²	*6.80* ³
↓ dVI	**13.18** ¹	13.93 ²	*13.99* ³

the overall (average over all DT frames) benchmark performance of the proposed algorithm ($DTAR3D + EM(e + pp)$) with postprocessing (pp) and robust trimmed initialization (e) with its alternative versions. The results demonstrate very good performance on all criteria with the exception of over-segmentation tendency and slightly worse variation of information criterion. We could not compare our results with few published alternative DT segmenters [1, 2, 4] because neither their code, nor their experimental segmentation data are publicly available, however the static single-frame (AR3D+EM) version of the method was extensively evaluated and compared with several alternative methods (22

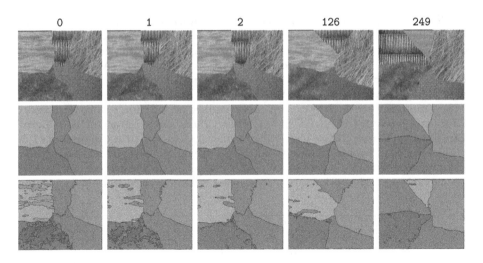

Fig. 1. Selected experimental dynamic texture mosaic frames (0, 1, 2, 126, 249), ground truth from the benchmark (middle row), and the corresponding segmentation results (DTAR3D+EM e+pp - bottom))

other leading unsupervised segmenters) in the segmentation benchmark. The static method proved its very good performance and outperformed most of these alternatives (see details in http://mosaic.utia.cas.cz). For example, the important correct region segmentation criterion (CS) is 25% better than for the HGS method [18], under-segmentation is low as well as missed and noise errors [19].

Fig.1 shows five selected (three from the beginning, one from the middle and one from the end of the sequence) 720×576 frames from the experimental benchmark mosaics created from five Dyntex dynamic colour textures (47fa110 - *curtain*, 54aa110 - *curly hair*, 54ac210 - *straw*, 54pd110 - *escalator*, and 571b110 - *water*). While the first frame suffers with over-segmentation the contextual information propagated from previous frames significantly improves the segmentation consistency. Hard natural Dyntex textures were chosen for comparison rather than synthesised (for example using the generative AR3D model or some other Markov random field model) ones because they are expected to be more difficult for the underlying segmentation model. Resulting segmentation results are promising even if we could not compare them with alternative DT segmentation methods. The time for an unoptimized parameter estimation is 170 s and segmentation time is 10 s per frame. Our results can be further improved by an appropriate more elaborate postprocessing or frame model initialization.

5   Conclusions

We proposed novel method for fast unsupervised dynamic texture or video segmentation with unknown variable number of classes based on the underlying three dimensional Markovian local image representation and the Gaussian mixture parametric space models. Single homogeneous texture regions can not only dynamically change their location but simultaneously also their shape. Textural regions can also disappear temporarily or permanently and new regions can appear at any time. Although the algorithm uses the random field type data model it is very fast because it uses efficient recursive parameter estimation of the model and therefore is much faster than the usual Markov chain Monte Carlo estimation approach needed for Markovian models. Segmentation methods typically suffer with lot of application dependent parameters to be experimentally estimated. Our method requires only a contextual neighbourhood selection and two additional thresholds all of them having an intuitive meaning. The algorithm's performance is demonstrated on the extensive benchmark objective tests on natural dynamic texture mosaics. The static version of our method outperforms several alternative unsupervised segmentation algorithms and it is also faster than most of them. These dynamic texture unsupervised segmentation test results are encouraging and we proceed with more elaborate post-processing and some modification of the texture representation model.

References

1. Doretto, G., Cremers, D., Favaro, P., Soatto, S.: Dynamic texture segmentation. In: Proceedings of the 9th IEEE International Conference on Computer Vision, vol. 2, pp. 1236–1242 (2003)
2. Péteri, R., Chetverikov, D.: Dynamic texture recognition using normal flow and texture regularity. In: Marques, J.S., Pérez de la Blanca, N., Pina, P. (eds.) IbPRIA 2005, Part II. LNCS, vol. 3523, pp. 223–230. Springer, Heidelberg (2005)
3. Chan, A.B., Vasconcelos, N.: Classifying video with kernel dynamic textures. In: IEEE Computer Society Conference on Computer Vision and Pattern Recognition (CVPR 2007), pp. 1–6. IEEE Computer Society (2007)
4. Chan, A.B., Vasconcelos, N.: Layered dynamic textures. IEEE Transactions on Pattern Analalysis and Machine Intelligence 31(10), 1862–1879 (2009)
5. Chen, J., Zhao, G., Salo, M., Rahtu, E., Pietikinen, M.: Automatic dynamic texture segmentation using local descriptors and optical flow. IEEE Transactions on Image Processing (2012)
6. Zhao, G., Pietikäinen, M.: Dynamic texture recognition using local binary patterns with an application to facial expressions. IEEE Transactions on Pattern Analysis and Machine Intelligence 29(6), 915–928 (2007)
7. Donoser, M., Urschler, M., Riemenschneider, H., Bischof, H.: Highly consistent sequential segmentation. In: Heyden, A., Kahl, F. (eds.) SCIA 2011. LNCS, vol. 6688, pp. 48–58. Springer, Heidelberg (2011)
8. Kashyap, R.L.: Image models. In: Young, T.Y., Fu, K.S. (eds.) Handbook of Pattern Recognition and Image Processing. Academic Press, New York (1986)
9. Haindl, M.: Texture synthesis. CWI Quarterly 4(4), 305–331 (1991)
10. Panjwani, D.K., Healey, G.: Markov random field models for unsupervised segmentation of textured color images. IEEE Transactions on Pattern Analysis and Machine Intelligence 17(10), 939–954 (1995)
11. Manjunath, B.S., Chellapa, R.: Unsupervised texture segmentation using Markov random field models. IEEE Transactions on Pattern Analysis and Machine Intelligence 13, 478–482 (1991)

12. Haindl, M.: Texture segmentation using recursive markov random field parameter estimation. In: Bjarne, K.E., Peter, J. (eds.) Proceedings of the 11th Scandinavian Conference on Image Analysis, Lyngby, Denmark, pp. 771–776. Pattern Recognition Society of Denmark (June 1999)

13. Haindl, M., Mikeš, S., Pudil, P.: Unsupervised hierarchical weighted multi-segmenter. In: Benediktsson, J.A., Kittler, J., Roli, F. (eds.) MCS 2009. LNCS, vol. 5519, pp. 272–282. Springer, Heidelberg (2009)

14. Haindl, M., Mikeš, S.: Unsupervised texture segmentation using multispectral modelling approach. In: Tang, Y.Y., Wang, S.P., Yeung, D.S., Yan, H., Lorette, G. (eds.) Proceedings of the 18th International Conference on Pattern Recognition, ICPR 2006, vol. II, pp. 203–206. IEEE Computer Society, Los Alamitos (2006)

15. Haindl, M., Šimberová, S.: A multispectral image line reconstruction method. In: Theory & Applications of Image Analysis, pp. 306–315. World Scientific Publishing Co., Singapore (1992)

16. Haindl, M., Mikeš, S.: Texture segmentation benchmark. In: Lovell, B., Laurendeau, D., Duin, R. (eds.) Proceedings of the 19th International Conference on Pattern Recognition, ICPR 2008, pp. 1–4. IEEE Computer Society (2008)

17. Péteri, R., Fazekas, S., Huiskes, M.J.: DynTex: A Comprehensive Database of Dynamic Textures. Pattern Recognition Letters 31(12), 1627–1632 (2010), http://projects.cwi.nl/dyntex/

18. Hoang, M.A., Geusebroek, J.M., Smeulders, A.W.M.: Color texture measurement and segmentation. Signal Processing 85(2), 265–275 (2005)

19. Hoover, A., Jean-Baptiste, G., Jiang, X., Flynn, P.J., Bunke, H., Goldgof, D.B., Bowyer, K., Eggert, D.W., Fitzgibbon, A., Fisher, R.B.: An experimental comparison of range image segmentation algorithms. IEEE Transaction on Pattern Analysis and Machine Intelligence 18(7), 673–689 (1996)

20. Kittler, J.V., Marik, R., Mirmehdi, M., Petrou, M., Song, J.: Detection of defects in colour texture surfaces. In: IAPR Workshop on Machine Vision Application, Tokyo, Japan, pp. 558–567 (1994)

21. Mitra, P., Murthy, C.A., Pal, S.K.: Unsupervised feature selection using feature similarity. IEEE Transactions on Pattern Analysis and Machine Intelligence 24, 301–312 (2002)

22. Mirmehdi, M., Marik, R., Petrou, M., Kittler, J.: Iterative morphology for fault detection in stochastic textures. Electronic Letters 32(5), 443–444 (1996)

Voting Clustering and Key Points Selection

Costas Panagiotakis[1] and Paraskevi Fragopoulou[2]

[1] Dept. of Commerce and Marketing, Technological Educational Institute (TEI)
of Crete, 72200 Ierapetra, Greece
`cpanag@staff.teicrete.gr`
[2] Dept. of Applied Informatics and Multimedia, TEI of Crete, PO Box 140, Greece
`fragopou@ics.forth.gr`*

Abstract. We propose a method for clustering and key points selection. We have shown that the proposed clustering based on the voting maximization scheme has advantages concerning the cluster's compactness, working well for clusters of different densities and/or sizes. Experimental results demonstrate the high performance of the proposed scheme and its application to video summarization problem.

Keywords: Clustering, Grouping, K-means, Video summarization.

1 Introduction

Clustering is one of the most fundamental problems of pattern recognition with many applications in different fields like computer vision, signal-image-video analysis, multimedia, networks and biology. The clustering task involves grouping N given objects (points of $d-$dimensional space) into a set of K subgroups (clusters) in such a manner that the similarity measure between the objects within a subgroup is higher than the similarity measure between the objects from other subgroups [1]. Clustering algorithms can be divided into two main categories: hierarchical and partitional [2]. Hierarchical clustering algorithms recursively find nested clusters either in agglomerative (bottom-up) mode or in divisive (top-down) mode. According to partitional clustering algorithms, the clusters are simultaneously computed as a partition of the data. The resulting clusters can be disjoint and nonoverlapping (crisp clustering), where an object belongs to one and only one cluster, or overlapping (fuzzy clustering), where an object may belong to more than one cluster.

During the last decades, thousands of clustering algorithms [2] have been published, so hereafter we briefly present some popular and widely used clustering algorithms. An extensive survey of various clustering algorithms can be found in [2]. The K-means clustering algorithm, is one of the simplest partitional clustering algorithms that solves the clustering problem for a given number of clusters. The goal of K-means is to minimize the sum of squared error (SSE)

---

* Paraskevi Fragopoulou is also with the Foundation for Research and Technology-Hellas, Institute of Computer Science, 70013 Heraklion, Crete, Greece.

R. Wilson et al. (Eds.): CAIP 2013, Part I, LNCS 8047, pp. 441–448, 2013.

over all clusters. In [3], a variant method (K-means++ algorithm) for centroid initialization has been proposed that chooses centers at random from the data points, but weights the data points according to their squared distance from the closest center already chosen. K-means++ usually outperforms K-means in terms of both accuracy and speed. A deterministic initialization scheme for K-means is given by the KKZ algorithm [4]. According to KKZ method, the first centroid is given as the data point with maximum norm, and the second centroid is the point farthest from the first centroid, the third centroid is the point farthest from its closest existing centroid and so on. An extension/variation of K-means is the K-medoid or Partitioning Around Medoids (PAM) [5], where the clusters are represented using the medoid of the data instead of the mean. Medoid is the object of the cluster with minimum distance to all others objects in the cluster. Most of the approaches from literature are heuristic or they try to optimize a criterion that may not be appropriate for clustering or they require a training set. On the contrary, in this paper, we have solved the crisp clustering problem via a voting maximization scheme that ensures high similarity between the points of the same cluster without any user defined parameter. In addition, the proposed method has been applied to video summarization problem [6].

2   The Clustering Problem

In this section the clustering problem is analyzed. Let us assume a dataset of N points, $x_i, i \in \{1, ..., N\}$, in the d dimensional space ($x_i \in \Re^d$) that are clustered into K non empty clusters, $p_k, k \in \{1, ..., K\}$, where p_k denotes the k-cluster indexes and $|p_k|$ denotes the number of points of cluster p_k. According to crisp clustering it holds that each point belongs to exactly one cluster.

One of the most widely used criteria for clustering and for other similar problems (e.g. see Microaggregation problem [7]) is the within-group squared error (SSE) minimization,for cases of almost equal sized clusters and almost the same variation, the minimization of SSE yields what the humans mean "optimal clustering". However, the clustering that corresponds to the minimization of SSE is not always appropriate even for the simple case of two clusters. According to the minimization of SSE, it is difficult to keep connected large clusters with high variation, that means that if there exists a large physical cluster with high variation it is possible to be divided into two or more clusters.

In this research, we introduce a new validity measure, the Voting Measure (VM) that can also work well for clusters with different densities and/or sizes. VM is invariant on scaling and number of data points and is bounded $VM \in [0, 1]$. In order to define VM, first we introduce the voting point problem. According to this problem, we have to define the function $V(i, j) \in [0, 1]$ that corresponds to the votes of point x_i, $i \in \{1, ..., N\}$ to point $x_j, j \in \{1, ..., N\}$. However, if we use a metric for points' density like the Gaussian similarity function in spectral clustering, then high density clusters will be favored. In order to overcome this problem, the voting function is defined so that it should satisfy the following conditions:

(a) $\sum_{j=1}^{N} V(i,j) = 1$,   (b) $V(i,i) = 0$,   (c) $V(i,j) \sim \frac{1}{d(x_i,x_j)}$,   (d) $V(i,j) \leq \frac{1}{2}$
where $d(x_i, x_j)$ denotes the Euclidean distance between the points x_i, x_j. The first two conditions ensure the point "equality" (each point have the same voting "power"). The third condition ensures the scale/density invariant property. According to the first three conditions it holds that

$V_3(i,j) = \frac{\frac{1}{d(x_i,x_j)}}{\sum_{k \in \{1,...,N\}-\{i\}} \frac{1}{d(x_i,x_k)}}$, where $V_3(i,j)$ denotes the voting matrix that

satisfy the first three conditions (the sub-index show the number of satisfied conditions). The last condition is added in order to ensure that each point is will vote the rest points, avoiding the special case of pairs of identical points that only vote each other resulting wrong voting descriptors (see at the end of the Section). When all the conditions are satisfied then $V_4(i,j)$ is given by:

$$V_4(i,j) = \begin{cases} V_3(i,j) & , \delta(i) \leq 0 \\ \min(\frac{V_3(i,j)}{1-\delta(i)}, \frac{1}{2}) & , \delta(i) > 0 \end{cases} \tag{1}$$

where $\delta(i) = \max_{j \in \{1,...,N\}} V_3(i,j) - \frac{1}{2}$. In our experimental results, the voting matrix is computed based on the four prementioned conditions. The voting descriptor $VD(j) = \sum_{i=1}^{N} V(i,j)$ of point x_j, $j \in \{1,...,N\}$ measures the votes that point x_j receives. Under any dataset, it holds that the mean value of VD is one ($E(VD) = 1$). VM is defined by the average value of voting descriptors per cluster taking into account only the intrinsic voting, dividing by the number of clusters K:

$$VM = \frac{1}{K} \cdot \sum_{k=1}^{K} \frac{\sum_{i \in p_k} \sum_{j \in p_k} V(j,i)}{|p_k|} \tag{2}$$

Fig. 1(a) depicts a dataset using a colormap according to voting descriptor (red for high values and blue for low values). It holds that the voting descriptor generally receives higher values on points that are closer to a cluster centroid, while it receives lower values on boundary points. Lower values (e.g. close to zero) are observed for outliers, since these points are quite far from clusters, thus it is difficult to receive votes.

3   The Proposed Algorithm

3.1   Voting-Based Clustering Algorithm

In this section, the proposed Clustering based on Voting Representativeness algorithm (CVR) is presented. This method requires as input the voting array V, the voting descriptor VD, and the K. The output of the method is the cluster indexes. The proposed Clustering based on Voting Representativeness algorithm (CVR) method consists of two phases:

- In the first phase, K iterations are performed selecting the K key points. In the kth-iteration of the method, we select a key point of the dataset to be the representative of the k-cluster and we discard it from the dataset. Therefore, at the end of the first phase, the each cluster has been initialized with one record.

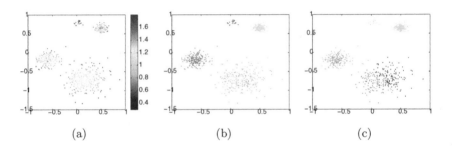

Fig. 1. (a) The dataset using a colormap according to voting descriptor. Results of clustering (b) $K = 4$, $SSE = 27.68$ and (c) $K = 4$, $SSE = 23.89$.

- Finally, in the second trivial phase the $N - K$ remaining unlabeled points are assigned to the cluster that corresponds to their "closest" representative point according to the voting formulation.

Hereafter, we analyze the first phase of the proposed method with more details, that has been used in video summarization problem (see Section 4). In the first iteration of the first phase, we detect the most representative (key) point of the dataset (p_1), where VD is maximized. This key point will be assigned to the first cluster and it will be discarded from the dataset (S).

For the selection of the next key points $p_k, k > 1$, we have to taken into account the already selected representative points. Therefore, the second key point $(p_k,\ k = 2)$ is selected taking into account the first one. This point should belong to a different cluster meaning that it should have low similarity with p_1 and vice versa. In order to satisfy this condition, we select the point with index i that minimizes the formula $v = \frac{V(i,p_{k-1})}{VD(p_{k-1})} + \frac{V(p_{k-1},i)}{VD(k)}$. This is the sum of percentages of votes that the point with index p_1 receives from the point with index i and vice versa.

We initialize a function $F(i) = 0$, $i \in S$. The next key points are selected by repeating the same procedure using the function F. When a point (x_{p_k}) is selected as a key point, we add it to the appropriate cluster and we discard it from the set S, where S denotes the domain of F. Finally, F is updated in order to ensure that the next key points will have low similarity with the already computed key points $F(i) = \max(F(i), v)$ as well as with x_{p_k}. The global minima of F will give the next key points. The total computational cost of the proposed CVR algorithm can be reduced from $O(N^2)$ to $O(N \cdot \log N + K \cdot N)$ when a sparse matrix and R-tree-like data structure are used.

3.2   Local Maximization of VM

This section presents an optional algorithm, inspired by the GSMS-T2 [7], that possibly improves a given initial clustering based on the local maximization of Voting Measure (VM). When we use as input the clustering of CVR method, the resulting algorithm is called CVR-LMV. Let's assume that two nearby located points x_i, x_j, $i, j \in \{1, ..., N\}$ that are misclassified by CVR in the same cluster, so that $V(i,j) \geq V(i,k), \forall k \in \{1, ..., N\}$ and $V(j,i) \geq V(j,k), \forall k \in \{1, ..., N\}$. Under this assumption, it is possible that if we separately check to reassign the point i (or the point j) to the true cluster, VM will be reduced, since the point x_j (or the point x_i) belongs to a different cluster.

In order to solve this problem without increasing the computation cost of the algorithm, we have introduced the median based VM $\widehat{VM}$, that estimates VM based on the median value of votes of points without affected by nearby points.

$$\widehat{VM} = \frac{1}{K} \cdot \sum_{k=1}^{K} \sum_{i \in p_k} median_{j \in p_k}(V(j,i)) \tag{3}$$

Let VM and VM' denote the validity measure before and after the possible reassignment. Let $\widehat{VM}$ and $\widehat{VM}'$ denote the median based VM before and after the possible reassignment. According to the proposed algorithm, we reassign the point with index i, if $VM' > VM$ or $\widehat{VM}' > \widehat{VM} \wedge \widehat{VM}' - \widehat{VM} + VM' - VM > 0$ is satisfied. The first condition ensures that VM increases. If only the second condition is true, this will cause an impermanent decrease of VM. Since the increase of $\widehat{VM}$ is higher than the decrease of VM means that the point with index i is closer to the examined cluster and we have to perform reassignment. In the next steps, we will also reassign the neighbors of point with index i and VM will increase.

Figs. 1(b) and 1(c) illustrate two different clustering results of the same dataset using the CVR-LMV and K-means clustering, respectively. The SSE of clustering depicted in Fig. 1(c) is 13.69% lower than the SSE of clustering depicted in Fig. 1(b). However the optimal solution of clustering is clearly depicted in Fig. 1(b).

4   Experimental Results

In this section, the experimental results of our performance study are presented. We have tested our methods (CVR and CVR-LMV) using the following six real datasets [8], where the number of records, the number of clusters, the data dimension, the cluster sizes and cluster densities are varied:

- the Iris (150 records in 4-dimensional space, $K = 3$).
- the Yeast (1484 records in 8-dimensional space, $K = 10$).
- the Segmentation (2100 records in 19-dimensional space, $K = 7$),
- the Wisconsin breast cancer (683 records in 30-dimensional space, $K = 2$).
- the Wine (178 records in 13-dimensional space, $K = 3$).
- the first 10^4 records of covtype (covtype10k) in 54-dimensional space, $K = 7$.

We have tested the proposed methods with 144 synthetic datasets generated by c random cluster centroids that are uniformly distributed over the d-dimensional hypercube ($c \in \{4, 8, 16\}$, $d \in \{4, 8\}$). The number of points n_i in cluster i is randomly selected from a uniform distribution between $\min n$ and $\max n$ ($\min n \in \{16, 128\}$, $\max n - \min n \in \{0, 128\}$). The n_i points in cluster i are randomly selected around the cluster centroid from a d-dimensional multivariate Gaussian distribution with covariance matrix $\Sigma_i = \sigma_i^2 I_d$ and mean value equal to the cluster centroid, where σ_i is randomly selected from a uniform distribution between $\min \sigma$ and $\max \sigma$, ($\min \sigma \in \{0.04, 0.08, 0.16\}$), ($\max \sigma - \min \sigma \in \{0, 0.08\}$). The parameters c and $\min \sigma$ receive three different values and the rest of the parameters receive two different values yielding $3^2 \cdot 2^4 = 144$ datasets.

In order to evaluate the accuracy of the proposed scheme, we have compared the proposed methods with seven other clustering methods: the K-means, the K-means KKZ algorithms [4], the hierarchical agglomerative algorithm based on the linkage metric of average link (HAC-AV) [9], spectral clustering using Nystrom method without orthogonalization (SCN) and with orthogonalization (SCN-O) [10], the K-means++ method [3] and the PAM algotithm [5]. For the non deterministic algorithms, 20 trials have been performed under any given dataset, getting the average value of the used performance metrics. We evaluate the performance using the clustering accuracy (Acc) [10]. $Acc \in [0, 1]$ is defined as the percentage of the correctly classified points.

Table 1. The accuracy (first 6 lines) and the average Acc (last line) of several clustering algorithms in 6 real and 144 synthetic datasets (144 S.D.), respectively

Dataset	CVR-LMV	CVR	K-means	K-means KKZ	HAC-AV	SCN	SCN-O	PAM	K-means++
Iris	**93.33%**	81.33%	84.20%	89.33%	90.67%	89.10%	88.87%	77.43%	85.77%
Yeast	39.22%	**42.39%**	36.04%	37.80%	32.35%	37.54%	37.10%	32.37%	35.15%
Segmentation	52.14%	37.43%	51.87%	35.62%	14.62%	47.35%	46.55%	**52.45%**	50.86%
Wisconsin	**91.04%**	90.51%	85.41%	85.41%	66.26%	73.15%	85.14%	84.97%	85.41%
Wine	**71.35%**	**71.35%**	68.20%	56.74%	61.24%	66.04%	60.17%	67.44%	65.65%
covtype10k	37.10%	**38.18%**	36.41%	35.95%	35.63%	36.20%	36.49%	35.90%	36.97%
144 S.D.	**98.71%**	97.85%	79.51%	97.51%	97.01%	94.04%	97.08%	78.61%	86.21%

Table 1 depicts the clustering accuracy measure of CVR-LMV, CVR, K-means, K-means KKZ, HAC-AV, SCN, SCN-O, PAM and K-means++ algorithms in real datasets (first six lines of the table) and the average clustering accuracy measure over the 144 synthetic datasets (144 S.D.) (last line of table). According to these results, the proposed methods CVR-LMV and CVR yield the highest performance results, outperforming the other methods from literature in five out of six real datasets. The highest performance results are achieved by CVR-LMV, since it holds that almost always, it gives the highest or the second highest performance results. According to the experiments on synthetic datasets, CVR-LMV yields the highest performance results, outperforming the other algorithms. CVR is the second highest performance method. High performance results are also obtained by K-means KKZ, HAC-AV and SCN-O methods. Concerning the probability that CVR-LMV reduces the clustering performance, this probability increases when CVR fails to find the true classes. In this case, CVR-LMV is possible to reduce or increase the clustering performance.

(a) #20   (b) #120   (c) #274   (d) #106   (e) #275

Fig. 2. Selected key frames of tennis ((a),(b),(c)) and foreman ((e),(f)) videos

(a) #7   (b) #68   (c) #119   (d) #182   (e) #262

Fig. 3. Selected key frames of hall monitor video

The proposed method can be used on several clustering based applications like the video summarization using key frames [6], where the goal is to select a subset of a video sequence (key frames) that can represent the video visual content. Similarly to [6], we have used the Color Layout Descriptor (CLD) which suffices to describe smoothly the changes in visual content. Then we apply the CVR algorithm using as input the CLD vectors and the desired number of key points K. The key points of the first phase of the CVR algorithm can be considered as the selected key frames, since they have the property to cover the video content space belonging to different clusters according to the CVR algorithm. An advantage of the proposed method is that ordering of the resulting key frames corresponds to their significance. Moreover, the proposed method does not assume that the video file has been segmented into shots as most of the key frame extraction algorithms done. The proposed method has been tested in several indoor and outdoor real life video sequences that have been used in [6] describing well the video content. Hereafter, we present the results of the proposed method on tennis, foreman and hall monitor videos[1] (see Figs. 2, 3) using three, two and five key frames, respectively. Under any case, it holds that the selected key frames are close to the humans' perception: In the tennis video, the first two selected key frames (#274, #120) belong to the two different shots of the video and the third one (#20) belongs on the first shot that has substantial visual content changes. In the foreman video, the selected key frames belong on the start and end of the sequence, describing well the two characteristics phases of the sequence (the interview and the buildings). In the hall monitor video the five selected key frames correspond to the five different "scenes" of the video (empty hall, a human with a bag in hall and so on).

5   Conclusions

In this paper, we propose a deterministic point clustering method that can be also used in video summarization problem. According to the proposed

---

[1] http://media.xiph.org/video/derf/

framework, the problem of clustering is reduced to the maximization of the sum of votes between the points of the same cluster. In addition, we have proposed the LMV algorithm that possibly improves a given initial clustering based on the local maximization of the proposed robust voting measure (VM). The proposed method can yield high performance results on clusters of different densities and/or sizes outperforming other methods from literature. In addition, the selected key frames describes well the visual content of the videos.

Acknowledgments. This research has been partially co-financed by the European Union (European Social Fund - ESF) and Greek national funds through the Operational Program "Education and Lifelong Learning" of the National Strategic Reference Framework (NSRF) - Research Funding Program ARCHIMEDE III-TEI-Crete-P2PCOORD.

References

1. Gupta, U., Ranganathan, N.: A game theoretic approach for simultaneous compaction and equipartitioning of spatial data sets. IEEE Transactions on Knowledge and Data Engineering 22, 465–478 (2010)
2. Jain, A.: Data clustering: 50 years beyond k-means. Pattern Recognition Letters 31, 651–666 (2010)
3. Arthur, D., Vassilvitskii, S.: k-means++: The advantages of careful seeding. In: Proceedings of the Eighteenth Annual ACM-SIAM Symposium on Discrete Algorithms, pp. 1027–1035 (2007)
4. Katsavounidis, I., Kuo, C.C.J., Zhang, Z.: A new initialization technique for generalized lloyd iteration. IEEE Signal Processing Letters 1, 144–146 (1994)
5. Theodoridis, S., Koutroumbas, K.: Pattern Recognition, 3rd edn. Elsevier (2006)
6. Panagiotakis, C., Doulamis, A., Tziritas, G.: Equivalent key frames selection based on iso-content principles. IEEE Transactions on Circuits and Systems for Video Technology 19, 447–451 (2009)
7. Panagiotakis, C., Tziritas, G.: Successive group selection for microaggregation. IEEE Trans. on Knowledge and Data Engineering 99 (accepted, 2011)
8. Blake, C., Keough, E., Merz, C.J.: UCI Repository of Machine Learning Database (1998), http://www.ics.uci.edu/~mlearn/MLrepository.html
9. Day, W., Edelsbrunner, H.: Efficient algorithms for agglomerative hierarchical clustering methods. Journal of Classification 1, 7–24 (1984)
10. Chen, W.Y., Song, Y., Bai, H., Lin, C.J., Chang, E.Y.: Parallel spectral clustering in distributed systems. IEEE Transactions on Pattern Analysis and Machine Intelligence 33, 568–586 (2011)

Motor Pump Fault Diagnosis with Feature Selection and Levenberg-Marquardt Trained Feedforward Neural Network

Thomas W. Rauber and Flávio M. Varejão

Departamento de Informática, Centro Tecnológico
Universidade Federal do Espírito Santo
29060-970 Vitória, Brazil
{thomas,fvarejao}@inf.ufes.br

Abstract. We present a system for automatic model-free fault detection based on a feature set from vibrational patterns. The complexity of the feature model is reduced by feature selection. We use a wrapper approach for the selection criteria, incorporating the training of an artificial neural network into the selection process. For fast convergence we train with the Levenberg-Marquardt algorithm. Experiments are presented for eight different fault classes.

Keywords: Fault diagnosis, feature selection, feedforward neural network, Levenberg-Marquardt.

The diagnosis of faults in expensive industrial equipment under production conditions is a valuable tool for improving the economic and security quality of its operation [1]. On the contrary to model-based diagnosis [2] where an analytical model of the machine has to be provided, we use a model-free approach based on supervised learning based on labeled data [3]. The sequence of processing steps to obtain a feature vector is raw data acquisition from several sensors, pre-processing on the level of the signal (filtering) and feature extraction. An additional information reduction step which we consider fundamental for an optimized performance of the fault diagnosis system is feature selection.

Since we are dealing with rotating machinery, the use of vibrational signals is indicated, positioning accelerometers at appropriate positions of motor and pump which deliver time domain signals that can be converted into dislocation, velocity and acceleration signals in the frequency domain [4]. For bearing faults, the envelope detection (or amplitude demodulation) [5] is an indicated tool that will be employed here to extract features from the raw signals. In [6], an overview of fault diagnosis of rotating machinery by empirical mode decomposition is given. Raw features are extracted from the vibrational signals, which are subjected to feature selection [7] and subsequently classified by a feedforward net trained by the Levenberg-Marquardt weight optimization method [8,9]. The equipment we are considering are motor pumps operating on offshore oil rigs. We work with 2000 examples of vibration signals obtained from operating partially faulty motor pumps, installed on 25 oil platforms off the Brazilian coast.

R. Wilson et al. (Eds.): CAIP 2013, Part I, LNCS 8047, pp. 449–456, 2013.

The signals were obtained during a period of five years. To generate the classified training data, experts in maintenance engineering provided a label for every fault present in each acquired example. Since several faults can simultaneously occur in a machine, we construct an independent classification task for each type of fault (one against all). Naturally the labelling process has been done by different persons and therefore the ground truth of the class membership is subject to model errors introduced a priori, i.e. it cannot be excluded that the provided label is erroneous in some cases.

1   Condition Monitoring of Oil Rig Motor Pumps

In real-world processes the availability of an analytical model is often unrealistic or inaccurate due to the complexity of the process. In this case model-free techniques are an alternative approach. This paper is concerned with model-free diagnosis of multiple faults in motor pumps, relying on supervised learning based techniques.

1.1   Motor Pump Equipment

Rotating machinery covers a wide range of mechanical equipment and plays an important role in industrial applications. In this work we focus on a specific rotating machine model, namely the horizontal motor pump with extended coupling between the electric motor and the pump. Accelerometers are placed at strategic positions along the main directions to capture specific vibrations of the main shaft which provides a multichannel time domain raw signal.

1.2   Considered Fault Categories

We build a predictor for individually detecting each of the following eight fault categories in an input pattern: shaft misalignment, pump blade unbalance, mechanical looseness of the pump, mechanical looseness of the motor, structural looseness of the pump, structural looseness of the motor, hydrodynamic fault (due to blade pass and vane pass, cavitation or flow turbulence) and resonance.

Fig. 1 illustrates how the frequency spectrum is associated with two of the faults, presenting the Fourier spectrum of the vibration signal (measured at the pump immediately behind the coupling and in horizontal direction) of a faulty motor pump with a misalignment fault and also an emerging hydrodynamic fault.

Each example in the database of 2000 machine signal acquisitions presented the occurrence of at least one fault. Examples presenting the occurrence of multiple faults are more common than examples in which just one fault is occurring. For each of the faults we built a one-against-the-rest classifier, i.e. a specialist for a certain kind of problem.

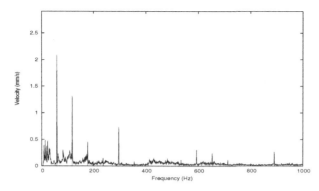

Fig. 1. Misalignment fault and its manifestation in the frequency spectrum at the first three harmonics of the shaft rotation frequency. The high energy in the fifth harmonic, as well as the noise in low frequencies indicate that additionally a hydrodynamic fault is emerging.

1.3   Extracted Features

Our general strategy is based on providing as much information as possible in the initial *feature extraction* stage. The available preprocessed signals are the frequency and the envelope spectrum of machine vibration signals. Hence we work with well-established signal processing techniques, namely the Fourier transform, envelope analysis based on the Hilbert transform [10] and median filtering. In this context, the extracted features correspond to the vibrational energy of predetermined frequency bands of the spectrum. We initially extract the same feature categories for building the predictor of every considered fault. Specifically, the initially extracted feature set is composed of a total of $D = 81$ features, with 68 of them from the Fourier spectrum and 13 of them from the Envelope spectrum.

2   Feature Selection

The main idea of feature selection is to obtain data that has a reduced dimensionality and more relevant information that can increase the classification performance. Feature selection is basically composed of a search algorithm and a selection criterion [11,12,7,13], Another important aspect of feature selection is the explication of the importance of each feature for the classification process. Previous work has investigated the problem of feature selection in the context of fault detection of rotating machines. In [14], features were ranked by their appraisal, using the sensitivity [3] during the training of a feedforward net with one hidden layer. Feature selection based on a individual threshold ranking in the context of tool condition monitoring can be found in [15]. A heuristic based on binary ant colony is used for feature selection in the context of a rotary kiln in [16]. Mutual information is the selection criterion proposed in [17] which also give a considerable overview of feature extraction and selection methods, also cf.

[18] where the minimum redundancy maximum relevancy (mRMR) criterion is proposed. The C4.5 decision tree machine learning algorithm presented in [19] implicitly performs feature selection by positioning those features with highest mutual information at the treetop.

We use a *Sequential Forward Selection (SFS)* [3] search algorithm which constitutes a good compromise between search space coverage and speed. As the selection criterion we use a *wrapper* approach with the estimated accuracy of a Levenberg-Marquardt trained feedforward net. For an application in human gait recognition that uses a multidimensional expansion of the mutual information theory and SFS, c.f. for instance [20]. This work is an example of a *filter* approach which do not use the final performance criterion as the selection criterion.

3   Feedforward Net and Weight Optimization

We follow the terminology of [8,9], to define the network calculus and the weight optimization. We expect the reader to be familiar with the basic concepts of a feedforward net and the principle of gradient descent.

3.1   Architecture

Consider as input to the net a R-dimensional pattern $\underline{p}$ from the Euclidean vector space $\mathbb{R}^R$. The net input with weights $w_{i,j}^{m+1}$ from the jth unit in layer m to the ith unit in layer $(m+1)$ and the biases b_i^{m+1} is

$$n_i^{m+1} = \sum_{j=1}^{S^m} w_{i,j}^{m+1} a_j^m + b_i^{m+1}. \tag{1}$$

Passing through an activation function f, the output of unit i becomes

$$a_i^{m+1} = f^{m+1}(n_i^{m+1}). \tag{2}$$

The network has M layers and the output of layer m in matrix form can be written as

$$\underline{a}^0 = \underline{p}, \quad \underline{a}^{m+1} = \underline{f}^{m+1}(W^{m+1}\underline{a}^m + \underline{b}^{m+1}), \quad m = 0, 1, \ldots, M-1, \quad \underline{a}^M = \underline{y}, \tag{3}$$

where $\underline{y}$ is the final output of the net. The $S^{m+1} \times S^m$ matrix W^{m+1} contains the weights of layer $(m+1)$. The activation function $f : \mathbb{R} \to \mathbb{R}$ is usually the logistic sigmoid function $f(n) = 1/(1 + \exp(-n))$, hyperbolic tangent sigmoid function $f(n) = \tanh n$ or the identity function $f(n) = n$. We consider a network with only one hidden layer, i.e. $M = 2$ and $m = 0, 1$, since empirically additional layers do not increase discriminative power.

3.2   Levenberg-Marquardt Training

For data sets with a reasonable number of patterns, this network training method is currently considered as state of the art due to its fast convergence and constitutes a strong motivation to use this technique for our purpose. The parameter vector $\underline{x} = \left[w_{1,1}^1 \ w_{1,2}^1 \cdots w_{S^1,R}^1 \ b_1^1 \cdots b_{S^1}^1 \cdots \ w_{1,1}^2 \cdots b_{S^M}^M \right]$ of dimension $n = \sum_{m=1}^M S^m(S^{m-1}+1)$ is assembled from all weights and biases and then subjected to the Levenberg-Marquardt (LM) optimization which is a modified second order approximator Gauss-Newton method. A control parameter μ determines how much steepest descent or how much Gauss-Newton the LM algorithm becomes.

For each of the $q = 1, \ldots, Q$ patterns and each of the S^M units of the final layer each component of the individual error $\underline{e}_q = \underline{t}_q - \underline{a}_q^M$ with targets $\underline{t}_q$ and final output vector $\underline{a}_q^M$ is

$$e_{k,q}, \quad k = 1, \ldots, S^M, \ q = 1, \ldots, Q. \tag{4}$$

There are $N = Q \cdot S^M$ such errors. Their gradient with respect to each of the weights and biases

$$\frac{\partial e_{k,q}}{\partial w_{i,j}^m}, \ \frac{\partial e_{k,q}}{\partial b_i^m}, \quad k = 1, \ldots, S^M, \ q = 1, \ldots, Q,$$

$$i = 0, \ldots, S^m, \ j = 1, \ldots, S^{m+1}, \ m = 0, \ldots, M-1 \tag{5}$$

is calculated and introduced into the $N \times n$ Jacobian matrix $J(\underline{x})$.

The sensitivity [9] of the i-th unit of the m-th layer s_i^m of the conventional backpropagation is replaced by the definition of the *Marquardt sensitivity* of unit i in layer m

$$\tilde{s}_{i,h}^m \equiv \frac{\partial e_{k,q}}{\partial n_{i,q}^m}, \tag{6}$$

where the index h over all N pattern-output unit pairs is calculated as $h = (q-1)S^M + k, \ q = 1, \ldots, Q, \ k = 1, \ldots, S^M$. The elements of the Jacobian can now be obtained as

$$[J]_{h,\ell} = \frac{\partial e_{k,q}}{\partial w_{i,j}^m} = \frac{\partial e_{k,q}}{\partial n_{i,q}^m} \cdot \frac{\partial n_{i,q}^m}{\partial w_{i,j}^m} = \tilde{s}_{i,h}^m a_{j,q}^{m-1}, \quad [J]_{h,\ell} = \frac{\partial e_{k,q}}{\partial b_i^m} = \tilde{s}_{i,h}^m. \tag{7}$$

The index ℓ over all network connections from layer m to layer $(m+1)$ is calculated as $\ell = j \cdot S^m + i, \ i = 1, \ldots, S^{m+1}, \ j = 0, \ldots, S^m, \ m = 0, \ldots, M-1$.

4   Experimental Results

The main objective is to illustrate the advantages of feature selection. With only a fraction of the original feature set it should be possible to obtain equivalent or better performance, compared to the complete feature set. As mentioned before, we use a combination of performance estimation and selection by taking the performance score as the proper criterion (wrapper).

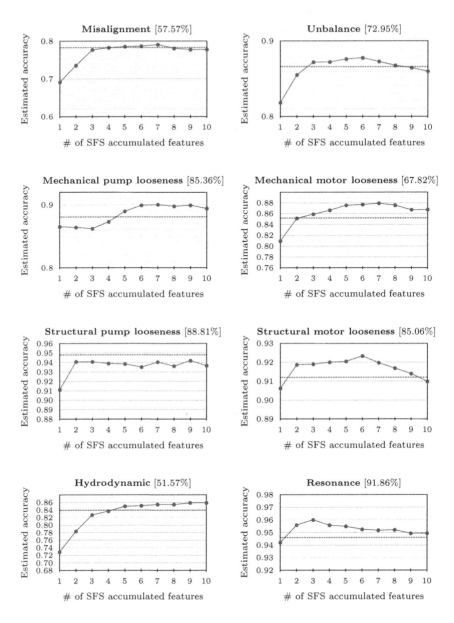

Fig. 2. Estimated classification accuracy [%] (y-axis) as a function of the cardinality of the selected feature set (x-axis) during the Sequential Forward Selection process. A blue dotted line shows the estimated accuracy when using all available 81 features. Each data set shows a qualitatively similar performance evolution. After a relatively small number of selected features the performance curve enters a saturation state with degrading performance.

4.1 Experimental Setup

As the selection algorithm the Sequential Forward Selection described in section 2 is used as a wrapper with the LM training of a feedforward net, cf. section 3.2. The number of units in the hidden layer is set as twice the current number of features plus one, for instance when the actual number of features in the SFS search is four, the number of neurons in the hidden layer is set to nine. As the performance criterion we choose the estimated error rate. The data is split randomly into 70% training data, 15% validation data and 15% test data. Training is interrupted if six consecutive validations perform worse than the corresponding training. The final score is taken as the mean of ten experiments.

From the total of 81 features we select ten features and plot the estimated performance for each cardinality of selected features. For instance during the SFS selection with the 'mechanical motor looseness' data set the best score for seven selected features was 87.96%. The results for all fault classes are plotted in fig. 2. Together with the estimated error for each cardinality, the estimated error for the total number of features is shown as a horizontal reference line.

4.2 Discussion

It can be clearly observed from the evolution of the estimated error in fig. 2 that the feature selection is able to reduce the complexity of the subsequent classification stage considerably. At the same time the performance is improved since noise is filtered out. Except for the 'structural pump looseness' fault, the estimated performance with only a fraction of the features is higher compared to the case when taking all available features for the training of the classifier. This clearly justifies the use of this important step in pattern recognition, also for this field of application.

5 Conclusion

We have presented a complete system for the diagnosis of faults in a real world scenario of rotating machinery installed on offshore oil rigs. A feature pool of frequency measurements is provided. From this pool, a subset is selected that achieves better performance with less complexity. Future work will concentrate on other sensors, feature models and performance estimation techniques.

Acknowledgments. This work was supported by Brazilian National Science Foundation CNPq (project 552630/2011-0) and the State Science Foundation of the State of Espírito Santo FAPES (project 48511579/2009).

References

1. Tavner, P.J., Ran, L., Penman, J., Sedding, H.: Conditiong Monitoring of Electrical Machines. The Institution of Engineering and Technology, London (2008)

2. Isermann, R.: Fault-Diagnosis Systems: An Introduction from Fault Detection to Fault Tolerance. Springer, Berlin (2006)
3. Theodoridis, S., Koutroumbas, K.: Pattern Recognition, 3rd edn. Academic Press, Inc., Orlando (2006)
4. Scheffer, C., Girdhar, P.: Pratical Machinery Vibration Analysis and Predictive Maintenance, 1st edn. Elsevier (2004)
5. McInerny, S.A., Dai, Y.: Basic vibration signal processing for bearing fault detection. IEEE Transactions on Education 46, 149–156 (2003)
6. Lei, Y., Lin, J., He, Z., Zuo, M.J.: A review on empirical mode decomposition in fault diagnosis of rotating machinery. Mechanical Systems and Signal Processing 35, 108–126 (2013)
7. Guyon, I., Elisseeff, A.: An introduction to variable and feature selection. J. Mach. Learn. Res. 3, 1157–1182 (2003)
8. Hagan, M., Menhaj, M.: Training feedforward networks with the marquardt algorithm. IEEE Transactions on Neural Networks 5, 989–993 (1994)
9. Hagan, M., Demuth, H., Beale, M.: Neural Network Design. Vikas Publishing House (2003)
10. Mendel, E., Rauber, T.W., Varejao, F.M.: Automatic bearing fault pattern recognition using vibration signal analysis. In: Proc. of the IEEE Int. Symp. on Ind. Electronics, ISIE 2008 (2008)
11. Devijver, P.A., Kittler, J.: Pattern Recognition: A Statistical Approach. Prentice/Hall Int., London (1982)
12. Kudo, M., Sklansky, J.: Comparison of algorithms that select features for pattern classifiers. Pattern Recognition Letters 33, 25–41 (2000)
13. Liu, H., Motoda, H.: Computational Methods of Feature Selection (Chapman & Hall/CRC Data Mining and Knowledge Discovery Series). Chapman & Hall/CRC (2007)
14. Matsuura, T.: An application of neural network for selecting feature parameters in machinery diagnosis. J. of Materials Processing Technol. 157–158, 203–207 (2004)
15. Jemielniak, K., Urbański, T., Kossakowska, J., Bombiński, S.: Tool condition monitoring based on numerous signal features. The International Journal of Advanced Manufacturing Technology 59, 73–81 (2012)
16. Kadri, O., Mouss, L.H., Mouss, M.D.: Fault diagnosis of rotary kiln using svm and binary aco. Journal of Mechanical Science and Technology 26, 601–608 (2012)
17. Tang, J., Chai, T., Yu, W., Zhao, L.: Feature extraction and selection based on vibration spectrum with application to estimating the load parameters of ball mill in grinding process. Control Engineering Practice 20, 991–1004 (2012); 4th Symposium on Advanced Control of Industrial Processes (ADCONIP)
18. Wang, J., Liu, S., Gao, R.X., Yan, R.: Current envelope analysis for defect identification and diagnosis in induction motors. Journal of Manufacturing Systems 31, 380–387 (2012); Selected Papers of 40th North American Manufacturing Research Conference
19. Amarnath, M., Sugumaran, V., Kumar, H.: Exploiting sound signals for fault diagnosis of bearings using decision tree. Measurement 46, 1250–1256 (2013)
20. Guo, B., Nixon, M.: Gait feature subset selection by mutual information. IEEE Transactions on Systems, Man and Cybernetics, Part A: Systems and Humans 39, 36–46 (2009)

Unobtrusive Fall Detection at Home Using Kinect Sensor

Michal Kepski[2] and Bogdan Kwolek[1]

[1] AGH University of Science and Technology, 30 Mickiewicza Av.,
30-059 Krakow, Poland
bkw@agh.edu.pl
[2] University of Rzeszow, 16c Rejtana Av., 35-959 Rzeszów, Poland
mkepski@univ.rzeszow.pl

Abstract. The existing CCD-camera based systems for fall detection require time for installation and camera calibration. They do not preserve the privacy adequately and are unable to operate in low lighting conditions. In this paper we show how to achieve automatic fall detection using only depth images. The point cloud corresponding to floor is delineated automatically using v-disparity images and Hough transform. The ground plane is extracted by the RANSAC algorithm. The detection of the person takes place on the basis of the updated on-line depth reference images. Fall detection is achieved using a classifier trained on features representing the extracted person both in depth images and in point clouds. All fall events were recognized correctly on an image set consisting of 312 images of which 110 contained the human falls. The images were acquired by two Kinect sensors placed at two different locations.

Keywords: Depth image and point cloud processing, fall detection.

1 Introduction

In almost all countries of the world the elderly population is continuously increasing. Improving the quality of life of increasingly elderly population is one of the most central challenges facing our society today. As humans become old, their bodies weaken and the risk of accidental falls raises noticeably [12]. A fall can lead to severe injuries such as broken bones, and a fallen person might need assistance at getting up again. Falls lead to losing self-confidence, a loss of independence and a higher risk of morbidity and mortality. Thus, in recent years a lot of research has been devoted to development of unobtrusive fall detection methods [15]. However, despite many efforts undertaken to achieve reliable and unobtrusive fall detection [16], the existing technology does not meet the seniors' needs [18]. The main reason is that it does not preserve the privacy and unobtrusiveness adequately. In particular, the current solutions generate too much false alarms, which in turn lead to considerable frustration of the seniors.

Most of the currently available techniques for fall detection are based on body-worn or built-in devices. They typically employ accelerometers or both accelerometers and gyroscopes [16]. However, on the basis of such sensors it is not

R. Wilson et al. (Eds.): CAIP 2013, Part I, LNCS 8047, pp. 457–464, 2013.

easy to separate real falls from fall-like activities [2]. They typically trigger significant number of false alarms. Moreover, the detectors that are typically worn on a belt around the hip, are obstructive and uncomfortable during the sleep [7]. What's more, their monitoring performance in critical phases like getting up from the bed or the chair is relatively poor.

In recent years, a lot of research has been done on detecting falls using a wide range of sensor types [16][18], including pressure pads [17], single CCD camera [1], multiple cameras [6], specialized omni-directional ones [14] and stereo-pair cameras [8]. Video cameras have several advantages over other sensors including the capability of recognition a variety of activities. Additional benefit is low intrusiveness and possibility of a remote verification of fall events. However, the solutions that are available at present require time for installation, camera calibration and in general they are not cheap. Additionally, the lack of 3D information can lead to lots of false alarms. Moreover, in vast majority of such systems the privacy is not preserved adequately.

Recently, the Kinect sensor was employed in fall detection systems [9][10][13]. It is the world's first low-cost device that combines an RGB camera and a depth sensor. Unlike 2D cameras, it allows tracking the body movements in 3D. Thus, if only depth images are used it preserves the privacy. Since it is equipped with an active light source it is independent of external light conditions. Owing to using the infrared light it is capable of extracting depth images in dark rooms.

In this work we demonstrate an approach to fall detection using only depth images. The person is detected on the basis of the depth reference image. We demonstrate a method for updating the depth reference image with a low computational cost. The ground plane is extracted automatically using the v-disparity images, Hough transform and the RANSAC algorithm. Fall detection is achieved using a classifier trained on features representing the extracted person both in depth images and in point clouds.

2   Person Detection in Depth Images

Depth is very useful cue to achieve reliable person detection because humans may not have consistent color and texture.but have to occupy an integrated region in space. The depth images were acquired by the Kinect sensor using OpenNI (Open Natural Interaction) library. The sensor has an infrared laser-based IR emitter, an infrared camera and a RGB camera. The IR camera and the IR projector form a stereo pair with a baseline of approximately 75 mm. Kinect depth measurement is based on structured light, making a triangulation between the dot pattern emitted and the pattern captured by the IR CMOS sensor. The pixels in the depth images indicate calibrated depth in the scene. Kinect's angular field of view is 57° horizontally and 43° vertically. The sensor has a practical ranging limit of about 0.6-5 m. It captures depth and color images simultaneously at a frame rate of about 30 fps. The default RGB video stream has size 640 × 480 and 8-bit for each channel. The depth stream is 640 × 480 resolution and with 11-bit depth, which provides 2048 levels of sensitivity.

Due to occlusions it is not easy to detect a person using only single camera and depth images. The software called NITE from PrimeSense offers skeleton tracking on the basis of images acquired by the Kinect sensor. However, this software is targeted for supporting the human-computer interaction, and not for detecting the person fall. Thus, in many circumstances it can have difficulties in extracting and tracking the person's skeleton [10].

The person was detected on the basis of a scene reference image, which was extracted in advance and then updated on-line. In the depth reference image each pixel assumes the median value of several pixels values from the past images. In the set-up stage we collect a number of the depth images, and for each pixel we assemble a list of the pixel values from the former images, which is then sorted in order to extract the median. Given the sorted lists of pixels the depth reference image can be updated quickly by removing the oldest pixels and updating the sorted lists with the pixels from the current depth image and then extracting the median value. We found that for typical human motions, good results can be obtained using 13 depth images. For the Kinect acquiring the images at 25 Hz we take every fifteenth image.

Figure 1 illustrates some example depth reference images, which were obtained using the discussed technique. In the image #500 we can see an office with the closed door, which was then opened to demonstrate how the algorithm updates the reference image. In frames #650 and #800 we can see that the opened door appears temporally in the binary image, and then it disappears in the frame #1000. As we can observe, the updated reference image is clutter free and allows us to extract the person's silhouette in the depth images. In order to eliminate small objects the depth connected components were extracted. Afterwards, small artifacts were eliminated. Otherwise, the depth images can be cleaned using morphological erosion. When the person does not move the reference image is not updated.

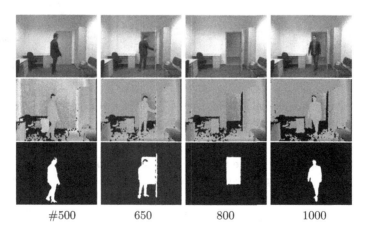

#500   650   800   1000

Fig. 1. Person segmentation using depth reference image. RGB images (upper row), depth (middle row) and binary images depicting the delineated person (bottom row).

In the detection mode the foreground objects are extracted through differencing the current image from such a reference depth map. Afterwards, the foreground object is determined through extracting the largest connected component in the thresholded difference map. Alternatively, the subject can be delineated using a pre-trained person detector. However, having in mind the privacy, the use of a person detector operating on depth images or point clouds leads to lower detection ratio and a higher computational cost.

3   V-Disparity Based Ground Plane Extraction

In [11] a method based on v-disparity maps between two stereo images has been proposed to achieve reliable obstacle detection. Given a depth map provided by the Kinect sensor, the disparity d can be determined in the following manner:

$$d = \frac{b \cdot f}{z} \tag{1}$$

where z is the depth (in meters), b is the horizontal baseline between the cameras (in meters), f is the (common) focal length of the cameras (in pixels). The IR camera and the IR projector form a stereo pair with a baseline of approximately $b = 7.5$ cm, whereas the focal length f is equal to 580 pixels.

Let H be a function of the disparities d such that $H(d) = I_d$. The I_d is the v-disparity image and H accumulates the pixels with the same disparity from a given line of the disparity image. Thus, in the v-disparity image each point in the line i represents the number of points with the same disparity occurring in the i-th line of the disparity image. Figure 2c illustrates the v-disparity image that corresponds to the depth image depicted on Fig. 2b.

Fig. 2. V-disparity map calculated on depth images from Kinect: RGB image a), corresponding depth image b), v-disparity map c)

The line corresponding to the floor pixels in the v-disparity map was extracted using the Hough transform. Assuming that the Kinect is placed at height about 1 m from the floor, the line representing the floor should begin in the disparities ranging from 15 to 25 depending on the tilt angle of the sensor. On Fig. 3 we can see some example lines extracted on the v-disparity images, which were obtained on the basis of images acquired in typical rooms, like office, see Fig. 2c, classroom, etc.

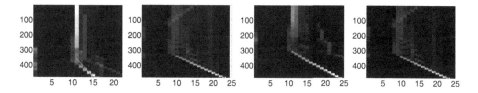

Fig. 3. Lines extracted by Hough transform on various v-disparity maps

The line corresponding to the floor was extracted using Hough transform (HT) operating o v-disparity values and a predefined range of parameters. The accumulator was incremented by v-disparity values, see Fig. 4a. It is worth noting that ordinary HT operating on thresholded v-disparity images often gives incorrect results, see Fig. 4b where the extremum is quite close to 0 deg.

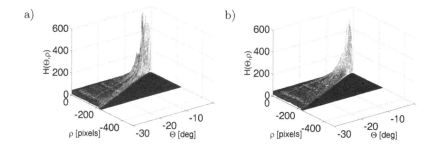

Fig. 4. Accumulator of the Hough transform: operating on v-disparity values a), thresholded v-disparity images b). The accumulator depicted on figure a) is divided by 100.

Given the extracted line in such a way, the pixels belonging to the floor areas were determined. Due to the measurement inaccuracies, pixels falling into some disparity extent d_t were also considered as belonging to the ground. Assuming that d_y is a disparity in the line y, which represents the pixels belonging to the ground plane, we take into account the disparities from the range $d \in (d_y - d_t, d_y + d_t)$ as a representation of the ground plane. Given the line extracted by the Hough transform, the points on the v-disparity image with the corresponding depth pixels were selected, and then transformed to the point cloud [10]. After the transformation of the pixels representing the floor to the 3D points cloud, the plane described by the equation $ax + by + cx + d$ was recovered. The parameters a, b, c and d were estimated using the RANSAC algorithm. The distance to the ground plane from the 3D centroid of points cloud corresponding to the segmented person was determined on the basis of the following equation:

$$D = \frac{|aX_c + bY_c + cZ_c + d|}{\sqrt{a^2 + b^2 + c^2}} \qquad (2)$$

where X_c, Y_c, Z_c stand for the coordinates of the centroid.

4   Experimental Results

A data-set consisting of normal activities like walking, sitting down, crouching
down and lying has been composed in order to train classifiers and to evaluate
the performance of the fall detection system. Thirty five volunteers with age
under 28 years attended in preparation of the data-set. The image sequences
were recorded using two Kinect devices. The first Kinect was placed at a height
of about one meter to the floor, whereas the second one was placed at a ceiling
corner of the room. Figure 5 shows example depth images seen from two different
views.

Fig. 5. Person in depth images seen from two different views

In total 312 images representing typical human actions were selected and then
utilized to extract the following features:

- h/w - a ratio of width to height of the person bounding box, calculated in
  the points cloud
- h/h_{max} - a ratio expressing the height of the person surrounding box in the
  current frame to the height of the person
- $dist$ - the distance of the person centroid to the floor, expressed in millimeters
- $max(\sigma_x, \sigma_z)$ - standard deviation from the centroid for the abscissa and the
  depth, respectively.

Figure 6 depicts a scatterplot matrix for the employed attributes, in which a collection of scatterplots is organized in a two-dimensional matrix simultaneously to
provide correlation information among the attributes. In a single scatterplot two
attributes are projected along the x-y axes of the Cartesian coordinates. As we
can observe, the overlaps in the attribute space are not too significant. We considered also another attributes, for instance, a filling ratio of the rectangles making
up the person bounding box. The worth of the features was evaluated on the basis
of the information gain [4], which measures the dependence between the feature
and the class label. In the evaluation we utilized the `InfoGainAttributeEval`
procedure from the Weka [5], which is a collection of machine learning algorithms.

The classification accuracy was evaluated in 10-fold cross-validation using
Weka software. The falls were classified using KStar [3], AdaBoost, SVM, multi-
layer perceptron (MLP), Naïve Bayes (NB) and k-NN classifiers. The KStar and

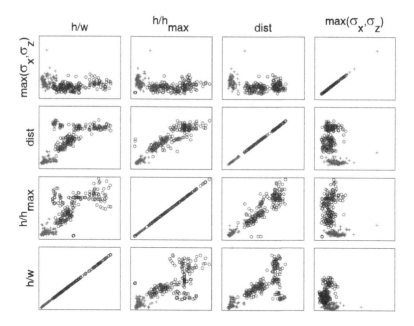

Fig. 6. Multivariate classification scatter plot

MLP classified all falls correctly, whereas the remaining algorithms incorrectly classified 2 instances. The number of images with person fall was equal to 110.

The system was implemented in C/C++ and runs at 25 fps on 2.4 GHz I7 (4 cores, Hyper-Threading) notebook powered by Linux. The most computationally demanding operation is extraction of the depth reference image. For images of size 640×480 the computation time needed for extraction of the depth reference image is about 9 milliseconds. At the PandaBoard, which is a low-power, low-cost single-board computer development platform, this operation can be completed in 0.15 sec. We are planning to implement the whole system on the PandaBoard.

5   Conclusions

In this work we demonstrated our approach to fall detection using Kinect. The fall detection is done on the basis of the segmented person in the depth images. The segmentation of the person takes place using updated depth reference image of the scene. For person extracted in such a way the corresponding points cloud is then extracted. The ground plane is determined automatically using the v-disparity images, Hough transform and the RANSAC algorithm. The fall is detected using a classifier built on features extracted both from the depth images as well as the points cloud corresponding to the extracted person. The system achieves high detection rate. On image set consisting of 312 images of which 110 contained human falls all fall events were recognized correctly.

Acknowledgment. This work has been supported by the National Science Centre (NCN) within the project N N516 483240.

References

1. Anderson, D., Keller, J., Skubic, M., Chen, X., He, Z.: Recognizing falls from silhouettes. In: Annual Int. Conf. of the Engineering in Medicine and Biology Society, pp. 6388–6391 (2006)
2. Bourke, A., O'Brien, J., Lyons, G.: Evaluation of a threshold-based tri-axial accelerometer fall detection algorithm. Gait & Posture 26(2), 194–199 (2007)
3. Cleary, J., Trigg, L.: An instance-based learner using an entropic distance measure. In: Int. Conf. on Machine Learning, pp. 108–114 (1995)
4. Cover, T.M., Thomas, J.A.: Elements of Information Theory. Wiley (1992)
5. Cover, T.M., Thomas, J.A.: Data Mining: Practical machine learning tools and techniques, 2nd edn. Morgan Kaufmann, San Francisco (2005)
6. Cucchiara, R., Prati, A., Vezzani, R.: A multi-camera vision system for fall detection and alarm generation. Expert Systems 24(5), 334–345 (2007)
7. Degen, T., Jaeckel, H., Rufer, M., Wyss, S.: Speedy: A fall detector in a wrist watch. In: Proc. of IEEE Int. Symp. on Wearable Computers, pp. 184–187 (2003)
8. Jansen, B., Deklerck, R.: Context aware inactivity recognition for visual fall detection. In: Proc. IEEE Pervasive Health Conference and Workshops, pp. 1–4 (2006)
9. Kepski, M., Kwolek, B., Austvoll, I.: Fuzzy inference-based reliable fall detection using kinect and accelerometer. In: Rutkowski, L., Korytkowski, M., Scherer, R., Tadeusiewicz, R., Zadeh, L.A., Zurada, J.M. (eds.) ICAISC 2012, Part I. LNCS, vol. 7267, pp. 266–273. Springer, Heidelberg (2012)
10. Kepski, M., Kwolek, B.: Human fall detection using kinect sensor. In: Burduk, R., Jackowski, K., Kurzynski, M., Wozniak, M., Zolnierek, A. (eds.) CORES 2013. AISC, vol. 226, pp. 743–752. Springer, Heidelberg (2013)
11. Labayrade, R., Aubert, D., Tarel, J.P.: Real time obstacle detection in stereovision on non flat road geometry through "v-disparity" representation. In: IEEE Intelligent Vehicle Symposium, vol. 2, pp. 646–651 (2002)
12. Marshall, S.W., Runyan, C.W., Yang, J., Coyne-Beasley, T., Waller, A.E., Johnson, R.M., Perkis, D.: Prevalence of selected risk and protective factors for falls in the home. American J. of Preventive Medicine 8(1), 95–101 (2005)
13. Mastorakis, G., Makris, D.: Fall detection system using Kinect's infrared sensor. J. of Real-Time Image Processing, 1–12 (2012)
14. Miaou, S.G., Sung, P.H., Huang, C.Y.: A customized human fall detection system using omni-camera images and personal information. Distributed Diagnosis and Home Healthcare, 39–42 (2006)
15. Mubashir, M., Shao, L., Seed, L.: A survey on fall detection: Principles and approaches. Neurocomputing 100, 144–152 (2013), special issue: Behaviours in video
16. Noury, N., Fleury, A., Rumeau, P., Bourke, A., ÓLaighin, G., Rialle, V., Lundy, J.: Fall detection - principles and methods. In: Annual Int. Conf. of the IEEE Engineering in Medicine and Biology Society, pp. 1663–1666 (2007)
17. Tzeng, H.W., Chen, M.Y., Chen, J.Y.: Design of fall detection system with floor pressure and infrared image. In: Int. Conf. on System Science and Engineering, pp. 131–135 (2010)
18. Yu, X.: Approaches and principles of fall detection for elderly and patient. In: 10th Int. Conf. on e-Health Networking, Applications and Services, pp. 42–47 (2008)

"BAM!" Depth-Based Body Analysis in Critical Care

Manuel Martinez, Boris Schauerte, and Rainer Stiefelhagen

Institute for Anthropomatics, Karlsruhe Institute of Technology,
Adenauerring 2, 76131 Karlsruhe, Germany
{name.surname}@kit.edu

Abstract. We investigate computer vision methods to monitor Intensive Care Units (ICU) and assist in sedation delivery and accident prevention. We propose the use of a Bed Aligned Map (BAM) to analyze the patient's body. We use a depth camera to localize the bed, estimate its surface and divide it into 10 cm × 10 cm cells. Here, the BAM represents the average cell height over the mattress. This depth-based BAM is independent of illumination and bed positioning, improving the consistency between patients. This representation allow us to develop metrics to estimate bed occupancy, body localization, body agitation and sleeping position. Experiments with 23 subjects show an accuracy in 4-level agitation tests of 88 % and 73 % in supine and fetal positions respectively, while sleeping position was recognized with a 100 % accuracy in a 4-class test.

Keywords: depth camera, critical care, monitoring, agitation, sleeping position.

1 Introduction

Effective control of sedation in Intensive Care Units (ICUs) is performed in a closed-loop to keep patients relaxed and mentally conscious [6]. Feedback is obtained from medical equipment that monitors vital signs and notes from medical staff who register the behavior of the patient. In contrast to vital signs, there is no objective method to measure behavioral cues. Each hospital has a different methodology for behavior monitoring making it difficult to translate the experiences from one hospital to another. This results in wide disparities between different medical wards (reports of *delirium* incidence range from 11 % to 80 % [14]).

Actigraphy, the measurement of physical activity, has been suggested as an objective indicator to be included in sedation scales [6]. Although actigraphy is extensively used in sleep monitoring laboratories, the procedure to attach all the required sensors to capture a meaningful actigraphic profile is costly. Additionally, some sensors are intrusive and therefore not used for critical care. Computer vision monitoring systems are increasingly used [2,5,8,13,16] as they are easy to install, non-intrusive, and the versatility of the sensor allows them to handle a wide variety of tasks [8,11]. Agitation is the most common actigraphic cue, however there is no "golden standard" to quantify it [4] and most computer vision algorithms provide view-dependent custom measurements.

To the best of our knowledge, there is no system able to work completely unattended in all lighting conditions (*e.g.*, during the night). Current approaches require markers [2, 8], active management by medical staff [5, 16] and/or color [2, 8].

R. Wilson et al. (Eds.): CAIP 2013, Part I, LNCS 8047, pp. 465–472, 2013.

Fig. 1. Left: the Medical Recording Device developed within the VIPSAFE project monitors the patient and the ICU environment. Right: The Bed Aligned Map (BAM) is a height based representation aligned to the surface of the bed (best viewed in color).

We identified the three main problems for computer vision ICU monitoring:

Occlusion: As most of the body is occluded by a blanket, high-level approaches that rely on the shape of the body, such as poselets [3] and bodypart detectors [12] are not effective.

Lack of Datasets: Due to privacy concerns, there is no public dataset to train data intensive models.

Night Monitoring: Night monitoring can be done under infrared illumination [10, 11], but color information is lost.

Depth cameras have been used successfully to automatically estimate breathing rate in clothing-occluded ICU patients [1,10]. Depth cameras allow us to overcome the night monitoring problems as they are independent of the light conditions, and volumetric information can be extracted even when the patient is covered by the bed clothing. Capturing a meaningful depth field requires an active depth camera like Kinect, as stereo cameras are unable to capture an accurate depth field due to the lack of texture in most medical clothing.

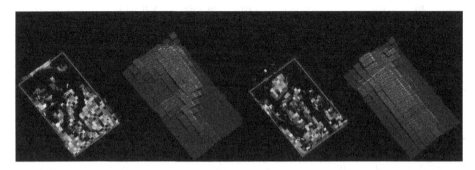

Fig. 2. Bed localiation even when a patient is sleeping on it (best viewed in color). From left to right: Post-filtered tiles from a patient lying in fetal position with the outline of the estimated bed position with his correspoding BAM. Same from a patient lying in supine position.

In this paper we go one step further and propose the Bed Aligned Map (BAM), a robust representation model aligned to the bed surface. To this end we develop a novel algorithm able to localize the bed even when somebody is sleeping on it.

Although some indicators (*e.g.*, bed occupancy, body location with respect to the bed) can be obtained directly from BAM, its main advantage is its capability to easily combine multiple observations of several patients, simplifying the development of machine learning based classifiers. We prove this capability by training a sleeping position classifier using data from only 23 subjects and achieving a 100% accuracy in a 4-class test.

2   Experimental Setup

Within the framework of the VIPSAFE[1] [11] project, we have developed a Medical Recording Device (Fig. 1) with a large variety of sensors and cameras. This project uses the depth camera (derived from Kinect) which provides a 640x480@30fps depth map. We recorded 23 male and female subjects from different ethnicities and ages between 14 and 50; and they were asked to perform a sequence of 45 actions divided in 5 scenarios. To capture a wider range of behaviors, subjects were given only minimal guidance, relying on their own interpretation. To evaluate sleeping positions they were asked to lie on their back, and then move to a lateral right position followed by lateral left position. To evaluate agitation they were asked to be relaxed, then to show small distress, followed by increased distress and strong distress. This minimal guidance resulted in strongly different interpretations of distress, which was our goal.

3   The Bed Aligned Map

Beds in critical care are wheeled, articulated and can be installed in a variety of configurations. Commonly a wall with medical equipment is behind the head of the patient, but having the wall along the side of the patient is not unheard of. Finally, in the most versatile medical wards, most equipment is also attached to mobile stands around the bed in order to accommodate the different requirements a patient may have. Therefore the location of the bed must be determined to accurately select the Region of Interest (ROI).

In most studies the ROI is fixed or manually defined [1, 5, 16]. Kittipanya-Ngam [8] suggest an automated algorithm which models the bed as rigid rectangular surface using edges and Hough transform for localization. However the articulated beds used in critical care are divided in several segments which can be adjusted at different inclinations to better suit the needs of the patient (Fig. 1). The baseline approach used in VIPSAFE [11] used region growing in the depth field to find a low curvature area, this approach was successful on articulated beds, but required the bed to be empty.

We present here an approach that improves our previous work by enabling the detection of non-empty articulated beds. The algorithm performs the following steps:

---

[1] VIPSAFE: Visual Monitoring for Improving Patient Safety
https://cvhci.anthropomatik.kit.edu/project/vipsafe

Prefiltering: Non-smooth pixels in the disparity image are discarded: pixels are considered smooth if the difference in disparity between itself and its neighbors is at most 1. This removes noisy pixels and pixels adjacent to edges.

Tile Splitting: Pixels are grouped in tiles of 16×16; the center and normal vector of each tile is estimated. The size is chosen to be small enough to offer good spatial resolution, but large enough to determine the direction of the normal vector with precision.

Tile Filtering: Tiles below the minimum height of the bed are discarded. Blocks tilted more than 45 degrees respect to the ground are discarded (usually walls and medical equipment). At this point most remaining blocks belong to the bed.

2D Estimation: Remaining tiles are projected to the ground plane. In the ground plane we fit the smallest 2D bounding box containing 95 % of the remaining tiles. The long side of the bounding box can have a varying size due to the bed articulation, but the shortest side is assumed to be fixed. If it is not close to the measured width of the bed, the estimation is discarded (Fig. 2).

3D Estimation: To compensate for the articulation of the bed, its height profile is estimated along the long side of the bounding box using the convex hull of the detected points. We assume that the bed is wide enough to not be covered entirely by the patient. Thus each horizontal cut of the bed will provide at least one measure showing its mattress height.

Normalization: The estimated 2D surface of the bed is divided in sections of 10x10cm and the average height above the mattress is calculated for each section (Fig. 2). Sections without height estimate (rare) are interpolated from the neighbors.

The resulting representation estimates the average height of the patient with respect to a planar bed mattress; we call it Bed Aligned Map (BAM). It is independent of bed localization and lighting conditions and allows us to compare the behavior of the patients in different medical institutions which was not possible until now.

We estimated the bed localization once every 10 seconds (a total of 2505 times). We accepted the bed estimations if the detected bed width lies within 5cm of the actual value. In total 91.8 % of the times the bed estimation was accepted, and the mean standard deviation measured was of 13.6 mm for width and 31.4 mm for length.

4   Body Analysis

4.1   Bed Occupancy and Body Localization

Bed occupancy is a common indicator extracted by visual monitoring systems. Since the body is generally occluded by the blanket, bed occupancy is estimated by detecting the patient's head with skin color models [9] or markers [2]. Neither approach is practical (color is not available by night). In contrast, bed occupancy can be trivially extracted from the BAM by estimating the volume under the blanket (Fig. 4).

BAM can also be used to estimate the body localization (Fig. 3), which combined with safety frameworks is used to predict if a patient is in danger of falling out of the bed.

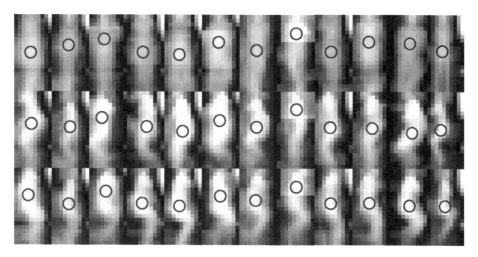

Fig. 3. BAM representations of subjects lying in supine position (top), on the left side (middle), and on the right side (bottom). The estimated center of gravity of the body is displayed as a circle. Best viewed in color.

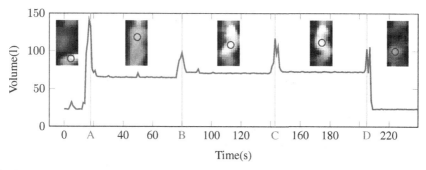

Fig. 4. Bed Occupancy: subject enters the bed (A), changes two times of sleeping position (B, C), and leaves the bed (D). Note how the volume never reaches zero as the pillow and the bed clothing occupy a significant amount of space.

4.2 Agitation

Agitation is the main indicator recorded in several computer vision ICU monitoring systems. Due to the difficulty of localizing precisely the body, it is usually quantifyed by analyzing the changes between consecutive images. This approach is not robust to changes in illumination [13], although light invariant feature descriptors have been used to compensate global illumination changes [16].

We propose one agitation measure defined as the mean difference between maximum and minimum cell height of all BAMs captured within one second. The resulting measure has volumetric units and is independent of the viewpoint used to capture it.

Lacking a standard procedure to measure agitation, we asked the subjects to show three different levels of distress in supine and fetal positions. To compare between

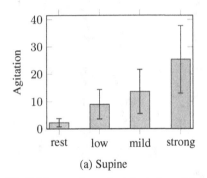

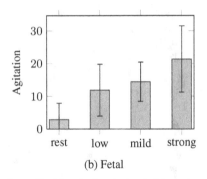

(a) Supine	(b) Fetal

Fig. 5. Mean and standard deviation of the agitation values of subjects when instructed to rest or show a low, mild and strong distress respectively

Table 1. Agitation classification within a subject using the suggested metric

(a) Supine

	rest	low	mild	strong
rest	23	0	0	0
low	0	21	2	0
mild	0	1	18	4
strong	0	1	3	19

(b) Fetal

	rest	low	mild	strong
rest	21	1	1	0
low	1	16	4	2
mild	1	3	14	5
strong	0	3	4	16

agitation levels we averaged the measurements corresponding to 5 seconds, and the BAM was extracted at 10 fps.

The only instructions our subjects received were to show *low*, *mild* and *strong* distress; this results in wide disparities between subjects but the average measured agitation showed a consistent progression between intensity levels (Fig. 5). Then we evaluated the effectiveness of this indicator within a subject, and the resulting confusion tables can be seen at Table 1.

4.3 Sleep Position

To prevent pressure ulcers, it is recommended to change the sleeping position of ICU patients every two hours. As most patients are too sedated to relocate on their own, the ICU crew must check often the sleeping position of the patients and relocate them if required. This is an unwieldy task and the adherence to the suggested guidelines is, in general, low [15].

Using classical pose estimation methods is not possible as the patient body is usually covered by a blanket, however the volumetric nature of BAM simplifies this task. We tested BAM ability to distinguish between an empty bed, a person lying on his back, a person lying to the left and a person lying to the right, from a single image. Using a naive Nearest Neighbor approach with euclidean distance we obtain a accuracy of 85.9 % (Table 2) using a leave-one-person-out cross-validation. This results were improved by using PCA to reduce BAM to 32 dimensions and Large Margin Nearest Neighbor [7]

Table 2. Confusion matrix of sleep position classification using BAM. The high accuracy obtained from the simple 1NN approach endorses the quality of the BAM as a robust representation. While using LMNN and PCA achieves 100 % accuracy.

(a) 1NN

	empty	supine	left	right
empty	21	2	0	0
supine	0	20	3	0
left	1	3	18	1
right	0	0	3	20

(b) PCA-LMNN

	empty	supine	left	right
empty	23	0	0	0
supine	0	23	0	0
left	0	0	23	0
right	0	0	0	23

as a classifier. LMNN uses semidefinite programming to learn a Mahalanobis distance metric for kNN classification. This combination achieves a 100 % accuracy.

5 Conclusions

We address two principal challenges that computer vision approaches face in critical care monitoring: First, bedridden patients in hospitals are often covered by a textureless blanket. This makes is hard for computer vision algorithms to estimate body parameters and articulation. But, it is possible to detect movements and rough shapes beneath the blanket, especially when depth information is available. Second, intensive care units are dynamic environments in which the location of the bed or sensor can be changed by the hospital personnel at any time.

We address these two challenges and introduce the Bed Aligned Map (BAM), which extracts and aligns the image patch that contains the bed. BAM is calculated from depth information, is view and light independent and does not require markers. We show some indicators that can be obtained directly from BAM (bed occupancy, body location with respect to the bed) and present a robust metric to quantify body agitation. Furthermore, the BAM facilitates the development of machine learning based classifiers, because the alignment allows us to combine observations of several patients. We use this property to develop a sleeping position classifier where we discern between an empty bed, a patient lying on his back, and a patient lying on his left and right sides. On this 4-class problem a naive nearest neighbor approach using BAM achieves a 85.9 % accuracy while a combined LMNN and PCA approach achieves 100 % accuracy on a 23 subject experiment.

Acknowledgements. This work is supported by the German Federal Ministry of Education and Research (BMBF) within the VIPSAFE project.

References

1. Aoki, H., Takemura, Y., Mimura, K., Nakajima, M.: Development of non-restrictive sensing system for sleeping person using fiber grating vision sensor. In: Micromechatronics and Human Science (2001)

2. Becouze, P., Hann, C., Chase, J., Shaw, G.: Measuring facial grimacing for quantifying patient agitation in critical care. In: Computer Methods and Programs in Biomedicine (2007)
3. Bourdev, L., Malik, J.: Poselets: Body part detectors trained using 3D human pose annotations. In: ICCV (2009)
4. Chanques, G., Jaber, S., Barbotte, E., Violet, S., Sebbane, M., Perrigault, P.F., Mann, C., Lefrant, J.Y., Eledjam, J.J.: Impact of systematic evaluation of pain and agitation in an intensive care unit* (2006)
5. Geoffrey Chase, J., Agogue, F., Starfinger, C., Lam, Z., Shaw, G.M., Rudge, A.D., Sirisena, H.: Quantifying agitation in sedated icu patients using digital imaging. In: Computer Methods and Programs in Biomedicine (2004)
6. Grap, M.J., Hamilton, V.A., McNallen, A., Ketchum, J.M., Best, A.M., Isti Arief, N.Y., Wetzel, P.A.: Actigraphy: Analyzing patient movement. Heart & Lung: The Journal of Acute and Critical Care (2011)
7. Weinberger, K., John Blitzer, L.K.S.: Distance metric learning for large margin nearest neighbor classification. In: NIPS (2006)
8. Kittipanya-Ngam, P., Guat, O., Lung, E.: Computer vision applications for patients monitoring system. In: FUSION (2012)
9. Mansor, M., Yaacob, S., Nagarajan, R., Che, L., Hariharan, M., Ezanuddin, M.: Detection of facial changes for ICU patients using knn classifier. In: ICIAS (2010)
10. Martinez, M., Stiefelhagen, R.: Breath rate monitoring during sleep using near-ir imagery and pca. In: ICPR (2012)
11. Martinez, M., Stiefelhagen, R.: Automated multi-camera system for long term behavioral monitoring in intensive care units. In: MVA (2013)
12. Mikolajczyk, K., Schmid, C., Zisserman, A.: Human detection based on a probabilistic assembly of robust part detectors. In: Pajdla, T., Matas, J(G.) (eds.) ECCV 2004. LNCS, vol. 3021, pp. 69–82. Springer, Heidelberg (2004)
13. Naufal Bin Mansor, M., Yaacob, S., Nagarajan, R., Hariharan, M.: Patient monitoring in ICU under unstructured lighting condition. In: ISIEA (2010)
14. Ouimet, S., Kavanagh, B.P., Gottfried, S.B., Skrobik, Y.: Incidence, risk factors and consequences of ICU delirium. Intensive Care Medicine (2007)
15. Paquay, L., Wouters, R., Defloor, T., Buntinx, F., Debaillie, R., Geys, L.: Adherence to pressure ulcer prevention guidelines in home care: a survey of current practice. Journal of Clinical Nursing (2008)
16. Reyes, M., Vitria, J., Radeva, P., Escalera, S.: Real-time activity monitoring of inpatients. In: MICCAT (2010)

3-D Feature Point Matching for Object Recognition Based on Estimation of Local Shape Distinctiveness

Masanobu Nagase, Shuichi Akizuki, and Manabu Hashimoto

Graduate School of Information Science and Technology Chukyo University
101-2 Yagoto honmachi, Showa-ku, Nagoya, Aichi, 466-8666, Japan
{nagase,mana}@isl.sist.chukyo-u.ac.jp

Abstract. In this paper, we propose a reliable 3-D object recognition method that can statistically minimize object mismatching. Our method basically uses a 3-D object model that is represented as a set of feature points with 3-D coordinates. Each feature point also has an attribute value for the local shape around the point. The attribute value is represented as an orientation histogram of a normal vector calculated by using several neighboring feature points around each point. Here, the important thing is this attribute value means its local shape. By estimating the relative similarity of two points of all possible combinations in the model, we define the distinctiveness of each point. In the proposed method, only a small number of distinctive feature points are selected and used for matching with all feature points extracted from an acquired range image. Finally, the position and pose of the target object can be estimated from a number of correctly matched points. Experimental results using actual scenes have demonstrated that the recognition rate of our method is 93.8%, which is 42.2% higher than that of the conventional Spin Image method. Furthermore, its computing time is about nine times faster than that of the Spin Image method.

Keywords: object recognition, 3-D feature point matching, robot vision, point cloud data, 3-D descriptor, bin-picking.

1 Introduction

Bin-picking systems are an important means for developing automated cell manufacturing systems. An important requirement for such systems is a reliable and high-speed means for recognizing the pose of an object in scenes that consist of a lot of randomly stacked same objects.

In the field of 3-D object recognition, a lot of model-based object recognition methods have been proposed. These methods estimate the pose parameters of objects by matching an object model to an input range image. The Spin Image method[1] is a typical model-based method. It uses pose-invariant features created by calculating the direction of normal vectors in each point of an object model. However, its computational cost is expensive because it is

R. Wilson et al. (Eds.): CAIP 2013, Part I, LNCS 8047, pp. 473–481, 2013.

necessary to calculate the feature values from all points of the object model. Other methods[2][3] using edge information with depth value have been proposed. These methods can achieve high-speed recognition because they use only local information of the object model. For randomly stacked objects, however, mismatchings may frequently occur due to pseudo-edges caused by objects that overlap other objects.

For other model-based approaches, several high-speed recognition methods have been proposed. These methods use only feature points for the matching process. For example, the DAI (Depth Aspect Image) matching method[4] and the Local Surface Patch method[5] are typical methods that use this approach. These methods use distinctive local shapes that have large curvature, so they are effective in some cases. However, for cases where there are a lot of local shapes that have large curvature, mismatching will be increased.

A recent study proposed a 3-D local descriptor called SHOT (Signature of Histograms of OrienTations)[6][7]. This method uses only one corresponding point with SHOT descriptors, so high-speed recognition is achieved. A problem with it, however, is that pose parameter calculation becomes difficult when the SHOT descriptor is disturbed by outliers due to multiple objects.

A more substantial problem is that no practical 3-D object recognition methods have yet been developed that achieve both high speed and reliability.

The purpose of our research, therefore, is to develop a new method that can achieve both reliability and high speed. From the viewpoint of efficient processing, our method can be categorized as a feature-point-based matching method using "point cloud data".

We assume that the object model in this study consists of point cloud data with 3-D coordinates. Each point of the object model has an attribute value that represents the local shape around the interest point. The attribute value is represented as an orientation histogram of a normal vector, which is calculated by using several neighboring feature points around the interest point. As mentioned above, the attribute value of a model point means its local shape. Before matching the model points to acquired data, we determine the distinctiveness of all points by calculating the relative similarity of two points of all possible combinations in the object model. Rather than all of the feature points, a small number of them with high distinctiveness are used in the matching process. Using this effective feature-point selection based on estimating distinctiveness, we achieve both reliable and high-speed recognition.

In Section 2 we explain the key idea of and concrete algorithm for the proposed method. In Section 3 we demonstrate, through experimental results acquired in testing a lot of real range images, that our method has better performance than conventional methods such as the Spin Image method.

2   Proposed Method

2.1   Basic Idea

In this study, we introduce two basic ideas.

The first is to calculate the distinctiveness of each feature point of an object model. The use of feature points that have high distinctiveness for the matching process reduces the risk of mismatching.

The second is to use only a small number of selected feature points for the matching process. Reducing the number of feature points used for the matching process achieves high-speed recognition.

2.2 Outline of Proposed Algorithm

Figure 1 shows a schematic block diagram of the proposed algorithm.

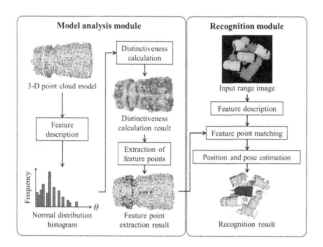

Fig. 1. Schematic block diagram of proposed algorithm

The proposed algorithm consists of two modules: an object model analysis module and a recognition module. In this study, we assume that the object model consists of feature points with 3-D coordinates.

In the object model analysis module, the attribute values of each feature point are described by a histogram created by the normal vector of several neighboring feature points. Next, the distinctiveness value of each point is calculated by the similarity between normal distribution histograms. Finally, the distinctive feature points used for matching are selected on the basis of high distinctiveness value.

In the recognition module, the position and pose of the object are estimated from a number of correctly corresponding points.

2.3 Normal Distribution Histogram

Figure 2 shows the method for creating a normal distribution histogram, which is the local shape descriptor we propose in this study.

First, the sphere region of radius r is set to interest point n. Next, angle θ is calculated between the normal vector $\mathbf{N}_n$ and another normal vector $\mathbf{N}_{m_t}$ that contains the sphere region. This creates the normal distribution histogram of θ. This histogram represents the local shapes of an interest point using neighboring points. Even if the input data contains outliers, stable feature description is possible because the proposed descriptor uses many neighboring points of the interest point for feature description. This process is applied for all points of the object model.

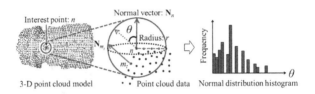

Interest point: n Normal vector: $\mathbf{N}_n$ Radius r Frequency θ

3-D point cloud model   Point cloud data   Normal distribution histogram

Fig. 2. Method for creating normal distribution histogram

2.4   Calculation of Distinctiveness Value of Feature Points

Next, we explain the method for calculating the distinctiveness value at each point of the object model.

The dissimilarity value B is calculated by the Bhattacharyya coefficient between the normal distribution histograms of the interest point and one of another point created as described in Subsection 2.3:

$$B(P,Q) = 1 - \sum_{u=1}^{U} \sqrt{P_u Q_u} \tag{1}$$

where P and Q are normal distribution histograms, U represents the number of bins in the histogram, and u represents the interest bin. The dissimilarity value will be nearest to 1 when the correlation between histograms is low.

Next, the distinctiveness value S_n is calculated by Equation (2):

$$S_n = \frac{1}{T} \sum_{t=1}^{T} B(p_n, q_t) \tag{2}$$

where p and q are normal distribution histograms, T represents the number of points of the object model, and n and t are the interest point and another model point. The distinctiveness value S_n is calculated, with its range lying between 0 and 1. When S_n is nearest to 1, it means the distinctiveness value of point n is high. In this study, feature points with a high distinctiveness value are extracted as feature points.

2.5 Position and Pose Estimation by Matching Feature Points

In this subsection we explain our pose recognition method, which uses distinctive feature points.

First, the Bhattacharyya coefficient is used to calculate the similarity between two normal distribution histograms calculated from all of the points in the input range image and the distinctive feature points extracted from the object model. Corresponding points are determined from the input range image and the object model. The pose parameters of the object model are calculated from the corresponding points of the input range image and the object model, which satisfies Equation (3):

$$(|d_{s_1,s_2} - d_{m_1,m_2}| < th_d) \wedge (|\theta_{s_1} - \theta_{m_1}| < th_t) \wedge (|\theta_{s_2} - \theta_{m_2}| < th_t) \qquad (3)$$

where m_1, m_2 are distinctive feature points of the object model, s_1, s_2 are points of an input range image, $\theta_{m_1}, \theta_{m_2}, \theta_{s_1}, \theta_{s_2}$ are the angles between these points and the normal vector of the interest feature point, d_{m_1,m_2}, d_{s_1,s_2} are the Euclidean distances between the two points of the model and those of the input range image, and th_d and th_t are the distance and angle thresholds.

We associate the vector to the centroid of the object model to the points of interest feature point m_1. The pose parameter is applied to the centroid vector.

Second, the transformation parameters calculated from all matching results are voted for in a voting space prepared on the input range image. An example matching that uses distinctive feature points is illustrated in Figure 3.

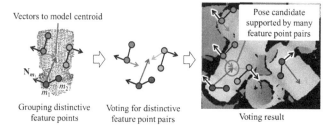

Fig. 3. Overview of pose recognition scheme using distinctive feature points extracted from object model

After the voting, the candidate parameters supported by many corresponding points are determined to be reasonable transformation parameters for the object model in an input range image. Finally, we carefully confirm the consistency between object model and input range image for all hypotheses by using many points other than the distinctive feature points. The parameter with the highest consistency is determined to be the recognition result.

Here, the consistency between a transformed object model and an input range image is calculated by Equation (4):

$$R = \frac{1}{T} \sum_{t=1}^{T} |m_t - f(i,j)| \qquad (4)$$

where m_t represents the t-th point in a transformed model object. The value R represents the difference between a transformed object model and an input range image. A low R value means high consistency.

3 Experiments and Discussion

3.1 Distribution of Extracted Distinctive Feature Points

In this section, we use various methods to explain the distribution of extracted distinctive feature points. Experiments were conducted to compare the proposed method with two conventional methods: the random method, in which distinctive feature points are randomly extracted, and the curvature method, in which distinctive feature points with large curvature are preferentially extracted.

In Figure 4, (a) is an overview of the model, (b) is the result obtained in calculating the distinctiveness of each point of the object model, and (c), (d), and (e) show the distinctive feature points extracted by the random, curvature, and proposed methods. Each method extracted 30 distinctive feature points.

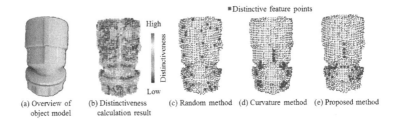

(a) Overview of   (b) Distinctiveness   (c) Random method   (d) Curvature method   (e) Proposed method
    object model   calculation result

Fig. 4. Overview of object model and distinctiveness calculation result

The random method extracted feature points from smooth shaped parts, which accounted for a large part of the object model. The curvature method extracted feature points from the recessed part of a large curvature shape; however, we thought that in this case the feature points might be easily hidden and thus correct matching could not be obtained for them if the model underwent a pose change. The proposed method, however, selects distinctive feature points that is selected for large curvature of characterizing the model continues in a straight line and planar shape of the object model. Therefore, the proposed method enables correct matching even if the object model undergoes a pose change.

3.2 Performance for Complicated Scenes

To verify the effectiveness of the proposed method, we compared its performance for randomly stacked objects with that of four conventional methods: (1) the

Spin Image method[1], (2) the Correspondence Grouping[8] method, which is contained in the Point Cloud Library[9] as a recognition module, (3) the random method, and (4) the curvature method. To estimate the versatility of our method, we evaluated its recognition performance by using four kinds of objects. The parameters of our approach are r=2.0mm, th_d=1.2mm, th_t=5°. The number of bins in the normal distribution histogram is 37.

Table 1 shows the recognition success rate P_r, the processing time T, and the number of distinctive feature points N of each method for four datasets that collectively consisted of about 130 real range images. These range images are captured by laser range finder. In this study, we considered recognition was successful if the alignment error of the input range image and the object model was within 1.5 mm. Figure 5 (a), (b), (c) and (d) show overviews of the input scenes, while (e), (f), (g) and (h) show recognition results that are superimposed transformed object models on the input data. The experiments were performed using an Intel ®CORE ™i7 3.40GHz with 8GB memory.

Table 1. Recognition success rate and processing time

		Object A	Object B	Object C	Object D	Mean
Spin	P_r[%]	49.6	50.8	35.2	70.6	51.6
Image[1]	T[sec]	24.95	55.34	31.21	20.68	33.05
Correspondence	P_r[%]	74.4	96.2	65.6	84.9	80.3
Grouping[8][9]	T[sec]	45.41	52.85	29.26	26.10	38.41
	N[point]	70	50	30	30	-
Random method	P_r[%]	89.1	96.9	85.2	69.8	85.3
	T[sec]	5.87	4.77	2.06	1.74	3.61
	N[point]	70	50	30	30	-
Curvature method	P_r [%]	86.8	76.9	18.0	54.8	59.1
	T[sec]	6.01	4.94	2.21	1.97	3.78
	N[point]	70	50	30	30	-
Proposed method	P_r [%]	89.1	97.7	94.5	93.7	93.8
	T[sec]	5.83	4.76	2.05	1.76	3.60

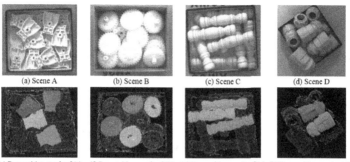

(a) Scene A   (b) Scene B   (c) Scene C   (d) Scene D

(e) Recognition result of (a) (f) Recognition result of (b) (g) Recognition result of (c) (h) Recognition result of (d)

Fig. 5. Example recognition results

Experiments confirmed that the proposed method achieves 93.8% recognition success rate to 51.6% for the Spin Image method. It is also about nine times faster since it uses only a small number of distinctive feature points for the matching process while the Spin Image method uses all points of the model.

Furthermore, since the Spin Image method creates spin images by selecting points at random from range images, correct matching cannot be achieved if the randomly selected points correspond to those in the object model. This is one of the reasons for the method's low recognition rate. The proposed method's recognition results were also superior to those for the Correspondence Grouping method, because the range of the reference frame can easily allow the inclusion of data from objects at a nearby object boundary in the input range data. Through experiments we also confirmed the amount of time it takes for the methods to create reference frames. The experiment results confirmed that the proposed method not only achieves higher recognition rates than the conventional methods, but also that its processing time is equal to or better than that of the other methods.

4   Conclusion

We proposed an object recognition system that achieves both reliable and high-speed recognition by using a small number of distinctive feature points.

Experimental results using actual scenes demonstrated that our method achieves 93.8% recognition rate, which is 42.2% higher than that of the conventional Spin Image method, and that its computing time is also about nine times faster. These results confirmed that the process our method uses to select distinctive feature points is an effective approach to object recognition.

In future work, we intend to further improve the method's processing time, optimize various parameters, and build a bin-picking system that implements the method.

Acknowledgment. This work was partially supported by Grant-in-Aid for Scientific Research (C) 23560512.

References

1. Johnson, A.E., Hebert, M.: Using Spin Images for Efficient Object Recognition in Cluttered 3D Scenes. Trans. IEEE Pattern Analysis and Machine Intelligence 21, 433–499 (1999)
2. Sumi, Y., Tomita, F.: 3D Object Recognition Using Segment-Based Stereo Vision. In: Chin, R., Pong, T.-C. (eds.) ACCV 1998. LNCS, vol. 1352, pp. 249–256. Springer, Heidelberg (1997)
3. Steder, B., Rusu, R.B., Konolige, K., Burgard, W.: Point Feature Extraction on 3D Range Scans Taking into Account Object Boundaries. In: IEEE International Conference on Robotics and Automation, pp. 2601–2608 (2011)

4. Takeguchi, T., Kaneko, S.: Depth Aspect Images for Efficient Object Recognition. In: Proc. SPIE Conference on Optomechatronic Systems IV, vol. 5264, pp. 54–65 (2003)
5. Chen, H., Bhanu, B.: 3D Free-form Object Recognition in Range Images Using Local Surface Patches. Pattern Recognition Letters 28, 1252–1262 (2007)
6. Tombari, F., Salti, S., Di Stefano, L.: Unique Signatures of Histograms for Local Surface Description. In: Daniilidis, K., Maragos, P., Paragios, N. (eds.) ECCV 2010, Part III. LNCS, vol. 6313, pp. 356–369. Springer, Heidelberg (2010)
7. Tombari, F., Salti, S., Stefano, L.D.: A Combined Texture-Shape Descriptor for Enhanced 3D feature Matching. In: IEEE International Conference on Image Processing, pp. 809–812 (2011)
8. Tombari, F., Stefano, L.D.: Object Recognition in 3D Scene with Occlusions and Clutter by Hough Voting. In: IEEE Proc. on 4th Pacific-Rim Symposium on Image and Video Technology, pp. 349–355 (2010)
9. Rusu, R.B., Cousins, S.: 3D is here: Point Cloud Library (PCL). In: IEEE International Conference on Robotics and Automation, pp. 1–4 (2011)

3D Human Tracking from Depth Cue in a Buying Behavior Analysis Context

Cyrille Migniot and Fakhreddine Ababsa

IBISC laboratory - University of Evry val d'Essonne, France
{Cyrille.Migniot,Fakhr-Eddine.Ababsa}@ufrst.univ-evry.fr

Abstract. This paper presents a real time approach to track the human body pose in the 3D space. For the buying behavior analysis, the camera is placed on the top of the shelves, above the customers. In this top view, the markerless tracking is harder. Hence, we use the depth cue provided by the kinect that gives discriminative features of the pose. We introduce a new 3D model that are fitted to these data in a particle filter framework. First the head and shoulders position is tracked in the 2D space of the acquisition images. Then the arms poses are tracked in the 3D space. Finally, we demonstrate that an efficient implementation provides a real-time system.

Keywords: Human tracking, kinect, particle filter, buying behavior.

1 Introduction

Behavior analysis based on artificial vision method offers a wide range of applications that are currently little developed in the marketing area. In the customer behavior analysis, the camera is often placed on the ceiling of the market. Only the top view of the person is also available. However, the great majority of the methods in the literature use a model adapted to a front view of the person because the shape of a person is much more discriminative on this orientation. The aim of the project ANR-10-CORD0016 ORIGAMI2 that supports this work is to develop real-time and non intrusive tools designed to analyze the shoppers buying act decisions. The approach is, in the first time, based on extracting and following the shoppers' gaze and gesture positions with computer vision algorithmic. It is then based on statistically analyzing the extracted data: the goal of this cognitive analysis is to measure the interaction between the shopper and their environment. This technology will provide consumer goods producers with non biased and exhaustive information on shoppers' behaviors during their buying acts.

To make the tracking possible, the depth cue is required. One of the more popular devices used to provide it is kinect, which has sensors that capture both rgb and depth data. In this paper we integrate the depth cue in a particle filter to track the body parts. The gesture recognition and the behavior of the customer could, in a second time, be analyzed using the Moeslund's taxinomy.

R. Wilson et al. (Eds.): CAIP 2013, Part I, LNCS 8047, pp. 482–489, 2013.

Pose estimation and 3D tracking have received a significant amount of attention in the computer vision research community in the past decade. To do this, the observation is fitted to a model that embodies the possible states. For an articulated target as a person, the particle filter [9] is mostly used. It estimates the current pose from a sample of possible states weighted from a likelihood function that represents the probability that a state of the model corresponds to the observation. A skeleton defines the states of the model. It comprises of a set of appropriately assembled geometric primitives [4,7,8] or 3D gaussians [15] to introduce the volume occupied by the body in the 3D space. The main variations on the framework come from the choice of the likelihood function. Skin color [6] and contour (matched to the chamfer distance [16]) are the most useful features. Kabayashi [11] inserts results of classifiers in the likelihood function. Some poses of the skeleton can not be executed by a human body. The sampling can be constrainted by a projection on the feasible configuration space [7] or by stochastic Nelder-Mead simplex search [12].

In the buying behavior analysis context, post treatment is not assesed and real time processing is also appreciated. In the particle filtering, the most expensive operation is the evaluation of the likelihood function because it has to be done once at every time step for every particle. Some adaptations are needed to obtain a real time processing. Gonzales [6] realizes a tracking for each sub-part of the body so as to use only simple models. A hierarchical particle filter [17] simplifies the likelihood function. The annealed particle filtering [4] reduces the required number of particles. Finally Kjellström [10] considers interaction with objects in the environment to constrain the pose of body and remove degrees of freedom.

In this paper, we propose a new human pose tracking by particle filtering in a top view. To obtain a real time processing, the model is broken it up a 2D model representing the head and the shoulders and an 3D model representing the arms. Using the depth cue provided by a kinect drastically reduces the complexity of the first one. For the second one, the pose is constrainted by the position of the shoulders.

Our main contributions are fisrt considering buying act conditions to optimize the tracking, then taking advantage of a recent data acquisition equipment and finally decomposing the model in two parts so as to reduce the filtering complexity and use simultaneously 2D and 3D models.

2   Particle Filter Implementation

We use the Xtion Pro-live camera produced by Asus for the acquisition. All the points that the sensor is not able to measure depth are offset to 0 in the output array. We regard it as a kind of noise. Moreover we only model the upper part of the body. Thus, we threshold the image to only take into consideration the pixels recognized as an element of the torso, the arms or the head. It gives a first segmentation of region of interest (ROI).

The Asus Xtion Pro-live provides simultaneously the color and the depth cues. Nevertheless the color cue is often degraded in practice. Indeed, persons on the

supermarket shelves are over-lit. The tracking must be robust and the depth cue is not disturbed by lighting. Thus we only take into consideration the depth cue.

2.1   The Particle Filter

Particle filtering has been a successful numerical approximation technique for Bayesian sequential estimation with non-linear, non-Gaussian models. At moment k, let x_k be the state of the model and y_k be the observation. Particle filter recursively approximates the posterior probability density $p(x_k|y_k)$ of the current state x_k evaluating observation likelihood based on a weighted particle sample set $\{x_k^i, \omega_k^i\}$. Each of the N particles x_k^i corresponds to a random state propagated by the dynamic model of the system and weighted by ω_k^i. There are 4 basic steps:

- **resampling:** N particles $\{x_k^{\prime i}, \frac{1}{N}\} \sim p(x_k|y_k)$ from sample $\{x_k^i, \omega_k^i\}$ are re-sampled. Particles are selected by their weight: large weight particles are duplicated while low weight particles are deleted.
- **propagation:** particles are propagated using the dynamic model of the system $p(x_{k+1}|x_k)$ to obtain
  $\{x_{k+1}^i, \frac{1}{N}\} \sim p(x_{k+1}|y_k)$.
- **weighting:** particles are weighted by a likelihood function related to the correspondence from the model to the new observation. The new weights ω_{k+1}^i are normalized so that : $\sum_{i=1}^{N} \omega_{k+1}^i = 1$. It provides the new sample $\{x_{k+1}^i, \omega_{k+1}^i\} \sim p(x_{k+1}|y_{k+1})$.
- **estimation:** the new pose is approximated by:

$$x_{k+1} = \sum_{i=1}^{N} \omega_{k+1}^i x_{k+1}^i \qquad (1)$$

2.2   The 2D Head-Shoulders Model

Top of the head and top of the shoulders make a variation of depth that is well descriptive of the human class [14]. Moreover, the shapes of this two parts in the top view is almost constant and make ellipses. Canton-Ferrer [3] defines the volume of the person by an ellipsoid. While he estimates the position of the person, we estimate its pose. Our model is also made of 2 ellipses whose the dimension is relative to the person stoutness and are computed in the initialization step. The state vector is defined by: $V^{hs} = \{x^h, y^h, \theta^h, x^s, y^s, \theta^s\}$ where $(x^\cdot, y^\cdot)$ gives the position of the center of the ellipse and $\theta^\cdot$ its orientation for the head (h) and the shoulders (s). We first threshold the depth image to separate the pixels that are likely to correspond to the head and the pixels that are likely to correspond to the shoulders. This map is our observation. To define the likelihood function, the ellipses given by a state vector (a particle) is matched to the chamfer distance map of the thresholded depth image. The interaction between the 2 ellipses at the neck level is introduced by constraints in the propagation step : the position of one part reduces the possible state space of the second.

2.3 The 3D Arms Model

For the arms tracking, we need to realize the tracking in the 3D space. A 3D model of the whole body could be used (figure 1(a)) but the shoulders are best tracked in the 2D space and a complete model is time consuming. A tracking is done for each arm hardly constrained by the 2D estimation of the shoulders position of section 2.2 as illustrated in figure 1(c). In our model, the arm has 5 degrees of freedom: 3 for the shoulder and 2 for the elbow. The pose of the skeleton is defined by the 5 angles of the state vector: $V^a = \{\theta_x^{sh}, \theta_y^{sh}, \theta_z^{sh}, \theta_x^{el}, \theta_z^{el}\}$. Geometrical primitives introduce the volume: arms and forearms are modeled by truncated cylinders, torso by an elliptic cylinder and finally the hands by rectangular planes.

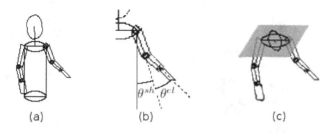

(a)   (b)   (c)

Fig. 1. The 3D models: (a) the 3D model is made of a skeleton with geometrical primitives, (b) the angles of the articulation defines the pose of the person, (c) in the 3D-2D processing the head and the shoulders are tracked in the 2D space of the recorded images whereas the arms are tracked in the 3D space.

The depth variation is well-descriptive of arm. The pixels of the foreground in the depth image are transposed in the 3D space. Then the model state is fitted to these 3D points.

Let Δ be the pixels of the foreground of the depth image excluding the head and the shoulders detected previously and $\mathcal{M}$ be the 3D model state given by a particle. The likelihood function related to particle i is defined by:

$$\omega_i = \underset{p \in \Delta}{average}(d_{3D}(p, \mathcal{M}^i)) \tag{2}$$

where d_{3D} is the euclidean shortest distance from a point to a 3D model.

3   Performances Analysis

We now present some experimental results. So as to control the movement of the person and to maximize the number of tested poses, we have simulated the behavior of customers in experimental conditions. In fact, the most important variation is the presence of shelves and goods. But, as the camera do not move, an estimation of the background is computed and can be removed to the frames of the sequence. Using experimental conditions is justified because the ROI also obtained are similar to the experimental ones.

The Xtion Pro live camera produced by Asus is installed at 2,9 m of the ground. It provides 7 frames per second. The dimension of a frame is 320×240 pixels. In the first experiment, we recorded two sequences $\mathcal{S}_1$ et $\mathcal{S}_2$ that are made of 450 frames (>1min) and 300 frames ($\approx$43s). The movement of the arms are various and representative of the buying behaviors. The depth cue is extracted with the OpenNI library. The distance of use of the Xtion Pro live camera is between 0,8m and 3,5m. Consequently it can not be used in at-a-distance video surveillance but is relevant for the buying behavior analysis context.

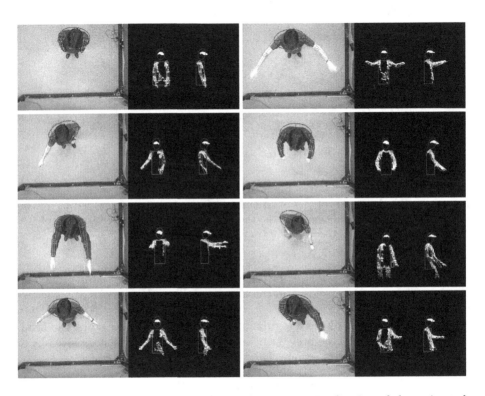

Fig. 2. The tracking provides the pose of the person: visualization of the estimated model state on the recorded frames (in left) and in the 3D space (in right) with the projection of the pixels of the depth image in white

We now estimate the quality of the arms tracking. We have manually annotated the pixels of the arms on the frames of the 2 sequences to create a groundtruth. Then we compute the average distance ε from the projection on the 3D space of each of these pixels to the model state estimated by our method. It has to be minimized to optimize the tracking. The mean variable of the particle filter is the number of particles. If it is increased, the tracking is improved but the computing time is increased too. The processing times are here obtained with a non-optimized C++ implementation running on a 3,1GHz processor. We give in the following the average processing times per frame. We can seen in figure 3 that there are no meaningful improvement over 50 particles (computed in 25 ms). With this configuration there are an average distance of less than 2,5cm between each pixel of the observation and the estimated model state. This processing is real time.

We compare our algorithm with the case where the 3D fitting presented in section 2.3 is applied on a complete 3D model (figure 1(a)) with 17 degrees of freedom. The figure 3 shows that the tracking is less efficient with this configuration. Indeed, the required number of particles is higher because the number of degrees of freedom is higher. Consequently the processing time increases. Moreover, as we realized a part-based treatment, each body part is tracked more efficiently.

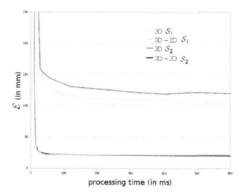

Fig. 3. Performances of the tracking with the various models on the 2 sequences: the tracking is the best with our 3D-2D method

In a second experiment, we evaluate the trajectories of the articulations of the arms. Two cameras ARTTRACK1 provides the 3D positions of reflecting balls with the software DTRACK. We have placed captors on the shoulder, the elbow and the wrist of the left arm of a person and we have recorded their positions simultaneously to the kinect acquisition in a sequence S_3 ($\approx$55s). The captors can not be placed accurately on the center of the articulations. The recorded positions are so not a groundtruth. However they can be used to evaluate the trajectories of the articulations that define the arm movement. We show in figure 4 that the our trajectories well fitted the ART ones. Then the difficult case where the person bends down (the sharp peak on the z coordinate) is much better estimated by our method. Finally our tracking is more robust when the movements are sharp (z coordinate of the wrist). This experiment validates the estimation of the arm movement by our method.

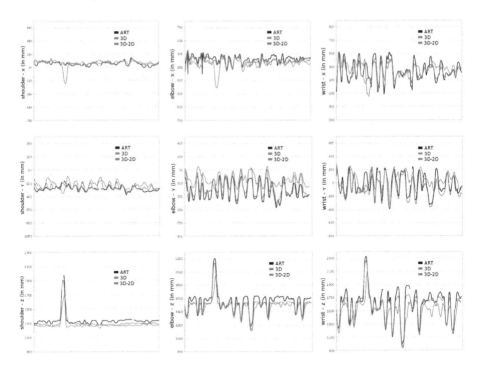

Fig. 4. Trajectories of the 3D coordinates (x,y and z) of the shoulder, the elbow and the wrist of the left arm in the sequence $\mathcal{S}_3$: our 3D-2D method well follows the articulation movements

4   Conclusion

In this paper we have presented a 3D gesture tracking method that uses the well known particle filter method. To be efficient in the buying behavior analysis context where the camera is placed above the customers, our treatment is adapted to the top view of the person and used the depth cue provided by the new Asus camera. To do this, we have introduced a top view model that simultaneously uses 2D and 3D fitting. The process is accurate and real-time.

In the future, our method could be inserted in an action recognition processing to analyse the customer behavior. Moreover, a camera pose estimation [5,2,1] could insert our work in a Augmented Reality context with a moving camera. Finally an additional camera placed at the head level could refine the behavior analysis by a gaze estimation [13].

References

1. Ababsa, F.: Robust Extended Kalman Filtering For Camera Pose Tracking Using 2D to 3D Lines Correspondences. In: IEEE/ASME Conference on Advanced Intelligent Mechatronics, pp. 1834–1838 (2009)

2. Ababsa, F., Mallem, M.: A Robust Circular Fiducial Detection Technique and Real-Time 3D Camera Tracking. International Journal of Multimedia 3, 34–41 (2008)
3. Canton-Ferrer, C., Salvador, J., Casas, J.R., Pardàs, M.: Multi-person Tracking Strategies Based on Voxel Analysis. In: Stiefelhagen, R., Bowers, R., Fiscus, J.G. (eds.) CLEAR 2007 and RT 2007. LNCS, vol. 4625, pp. 91–103. Springer, Heidelberg (2008)
4. Deutscher, J., Reid, I.: Articulated Body Motion Capture by Stochastic Search. International Journal of Computer Vision 2, 185–205 (2005)
5. Didier, J.Y., Ababsa, F., Mallem, M.: Hybrid Camera Pose Estimation Combining Square Fiducials Localisation Technique and Orthogonal Iteration Algorithm. International Journal of Image and Graphics 8, 169–188 (2008)
6. Gonzalez, M., Collet, C.: Robust Body Parts Tracking using Particle Filter and Dynamic Template. In: IEEE International Conference on Image Processing, pp. 529–532 (2011)
7. Hauberg, S., Sommer, S., Pedersen, K.S.: Gaussian-like Spatial Priors for Articulated Tracking. In: Daniilidis, K., Maragos, P., Paragios, N. (eds.) ECCV 2010, Part I. LNCS, vol. 6311, pp. 425–437. Springer, Heidelberg (2010)
8. Horaud, R., Niskanen, M., Dewaele, G., Boyer, E.: Human Motion Tracking by Registering an Articulated Surface to 3D Points and Normals. IEEE Transaction on Pattern Analysis and Machine Intelligence 31, 158–163 (2009)
9. Isard, M., Blake, A.: CONDENSATION - Conditional Density Propagation for Visual Tracking. International Journal of Computer Vision 29, 5–28 (1998)
10. Kjellström, H., Kragic, D., Black, M.J.: Tracking People Interacting with Objects. In: IEEE Conference on Computer Vision and Pattern Recognition (2010)
11. Kobayashi, Y., Sugimura, D., Sato, Y., Hirasawa, K., Suzuki, N., Kage, H., Sugimoto, A.: 3D Head Tracking using the Particle Filter with Cascaded Classifiers. In: British Machine Vision Conference, pp. 37–46 (2006)
12. Lin, J.Y., Wu, Y., Huang, T.S.: 3D Model-based Hand Tracking using Stochastic Direct Search Method. In: IEEE International Conference on Automatic Face and Gesture Recognition, pp. 693–698 (2004)
13. Funes-Mora, K.A., Odobez, J.: Gaze Estimation from Multimodal Kinect Data. In: IEEE Conference on Computer Vision and Pattern Recognition, pp. 25–30 (2012)
14. Micilotta, A., Bowden, R.: View-Based Location and Tracking of Body Parts for Visual Interaction. In: British Machine Vision Conference, pp. 849–858 (2004)
15. Stoll, C., Hasler, N., Gall, J., Seidel, H.P., Theobalt, C.: Fast Articulated Motion Tracking using a Sums of Gaussians Body Model. In: International Conference on Computer Vision, pp. 951–958 (2011)
16. Xia, L., Chen, C.C., Aggarwal, J.K.: Human Detection Using Depth Information by Kinect. In: International Workshop on Human Activity Understanding from 3D Data (2011)
17. Yang, C., Duraiswami, R., Davis, L.: Fast Multiple Object Tracking via a Hierarchical Particle Filter. In: International Conference on Computer Vision, pp. 212–219 (2005)

A New Bag of Words LBP (BoWL) Descriptor for Scene Image Classification

Sugata Banerji*, Atreyee Sinha, and Chengjun Liu

Department of Computer Science,
New Jersey Institute of Technology,
Newark, NJ 07102, USA
{sb256,as739,cliu}@njit.edu

Abstract. This paper explores a new Local Binary Patterns (LBP) based image descriptor that makes use of the bag-of-words model to significantly improve classification performance for scene images. Specifically, first, a novel multi-neighborhood LBP is introduced for small image patches. Second, this multi-neighborhood LBP is combined with frequency domain smoothing to extract features from an image. Third, the features extracted are used with spatial pyramid matching (SPM) and bag-of-words representation to propose an innovative Bag of Words LBP (BoWL) descriptor. Next, a comparative assessment is done of the proposed BoWL descriptor and the conventional LBP descriptor for scene image classification using a Support Vector Machine (SVM) classifier. Further, the classification performance of the new BoWL descriptor is compared with the performance achieved by other researchers in recent years using some popular methods. Experiments with three fairly challenging publicly available image datasets show that the proposed BoWL descriptor not only yields significantly higher classification performance than LBP, but also generates results better than or at par with some other popular image descriptors.

Keywords: BoWL descriptor, Bag of Words, LBP, Scene Image Classification, Spatial Pyramid.

1 Introduction

Content-based image classification, search and retrieval is a rapidly-expanding research area. The large volume of digital images taken worldwide every year necessitates the development of automated classification systems. Apart from classifying large volume of uncategorized images, image recognition has a variety of uses such as weather forecasting, medical diagnostics and robot vision.

The Local Binary Patterns (LBP) descriptor, which captures the variation in intensity between neighboring pixels, was originally introduced to encode the texture from images [1]. Due to its computational efficiency, the LBP feature has been used alone or in conjunction with other features to develop new image descriptors suitable for content-based classification tasks [2], [3], [4].

---

* Corresponding author.

R. Wilson et al. (Eds.): CAIP 2013, Part I, LNCS 8047, pp. 490–497, 2013.

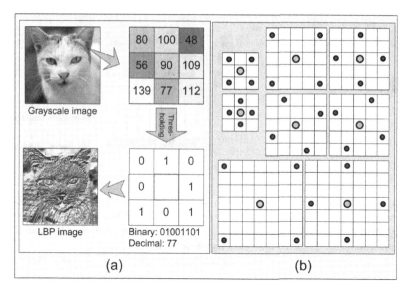

Fig. 1. (a) shows a grayscale image, its LBP image, and the illustration of the computation of the LBP code for a center pixel with gray level 90. (b) shows the eight 4-neighborhood masks used for computing the proposed BoWL descriptor.

Lately, part-based methods have been very popular among researchers due to their accuracy in image classification tasks [5]. Here the image is considered as a collection of sub-images or parts. After features are extracted from all the parts, similar parts are clustered together to form a visual vocabulary and a histogram of the parts is used to represent the image. This approach is known as a "bag-of-words model", with features from each part representing a "visual word" that describes one characteristic of the complete image [6].

This paper explores a new bag-of-words based image descriptor that makes use of the multi-neighborhood LBP concept from [7], but significantly improves the classification accuracy.

2 An Innovative Bag of Words LBP (BoWL) Descriptor for Scene Image Classification

In this section, we review the LBP descriptor, and then describe the process of computing the proposed Bag of Words LBP (BoWL) descriptor from an image.

2.1 Local Binary Patterns (LBP)

The Local Binary Patterns (LBP) method derives the texture description of a grayscale i.e. intensity image by comparing a center pixel with its neighbors [1]. LBP tends to achieve grayscale invariance because only the signs of the differences between the center pixel and its neighbors are used to define the value of the LBP code. Figure 1(a)

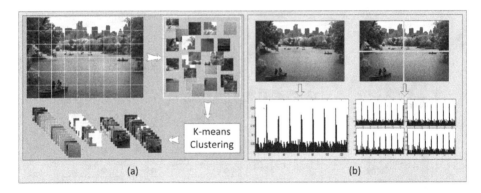

Fig. 2. (a) A grayscale image is broken down into small image patches which are then quantized into a number of visual words and the image is represented as a histogram of words. (b) The spatial pyramid model for image representation. The image is successively tiled into different regions and features are extracted from each region and concatenated.

shows a grayscale image on the top left and its LBP image on the bottom left. The two 3×3 matrices on the right illustrate how the LBP code is computed for the center pixel whose gray level is 90.

2.2   Dense Sampling: Image to Bag of Features

The first step while computing the new BoWL descriptor is sampling. Some image descriptors like SIFT [8] use multiscale keypoint detectors to select regions of interest within the image, but dense or even random sampling often outperforms the keypoint-based sampling methods [9]. In the method proposed here, the image is divided into a large number of equal sized blocks using a uniform grid and each block is used as a separate region for feature extraction. To increase classification performance, overlapping image blocks are used. This process is explained in Figure 2(a).

2.3   A Modified LBP for Small Image Patches

Different forms of the LBP descriptor have resulted from different styles of selecting the neighborhood by different researchers [10], [7], [11]. Figure 1(b) shows the eight 4-pixel neighborhoods used for generating the multi-neighborhood LBP descriptor used here. The traditional LBP process assigns one out of 2^8 possible intensity values to each pixel forming a 256 bin histogram. However, if this technique is applied to a small image patch with ~256 pixels the histogram becomes sparse. To solve this problem, eight smaller neighborhoods of four pixels each are used. These neighborhoods produce a more dense 16-bin histogram, and eight such histograms from different neighborhoods are concatenated to generate the 128-dimensional feature vector describing each image patch.

The Discrete Cosine Transform (DCT) can be used to transform an image from the spatial domain to the frequency domain. DCT is thus able to extract the features in the frequency domain to encode different image details that are not directly accessible in the spatial domain. In the proposed method, the original image is transformed to the frequency domain and the highest 25%, 50% and 75% frequencies are eliminated, respectively. The original image and the three images thus formed undergo the same process of dense sampling and eight-mask LBP feature extraction.

2.4 Bag of Features to Histogram of Visual Words

As demonstrated in the lower part of Figure 2(a), the bag of features extracted from the training images are quantized into a visual vocabulary with discrete visual words using the popular k-means clustering method. The vocabulary size used by other researchers varies from a few hundreds [12] to several thousands and tens of thousands [13]. For the BoWL features, experiments were performed with vocabularies of varying sizes and a 1000-word vocabulary was found to be optimum. After the formation of the visual vocabulary, each image patch from each training and test image is mapped to one specific word in the vocabulary and the image, therefore, can be represented by a histogram of visual words.

Using the image pyramid representation of [12], a descriptor is able to represent local image features and their spatial layout. In this method, an image is tiled into successively smaller blocks at each level and descriptors are computed for each block and concatenated. This technique is explained in Figure 2(b). For this work, only the second level of this pyramid has been used to keep the computational complexity low. This creates a 4000 dimensional BoWL feature vector for each image.

For classification, a Support Vector Machine (SVM) with a Hellinger kernel is trained independently for each class (one-vs-all). The SVM implementation used here is the one that is distributed with the VlFeat package [14].

3 Experiments

This section first introduces the three scene image datasets used for testing the new BoWL image descriptor and then does a comparative assessment of the classification performances of the LBP, the BoWL and some other popular descriptors.

3.1 Datasets Used

Three publicly available and widely used image datasets are used in this work for assessing the classification performance of the proposed descriptor.

The UIUC Sports Event Dataset. The UIUC Sports Event dataset [15] contains 1,574 images from eight sports event categories. These images contain both indoor and outdoor scenes where the foreground contains elements that define the category. The background is often cluttered and is similar across different categories. Some sample images are displayed in Figure 3(a).

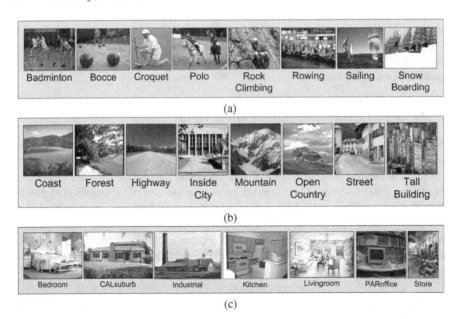

Fig. 3. Some sample images from (a) the UIUC Sports Event dataset, (b) the MIT Scene dataset, and (c) the Fifteen Scene Categories dataset

The MIT Scene Dataset. The MIT Scene dataset (also known as OT Scenes) [16] has 2,688 images classified as eight categories. There is a large variation in light, content and angles, along with a high intra-class variation [16]. Figure 3(b) shows a few sample images from this dataset.

The Fifteen Scene Categories Dataset. The Fifteen Scene Categories dataset [12] is composed of 15 scene categories with 200 to 400 images: thirteen were provided by [5], eight of which were originally collected by [16] as the MIT Scene dataset, and two were collected by [12]. Figure 3(c) shows one image each from the newer seven classes of this dataset.

3.2   Comparative Assessment of the LBP, the BoWL and other Popular Descriptors on Scene Image Datasets

In this section, a comparative assessment of the LBP and the proposed BoWL descriptor is made using the three datasets described earlier to evaluate classification performance. To compute the BoWL and the LBP, first each training image, if color, is converted to grayscale. For evaluating the relative classification performances of the LBP and the BoWL descriptors, a Support Vector Machine (SVM) classifier with a Hellinger kernel [17], [14] is used.

For the UIUC Sports Event dataset, 70 images are used from each class for training and 60 from each class for testing of the two descriptors. The results are obtained over five random splits of the data. As shown in Figure 4, the BoWL outperforms the LBP

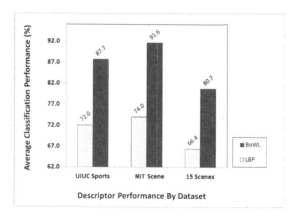

Fig. 4. The mean average classification performance of the LBP and the proposed BoWL descriptors using an SVM classifier with a Hellinger kernel on the three datasets

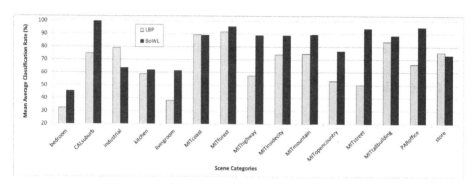

Fig. 5. The comparative mean average classification performance of the LBP and the BoWL descriptors on the 15 categories of the Fifteen Scene Categories dataset

by a big margin of over 15%. In fact, on this dataset the BoWL not only outperforms the LBP, but also provides a decent classification performance on its own.

From both the MIT Scene dataset and the Fifteen Scene Categories dataset five random splits of 100 images per class are used for training, and the rest of the images are used for testing. Again, the BoWL produces decent classification performance on its own apart from beating the LBP by a fair margin. Figure 4 displays these results on the MIT Scene dataset and Fifteen Scene Categories dataset. The highest classification rate for the MIT Scene dataset is as high as 91.6% for the BoWL descriptor. The classification performance of BoWL beats that of LBP by a margin of over 17%.

On the Fifteen Scene Categories dataset, the overall success rate for BoWL is 80.7% which is again over 14% higher than LBP. This is also shown in Figure 4. In Figure 5, the category wise classification rates of the grayscale LBP and the grayscale BoWL descriptors for all 15 categories of this dataset are shown. The BoWL here is shown to better the LBP classification performance in 12 of the 15 scene categories.

Table 1. Comparison of the Classification Performance (%) of the Proposed Grayscale BoWL Descriptor with Other Popular Methods on the Three Image Datasets

Method		UIUC	MIT Scene	15 Scenes
SIFT+GGM	[15]	73.4	-	-
OB	[18]	76.3	-	-
KSPM	[19]	-	-	76.7
KC	[20]	-	-	76.7
CA-TM	[21]	78.0	-	-
ScSPM	[19]	-	-	80.3
SIFT+SC	[22]	82.7	-	-
SE	[16]	-	83.7	-
HMP	[22]	85.7	-	-
C4CC	[23]	-	86.7	-
BoWL+SVM (Proposed)		**87.7**	**91.6**	**80.7**

The classification performance of the proposed BoWL descriptor is also compared with some popular image descriptors and classification techniques as reported by other researchers. The detailed comparison is shown in Table 1.

4   Conclusion

In this paper, a variation of the LBP descriptor is used with a DCT and bag-of-words based representation to form the novel Bag of Words-LBP (BoWL) image descriptor. The contributions of this paper are manifold. First, a new multi-neighborhood LBP is proposed for small image patches. Second, this multi-neighborhood LBP is coupled with a DCT-based smoothing to extract features at different scales. Third, these features are used with a spatial pyramid image representation and SVM classifier to prove that the BoWL descriptor significantly improves image classification performance over LBP. Finally, experimental results on three popular scene image datasets show that the BoWL descriptor also yields classification performance better than or comparable to several recent methods used by other researchers.

References

1. Ojala, T., Pietikainen, M., Harwood, D.: A comparative study of texture measures with classification based on feature distributions. Pattern Recognition 29(1), 51–59 (1996)
2. Banerji, S., Sinha, A., Liu, C.: New image descriptors based on color, texture, shape, and wavelets for object and scene image classification. Neurocomputing (2013)
3. Banerji, S., Sinha, A., Liu, C.: Scene image classification: Some novel descriptors. In: IEEE International Conference on Systems, Man, and Cybernetics, Seoul, Korea, October 14-17, pp. 2294–2299 (2012)
4. Sinha, A., Banerji, S., Liu, C.: Novel color gabor-lbp-phog (glp) descriptors for object and scene image classification. In: The Eighth Indian Conference on Vision, Graphics and Image Processing, Mumbai, India, December 16-19, p. 58 (2012)

5. Fei-Fei, L., Perona, P.: A bayesian hierarchical model for learning natural scene categories. In: Conference on Computer Vision and Pattern Recognition, pp. 524–531 (2005)
6. Yang, J., Jiang, Y., Hauptmann, A., Ngo, C.: Evaluating bag-of-visual-words representations in scene classification. In: Multimedia Information Retrieval, pp. 197–206 (2007)
7. Banerji, S., Verma, A., Liu, C.: Novel color LBP descriptors for scene and image texture classification. In: 15th International Conference on Image Processing, Computer Vision, and Pattern Recognition, Las Vegas, Nevada, July 18-21, pp. 537–543 (2011)
8. Lowe, D.: Distinctive image features from scale-invariant keypoints. International Journal of Computer Vision 60(2), 91–110 (2004)
9. Nowak, E., Jurie, F., Triggs, B.: Sampling strategies for bag-of-features image classification. In: Leonardis, A., Bischof, H., Pinz, A. (eds.) ECCV 2006. LNCS, vol. 3954, pp. 490–503. Springer, Heidelberg (2006)
10. Zhu, C., Bichot, C., Chen, L.: Multi-scale color local binary patterns for visual object classes recognition. In: International Conference on Pattern Recognition, Istanbul, Turkey, August 23-26, pp. 3065–3068 (2010)
11. Gu, J., Liu, C.: Feature local binary patterns with application to eye detection. Neurocomputing (2013)
12. Lazebnik, S., Schmid, C., Ponce, J.: Beyond bags of features: Spatial pyramid matching for recognizing natural scene categories. In: IEEE Conference on Computer Vision and Pattern Recognition, New York, NY, USA (2006)
13. Sivic, J., Zisserman, A.: Video google: a text retrieval approach to object matching in videos. In: Ninth IEEE International Conference on Computer Vision, pp. 1470–1477 (2003)
14. Vedaldi, A., Fulkerson, B.: Vlfeat – an open and portable library of computer vision algorithms. In: The 18th Annual ACM International Conference on Multimedia (2010)
15. Li, L.J., Fei-Fei, L.: What, where and who? classifying event by scene and object recognition. In: IEEE International Conference in Computer Vision (2007)
16. Oliva, A., Torralba, A.: Modeling the shape of the scene: A holistic representation of the spatial envelope. International Journal of Computer Vision 42(3), 145–175 (2001)
17. Vapnik, Y.: The Nature of Statistical Learning Theory. Springer (1995)
18. Li, L.J., Su, H., Xing, E.P., Fei-Fei, L.: Object bank: A high-level image representation for scene classification & semantic feature sparsification. In: Neural Information Processing Systems, Vancouver, Canada (December 2010)
19. Yang, J., Yu, K., Gong, Y., Huang, T.: Linear spatial pyramid matching using sparse coding for image classification. In: IEEE Conference on Computer Vision and Pattern Recognition, Singapore, December 4-6, pp. 1794–(1801)
20. Van Gemert, J., Veenman, C., Smeulders, A., Geusebroek, J.M.: Visual word ambiguity. IEEE Transactions on Pattern Analysis and Machine Intelligence 32(7), 1271–1283 (2010)
21. Niu, Z., Hua, G., Gao, X., Tian, Q.: Context aware topic model for scene recognition. In: IEEE Conference on Computer Vision and Pattern Recognition, Providence, RI, USA, June 16-21, pp. 2743–2750 (2012)
22. Bo, L., Ren, X., Fox, D.: Hierarchical matching pursuit for image classification: Architecture and fast algorithms. In: Advances in Neural Information Processing Systems (December 2011)
23. Bosch, A., Zisserman, A., Muñoz, X.: Scene classification via pLSA. In: Leonardis, A., Bischof, H., Pinz, A. (eds.) ECCV 2006. LNCS, vol. 3954, pp. 517–530. Springer, Heidelberg (2006)

Accurate Scale Factor Estimation
in 3D Reconstruction*

Manolis Lourakis and Xenophon Zabulis

Institute of Computer Science,
Foundation for Research and Technology - Hellas (FORTH)
Vassilika Vouton, P.O.Box 1385, GR 711 10, Heraklion, Crete, Greece

Abstract. A well-known ambiguity in monocular structure from motion estimation is that 3D reconstruction is possible up to a similarity transformation, i.e. an isometry composed with isotropic scaling. To raise this ambiguity, it is commonly suggested to manually measure an absolute distance in the environment and then use it to scale a reconstruction accordingly. In practice, however, it is often the case that such a measurement cannot be performed with sufficient accuracy, compromising certain uses of a 3D reconstruction that require the acquisition of true Euclidean measurements. This paper studies three alternative techniques for obtaining estimates of the scale pertaining to a reconstruction and compares them experimentally with the aid of real and synthetic data.

Keywords: structure from motion, scale ambiguity, pose estimation.

1   Introduction

Structure from motion with a single camera aims at recovering both the 3D structure of the world and the motion of the camera used to photograph it. Without any external knowledge, this process is subject to the inherent scale ambiguity [9,17,5], which consists in the fact that the recovered 3D structure and the translational component of camera motion are defined up to an unknown scale factor which cannot be determined from images alone. This is because if a scene and a camera are scaled together, this change would not be discernible in the captured images. However, in applications such as robotic manipulation or augmented reality which need to interact with the environment using Euclidean measurements, the scale of a reconstruction has to be known quite accurately.

Albeit important, scale estimation is an often overlooked step by structure from motion algorithms. It is commonly suggested that scale should be estimated by manually measuring a single absolute distance in the scene and then using it to scale a reconstruction to its physical dimensions [5,12]. In practice, there are two problems associated with such an approach. The first is that it favors certain elements of the reconstruction, possibly biasing the estimated scale. The second, and more important, is that the distance in question has to be measured

---

* Work funded by the EC FP7 programme under grant no. 270138 DARWIN.

R. Wilson et al. (Eds.): CAIP 2013, Part I, LNCS 8047, pp. 498–506, 2013.

accurately in the world and then correctly associated with the corresponding distance in the 3D reconstruction. Such a task can be quite difficult to perform and is better suited to large-scale reconstructions for which the measurement error can be negligible compared to the distance being measured. However, measuring distances for objects at the centimeter scale has to be performed with extreme care and is therefore remarkably challenging. For example, [1] observes that a modeling error of $1mm$ in the scale of a coke can, gives rise to a depth estimation error of up to $3cm$ at a distance of $1m$ from the camera, which is large enough to cause problems to a robotic manipulator attempting to grasp the object.

This work investigates three techniques for obtaining reliable scale estimates pertaining to a monocular 3D reconstruction and evaluates them experimentally. These techniques differ in their required level of manual intervention, their flexibility and accuracy. Section 2 briefly presents our approach for obtaining a reconstruction whose scale is to be estimated. Scale estimation techniques are detailed in Sections 3-5 and experimental results from their application to real and synthetic datasets are reported in Sect. 6. The paper concludes in Sect. 7.

2   Obtaining a 3D Reconstruction

In this work, 3D reconstruction refers to the recovery of sparse sets of points from an object's surface. To obtain a complete and view independent representation, several images depicting an object from multiple unknown viewpoints are acquired with a single camera. These images are used in a feature-based structure from motion pipeline to estimate the interimage camera motion and recover a corresponding 3D point cloud [16]. This pipeline relies on the detection and matching of SIFT keypoints across images which are then reconstructed in 3D. The 3D coordinates are complemented by associating with each reconstructed point a SIFT feature descriptor [11], which captures the local surface appearance in the point's vicinity. A SIFT descriptor is available from each image where a particular 3D point is seen. Thus, we select as its most representative descriptor the one originating from the image in which the imaged surface is most frontal and close enough to the camera. This requires knowledge of the surface normal, which is obtained by gathering the point's 3D neighbours and robustly fitting to them a plane. As will become clear in the following, SIFT descriptors permit the establishment of putative correspondences between an image and an object's 3D geometry. Combined together, 3D points and SIFT descriptors of their image projections constitute an object's representation.

3   Scale Estimation from Known Object Motion

The simplest approach to estimate an object's scale employs a single static camera to acquire two views of the object in different poses with known relative displacement. Then, the pose of the object in each view is determined. Since the camera is static, the two poses estimated can be used to compute the object's displacement up to the unknown scale. The sought scale is simply the ratio of known over recovered displacement. To ease the task of measuring 3D displacements, the object is placed so that it is aligned with the checkers of a checkerboard grid. Such a guided placemement allows the distance between the object's locations to be known through the actual size of each checker. An advantage of the known motion approach is that it does not involve a special camera setup. On the other hand, it suffers from two disadvantages. First, it relies on careful object placement on the grid and is, therefore, susceptible to human error. Second, it treats images separately and thus does not avail any opportunities for combining them and in so doing increase the overall accuracy.

A key ingredient of the method outlined above is the estimation of the pose of a known object in a single image, therefore more details regarding this computation are provided next. Given an image of the object, SIFT keypoints are detected in it and then matched against those contained in its reconstructed representation (cf. Sect. 2). The invariance of SIFT permits the reliable identification of features that have undergone large affine distortions in the image. The established correspondences are used to associate the 2D image locations of detected features with the 3D coordinates of their corresponding points on the object's surface. The procedure adopted for point matching is the F2P strategy from [8]. Compared to the standard test defined by the ratio of the distances to the closest and second closest neighbors [11], F2P was found to yield fewer erroneous matches. An important detail concerns the quantification of distances among SIFT descriptors, which are traditionally computed with the Euclidean (L_2) norm. Considering that the SIFT descriptor is a weighted histogram of gradient orientations, improvements in matching are attained by substituting L_2 with histogram norms such as the Chi-squared (χ^2) distance [15]. This is a histogram distance that takes into account the fact that in many natural histograms, the difference between large bins is less important than the difference between small bins and should therefore be reduced. Keypoint matching provides a set of 3D-2D correspondences from which pose is estimated as explained below.

Pose estimation concerns determining the position and orientation of an object with respect to a camera given the camera intrinsics and a set of n correspondences between known 3D object points and their image projections. This problem, also known as the Perspective-n-Point (PnP) problem, is typically solved using non-iterative approaches that involve small, fixed-size sets of correspondences. For example, the basic case for triplets ($n = 3$, known as the P3P problem), has been studied in [3] whereas other solutions were later proposed in [2,7]. P3P is known to admit up to four different solutions, whereas in practice it usually has just two. Our approach for pose estimation in a single image uses a set of 2D-3D point correspondences to compute a preliminary pose estimate and then refine it iteratively. This is achieved by embedding the P3P solver [3] into a RANSAC [2] framework and computing an initial pose estimate along with a classification of correspondences into inliers and outliers. The pose computed by RANSAC is next refined to take into account all inlying correspondences by minimizing a non-linear cost function corresponding to their total reprojection error. The minimization is made more immune to noise caused by mislocalized image points by substituting the squared reprojection error with a robust cost function (i.e., M-estimator). Our pose estimation approach is detailed in [10].

4   Scale Estimation from 3D Reconstruction and Absolute Orientation

Another way of approaching the scale estimation problem is to resort to stereo. More specifically, a strongly calibrated stereo pair is assumed and two-view triangulation is employed to estimate the 3D coordinates of points on the surface of the object. These points are then matched to points from the object's representation. The scale factor is estimated by finding the similarity aligning the triangulated 3D points with their counterparts from the representation. This is achieved by solving the absolute orientation problem, which also accounts for the unknown scale. To safeguard against possible outliers, the calculation is embedded in a RANSAC robust estimation scheme that seeks the transformation aligning together a fraction of the available 3D matches. More details regarding the solution of the absolute orientation problem are given next.

Starting with a stereo image pair depicting the object whose scale is to be estimated, sparse correspondences between the two images are established. This is achieved by detecting SIFT features in each image and then matching them through their descriptors. For each pair of corresponding points, stereo triangulation is used to estimate the 3D coordinates of the imaged world point [4]. Knowledge of the extrinsic calibration of the stereo rig permits the triangulated points to be expressed in their true scale. Further to their matching in the stereo images, SIFT descriptors are also matched against the descriptors stored in the representation. In other words, three-way correspondences are established between object points in the two images and the representation. In this manner, the triangulated points are associated with 3D points from the object's representation. The sought scale factor is then computed by determining the similarity between the triangulated 3D points and their counterparts, as follows.

Let $\{\mathbf{M}_i\}$ be a set of $n \geq 3$ reference points from the representation expressed in an object-centered reference frame and $\{\mathbf{N}_i\}$ a set of corresponding camera-space triangulated points. Assume also that the two sets of points are related by a similarity transformation as $\mathbf{N}_i = \lambda \, \mathbf{R} \, \mathbf{M}_i \, + \, \mathbf{t}$, where λ is the sought scale factor and $\mathbf{R}, \mathbf{t}$ a rotation matrix and translation vector defining an isometry. As shown by Horn [6], absolute orientation can be solved using at least three non-collinear reference points and singular value decomposition (SVD). The solution proceeds by defining the centroids $\overline{\mathbf{M}}$ and $\overline{\mathbf{N}}$ and the locations $\{\mathbf{M}'_i\}$ and $\{\mathbf{N}'_i\}$ of 3D points relative to them:

$$\overline{\mathbf{M}} = \frac{1}{n}\sum_{i=1}^{n}\mathbf{M}_i \, , \ \ \overline{\mathbf{N}} = \frac{1}{n}\sum_{i=1}^{n}\mathbf{N}_i \, , \ \ \mathbf{M}'_i = \mathbf{M}_i - \overline{\mathbf{M}} \, , \ \mathbf{N}'_i = \mathbf{N}_i - \overline{\mathbf{N}}.$$

Forming the cross-covariance matrix $\mathbf{C}$ as $\sum_{i=1}^{n} \mathbf{N}'_i \, \mathbf{M}'^t_i$, the rotational component of the similarity is directly computed from $\mathbf{C}$'s decomposition $\mathbf{C} = \mathbf{U} \, \mathbf{\Sigma} \, \mathbf{V}^t$

as $\mathbf{R} = \mathbf{V}\,\mathbf{U}^t$. The scale factor is given by

$$\lambda = \sqrt{\sum_{i=1}^{n}||\mathbf{M}'_i||^2 \Big/ \sum_{i=1}^{n}||\mathbf{N}'_i||^2}\,, \tag{1}$$

whereas the translation follows as $\mathbf{t} = \overline{\mathbf{N}} - \lambda\,\mathbf{R}\,\overline{\mathbf{M}}$.

The primary advantages of this method over the one of Sect. 3 are that it does not require a particular object positioning strategy nor the measurement of any distances. Any object placement, provided that it is well imaged and avails sufficient correspondences, is suitable for applying the method. On the other hand, 3D reconstruction of points based on binocular stereo is often error-prone [13] and such inaccuracies can significantly affect the final estimation result.

5   Scale Estimation from Binocular Reprojection Error

Similarly to that in Sect. 4, this method also employs an extrinsically calibrated stereo pair. Given an object's 3D representation, its scale is determined by considering the reprojection error pertaining to the object's projections in the two images. Using the same coordinate system for both cameras, the reprojection error is expressed by an objective function which also includes scale in addition to rotation and translation. Then, the object's scale and pose are jointly estimated by minimizing the total reprojection error in both images, as follows.

The method starts by detecting SIFT keypoints in both stereo images. Independently for each image, the extracted keypoints are matched against the points of the representation through their descriptors. For each image, monocular pose estimation is carried out as described in Sect. 3 to determine the object's pose in it. Knowledge of the camera extrinsics allows us to express both of these poses in the same coordinate system, for example that of the left camera. Indeed, if the pose of the object in the left camera is defined by $\mathbf{R}$ and $\mathbf{t}$, its pose in the right camera equals $\mathbf{R_s}\mathbf{R}$ and $\mathbf{R_s}\mathbf{t} + \mathbf{t_s}$, where $\mathbf{R_s}$ and $\mathbf{t_s}$ correspond to the pose of the right camera with respect to the left. Due to the stereo rig being rigid, $\mathbf{R_s}$ and $\mathbf{t_s}$ remain constant and can be estimated offline via extrinsic calibration. The most plausible scale and left camera pose are determined via the minimization of the cumulative reprojection error in both images. The binocular reprojection error consists of two additive terms, one for each image. More specifically, denoting the intrinsics for the left and right images by $\mathbf{K}^L$ and $\mathbf{K}^R$, the binocular reprojection error for n points in the left image and m in the right is defined as:

$$\sum_{i=1}^{n} d(\mathbf{K}^L \cdot [\lambda\,\mathbf{R(r)}\,|\,\mathbf{t}]\cdot\mathbf{M}_i - \mathbf{m}_i^L)^2 + \sum_{j=1}^{m} d(\mathbf{K}^R \cdot [\lambda\,\mathbf{R_s}\mathbf{R(r)}\,|\,\mathbf{R_s}\mathbf{t} + \mathbf{t_s}]\cdot\mathbf{M}_j - \mathbf{m}_j^R)^2, \tag{2}$$

where λ, $\mathbf{t}$ and $\mathbf{R(r)}$ are respectively the sought scale factor, translation vector and rotation matrix parameterized using the Rodrigues rotation vector $\mathbf{r}$, $\mathbf{K}^L \cdot$

$[\lambda \mathbf{R}(\mathbf{r}) \mid \mathbf{t}] \cdot \mathbf{M}_i$ is the projection of homogeneous point $\mathbf{M}_i$ in the left image, $\mathbf{K}^R \cdot [\lambda \mathbf{R}_s \mathbf{R}(\mathbf{r}) \mid \mathbf{R}_s \mathbf{t} + \mathbf{t}_s] \cdot \mathbf{M}_j$ is the projection of homogeneous point $\mathbf{M}_j$ in the right image, $\mathbf{m}_i^L$ and $\mathbf{m}_j^R$ are respectively the 2D points corresponding to $\mathbf{M}_i$ and $\mathbf{M}_j$ in the left and right images and $d(\mathbf{x}, \mathbf{y})$ denotes the reprojection error, i.e. the Euclidean distance between the image points represented by vectors $\mathbf{x}$ and $\mathbf{y}$. The expression in (2) can be extended to an arbitrary number of cameras and is minimized with respect to λ, $\mathbf{r}$, $\mathbf{t}$ with the Levenberg-Marquardt non-linear least squares algorithm, employing only the inliers of the two monocular estimations to ensure resilience to outliers. Similarly to the monocular case, a M-estimate of the reprojection error is minimized rather than the squared Euclidean norm. One possible initialization is to start the minimization from the monocular pose computed for the left camera. Still, this initialization does not treat images symmetrically as it gives more importance to the left image. Therefore, if the pose with respect to the left camera has been computed with less precision than that in the right, there is a risk of the binocular refinement also converging to a suboptimal solution. To remedy this, the refinement scheme is extended by also using the right image as reference and refining pose in it using both cameras, assuming a constant transformation from the left to the right camera. Then, the pose yielding the smaller overall binocular reprojection error is selected.

This method has several attractive features: It does not require a particular object placement strategy. There is no need for a short baseline as correspondences are not established across the two views but, rather, between each individual view and the reconstruction. Because no attempt is made to reconstruct in 3D, the experimental setup is relieved from the constraints related to the binocular matching of points and the inaccuracies associated with their reconstruction. A direct consequence of this is that the two cameras may have very different viewpoints. In fact, employing large baselines favours the method as it better constrains the problem of scale factor estimation.

6   Experiments

Each of the three methods previously described provides a means for computing a single estimate of the pursued scale factor through monocular or binocular measurements. It is reasonable to expect that such estimates will be affected by various errors, therefore basing scale estimation on a single pair of images should be avoided. Instead, more accurate estimates can be obtained by employing multiple images in which the object has been moved to different positions and collecting the corresponding estimates. Then, the final scale estimate is obtained by applying a robust location estimator such as their sample median [14]. In the following, the methods of Sect. 3, 4 and 5 will be denoted as MONO, ABSOR and REPROJ, respectively. Due to limited space, two sets of experiments are reported.

An experiment with synthetic images was conducted first, in which the baseline of the stereo pair imaging the target object was varied. A set of images was generated, utilizing a custom OpenGL renderer. A 1:1 model of a textured rectangular cuboid (sized $45 \times 45 \times 90 \, mm^3$), represented by a 3D triangle mesh (with 14433 vertices & 28687 faces), was rendered in 59 images. These images correspond to a virtual camera (1280 × 960 pixels, 22.2° × 16.7° FOV) circumventing the object in a full circle of radius 500 mm perpendicular to its major symmetry axis. At all simulated camera locations, the optical axis was oriented so that it pointed towards the object's centroid. The experiment was conducted in 30 conditions, each employing an increasingly larger baseline. In condition n, the ith stereo pair comprised of images i and $i+n$. Hence, the baseline increment in each successive condition was ≈ 52mm. In Fig. 1(a) and (b), an image from the experiments and the absolute error in the estimated scale factor are shown. Notice that the plot for ABSOR terminates early at a baseline of ≈ 209mm. This is because as the baseline length increases, the reduction in overlap between the two images of the stereo pair results in fewer correspondences. In conditions of the experiment corresponding to larger baselines, some stereo pairs did not provide enough correspondences to support a reliable estimate by ABSOR. As a result, the estimation error for these pairs was overly large.

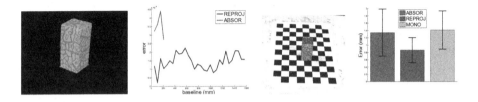

Fig. 1. Experiments. Left to right: (a) sample image from the experiment with synthetic stereo images and (b) scale factor estimation error (in milli scale), (c) sample image from the experiment with real images and (d) translational pose estimation error.

The three methods are compared next with the aid of real images. Considering that the task of directly using the estimated scales to assess their accuracy is cumbersome, it was chosen to compare scales indirectly through pose estimation. More specifically, an arbitrarily scaled model of an object was re-scaled with the estimates provided by MONO, ABSOR and REPROJ. Following this, these re-scaled models were used for estimating poses of the object as explained in Sect. 3, which were then compared with the true poses. In this manner, the accuracy of a scale estimate is reflected on the accuracy of the translational components of the estimated poses. To obtain ground truth for object poses, a checkerboard was used to guide the placement of the object that was systematically moved at locations aligned with the checkers. The camera pose with respect to the checkerboard was estimated through conventional extrinsic calibration, from which the locations of the object on the checkerboard were transformed to the camera reference frame. The object and the experimental setup are shown in Fig. 1(c). Note that these presumed locations include minute calibration inaccuracies as well as human errors in object placement. The object was placed and aligned upon every checker of the 8 × 12 checkerboard in the image. The checkerboard was at a distance of approximately 1.5 m from the camera, with each checker being 32 × 32 mm^2.

Camera resolution was 1280×960 pixels, and its FOV was $16° \times 21°$. The mean translational error in these 96 trials was $1.411\,mm$ with a deviation of $0.522\,mm$ for MONO, $1.342\,mm$ with a deviation of $0.643\,mm$ for ABSOR and $0.863\,mm$ with a deviation of $0.344\,mm$ for REPROJ. The mean translational errors of the pose estimates are shown graphically in Fig. 1(d).

7 Conclusion

The paper has presented one monocular and two binocular methods for scale factor estimation. Binocular methods are preferable due to their flexibility with respect to object placement. Furthermore, the binocular method of Sect. 5 is applicable regardless of the size of the baseline and was shown to be the most accurate, hence it constitutes our recommended means for scale estimation.

References

1. Collet Romea, A., Srinivasa, S.: Efficient Multi-View Object Recognition and Full Pose Estimation. In: Proc. of ICRA 2010 (May 2010)
2. Fischler, M., Bolles, R.: RanSaC: A Paradigm for Model Fitting with Applications to Image Analysis and Automated Cartography. In: CACM, vol. 24, pp. 381–395 (1981)
3. Grunert, J.: Das pothenotische Problem in erweiterter Gestalt nebst über seine Anwendungen in Geodäsie. Grunerts Archiv für Mathematik und Physik (1841)
4. Hartley, R., Sturm, P.: Triangulation. CVIU 68(2), 146–157 (1997)
5. Hartley, R., Zisserman, A.: Multiple View Geometry in Computer Vision, 2nd edn. Cambridge University Press (2004) ISBN: 0521540518
6. Horn, B.: Closed-form Solution of Absolute Orientation Using Unit Quaternions. J. Optical Soc. Am. A 4(4), 629–642 (1987)
7. Kneip, L., Scaramuzza, D., Siegwart, R.: A Novel Parametrization of the Perspective-three-Point Problem for a Direct Computation of Absolute Camera Position and Orientation. In: Proc. of CVPR 2011, pp. 2969–2976 (2011)
8. Li, Y., Snavely, N., Huttenlocher, D.P.: Location Recognition Using Prioritized Feature Matching. In: Daniilidis, K., Maragos, P., Paragios, N. (eds.) ECCV 2010, Part II. LNCS, vol. 6312, pp. 791–804. Springer, Heidelberg (2010)
9. Longuet-Higgins, H.: A Computer Algorithm for Reconstructing a Scene From Two Projections. Nature 293(5828), 133–135 (1981)
10. Lourakis, M., Zabulis, X.: Model-Based Pose Estimation for Rigid Objects. In: Chen, M., Leibe, B., Neumann, B. (eds.) ICVS 2013. LNCS, vol. 7963, pp. 83–92. Springer, Heidelberg (2013)
11. Lowe, D.: Distinctive Image Features from Scale-Invariant Keypoints. Int. J. Comput. Vis. 60(2), 91–110 (2004)
12. Moons, T., Gool, L.V., Vergauwen, M.: 3D Reconstruction from Multiple Images Part 1: Principles. Found. Trends. Comput. Graph. Vis. 4(4), 287–404 (2009)
13. Nistér, D., Naroditsky, O., Bergen, J.: Visual Odometry for Ground Vehicle Applications. J. Field Robot. 23, 3–20 (2006)
14. Rousseeuw, P.: Least Median of Squares Regression. J. Am. Stat. Assoc. 79, 871–880 (1984)

15. Rubner, Y., Puzicha, J., Tomasi, C., Buhmann, J.: Empirical Evaluation of Dissimilarity Measures for Color and Texture. Comput. Vis. Image Und. 84(1), 25–43 (2001)
16. Snavely, N., Seitz, S., Szeliski, R.: Photo Tourism: Exploring Photo Collections in 3D. ACM Trans. Graph. 25(3), 835–846 (2006)
17. Szeliski, R., Kang, S.: Shape Ambiguities in Structure from Motion. In: Buxton, B.F., Cipolla, R. (eds.) ECCV 1996. LNCS, vol. 1064, pp. 709–721. Springer, Heidelberg (1996)

Affine Colour Optical Flow Computation

Ming-Ying Fan[1], Atsushi Imiya[2], Kazuhiko Kawamoto[3], and Tomoya Sakai[4]

[1] School of Advanced Integration Science, Chiba University
[2] Institute of Management and Information Technologies, Chiba University
[3] Academic Link Center, Chiba University
Yayoicho 1-33, Inage-ku, Chiba 263-8522, Japan
[4] Department of Computer and Information Sciences, Nagasaki University
Bunkyo-cho 1-14, Nagasaki 852-8521, Japan

Abstract. The purpose of this paper is three-fold. First, we develop an algorith for the computation a locally affine optical flow field from multichannel images as an extension of the Lucus-Kanade (LK) method. The classical LK method solves a system of linear equations assuming that the flow field is locally constant. Our method solves a collection of systems of linear equations assuming the flow field is locally affine. For autonomous navigation in a real environment, the adaptation of the motion and image analysis algorithm to illumination changes is a fundamental problem, because illumination changes in an image sequence yield counterfeit obstacles. Second, we evaluate the colour channel selection of colour optical flow computation. By selecting an appropriate colour channel, it is possible to avoid these counterfeit obstacle regions in the snapshot image in front of a vehicle. Finally, we introduce an evaluation criterion for the computed optical flow field without ground truth.

1 Introduction

The theoretical aim of this paper is to introduce the affine tracker [10] for multichannel temporal image sequences. Furthermore, we also introduce an evaluation criterion for the computed optical flow field without ground truth.

Optical flow provides fundamental features for motion analysis and motion understanding. In ref. [10], using local stationariness of visual motion, a linear method for motion tracking was introduced. The colour optical flow method computes optical flow from a multichannel image sequence, assuming the multichannel optical flow constraint that, in a short duration, the illumination of an image in each channel is locally constant [4]. This assumption is an extension of the classical optical flow constraint to the multichannel case. This colour optical flow constraint derives a multichannel version of KLT tracker [8].

The colour optical flow constraint yields an overdetermined or redundant system of linear equations [4], although the usual optical flow constraint for a single channel image yields a singular linear equation. Therefore, the colour optical flow constraint provides a simple method to compute optical flow without either regularisation [1] or multiresolution analysis [2]. The other method to use multichannel image is to unify features on each channel.

R. Wilson et al. (Eds.): CAIP 2013, Part I, LNCS 8047, pp. 507–514, 2013.

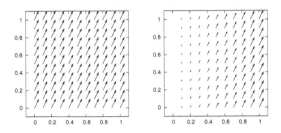

Fig. 1. Order of planar vector fields. (a) A constant vector field $\boldsymbol{u}(x,y) = (1,1)^{\top}$. (b) A linear vector field $\boldsymbol{u}(x,y) = (x,x)^{\top}$.

Barron and Klette [7] experimentally examined combinations of channels for the accurate computation of optical flow using Golland and Bruckstein method [4]. Barron and Klette concluded that the Y-channel image has advantages for the accurate and robust computation. Mileva et. al. [9] showed the H-channel image has advantages for robust optical flow computation in illumination changing environment. Andrews and Lovell [5] examined combinations of colour models and optical-flow computation algorithms. In ref. [6] van de Weijer and Gevers examined photometric invariant for optical flow computation. These references were devoted to the accurate and robust optical flow computation from multichannel images. For the computation of photometric invariant optical flow, performance of both single channel and multichannel methods were compared [7,6]. They experimentally showed that the effects of brightness component and colour components are different for the results of optical flow vector detection.

In ref. [10], using local statinonarity of visual motion, a linear method for motion tracking was introduced. As a sequel to refs. [10,6,7], we develop a local-affine method of motion tracking for multichannel image sequence.

Figure 1 show locally constant and linear displacement fields in a region. The LK method derives an optical flow field assuming that the field is constant in a windowed region as shown in Fig 1 (a). Our method assumes that the optical flow filed linearly depends on the location of pixels as shown in Fig 1 (b). This assumption allows us to compute a globally smooth optical flow filed.

2   Colour Optical Flow

A colour image is expressed as a triplet of gray-valued images such that $\boldsymbol{f}^{\alpha} = (f^{\alpha 1}, f^{\alpha 2}, f^{\alpha 3})^{\top}$, where α is the index to identify the colour space. The triplets $\boldsymbol{f}^{\alpha}$ and $\boldsymbol{f}^{\beta}$, which are derived in different colour spaces, are combined by a one-to-one transform as $\boldsymbol{f}^{\alpha} = \boldsymbol{\Phi}^{\alpha\beta}(\boldsymbol{f}^{\beta})$, where $f^{\alpha i} = \phi_i^{\alpha\beta}(f^{\beta 1}, f^{\beta 2}, f^{\beta 3})$ for $i = 1,2,3$. For a temporal sequence of colour images, we have the relation

$$\frac{d}{dt}\boldsymbol{f}^{\alpha} = \nabla\boldsymbol{\Phi}^{\alpha\beta}\left(\frac{d}{dt}\boldsymbol{f}^{\beta}\right), \tag{1}$$

where $\nabla\boldsymbol{\Phi}^{\alpha\beta}$ is the Jacobian matrix of $\phi^{\alpha\beta}$, since

$$\frac{df^{\alpha i}}{dt} = \frac{\partial\phi_i^{\alpha\beta}}{\partial f^{\beta 1}}\frac{df^{\beta 1}}{dt} + \frac{\partial\phi_i^{\alpha\beta}}{\partial f^{\beta 2}}\frac{df^{\beta 2}}{dt} + \frac{\partial\phi_i^{\alpha\beta}}{\partial f^{\beta 3}}\frac{df^{\beta 3}}{dt}. \tag{2}$$

Since the matrix $\nabla\boldsymbol{\Phi}^{\alpha\beta}$ is invertible, we have the following Lemma.

Lemma 1 Iff $\frac{d}{dt}\boldsymbol{f}^\alpha = 0$, $\frac{d}{dt}\boldsymbol{f}^\beta = 0$ and $\frac{d}{dt}\boldsymbol{f}^\alpha = 0$, $\frac{d}{dt}f^{\alpha i} = 0$ for all $i = 1, 2, 3$.

We call

$$\frac{d}{dt}\boldsymbol{f}^\alpha = \left(\frac{d}{dt}f^{\alpha 1}, \frac{d}{dt}f^{\alpha 2}, \frac{d}{dt}f^{\alpha 3}\right)^\top = 0 \tag{3}$$

the colour brightness consistency. Lemma 1 implies that colour brightness consistency is satisfied for all colour spaces. Therefore, hereafter, we set the spatio-temporal multichannel colour image as $\boldsymbol{f}(\boldsymbol{x}) = (f^1(\boldsymbol{x}), f^2(\boldsymbol{x}), f^3(\boldsymbol{x}))^\top$. Then, equation (3) becomes

$$\boldsymbol{J}\boldsymbol{u} + \boldsymbol{f}_t = 0 \tag{4}$$

for $\boldsymbol{f}_t = (f_t^1, f_t^2, f_t^3)^\top$ and the optical flow $\boldsymbol{u} = (\frac{dx}{dt}, \frac{dy}{dt})^\top = (\dot{x}, \dot{y})^\top = \dot{\boldsymbol{x}}$ of the point $\boldsymbol{x}$, where $\boldsymbol{J} = (\nabla f^1, \nabla f^2, \nabla f^3)^\top$.

3 Colour Affine Method

Assuming that the optical flow vector $\boldsymbol{u}$ is constant in the neighbourhood $\Omega(\boldsymbol{x})$ of point $\boldsymbol{x}$, the optical flow vector is the minimiser of

$$E_0 = \frac{1}{2} \cdot \frac{1}{|\Omega(\boldsymbol{x})|} \int_{\Omega(\boldsymbol{x})} |\boldsymbol{J}\boldsymbol{u} + \boldsymbol{f}_t|^2 d\boldsymbol{x} = \frac{1}{2}\boldsymbol{u}^\top\bar{\boldsymbol{G}}\boldsymbol{u} + \bar{\boldsymbol{e}}\boldsymbol{u} + \frac{1}{2}\bar{c} \tag{5}$$

where

$$\bar{\boldsymbol{G}} = \frac{1}{|\Omega(\boldsymbol{x})|} \int_{\Omega(\boldsymbol{x})} \boldsymbol{J}^\top\boldsymbol{J}d\boldsymbol{x} = \sum_{i=1}^{3}\boldsymbol{G}^i, \quad \boldsymbol{G}^i = \frac{1}{|\Omega(\boldsymbol{x})|} \int_{\Omega(\boldsymbol{x})} \nabla f^i\nabla f^{i\top}d\boldsymbol{x}, \tag{6}$$

$$\bar{\boldsymbol{e}} = \frac{1}{|\Omega(\boldsymbol{x})|} \int_{\Omega(\boldsymbol{x})} \boldsymbol{J}^\top\boldsymbol{f}_t d\boldsymbol{x} = \sum_{i=1}^{3}\boldsymbol{e}^i, \quad \boldsymbol{e}^i = \frac{1}{|\Omega(\boldsymbol{x})|} \int_{\Omega(\boldsymbol{x})} f_t^i\nabla f^{i\top}d\boldsymbol{x}, \tag{7}$$

$$\bar{c} = \frac{1}{|\Omega(\boldsymbol{x})|} \int_{\Omega(\boldsymbol{x})} |\boldsymbol{f}_t^i|^2 d\boldsymbol{x} = \sum_{i=1}^{3}c_i, \quad c_i = \frac{1}{|\Omega(\boldsymbol{x})|} \int_{\Omega(\boldsymbol{x})} (f_t^i)^2 d\boldsymbol{x}. \tag{8}$$

Equation (5) implies that the solution of the system of the linear equations

$$\frac{\partial E_0}{\partial\boldsymbol{u}} = \bar{\boldsymbol{G}}\boldsymbol{u} + \bar{\boldsymbol{e}} = 0 \tag{9}$$

is the optical flow field vector $\boldsymbol{u}$ of the point $\boldsymbol{x}$.

If the displacement is locally affine such that $u = Dx + d$, where D and d are a 2×2 matrix and a two-dimensional vector, respectively, we estimate D and d which minimise the criterion

$$E_1 = \frac{1}{2} \cdot \frac{1}{|\Omega(x)|} \int_{\Omega(x)} |J(Dx + d) + f_t|^2 dy$$

$$= \frac{1}{2} \cdot \frac{1}{|\Omega(x)|} \int_{\Omega(x)} \left|(J, (x^\top \otimes J)) \begin{pmatrix} d \\ vecD \end{pmatrix} + f_t\right|^2 dy. \qquad (10)$$

as an extension of eq. (5)[1].

Solving the system of linear equations

$$\frac{\partial E_1}{\partial(d^\top, (vecD)^\top)^\top} = \begin{pmatrix} \bar{G}, & x^\top \otimes \bar{G} \\ x \otimes \bar{G}, & (xx^\top) \otimes \bar{G} \end{pmatrix} \begin{pmatrix} d \\ vecD \end{pmatrix} + \begin{pmatrix} \bar{e} \\ x \otimes \bar{e} \end{pmatrix} = 0 \qquad (11)$$

for the point x, we have an affine optical flow field vector u at the point x. Since $rank\bar{G} \le 2$ and $rank(xx)^\top = 1$,

$$\begin{pmatrix} d \\ vecD \end{pmatrix} = -\begin{pmatrix} \bar{G}, & x^\top \otimes \bar{G} \\ x \otimes \bar{G}, & (xx^\top) \otimes \bar{G} \end{pmatrix}^\dagger \begin{pmatrix} \bar{e} \\ x \otimes \bar{e} \end{pmatrix}. \qquad (12)$$

Furthermore, for the accurate computation of D and d, we employ the pyramid-based method shown in Algorithm 1.

Algorithm 1. Colour Affine TLK tracker with Gaussian Pyramid

Data: $u^{L+1} := 0, L \ge 0, l := L$
Data: $f_k^L \cdots f_k^0$
Data: $f_{k+1}^L \cdots f_{k+1}^0$
Result: optical flow u_k^0
while $l \ge 0$ **do**

> $f_{k+1}^l := f_{k+1}^l(\cdot + E(u_k^{l+1}), k + 1)$;
> compute D_k^l and d_k^l ;
> $u_k^l := D_k^l x^l + d_k^l$;
> $l := l - 1$

end

In Algoritm 1, for the sampled vector function $f_{ij}^k = f(i, j, k)$, the pyramid transform R and its dual transform E are expressed as

$$Rf_{mn}^k = \sum_{i,j=-1}^{1} w_i w_j f_{2m-i,\, 2n-j}^k, \quad Ef_{mn}^k = 4\sum_{i,j=-2}^{2} w_i w_j f_{\frac{m-i}{2},\, \frac{n-j}{2}}^k, \qquad (13)$$

where $w_{\pm1} = \frac{1}{4}$ and $w_0 = \frac{1}{2}$, and the summation is achieved for $(m - i)/2$ and $(n - j)/2$ are integers.

---

[1] The matrix equation $AXB = C$ is replaced to the linear system of equations $(B^\top \otimes A)vecX = vecC$.

4 Numerical Experiments

Colour Space. There are several standard and nonstandard colour spaces for the representation of colour images. Selection of the most relevant colour space is a fundamental issue for colour optical flow computation. We use the following spaces.

Primary colour systems RGB, CMY, XYZ.
Luminance-chrominance colour systems $YUV, YIQ, YCbCr, HSV, HSL$.
Perceptual colour systems $L*a*b*$.
Usual noncorrelated colour system $I1I2I3$.

For the selection of the window size in the affine colour optical flow computation, we evaluate the spatial angle error $\psi_E = arccos(\boldsymbol{u}_c, \boldsymbol{u}_e)$ between the ground truth $\boldsymbol{u}_c$ and the estimation $\boldsymbol{u}_e$ for Middlebury sequences.

Figure 2 shows errors of computed colour optical flow vectors for various window sizes. Left and right columns shows average angle errors and least mean square errors, respectively, for hydra, grove3, dimetrodon, and urban3 sequences.

Results in Fig. 2 suggest that for accurate colour optical flow computation, we are required to use a window larger than 5×5. In Fig. 3, we show the results of colour optical flow computation using the 7×7 window for Hydra and Grove3 sequences, respectively. In Fig. 3, (a) and (e) are original image. (b) and (f) are the ground truths of optical flow fields. Furthermore, (c) and (g) are the optical flow fields computed with 7×7 window.

For the flow vector $\boldsymbol{v}(x, y, t) = (u, v)^\top$, setting $f'(x, y, t) = f(x - u, y - v, t + 1)$, we define

$$RMS\ error = \sqrt{\frac{1}{\Omega} \int \int_\Omega (f(x, y, t) - f'(x, y, t))^2 dx dy} \qquad (14)$$

for images in the region of interest Ω at time t. We use the sequential error

$$\epsilon(t) = \sqrt{\frac{1}{\Omega} \int_\Omega |\boldsymbol{u}(\boldsymbol{x}, t) - \boldsymbol{u}(\boldsymbol{x}', t + 1)|^2 d\boldsymbol{x}} \qquad (15)$$

for sequential computation without ground truth.

For the evaluation using the DIPLODOC sequence, we compute the optical flow from the 120th to 142th frames. We work with a pyramid of level 2 or 3 and use 10 iteration at every levels.

Although between frame 130 and frame 132, shading causes counterfeit obstacles in the RGB space, optical flow in the Lab space detected accurately as shown in Fig. 4(a). Figure 4(b) again suggests that for accurate colour optical flow computation, we are required to use a window larger than 5×5.

The above results imply that for the application of colour optical flow to vehicle vision systems, adaptive selection of the colour space and unification of the results computed using several colour spaces are essential.

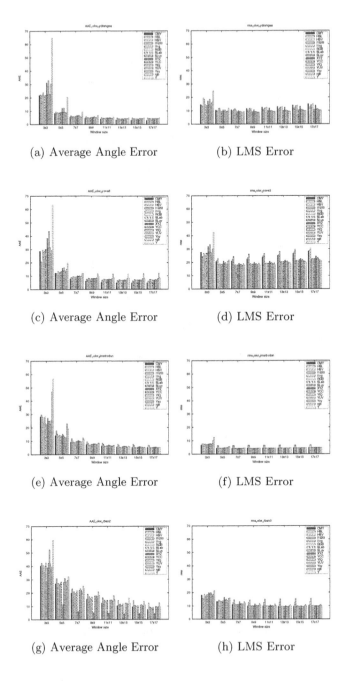

(a) Average Angle Error   (b) LMS Error

(c) Average Angle Error   (d) LMS Error

(e) Average Angle Error   (f) LMS Error

(g) Average Angle Error   (h) LMS Error

Fig. 2. Computed optical flow. Errors for various window sizes. Left: Average angle error. Right: Reast mean square error. From top to bottom: results for hydra, grove3, dimetrodon and urban3 sequences.

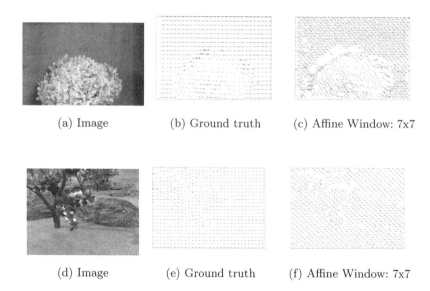

(a) Image   (b) Ground truth   (c) Affine Window: 7x7

(d) Image   (e) Ground truth   (f) Affine Window: 7x7

Fig. 3. Computed optical flow: (a) (e) Image. (b) (f) Ground truth of optical flow. (c) Optical flow field computed with 7 window. (g) Optical flow field computed with 7 window.

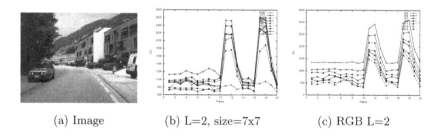

(a) Image   (b) L=2, size=7x7   (c) RGB L=2

Fig. 4. Result of DIPLODOC Sequence. (a) Image from the sequence. (b) Sequential error eq. (15) of various colour channels for the window 7×7. (c) Sequential error eq. (15) for various windows for the RGB channel. We used the pyramid of two layers.

5   Conclusions

For autonomous navigation in a real environment, the adaptation of the motion and image analysis algorithms to illumination changes is a fundamental problem, because illumination changes in an image sequence yield counterfeit obstacles. In this paper, extending KLT-tracker, we develop the colour affine tracker for motion analysis of outdoor long image sequences. The method computes a locally affine optical flow filed using a shift-variant linear equation.

We evaluated the performance of affine colour optical flow computation using Middlebury colour sequences. The results show that our method for multichannel images improves the average angle errors against optical flow computed from monochrome and single channel images. We evaluated the temporal stability of the optical flow field sequences, which are common as images captured by vehicle-mounted imaging systems. The result is a combination of the previous results in refs. [7,9,6,8].

Numerical results shows that for the computation of affine optical flow, we are required to use windows larger than 7×7. Furthermore, the computation with the 5 window derives stable results for the Lucus-Kanade method. Therefore, we have the following conjuncture.

Conjuncture 1. *For the computation of the locally n-th order flow field, we are required to use windows larger than $(5 + n) \times (5 + n)$.*

References

1. Horn, B.K.P., Schunck, B.G.: Determining optical flow. Artificial Intelligence 17, 185–204 (1981)
2. Bouguet, J.-Y.: Pyramidal implementation of the Lucas Kanade feature tracker description of the algorithm, In: Intel Corporation. Microprocessor Research Labs, OpenCV Documents (1999)
3. Lucas, B.D., Kanade, T.: An iterative image registration technique with an application to stereo vision. In: International Joint Conference on Artificial Intelligence, pp. 674–679 (1981)
4. Golland, P., Bruckstein, A.M.: Motion from color CVIU, vol. 68, pp. 346–362 (1997)
5. Andrews, R.J., Lovell, B.C.: Color optical flow. In: Proc. Workshop on Digital Image Computing, pp. 135–139 (2003)
6. van de Weijer, J., Gevers, T.: Robust optical flow from photometric invariants. In: Proc. ICIP, pp. 1835–1838 (2004)
7. Barron, J.L., Klette, R.: Quantitative color optical flow. In: Proceedings of 16th ICPR, vol. 4, pp. 251–255 (2002)
8. Heigl, B., Paulus, D., Niemann, H.: Tracking points in sequences of color images. In: Proceedings 5th German-Russian Workshop on Pattern Analysis, pp. 70–77 (1998)
9. Mileva, Y., Bruhn, A., Weickert, J.: Illumination-robust variational optical flow with photometric invariants. In: Hamprecht, F.A., Schnörr, C., Jähne, B. (eds.) DAGM 2007. LNCS, vol. 4713, pp. 152–162. Springer, Heidelberg (2007)
10. Shi, J., Tomasi, C.: Good features to track. In: CVPR 1994, pp. 593–600 (1994)

Can Salient Interest Regions Resume Emotional Impact of an Image?

Syntyche Gbèhounou[1], François Lecellier[1],
Christine Fernandez-Maloigne[1], and Vincent Courboulay[2]

[1] Department SIC of XLIM Laboratory, UMR CNRS 7252 - University of Poitiers,
Bât. SP2MI, Téléport 2, Boulevard Marie et Pierre Curie, BP 30179
86962 Futuroscope Chasseneuil cedex, France
`firstname.lastname@univ-poitiers.fr`
[2] L3i - University of La Rochelle, Avenue M. Crépeau
17042 La Rochelle Cedex 01, France
`vcourbou@univ-lr.fr`

Abstract. The salient regions of interest are supposed to contain the interesting keypoints for analysis and understanding. We studied in this paper the impact of image reduction to the region of interest on the emotion recognition. We chose a bottom-up visual attention model because we addressed emotions on a new low-semantic data set SENSE (Studies of Emotion on Natural image databaSE). We organized two experimentations. The first one has been conducted on the whole images called SENSE1 and the second on reduced images named SENSE2. These latter are obtained with a visual attention model and their size varies from 3% to 100% of the size of the original ones. The information collected during these evaluations are the nature and the power of emotions. For the nature observers have choice between "Negative", "Neutral" and "Positive" and the power varies from "Weak" to "Strong". On the both experimentations some images have ambiguous categorization. In fact, the participants were not able to decide on their emotional class (Negative, Neutral ans Positive). The evaluations on reduced images showed that average 79% of the uncategorised images during SENSE1 are categorized during SENSE2 in one of the both major classes. Reducing the size of the area to be observed leads to a better evaluation maybe because some semantic content are attenuated.

Keywords: bottom-up saliency, regions of interest, emotions, psycho-visual tests.

1 Introduction

Many achievements have been made in computer vision in order to replicate the most amazing capabilities of the human brain. However, some aspects of our behaviour remain unsolved, for example emotions prediction for images and videos. Emotions extraction has several applications, for example for films classification or road safety education by choosing the adequate images to the situation.

R. Wilson et al. (Eds.): CAIP 2013, Part I, LNCS 8047, pp. 515–522, 2013.

Trying to extract the emotional impact in images is an ambitious task. In fact, different information in an image (content, textures, colours, semantic, ...) can be emotional vector and emotions are complex reactions. Many factors, like cultural aspects, are more complex than content or overall colour and must be considered in the emotional interpretation of an image.

Several papers explore emotions extraction domain [4,5,7,8,12] and propose different approaches to extract emotion of the images. The principal strategy is based on faces detection, an emotion is then associated with facial features (such as eyebrows, lips). The other major approach is the detection of emotions from the characteristics of the image [1,4,5,7,12]. Considering these two approaches, it is interesting to compute the model on a part of images for many reasons. The first one is reducing of the size of the features computed. The limitation of the viewed images to the salient regions can reduce the semantic interpretation. Then can allow easy classification by observers and so a good ratings of our database. Saliency appears to be a good strategy to reduce the information and to conserve the main attractive ones. For example, in a faces characteristics based strategy, visual attention models can detect the different faces if they are the salient information and in another strategies the analysis can be based only on the features of the salient regions.

In this paper, we considered bottom-up visual attention model because we addressed "primary-emotions" and they are felt in the first seconds. This requires a short observation period. In fact, the viewing duration is important during an evaluation of an image regardless the task. This duration involved the process of bottom-up and top-down saliency. Our goal is to study the impact of the reduction of the size of the observed image on the emotions evaluation. This reduction can allow to focus the emotions extraction model on the most relevant regions.

2   The Bottom-Up Visual Attention Model

Recenlty, Perreira Da Silva et al. [10] proposes a new hybrid model which allows modeling the temporal evolution of the visual focus of attention and its validation. As shown in figure 1, it is based on the classical algorithm proposed by Itti [2], in which the first part of its architecture relies on the extraction of three conspicuity maps based on low level characteristics computation. These three conspicuity maps are representative of the three main human perceptual channels: color, intensity and orientation. In[9] Perreira Da Silva et al. propose to substitute the second part of Itti's model by an optimal competitive approach: a preys/predators system. They have demonstrated that it is an optimal way of extracting information.

Besides, this optimal criteria, preys/predators equations are particularly well adapted for such a task:

- preys / predators systems are dynamic, they include intrinsically time evolution of their activities. Thus, the visual focus of attention , seen as a predator, can evolve dynamically;

– without any objective (top-down information or pregnancy), choosing a method for conspicuity maps fusion is hard. A solution consists in developing a competition between conspicuity maps and waiting for a natural balance in the preys/predators system, reflecting the competition between emergence and inhibition of elements that engage or not our attention;
– discrete dynamic systems can have a chaotic behaviour. Despite the fact that this property is not often interesting, it is an important one in this case. Actually, it allows the emergence of original paths and exploration of visual scene, even in non salient areas, reflecting something like curiosity or emotion.

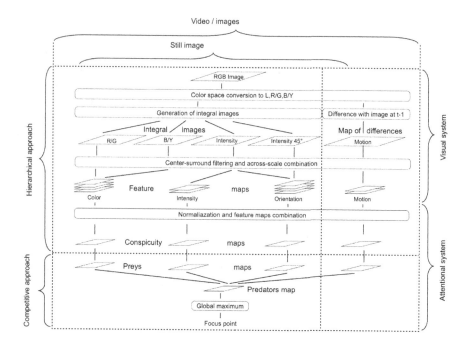

Fig. 1. Architecture of the computational model of attention

Perreira Da Silva et al. [10] shows that despite the non deterministic behaviour of preys/predators equations, the system exhibits interesting properties of stability, reproducibility and reactiveness while allowing a fast and efficient exploration of the scene. We applied the same optimal parameters used by Perreira Da Silva to evaluate our approach.

The attention model presented in this section is computationally efficient and plausible [9]. It provides many tuning possibilities (adjustment of curiosity, central preferences, etc.) that can be exploited in order to adapt the behavior of the system to a particular context.

3   Experimentations

3.1   Image Database

There are many image databases for emotions studies; the most known is International Affective Picture System (IAPS) [3] from the Center for Emotion and Attention (CSEA) at the University of Florida. In general they are highly semantic and this aspect justifies our choice to create a new low-semantic database for emotions study and research purpose in general way. In this paper, "low-semantic" means, that the images do not shock and do not force a strong emotional response. We also choose low semantic images to minimize the potential interactions between emotions on following images during subjective evaluations. This aspect is important to ensure that the emotions indicated for an image is really related to its content and not to the emotional impact of the previous one.

For these experimentations the data set used in [1] has been expanded to 350 images and is now called SENSE (Studies of Emotion on Natural image databaSE) and is free to use. It is a diversified set of images which contains landscapes, animals, food and drink, historic and touristic monuments.

This data set has also the advantage to be composed of natural images except some non-natural transformations (rotations and colour balance modification) on a few images. These transformations are performed to measure their impact on emotions recognition system based on low-level images features [1].

3.2   Experimentations

Our goal during psycho-visual evaluations is to assess the different images according to the nature of the emotional impact during a short viewing duration. For evaluations of emotional impact of an image, viewing duration is really important. In fact, if the observation time extends observers access more to the semantic and their ratings are semantic interpretations and not really "primary emotions".

Usually two methodologies of emotion classification are found [4]:

- Discrete approach;
- Dimensional approach.

In the discrete modelling, emotional process is explained with a set of basic or fundamental emotions, innate and common to all human. There is no consensus about the nature and the number of these fundamental emotions [4]. It can be difficult to score our images with this approach. For example, scoring an image like "Happy" or "Sad" on a low semantic database needs a real semantic interpretation and we prefer a "primary" emotion after a short observation time.

In the dimensional approach, emotions are the result of fixed number of concepts represented in a dimensional space [4]. The dimensions can be pleasure, arousal and power. They vary depending the needs of the application or the researches.

The images of IAPS are scored according to the affective ratings: pleasure, arousal and dominance.

During our experimentations we asked participants to indicate the nature of the emotions; "Positive", "Negative" or "Neutral" and the power varies from "Weak" to "Strong". According to us, it seems easier to rate our images by this way specially in a short observation duration.

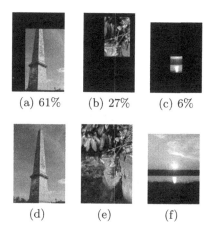

(a) 61%   (b) 27%   (c) 6%

(d)   (e)   (f)

Fig. 2. (a)-(c)Some images assessed during SENSE2 with the percentage of the original image conserved and (d)-(f) their corresponding in SENSE1

Because our tests were applied on a low semantic database we do not need to worry about the potential interactions between emotions on following images. These interactions are really minimized.

We conducted two different tests:

- First evaluations on the full images, an example is shows on Fig. 2(d)-2(f). 1741 participants, including 848 men (48.71%) and 893 women (51.29%), around the world, scored the database. These evaluations are named SENSE1.
- Second tests on the regions of interest obtained with the visual attention model described in the previous section. 1166 participants including 624 women (53.49%) and 542 men (46.51%) scored the 350 images. Their size varies from 3% to 100% of the size of the original ones. Fig.2(a)-2(c) are some examples. These experimentations are named SENSE2.

The two experimentations were successively accessible via the Internet. In fact, SENSE1 were made several months before SENSE2. The participants take voluntarily the one or two evaluations and can also stop it when they want. Even if we cannot control the observation conditions (concentration, displaying, humour), it is not a problem for emotional impact evaluations as these are the daily viewing conditions. Participants were asked not to take a long time to score images. The average time of observation is 6.6 seconds so we considered the responses as "primary" emotions . Each observer evaluated at most 24 randomly selected images if he makes the full test.

4   Results and Discussions

Each image was assessed by an average of 104.81 observers during SENSE1 and 65.40 during SENSE2.

- During SENSE1, only 21 images (6% of the all database) were scored by less than 100 persons. The less assessed image was evaluated by 86 different participants, both genders combined.
- During SENSE2, the less rated image was seen by 47 participants. Only 2 images were rated by less than 50 persons.

Despite these diversified evaluations, some images are not really categorized. We considered that an image is categorized (in some emotion nature class Negative, Neutral or Positive) if the difference of the percentages (of observers) between the two most important emotions is greater than or equal to 10%.

The results from SENSE1 are considered like the reference for this study and the analysis of the impact of the reduction of the size will be interpreted with the rate of good categorization.

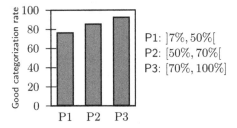

Fig. 3. Good categorization rates during SENSE2 for categorized images during SENSE1

If we considered the results of SENSE2 according to the percentage of the original represented by the visual region of the interest, we noticed that when the percentage of the image is less than or equal to 7%, the images (18 of the 20 concerned) are "Neutral" or "Uncategorised" excepted 2 images. These latter including the image 2(c) have the particularity to have been resumed with the main colours and their emotional impact can essentially be resume with colours.

Fig. 3 represents the rate of images categorized during SENSE1 and SENSE2 in the same class of emotions. Regarding the different results on the SENSE1, reduce the size of the images according to a bottom-up visual attention is a good solution to evaluate the primary emotions. In fact, these emotions must be uncorrelated as possible to the semantic. They appear in the first seconds of viewing before the top-down process. The main errors of categorization during SENSE2 concern neutral images. In fact, neutral images are ambiguous. We proposed the nature "Neutral" to our participants not to force them to score an image as positive or negative if they are not sure about its emotional impact.

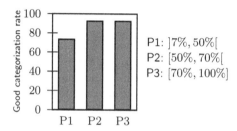

P1:]7%, 50%[
P2: [50%, 70%[
P3: [70%, 100%]

Fig. 4. Rate of uncategorised images during SENSE1 now categorized during SENSE2

Sometimes some images can be rated neutral because there are found positive or negative but not enough.

Fig. 4 shows images uncategorised[1] during SENSE1 and definitively classified during SENSE2 classify in one of the two major classes of emotion found SENSE1. On SENSE1, 61 images are "Uncategorised", the main contribution of this paper concerns these kind of images. In fact, Figure 4 shows that a large part of them (79%) is now categorized; often in one of the two major classes of SENSE1. Reduce the viewing region has probably reduced the semantic and the analysis time.

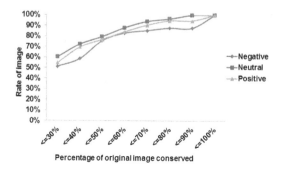

Fig. 5. Rate of good categorization during SENSE2 according to the percentage of original image viewed

Fig. 5 represents the rate of images with good categorization during SENSE2 acording to the percentage of observed thumbnails. It shows that for the three classes of emotions; from 50%, 77% of the images are correctly categorized. This notice answers to our hypothesis that the idea of reduction of the image with a bottom-up visual attention model can offer similar results compare to the full images.

---

[1] To be considered categorized the major class of an image must have a percentage of at least 10% higher than the other.

5   Conclusions and Future Work

In this paper we study the impact of salient regions of an image on its emotion perception. We have shown that when the interest regions are too small they cannot allow an adequate evaluation of the emotional impact. But the results prove that a bottom-up visual attention model could be very helpful to reduce the size of the evaluated image to a pertinent regions that allow "primary emotions" recognition.

We plan to test another visual attention models and compare the different results with those of subjective experimentations with an eye-tracker. Another future work is description of the salient regions by colours, textures, contours and positions features in order to determine the characteristics of these thumbnails which resume the emotions.

References

1. Gbèhounou, S., Lecellier, F., Fernandez-Maloigne, C.: Extraction of emotional impact in colour images. In: Proc. CGIV, vol. 6, pp. 314–319 (2012)
2. Itti, L., Koch, C., Niebur, E.: A model of saliency-based visual attention for rapid scene analysis. IEEE Transactions on Pattern Analysis and Machine Intelligence 11(20), 1254–1259 (1998)
3. Lang, P.J., Bradley, M.M., Cuthbert, B.N.: International affective picture system (IAPS): Affective ratings of pictures and instruction manual. Technical report A-8, University of Florida (2008)
4. Liu, N., Dellandréa, E., Chen, L.: Evaluation of features and combination approaches for the classification of emotional semantics in images. In: International Conference on Computer Vision Theory and Applications (2011)
5. Lucassen, M., Gevers, T., Gijsenij, A.: Adding texture to color: quantitative analysis of color emotions. In: Proc. CGIV (2010)
6. Machajdik, J., Hanbury, A.: Affective image classification using features inspired by psychology and art theory. In: Proc. International Conference on Multimedia, pp. 83–92 (2010)
7. Ou, L., Luo, M.R., Woodcock, A., Wright, A.: A study of colour emotion and colour preference. part i: Colour emotions for single colours. Color Research & Application 29(3), 232–240 (2004)
8. Paleari, M., Huet, B.: Toward emotion indexing of multimedia excerpts. In: Proc. Content-Based Multimedia Indexing, International Workshop, pp. 425–432 (2008)
9. Perreira Da Silva, M., Courboulay, V., Prigent, A., Estraillier, P.: Evaluation of preys/predators systems for visual attention simulation. In: International Conference on Computer Vision Theory and Applications, VISAPP 2010, pp. 275–282 (2010)
10. Perreira Da Silva, M., Courboulay, V.: Implementation and evaluation of a computational model of attention for computer vision. In: Developing and Applying Biologically-Inspired Vision Systems: Interdisciplinary Concepts, pp. 273–306 (2012)
11. Wang, W., Yu, Y.: Image emotional semantic query based on color semantic description. In: Proc. The Fourth International Conference on Machine Leraning and Cybernectics, vol. 7, pp. 4571–4576 (2005)
12. Wei, K., He, B., Zhang, T., He, W.: Image Emotional Classification Based on Color Semantic Description. In: Tang, C., Ling, C.X., Zhou, X., Cercone, N.J., Li, X. (eds.) ADMA 2008. LNCS (LNAI), vol. 5139, pp. 485–491. Springer, Heidelberg (2008)

Contraharmonic Mean Based Bias Field Correction in MR Images

Abhirup Banerjee and Pradipta Maji

Machine Intelligence Unit, Indian Statistical Institute, Kolkata, India
{abhirup_r,pmaji}@isical.ac.in

Abstract. One of the key problems in magnetic resonance (MR) image analysis is to remove the intensity inhomogeneity artifact present in MR images, which often degrades the performance of an automatic image analysis technique. In this regard, the paper presents a novel approach for bias field correction in MR images using the merit of contraharmonic mean, which is used in low-pass averaging filter to estimate the near optimum bias field in multiplicative model. A theoretical analysis is presented to justify the use of contraharmonic mean for bias field estimation. The performance of the proposed approach, along with a comparison with other bias field correction algorithms, is demonstrated on a set of MR images for different bias fields and noise levels.

Keywords: Magnetic resonance imaging, intensity inhomogeneity, bias field, contraharmonic mean filter.

1 Introduction

Magnetic resonance (MR) images are often corrupted by a specific inhomogeneity artifact, called intensity inhomogeneity or bias field, which creates a shading effect in the images [1]. Because of this slow spatially varying artifact, the intensity values of a specific tissue class vary in different locations, which result in increase of overall variation of the tissue class. Although this inhomogeneity artifact is hardly visible in human eyes, it is enough to degrade the performance of any automatic image analysis tool such as segmentation or registration. Hence, a preprocessing step is often required to remove such inhomogeneity artifacts from the MR images before applying these tools.

Several retrospective methods exist in the literature that try to remove this artifact depending on the information of the acquired image. While some histogram based methods such as N3 [2] try to estimate the bias field by maximizing high frequency information of the tissue intensity distribution, others try to remove it by simultaneously estimating the bias field and segmenting the image into meaningful tissue classes [3,4]. Pham and Prince [5] and Ahmed et al. [6] proposed fuzzy-c-means based bias field correction approach, while Ashburner and Friston [7] developed a probabilistic framework for simultaneous image registration, tissue classification, and bias correction.

R. Wilson et al. (Eds.): CAIP 2013, Part I, LNCS 8047, pp. 523–530, 2013.

The simplest and computationally inexpensive method to remove intensity inhomogeneity is filtering method, which depends only on the information of the acquired image. Assuming that intensity inhomogeneity is a low-frequency component in the high-frequency structure of the image, these methods try to remove it by low-pass filtering the image. One of the popular filtering methods is homogeneous unsharp masking (HUM) [8], which is an improvement of classical homomorphic filtering. The HUM is generally implemented either after masking out the background pixels from the image or by replacing the background pixels with average intensity values. However, Zhou et al. [9] also removed the high-intensity structures such as grease and cerebro-spinal fluid and replaced them by the average intensity in their neighborhood. Some other methods also exist in the literature that use median filter instead of mean filter to estimate the intensity inhomogeneity component [10,11]. However, Brinkmann et al. [12] showed experimentally that the mean filter outperforms median filter in estimating the bias field from the MR images. In [12], they also tried to find the optimum window size or the optimum range of window size for the low-pass filter.

In general, arithmetic mean (AM) filter is used as a low-pass filter in the HUM. But, it only computes simple arithmetic mean of the intensity values of the pixels in the neighborhood area of a specific pixel. Hence, all pixels in the neighborhood contribute equally in calculating the local average. In effect, this causes a problem in calculating the bias field component of the pixels in object-background edge area. In [12], Brinkmann et al. used a thresholding technique to distinguish background pixels from the object pixels.

In this regard, the paper presents a bias field estimation technique, using the merit of contraharmonic mean (CHM), which is used in low-pass filtering to estimate the bias field. A theoretical analysis is presented to justify the use of contraharmonic mean for bias field estimation. The effectiveness of the proposed algorithm, along with a comparison with the HUM and N3 algorithms, is demonstrated on a set of benchmark MR images both qualitatively and quantitatively for different bias fields and noise levels.

2   Basics of HUM

The HUM assumes that intensity inhomogeneity is a low-frequency component in the high-frequency structure of the image. It is usually implemented with a noise threshold to prevent background pixels from distorting the bias field estimation.

The model of the HUM assumes that intensity inhomogeneity is multiplicative. If the ith pixel of the inhomogeneity-free image is u_i, and corresponding intensity inhomogeneity field and noise are b_i and n_i, respectively, then the ith pixel v_i of the acquired image is obtained as follows:

$$v_i = u_i b_i + n_i. \tag{1}$$

In general, the bias field can be estimated either from the noise-free image or from the noisy image. However, Guillemaud and Brady [4] showed that post-filtering is more preferable than pre-filtering. Also, intensity inhomogeneity is a low-frequency component. Hence, the model of the HUM can be rewritten as

$$u_i = \frac{v_i}{b_i} = \frac{v_i C_N}{LPF(v_i)},$$ (2)

where $LPF(.)$ is the low-pass filter and C_N represents the normalizing constant that depends on the low-pass filter. If the low-pass filter is an averaging filter, then the constant C_N is used to preserve the average intensity of the image.

3   Proposed Method

This section presents a new approach, using the merits of contraharmonic mean, for estimating bias field present in the MR images.

3.1   Contraharmonic Mean for Bias Field Estimation

Generally, it is assumed that the bias field is multiplicative. So, if fixed amount of bias field is applied to two different pixels, then the pixel with higher intensity value will suffer the effect of bias field much more than the pixel with lower intensity value. Hence, the pixel with higher intensity value should be given higher priority while estimating the bias field. Hence, instead of using simple AM filter, weighted AM filter should be used as a low-pass filter, where higher intensity value gets higher weightage. To achieve this goal, contraharmonic mean (CHM) filter with order $p > 0$ is a favourable choice as a low-pass filter, because it gives higher weightage to higher intensity values and lower weightage to lower intensity values while calculating the mean.

The CHM filter of order p, for any coordinate i of the filtered image $\hat{f}$, is defined as follows:

$$\hat{f}_i = \frac{\sum\limits_{j \in N_i} v_j^{p+1}}{\sum\limits_{j \in N_i} v_j^{p}}$$ (3)

where N_i denotes the set of pixels in a square window centered at coordinate i. The CHM filter reduces to the AM filter for $p = 0$ and to the harmonic mean filter in case of $p = -1$.

Hence, the model of the HUM using the CHM filter can be rewritten as

$$u_i'' = \frac{v_i}{b_i''}$$ (4)

where b_i'' is the estimated bias field at coordinate i of the acquired image v and is given by

$$b_i'' = \left\{ \frac{\sum\limits_{j \in N_i} v_j^{p+1}}{\sum\limits_{j \in N_i} v_j^{p}} \right\} \left\{ \frac{\sum\limits_{j \in I} v_j^{p+1}}{\sum\limits_{j \in I} v_j^{p}} \right\}^{-1}$$ (5)

where I denotes the set of all pixels in the image and the normalizing constant C_N is estimated by the global CHM of the intensity values of all the pixels in the image.

3.2 Importance of CHM

The following discussion constitutes the fact that the CHM of order $p > 0$ estimates the intensity inhomogeneity component more efficiently than the AM.

Let the original intensity and reduced intensity of the ith pixel of an image be denoted by u_i and v_i, respectively, and the intensity of that pixel restored by the HUM using the AM filter and CHM filter of order $p > 0$ be denoted by u_i' and u_i'', respectively. The CHM filter will provide better restoration than the AM filter if the error in estimating the intensity value of the restored pixel is minimum, that is, if

$$(u_i - u_i'')^2 < (u_i - u_i')^2. \tag{6}$$

So, better restoration can be achieved by the CHM filter of order $p > 0$ if

$$u_i' < u_i'' \quad \text{and} \quad u_i'' < 2u_i - u_i'. \tag{7}$$

$$\text{Now,} \quad u_i' < u_i'' \quad \Leftrightarrow \quad \frac{v_i}{b_i'} < \frac{v_i}{b_i''} \quad \Leftrightarrow b_i'' < b_i'$$

$$\Leftrightarrow \left\{ \frac{\sum\limits_{j \in N_i} v_j^{p+1}}{\sum\limits_{j \in N_i} v_j^p} \right\} \left\{ \frac{\sum\limits_{j \in I} v_j^p}{\sum\limits_{j \in I} v_j^{p+1}} \right\} < \left\{ \frac{\sum\limits_{j \in N_i} v_j}{|N_i|} \right\} \left\{ \frac{|I|}{\sum\limits_{j \in I} v_j} \right\}$$

$$\Leftrightarrow \frac{|N_i| \sum\limits_{j \in N_i} v_j^{p+1}}{\sum\limits_{j \in N_i} v_j \sum\limits_{j \in N_i} v_j^p} < \frac{|I| \sum\limits_{j \in I} v_j^{p+1}}{\sum\limits_{j \in I} v_j \sum\limits_{j \in I} v_j^p} \tag{8}$$

Subtracting 1 from both sides of (8) and multiplying the numerator by 2, we get

$$\Leftrightarrow \frac{\sum\limits_{j \in N_i} \sum\limits_{k \in N_i} (v_j - v_k)(v_j^p - v_k^p)}{\sum\limits_{j \in N_i} v_j \sum\limits_{j \in N_i} v_j^p} < \frac{\sum\limits_{j \in I} \sum\limits_{k \in I} (v_j - v_k)(v_j^p - v_k^p)}{\sum\limits_{j \in I} v_j \sum\limits_{j \in I} v_j^p}$$

$$\Leftrightarrow \eta_{N_i} < \eta_I, \quad \text{where} \quad \eta_R = \frac{\sum\limits_{j \in R} \sum\limits_{k \in R} (v_j - v_k)(v_j^p - v_k^p)}{\sum\limits_{j \in R} v_j \sum\limits_{j \in R} v_j^p}$$

The numerator of η_R denotes a measure of dispersion and the denominator is used to remove the effect of the sample from the expression and make it unit-free. Hence, the quantity η_R denotes a measure of relative dispersion. In case of $p = 1$, η_R is twice the square of coefficient of variation.

The analysis reported above establishes the fact that the better restoration can be achieved by the CHM filter of order $p > 0$ than the AM filter if the measure of relative dispersion η_{N_i} within the filtered area N_i is less than the measure of relative dispersion η_I in the whole image I. Now, this is quite trivial as the filtered area N_i is much smaller than the whole image I. Also, there are smaller number of tissue classes present within a specified filtered area, which makes the value of η_{N_i} smaller than that of η_I. This shows that the CHM filter of order $p > 0$ provides better restoration of MR images than that of the AM filter if the condition $u_i'' < 2u_i - u_i'$ is satisfied. Hence, as p increases, the HUM using the CHM filter provides better restoration than that of the AM filter if the condition $u_i'' < 2u_i - u_i'$ is satisfied. The CHM filter attains its best performance at p_{optimum}, and after that the performance decreases with the increase in p as the above condition will not be satisfied for large value of p.

4 Experimental Results and Discussion

The performance of the proposed bias field estimation method is extensively studied and compared with the AM based HUM [8,12] and N3 [2] algorithms. In [12], Brinkmann et al. showed that the optimal window size of the low-pass filter lies in the range 65 to 127. Hence, the optimal window size is fixed at 121 for all the experiments.

To analyze the performance of different algorithms, the experimentation is done on some benchmark images obtained from "BrainWeb: Simulated Brain Database" (http://www.bic.mni.mcgill.ca/brainweb/). The results are reported for different noise levels and intensity inhomogeneity. The noise is calculated relative to the brightest tissue. The performance of different methods is evaluated using the RMSE value. A good bias field correction procedure should make the value of RMSE as low as possible.

4.1 Performance of Different Algorithms

Fig. 1 presents the performance of the proposed, HUM and N3 bias field correction methods, in terms of RMSE value. From the results reported in Fig. 1, it is observed that the proposed algorithm provides optimum restoration in the 7 cases out of total 12 cases, in terms of RMSE value, while optimum restoration is achieved in the remaining 5 cases using the N3 algorithm. The second, third, and fourth columns of Fig. 2 and 3 compare the reconstructed images produced by the proposed, HUM, and N3 algorithms for different bias fields and noise levels. All the results reported in Fig. 2 and 3 establish the fact that the proposed method estimates the bias field more accurately than the existing HUM and N3 algorithms irrespective of the bias fields and noise levels.

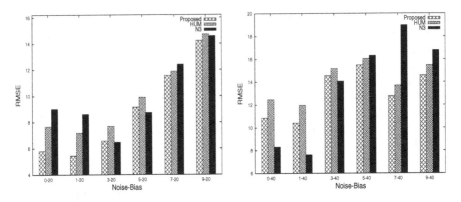

Fig. 1. Performance of proposed, HUM, and N3 algorithms for bias affected images

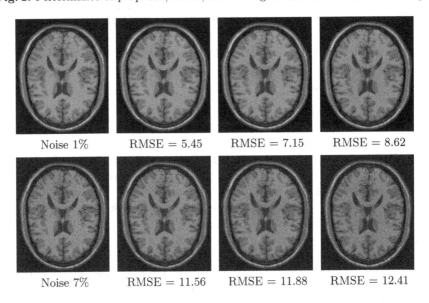

| Noise 1% | RMSE = 5.45 | RMSE = 7.15 | RMSE = 8.62 |
| Noise 7% | RMSE = 11.56 | RMSE = 11.88 | RMSE = 12.41 |

Fig. 2. Input image with 20% bias field and images restored by the proposed algorithm (using CHM filter), the HUM algorithm of Brinkmann et al., and the N3 algorithm

4.2 Unbiased Estimation

One of the caveats about the HUM algorithm is that it can alter an image even when no inhomogeneity is present, while a perfect correction algorithm should be expected to leave the image unchanged.

From the results reported in Fig. 4, it is observed that the proposed algorithm provides better restoration in all of the 6 cases, in terms of lowest RMSE value. The HUM algorithm of Brinkmann et al. and the N3 algorithm severely change the input image in spite of absence of intensity inhomogeneity artifacts, whereas the proposed algorithm leaves the input image more or less unchanged.

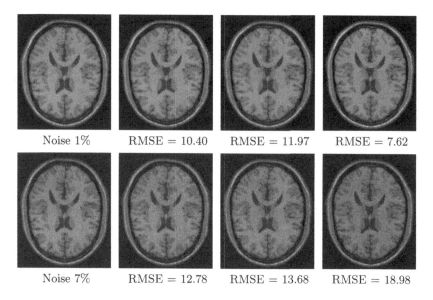

Fig. 3. Input image with 40% bias field and images restored by the proposed algorithm (using CHM filter), the HUM algorithm of Brinkmann et al., and the N3 algorithm

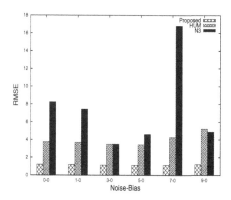

Fig. 4. Performance of proposed, HUM, and N3 methods for bias-free images

5   Conclusion

The contribution of the paper is two fold, namely, the development of a bias field correction algorithm, using the merits of contraharmonic mean filter; and demonstrating the effectiveness of the proposed algorithm, along with a comparison with other algorithms, on a set of MR images obtained from "BrainWeb: Simulated Brain Database" for different bias fields and noise levels. A theoretical analysis is presented to justify the use of contraharmonic mean for bias field estimation. The algorithm using the contraharmonic mean filter instead of arithmetic mean filter provides better restoration of the MR images than the convensional AM based HUM.

Acknowledgment. This work is partially supported by the Indian National Science Academy, New Delhi (grant no. SP/YSP/68/2012).

References

1. Suetens, P.: Fundamentals of Medical Imaging. Cambridge University Press (2002)
2. Sled, J.G., Zijdenbos, A.P., Evans, A.C.: A Nonparametric Method for Automatic Correction of Intensity Nonuniformity in MRI Data. IEEE Transactions on Medical Imaging 17(1), 87–97 (1998)
3. Wells III, W.M., Grimson, W.E.L., Kikins, R., Jolezs, F.A.: Adaptive Segmentation of MRI Data. IEEE Transactions on Medical Imaging 15(8), 429–442 (1996)
4. Guillemaud, R., Brady, M.: Estimating the Bias Field of MR Images. IEEE Transactions on Medical Imaging 16(3), 238–251 (1997)
5. Pham, D.L., Prince, J.L.: Adaptive Fuzzy Segmentation of Magnetic Resonance Images. IEEE Transactions on Medical Imaging 18(9), 737–752 (1999)
6. Ahmed, M.N., Yamany, S.M., Mohamed, N., Farag, A.A., Moriarty, T.: A Modified Fuzzy C-Means Algorithm for Bias Field Estimation and Segmentation of MRI Data. IEEE Transactions on Medical Imaging 21(3), 193–199 (2002)
7. Ashburner, J., Friston, K.J.: Unified Segmentation. NeuroImage 26(3), 839–851 (2005)
8. Axel, L., Costantini, J., Listerud, J.: Intensity Correction in Surface-Coil MR Imaging. American Journal of Roentgenology 148, 418–420 (1987)
9. Zhou, L.Q., Zhu, Y.M., Bergot, C., Laval-Jeantet, A.M., Bousson, V., Laredo, J.D., Laval-Jeantet, M.: A Method of Radio-Frequency Inhomogeneity Correction for Brain Tissue Segmentation in MRI. Computerized Medical Imaging and Graphics 25(5), 379–389 (2001)
10. Narayana, P.A., Borthakur, A.: Effect of Radio Frequency Inhomogeneity Correction on the Reproducibility of Intra-Cranial Volumes Using MR Image Data. Magnetic Resonance in Medicine 33, 396–400 (1994)
11. Bedell, B.J., Narayana, P.A., Wolinsky, J.S.: A Dual Approach for Minimizing False Lesion Classifications on Magnetic-Resonance Images. Magnetic Resonance in Medicine 37(1), 94–102 (1997)
12. Brinkmann, B.H., Manduca, A., Robb, R.A.: Optimized Homomorphic Unsharp Masking for MR Grayscale Inhomogeneity Correction. IEEE Transactions on Medical Imaging 17(2), 161–171 (1998)

Correlation between Biopsy Confirmed Cases and Radiologist's Annotations in the Detection of Lung Nodules by Expanding the Diagnostic Database Using Content Based Image Retrieval

Preeti Aggarwal[1], H.K. Sardana[2], and Renu Vig[1]

[1] UIET, Panjab University, Chandigarh, India
[2] CSIO, Chandigarh, India
pree_agg2002@yahoo.com, renuvig@hotmail.com,
hk_sardana@csio.res.in

Abstract. In lung cancer computer-aided diagnosis (CAD) systems, having an accurate and available ground truth is critical and time consuming. In this study, we have explored Lung Image Database Consortium (LIDC) database containing pulmonary computed tomography (CT) scans, and we have implemented content-based image retrieval (CBIR) approach to exploit the limited amount of diagnostically labeled data in order to annotate unlabeled images with diagnoses. By applying CBIR method iteratively and using pathologically confirmed cases, we expand the set of diagnosed data available for CAD systems from 17 nodules to 121 nodules. We evaluated the method by implementing a CAD system that uses various combinations of lung nodule sets as queries and retrieves similar nodules from the diagnostically labeled dataset. In calculating the precision of this system Diagnosed dataset and computer-predicted malignancy data are used as ground truth for the undiagnosed query nodules. Our results indicate that CBIR expansion is an effective method for labeling undiagnosed images in order to improve the performance of CAD systems. It also indicated that little knowledge of biopsy confirmed cases not only assist the physician's as second opinion to mark the undiagnosed cases and avoid unnecessary biopsies too.

Keywords: Chest CT scan, computer-aided diagnosis, LIDC, cancer detection and diagnosis, biopsy.

1 Introduction

Lung cancer is the leading cause of cancer death in the United States. Early detection and treatment of lung cancer is important in order to improve the five year survival rate of cancer patients. Medical imaging plays an important role in the early detection and treatment of cancer. It provides physicians with information essential for efficient and effective diagnosis of various diseases. In order to improve lung nodule detection, CAD is effective as a second opinion for radiologists in clinical settings [1]. To assess the high-quality of the data, several researchers and physicians have to be involved in

R. Wilson et al. (Eds.): CAIP 2013, Part I, LNCS 8047, pp. 531–538, 2013.

the case selection process and the delineation of regions of interest (ROIs) to cope with the inter- and intra-observer variability, the latter being particularly important in radiology [2]. Efforts for building a resource for the lung imaging research community are detailed in [3]. In almost all the CAD studies, most authors created their own datasets with their own ground truth for evaluation. The use of different datasets makes the comparison of these CAD systems not feasible and therefore, there is an immediate need for reference datasets that can provide a common ground truth for the evaluation and validation of these systems.

The pulmonary CT scans used in this study were obtained from the LIDC [3], and we refer to the nodules in this dataset as the LIDC Nodule Dataset. Recently, diagnosis data for some of the nodules were released by the LIDC; however, because the diagnosis is available patient-wise not nodule-wise, only the diagnoses belonging to patients with a single nodule could be reliably matched with the nodules in the LIDC Nodule Dataset, resulting in 18 diagnosed nodules (eight benign, six malignant, three metastases and one unknown). The 17 nodules with known diagnoses comprise the initial Diagnosed Subset as one case with unknown diagnose cannot be considered as ground truth. Since the diagnoses in the LIDC Diagnosis Dataset are the closest thing to a ground truth available for the malignancy of the LIDC nodules, our goal is to expand the Diagnosed Subset by adding nodules similar to those already in the subset.

To identify these similar nodules and to predict their diagnoses, CBIR with classification is employed. The radiologist's annotation along with LIDC data is also considered as semantic rating to prepare the ground truth from LIDC data. Increasing the number of nodules for which a diagnostic ground truth is available is important for future CAD applications of the LIDC database. With the aid of similar images, radiologists' diagnoses of lung nodules in CT scans can be significantly improved [4]. Having diagnostic information for medical images is an important tool for datasets used in clinical CBIR; however, any CAD system would benefit from a larger Diagnosed Subset as well as the semantic rating, since the increased variability in this set would result in more accurately predicted diagnoses for new patients.

1.1   State of the Art

Only a limited number of CAD studies have used a pathologically confirmed diagnostic ground truth, since there are few publically available databases with pathological annotations [5]. Even with LIDC data where biopsy confirmed cases are available still due to the variability in the opinion of four different radiologists made the LIDC data more complex and redundant. In exploring the relationship between content-based similarity and semantic-based similarity for LIDC images, Jabon et al. found that there is a high correlation between image features and radiologists' semantic ratings [6]. Though in this study, the malignancy rating is also considered for patients having multiple nodules by taking the mean of all the four radiologists rating. McNitt-Gray et al. [7] used nodule size, shape and co-occurrence texture features as nodule characteristics to design a linear discriminant analysis (LDA) classification system for malignant versus benign nodules. Armato et al. [8] used nodule appearance and shape to build an LDA classification system to classify pulmonary nodules into malignant versus benign classes. Takashima et al. [9] used shape information to characterize malignant versus benign lesions in the lung. Samuel et al. [10] developed a system for lung nodule diagnosis using Fuzzy Logic. Although the work cited here provides convincing evidence that a combination of image features can indirectly encode radiologists' knowledge about indicators of malignancy the precise mechanism by which this correspondence happens is unknown. To understand this mechanism, there is a need to explore and find the correlation between all these is required to prepare the ground truth of LIDC data. Also, in all these systems the major concern was to distinguish benign nodules from malignant one where as in the current study we have assigned a new class to the nodules metastasis, which indicates that the nodule is malignant however the primary cancer is not lung cancer and adding this new class will definitely help the physicians in better understanding of cause and diagnosis for those patients. The third class metastasis has not been introduced in the history of CBIR and medical imaging. In the current study, we adopted a semi-supervised approach for labeling undiagnosed nodules in the LIDC. CBIR is used to label nodules most similar to the query with respect to Euclidean distance of image features.

2   Materials

2.1   Lung Image Database Consortium (LIDC) Dataset; A Benchmark

The NIH LIDC has created a dataset to serve as an international research resource for development, training, and evaluation of CAD algorithms for detecting lung nodules on CT scans. The LIDC database, released in 2009, contains 399 pulmonary CT scans. Up to four radiologists analyzed each scan by identifying nodules and rating the malignancy of each nodule on a scale of 1-5. The boundaries provided in the XML files are already marked using manual as well as semi-automated methods [1] [4]. Both cancerous and non-cancerous regions appear with little distinction on CT scan image. The nine characteristics are presented in [11] are the common terms physicians consider for a nodule to be benign or malignant. To our best knowledge, this is the first use of the LIDC dataset for the purpose of validating and classifying lung nodule using biopsy report as well as the semantics attached.

2.2   Lung Nodule Detection and Selection of Slices

Lung nodules are volumetric and almost available in each slice of patient. CT scan of chest is the better method to analyze these nodules for detection as well as for diagnosis. Due to multiple slices in CT, the physician has to see each and every slice for better understanding of each nodule, if present. This task is time consuming as well as not deterministic in any way. We presented a CAD system which considers a nodule as qualifying nodule if and only if it is visible in three consecutive slices. This method can further lead to decrease in time needed to examine the patient's scan by a radiologist. In this work, radiologist's markings are considered for the nodule detection and segmentation from chest CT scan. For better results as well to prepare the ground truth the values of annotations are averaged for all the four radiologists. No automatic segmentation is considered in this study as manual segmentation in medical imaging provided better results; see Fig. 1 [12].

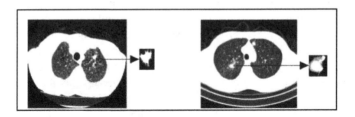

Fig. 1. Radiologist segmentation of nodules

Fig. 1 presents the radiologist's segmentation of nodule and hence manual segmentation is considered as "gold standard". Each slice is read independently to identify its area marked by all the four radiologists and only those slices per nodule is considered to be in the database whose area is maximum [13].

2.3   Final Extracted Nodule Dataset

CT scan of 80 biopsy confirmed patients with solitary pulmonary nodules mostly less than 3 cm have been taken from. All the images are of size 512*512 and each having 16 bit resolution. All images are in DICOM (Digital Imaging and Communication in Medicine) format which is well known standard used in medical field. Total of 1737 nodules are marked in 80 patients considering each slice of a patient having area greater than all those marked by four different radiologists. Out of 80 biopsy confirmed cases only 18 cases were available with single nodule. From these 18, only 17 cases were considered further to prepare the ground truth as diagnosis for one patient was unknown and this set will be referred to as the Diagnosed17. The classes assigned to these nodules were malignant, benign and metastasis based on the diagnosis report available. Rest 62 patients were assigned the class based on the mean of malignancy rating provided by four different radiologists as no ground truth is available for these 62 patients with multiple nodules and this set will be referred as RadioMarked62, see section 3. It contains 1677 nodules from 62 patients. 83 well known image features were extracted for each nodule based on texture, size, shape, and intensity [11]. The four feature extraction methods used to obtain these 83 features from the LIDC images were Haralick co-occurrence, Grey level difference method (GLDM), Gabor filters, and Intensity [11]. The number of nodules was reduced to 210 by removing nodules smaller than five-by-five pixels and multiple slices per nodules considering slice with largest area of nodule because features extracted from these smaller nodules are imprecise. Four different "undiagnosed" query sets containing subsets of the LIDC Nodule Dataset were used, since neither computer-predicted nor radiologist-predicted malignancy ratings can be considered ground truth due to high variability between radiologists' ratings. Each of these query sets differed in diagnostic ground truth. The first query set (Rad210) used the radiologist-predicted malignancy, the second set (Comp210) used the computer-predicted malignancy, the third set (Comp_Rad_biopsy57) used only those nodules for which the radiologist, computer-predicted as well as biopsy confirmed malignancies agreed and the fourth set used only those nodules for which the radiologist- and computer-predicted malignancies agreed. The radiologist-predicted and computer-predicted contained equal number of nodules i.e. 210 and radiologist-computer-biopsy-agreement query set contained 57, and Rad_Comp92 contained 92 nodules after all modifications.

3   Methods

3.1   Labeling of the Nodules

Nodules are labeled according to single nodule per patient and patients with multiple nodules. Following sections show the details:

Patients with Single Nodule.
Out of 80, only 18 patient cases were having one nodule whereas 62 patients were having more than one nodule.   Biopsy report for those patients has four classes identified as 0, 1, 2 and 3. 17 out of 18 biopsy confirmed cases were having the diagnosis as 1, 2 and 3 whereas only one patient was having the diagnosis as 0 which means unknown or indeterminate. This can decrease the classification results, so was not considered in this study. Consequently, 17 pathologically confirmed cases were assigned three classes malignant (M), benign (B) and metastases (MT). There are eight benign (B) nodules, six malignant (M) nodules and three metastases (MT) nodules present in the initial Diagnosed17 set.

Patients with Multiple Nodules.
62 out of 80 biopsy confirmed cases with multiple nodules are assigned classes on the basis of radiologist's malignancy characteristics [11]. Out of nine annotations only malignancy feature is used to assign the class to each nodule marked by radiologists as this is most promising feature to determine the malignancy of a nodule. The method used to label each nodule is as follows

```
Nodules with malignancy rating >=3 assigned class Malig-
nant (M) whereas
Nodules with malignancy rating <3 assigned class Benign
(B)
```

In this way, 1677 nodules from 62 patients were assigned the malignancy class as above. These 1677 nodules contain multiple slices per nodule and assigned to RadioMarked62 set, which further have been reduced to 210 and assigned to QueryNoduleSet210. QueryNoduleSet210 further assigned to various categories like Rad210, Comp210 and Comp_Rad_biopsy210 as explained earlier.

3.2   Summary of CBIR Method of Expanding the Diagnosed Subset17; CBIR Expansion Occurs Iteratively

In the absence of diagnostic information, labels can be applied to unlabeled data using semi-supervised learning (SSL) approaches. In SSL, unlabeled data is exploited to improve learning when the dataset contains an insufficient amount of labeled data [14]. Using available datasets and by evaluating the method with a CAD application, we determined how to effectively expand the Diagnosed17 with CBIR and assist the physicians in the final diagnosis. Each nodule in the QueryNoduleSet210 was then used as a query to retrieve the ten most similar images from the remaining nodules in the Diagnosed17 using CBIR with Euclidean distance. The query nodule was assigned predicted malignancy ratings based on the retrieved nodules (e.g., if the maximum retrieved nodules belong to class malignant then the query nodule was assigned the class M), Fig. 2. The newly identified nodule was considered candidates for addition to the Diagnosed17.

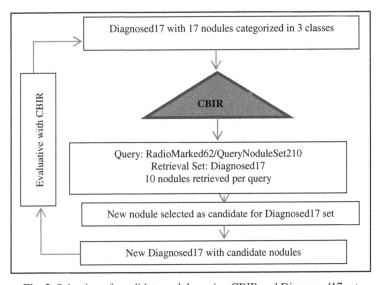

Fig. 2. Selection of candidate nodules using CBIR and Diagnosed17 set

3.3   Diagnosed   Subset Evaluation

Nodules to be added to the Diagnosed17 were selected from the candidates described above. For verifying the addition of a candidate nodule in the Diagnosed17, a reverse mechanism is adopted. Diagnosed17 nodules acted as query and nodules to be retrieved are from QueryNoduleSet210, see Fig. 2. The first three similar nodules are assigned the same malignancy as the query nodule if they were previously assigned as candidate nodules (i.e. if the query nodule is benign then the top three retrieved nodules are also assigned the class benign if previously are assigned as candidate nodule). With this mechanism Diagnosed17 in expanded to Diagnosed74 and then to

Diagnosed121. This process repeated until no candidate nodules were added to the Diagnosed17 following an iteration. Since neither computer-predicted nor radiologist-predicted malignancy ratings can be considered ground truth due to high variability between radiologists' ratings [5]. This mechanism guarantees the preparation of LIDC ground truth and accuracy of CBIR based diagnostic labeling. All the nodules can be classified in three class benign, malignant and metastasis.

4   Results and Discussion

Using the query and retrieval sets as described above, average precision after 3, 5, 10, and 15 images retrieved was calculated. A retrieved nodule was considered relevant if its diagnosis matched the malignancy rating (either radiologist-predicted, computer-predicted, or both) of the query nodule. Initial precision values were obtained by using the 17 nodules in the initial Diagnosed17 as the retrieval set. Then, nodules were added to this set as described in sections 2.2 and 2.3. Precision was recalculated, and the nodule addition process was repeated iteratively using the new Diagnosed17.

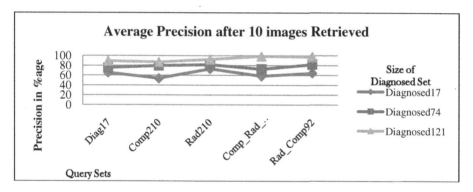

Fig. 3. Comparison of precision for different query sets at x-axis and different retrieval sets at y-axis

Various experiments were setup for the validation of nodules examined. Fig. 3 shows that with five query sets and three retrieval sets Diagnosed17, Diagnosed74 and Diagnosed121, the precision increases respectively. Nodules in Comp_Rad_biopsy57 have provided the best precision i.e. 98% which is the best precision achieved in the history of medical CBIR with best of our knowledge.

CBIR is an effective method for expanding the Diagnosed Subset by labeling nodules which do not have associated diagnoses. As LIDC is having lack of ground truth, CBIR techniques works tremendously better to prepare the ground truth. This method outperforms control expansion, yielding higher precision values when tested with a potential CAD application [12] that requires a diagnostically accurate ground truth. By increasing the size of the Diagnosed Subset from 17 to 74 and finally to 121 nodules, CBIR expansion provides greater variability in the retrieval set, resulting in retrieved nodules that are more similar to undiagnosed queries.

References

1. Wormanns, D., Fiebich, M., Saidi, M., Diederich, S., Heindel, W.: Automatic detection of pulmonary nodules at spiral CT: clinical application of a computer-aided diagnosis system. European Radiology 12, 1052–1057 (2002)
2. Blum, A., Mitchell, T.: Combining Labelled and Unlabelled Data with Co-Training. In: Proceedings of the 11th Annual Conference on Computational Learning Theory, COLT 1998, pp. 92–100 (1998)
3. McNitt-Gray, M.F., Armato, S.G., Meyer, C.R., Reeves, A.P., McLennan, G., Pais, R.C., et al.: The lung image database consortium (LIDC) data collection process for nodule detection and annotation. Academic Radiology 14(12), 1464–1474 (2007)
4. Armato III, S.G., McLennan, G., Bidaut, L., McNitt-Gray, M.F., Meyer, C.R., Reeves, A.P., Zhao, B., Aberle, D.R., Henschke, C.I., Hoffman, E.A., Kazerooni, E.A., MacMahon, H., van Beek, E.J.R., Yankelevitz, D., et al.: The Lung Image Database Consortium (LIDC) and Image Database Resources Initiative (IDRI): A completed reference database of lung nodules on CT scans. Medical Physics 38, 915–931 (2011)
5. Horsthemke, W.H., Raicu, D.S., Furst, J.D., Armato III, S.G.: Evaluation Challenges for Computer-Aided Diagnostic Characterization: Shape Disagreements in the Lung Image Database Consortium Pulmonary Nodule Dataset. In: Tan, J. (ed.) New Technologies for Advancing Healthcare and Clinical Practices, pp. 18–43. IGI Global, Hershey PA (2011)
6. Jabon, S.A., Raicu, D.S., Furst, J.D.: Content-based versus semantic-based similarity retrieval: a LIDC case study. In: SPIE Medical Imaging Conference, Orlando (February 2009)
7. McNitt-Gray, M.F., Hart, E.M., Wyckoff, N., Sayre, J.W., Goldin, J.G., Aberle, D.R.: A pattern classification approach to characterizing solitary pulmonary nodules imaged on high resolution CT: Preliminary results. Med. Phys. 26, 880–888 (1999)
8. Armato III, S.G., Altman, M.B., Wilkie, J., Sone, S., Li, F., Doi, K., Roy, A.S.: Automated lung nodule classification following automated nodule detection on CT: A serial approach. Med. Phys. 30, 1188–1197 (2003)
9. Takashima, S., Sone, S., Li, F., Maruyama, Y., Hasegawa, M., Kadoya, M.: Indeterminate solitary pulmonary nodules revealed at population-based CT screening of the lung: using first follow-up diagnostic CT to differentiate benign and malignant lesions. Am. J. Roentgenol. 180, 1255–1263 (2003)
10. Samuel, C.C., Saravanan, V., Vimala, D.M.R.: Lung nodule diagnosis from CT images using fuzzy logic. In: Proceedings of International Conference on Computational Intelligence and Multimedia Applications, Sivakasi, Tamilnadu, India, December 13-15, pp. 159–163 (2007)
11. Raicu, D.S., Varutbangkul, E., Furst, J.D.: Modelling semantics from image data: opportunities from LIDC. International Journal of Biomedical Engineering and Technology 3(1-2), 83–113 (2009)
12. Giuca, A.-M., Seitz Jr., K.A., Furst, J., Raicu, D.: Expanding diagnostically labeled datasets using content-based image retrieval. In: IEEE International Conference on Image Processing 2012, Lake Buena Vista, Florida, September 30-October 3 (2012)
13. Aggarwal, P., Vig, R., Sardana, H.K.: Largest Versus Smallest Nodules Marked by Different Radiologists in Chest CT Scans for Lung Cancer Detection. In: International Conference on Image Engineering, ICIE 2013 Organized by IAENG at Hong Kong (in press, 2013)
14. Zhou, Z.-H.: Learning with Unlabeled Data and Its Application to Image Retrieval. In: Yang, Q., Webb, G. (eds.) PRICAI 2006. LNCS (LNAI), vol. 4099, pp. 5–10. Springer, Heidelberg (2006)

Enforcing Consistency of 3D Scenes with Multiple Objects Using Shape-from-Contours

Matthew Grum and Adrian G. Bors

Dept. of Computer Science, University of York, York YO10 5GH, UK

Abstract. In this paper we present a new approach for modelling scenes with multiple 3D objects from images taken from various viewpoints. Such images are segmented using either supervised or unsupervised algorithms. We consider the mean-shift and support vector machines for image segmentation using the colour and texture as features. Back-projections of segmented contours are used to enforce the consistency of the segmented contours with initial estimates of the 3D scene. A study for detecting merged objects in 3D scenes is provided as well.

Keywords: 3D scene reconstruction, multi-view images, Shape-from-contours, image segmentation.

1 Introduction

Single 3D object reconstruction from several images has attracted considerable research interest using various approaches such as multi-view stereo, shape-from-silhouettes, shape-from-shading, etc. Various 3D object representations are used including voxels [1], radial basis functions (RBF) [2] and meshes [3]. Space carving is a form of multi-view stereo which assigns voxels to a 3D object or carves them away from its volume according to their photoconsistency [1]. Implicit RBFs have been shown to represent well surfaces of 3D objects in [2]. Object reconstruction from its silhouettes was based on the principle of duality between the tangent planes and their corresponding object space [4,5] or by using visual hulls of the object [6]. In [7] disparities between projections of 3D patches from various images, are used to correct the 3D scene modelled using RBFs.

The methodology described in this paper aims to robustly enforce the consistency of scenes of multiple objects with their corresponding contours segmented from images. We consider a certain approximate representation of the 3D scene as the initialization. The surface representation elements, which may be voxels, RBF centers or vertices, are displaced according to their consistency with segmented contours. We consider both supervized and unsupervized segmentation for extracting object contours from images from various views. The shape-from-contours approach for correcting 3D scenes of multiple objects by using object contour consistency is described in Section 2. A study of identifying

R. Wilson et al. (Eds.): CAIP 2013, Part I, LNCS 8047, pp. 539–547, 2013.
© Springer-Verlag Berlin Heidelberg 2013

wrongly merged objects in 3D scenes is provided in Section 3. Experimental results and the conclusions of this study are described in Section 4 and Section 5, respectively.

2   3D Scene Correction Using Shape-from-Contours

Let us assume that we have a set of images $\mathcal{I} = \{\mathbf{I}_i | i = 1, \ldots, n\}$, each taken from a different viewing angle, which are characterized by their projection matrices $\mathcal{P} = \{\mathbf{P}_i | i = 1, \ldots, n\}$. In the following we assume that we have an initial approximate representation of a scene $\mathcal{S}$ with multiple objects. Correcting such scenes using image disparities in the projections of 3D patches was discussed in [7]. That approach relies on good textures but does not provide good results in areas of uniform color. Nevertheless, such areas can be easily segmented.

Let us assume that the scene contains at least two distinct objects $\{\mathbf{A}, \mathbf{B}\} \in \mathcal{S}$ closely located to each other. We consider that each object outline from the 3D scene is projected onto segmented contours, of their corresponding projections from the input images, denoted as $\{\mathbf{a}_i, \mathbf{b}_i\} \in \mathbf{I}_i, i = 1, \ldots, n$ where:

$$\mathbf{a}_i = \mathbf{P}_i\mathbf{A} \quad ; \quad \mathbf{b}_i = \mathbf{P}_i\mathbf{B} \tag{1}$$

where $\mathbf{P}_i$ represents the projection matrix from the 3D scene to the ith image. In this paper we consider image segmentation for defining the contours of objects, such as $\mathbf{A}$ and $\mathbf{B}$ in 3D or $\{\mathbf{a}_i, \mathbf{b}_i\}$ in the 2D images from $\mathcal{I}$. By comparing the projections of the segmented objects in 3D with their corresponding image segmentations we can detect any inconsistencies and use these to correct $\mathcal{S}$.

In the following we consider both unsupervized and supervized image segmentation for extracting object contours. We consider a feature space for each pixel represented by a vector $\mathbf{z} = [r, g, b, \zeta t]^T$, containing the three color components and a texture feature t, weighted by ζ, provided by the output of the Harris corner detector. For the unsupervized image segmentation we use the mean shift algorithm which was employed for image segmentation in [8]. The local maxima in the probability density function of the features are found by the mean-shift algorithm. Pixels with features closest to each of these local maxima are assigned to the corresponding segmented regions. For the supervized segmentation we use support vector machines (SVM) [9]. SVM requires a training set which is created by sampling a set of pixels from one or more images from the set $\mathcal{I}$. Each of these pixels is labelled according to their class which may correspond to an object or to the background. SVM using quadratic programming techniques finds the boundary which optimally divides the training data set into classes, each corresponding to an object.

The goal of the segmentation is to extract a set of object boundaries from images. The initial estimates of the object boundaries are refined by using active contours such as snakes, in order to join edge maps, representing boundaries of segmented objects from images, into continuous contours of objects $\mathbf{C}_i$. The consistency of the object contours, resulting after projecting the 3D object outlines $\mathcal{C}_{\mathcal{S}}$ is verified with that corresponding to segmented object contours from images. Any inconsistencies between the projected contours of the 3D scene $\mathbf{P}_i\mathcal{C}_{\mathcal{S}}$

and the contours $\mathbf{C}_i$ segmented from the image of the corresponding view are detected and then used to correct the 3D scene. The visual hull, denoted by $\mathcal{H}$, is the outer bound of the scene based on its appearance in several images and was used for modelling 3D scenes from images in shape-from-silhouettes [4,6,5,11]. If a point lies within the visual hull then its projection falls inside the scene silhouette in each image. However, the visual hull will not be able to represent certain regions in multi-object scenes, such as for example the region from the middle of the scene, due to the fact that objects will invariably occlude each other in several images in such scenes.

In shape-from-contours, the concept of the visual hull is applied to individual objects from the scene. In this case, the visual hull of objects, denoted as $\mathcal{H}(\mathbf{a}_i)$ and $\mathcal{H}(\mathbf{b}_i)$ is provided by the object contours such as $\mathbf{a}_i$ or $\mathbf{b}_i$ from each image $i = 1, \ldots, n$, where these objects are visible. After comparing the sets of pixels corresponding to 2D contours and those from the projected 3D contours we identify the regions corresponding to the undesired difference sets as :

$$\{\mathbf{c} | \mathbf{P}_i\mathbf{c} = (\mathbf{S}(\mathbf{P}_i\mathcal{C}_\mathcal{S})\backslash\mathbf{S}(\mathbf{C}_i)) \cup (\mathbf{S}(\mathbf{C}_i)\backslash\mathbf{S}(\mathbf{P}_i\mathcal{C}_\mathcal{S}))\} \qquad (2)$$

where $\mathbf{S}(\mathbf{C}_i)$ represents the set of pixels located in the interior of contour $\mathbf{C}_i$, $i = 1, \ldots, n$ and $\mathbf{c} \in \mathcal{S}$ is a point from the 3D scene, whose projection $\mathbf{P}_i\mathbf{c}$ lies among the pixels from the area between the sets $\mathbf{P}_i\mathcal{C}_\mathcal{S}$ and $\mathbf{C}_i$ from each image. Such points are displaced to their nearest surface in 3D along its surface normal:

$$\hat{\mathbf{c}} = \mathbf{c} - \gamma\frac{1}{m}\sum_{i=1}^{m}\mathbf{P}_i^{-1}\,\overrightarrow{\nabla_{\mathbf{z}_j}\mathbf{C}_i}, \qquad (3)$$

where $m \leq n$ represents all the images in which the inconsistency between the 3D scene projections and the actual object contours is identified, γ is a correction factor, and $\overrightarrow{\nabla_{\mathbf{z}_j}\mathbf{C}_i}$ represents the correction vector which is perpendicular on the object contour calculated in the location $\mathbf{z}_j$. Eventually, such points would be located in $\mathbf{S}(\mathbf{P}_i\mathcal{C}_\mathcal{S})\cap\mathbf{S}(\mathbf{C}_i)$ ensuring the consistency of $\mathcal{H}(\mathbf{a}_i)$ and $\mathcal{H}(\mathbf{b}_i)$ with the 3D scene $\mathcal{S}$. This methodology can be applied to various surface representations such as voxels, parametric (including RBFs) and meshes, where surface self-intersections would have to be avoided [3].

3   Analysis of Object Separability When Reconstructing Scenes with Multiple Objects

In the following we consider the case when two objects from the scene are wrongly merged together in the initial stages of the 3D modelling of the scene. Such situations may arise due to object occlusion, uncertainty in camera parameters, illumination conditions, image noise, etc, [3]. We consider a simple artificial scene consisting of two identical objects, considered as either a pair of cylinders or a pair of cuboids with square base. A circular configuration of n cameras is considered located evenly spaced on a circle located at a height corresponding to $\theta = 0.85$ radians.

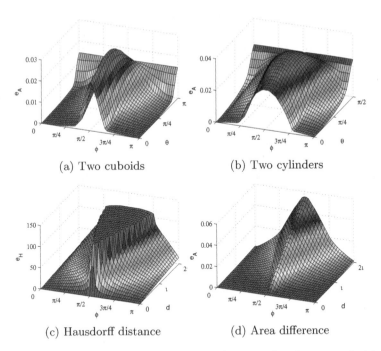

(a) Two cuboids   (b) Two cylinders

(c) Hausdorff distance   (d) Area difference

Fig. 1. Detecting inconsistencies between the merged and separated objects

We assess the influence of the shape when attempting to detect wrongly merged objects in 3D scenes, which are shown as separate in their image projections. The distance between the objects is set as equal to their width and we consider the normalized area error, calculated from the image projections as:

$$e_A(F,G) = \frac{|(\mathbf{S}(F) \cup \mathbf{S}(G)) \setminus (\mathbf{S}(F) \cap \mathbf{S}(F))|}{|\mathbf{S}(G)|} \tag{4}$$

where $\mathbf{S}(F)$ and $\mathbf{S}(G)$ are the areas corresponding to the projections of the 3D objects in the hypotheses of fused and separated objects. Figs. 1(a) and 1(b) show the plots of the normalized area error $e_A(F,G)$ when varying both the elevation θ and the azimuth ϕ angles of the camera while the distance between

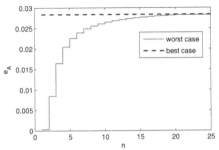

Fig. 2. Surface error $e_{\mathbf{A}}(\mathcal{F},\mathcal{G})$ plotted against the number of cameras n

the objects is kept constant. We also consider varying the distance between the objects d by moving them away from each other. Plots of both Hausdorff distance [10] and the area error $e_A(F, G)$ are shown when varying ϕ and d in Figs. 1(c) and 1(d) for the scene showing two cuboids. These plots clearly show the width of the peak getting smaller as the intra-object gap is reduced.

Large numbers of input images do not necessarily improve 3D scene reconstruction proportionally [11]. We estimate the necessary number of cameras for detecting when two cuboids are merged. For each number of given cameras n, we record the minimum and maximum area errors $e_A(F, G)$, measured between the fused and separate case hypotheses when considering all possible offsets. The results for the best and worse cases when detecting the separation for each cameras configuration are shown in Figure 2. It can be observed that when using more than 10 cameras, the error $e_A(F, G)$ from (4) provides a good assessment of the inconsistencies between the 3D scene and the objects shown in images.

4   Experimental Results

The proposed methodology of correcting 3D scenes of multiple objects using the consistency with object contours was applied on various image sets. Four images, from a set of $n = 12$ images of a scene with 5 main objects captured from various viewpoints, are shown in Figs. 3a-e. We initialize the 3D scene using space carving [1], represent its surface with implicit RBFs [2], and correct the image disparities from projections of 3D patches as in [7]. The resulting 3D scene is shown from two different angles in Figs. 4a and 7a. It can be observed that two of the objects representing a knife-block and a kettle are merged together as shown in the closer view from Fig. 4b. The results provided by shape-from-silhouettes (SFS) [5,6] when applied on the original set of 12 images is shown in Fig. 5a. In Fig. 5b we apply SFS onto the result of the 3D scene from Fig. 4a.

(a)   (b)   (c)   (d)   (e)

Fig. 3. Five images from the image set showing multiple objects

In the following we apply the proposed shape-from-contours (SFC) methodology, described in Section 2. The main difference between SFC and SFS occurs in the regions where two or more objects are located close or in contact with each other. Individual 3D objects from the scene are separated by thresholding the scene with a plane parallel with their horizontal base. Object contours are extracted from the image set and compared with the contours resulting from projecting the current 3D scene onto the image planes using identical camera

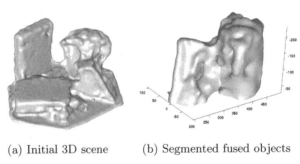

(a) Initial 3D scene   (b) Segmented fused objects

Fig. 4. 3D scene representations using implicit RBFs

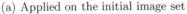

(a) Applied on the initial image set   (b) Applied on the 3D initial estimate

Fig. 5. Shape-from-silhouettes results

parameters $\mathcal{P}$ with those of the original images. We consider a weight of $\zeta = 2$ for the Harris corner output from the feature vector $\mathbf{z}$. Both unsupervised and supervised image segmentation are considered for extracting the object contours from the images. Mean shift clustering is used for unsupervised segmentation while SVM was employed for supervised segmentation as described in Section 2. The training for SVM considers only a few pixels from the objects and background of a single image, shown in Fig. 3b.

The merged object segmentation in four different images is shown in blue in Figs. 6a-d and 6e-h, when using unsupervised and supervised segmentation, respectively, while the projection of the fused object surface from Fig. 4b, is shown in red. We can observe a large discrepancy in Figs. 6c and 6g and a smaller one in Figs. 6a, 6b, 6e and 6f. The regions between the two contours, displayed using red and blue, are back-projected into the 3D scene and their corresponding volumes corrected. For the RBF representation, the corresponding centers are displaced according to (3) or their weights are switched from positive to negative. The initial 3D scene is shown in Fig. 7a, while the 3D updated scene results are provided in Figs. 7b and 7c after the correction by using unsupervised and supervised segmented contours, respectively. There is a significant improvement in the 3D reconstruction of the area between the kettle and knife block, with both methods achieving a complete separation of the two objects. In the updated results, regions from the middle of the scene are now visible through the gap

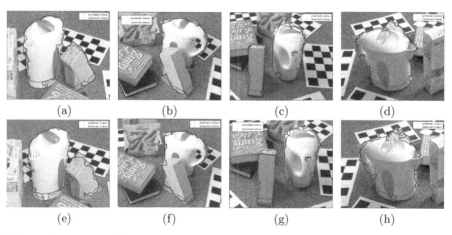

Fig. 6. Projections of the 3D scene onto image planes, shown with red, and object contours resulting from image segmentation, shown with blue, using mean-shift in (a)-(d) and SVM in (e)-(h). Some segmentation errors due to shading and specularities can be observed in the segmented contours.

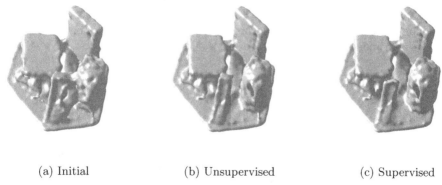

(a) Initial   (b) Unsupervised   (c) Supervised

Fig. 7. 3D scene correction results by using the discrepancy in the contours resulting from the projection of the 3D scene and those segmented from the actual images

between the kettle and knife-block. These results are definitely better than those provided by SFS from Figs. 5a and 5b.

Numerical errors are evaluated for assessing the improvement in the 3D scene when using SFC from either unsupervized or supervized image segmentations. We consider two error measures as in the study from Section 3: the Hausdorff distance [10] and area error $e_A(F, G)$ from (4). These measures assess the differences between the projected contours of objects and their corresponding image segmented contours. Numerical results are shown in Figs. 8a and 8b when varying the azimuth angle ϕ. An error peak, which corresponds to the region located between the kettle and the knife-block, can be seen in all four curves from both plots from Fig. 8.

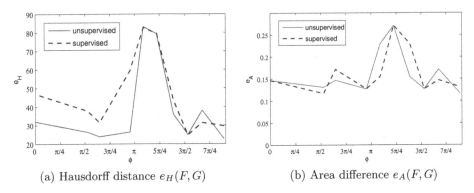

(a) Hausdorff distance $e_H(F, G)$ (b) Area difference $e_A(F, G)$

Fig. 8. Numerical accuracy of extracted contours for the entire image set

In the following, we evaluate the PSNR, for a region as shown inside the black rectangle from Fig. 3e, between the original image and the corresponding projections from the corrected 3D scene. For this region, the initial PSNR of 11.17 dB is improved to 13.91 dB and to 13.75 dB, when using unsupervized and supervised segmentations for SFC. Three different views of the entire 3D scene reconstruction are shown in Fig. 9 after enforcing unsupervised shape-from-contours consistency, considering the same projection parameters $\mathcal{P}$ as in the original image set.

Fig. 9. Views of the 3D scene corrected using unsupervised shape-from-contours

5   Conclusions

This paper proposes to use shape-from-contours (SFC) for modelling scenes of multiple objects. SFC use back-projections of segmented contours of objects from multi-view images in order to improve the 3D scene with multiple objects. Both supervised and unsupervised segmentation using the mean-shift and support vector machines (SVM), respectively, are used for segmenting the image set. A study analyzing the detection of merged objects in reconstructed 3D scenes is provided together with the analysis of the number of cameras required for detecting such errors. The proposed methodology can be applied for correcting various 3D scene representations including those using voxels, meshes or parametric models.

References

1. Broadhurst, A., Drummond, T.W., Cipolla, R.: A probabilistic framework for space carving. In: Proc. Int. Conf. on Comp. Vision, vol. 1, pp. 388–393 (2001)
2. Dinh, H.Q., Turk, G., Slabaugh, G.: Reconstructing surfaces by volumetric regularization using radial basis functions. IEEE Trans. on Pattern Analysis and Machine Intelligence 24(10), 1358–1371 (2002)
3. Zaharescu, A., Boyer, E., Horaud, R.: Topology-Adaptive Mesh Deformation for Surface Evolution, Morphing, and Multiview Reconstruction. IEEE Trans. on Pattern Analysis and Machine Intelligence 33(4), 823–837 (2011)
4. Liang, C., Wong, K.-Y.: Robust recovery of shapes with unknown topology from the dual space. IEEE Trans. on Pat. Anal. and Machine Intell. 29(12), 2205–2216 (2007)
5. Lazebnik, Z., Furukawa, Y., Ponce, J.: Projective visual hulls. Int. Jour. of Comp. Vision 74(2), 137–165 (2007)
6. Koenderink, J.: What does the occluding contour tell us about solid shape. Perception 13(3), 321–330 (1984)
7. Grum, M., Bors, A.G.: Enforcing image consistency in multiple 3-D object modelling. In: Proc. Int. Conf. on Pattern Recog., Tampa, FL, USA, pp. 3354–3357 (2008)
8. Comaniciu, D., Meer, D.: Mean shift: a robust approach toward feature space analysis. IEEE Trans. on Pattern Analysis and Machine Intell. 24(5), 603–619 (2002)
9. Scholkopf, B., Sung, K.-K., Burges, C., Girosi, F., Niyogi, P., Poggio, T., Vapnik, V.: Comparing support vector machines with Gaussian kernels to Radial Basis Function Classifiers. IEEE Trans. on Signal Processing 45(11), 2758–2765 (1997)
10. Huttenlocher, D., Klanderman, G., Rucklidge, W.: Comparing images using the Hausdorff distance. IEEE Trans. on Pattern Analysis and Machine Intelligence 15(9), 850–863 (1993)
11. Chaurasia, G., Sorkine, O., Drettakis, G.: Silhouette-Aware Warping for Image-Based Rendering. Computer Graphics Forum 30(4), 1223–1232 (2011)

Expectation Conditional Maximization-Based Deformable Shape Registration

Guoyan Zheng

Institute for Surgical Technology and Biomechanics, University of Bern, Switzerland
guoyan.zheng@ieee.org

Abstract. This paper addresses the issue of matching statistical and non-rigid shapes, and introduces an Expectation Conditional Maximization-based deformable shape registration (ECM-DSR) algorithm. Similar to previous works, we cast the statistical and non-rigid shape registration problem into a missing data framework and handle the unknown correspondences with Gaussian Mixture Models (GMM). The registration problem is then solved by fitting the GMM centroids to the data. But unlike previous works where equal isotropic covariances are used, our new algorithm uses heteroscedastic covariances whose values are iteratively estimated from the data. A previously introduced virtual observation concept is adopted here to simplify the estimation of the registration parameters. Based on this concept, we derive closed-form solutions to estimate parameters for statistical or non-rigid shape registrations in each iteration. Our experiments conducted on synthesized and real data demonstrate that the ECM-DSR algorithm has various advantages over existing algorithms.

Keywords: Expectation conditional maximization, deformable shape registration, Gaussian mixture models, heteroscedastic covariances.

1 Introduction

Registration of a set of model points to the observation data is a frequently encountered problem in several fields namely, computer vision and pattern recognition [1-9], as well as medical imaging [10-17]. The iterative closest point (ICP) algorithm [1] is one of the most well-known algorithms. It works by alternating between correspondence establishment and parameter estimation until convergence. Disadvantages of the ICP algorithm include the requirement of a good initial guess, the convergence to local minima and the sensitivity to outliers. This has motivated the introduction of various robust methods based on Gaussian Mixture Models (GMM) fitting which is then solved by the Expectation Maximization (EM) algorithm [18]. Common to all these previous works, however, is that equal isotropic covariances are used. Horaud *et al.* introduce the Expectation Conditional Maximization (ECM) for Point Registration algorithm [9] which replaces the maximization step in the EM algorithm with Conditional Maximization (CM) steps that consist of first estimation of the registration parameters by maximizing the expectation and then computing the covariance matrices conditioned by the newly estimated registration parameters. They have shown that

R. Wilson et al. (Eds.): CAIP 2013, Part I, LNCS 8047, pp. 548–555, 2013.

their algorithm allows the use of general covariance matrices for the mixture model components and improves over the equal isotropic covariance case, but they only applied their algorithm to solve rigid and articulated point registration problems. Recently Xie *et al.* [14] used the ECM algorithm to solve the statistical shape registration problem but the shape coefficients were estimated asynchronously.

In this paper, we extend the ECM algorithm [9, 19] to solve the statistical and non-rigid shape registration problems and introduce the ECM-based deformable shape registration (ECM-DSR) algorithm. Unlike previous works where equal isotropic covariances are used, our new algorithm allows uses heteroscedastic covariances whose values are iteratively estimated. Furthermore, a previously introduced virtual observation concept is adopted here to simplify the estimation of the registration parameters. Based on this concept, we derive closed-form solutions to estimate parameters for statistical or non-rigid shape registration in iteration. We conducted comprehensive experiments on synthesized and real data to demonstrate the advantages of the ECM-DSR algorithm over existing algorithms.

Details about the ECM-DSR algorithm will be described in Section 2, followed by experimental results in Section 3. We conclude the paper in Section 4.

2   The ECM-DSR Algorithm

2.1   Mathematical Notations

Throughout the paper, we use following notations. The superscript "T" means "transpose". D is the dimension of the point sets; N, M are the number of points in the two point sets: $\mathbf{Y}_{N \times D} = [\mathbf{y}_1, \mathbf{y}_2, ..., \mathbf{y}_N]^T$ is the data matrix for the data points and $\mathbf{X}_{M \times D} = [\mathbf{x}_1, \mathbf{x}_2, ..., \mathbf{x}_M]^T$ is the data matrix for the GMM centroids; $\mathbf{T}_{M \times D} = \Phi(\mathbf{X}, \theta)$ is the transformation Φ applied to $\mathbf{X}$ to get the new positions $\mathbf{T}$ of the GMM centroids (more specifically, $\mathbf{t}_i = \Phi(\mathbf{x}_i, \theta)$), where θ is the set of the transformation parameters. $||\mathbf{L}(\Phi)||^2$ is a regularization over the transformation. For a statistical shape model, we also use $\mathbf{X}_{M \times D}$ to indicate the mean model. Giving a cutoff number K, $\{\delta_k^2, k = 1, 2, ..., K\}$ are the set of eigenvalues that are sorted in descending order and $\{\mathbf{p}_k, k = 1, 2, ..., K\}$ are their corresponding normalized eigenvectors of the statistical shape model, where each eigenvector is $(\mathbf{p}_k)_{M \times D} = [\mathbf{p}_k(1), ..., \mathbf{p}_k(M)]^T$. Furthermore, dot product between two vectors $\mathbf{a}$ and $\mathbf{b}$ is written as either $\mathbf{a} \cdot \mathbf{b}$ or $\mathbf{a}^T \mathbf{b}$, depending on the context. $\mathbf{I}$ is an identity matrix and $diag(\mathbf{a})$ means a diagonal matrix constructed from the vector $\mathbf{a}$; $trace(\mathbf{W})$ means to compute the trace of a matrix $\mathbf{W}$.

2.2   ECM for Shape Registration

The shape registration problem is cast into a missing data framework and the unknown correspondences are handled with GMM. We consider the points in $\mathbf{X}$ as the GMM centroids and the points in $\mathbf{Y}$ as the data points generated by the GMM. The problem is solved by minimizing the negative log-likelihood function

$$E(\theta, \Sigma_1, ..., \Sigma_M) = - \sum_{n=1}^{N} log \sum_{m=1}^{M} P(\mathbf{x}_m) P_{\Sigma_m}(\mathbf{y}_n | \Phi(\mathbf{x}_m, \theta)) \tag{1}$$

where $\{\Sigma_m, m = 1, 2, \dots, M\}$ is the M covariance matrices and $P_{\Sigma_m}(\mathbf{y}_n | \Phi(\mathbf{x}_m, \theta)) = \mathcal{N}(\mathbf{y}_n | \Phi(\mathbf{x}_m, \theta), \Sigma_m)$ is the likelihood of an observation n given its assignment to GMM centroid m, which is drawn from a Gaussian distribution with mean $\Phi(\mathbf{x}_m, \theta)$ and covariance Σ_m. Although the original ECM algorithm [9] allows the use of general covariance matrices, we choose to use heteroscedastic covariance for each GMM centroid. Thus, we have $\Sigma_m = \sigma_m^2 \mathbf{I}$. Our unknowns now are $\psi = (\theta, \sigma_1^2, \dots, \sigma_M^2)$ that can be found by the ECM algorithm [19]. The expectation step computes the posterior probability of the GMM components:

$$p_{mn} = P(m | \mathbf{y}_n) = \frac{\sigma_m^{-D} \exp\left(-\frac{\|\mathbf{y}_n - \Phi(\mathbf{x}_m, \theta)\|^2}{2\sigma_m^2}\right)}{\sum_{i=1}^{M} \sigma_i^{-D} \exp\left(-\frac{\|\mathbf{y}_n - \Phi(\mathbf{x}_i, \theta)\|^2}{2\sigma_i^2}\right) + c} \tag{2}$$

where c as suggested by Horaud $et\ al.$ [9] corresponds to the outlier component.

The unknowns ψ are estimated by minimizing following objective function:

$$\varepsilon(\psi) = \frac{1}{2} \sum_{n=1}^{N} \sum_{m=1}^{M} \frac{p_{mn}}{\sigma_m^2} \left[\left(\|\mathbf{y}_n - \Phi(\mathbf{x}_m, \theta)\|^2 \right) + D\sigma_m^2 \log(\sigma_m^2) \right] + \frac{\rho}{2} \|L(\Phi)\|^2 \tag{3}$$

where ρ is the parameters controlling the contribution of the regularization and the problem is solved by two conditional minimization steps, using p_{mn} given by (2):

A. Estimating the registration parameters by minimizing

$$\theta^{q+1} = \operatorname{argmin}_\theta \frac{1}{2} \sum_{n=1}^{N} \sum_{m=1}^{M} \frac{p_{mn}}{\sigma_m^2} \left(\|\mathbf{y}_n - \Phi(\mathbf{x}_m, \theta)\|^2 \right) + \frac{\rho}{2} \|L(\Phi)\|^2 \tag{4}$$

Details about how to estimate the registration parameters will be given in section **2.3**.

B. For all $m = 1, 2, \dots, M$, estimate covariances using following closed-form solution

$$\sigma_m^2 = \frac{\sum_{n=1}^{N} p_{mn} \|\mathbf{y}_n - \Phi(\mathbf{x}_m, \theta)\|^2}{D \sum_{n=1}^{N} p_{mn}} \tag{5}$$

2.3   Virtual Observation Concept for Estimating the Registration Parameters

Virtual observation concept has been implicitly or explicitly used by several authors such as in [3] and [9] to simplify the point matching problem. We also adopted this concept to simplify the solution to our problem. The so-called virtual observation $\mathbf{o}_m$ and its weight λ_m are defined as $\lambda_m = \sum_{n=1}^{N} \frac{p_{mn}}{\sigma_m^2}$, and $\mathbf{o}_m = \frac{1}{\lambda_m} \sum_{n=1}^{N} \frac{p_{mn}}{\sigma_m^2} \mathbf{y}_n$, respectively. With these two definitions, now Eq. (4) can be simplified as

$$\theta^{q+1} = \operatorname{argmin}_\theta \frac{1}{2} \sum_{m=1}^{M} \lambda_m^q \|\mathbf{o}_m^q - \Phi(\mathbf{x}_m, \theta)\|^2 + \frac{\rho}{2} \|L(\Phi)\|^2 \tag{6}$$

Eq. (6) and Eq. (4) has exactly the same solution. This can be proved by expanding the first term of the right side of the Eq. (4) and neglect the constant coefficient $\frac{1}{2}$ as:

$$\sum_{m=1}^{M} \left[\sum_{n=1}^{N} \frac{p_{mn}}{\sigma_m^2} \mathbf{y}_n^T \mathbf{y}_n - 2 \sum_{n=1}^{N} \frac{p_{mn}}{\sigma_m^2} \mathbf{y}_n^T \Phi(\mathbf{x}_m, \theta) + \sum_{n=1}^{N} \frac{p_{mn}}{\sigma_m^2} \Phi(\mathbf{x}_m, \theta)^T \Phi(\mathbf{x}_m, \theta) \right] \tag{7}$$

Since the first term of Eq. (7) does not depend on the registration parameters θ, replacing it with $\lambda_m[\mathbf{o}_m^T\mathbf{o}_m]$ will not change the original optimization problem of Eq. (4). The second term of Eq. (7) is $-2\lambda_m\mathbf{o}_m^T\Phi(\mathbf{x}_m,\theta)$, and the third term is $\lambda_m\Phi(\mathbf{x}_m,\theta)^T\Phi(\mathbf{x}_m,\theta)$. Combining all three terms we have it as $\sum_{m=1}^M \lambda_m^q||\mathbf{o}_m^q - \Phi(\mathbf{x}_m,\theta)||^2$. This proves that Eq. (6) and Eq. (4) has the same solution.

With the virtual observation concept, we can now discuss how to solve Eq. (6). The solution depends on how we parameterize the transformation Φ.

- **When Φ is a rigid or a scaled rigid transformation.** In this case, $||\mathbf{L}(\Phi)||^2 = 0$. Previous works such as [9], [14] and [15] have discussed its solution. Thus, we will not address it here. We invited the interested reader to refer to these works.
- **When Φ is a statistical shape model instantiation.** In this case, Φ can be parameterized as $\Phi(\mathbf{X},\theta) = \mathbf{X} + \sum_{k=1}^K b_k\,\mathbf{p}_k$ and $||\mathbf{L}(\Phi)||^2 = \sum_{k=1}^K \frac{b_k^2}{\delta_k^2}$ is the Mahalanobis distance [20]. All the shape coefficients can be solved with a closed-form solution:

$$\mathbf{b} = \mathbf{A}^{-1}\mathbf{d} \qquad (8)$$

where $\mathbf{b} = [b_1, \ldots, b_K]^T$ are the shape coefficients vector to be determined; $\mathbf{A}$ is

$$\mathbf{A}_{K\times K} = \begin{bmatrix} \sum_{i=1}^M \lambda_i(\mathbf{p}_1(i)\cdot\mathbf{p}_1(i)) + \frac{\rho}{\delta_1^2} & \cdots & \sum_{i=1}^M \lambda_i(\mathbf{p}_k(i)\cdot\mathbf{p}_1(i)) & \cdots & \sum_{i=1}^M \lambda_i(\mathbf{p}_K(i)\cdot\mathbf{p}_1(i)) \\ \vdots & \cdots & \vdots & \cdots & \vdots \\ \sum_{i=1}^M \lambda_i(\mathbf{p}_1(i)\cdot\mathbf{p}_k(i)) & \cdots & \sum_{i=1}^n \lambda_i(\mathbf{p}_k(i)\cdot\mathbf{p}_k(i)) + \frac{\rho}{\delta_k^2} & \cdots & \sum_{i=1}^M \lambda_i(\mathbf{p}_K(i)\cdot\mathbf{p}_k(i)) \\ \vdots & \cdots & \vdots & \cdots & \vdots \\ \sum_{i=1}^M \lambda_i(\mathbf{p}_1(i)\cdot\mathbf{p}_K(i)) & \cdots & \sum_{i=1}^M \lambda_i(\mathbf{p}_k(i)\cdot\mathbf{p}_K(i)) & \cdots & \sum_{i=1}^M \lambda_i(\mathbf{p}_K(i)\cdot\mathbf{p}_K(i)) + \frac{\rho}{\delta_K^2} \end{bmatrix}$$

and $\mathbf{d}$ is computed as

$$\mathbf{d} = \begin{bmatrix} \sum_{i=1}^m \lambda_i((\mathbf{o}_i - \mathbf{x}_i)\cdot\mathbf{p}_1(i)) \\ \vdots \\ \sum_{i=1}^m \lambda_i((\mathbf{o}_i - \mathbf{x}_i)\cdot\mathbf{p}_k(i)) \\ \vdots \\ \sum_{i=1}^m \lambda_i((\mathbf{o}_i - \mathbf{x}_i)\cdot\mathbf{p}_K(i)) \end{bmatrix}$$

- **When Φ is a non-rigid transformation.** There are different ways to parameterize a non-rigid transformation Φ. One example is to use thin-plate splines [3, 6]. Here we choose to use the coherent point drift (CPD) that was introduced by Myronenko and Song [7] to parameterize Φ. In CPD, the non-rigid transformation is modeled as a displacement field defined over each GMM centroid that can be expressed as:

$$\mathbf{T} = \Phi(\mathbf{X},\theta) = \mathbf{X} + \mathbf{G}\mathbf{W} \qquad (9)$$

where $\mathbf{W}_{M\times D}$ is a matrix of coefficients to be determined, $\mathbf{G}_{M\times M}$ is a symmetric kernel matrix with elements $\mathbf{G}(i,j) = \exp\left(-\frac{||\mathbf{x}_i-\mathbf{x}_j||^2}{2\beta^2}\right)$. With this parameterization, the regularization over the transformation is: $||\mathbf{L}(\Phi)||^2 = trace(\mathbf{W}^T\mathbf{G}\mathbf{W})$. If we represent all the virtual observation weights as a vector $\boldsymbol{\lambda} = [\lambda_1, \ldots, \lambda_M]^T$ and compute the partial derivatives of Eq. (6) with respect to $\mathbf{W}$, we can get a closed-form solution:

$$\mathbf{W} = (diag(\boldsymbol{\lambda})\mathbf{G} + \rho\mathbf{I})^{-1}(diag(\boldsymbol{\lambda})(\mathbf{O} - \mathbf{X})) \qquad (10)$$

where $\mathbf{O}_{M \times D} = [\mathbf{o}_1, \mathbf{o}_2, ..., \mathbf{o}_M]^T$ is the data matrix of all virtual observations.

3   Experimental Results

Qualitative and quantitative experiments are conducted to evaluate the performance of the present approach.

3.1   Qualitative Experiments

We first conducted a qualitative experiment on 2D synthesized data with outliers by Chui and Rangarajan [3] to evaluate the performance and the efficacy of our non-rigid registration algorithm taking the CPD algorithm as the reference method[1]. Fig. 1 shows qualitatively how these two algorithms perform when tested on a synthesized data with outliers. In this figure, we also depict the final covariances that are estimated automatically by these two algorithms. From this depiction, one can observe that our algorithm uses heteroscedastic covariances which are helpful in effectively handling outliers while the CPD algorithm uses equal covariances, leading to poor results in handling outliers. Furthermore, it took 42 steps for our algorithm to converge while this number changed to 87 when the CPD algorithm was used.

To better illustrate how the heteroscedastic covariances that are automatically estimated by the ECM-DSR algorithm can tell us more information about the uncertainty of the results, we conducted a second study on registering a pair of corpus callosum shapes (Fig. 2). For this study, it took the ECM-DSR algorithm 21 iterations to converge and the CPD algorithm converged after 31 iterations. Both algorithms achieved reasonably good results but we can identify three regions where the uncertainty of the registration is high by looking into the heteroscedastic covariances estimated by the ECM-DSR algorithm. Such information cannot be obtained from the CPD algorithm.

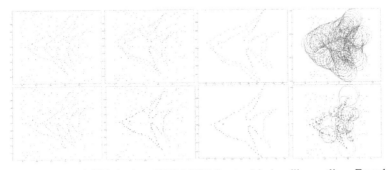

Fig. 1. Performance of CPD (top) and ECM-DSR (bottom) in handling outliers. From left to right: inputs, results, overlap the results with ground truth, and estimated covariances depicted as black circles around GMM centroids whose radii equal to the corresponding covariances.

---

[1] From `http://www.umiacs.umd.edu/~zhengyf/PointMatchDemo/DataChui.zip`, we got the synthesized data, and from `https://sites.google.com/site/myronenko/research/cpd`, we got the reference implementation of the CPD algorithm and the bunny model data shown in Fig. 3.

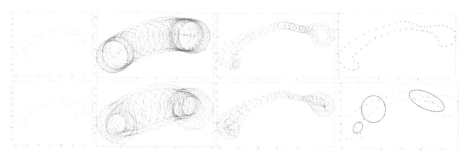

Fig. 2. Equal covariances estimated by the CPD algorithm (top) and the heteroscedastic covariances estimated by the ECM-DSR algorithm (bottom) during iterations. The rightmost column shows the estimated covariances after convergence. Three regions of high uncertainty (depicted with red ellipses) can be identified for the ECM-DSR but not for the CPD.

The third qualitative experiment was conducted on non-rigid registration of two 3D bunny models. Fig. 3. shows the results achieved by our approach.

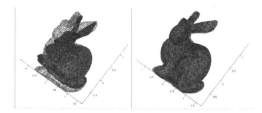

Fig. 3. Qualitative experiment conducted on non-rigid registration of two 3D bunny models. Left: before registration; right: after registration.

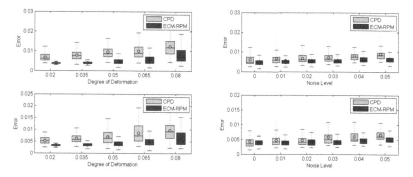

Fig. 4. Boxplots of the comparison of the ECM-DSR with those of the CPD on the Chui-Rangarajan synthesized data sets. Top: the Chinese Character shape, bottom: the fish shape.

3.2 Quantitative Experiments on Chui-Rangarajan Synthesized Data

With synthesized data, we know the ground truth. Thus, it can be used to test an algorithm. More details about the synthesized data are explained in [3], which contains three sets of data designed on two shape templates (Chinese Character shape and fish shape) to measure the robustness of an algorithm under different degrees of deformation, noise levels and outliers. Fig. 4 demonstrates the quantitative comparison results between our non-rigid registration algorithm and the CPD algorithm.

3.3   Scapula Data

In this experiment, we applied the ECM-DSR algorithm to a challenging task that is to instantiate a surface model of the scapula from a statistical shape model (SSM) and sparse point set.

To this end, we construct a statistical shape model of the scapula from 24 segmented CT models. Additionally, we have 9 segmented CT models of complete scapula. Each time about 500 to 1000 points are randomly generated from each segmented CT model which will be used as the input to instantiate a surface model of the scapula. We conducted quantitative study on the 9 complete scapula data to evaluate the reconstruction accuracy of the ECM-DSR algorithm. The reconstruction accuracy was estimated by computing the distances between the reconstructed surface models and the ground truth surface models segmented from CT data.

Fig. 5 shows the quantitative reconstruction results by our algorithm. A mean reconstruction error of 0.66 mm was found.

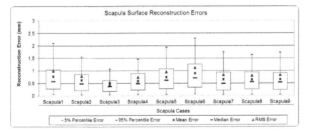

Fig. 5. Quantitative reconstruction results by the ECM-DSR algorithm

4   Conclusions

In this paper we presented a robust point matching algorithm for statistical and non-rigid shape registration based on the Expectation Conditional Maximization algorithm. Our experiments conducted on synthesized and real data demonstrate that ECM-DSR has various advantages over existing algorithms, including less iteration steps required for convergence, higher accuracy, more robust to outliers and providing more information about the uncertainty of the registration results.

Acknowledgements. This work was partially supported by the Swiss National Science Foundation (SNSF) via Project 205321_138009.

References

1. Besl, P., McKay, N.: A method for registration of 3-d shapes. IEEE Trans. Pat. Anal. and Machine Intel. 14, 239–256 (1992)
2. Granger, S., Pennec, X.: Multi-scale EM-ICP: A fast and robust approach for surface registration. In: Heyden, A., Sparr, G., Nielsen, M., Johansen, P. (eds.) ECCV 2002, Part IV. LNCS, vol. 2353, pp. 418–432. Springer, Heidelberg (2002)
3. Chui, H., Rangarajan, A.: A new point matching algorithm for nonrigid registration. Comput. Vis. Image Understand. 89(2-3), 114–141 (2003)
4. Luo, B., Hancock, E.: A unified framework for alignment and correspondence. Comp. Vis. and Image Underst. 92(1), 26–55 (2003)
5. Tsin, Y., Kanade, T.: A correlation-based approach to robust point set registration. In: Pajdla, T., Matas, J(G.) (eds.) ECCV 2004. LNCS, vol. 3023, pp. 558–569. Springer, Heidelberg (2004)
6. Zheng, Y., Doermann, D.S.: Robust Point Matching for Nonrigid Shapes by Preserving Local Neighborhood Structures. IEEE Trans. Pattern Anal. Mach. Intell. 28(4), 643–649 (2006)
7. Myronenko, A., Song, X.: Point set registration: coherent point drift. IEEE Trans. Pattern Anal. Mach. Intell. 32(12), 2262–2275 (2010)
8. Jian, B., Vemuri, B.C.: Robust Point Set Registration Using Gaussian Mixture Models. IEEE Trans. Pattern Anal. Mach. Intell. 33(8), 1633–1645 (2011)
9. Horaud, R., Forbes, F., Yguel, M., Dewaele, G., Zhang, J.: Rigid and Articulated Point Registration with Expectation Conditional Maximization. IEEE Trans. Pattern Anal. Mach. Intell. 33(3), 587–602 (2011)
10. Chui, H., Rangarajan, A., Zhang, J., Leonard, C.M.: Unsupervised learning of an atlas from unlabeled point-sets. IEEE Trans. Pattern Anal. Mach. Intell. 26(2), 160–172 (2004)
11. Hufnagel, H., Pennec, X., Ehrhardt, J., Ayache, N., Handels, H.: Generation of a statistical shape model with probabilistic point correspondences and the expectation maximization-iterative closest point algorithm. Int. J. CARS 2(5), 265–273 (2008)
12. Abi-Nahed, J., Jolly, M., Yang, G.Z.: Robust active shape models: A robust, generic and simple automatic segmentation tool. In: Larsen, R., Nielsen, M., Sporring, J. (eds.) MICCAI 2006. LNCS, vol. 4191, pp. 1–8. Springer, Heidelberg (2006)
13. Shen, K., Bourgeat, P., Fripp, J., Meriaudeau, F., Salvado, O.: Consistent estimation of shape parameters in statistical shape model by symmetric EM algorithm. In: SPIE Medical Imaging 2012: Image Processing, vol. 8134, p. 83140R (2012)
14. Xie, W., Schumann, S., Franke, J., Grützner, P.A., Nolte, L.P., Zheng, G.: Finding Deformable Shapes by Correspondence-Free Instantiation and Registration of Statistical Shape Models. In: Wang, F., Shen, D., Yan, P., Suzuki, K. (eds.) MLMI 2012. LNCS, vol. 7588, pp. 258–265. Springer, Heidelberg (2012)
15. Kang, X., Taylor, R.H., Armand, M., Otake, Y., Yau, W.P., Cheung, P.Y.S., Hu, Y.: Correspondenceless 3D-2D registration based on expectation conditional maximization. In: Proc. SPIE, vol. 7964, p. 79642Z (2011)
16. Chen, T., Vemuri, B.C., Rangarajan, A., Eisenschenk, S.J.: Groupwise point-set registration using a novel CDF-based Havrda-Charvat divergence. IJCV 86(1), 111–124 (2010)
17. Rasoulian, A., Rohling, R., Abolmaesumi, P.: Group-wise registration of point sets for statistical shape models. IEEE Trans. Med. Imaging 31(11), 2025–2034 (2012)
18. Dempster, A.P., Laird, N.M., Rubin, D.B.: Maximum likelihood estimation from in complete data via the EM algorithm (with discussion). J. Royal Statistical Soc.(B) 39, 1–38 (1877)
19. Meng, X.-L., Rubin, D.B.: Maximum likelihood estimation via the ECM algorithm: A general framework. Biometrika 80(2), 267–278 (1993)

Facial Expression Recognition with Regional Features Using Local Binary Patterns

Anima Majumder, Laxmidhar Behera, and Venkatesh K. Subramanian

Department of Electrical Engineering,
Indian Institute of Technology Kanpur, India
{animam,lbehera,venkats}@iitk.ac.in

Abstract. This paper presents a simple yet efficient and completely automatic approach to recognize six fundamental facial expressions using Local Binary Patterns (LBPs) texture features. A system is proposed that can automatically locate four important facial regions from which the uniform LBPs features are extracted and concatenated to form a 236 dimensional enhanced feature vector to be used for six fundamental expressions recognition. The features are trained using three widely used classifiers: Naive bayes, Radial Basis Function Network (RBFN) and three layered Multi-layer Perceptron (MLP3). The notable feature of the proposed method is the use of few preferred regions of the face to extract the LBPs features as opposed to the use of entire face. The experimental results obtained from MMI database show proficiency of the proposed features extraction method.

Keywords: Facial expression recognition, local binary pattern, facial features extraction, radial basis function network, multilayer perceptron, naive bayes.

1 Introduction

Communication plays a very important role in our day to day life. Facial expressions those come under the category of nonverbal communication are considered to be one of the most powerful and immediate means of recognizing one's emotion, intentions and opinion about each other. A study of Mehrabian [1] has found that while communicating feelings and attitudes, a person convey 55% of the message through facial expression alone, 38% via vocal cues and the remaining 7% is through verbal cues. The goal of facial expression recognition system is to have an automatic system that can recognition expressions like Happiness, Sadness, Disgust, Anger, Surprise and Fear regardless of the person's identity. Since last few decades [2,3,4,5], researchers have been working on facial expression recognition and a lot of advancements have been made in recent years. But recognizing facial expressions with high accuracy is still a challenging area because of it's subtlety, complexity and variability of expressions.

Generally, techniques to represent facial features needed for expressions recognition are broadly categorized into two types: Geometric based method and

R. Wilson et al. (Eds.): CAIP 2013, Part I, LNCS 8047, pp. 556–563, 2013.

Appearance based method. Geometric features such as eyes, mouth, nose etc., contain location and shape information of those features, whereas, appearance features examines the appearance change of face like wrinkle, bulges and furrows [6]. In this presented work, we use both information of facial geometry and appearance based method to represent facial features for six fundamental expressions (Happiness, Sadness, Disgust, Anger, Surprise, Fear). Facial geometry is used for automatic localization of 4 important facial regions like eyes regions, Nose region and Lips region. Those regions are extracted in a way that the regions cover nearby regions containing important information needed for expressions recognition. LBPs have already been presented to be a successful texture descriptor in many computer vision applications [7,8,3]. LBPs are used over Gabor filters because of its simplicity and much lower dimensionality. Many researchers applied LBPs for Facial expressions recognition but, mostly they either applied over whole face image or after dividing the face region into $M \times N$ sub-blocks [6,3]. Holistic representation of features loses information related to the location of the features. Moreover, dividing the whole facial region into different sub-blocks and then taking LBPs from each sub-block needs more computation time, which is unnecessary. Not all the blocks within the face region contains useful informations needed for expression recognition. We introduce a new method that reduces such unnecessary computation cost by localizing required facial zones needed for expression recognition. Uniform LBPs obtained from each of the 4 facial regions are concatenated to form a feature vector of dimension 236. We apply three widely used classifiers: Naive Bayes, Radial Basis Function Network, and three layered MLP [9,10].

Rest of the paper is organized as follows. Section 2 demonstrates the different facial regions extraction techniques. Section 3 gives a brief overview about the local binary pattern and proposed method. Section 4 shows the experimental results obtained after applying 3 different classifiers: Naive bayes, RBFN and MLP3. Finally, in section 5 conclusions are drawn.

2 Different Facial Region Extraction Techniques

Automatic facial expression recognition techniques require two most important aspects:

- Features representation
- Modeling of appropriate classifier [3].

Extraction of features those can represent the facial expressions effectively, are the key to have an accurate facial expression recognition system. In this paper, we introduce a new mechanism for automatic extraction of appearance features from different facial regions, using local binary pattern. Fig. 1 shows the 4 important localized regions from where LBP features are extracted.

The flow diagram shown in Fig. 2 demonstrates the steps involved in automatic facial regions extraction techniques.

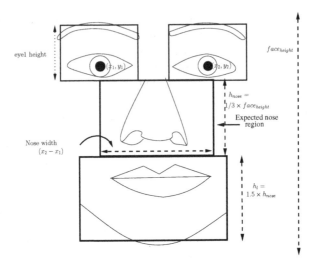

Fig. 1. Pictorial description of the 4 key facial regions extraction technique

2.1 Facial Regions Extraction

The foremost important part to have better facial expression recognition results is to have automatic and accurate face and facial regions detection methods. Accurate extraction of facial features is the key to have successful classification results. Most of the facial expression recognition techniques using Local binary patterns applies the LBP over each sub-block covering the whole face image [3,6,11]. Caifeng Shah et.al [3] divided the whole face image into small sub-block regions, extracted the LBPs from each region and then assigned weights to each sub-region based on importance of that region. But, not all the facial regions contain useful informations for expression recognition. Some regions contain almost no information for any expression. Thus, calculation of LBPs over whole facial region leads to unnecessary computational cost. In this work we demonstrate a completely automatic facial regions extraction method. The four important regions where most of the informations available are: Two eyes region enclosing eyebrow regions, nose region, lips region enclosing chin region. Fig. 1 shows a pictorial explanation for the calculation of estimated facial regions based on actual face height and width. The steps involved in this process is given in the block diagram shown in Fig. 2. Face detection is followed by eyes detection. We apply Paul Viola and Michael Jones' face detection algorithm [12] to detect the face region from the image. They use simple rectangular (Haar-like) features which are equivalent to intensity difference readings and are quite easy to compute. The face detection using Viola Jones' method is 15 times quicker than any technique. It gives 95% detection accuracy at around 17 fps.

The next important step after face detection is detection of two eyes. The eyes' centers play a vital role in face alignment, scaling and location estimation of other

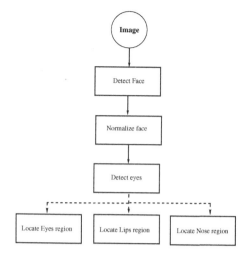

Fig. 2. Basic block diagram to extract important facial regions

facial features, like lips, eyebrows, nose, etc. Thus, accurate detection of eyes are very much desirable. We estimate the expected regions of eyes using basic facial geometry [13]: for frontal face images, the eyes are located in the upper facial region. We remove $(1/5)^{th}$ upper facial region and extract $(1/3)^{rd}$ vertical part as the expected eyes regions. We apply Haar-like cascaded features and Viola-Jones' object detection algorithm to detect two eyes within the expected eyes region. Nose lies below the two eyes' region and above lips region in frontal face images. Fig. 1 shows a pictorial description about the nose region. We calculate the two eyes' centers as (x_1, y_1) and (x_2, y_2)(centroid of the eye rectangular region) respectively. The expected nose region starts from the left eye's center with width $(x_2 - x_1)$ and height $(\frac{1}{3})^{rd}$ of the face height. Similarly, we calculate the expected lip region that also covers the chin region. The lip region starts after the nose region. We take lip regions with x coordinate same as eyes' center's x coordinate and width as distance between two eye's centers. To cover the extra region near the lips that usually contain some wrinkles during certain expression, we add $(1/4)^{th}$ of lips width in both left and right side. Lips region height is taken as last $(1/3)^{rd}$ region that also includes chin region. Eyes' regions are also extended using facial geometry that cover the regions near eyebrows and eyes' crow's feet.

3   Local Binary Patterns

We perform person independent facial expression recognition using Local Binary Patterns (LBPs). Initially, the LBPs was introduced by Ojala et.al [14] and it is proven to be a very powerful means of texture description. Given a monochrome image $I(x, y)$ let, g_c be the center pixel within a 3×3 neighborhood. The pixels within the neighborhood are labeled by thresholding each pixel with the value of the center pixel g_c. For a gray value g_p in an evenly spaced circular neighborhood with maximum of P pixels and radius R around point (x, y), coordinates of the point can be found as

$$x_p = x + R\,cos(2\pi p/P), y_p = y - R\,sin(2\pi p/P). \tag{1}$$

The binary operator $S(g_p - g_c)$ can be defined as

$$S(g_p - g_c) = \begin{cases} 1 & \text{if } g_p \geq g_c \\ 0 & \text{otherwise.} \end{cases}$$

The LBP_{PR} operator is computed by applying a binomial factor to each of the $S(g_p - g_c)$. The method can be stated as

$$LBP_{P,R}(x_c, y_c) = \sum_{p=0}^{P-1} S(g_p - g_c)2^p. \tag{2}$$

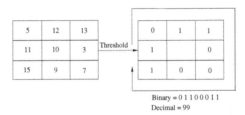

Binary = 0 1 1 0 0 0 1 1
Decimal = 99

Fig. 3. An example of basic LBP operation. Neighborhood pixels are thresholded with center pixel and followed by generation of decimal value for the binary coded data.

Fig. 3 shows an example of a basic LBPs operator. Each pixel around the center pixel is thresholded. A binary pattern is extracted and the corresponding decimal equivalent is calculated. The prominent properties of LBPs features are: robustness for change in illumination and computational simplicity. The texture primitives like spot, line end, edge and corner are detected by operators. Fig. 4 shows examples of texture primitives can be detected on applying LBPs. The notation LBP_{PR} indicates P sampling points each at equal distance R from the center pixel.

Ojala et.al [14] verified that only a subset of the 2^P patterns is sufficient enough to describe most of the texture information with in the image. The patterns for $LBP(8, 1)$ with bit-wise transitions not more than 2, called uniform patterns contains more than 90% of the texture informations. The uniform patterns contains in total of 58 different patterns for $LBP(8, 1)$ with 58 binary

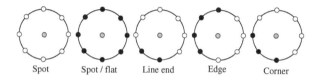

Spot   Spot / flat   Line end   Edge   Corner

Fig. 4. Examples of texture primitives those can be detected by LBP. White circles shows ones and the black circles shows zeros.

patterns (56 rotational patterns and 2 non-rotational patterns). The patterns with transitions $U(x) \geq 2$ is called non-uniform patterns and is assigned to a single label, totally 59 patterns for $LBP_{8,1}^{u2}$. Fig. 3 shows an example of the LBPs and corresponding histogram for an extracted lips region.

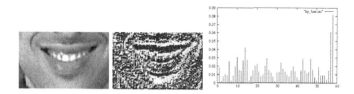

Fig. 5. Images showing lips region, corresponding uniform local binary code and the feature histogram for the lips region

4   Experimental Results

Experiments are conducted on publicly available MMI facial expression database [15]. The results present classification accuracy of six basic facial expressions (happiness (H), sadness (Sa), disgust (D), anger (A), surprise (Sur), fear (F)). In our experiment, we use 81 different video clips taken from MMI facial expression database. The video clips comprises of 12 different characters and each character shows all the 6 basic expressions separately. The uniform LBP features of dimension 59 obtained from each of the 4 facial zones are concatenated

Table 1. Confusion matrix of emotions detection for the 236 dimensional LBP features data using Naive Bayes. The emotion classified with maximum percentage is shown to be the detected emotion.

	H	Sa	D	A	Sur	F
H	**91.9**	5.12	0	2.56	0	1.28
Sa	0.9	**45.9**	4.5	1.8	29.7	17.1
D	3.84	3.84	**75.0**	11.53	3.84	1.92
A	1.61	0	11.29	**61.3**	20.96	4.83
Sur	0	1.36	0	0	**90.4**	8.21
F	1.47	5.88	1.47	2.94	35.29	**52.9**

Table 2. Confusion matrix of emotions detection for the 236 dimensional LBP features data using Radial Basis Function. The emotion classified with maximum percentage is shown to be the detected emotion.

	H	Sa	D	A	Sur	F
H	**87.2**	3.84	5.12	3.84	0	0
Sa	0	**90.1**	0	1.8	5.4	2.7
D	5.7	5.7	**80.8**	5.7	1.9	0
A	0	0	3.2	**96.8**	0	0
Sur	0	5.48	0	2.74	**91.8**	0
F	1.47	5.88	0	5.88	0	**86.8**

Table 3. Confusion matrix of emotions detection for the 236 dimensional LBP features data using MLP3. The emotion classified with maximum percentage is shown to be the detected emotion.

	H	Sa	D	A	Sur	F
H	**89.7**	3.8	5.13	0	0	1.28
Sa	2.7	**88.3**	0	0	0	9.0
D	1.92	5.77	**84.6**	0	0	7.7
A	0	4.84	11.29	**74.2**	0	9.7
Sur	0	2.73	2.73	0	**94.52**	0
F	1.47	8.82	1.47	0	0	**88.2**

together to form a feature vector of dimension 236. Neighborhood size of 3×3 is considered to extract LBP features for each of the four regions. We apply 3 widely used classifiers: Naive Bayes, RBFN and MLP3 for facial expression recognition. The experimental results are shown in tables 1, 2 and 3 respectively. The average recognition accuracy of Naive bayes classifier is 69.41% with training time 0.7 second and for MLP3 it is 86.05% with training time much higher (3155 seconds). It is observed that, RBFN gives best performance among the three classifiers with average classification accuracy 88.91% and training time 12.8 seconds.

5   Conclusions

The paper present an empirical study of facial expression recognition system based on Local binary patterns features. We propose an automatic method of extracting 4 important facial regions those includes two eyes, nose, mouth region and near by region of theses features like chin region, crows-feet region, check region, some portion of eyebrows region. Thus the method avoids unnecessary computation cost by applying LBPs over whole face image and yet preserves location information. Moreover, features dimension is much smaller (only 4 times LBPs from each block) as opposed to the method in which whole face image is divided into $M \times N$ sub-blocks. The experiments are performed over MMI facial expression database. Three well-known classifiers: Naive Bayes, RBFN and MLP-3 are used to classify the LBPs features into six basic facial expressions.

The recognition results show the accuracy of our proposed facial expression recognition system. It is observed that RBFN outperforms the other two classifiers. As future works, we can conduct experiments using different neighborhood sizes. Also, a comparative analysis can be done by applying LBPs over whole face image.

References

1. Mehrabian, A.: Nonverbal communication. Aldine (2007)
2. Sun, Y., Yin, L.: Facial expression recognition based on 3D dynamic range model sequences. In: Forsyth, D., Torr, P., Zisserman, A. (eds.) ECCV 2008, Part II. LNCS, vol. 5303, pp. 58–71. Springer, Heidelberg (2008)
3. Shan, C., Gong, S., McOwan, P.: Facial expression recognition based on local binary patterns: A comprehensive study. Image and Vision Computing 27, 803–816 (2009)
4. Tsalakanidou, F., Malassiotis, S.: Real-time 2d+ 3d facial action and expression recognition. Pattern Recognition 43, 1763–1775 (2010)
5. Moridis, C., Economides, A.: Affective learning: Empathetic agents with emotional facial and tone of voice expressions. IEEE Transactions on Affective Computing 3, 260–272 (2012)
6. Moore, S., Bowden, R.: Local binary patterns for multi-view facial expression recognition. Computer Vision and Image Understanding 115, 541–558 (2011)
7. Chan, C.-H., Kittler, J., Messer, K.: Multi-scale local binary pattern histograms for face recognition. In: Lee, S.-W., Li, S.Z. (eds.) ICB 2007. LNCS, vol. 4642, pp. 809–818. Springer, Heidelberg (2007)
8. Ahonen, T., Hadid, A., Pietikäinen, M.: Face recognition with local binary patterns. In: Pajdla, T., Matas, J(G.) (eds.) ECCV 2004. LNCS, vol. 3021, pp. 469–481. Springer, Heidelberg (2004)
9. Zhang, Z., Zhang, Z.: Feature-based facial expression recognition: Sensitivity analysis and experiments with a multilayer perceptron. International Journal of Pattern Recognition and Artificial Intelligence 13, 893–911 (1999)
10. Rosenblum, M., Yacoob, Y., Davis, L.: Human expression recognition from motion using a radial basis function network architecture. IEEE Transactions on Neural Networks 7, 1121–1138 (1996)
11. Zhao, G., Pietikainen, M.: Dynamic texture recognition using local binary patterns with an application to facial expressions. IEEE Transactions on Pattern Analysis and Machine Intelligence 29, 915–928 (2007)
12. Viola, P., Jones, M.: Robust real-time object detection. International Journal of Computer Vision 57, 137–154 (2002)
13. Majumder, A., Behera, L., Venkatesh, K.S.: Automatic and Robust Detection of Facial Features in Frontal Face Images. In: Proceedings of the 13th International Conference on Modelling and Simulation. IEEE (2011)
14. Ojala, T., Pietikäinen, M., Harwood, D.: A comparative study of texture measures with classification based on featured distributions. Pattern Recognition 29, 51–59 (1996)
15. Pantic, M., Valstar, M.F., Rademaker, R., Maat, L.: Web-based database for facial expression analysis. In: Proceedings of IEEE Int'l Conf. Multimedia and Expo, ICME 2005, Amsterdam, The Netherlands, pp. 317–321 (2005)

Global Image Registration Using Random Projection and Local Linear Method

Hayato Itoh[1], Tomoya Sakai[2], Kazuhiko Kawamoto[3], and Atsushi Imiya[4]

[1] Graduate School of Advanced Integration Science, Chiba University,
Yayoicho 1-33, Inage-ku, Chiba 263-8522, Japan
[2] Graduate School of Engineering, Nagasaki University,
Bunkyo-cho 1-14, Nagasaki 852-8521, Japan
[3] Academic Link Center, Chiba University,
Yayoicho 1-33, Inage-ku, Chiba 263-8522, Japan
[4] Institute of Management and Information Technologies, Chiba University,
Yayoicho 1-33, Inage-ku, Chiba 263-8522, Japan

Abstract. The purpose of this paper is twofold. First, we introduce fast global image registration using random projection. By generating many transformed images as entries in a dictionary from a reference image, nearest-neighbour-search (NNS)-based image registration computes the transformation that establishes the best match among the generated transformations. For the reduction in the computational cost for NNS without a significant loss of accuracy, we use random projection. Furthermore, for the reduction in the computational complexity of random projection, we use the spectrum-spreading technique and circular convolution. Second, for the reduction in the space complexity of the dictionary, we introduce an interpolation technique into the dictionary using the linear subspace method and a local linear property of the pattern space.

1 Introduction

Image registration overlays two or more template images with the same observed at different times, from different viewpoints, or by different sensors, on a reference image. Image registration is a process of estimating geometric transformations that transform all or most points on template images to corresponding points on a reference image.

Setting Π to be an appropriate parameter space for image generation, we assume that images are expressed as $f(\boldsymbol{x}, \boldsymbol{\theta})$ for $\exists \boldsymbol{\theta} \in \Pi$, $\boldsymbol{x} \in \mathbb{R}^l$. We call the set of generated images $f(\boldsymbol{x}, \boldsymbol{\theta}_i)$ and the parameter $\boldsymbol{\theta}_i$ a dictionary. Here, $i = 1, \ldots, N$. Image registration methods are generally classified into local image registration and global image registration. For the global alignment of images, the linear transformation $\boldsymbol{x}' = \boldsymbol{A}\boldsymbol{x} + \boldsymbol{t}$ that minimises the criterion

$$R(f, g) = \sqrt{\int_{\Omega} |f(\boldsymbol{x}') - g(\boldsymbol{x})|^2 d\boldsymbol{x}} \tag{1}$$

R. Wilson et al. (Eds.): CAIP 2013, Part I, LNCS 8047, pp. 564–571, 2013.

for the reference image $f(\boldsymbol{x})$ and the template image $g(\boldsymbol{x})$ is used to relate two images. In image registration, we assume that the parameter $\boldsymbol{\theta}$ in Π generates the affine coefficients $\boldsymbol{A}$ and $\boldsymbol{t}$. Solving the nearest-neighbour search (NNS) problem using the dictionary, we can estimate the transformation $\boldsymbol{A}, \boldsymbol{t}$ as $\boldsymbol{\theta}_i$.

The simplest solution to the NNS problem is to compute the distance from the query point to every other point in the database, preserving a track of the "best so far". This algorithm, sometimes referred to as the naive approach, has a computational cost of $\mathcal{O}(Nd)$. Here, N and d are the cardinality of a set of points in a metric space and the dimensionality of the metric space, respectively.

The NNS-based image registration requires the storage of reference images in the dictionary, since the method finds the best matched image from the dictionary. Since this mathematical property leads to the conclusion that we are required to store a large number of images in the dictionary, for the robust image registration, the space complexity of the dictionary becomes large. Fast global image registration algorithms using random projection have been developed [1–3]. In these methods, using random projection, we can reduce d in NNS[4].

In addition to random projection, using a local linear property of the pattern space, we interpolate entries in a sparse dictionary by generating an image and estimating the parameter. Using such an interpolation, we can reduce N in NNS. Generally, the pattern space generated by the affine motion of the image data is a curved manifold in the higher-dimensional Euclidean space. However, if the motion is relatively small and can be approximated by linear perturbation to a sampled image, it is possible to approximate transformed images as a linear combination of sampled images in the neighbourhood of the reference image. Using this approximation property, we generate new reference images that are similar to the target image using images in the sparse dictionary. Furthermore, using the local linear property, we can estimate the parameter of the generated image. This strategy reduces the space complexity of the dictionary.

In this paper, using an efficient random projection[3] and the local linear property of the images, we introduce a method of reducing the time and space computational costs of this naive NNS-based image registration.

2 Local Linear Property

2.1 Linear Subspace of Pattern

Setting the Hilbert space H to be the space of patterns, we assume that in H, the inner product (f, g) is defined. Furthermore, we define the Schatten product $\langle f, g \rangle$, which is the operator from H to H. Let $f \in H$ and P be a pattern and an operator for a class, respectively; thus, we define the class $\mathcal{C} = \{ f \mid Pf = f, \ P^*P = I \}$. For recognition, we construct P for $f \in \mathcal{C}$ while minimising $E[\|f - Pf\|_2]$ with respect to $P^*P = I$, where $f \in \mathcal{C}$ is the pattern for a class, I is the identity operator, and E is the expectation in H. This methodology is well known as the subspace method [5–7].

For the practical calculation of P, we adopt the Karhunen-Loeve expansion. The Karhunen-Loeve expansion approximates the subspace of data in H.

We set $\{\varphi_j\}_{j=1}^n$ to be the eigenfunction of $M = \mathrm{E}[\langle f, f \rangle]$. We define the eigenfunction of M as $\|\varphi_j\|_2 = 1$ for eigenvalues $\lambda_1 \geq \lambda_2 \geq \cdots \geq \lambda_j \geq \cdots \geq \lambda_n$. Therefore, P is defined as $P_{n'} = \sum_{j=1}^{n'} \langle \varphi_j, \varphi_j \rangle$ for $n' \leq n$.

2.2 Geometric Perturbation in Local Linear Space

If the image $f(\boldsymbol{x})$ defined in the two-dimensional Euclidean plane $\boldsymbol{x} = (x, y)^\top \in \mathbb{R}^2$ is geometrically perturbed, we can accept the relation

$$f(\boldsymbol{x} + \boldsymbol{\delta}) = f(\boldsymbol{x}) + \boldsymbol{\delta}^\top \nabla f(x, y), \tag{2}$$

where $\boldsymbol{\delta}$ is a perturbation vector. Since

$$\int_{\mathbb{R}^2} f(\boldsymbol{x}) \partial_x f(\boldsymbol{x}) d\boldsymbol{x} = 0, \quad \int_{\mathbb{R}^2} f(\boldsymbol{x}) \partial_y f(\boldsymbol{x}) d\boldsymbol{x} = 0, \quad \int_{\mathbb{R}^2} \partial_x f(\boldsymbol{x}) \partial_y f(\boldsymbol{x}) d\boldsymbol{x} = 0, \tag{3}$$

images $g(\boldsymbol{x}) = f(\boldsymbol{R}\boldsymbol{x} + \boldsymbol{t})$ for a small angle rotation $\boldsymbol{R}$ and a small translation vector $\boldsymbol{t}$, we can assume the relation

$$g(\boldsymbol{x}) = a_0 f(\boldsymbol{x}) + a_1 \partial_x f(\boldsymbol{x}) + a_2 \partial_y f(\boldsymbol{x}). \tag{4}$$

Equation (4) implies that the number of independent images in the collected images,

$$L(f) = \{f_{ij} | f_{ij}(\boldsymbol{x}) = \lambda f(\boldsymbol{R}_i \boldsymbol{x} + \boldsymbol{t}_j)\}_{i,j=1}^{p,q}, \tag{5}$$

is 3. Setting $f \otimes g$ to be a linear operation such that $(f \otimes g)h = (h, g)$, where $(\cdot, \cdot)$ is the inner product of the image space, the covariance of $L(f)$ is defined as $\boldsymbol{L}_f = \mathrm{E}_{ijuv}^{pqpq}[f_{ij} \otimes f_{uv}]$, where $\mathrm{E}_i^n[f_i]$ is the expectation of $\{f_i\}_{i=1}^n$. We can use the first 3 principal vectors of $\boldsymbol{L}_f$ as the local bases for image expression.

3 Local Linear Method

For a two-dimensional image, we introduce a method of reducing the number N of an image dictionary. Using the local linear property of images in the image space, we first generate an image in a sparse dictionary[8, 9]. For the registration of a template g, using the generated image, we next estimate the parameters in the dictionary. From the generated image and estimated parameters, the local linear method (LLM) can generate new entries in the dictionary as an interpolation among entries. Figures 1(a)-(c) show the generation of an image, the estimation of parameters and the interpolation of elements in a dictionary, respectively.

3.1 Generation of Image in Dictionary

For image generation, we use the k-nearest neighbours (k-NNs) of g in the dictionary. Let $f^r \in \mathcal{L}$, $r = 1, 2, \cdots k$, be the rth neighbour of g. The random projection preserves the pairwise distances of vectorised images. Therefore, f^r

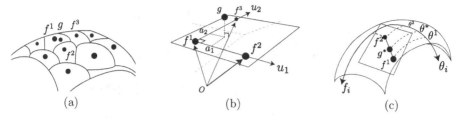

Fig. 1. (a) Nearest neighbours of g searched for by k-NNS on manifold. (b) Generation of image in dictionary. The input image g is projected onto the subspace spanned by three-nearest neighbours. (c) Interpolation of dictionary. For the template g, we firstly generate the image g^*. Next, we estimate the parameter θ^* of $g*$. Here, dim $\theta = 1$.

is searched for in a random projected space. Using the local linear property, we can approximate the space spanned by $\{u_i\}_{i=1}^3$ using one by $\{g\} \cup \{f^r\}_{r=1}^3$ if the data space $\mathcal{L}$ is not extremely sparse. Using the Gram-Schmidt orthonormalisation for f^1, f^2 and f^3, we obtain the bases $\{u_i\}_{i=1}^3$. Projecting the template to the space spanned by $\{u_i\}_{i=1}^3$, we obtain a new image,

$$g^* = \sum_{i=1}^3 a_i u_i, \tag{6}$$

from a triplet of pre-prepared entries in the dictionary. Here, α_i represents the coefficient of a linear combination. We assume that a small perturbation of the parameter causes a small geometrical transformation on the image pattern, that is, we accept the relation $f(\boldsymbol{x} + \boldsymbol{\delta}, \boldsymbol{\theta}) = f(\boldsymbol{x}, \boldsymbol{\theta} + \boldsymbol{\psi})$. Therefore, the linear approximation of the left-hand-side of the equation is

$$f(\boldsymbol{x}, \boldsymbol{\theta} + \boldsymbol{\psi}) = f(\boldsymbol{x}, \boldsymbol{\theta}) + \boldsymbol{\psi}^\top \nabla_{\varPi} f(\boldsymbol{x}, \boldsymbol{\theta}), \tag{7}$$

where $\nabla_{\varPi}$ is the gradient operation in the parameter space $\varPi$. Equations (2) and (7) derive the relation

$$\boldsymbol{\psi}^\top \nabla_{\varPi} f(\boldsymbol{x}, \boldsymbol{\theta}) = \boldsymbol{\delta}^\top \nabla f(\boldsymbol{x}, \boldsymbol{\theta}). \tag{8}$$

3.2   Parameter Estimation

For rotation transform with angle α in a counterclockwise direction and translation $\boldsymbol{a} = (a, b)^\top$, setting $\boldsymbol{\theta}_i = (\alpha_i, a_i, b_i)^\top$ and $\{\boldsymbol{\theta}_i\}_{i=1}^N = \varPi_N \in \varPi$, we express images $f_i = f(\boldsymbol{x}, \boldsymbol{\theta}_i)$ in a dictionary. Furthermore, let $f^1 = f(\boldsymbol{x}, \boldsymbol{\theta}^1)$ be the nearest neighbour of the template $f(\boldsymbol{x}, \boldsymbol{\theta})$ in the dictionary.

Setting $\boldsymbol{\theta}_\alpha^1 = (\alpha^2, a^1, b^1)^\top$, $\boldsymbol{\theta}_a^1 = (\alpha^1, a^2, b^1)^\top$ and $\boldsymbol{\theta}_b^1 = (\alpha^1, a^1, b^2)^\top$, we obtain the partial differential

$$\nabla_{\varPi} f(\boldsymbol{x}, \boldsymbol{\theta}) = \begin{pmatrix} \frac{f(\boldsymbol{x}, \boldsymbol{\theta}^1) - f(\boldsymbol{x}, \boldsymbol{\theta}_\alpha^1)}{\alpha^2 - \alpha^1} \\ \frac{f(\boldsymbol{x}, \boldsymbol{\theta}^1) - f(\boldsymbol{x}, \boldsymbol{\theta}_a^1)}{a^2 - a^1} \\ \frac{f(\boldsymbol{x}, \boldsymbol{\theta}^1) - f(\boldsymbol{x}, \boldsymbol{\theta}_b^1)}{b^2 - b^1} \end{pmatrix} = \begin{pmatrix} h_1 \\ h_2 \\ h_3 \end{pmatrix} \tag{9}$$

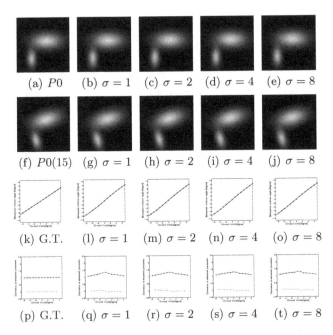

Fig. 2. Parameter estimation for phantom image. From top to bottom, original images, rotated images, estimated parameters and the differential curves of the estimated parameters are shown for $\sigma = 1, 2, 4$ and 8. In Figs. 2(p)-2(t), the solid and dashed lines represent the first- and second-order differentials, respectively.

as the difference among images. Here, $f(\boldsymbol{x}, \boldsymbol{\theta}_\alpha^1)$, $f(\boldsymbol{x}, \boldsymbol{\theta}_a^1)$ and $f(\boldsymbol{x}, \boldsymbol{\theta}_b^1)$ are the 2nd, 3rd and 4th nearest neighbours in the dictionary. From Eqs. (8) and (9), we obtain the relation

$$\boldsymbol{\psi} = -\frac{f(\boldsymbol{x}, \boldsymbol{\theta}^1) - f(\boldsymbol{x}, \boldsymbol{\theta})}{|\nabla_\Pi f(\boldsymbol{x}, \boldsymbol{\theta})|^2} \nabla_\Pi f(\boldsymbol{x}, \boldsymbol{\theta}) \tag{10}$$

at each point[1]. Here, $\boldsymbol{\psi} = (\psi_1, \psi_2, \psi_3)^\top$. Next, by computing the square of the average of both sides of Eq. (10), we obtain the relation

$$\mathrm{E}[\psi_i] = \sqrt{\int_\Omega \frac{|(f(\boldsymbol{x}, \boldsymbol{\theta}) - f(\boldsymbol{x}, \boldsymbol{\theta}^1))\, h_i|^2}{|\nabla_\Pi f(\boldsymbol{x}, \boldsymbol{\theta})|^4} d\boldsymbol{x}} \tag{11}$$

for the image. Therefore, we obtain the equation $\boldsymbol{\theta}^* = \boldsymbol{\theta}^1 + \mathrm{E}\,[\boldsymbol{\psi}]$ for parameter estimation, where $\mathrm{E}(\boldsymbol{\psi}) = (\mathrm{E}[\psi_1], \mathrm{E}[\psi_2], \mathrm{E}[\psi_3])^\top$.

4   Numerical Examples

For rotation transform, we show results of registration using the LLM. We evaluated our method both for phantom and real images. Phantom images are

---

[1] The least-mean-squares solution of $\boldsymbol{x}^\top \boldsymbol{a} + c = 0$ is $\boldsymbol{x} = -c\boldsymbol{a}/|\boldsymbol{a}|^2$.

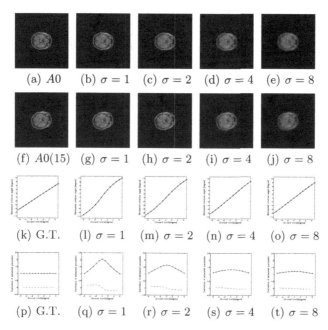

(a) $A0$ (b) $\sigma = 1$ (c) $\sigma = 2$ (d) $\sigma = 4$ (e) $\sigma = 8$

(f) $A0(15)$ (g) $\sigma = 1$ (h) $\sigma = 2$ (i) $\sigma = 4$ (j) $\sigma = 8$

(k) G.T.   (l) $\sigma = 1$ (m) $\sigma = 2$ (n) $\sigma = 4$ (o) $\sigma = 8$

(p) G.T.   (q) $\sigma = 1$ (r) $\sigma = 2$ (s) $\sigma = 4$ (t) $\sigma = 8$

Fig. 3. Parameter estimation for MRI slice image of human brain. From top to bottom, original images, rotated images, estimated parameters and the differential curves of the estimated parameters are shown for $\sigma = 1, 2, 4$ and 8. In Figs. 3(p)-3(t), the solid and dashed lines represent the first- and second-order differentials, respectively.

generated from a two-dimensional Gaussian function. Real images are MRI slice images of a simulated human brain. Figures 2(a) and 3(a) show the phantom image $P0$ and the slice image $A0$, respectively. For the generation of entries in the dictionary, we rotated the original image with angles $\frac{\pi}{12}i, i = 0, 1, 2, \cdots, 23$. We use the original image as reference and the rotated images as targets. Figures 2(f) and 3(f) show the sample images of the dictionary, respectively. For phantom images, we generate rotated phantom images with angles of $-6, -5, \ldots, 6$ degrees as template images. For real images, our template images are selected from several slice images different from the original slice image. Figures 4(a), (b), (c) and (d) show the MRI volume data and the images of slice $A0$, slice $B0$ and slice $C0$, respectively. As template images, we generate the rotated images $A0, B0$ and $C0$ with angles of $-6, -5, \ldots, 6$ degrees. For the stable computation, we first select images using the NNS, then we apply the Gaussian smoothing for selected images. We set the standard deviation of the Gaussian function to be $\sigma = 1, 2, 4$ and 8. Figures 2(b)-(e), 2(g)-(j), 3(b)-(e) and 3(g)-(j) show the smoothed images. In all registrations, the dimensions of vectorised images are reduced to 1024 dimensions by the efficient random projection.

Selecting a template image from the generated template set, we apply our registration algorithm to reference images in the dictionary. For phantom images, Figs. 2(k)-(o) show the estimated parameters for each σ. Furthermore,

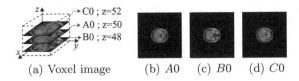

(a) Voxel image   (b) $A0$ (c) $B0$ (d) $C0$

Fig. 4. Extracted slice images from three-dimensional volume data. The volume data is the MRI simulation data of a human brain[10]. The size of the volume data is $181 \times 217 \times 181$ pixels. The slice images $A0$, $B0$ and $C0$ are extracted from the $z = 50$, $z = 48$ and $z = 52$ planes, repectively. The size of $A0$, $B0$, and $C0$ is 543×543 pixels.

Figs. 3(k)-(o) show the estimated parameters for real images. For phantom images, in Figs. 2(p)-(t), the solid and dashed lines show the first- and second-order differentials for the curves of the estimated parameters, respectively. For real images, in Figs. 3(p)-(t), the solid and dashed lines show the first- and second-order differentials for the curves of the estimated parameters, respectively.

Next, selecting a template image from the generated template set using several slice images, we apply our registration algorithm to reference images in the dictionary smoothing images with $\sigma = 0, 1$ and 2. The results of image generation and parameter estimation are shown in Tabs. 1 and 2, respectively. In Tab. 1, we evaluate the accuracy of the generation errors using the distance between the template and the generated images.

In Figs. 2(q)-2(t), the second-order differentials of the estimation curves are almost flat, that is, the rotation angle is linearly estimated for a potentially smooth image. In Figs. 3(q)-3(t), for $\sigma \geq 4$, the second-order differentials of the estimation curves are almost flat. These results indicate that, for $|\theta - \theta_i| < 6$, our method accurately estimates the parameters. From Tab. 1, the registration errors of the LLM are smaller than those of the NNS method. Table 2 shows that, for $\sigma = 1$, the estimated rotation angle satisfies $G.T - 0.3 \leq \theta^* \leq G.T + 0.5$. Tables 1 and 2 show that the LLM generates image in the dictionary using the local linear property of images in the pattern space.

These experiments show that our algorithm achieves the medical image registration with a sparse dictionary. The errors of our algorithm are less than 1 degree, while the maximum error of NNS is 6 degree. Using the random projection, we can compute the global image registration using the LLM with only 8.3% of the memory storage size of the NNS method.

5   Conclusions

We introduced the interpolation of entries in a dictionary to reduce the computational cost of preprocessing and the size of the dictionary used in the nearest-neighbour search. Using the random projection and interpolation techniques for the dictionary, we developed an algorithm that efficiently establishes a global image registration. From numerical examples, we show that our method can perform the registration with high accuracy using a small-memory-storage-size dictionary compared with the naive nearest-neighbour-search-based method.

Table 1. Registration errors

	θ	NNS	Registration error [×10³] LLM (3 bases)	LLM (4 bases)
A0	1	1.37	1.30	1.29
	2	2.41	2.22	2.21
	3	3.26	2.87	2.86
	4	3.95	3.30	3.30
	5	4.54	3.55	3.55
	6	5.03	3.63	3.63
B0	1	3.40	3.27	3.27
	2	3.78	3.52	3.52
	3	4.23	3.79	3.80
	4	4.69	4.03	4.03
	5	5.13	4.18	4.17
	6	5.35	4.23	4.23
C0	1	3.29	3.12	3.08
	2	3.63	3.35	3.33
	3	4.05	3.60	3.59
	4	4.47	3.81	3.80
	5	4.87	3.93	3.92
	6	5.22	3.96	3.95

Table 2. Estimated angles

	G.T θ	Estimated θ* $\sigma = 0$	$\sigma = 1$	$\sigma = 2$
A0	1	0.77	1.06	2.06
	2	1.68	1.76	2.38
	3	2.72	2.73	3.10
	4	3.82	3.83	4.07
	5	4.97	4.98	5.17
	6	6.07	6.07	5.58
B0	1	1.69	1.69	2.22
	2	2.41	2.39	2.76
	3	3.28	3.26	3.52
	4	4.22	4.22	4.43
	5	5.22	5.24	5.43
	6	6.23	6.21	6.03
C0	1	1.99	1.93	2.30
	2	2.52	2.46	2.71
	3	3.27	3.21	3.38
	4	4.13	4.01	4.22
	5	5.04	5.02	5.14
	6	5.96	5.98	6.10

This research was supported by the "Computational anatomy for computer-aided diagnosis and therapy: Frontiers of medical image sciences" project funded by a Grant-in-Aid for Scientific Research on Innovative Areas from MEXT, Japan, by Grants-in-Aid for Scientific Research funded by the Japan Society for the Promotion of Science, and by a Grant-in-Aid for Young Scientists (A) from MEXT.

References

1. Healy, D.M., Rohge, G.K.: Fast global image registration using random projections. In: Proc. Biomedical Imaging: From Nano to Macro, pp. 476–479 (2007)
2. Itoh, H., Lu, S., Sakai, T., Imiya, A.: Global image registration by fast random projection. In: Bebis, G. (ed.) ISVC 2011, Part I. LNCS, vol. 6938, pp. 23–32. Springer, Heidelberg (2011)
3. Sakai, T., Imiya, A.: Practical algorithms of spectral clustering: Toward large-scale vision-based motion analysis. In: Machine Learning for Vision-Based Motion Analysis, pp. 3–26. Springer (2011)
4. Vempala, S.S.: The Random Projection Method, vol. 65. American Mathematical Society (2004)
5. Iijima, T.: Theory of pattern recognition. Electronics and Communications in Japan, 123–134 (1963)
6. Watanabe, S., Labert, P.F., Kulikowski, C.A., Buxton, J.L., Walker, R.: Evaluation and selection of variables in pattern recognition. In: Computer and Information Science II, pp. 91–122 (1967)
7. Oja, E.: Subspace methods of pattern recognition. Research Studies Press (1983)
8. Hartley, R.I., Zisserman, A.: Multiple View Geometry in Computer Vision. Cambridge University Press (2004)
9. Mahajan, D., Huang, F.C., Matusik, W., Ramamoorthi, R., Belhumeur, P.: Moving gradients: A path-based method for plausible image interpolation. ACM Transactions on Graphics 28, 42:1–42:11 (2009)
10. Cocosco, C., Kollokian, V., Kwan, R.S., Evans, A.: Brainweb. online interface to a 3D MRI simulated brain database. NeuroImage 5, 425 (1997)

Image Segmentation
by Oriented Image Foresting Transform
with Geodesic Star Convexity

Lucy A.C. Mansilla and Paulo A.V. Miranda

Department of Computer Science, University of São Paulo (USP),
05508-090, São Paulo, SP, Brazil
{lucyacm,pmiranda}@vision.ime.usp.br

Abstract. Anatomical structures and tissues are often hard to be segmented in medical images due to their poorly defined boundaries, i.e., low contrast in relation to other nearby false boundaries. The specification of the boundary polarity and the usage of shape constraints can help to alleviate part of this problem. Recently, an Oriented Image Foresting Transform (OIFT) has been proposed. In this work, we discuss how to incorporate Gulshan's geodesic star convexity prior in the OIFT approach for interactive image segmentation, in order to simultaneously handle boundary polarity and shape constraints. This convexity constraint eliminates undesirable intricate shapes, improving the segmentation of objects with more regular shape. We include a theoretical proof of the optimality of the new algorithm in terms of a global maximum of an oriented energy function subject to the shape constraints, and show the obtained gains in accuracy using medical images of thoracic CT studies.

Keywords: graph search algorithms, image foresting transform, graph-cut segmentation, geodesic star convexity.

1   Introduction

Image segmentation, such as to extract an object from a background, is very useful for medical and biological image analysis. However, in order to guarantee reliable and accurate results, user supervision is still required in several segmentation tasks, such as the extraction of poorly defined structures in medical imaging, due to their intensity non-standardness among images, field inhomogeneity, noise, partial volume effects, and their interplay [1]. The high-level, application-domain-specific knowledge of the user is also often required in the digital matting of natural scenes, because of their heterogeneous nature [2]. These problems motivated the development of several methods for semi-automatic segmentation [3,4,5,6], aiming to minimize the user involvement and time required without compromising accuracy and precision.

One important class of interactive image segmentation comprises seed-based methods, which have been developed based on different theories, supposedly not related, leading to different frameworks, such as watershed [6], random

R. Wilson et al. (Eds.): CAIP 2013, Part I, LNCS 8047, pp. 572–579, 2013.

walks [7], fuzzy connectedness [8], graph cuts [4], distance cut [2], image forest-ing transform [9], and grow cut [10]. The study of the relations among different frameworks, including theoretical and empirical comparisons, has a vast litera-ture [11,12,13,14]. These methods can also be adapted to automatic segmentation whenever the seeds can be automatically found [15].

In this paper, we pursue our previous work on *Oriented Image Foresting Transform* (OIFT) [16], which extends popular methods [9,8], by incorporat-ing the boundary orientation (boundary polarity) to resolve between very sim-ilar nearby boundary segments by exploring directed weighted graphs. OIFT presents an excellent trade-off between time efficiency and accuracy, and is ex-tensible to multidimensional images. In this work, we discuss how to incorpo-rate Gulshan's geodesic star convexity (GSC) prior in the OIFT approach. This convexity constraint eliminates undesirable intricate shapes, improving the seg-mentation of objects with more regular shape. We include a theoretical proof of the optimality of the new algorithm in terms of a global maximum of an energy function subject to the shape constraints. The proposed method GSC-OIFT can simultaneously handle boundary polarity and shape constraints with improved accuracy for targeted image segmentation [17].

The next sections give a summary of the relevant previous work of the *Image Foresting Transform* [9] and OIFT [16]. The proposed extensions are presented in Section 5. In Section 6, we evaluate the methods, and state our conclusions.

2   Image Foresting Transform

An image can be interpreted as a weighted graph $G = (\mathcal{I}, \mathcal{A}, w)$ whose nodes are the image pixels in its image domain $\mathcal{I} \subset Z^n$, and whose arcs are the pixel pairs (s, t) in $\mathcal{A}$ (e.g., 4-neighborhood, or 8-neighborhood, in case of 2D images). The *adjacency relation* $\mathcal{A}$ is a binary relation on $\mathcal{I}$. We use $t \in \mathcal{A}(s)$ and $(s, t) \in \mathcal{A}$ to indicate that t is adjacent to s. Each arc $(s, t) \in \mathcal{A}$ has a fixed weight $w(s, t) \geq 0$. In this work, higher arc weights across the object's boundary should be considered, such as a dissimilarity measure between pixels s and t (e.g., $w(s, t) = |I(t) - I(s)|$ for a single channel image with values given by $I(t)$). The graph is undirected weighted if $w(s, t) = w(t, s)$ for all $(s, t) \in \mathcal{A}$, otherwise we have a directed weighted graph.

For a given image graph $G = (\mathcal{I}, \mathcal{A}, w)$, a path $\pi_t = \langle t_1, t_2, \ldots, t \rangle$ is a sequence of adjacent pixels with terminus at a pixel t. A path is *trivial* when $\pi_t = \langle t \rangle$. A path $\pi_t = \pi_s \cdot \langle s, t \rangle$ indicates the extension of a path π_s by an arc (s, t). A *predecessor map* is a function P that assigns to each pixel t in $\mathcal{I}$ either some other adjacent pixel in $\mathcal{I}$, or a distinctive marker nil not in $\mathcal{I}$ — in which case t is said to be a *root* of the map. A *spanning forest* is a predecessor map which contains no cycles — i.e., one which takes every pixel to nil in a finite number of iterations. For any pixel $t \in \mathcal{I}$, a spanning forest P defines a path π_t recursively as $\langle t \rangle$ if $P(t) = nil$, and $\pi_s \cdot \langle s, t \rangle$ if $P(t) = s \neq nil$.

A *connectivity function* computes a value $f(\pi_t)$ for any path π_t, usually based on arc weights. A path π_t is *optimum* if $f(\pi_t) \leq f(\tau_t)$ for any other path τ_t in G. By taking to each pixel $t \in \mathcal{I}$ one optimum path with terminus t, we obtain the optimum-path value $V(t)$, which is uniquely defined by $V(t) = \min_{\forall \pi_t \text{ in } G}\{f(\pi_t)\}$. The *image foresting transform* (IFT) [9] takes an image graph $G = (\mathcal{I}, \mathcal{A}, w)$, and a path-value function f; and assigns one optimum path π_t to every pixel $t \in \mathcal{I}$ such that an *optimum-path forest* P is obtained — i.e., a spanning forest where all paths are optimum. However, f must be *smooth* [9], otherwise, the paths may not be optimum.

The cost of a trivial path $\pi_t = \langle t \rangle$ is usually given by a handicap value $H(t)$, while the connectivity functions for non-trivial paths follow a path-extension rule. For example:

$$f_{max}(\pi_s \cdot \langle s, t \rangle) = \max\{f_{max}(\pi_s), w(s, t)\} \tag{1}$$

$$f_{sum}(\pi_s \cdot \langle s, t \rangle) = f_{sum}(\pi_s) + \delta(s, t) \tag{2}$$

$$f_{euc}(\pi_s \cdot \langle s, t \rangle) = \|t - R(\pi_s)\|^2 \tag{3}$$

$$f_w(\pi_s \cdot \langle s, t \rangle) = w(s, t) \tag{4}$$

where $w(s, t) \geq 0$ is a fixed arc weight, $\delta(s, t) \geq 0$ is a dissimilarity measure, $R(\pi_t)$ is the origin/root of a path π_t, and f_w is a non-smooth function, which has important relations with the f_{max} smooth function [18,12].

We consider image segmentation from two seed sets, $\mathcal{S}_o$ and $\mathcal{S}_b$ ($\mathcal{S}_o \cap \mathcal{S}_b = \emptyset$), containing pixels selected inside and outside the object, respectively. The search for optimum paths (usually considering f_{max}) is constrained to start in $\mathcal{S} = \mathcal{S}_o \cup \mathcal{S}_b$ (i.e., $H(t) = -1$ for all $t \in S$, and $H(t) = +\infty$ otherwise). The image is partitioned into two optimum-path forests — one rooted at the internal seeds, defining the object, and the other rooted at the external seeds, representing the background [18]. A label, $L(t) = 1$ for all $t \in \mathcal{S}_o$ and $L(t) = 0$ for all $t \in \mathcal{S}_b$, is propagated to all unlabeled pixels during the computation [9].

In the case of undirected weighted graphs, the connectivity functions f_{max} (under the conditions stated in [18]) and f_w give a global optimum segmentation according to an energy function of the cut boundary [13,14]. They maximize the graph-cut measure E defined by Equation 5 among all possible segmentation results satisfying the hard constraints (seeds).

$$E(L, G = (\mathcal{I}, \mathcal{A}, w)) = \min_{\forall (s,t) \in \mathcal{A} \mid L(s) \neq L(t)} w(s, t) \tag{5}$$

3   Oriented Image Foresting Transform (OIFT)

In the case of directed graphs, an important thing to note is that there are two different types of cut for each object boundary: an inner-cut boundary composed by edges that point toward object pixels $\mathcal{C}_i(L) = \{\forall (s, t) \in \mathcal{A} \mid L(s) = 0, L(t) = 1\}$, and an outer-cut boundary with edges from object to background pixels $\mathcal{C}_o(L) = \{\forall (s, t) \in \mathcal{A} \mid L(s) = 1, L(t) = 0\}$. Consequently, we have two different kinds of energy, $E_i(L, G)$ and $E_o(L, G)$:

$$E_i(L, G = (\mathcal{I}, \mathcal{A}, w)) = \min_{\forall (s,t) \in \mathcal{C}_i(L)} w(s, t) \tag{6}$$

$$E_o(L, G = (\mathcal{I}, \mathcal{A}, w)) = \min_{\forall (s,t) \in \mathcal{C}_o(L)} w(s, t) \tag{7}$$

As demonstrated in [16], the following non-smooth connectivity functions $f_{i,\max}^{bkg}$ and $f_{o,\max}^{bkg}$ in the IFT algorithm (which we denote as OIFT) lead to optimum cuts that maximize Eq. 6 and Eq. 7, respectively. The handicap values of $f_{i,\max}^{bkg}$ and $f_{o,\max}^{bkg}$ for trivial paths are defined as before (i.e., $H(t) = -1$ for all $t \in S$, and $H(t) = +\infty$ otherwise). The undirected weights $w(s,t)$ are converted to directed arcs by multiplying them by an orientation factor $(1+\alpha)$ if $I(s) > I(t)$, and by $(1 - \alpha)$ otherwise (e.g., $\alpha = 0.5$).

$$f_{i,\max}^{bkg}(\pi_s \cdot \langle s,t \rangle) = \begin{cases} \max\{f_{i,\max}^{bkg}(\pi_s), 2 \times w(t,s) + 1\} & \text{if } R(\pi_s) \in \mathcal{S}_o \\ \max\{f_{i,\max}^{bkg}(\pi_s), 2 \times w(s,t)\} & \text{if } R(\pi_s) \in \mathcal{S}_b \end{cases} \quad (8)$$

$$f_{o,\max}^{bkg}(\pi_s \cdot \langle s,t \rangle) = \begin{cases} \max\{f_{o,\max}^{bkg}(\pi_s), 2 \times w(s,t) + 1\} & \text{if } R(\pi_s) \in \mathcal{S}_o \\ \max\{f_{o,\max}^{bkg}(\pi_s), 2 \times w(t,s)\} & \text{if } R(\pi_s) \in \mathcal{S}_b \end{cases} \quad (9)$$

4   Geodesic Star Convexity (GSC)

A point p is said to be visible to c via a set $\mathcal{O}$ if the line segment joining p to c lies in the set $\mathcal{O}$. An object $\mathcal{O}$ is star-convex with respect to center c, if every point $p \in \mathcal{O}$ is visible to c via $\mathcal{O}$ [19]. It is also possible to define a discrete version of this constraint directly in the image domain, by considering a shortest path in the image graph, returned by the IFT (e.g., using f_{euc}, 8-connected adjacency, $H(c) = 0$, and $H(t) = +\infty$ for all $t \neq c$), as the line segment.

In the case of multiple stars, a computationally tractable definition, was proposed in [20]. The previous notion of the line segment (shortest path) joining the single star center c to p, is extended to a line segment joining the set of star centers $C = \{c_1, c_2, \ldots, c_n\}$ to p, which is taken as the shortest path between the point p and set C. In interactive segmentation, the set of star centers is usually taken to coincide with the internal seeds (i.e., $C = \mathcal{S}_o$), and, in the discrete version, the line segments form a spanning forest rooted at the internal seeds, where each line segment corresponds to a path in the graph.

In [20], the authors proposed the usage of a different notion of star convexity with shortest path from Euclidean to geodesic (f_{sum}). We use $H(t) = -1$ for all $t \in \mathcal{S}_o$ ($H(t) = +\infty$ otherwise), and $\delta(s,t) = [w(s,t) + 1]^\beta - 1 + \|t - s\|$ in the path-extension rule for f_{sum}, where $\|t - s\|$ is the Euclidean distance between pixels s and t, and β controls the forest topology in the returned predecessor map, which we will denote by P_{sum}. For lower values of β ($\beta \approx 0.0$), $\delta(s,t)$ approaches $\|t - s\|$, and it imposes more star regularization to the object's boundary. For higher values, $[w(s,t)+1]^\beta$ dominates the expression, allowing a better fit to the curved protrusions and indentations of the boundary.

5   OIFT with Geodesic Star Convexity (GSC-OIFT)

An object $\mathcal{O}$ is geodesic star convex (GSC) with respect to a set of centers C, if every point $p \in \mathcal{O}$ is visible to C via $\mathcal{O}$ (i.e., the shortest path joining p to

C in P_{sum} lies in the set $\mathcal{O}$). In this work, we want to constrain the search for optimum results, that maximize the graph-cut measures $E_i(L,G)$ (Eq. 6) and $E_o(L,G)$ (Eq. 7), only to segmentations that satisfy the geodesic star convexity constraint.

First, we compute the optimum forest P_{sum} for f_{sum} by the regular IFT algorithm, using only $\mathcal{S}_o$ as seeds, for the given directed graph $G = (\mathcal{I}, \mathcal{A}, w)$. Let's consider the following two sets of arcs $\xi^i_{P_{sum}} = \{\forall(s,t) \in \mathcal{A}|\; s = P_{sum}(t)\}$ and $\xi^o_{P_{sum}} = \{\forall(s,t) \in \mathcal{A}|\; t = P_{sum}(s)\}$. We have the following Lemma 1:

Lemma 1. *For a given segmentation L, we have $\mathcal{C}_o(L) \cap \xi^o_{P_{sum}} \neq \emptyset$, if and only if there is a violation of the geodesic star convexity constraint. We have $\mathcal{C}_i(L) \cap \xi^i_{P_{sum}} \neq \emptyset$, if and only if there is a violation of the geodesic star convexity constraint.*

Proof. We will demonstrate it for $\mathcal{C}_o(L) \cap \xi^o_{P_{sum}} \neq \emptyset$, but the demonstration for $\mathcal{C}_i(L) \cap \xi^i_{P_{sum}} \neq \emptyset$ is essentially identical. By definition, a violation of geodesic star convexity constraint with respect to a set of centers $C = \mathcal{S}_o$, will be given if there exists a point $p \in \mathcal{O} = \{\forall t|L(t) = 1\}$ that is not visible to C via $\mathcal{O}$ (i.e., there is a pixel r in the shortest path joining p to C in P_{sum}, and $r \notin \mathcal{O}$).

By the definitions of $\xi^o_{P_{sum}}$ and $\mathcal{C}_o(L)$, we have $\mathcal{C}_o(L) \cap \xi^o_{P_{sum}} = \{\forall(s,t) \in A|L(s) = 1, L(t) = 0 \text{ and } t = P_{sum}(s)\}$. For any edge $(s,t) \in \mathcal{C}_o \cap \xi^o_{P_{sum}}$ we have $t = P_{sum}(s)$, which means that there exists a shortest path $\pi_s = \pi_t \cdot \langle t,s \rangle$ in P_{sum} rooted at the internal seeds $\mathcal{S}_o$ (i.e., line segment between s and $\mathcal{S}_o$). But $(s,t) \in \mathcal{C}_o(L)$ implies that $L(t) = 0$ (i.e., $t \notin \mathcal{O}$), and hence s is not visible to $\mathcal{S}_o$ through $\pi_s = \pi_t \cdot \langle t,s \rangle$ in P_{sum}. Thus, $\mathcal{C}_o \cap \xi^o_{P_{sum}} \neq \emptyset$ implies in a violation of the geodesic star convexity constraint.

On the other hand, if we have a violation of the geodesic star convexity constraint, it means that $\exists s \in \mathcal{O}$ (i.e., $L(s) = 1$), which is not visible to $\mathcal{S}_o$ via the shortest path π_s in P_{sum}, so that there is a pixel $p_i \notin \mathcal{O}$ in $\pi_s = \langle p_1, \ldots, p_i, \ldots, p_n = s \rangle$, with $P_{sum}(p_{i+1}) = p_i$ and $p_{i+1} \in \mathcal{O}$. Hence, $(p_{i+1}, p_i) \in \mathcal{C}_o \cap \xi^o_{P_{sum}}$, which implies that $\mathcal{C}_o \cap \xi^o_{P_{sum}} \neq \emptyset$.

Therefore, we have $\mathcal{C}_o \cap \xi^o_{P_{sum}} \neq \emptyset$, if and only if there is a violation of the geodesic star convexity constraint. $\qquad\blacksquare$

Theorem 1 (Inner/outer-cut boundary optimality). *For a given image graph $G = (\mathcal{I}, \mathcal{A}, w)$, consider a modified weighted graph $G' = (\mathcal{I}, \mathcal{A}, w')$, with weights $w'(s,t) = -\infty$ for all $(s,t) \in \xi^o_{P_{sum}}$, and $w'(s,t) = w(s,t)$ otherwise. For two given sets of seeds $\mathcal{S}_o$ and $\mathcal{S}_b$, the segmentation computed over G' by the IFT algorithm for function $f^{bkg}_{o,\max}$ defines an optimum cut in the original graph G, that maximizes $E_o(L,G)$ among all possible segmentation results satisfying the shape constraints by the geodesic star convexity, and the seed constraints.*

Similarly, the segmentation computed by the IFT algorithm for function $f^{bkg}_{i,\max}$, over a modified graph $G' = (\mathcal{I}, \mathcal{A}, w')$; with weights $w'(s,t) = -\infty$ for all $(s,t) \in \xi^i_{P_{sum}}$, and $w'(s,t) = w(s,t)$ otherwise; defines an optimum cut in the original graph G, that maximizes $E_i(L,G)$ among all possible segmentation results satisfying the shape constraints by the geodesic star convexity, and the seed constraints.

Proof. We will prove the theorem in the case of function $f^{bkg}_{o,\max}$ the other case having essentially identical proof. Since we assign the worst weight to all arcs $(s,t) \in \xi^o_{P_{sum}}$ in G' (i.e., $w'(s,t) = -\infty$), any segmentation $\tilde{L}$ with $\mathcal{C}_o(\tilde{L}) \cap \xi^o_{P_{sum}} \neq \emptyset$ will receive the worst energy value $(E_o(\tilde{L}, G') = -\infty)$ [1]. From the Theorem in [16], we know that the IFT with $f^{bkg}_{o,\max}$ over G' maximizes the energy $E_o(L, G')$ in the graph G', consequently, it will naturally avoid in its outer-cut boundary any edge from $\xi^o_{P_{sum}}$. Since, there is always a solution that does not violate the GSC constraint (e.g., we could take $\mathcal{O} = \mathcal{S}_o$), and from Lemma 1, we have that the computed solution cannot violate the GSC constraint.

Since $w(s,t) \geq 0$, $\forall (s,t) \in \mathcal{A}$, and from Lemma 1, we have that any candidate segmentation $\tilde{L}$ satisfying the GSC constraint must have $E_o(\tilde{L}, G') \geq 0$. Moreover, since its weights for the arcs in $\mathcal{C}_o(\ddot{L})$ were not changed in G', we also have that $E_o(\ddot{L}, G') = E_o(\ddot{L}, G)$. Hence, all results satisfying the GSC constraint were considered in the optimization, and therefore Theorem 1 holds, as we wanted to prove.

6   Experiments and Conclusions

We conducted quantitative experiments, using a total of 40 image slices of 10 thoracic CT studies to segment the liver. All methods, including the power watershed algorithm ($PW_{q=2}$) [14], were assessed for accuracy employing the mean performance curve (Dice coefficient) and ground truth data obtained from an expert of the radiology department at the University of Pennsylvania.

Figure 1a shows the mean accuracy curves for all the images assuming different seed sets obtained by eroding and dilating the ground truth. The undirected arc weights were computed as $w(s,t) = |I(t) - I(s)|$. For the directed weighted graphs we considered $\alpha = 0.5$, and we used $\beta = 0.0$. For higher values of β, GSC-OIFT imposes less shape constraints, so that the accuracy tends to decrease (Fig. 1b-d). Figure 2 shows some results in the case of user-selected markers for the liver, and Figure 3 shows one example in 3D.

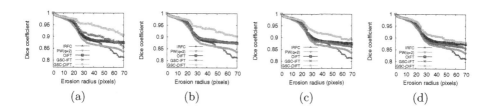

Fig. 1. (a) The mean accuracy curves of all methods for the liver segmentation for various values of β: (a) $\beta = 0.0$, (b) $\beta = 0.2$, (c) $\beta = 0.5$, and (d) $\beta = 0.7$

---

[1] The GSC restrictions are embedded directly into the graph G'.

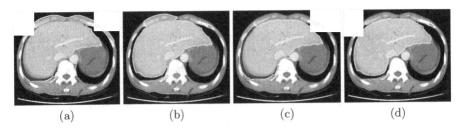

(a)	(b)	(c)	(d)

Fig. 2. Results for user-selected markers: (a) IRFC (IFT with $f_{\max}$), (b) OIFT ($f_{o,\max}^{bkg}$ with $\alpha = 0.5$), (c) GSC-IFT ($\beta = 0.7$, $\alpha = 0.0$), and (d) GSC-OIFT ($\beta = 0.7$, $\alpha = 0.5$)

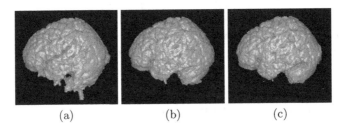

(a)	(b)	(c)

Fig. 3. Example of 3D skull stripping in MRI: (a) IRFC (IFT with $f_{\max}$), (b) GSC-IFT ($\beta = 0.3$, $\alpha = 0.0$), and (c) GSC-OIFT ($\beta = 0.3$, $\alpha = 0.5$), for the same user-selected markers

In conclusion, we developed extensions to the OIFT algorithm [16], by incorporating the geodesic star convexity constraint in its formulation. The results were proved to be optimum according to an energy functional of the cut boundary, and were shown to improve the accuracy in practice. GSC-OIFT only requires twice the computational time of a conventional IFT. As future work, we intend to combine it with statistical models for automatic segmentation.

Acknowledgment. The authors thank FAPESP (2012/06911-2), CNPq (305381/2012-1), and CAPES for the financial support, and Dr. J. K. Udupa (MIPG-UPENN) for the images.

References

1. Madabhushi, A., Udupa, J.: Interplay between intensity standardization and inhomogeneity correction in MR image processing. IEEE Transactions on Medical Imaging 24(5), 561–576 (2005)
2. Bai, X., Sapiro, G.: Distance cut: Interactive segmentation and matting of images and videos. In: Proc. of the IEEE Intl. Conf. on Image Processing, vol. 2, pp. II-249–II-252 (2007)
3. Falcão, A., Udupa, J., Samarasekera, S., Sharma, S., Hirsch, B., Lotufo, R.: User-steered image segmentation paradigms: Live-wire and live-lane. Graphical Models and Image Processing 60(4), 233–260 (1998)

4. Boykov, Y., Funka-Lea, G.: Graph cuts and efficient N-D image segmentation. Intl. Journal of Computer Vision 70(2), 109–131 (2006)
5. Kass, M., Witkin, A., Terzopoulos, D.: Snakes: Active contour models. Intl. Journal of Computer Vision 1, 321–331 (1987)
6. Cousty, J., Bertrand, G., Najman, L., Couprie, M.: Watershed cuts: Thinnings, shortest path forests, and topological watersheds. Trans. on Pattern Analysis and Machine Intelligence 32, 925–939 (2010)
7. Grady, L.: Random walks for image segmentation. IEEE Trans. Pattern Anaysis and Machine Intelligence 28(11), 1768–1783 (2006)
8. Ciesielski, K., Udupa, J., Saha, P., Zhuge, Y.: Iterative relative fuzzy connectedness for multiple objects with multiple seeds. Computer Vision and Image Understanding 107(3), 160–182 (2007)
9. Falcão, A., Stolfi, J., Lotufo, R.: The image foresting transform: Theory, algorithms, and applications. IEEE Transactions on Pattern Analysis and Machine Intelligence 26(1), 19–29 (2004)
10. Vezhnevets, V., Konouchine, V.: "growcut" - interactive multi-label N-D image segmentation by cellular automata. In: Proc. Graphicon., pp. 150–156 (2005)
11. Sinop, A., Grady, L.: A seeded image segmentation framework unifying graph cuts and random walker which yields a new algorithm. In: Proc. of the 11th International Conference on Computer Vision, ICCV, pp. 1–8. IEEE (2007)
12. Miranda, P., Falcão, A.: Elucidating the relations among seeded image segmentation methods and their possible extensions. In: XXIV Conference on Graphics, Patterns and Images, Maceió, AL (August 2011)
13. Ciesielski, K., Udupa, J., Falcão, A., Miranda, P.: Fuzzy connectedness image segmentation in graph cut formulation: A linear-time algorithm and a comparative analysis. Journal of Mathematical Imaging and Vision (2012)
14. Couprie, C., Grady, L., Najman, L., Talbot, H.: Power watersheds: A unifying graph-based optimization framework. Trans. on Pattern Anal. and Machine Intelligence 99 (2010)
15. Miranda, P., Falcão, A., Udupa, J.: Cloud bank: A multiple clouds model and its use in MR brain image segmentation. In: Proc. of the IEEE Intl. Symp. on Biomedical Imaging, Boston, MA, pp. 506–509 (2009)
16. Miranda, P., Mansilla, L.: Oriented image foresting transform segmentation by seed competition. IEEE Transactions on Image Processing (accepted, to appear, 2013)
17. Lézoray, O., Grady, L.: Image Processing and Analysis with Graphs: Theory and Practice. CRC Press, California (2012)
18. Miranda, P., Falcão, A.: Links between image segmentation based on optimum-path forest and minimum cut in graph. Journal of Mathematical Imaging and Vision 35(2), 128–142 (2009)
19. Veksler, O.: Star shape prior for graph-cut image segmentation. In: Forsyth, D., Torr, P., Zisserman, A. (eds.) ECCV 2008, Part III. LNCS, vol. 5304, pp. 454–467. Springer, Heidelberg (2008)
20. Gulshan, V., Rother, C., Criminisi, A., Blake, A., Zisserman, A.: Geodesic star convexity for interactive image segmentation. In: Proc. of Computer Vision and Pattern Recognition, pp. 3129–3136 (2010)

Multi-run 3D Streetside Reconstruction from a Vehicle

Yi Zeng and Reinhard Klette

The .enpeda.. Project, Department of Computer Science
The University of Auckland, New Zealand

Abstract. Accurate 3D modellers of real-world scenes are important tools for visualizing or understanding outside environments. The paper considers a camera-based 3D reconstruction system where stereo cameras are mounted on a mobile platform, recording images while moving through the scene. Due to the limited viewing angle of the cameras, resulting reconstructions often result in missing (e.g. while occluded) components of the scene. In this paper, we propose a stereo-based 3D reconstruction framework for merging multiple runs of reconstructions when driving in different directions through a real-world scene.

1 Introduction

Current large-scale camera-based reconstruction techniques can be subdivided into aerial reconstruction or ground-level reconstruction techniques. Although a large amount of user interaction is needed, the resulting model is often of high quality and visually compelling. There are various commercial products available in the market, demonstrating high quality, such as 3D RealityMaps [1], for example. However, reconstruction methods using aerial images only cannot produce models with photo-realistic details at ground level. There is an extensive literature on ground-level reconstruction; see, for example, [5,9,17]. In both aerial and ground-level reconstructions, cameras capture input images as they travel through the scene. Standard cameras only have limited viewing angles. Thus, a large number of blind spots of the scene exist, resulting in incomplete 3D models, and this is inevitable for a *single run reconstruction* (i.e. when moving cameras on a "nearly straight" path, without any significant variations in the path). A single run has a defined *direction*, being the vector from start and end point of the run.

In this paper, we propose a stereo-based reconstruction framework for automatically merging reconstruction results from multiple single runs in different directions. For each single run, we perform binocular stereo analysis on pairs of *left* and *right* images. We use the left image and the generated disparity map for a bundle-adjustment-based visual odometry algorithm. Then, applying the estimated changes in camera poses, a 3D point cloud of the scene is accumulated frame by frame. Finally, we triangulate the 3D point cloud using an α-shape algorithm to generate a surface model. Up to this stage we apply basically existing techniques. The novelty of this paper is mainly in the merging step, and we

R. Wilson et al. (Eds.): CAIP 2013, Part I, LNCS 8047, pp. 580–588, 2013.

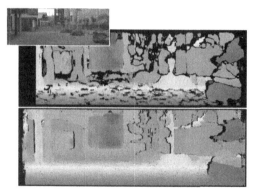

Fig. 1. From top to bottom: original image of a used stereo frame sequence, and colour-coded disparity maps using OpenCV (May 2013) block matching or iSGM

detail the case where two surface models are merged generated from single runs in opposite directions. Input data are recorded stereo sequences from a mobile platform. In this paper we discuss greyscale sequences recorded at Tamaki campus, The University of Auckland, at a resolution of 960 × 320 at 25 Hz, with 10 bit per pixel. Each recorded sequence consists of about 1,800 stereo frames. For an example of an input image, see the top of Fig. 1.

The quality of the used stereo matcher has crucial impact on the accuracy of our 3D reconstruction. We decided for iterative semi-global matching (iSGM), see [8], mainly due to its performance at ECCV 2012 [7]. A comparison with the block-matching stereo procedure in OpenCV (see Fig. 1, middle) illustrates the achieved improvement by using iSGM.

The rest of the paper is structured as follows. In Section 2, we estimate the ego-motion of the vehicle using some kind of bundle adjustment. Section 3 discusses alpha-shape, as used for the surface reconstruction algorithm applied in the system. Finally, the merging step is discussed in Section 4, also showing experimental results. Section 5 concludes the paper.

2 Visual Odometry

Visual Odometry [13], the estimation of position and direction of the camera, is achieved by analysing consecutive images in the recorded sequence. The quality of our reconstructed 3D scene is directly related to the result of visual odometry. Drift in visual odometry [10] often leads to a twist in the 3D model. The basic algorithm is usually: (1) Detect feature points in the image. (2) Track the features across consecutive frames. (3) Calculate the camera's motion based on the tracked features. In this paper, since we focus on quality, an algorithm [15] based on *Bundle Adjustment* (BA) is used for visual odometry.

We tested a basic algorithm for comparison. 2-dimensional (2D) feature points are detected and tracked across the left sequence only. The *speeded-up robust feature detector* (SURF), see [2], is used to extract feature points in the first frame. We chose SURF over the Harris corner detector [6] (which is a common choice in visual odometry) because corner points may not be evenly distributed depending on the geometry of the scene. The Lucas-Kanade [12] algorithm is used to track these detected features in the subsequent frame. Tracked feature points serve then as input, and are again tracked in the following frame, and so on. Since the same set of feature points is tracked, the total number of features decays over frames. When the total number of features drops below a threshold τ then a new set of features is detected using again the SURF detector. After calculating a relative transformation between Frames $t-1$ and t, the global pose of the cameras at time t is obtained by keeping a global accumulator, assuming that the pose of the camera at time 1 is a 4×4 identity matrix for initialization. However, in our experiments, when applying this basic algorithm, the estimation of camera pose transformations was inaccurate, and became less stable as errors accumulate along the sequence. In order to improve the accuracy, we apply a sliding-window bundle adjustment.

Bundle adjustment [16] is the problem of refining the 3D structure as well as the camera parameters. Mathematically, assume that n 3D points b_i are seen from m cameras with parameters a_j, and X_{ij} is the projection of the ith point on camera j. Bundle adjustment is the task to minimize the *reprojection error* with respect to 3D points b_i and cameras' parameters a_j. In formal representation, determine the minimum

$$\min_{a_j, b_i} \sum_{i=1}^{n} \sum_{j=1}^{m} d(Q(a_j, b_i), X_{ij})^2$$

where $Q(a_j, b_i)$ is the function projecting point i on camera j, and d is the Euclidean distance between points in the image plane. Bundle adjustment is a non-linear minimization problem which can be solved by using iterative methods such as Levenberg-Marquardt.

Ideally, the best result can be obtained by applying bundle adjustment to all the recorded frames. But, considering its complexity and the limited computing power we have, we use a sliding window bundle adjustment (similar to the method used in [15]), i.e. only optimizing the camera poses within a window of k frames, and moving this window across the whole sequence (only the left images are used for bundle adjustment).

Starting from frame F_1, a window of k images is constructed and the estimated camera poses are used as initial estimates. Then, bundle adjustment is applied for the window using the tracked features. In the next iteration, the window advances by one frame, i.e. we estimate now the camera pose for frame F_{k+1}, as described in the previous subsection. The estimated pose for F_{k+1} plus bundle-adjusted poses for F_2 to F_k, serve then as initial estimates for the camera pose for frame F_{k+2}, and so on.

3   Surface Reconstruction

In this section, we build a 3D model of the scene using results of visual odometry. The final surface representation is polygonal, but in order to build it we construct a point cloud model first. Once we calculate the pose for cameras for all frames, building a 3D point cloud model can be as easy as projecting all 3D points derived from pixels with valid disparities into a global coordinate system. However, we did not accumulate pixels for all the frames, because the number of points grows exponentially, and a large percentage of points is actually redundant information. (The vehicle was driving at 10 km/h only, and recall that images were captured at 25 Hz.) For each frame, only pixels within a specified disparity range are used, due to the non-linear property of the Z-function. See Fig. 2 for an example.

Point-cloud data usually contain large portion of noise and outliers, and the density of points varies across the 3D space. Two additional steps are to be carried out to refine the quality of the point cloud.

Down-Sampling. A voxel grid filter is applied to simplify cloud data, thus improving the efficiency of subsequent processing. The filter creates a 3D voxel grid spanning over the cloud data. Then, for each voxel, all the points within are replaced by their centroid.

Outlier Removal. Errors in stereo matching and visual odometry lead to sparse outliers which corrupt the cloud data. Some of these errors can be eliminated by

Fig. 2. A generated point cloud model. Yellow cubes indicate detected camera poses.

Fig. 3. A created surface model. Yellow cubes indicate camera poses.

applying a statistical filter on the point set, i.e. for each point, we compute the mean distance from it to all of its neighbours. If this mean distance of the point is outside a predefined interval, then the point can be treated as an outlier and is removed from the set. The order of these steps affects the overall performance of the process. The down-sampling process is significantly faster than outlier removal. Thus we decided to perform these two processes in the listed order.

Given a set S of points in 3D, the *α-shape* [4] was designed for answering questions such as "What is the shape formed by these points?" Edelsbrunner and Mücke mention in [4] an intuitive description of 3D α-shape: Imagine that a huge ice-cream fills space $\mathbb{R}^3$ and contains all points of S as "hard" chocolate pieces. Using a sphere-formed spoon, we carve out all possible parts of the ice-cream block without touching any of the chocolate pieces, even carving out holes inside the block. The object we end up with is the α-shape of S, and the value $α$ is the squared radius of the carving spoon.

To formally define the α-shape, we first define an α-complex. An α-complex of a set S of points is a subcomplex of the 3D Delaunay triangulation of S, which is a tetrahedrization such that no point in S is inside the circumsphere of any of the created tetrahedra. Given a value of $α$, the α-complex contains all the simplexes in the Delaunay triangulation which have an empty circumscribing sphere with squared radius equal to, or smaller than $α$. The α-shape is the topological frontier of the α-complex.

In our reconstruction pipeline, after obtaining and refining a point-cloud model, the α-shape is calculated and defines a 3D surface model of the scene. See Fig. 3 for an example. Compared to Fig. 2, the reader might agree with our general observation that the surface model looks in general "better" than the point-cloud visualization.

4   Merging Models from Opposite Runs

Now we are ready to discuss our proposed merger of point-cloud or surface data obtained from multiple runs through a 3D scene.

The 3D model reconstructed from a single run (i.e. driving through the scene in one direction) contains a large number of "blind spots" (e.g. due to occlusions, e.g. the "other side of the wall", or the limited viewing angle of the cameras, but also due to missing depth data, if disparities were rated "invalid"). By combining the results from opposite runs, we aim at producing a more accurate and more complete model of the scene.

The task of aligning consistently models from different views is know as *registration*. Fully automatic pairwise registration methods exist for laser-scanner data, and the main steps are listed below

1. Identify a set of interest points (e.g. SIFT [11]) that best represent both 3D point sets.
2. Compute a feature descriptor at each interest point, using methods such as *fast point feature histograms* (FPFH); see [14].

Fig. 4. Bird's-eye view of an initial alignment of two opposite runs. Results of each run are shown in different colours.

3. Estimate the correspondence between two sets of feature points based on their similarities. The simplest method is brute-force matching.
4. Assuming that the data is noisy, invalid correspondences are rejected to improve the registration.
5. Compute the pose transformation from the remaining correspondences.
6. Use the resulting estimation as an initial alignment; then apply an *iterative closest points technique* (ICP) to further align two point sets; see [3].

However, compared to laser-scanner data, stereo data is more inaccurate and contains a significant amount of noise, especially around the edge areas of scene objects. Therefore, the method stated above is not applicable for our system in this form. Considering the complexity of the scene (i.e. objects may look completely different from opposite directions) and the inaccuracy of stereo data, we propose the following semi-automatic method to align the two stereo point clouds.

Initial Alignment. We let the user manually select a set of corresponding points from both models. Then, a rough estimation of alignment is calculated by applying the least-square method. See Fig. 4 for an example.

Adjustment. Due to (not fully avoidable) errors in the visual odometry process and the considerable dimension (length) of the recorded scene, both point-cloud

Fig. 5. Bird's-eye views of individual and merged surface models

Fig. 6. Street views illustrating the benefit of merging 3D data

models cannot be perfectly aligned as a whole. (Both models are twisted to a certain degree in 3D space.) Therefore, we break the point cloud models into a few segments along the Z direction (the main driving direction). Then we loop through each segment, apply feature matching across the two point-cloud models using 3D feature detectors, such as SIFT. A more precise alignment for this segment is calculated by matching the two feature sets. If the new alignment does not differ from the initial alignment more than a threshold τ, the new alignment is applied to the cloud segment.

Post Processing. Since we merged two (very extensive) point clouds, the point density is not uniform any more. We need to down-sample the merged point cloud again (as described in the previous section), for the convenience of subsequent processing. After the merged point cloud is simplified, a surface model can be created using the α-shape algorithm. See Fig. 5 for surface models of two separate runs, and for the merged point cloud.

The street views in Fig. 6 show clearly the benefit of merging: many of the missing parts in one run are filled-in by reconstruction results of the second run. The facades of buildings and other details of the scene are getting more complete, with an accuracy as defined by stereo matching and visual odometry. We will not further illustrate the obvious positive effects, but like to point on two detected issues when merging. Figure 7 reveals that occlusions walls from opposite directions intersect each other. Due to the inaccurate disparities around the edge area, a wall structure can be formed along the viewing direction on the

Fig. 7. Occlusion walls from opposite directions intersect each other

edge. When merging models from opposite runs, the occlusion walls from the two models intersect each other.

5   Conclusions and Future Work

In this paper we described a stereo-based 3D reconstruction pipeline for modelling street scenes. We proposed a semi-automatic method for aligning models reconstructed from opposite directions, to fill-in missing components. Our proposed system is certainly useful for improving the completeness of ground-level 3D reconstruction. It might also be useful for combining results of aerial and ground-level large-scale 3D reconstruction. For future improvements we see needs to increase the accuracy of the visual odometry process, and to enhance the quality of the point cloud model. Evaluation on the quality and performance of the reconstruction system also needs to be done.

Acknowledgment. The authors thank Simon Hermann for the provision of iSGM for stereo matching.

References

1. 3D Reality Maps, www.realitymaps.de/en/ (last visited in April 2013)
2. Bay, H., Tuytelaars, T., Van Gool, L.: SURF: Speeded up robust features. In: Leonardis, A., Bischof, H., Pinz, A. (eds.) ECCV 2006, Part I. LNCS, vol. 3951, pp. 404–417. Springer, Heidelberg (2006)
3. Besl, P.J., McKay, N.D.: A method for registration of 3-D shapes. IEEE Trans. Pattern Analysis Machine Intelligence 14, 239–256 (1992)
4. Edelsbrunner, H., Mücke, E.P.: Three-dimensional alpha shapes. ACM Trans. Graphics 13, 43–72 (1994)
5. Geiger, A., Ziegler, J., Stiller, C.: StereoScan: Dense 3d reconstruction in real-time. In: Proc. IEEE IV, pp. 963–968 (2011)
6. Harris, C., Stephens, M.J.: A combined corner and edge detector. In: Proc. Alvey Vision Conf., pp. 147–151 (1988)
7. Heidelberg Robust Vision Challenge at ECCV 2012 (2012), http://hci.iwr.uni-heidelberg.de/Static/challenge2012/
8. Hermann, S., Klette, R.: Iterative semi-global matching for robust driver assistance systems. In: Lee, K.M., Matsushita, Y., Rehg, J.M., Hu, Z. (eds.) ACCV 2012, Part III. LNCS, vol. 7726, pp. 465–478. Springer, Heidelberg (2013)
9. Huang, F., Klette, R.: City-scale modeling towards street navigation applications. J. Information Convergence Communication Engineering 10 (2012)
10. Jiang, R., Klette, R., Wang, S.: Statistical modeling of long-range drift in visual odometry. In: Koch, R., Huang, F. (eds.) ACCV 2010 Workshops, Part II. LNCS, vol. 6469, pp. 214–224. Springer, Heidelberg (2011)
11. Lowe, D.G.: Distinctive image features from scale-invariant keypoints. Int. J. Computer Vision 60, 91–110 (2004)
12. Lucas, B.D., Kanade, T.: An iterative image registration technique with an application to stereo vision. Proc. IJCAI 2, 674–679 (1981)

13. Nister, D., Naroditsky, O., Bergen, J.: Visual odometry. In: Proc. CVPR, vol. 1, pp. 652–659 (2004)
14. Rusu, R.B., Blodow, N., Beetz, M.: Fast point feature histograms (FPFH) for 3D registration. In: Proc. IEEE ICRA, pp. 3212–3217 (2009)
15. Sünderhauf, N., Konolige, K., Lacroix, S., Protzel, P.: Visual odometry using sparse bundle adjustment on an autonomous outdoor vehicle. In: Proc. Autonome Mobile Systems, pp. 157–163 (2005)
16. Triggs, B., McLauchlan, P.F., Hartley, R.I., Fitzgibbon, A.W.: Bundle adjustment – A modern synthesis. In: Triggs, B., Zisserman, A., Szeliski, R. (eds.) ICCV-WS 1999. LNCS, vol. 1883, pp. 298–375. Springer, Heidelberg (2000)
17. Xiao, J., Fang, T., Zhao, P., Lhuilier, M., Quan, L.: Image-based street-side city modeling. In: Proc. SIGGRAPH, pp. 114:1–114:12 (2009)

Interactive Image Segmentation via Graph Clustering and Synthetic Coordinates Modeling

Costas Panagiotakis[1], Harris Papadakis[2], Elias Grinias[3], Nikos Komodakis[4], Paraskevi Fragopoulou[2], and Georgios Tziritas[5]

[1] Dept. of Commerce and Marketing, Technological Educational Institute (TEI) of Crete, 72200 Ierapetra, Greece
cpanag@staff.teicrete.gr

[2] Dept. of Applied Informatics and Multimedia, TEI of Crete, PO Box 140, Greece
adanar@epp.teicrete.gr, fragopou@ics.forth.gr*

[3] Dept. of Geoinformatics and Surveying, TEI of Serres, 62124 Serres, Greece
elgrinias@gmail.com

[4] Dept. of Computer Science and Applied Math, Ecole des Ponts ParisTech, France
nikos.komodakis@enpc.fr

[5] Dept. of Computer Science, University of Crete, P.O. Box 2208, Greece
tziritas@csd.uoc.gr

Abstract. We propose a method for interactive image segmentation. We construct a weighted graph that represents the superpixels and the connections between them. An efficient algorithm for graph clustering based on synthetic coordinates is used yielding an initial map of classified pixels. The proposed method minimizes a min-max Bayesian criterion that has been successfully used on image segmentation problem taking into account visual information as well as the given markers. Experimental results and comparisons with other methods demonstrate the high performance of the proposed scheme.

Keywords: image segmentation, network coordinates, graph clustering.

1 Introduction

Image segmentation is a key step in many image-video analysis and multimedia applications. According to interactive image segmentation, which is a special case of image segmentation, unambiguous solutions, or segmentations satisfying subjective criteria, could be obtained, since the user gives some markers on the regions of interest and on the background. Fig. 1 illustrates an example of an original image, two types of markers and the segmentation ground truth.

During the last decade, a large number of interactive image segmentation algorithms have been proposed in the literature. In [1], a new shape constraint based method for interactive image segmentation has been proposed using Geodesic paths. The authors introduce Geodesic Forests, which exploit the structure of

---

* Paraskevi Fragopoulou is also with the Foundation for Research and Technology-Hellas, Institute of Computer Science, 70013 Heraklion, Crete, Greece.

R. Wilson et al. (Eds.): CAIP 2013, Part I, LNCS 8047, pp. 589–596, 2013.

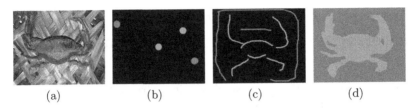

(a)   (b)   (c)   (d)

Fig. 1. (a) Original image, (b), (c) given markers and (d) the ground truth image

shortest paths in implementing extended constraints. In [2], discriminative learning methods have been used to train conditional models for both region and boundary based on interactive scribbles. In the region model, the authors use two types of local histograms with different window sizes to characterize local image statistics around a specific pixel. In the boundary model, the authors use 12-bin boundary features by applying gradient filters to each color component. In [3], a two step segmentation algorithm has been proposed that first obtains a binary segmentation and then applies matting on the border regions to obtain a smooth alpha channel. The proposed segmentation algorithm is based on the minimization of the Geodesic Active Contour energy.

According to the interactive segmentation algorithm proposed in [4], first, all the labeled seeds are independently propagated for obtaining homogeneous connected components for each of them. Then, the image is divided into blocks which are classified according to their probabilistic distance from the classified regions, and a topographic surface for each class is obtained. Finally, two algorithms for regularized classification based on the topographic surface have been proposed.

The proposed method can be divided into several steps. In the first step, we partition the image into superpixels using the oversegmentation algorithm proposed in [5]. Then, we construct a weighted graph that represents the superpixels and the connections between them, taking into account the given markers and visual information (see Sections 2). Next, we use the Vivaldi algorithm [6] that generates the superpixels' synthetic coordinates (see Section 3). An initial map of classified pixels is provided by an efficient algorithm for graph clustering based on synthetic coordinates (see Section 4). Thus, we solve the graph clustering problem using the synthetic network coordinates that are automatically estimated by a distributed algorithm based on interactions between neighboring nodes. Finally, the image segmentation is provided by a Markov Random Field (MRF) model or a flooding algorithm minimizing a min-max Bayesian criterion (see Section 5). Hereafter we present the proposed methodology, a more detailed analysis of the proposed method is given in [7].

2   Graph Generation

Initially, we partition the image into superpixels using the oversegmentation algorithm proposed in [5]. In this work, the description of visual content consists of

Lab color components for color distribution and textureness for texture content. This approach has been also used in [8]. The visual distance $d_v(s_i, s_j)$ between two superpixels s_i and s_j is given by the Mallows distance [9] of the three color components in Lab color space and for the textureness measure of the corresponding superpixels. Let G' be the weighted graph of superpixels, so that two superpixels s_i and s_j are connected with an edge of weight $d_v(s_i, s_j)$ if and only if they are neighbors, meaning that they share a common boundary. Then, the proximity distance $d_p(s_i, s_j)$ between superpixels s_i and s_j is given by the length of the shortest path from s_i to s_j in graph G'. The proposed distance between superpixels s_i and s_j that efficiently combines the visual and proximity distances is given by Equation 1:

$$d(s_i, s_j) = \sqrt{d_p(s_i, s_j)} \cdot d_v(s_i, s_j) \tag{1}$$

The use of the square root on the proximity distance is explained by the fact that the visual distance is more important than the proximity distance. The graph G' is used in order to compute the graph G that is defined hereafter.

In the next step, we construct a graph G that represents the superpixels and the connections between them, taking into account the given markers and visual information. According to the given markers, two superpixels can either be connected, meaning that they belong to the same class or be disconnected, meaning that they belong to different classes. Thus, the nodes (superpixels) in this graph are connected with edges of two types:

- the E_C edges that connect two superpixels belonging to the same class,
- the E_D edges that connect two superpixels belonging to different classes,

taking into account the two types of relations between superpixels. In the second step of the algorithm, the visual distance and the superpixels' proximity are used to create the set of edges E_C until G becomes a connected graph.

Hereafter, we present the procedure that computes the two sets of edges, E_C and E_D for graph G. E_C and E_D are initialized to the corresponding edges according to the given markers. Then, the $\frac{N \cdot (N-1)}{2}$ pairs of distances $d(.,.)$ are sorted and stored in vector v, where N denotes the number of superpixels. We add the sorted edges of v on E_C set until G becomes a connected graph in order to be able to execute the Vivaldi algorithm [6] that generates the superpixels' synthetic coordinates (see Section 3). In addition, we keep the graph balanced (almost equal degree per node) using an upper limit on node degree ($MaxConn = 10$).

3   Synthetic Coordinates

In this work, we have used Vivaldi [6] to position the superpixels in a virtual space (the $n-$dimensional Euclidean space $\Re^n$, e.g. $n = 20$). Vivaldi [6] is a fully decentralized, light-weight, adaptive network coordinate algorithm that predicts Internet latencies with low error. Recently, we have successfully applied

Vivaldi on the problem of locating communities on real and synthetic dataset graphs [10, 11]. In the current work, the input to the Vivaldi algorithm is a weighted graph, where the weights correspond to the nodes distances in $\Re^n$. We have used the weights 0.0 and 1000.0 for E_C and E_D, respectively. These weights correspond to the Euclidean distance between the virtual position of superpixels, that is used by the Vivaldi algorithm to position the superpixels in $\Re^n$ generating synthetic coordinates so that the Euclidean distance of any two superpixel positions approximates the actual distance (edge weight) between those superpixels. This means that superpixels of the same class will be placed closer in space than superpixels of different classes, forming natural clusters in space.

4   Graph Clustering

Having estimated a synthetic coordinate (position) $p(s_i) \in \Re^n$ for each superpixel $s_i, i \in \{1, ..., N\}$ of the graph, we can use a clustering algorithm in order to cluster a subset of superpixels into foreground and background classes, providing this way an initial map of classified pixels Map. The proposed algorithm creates the initial map by merging the superpixels that have been placed in proximity in $\Re^n$, meaning that they should belong to the same class. In this research, we have used a hierarchical clustering algorithm that recursively finds clusters in an agglomerative (bottom-up) mode. We successively merge a cluster c_1 with "UNKNOWN" label with the closest labeled cluster c_2, if the distance between c_1 and c_2 is lower than a predefined threshold T according to their synthetic coordinates. If no such pair of clusters exists, the algorithm terminates. T is automatically computed by the histogram of distances between all points' pairs. T is given by the value that better discriminates the two distributions (distances between points of the same class and between points of different classes) from the histogram of distances.

Usually, it holds that the image borders and especially the pixels close to the four image corners belong to the background class, so we have used the following simple rule so that a pixel is classified to background class if it belongs to an unclassified superpixel and its distance

– from the closest image border is less than 1% of the image diagonal
– from the closest image corner is less than 7% of the image diagonal.

Using the criterion of "unclassified superpixel" the proposed heuristic works well in cases where an object intersects the image boundary. Finally, we perform erosion on the classified superpixels using a disk of 2 pixels radius, in order to be able to correct some boundary errors of the oversegmentation algorithm.

5   Image Segmentation

Hereafter, we briefly describe the image segmentation method. The proposed criterion has been proposed in [4,8]. Let $S = \bigcup_{l=1}^{L} S_l$ be the set of those initially classified pixels estimated by the graph clustering algorithm. For any unclassified pixel s we can consider all the paths linking it to a classified set or region. A path $C_l(s)$ is a sequence of adjacent pixels $\{s_0, ..., s_{n-1}, s_n = s\}$. It holds that all pixels of the sequence are unlabeled, except s_0 which has label l. The cost of a particular path is defined as the maximum cost of a pixel classification according to the Bayesian rule and along the path

$$Cost(C_l(s)) = \max_{i=1...n} d_l^B(s_i) \tag{2}$$

Finally, the classification problem becomes equivalent to a search for the shortest path given the above cost. Two algorithms based on the principle of the $min - max$ Bayesian criterion for classification, have been used. These algorithms have been proposed in [4, 8].

- According to the Independent Label Flooding MRF-based minimization Algorithm (ILFMA), we use the primal-dual method proposed in [12], which casts the MRF optimization problem as an integer program and then makes use of the duality theory of linear programming in order to derive solutions that have been proved to be almost optimal.
- The Priority Multi-Class Flooding Algorithm (PMCFA), that is analytically described in [8], imposes strong topology constraints. All the contours of initially classified regions are propagated towards the space of unclassified image pixels, according to similarity criteria, which are based on the class label and the segmentation features.

In what follows, the proposed methods using the MRF model and the flooding algorithm are denoted as SGC-ILFMA and SGC-PMCFA, respectively.

6 Experimental Results

SGC-ILFMA and SGC-PMCFA have been compared with algorithms from the literature according to the reported results of [2] and [13], using the following two datasets:

- The LHI interactive segmentation benchmark [14]. This benchmark consists of 21 natural images with ground-truths and three types of users' scribbles for each image.
- The Zhao interactive segmentation benchmark [13]. This benchmark consists of 50 natural images with ground-truths and four types of users' scribbles (levels) for each image. The higher the level, the more markers are added.

In order to measure the algorithms' performance, we use the Region precision criterion (RP) [2]. RP measures an overlap rate between a result foreground and the corresponding ground truth foreground. A higher RP indicates a better segmentation result.

Fig. 2 depicts intermediate (initial map) and final segmentation results of the proposed methods (SGC-ILFMA and SGC-PMCFA) on an image of LHI dataset (see Fig. 2(a)) and three images of Zhao dataset. We graphically depict the given markers on the original images using red color for foreground and green color for background, respectively. The red, blue and white coloring of intermediate results correspond to foreground, background and unclassified pixels, respectively. Under any case, the results of the proposed algorithms are almost the same, yielding high performance results. In Figs. 2(f), 2(f) and 2(j) the initial marker information suffices for the segmentation. Although in Fig. 2(n) the low number of given markers does not suffice to discriminate the foreground and background classes, the proposed methods give good performance results. A demonstration of the proposed method with experimental results is given in [1].

Using the LHI dataset, we have compared the proposed methods with three other algorithms from the literature: CO3 [2], Unger et al. [3] based on the reported results of [2]. The proposed methods SGC-ILFMA and SGC-PMCFA yield RP 85.4% and 85.2%, respectively, outperforming the other methods. The third and the fourth highest performance results are given by the CO3 [2] method with $RP = 79\%$ and Unger et al. with $RP = 73\%$.

In addition, we have compared the proposed methods with three other algorithms from the literature Couprie et al. [15], Grady [16] and Noma et al. [17] using the reported results of [13] on Zhao dataset. Table 1 depicts the mean region precision (RP) on four different simulation levels of SGC-ILFMA, SGC-PMCFA, Bai et al., Couprie et al., Grady and Noma et al. algorithms. The highest performance results are clearly obtained by the SGC-ILFMA and SGC-PMCFA algorithms, while the third highest performance results are given by the Couprie et al. [15] method that gives similar results with the Grady and Noma et al. method.

Table 1. The region precision (RP) over the Zhao dataset

Method	SGC-ILFMA	SGC-PMCFA	Couprie et al.	Grady	Noma et al.
1	66.7%	**68.4%**	50%	46%	49%
2	84.1%	**84.5%**	72%	71%	69%
3	85.3%	**85.7%**	84%	84%	82%
4	88.1%	**88.6%**	88%	88%	87%

7 Conclusion

In this paper, a two-step algorithm is proposed for interactive image segmentation taking into account image visual information, proximity distances as well as the given markers. In the first step, we constructed a weighted graph of superpixels and we clustered this graph based on a synthetic coordinates algorithm. In the second step, we have used a MRF or a flooding algorithm for getting the final image segmentation. The proposed method yields high performance results under different types of images and shapes of the initial markers.

---

[1] http://www.csd.uoc.gr/~cpanag/DEMOS/intImageSegmentation.htm

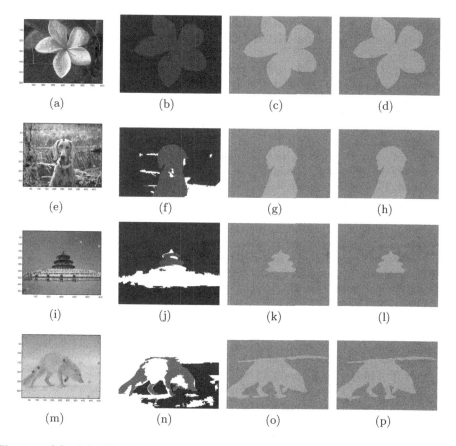

Fig. 2. (a), (e), (i), (m) Original images with markers from the LHI and Zhao datasets. (b), (f), (j), (n) Initial map of classified pixels. (c), (g), (k), (o) Final segmentation results of the SGC-ILFMA method. (d), (h), (l), (p) Final segmentation results of the SGC-PMCFA method.

Acknowledgments. This research has been partially co-financed by the European Union (European Social Fund - ESF) and Greek national funds through the Operational Program "Education and Lifelong Learning" of the National Strategic Reference Framework (NSRF) - Research Funding Programs: ARCHIMEDE III-TEI-Crete-P2PCOORD, THALIS-NTUA-UrbanMonitor and THALIS-UOA- ERASITECHNIS.

References

1. Gulshan, V., Rother, C., Criminisi, A., Blake, A., Zisserman, A.: Geodesic star convexity for interactive image segmentation. In: IEEE Conference on Computer Vision and Pattern Recognition, CVPR, pp. 3129–3136 (2010)

2. Zhao, Y., Zhu, S., Luo, S.: Co3 for ultra-fast and accurate interactive segmentation. In: Proceedings of the International Conference on Multimedia, pp. 93–102. ACM (2010)

3. Unger, M., Pock, T., Trobin, W., Cremers, D., Bischof, H.: Tvseg-interactive total variation based image segmentation. In: British Machine Vision Conference, BMVC (2008)

4. Grinias, I., Komodakis, N., Tziritas, G.: Flooding and MRF-based algorithms for interactive segmentation. In: International Conference on Pattern Recognition, ICPR, pp. 3943–3946 (2010)

5. Felzenszwalb, P., Huttenlocher, D.: Efficient graph-based image segmentation. International Journal of Computer Vision 59, 167–181 (2004)

6. Dabek, F., Cox, R., Kaashoek, F., Morris, R.: Vivaldi: A decentralized network coordinate system. In: Proceedings of the ACM SIGCOMM 2004 Conference, vol. 34, pp. 15–26 (2004)

7. Panagiotakis, C., Papadakis, H., Grinias, I., Komodakis, N., Fragopoulou, P., Tziritas, G.: Interactive image segmentation based on synthetic graph coordinates. In: Pattern Recognition (accepted, 2013)

8. Panagiotakis, C., Grinias, I., Tziritas, G.: Natural image segmentation based on tree equipartition, bayesian flooding and region merging. IEEE Transactions on Image Processing 20, 2276–2287 (2011)

9. Mallows, C.: A note on asymptotic joint normality. The Annals of Mathematical Statistics 43, 508–515 (1972)

10. Papadakis, H., Panagiotakis, C., Fragopoulou, P.: Local community finding using synthetic coordinates. In: Park, J.J., Yang, L.T., Lee, C. (eds.) FutureTech 2011, Part II. CCIS, vol. 185, pp. 9–15. Springer, Heidelberg (2011)

11. Papadakis, H., Panagiotakis, C., Fragopoulou, P.: Locating communities on real dataset graphs using synthetic coordinates. Parallel Processing Letters, PPL 20 (2012)

12. Komodakis, N., Tziritas, G.: Approximate labeling via graph cuts based on linear programming. IEEE Transactions on Pattern Analysis and Machine Intelligence 29, 1436–1453 (2007)

13. Zhao, Y., Nie, X., Duan, Y., Huang, Y., Luo, S.: A benchmark for interactive image segmentation algorithms. In: IEEE Workshop on Person-Oriented Vision, POV, pp. 33–38 (2011)

14. Yao, B., Yang, X., Zhu, S.-C.: Introduction to a large-scale general purpose ground truth database: Methodology, annotation tool and benchmarks. In: Yuille, A.L., Zhu, S.-C., Cremers, D., Wang, Y. (eds.) EMMCVPR 2007. LNCS, vol. 4679, pp. 169–183. Springer, Heidelberg (2007)

15. Couprie, C., Grady, L., Najman, L., Talbot, H.: Power watersheds: A new image segmentation framework extending graph cuts, random walker and optimal spanning forest. In: International Conference on Computer Vision, pp. 731–738 (2009)

16. Grady, L.: Random walks for image segmentation. IEEE Transactions on Pattern Analysis and Machine Intelligence 28, 1768–1783 (2006)

17. Noma, A., Graciano, A., Consularo, L., Cesar Jr., R., Bloch, I.: A new algorithm for interactive structural image segmentation. arXiv preprint arXiv:0805.1854 (2008)

Author Index